A Leonard E. Boyle Book

Father Leonard E. Boyle, OP, Dominican friar, quondam Senior Fellow at the Pontifical Institute of Mediaeval Studies, and Prefect of the Biblioteca Apostolica Vaticana under Pope John Paul II, touched a generation of scholars through his life and work. Following his death, the Pontifical Institute endowed a chair in Father Boyle's name, to ensure that his legacy lived on: the Leonard E. Boyle Book imprint has been developed as part of that mission. It represents an undertaking to provide financial support for books published through the Institute press reflecting disciplines, themes, and methodologies that resonate with Father Boyle's own interests, stretching as they did from Latin palaeography and the technical fields that comprise manuscript studies, to the history of his own order, medieval education, and pastoral care, to canon law, the theology of Thomas Aquinas and beyond. *Omnia disce. Videbis postea nihil esse superfluum.*

M. MICHÈLE MULCHAHEY
Leonard E. Boyle Professor of Manuscript Studies

Saint Michael's College Mediaeval Translations

General Editors
JOSEPH GOERING
GIULIO SILANO

MEDIAEVAL SOURCES IN TRANSLATION 58

Women's History in the Age of Reformation

Johannes Meyer's Chronicle of the Dominican Observance

Translated by

CLAIRE TAYLOR JONES

PONTIFICAL INSTITUTE OF MEDIAEVAL STUDIES

Acknowledgements

This publication is made possible in part by support from the Institute for Scholarship in the Liberal Arts, College of Arts and Letters, University of Notre Dame.

Library and Archives Canada Cataloguing in Publication

Title: Women's history in the age of Reformation : Johannes Meyer's chronicle of the Dominican observance / translated by Claire Taylor Jones.
Other titles: Buch der Reformacio Predigerordens. English | Johannes Meyer's chronicle of the Dominican observance
Names: Meyer, Johannes, 1422–1485, author. | Jones, Claire Taylor, translator. | Pontifical Institute of Mediaeval Studies, publisher.
Series: Saint Michael's College mediaeval translations. | Mediaeval sources in translation ; 58.
Description: Series statement: Saint Michael's College mediaeval translations | Mediaeval sources in translation ; 58. | Translation of: Buch der Reformacio Predigerordens. | Includes bibliographical references and indexes.
Identifiers: Canadiana (print) 20190105607 | Canadiana (ebook) 2019010662X | ISBN 9780888443083 (softcover) | ISBN 9781771104029 (PDF)
Subjects: LCSH: Dominicans – Germany, Southern – History – 15th century – Early works to 1800. | LCSH: Church renewal – Germany, Southern – History – 15th century – Early works to 1800. | LCSH: Dominican sisters – Germany, Southern – History – 15th century – Early works to 1800. | LCSH: Germany, Southern – Church history – 15th century – Early works to 1800.
Classification: LCC BX3535.S6 M4913 2019 | DDC 271/.2043—dc23

Pontifical Institute of Mediaeval Studies
59 Queen's Park Crescent East
Toronto, Ontario M5S 2C4
Canada
www.pims.ca

PRINTED IN CANADA

Contents

Acknowledgements

I have great affection for the stiff and pontificating, yet also deeply compassionate personality that comes through in the writings of Johannes Meyer, and this translation has been a labour of love. Nevertheless, I owe a debt of gratitude to several people who have assisted or encouraged me along the way. First and foremost, I thank Sara S. Poor for first making me aware of *The Book of the Reformation* in a graduate seminar a decade ago. However, this translation is above all a product of my time at the Pontifical Institute of Mediaeval Studies in Toronto. After patiently listening to me sing Meyer's praises, it was Markus Stock who first encouraged me to undertake a translation of this work. I am grateful that my editor, Fred Unwalla, took the time to talk the idea over with me and help me formulate the project's importance. He has also provided unflagging support and valuable advice throughout the process.

Some of the revisions were undertaken during a sabbatical at the Notre Dame Institute for Advanced Study. The maps were created by Matthew Sisk of the Navari Family Center for Digital Scholarship at the University of Notre Dame. The Notre Dame Institute for Scholarship in the Liberal Arts supported this volume with a publication subvention. I am grateful for all the collegial and institutional support I have found at Notre Dame.

Christian Seebald, who is preparing a new critical edition of the work, gave me excellent advice about the manuscripts and generously shared his resources with me. I thank Sarah DeMaris, whose inimitable edition of *Das Amptbuch* was an inspiration, for her encouragement (and warnings) along the way, and Christopher Liebtag Miller for his patient support. Several friends helped me decipher puzzling passages and phrases in the translation, and my writing group through the Society for Medieval Feminist Scholarship (Dana Oswald and Kathryn Maude) gave me invaluable feedback for improving the Introduction. I also owe immense gratitude to the press's anonymous readers for their careful and thoughtful recommendations through several drafts. I am also grateful for Ian Drummond's careful eye and painstaking work during the copy-editing process. All remaining errors and infelicities are my own.

Abbreviations

AFP	*Archivum Fratrum Praedicatorum*
DDS	Petra Zimmer and Brigitte Degler-Spengler (eds), *Die Dominikaner und Dominikanerinnen in der Schweiz,* Helvetia Sacra 4.5 (Basel: Schwabe, 1999).
SOPMA	Thomas Kaeppeli, *Scriptores Ordinis Praedicatorum medii aevi,* 4 vols (Rome: Ad S. Sabinae, 1970–1993).
VL[2]	Kurt Ruh et al. (eds), *Verfasserlexikon: Die deutsche Literatur des Mittelalters,* 2nd ed., 14 vols (Berlin: De Gruyter, 1978–2008).
ZfdA	*Zeitschrift für deutsches Altertum und deutsche Literatur*

Map of Dominican Communities in the Province of Teutonia, by Nation

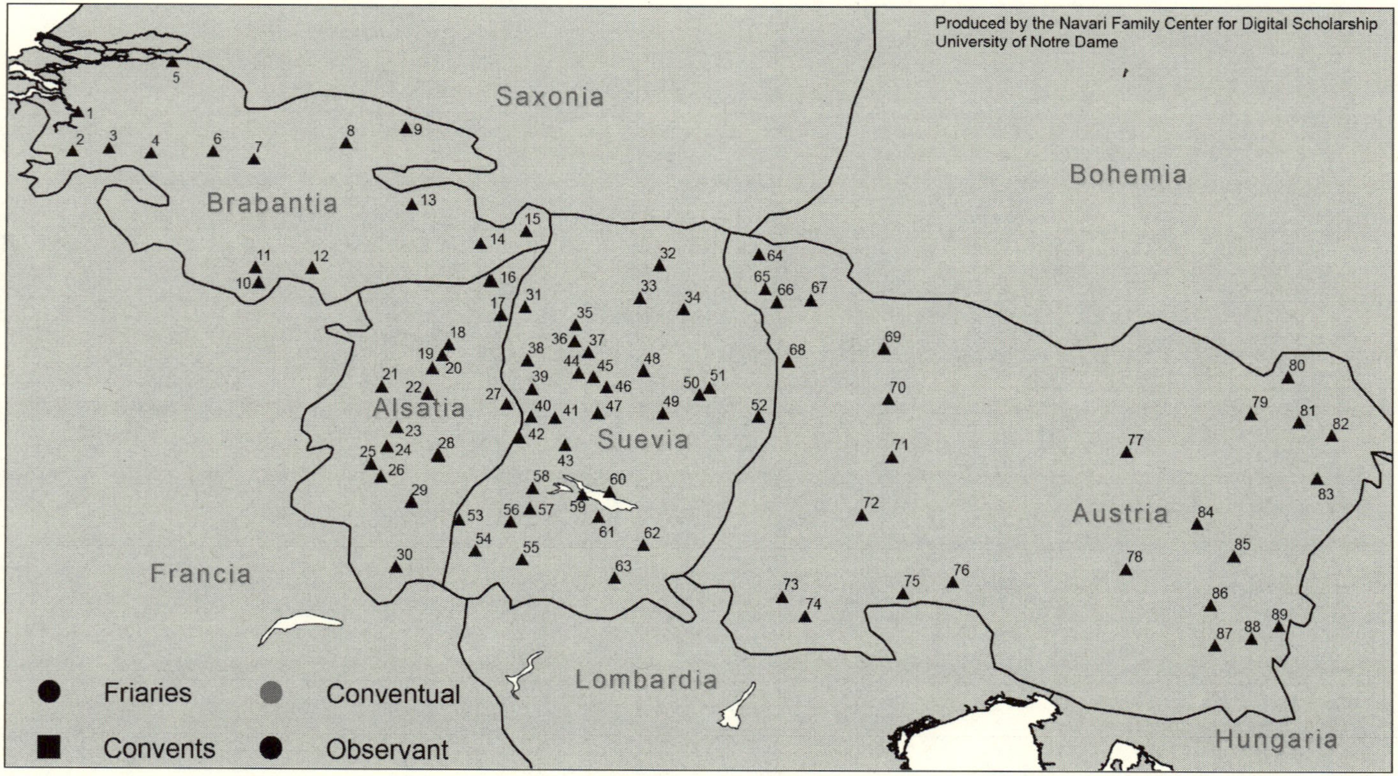

Brabantia

◍ 1 Antwerp
● 2 Brussels
▩ Herzogental
◍ 3 Leuven
● 4 Zoutleeuw
● 5 's Hertogenbosch
● 6 Maastricht
● 7 Aachen
● 8 Cologne
■ St Gertrude
● 9 Marienheide
◍ 10 Luxembourg
▩ 11 Mariental (Mersch)
◍ 12 Trier
▩ St Catherine
▩ St Barbara
◍ 13 Koblenz
● 14 Mainz
● 15 Frankfurt

Alsatia

● 16 Worms
■ Himmelkron
■ Liebenau
◍ 17 Speyer
■ Hasenpfuhl
▩ St Lambrecht
◍ 18 Weissenburg
▩ 19 Marienbrunn
◍ 20 Haguenau
■ 21 Obersteigen
◍ 22 Strasbourg
▩ St Marx
■ St Agnes
■ St Nicholas-in-Undis
▩ St John the Evangelist
▩ St Catherine
■ St Margaret
■ Penitents of Mary Magdalene
◍ 23 Schlettstadt
■ Sylo
● 24 Colmar
■ Unterlinden
■ St Catherine
● 25 Gebweiler
■ Engelport
■ 26 Schönensteinbach
▩ 27 Engelthal (Hallwangen)
◍ 28 Freiburg im Breisgau
■ Adelhausen
■ St Agnes
■ Penitents of Mary Magdalene
▩ St Catherine (Wiehre)
● 29 Basel
■ Mary Magdalene an den Steinen
▩ Klingental
● 30 Bern
■ St Michael's Island

Suevia

● 31 Heidelberg
◍ 32 Würzburg
▩ St Mark
◍ 33 Mergentheim
▩ 34 Rothenburg ob der Tauber
● 35 Wimpfen
▩ 36 Lauffen
■ 37 Steinheim
● 38 Pforzheim
■ Mary Magdalene
■ 39 Reuthin (Wildberg)
▩ 40 Kirchberg
▩ 41 Stetten in Gnadental
◍ 42 Rottweil
▩ 43 Neidingen
● 44 Stuttgart
● 45 Esslingen
■ Weiler
■ 46 Kirchheim unter Teck
■ 47 Gnadenzell (Offenhausen)
● 48 Schwäbisch Gmünd
■ Gotteszell
● 49 Ulm
■ 50 Medlingen
■ 51 Maria Medingen
◍ 52 Augsburg
▩ St Catherine
▩ St Margaret
▩ 53 Aarau
▩ 54 Neuenkirch
▩ 55 Schwyz
◍ 56 Zurich
▩ Ötenbach
▩ 57 Töss
▩ 58 St Katharinental (Diessenhofen)
◍ 59 Constance
■ Zoffingen
▩ St Walburga (Münsterlingen)
▩ 60 Löwental
■ 61 St Catherine (St Gallen)
▩ 62 St Peter (Bludenz)
● 63 Chur

Austria

● 64 Bamberg
■ Holy Sepulchre
▩ 65 Frauenaurach
● 66 Nuremberg
■ St Catherine
▩ 67 Engelthal
● 68 Eichstätt
● 69 Regensburg
■ Holy Cross
▩ Pettendorf
● 70 Landshut
■ 71 Altenhohenau
■ 72 Marienthal (Voldöpp)
▩ 73 Steinach (Merano)
● 74 Bolzano
▩ 75 St Catherine (Innichen)
▩ 76 Lienz
● 77 Steyr
◍ 78 Friesach
● 79 Krems
■ Imbach
● 80 Retz
● 81 Tulln
■ Tulln Convent
● 82 Vienna
● 83 Wiener Neustadt
● 84 Leoben
● 85 Graz
▩ 86 Mahrenberg
● 87 Neukloster near Celje (Vallis Senarum)
▩ 88 Studenitz
● 89 Pettau (Ptuj)

Map of the Region surrounding Schönensteinbach

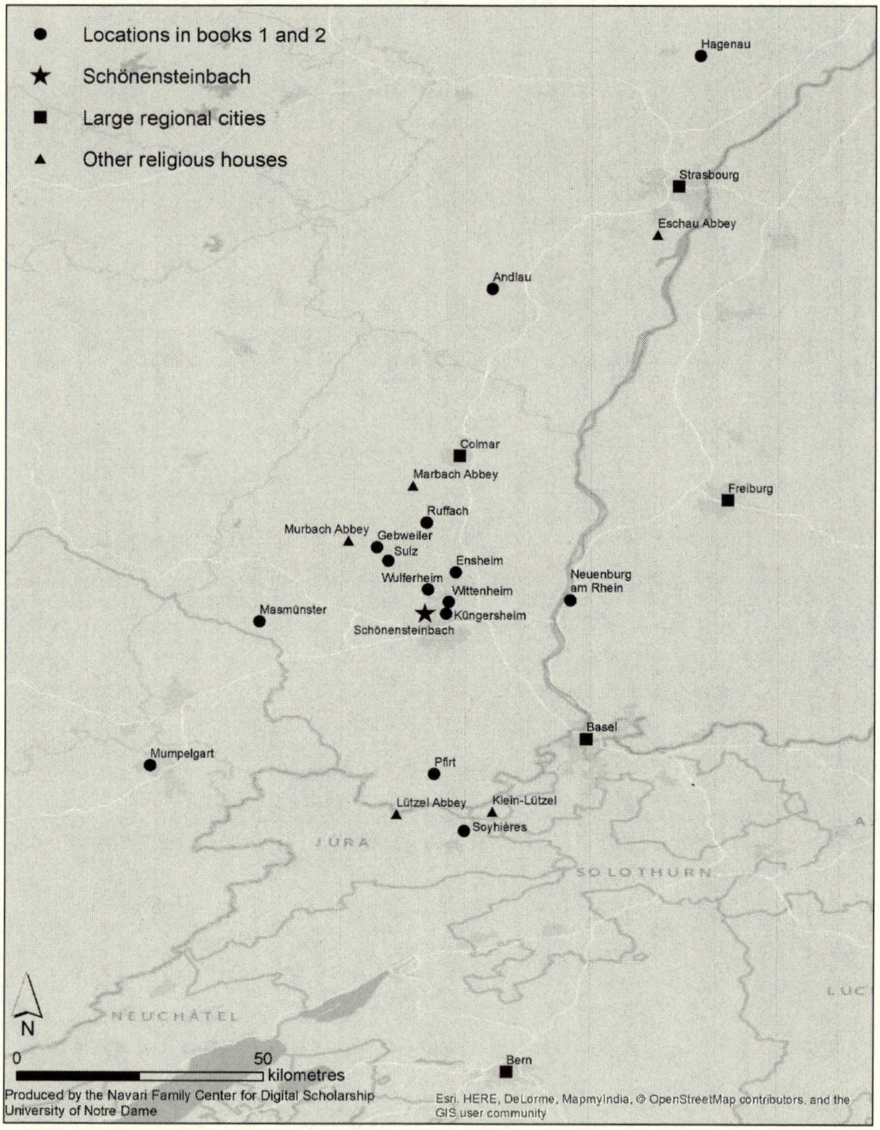

Introduction

"Honourable, dear, spiritual sisters in God, know that I, your poor brother Johannes, have laboured in your service for more than sixteen years by writing books." These words open the *Letter to Dominican Sisters,* in which the Dominican friar Johannes Meyer (1422–1485) lists and describes the German and Latin works he composed during the period from 1454 to 1470, including the work that is translated in this volume, *Das Buch der Reformacio Predigerordens,* or *The Book of the Reformation of the Order of Preachers,* finished in 1468.[1] In this work, Meyer drew on letters, treatises, and other written records, as well as interviews, oral accounts, and his own personal experience, to record the blossoming of the greatest reform movement to sweep through Germany before the Protestant Reformation: the Observant reform. The result is this sprawling, eclectic, yet curiously intimate account of the men – but mostly of the women – who devoted their lives to revitalizing the Dominican order in southern Germany. It is noteworthy, and entirely characteristic of Meyer, that in the *Letter to Dominican Sisters* he proclaims his dedication and service to women readers. Although he greatly admired the scholastic achievements for which his Dominican order is best known, his path did not lead through the university. Meyer lived during an age of vibrant piety and spiritual renewal, and he devoted his entire life to promoting religious practice through the Observant reform, a movement that he fostered by writing histories for and about women.

The *Book of the Reformation* provides an historical account, with a distinct positive slant, of the Observant reform as it played out among the Dominicans in southern Germany. In this Introduction I will contextualize Meyer's celebratory work within a more objective historical background. The circumstances that gave

1. The bulk of the work was completed by 1468, but additions cover the period up to 1477. The circumstances of composition are treated in more detail later in this Introduction. For more on the *Open Letter* and Meyer's authorial identity, see Christian Seebald, "Schreiben für die Reform: Reflexionen von Autorschaft in den Schriften des Dominikaners Johannes Meyer," in *Schriftstellerische Inszenierungspraktiken: Typologie und Geschichte,* ed. Christoph Jürgensen and Gerhard Kaiser (Heidelberg, 2011), 33–53.

rise to the reforms of the fifteenth century were not mere symptoms of decline, but complex social, political, and economic shifts. Correspondingly, the Observant reform, even within the Dominican order, was not a clear and unified programme, but a loose network of people who negotiated their different goals, interests, commitments, and processes in ways that varied over the century and a half of the movement. Meyer's own life and his career as a convent reformer coincided with a period of Observant success, which he both celebrated and furthered in his writing. So that the reader may better understand the spheres of authority exercised by the individual figures in Meyer's narrative, I provide an overview of the governing structures of the Dominican order and summarize the steps and the support needed to reform an individual convent. Despite the partisan nature of the *Book of the Reformation*, Meyer's treatment of medieval Dominican women provides a model from which today's historians stand to learn, in his reliance on their accounts and archives, his adoption of a female literary genre, and, importantly, his evident respect for their intellectual abilities and spiritual resolve. These features make the *Book of the Reformation* both a valuable historical record and a model for the sensitive treatment of women's capabilities and agency within historical contexts.

This historical introduction concludes with a review of the surviving manuscripts and a few words regarding the principles that guided my translation. These final reflections include some notes on Meyer's specialized vocabulary, which are intended as help in reading the translation but may also aid scholars who wish to use German primary sources from Observant contexts. Although the main purpose of this translation is to make this remarkable history available to English-speaking readers, I hope that it will inspire some to learn the languages and skills they will need to delve more deeply into the lives and struggles of religious women and the men who supported (or harassed) them in the late Middle Ages.

The Age of Reformation

To speak of "the Observant reform" is rather like speaking of "the Reformation," in that it lends a false unity to a religious phenomenon that manifested itself in an enormous variety of forms, which themselves changed over the century and a half of its influence. Over the course of the long fifteenth century, reforming movements affected almost every religious order, including even the military orders (albeit to a lesser extent). The term "Observance" usually refers only to the reform movements of the friars – that is, the Dominicans, the Franciscans, and the Augustinians – but the reforms of these orders were closely connected to reforming movements within the Benedictine order, in the universities, and at the church councils. Indeed, the fifteenth century was a vibrant "age of reform," to use Steven Ozment's phrase, and the Observance was only one of the many reform initiatives that affected both the church and the Holy Roman Empire.[2] Meyer's focus on southern German Dominicans in the *Book of the Reformation* is an accident of his own experience and interests. The events he recounts were part of a broad and diverse cultural renewal that permeated the monastic, domestic, and political spheres, although it manifested itself in various ways in response to political pressures, economic interests, and forceful personalities. The *Book of the Reformation* encompasses only one sphere of a pan-European cultural moment.

While the specific demands of reforming Franciscan friars may have had little in common with the programme of reforming Benedictine monks, all of the reform groups shared a commitment to a more rigorous observance of their respective rules and constitutions. The demand for renewed strictness was often accompanied by rhetoric about returning to the order's origins and living as each order's "first fathers" had lived.[3] The term "Observance" has come to be used because these reformers urged their fellows to observe their order's legislation more strictly.[4] This is not to say that "Observant" is in each case a term that mod-

2. See Steven Ozment, *The Age of Reform (1250–1550)* (New Haven, 1980); Ivan Hlaváček and Alexander Patschovsky (eds), *Reform von Kirche und Reich: Zur Zeit der Konzilien von Konstanz (1414–1418) und Basel (1431–1449)* (Konstanz, 1996); Duncan Hardy, *Associative Political Culture in the Holy Roman Empire: Upper Germany, 1346–1521* (Oxford, 2018), ch. 12.

3. Michael Vargas and John Van Engen have shown that the first fathers were likely not as exemplary as the Observant reformers imagined: see Michael A. Vargas, "Weak Obedience, Undisciplined Friars, and Failed Reforms in the Medieval Order of Preachers," *Viator* 42 (2011): 283–308; John Van Engen, "From Canons to Preachers: A Revolution in Medieval Governance," in *Domenico di Caleruega e la nascita dell'ordine dei frati predicatori* (Spoleto, 2005), 261–295.

4. Two major companion volumes exist, which approach this period in different ways. The volume edited by Kaspar Elm provides a comprehensive introduction, but is organized by order, and many of the contributions are further restricted by region. The newer volume edited by James Mixson and Bert Roest is organized thematically and better represents broader issues and common concerns, but does not supersede the historical background provided by the older volume. See Kaspar Elm (ed.), *Reformbemühungen und Observanzbestrebungen im spätmittelalterlichen Ordenswesen* (Berlin, 1989) and James D. Mixson and Bert Roest (eds), *A Companion to Observant Reform in the Late Middle Ages and Beyond* (Leiden, 2015). See also Mixson's and Roest's review essays: James D. Mixson, "Religious Life and Observant Reform in the Fifteenth Century," *History Compass* 11 (2013): 201–214; Bert Roest, "Observant Reform in Religious Orders," in *The Cambridge History of Christianity*, vol. 4: *Christianity in Western Europe, c. 1100–c. 1500*, ed. Miri Rubin and Walter Simons (Cambridge, 2009), 446–457.

ern historians have anachronistically applied to the past. Within the Dominican order, the reformers in the fifteenth century were already calling their own movement the Observance. At least in Meyer's case this seems to result less from self-branding than from a slippage in meaning from the goal of the movement (observance) to the movement itself (the Observance); it is therefore often difficult to know whether the word should be capitalized in my translation or not. Despite Meyer's unclear use of the term, the historical Observant movement in fact possessed a well-organized political structure that set it clearly apart from the "Conventual" branch of the order, which was just as capable of pursuing reform. The difference was in kind and degree.

The widespread reforming energy of the fifteenth century was inspired by a series of events in the fourteenth century that required resolution or spurred change. Although these circumstances have been characterized as disasters that led to a decline in all spheres of life, the lived historical reality was far more complex. Phenomena that were catastrophic for some could be neutral or even beneficial for others living at that time or in the next generation. The most notable of these events were the Hundred Years War between England and France (1337–1453),[5] the Black Death (in waves from 1347 on),[6] and the Great Western Schism that split Latin Christendom between a pope in Avignon and a pope in Rome (1378–1417).[7] Each of these long-term disruptions is reflected in the *Book of the Reformation*, and Meyer himself explains religious decline in the concrete terms that historians have long found appealing. In book 1, chapters 20–21, for example,[8] Meyer recounts how a series of military campaigns devastated the convent of Schönensteinbach along with its grounds and holdings. Hit subsequently by economic inflation and a mass illness (probably the Black Death), the community was unable to protect itself from the neighbouring friars and families, who seized Schönensteinbach's property in their own attempt to survive. No longer possessing either the personnel or the material support for a religious community, the convent passed into decay.

Though the catastrophes of the fourteenth century did bring crisis to Schönensteinbach, they led indirectly to vibrant renewal across Europe. The Schism was certainly a crisis for the papacy, but it could be argued that the conciliar

5. See Jonathan Sumption, *The Hundred Years War*, 4 vols (Philadelphia, 1991–2015).

6. See Bruce M.S. Campbell, *The Great Transition: Climate, Disease and Society in the Late-Medieval World* (Cambridge, 2016), 289–329.

7. See Joelle Rollo-Koster and Thomas M. Izbicki (eds), *A Companion to the Great Western Schism (1378–1417)* (Leiden, 2009).

8. Parenthetical references to the translation, as well as references in footnotes, will take the form **1.20–21**.

movement, which advocated placing governance in the hands of a council instead of the pope, was healthier for the church at large.[9] While Philip III of Burgundy was switching sides in the Hundred Years War, his court became one of the most renowned centres of artistic production in the history of European art and music.[10] Even the decimation wrought by the Black Death meant that the survivors could appropriate a greater share of the economic resources.[11] In just this way, Schönensteinbach's decline enriched the surrounding religious houses and secular lordships, some of whom stiffly resisted the foundation of the Observant Dominican convent, since it meant relinquishing the income from the holdings they had appropriated (see **2.3–4**).

The misfortunes of the late medieval period did not have simple effects, nor did the reforming efforts have simple causes, despite the grand narrative Meyer and later historians painted of reform as a cosmic battle against the nefarious forces of laziness and lechery. The Observant reform movement was indeed one of the new growths that sprouted from the tilled earth of the fourteenth century, but there is no single crisis of religious life that resulted in its ascendance, and various levels of politics exercised far greater influence than the moralizing grand narrative allows. Each individual convent entered the reform for different reasons and under particular influences. Because convent reform was so dependent on the support of secular authorities, very different kinds of "crises" completely external to the convent could result in the introduction of the Observance.

For example, as Sigrid Hirbodian has shown, the scandalous misbehaviour in the convent of St Agnes in Strasbourg had been largely resolved by an initial reform even before the Observance was introduced. This second reform resulted from a power struggle among the city's elite families, to which many of the nuns belonged.[12] Bernhard Neidiger describes a similar shift in political power in Basel

9. See Gerald Christianson, Thomas M. Izbicki, and Christopher M. Bellitto (eds), *The Church, the Councils, and Reform: The Legacy of the Fifteenth Century* (Washington, DC, 2008).

10. See Wim Blockmans and Anne van Oosterwijk (eds), *Staging the Court of Burgundy* (Turnhout, 2013).

11. Howard Kaminsky, "From Lateness to Waning to Crisis: The Burden of the Later Middle Ages," *Journal of Early Modern History* 4 (2000): 85–125, at 112–120.

12. Sigrid Hirbodian, "Dominikanerinnenreform und Familienpolitik: Die Einführung der Observanz im Kontext städtischer Sozialgeschichte," in *Schreiben und Lesen in der Stadt: Literaturbetrieb im spätmittelalterlichen Straßburg*, ed. Stephen Mossman, Nigel F. Palmer, and Felix Heinzer (Berlin, 2012), 1–16. For a consideration of this episode within a long-view historical context, see Sigrid Hirbodian, "Pastors and Seducers: The Practice of the *Cura monialium* in Mendicant Convents in Strasbourg," in *Partners in Spirit: Women, Men, and Religious Life in Germany, 1100–1500*, ed. Fiona Griffiths and Julie Hotchin (Turnhout, 2014), 303–337, at 314–319.

prior to the 1423 reform of the convent of St Mary Magdalene an den Steinen. The reorganization of power facilitated Basel's contact with the Observant Dominicans when the new city council improved Basel's relationship with the Habsburg noble family, who supported the Observants in nearby Alsace. Reforming the convent of St Mary Magdalene also gave Basel's new authorities the opportunity to exercise greater control over the community. Nevertheless, the new elites framed their initiative as a votive offering to counteract the wars and disturbances of the times through the prayers of the religious women.[13] In a similar case, the Nuremberg city council requested that the city's Dominican friary be reformed to the Observance in 1396. There had been a wave of illness in Nuremberg the year before, but it does not seem to have been the Black Death and was not as devastating as outbreaks of that plague tended to be.[14] A sudden disease-induced crisis in the friary cannot have necessitated the 1396 reform, but it would be fully in line with late medieval practice if the (comparatively mild) wave of "pestilence" prompted the council members to request the reform as an apotropaic measure that would invite God's pleasure and protect them from further disasters.[15] Religious institutions in fact often profited enormously from such incidents by receiving votive gifts and donations or inheritances.[16] Where Meyer presents the spread of the Observance as a pious battle against depravity and deprivation, he is obscuring complex motivations and intersecting circumstances underneath a grand narrative of decline and renewal that is too simple to be true. Pious intentions certainly played a role in the growth of the Obser-

13. Bernhard Neidiger, "Standesgemäßes Leben oder frommes Gebet? Die Haltung der weltlichen Gewalt zur Reform von Frauenklöstern im 15. Jahrhundert," *Rottenburger Jahrbuch für Kirchengeschichte* 22 (2003): 201–220, at 204–205.

14. Amalie Fößel, "Der 'Schwarze Tod' in Franken 1348–1350," *Mitteilungen des Vereins für Geschichte der Stadt Nürnberg* 74 (1987): 1–75, at 12–17.

15. Connecting this reform intention to the plague must remain pure speculation. No record survives in which the Nuremberg city council explains its motivation for requesting the reform. See Bernhard Neidiger, "Selbstverständnis und Erfolgschancen der Dominikanerobservanten: Beobachtungen in der Provinz Teutonia und im Basler Konvent," *Rottenburger Jahrbuch für Kirchengeschichte* 17 (1998): 67–122, at 79–80.

16. Bernhard Neidiger demonstrated this phenomenon in Basel through a careful study of the financial records of the Dominicans and Franciscans in that city. Despite dramatic declines in the population, donations to the religious houses increased markedly in each year following a plague year. See Bernhard Neidiger, *Mendikanten zwischen Ordensideal und städtischer Realität: Untersuchungen zum wirtschaftlichen Verhalten der Bettelorden in Basel* (Berlin, 1981), 157–159.

vance, but it was above all a political movement both within the Dominican order (as I shall discuss further below) and in the secular governments and families that supported it materially.[17]

Aside from these phenomena of "decline" and the political networks to which the convents belonged, the Observance participated in and contributed directly to two other widespread cultural moments of the fifteenth century: the explosion of lay piety and the rise of Renaissance humanism. Increasing lay piety in the late Middle Ages may have been a response to the natural and economic challenges of the fourteenth century, but it was certainly supported by a rise in the literacy rate.[18] Observant convents enjoyed reciprocal benefits with both urban elites and regional nobility, who were increasingly interested in devotional literature; the convents both received book donations and sold or gave books to laypeople.[19] Perhaps contrary to expectations, the intensification of lay piety in the late Middle Ages also influenced the learned sphere with a movement among university scholars known in German scholarship as *Frömmigkeitstheologie* (the

17. They may also have benefited from it materially, since as Amy Leonard points out, the introduction of the Observance with its ideals of voluntary poverty could give the city council an opportunity to extend financial oversight of the convent. Amy Leonard, *Nails in the Wall: Catholic Nuns in Reformation Germany* (Chicago, 2005), 36–37.

18. Werner Williams-Krapp, "The Erosion of a Monopoly: German Religious Literature in the Fifteenth Century," in *The Vernacular Spirit: Essays on Medieval and Religious Literature*, ed. Renate Blumenfeld-Kosinski, Duncan Robertson, and Nancy Bradley Warren (New York, 2002), 239–259.

19. Bert Roest and Johanneke Uphoff pithily summarize the vibrant culture of piety driven by cooperation between the laity and reformers of various religious orders in their Introduction to *Religious Orders and Religious Identity Formation, ca. 1420–1620: Discourses and Strategies of Observance and Pastoral Engagement* (Leiden, 2016), 1–12, at 2–4. For examples of book exchange, see Antje Willing (ed.), *Die Bibliothek des Klosters St. Katharina zu Nürnberg: Synoptische Darstellung der Bücherverzeichnisse* (Berlin, 2012), xxv–xxx; Balázs J. Nemes, "*Dis buch ist iohannes schedelin*: Die Handschriften eines Colmarer Bürgers aus der Mitte des 15. Jahrhunderts und ihre Verflechtungen mit dem Literaturangebot der Dominikanerobservanz," in *Kulturtopographie des deutschsprachigen Südwestens im späteren Mittelalter: Studien und Texte*, ed. Barbara Fleith and René Wetzel (Berlin, 2009), 157–214; Klaus Graf, "Ordensreform und Literatur in Augsburg während des 15. Jahrhunderts," in *Literarisches Leben in Augsburg während des 15. Jahrhunderts*, ed. Johannes Janota and Werner Williams-Krapp (Tübingen, 1995), 100–159; Karin Schneider, "Die Bibliothek des Katharinenklosters in Nürnberg und die städtische Gesellschaft," in *Studien zum städtischen Bildungswesen des späten Mittelalters und der frühen Neuzeit: Bericht über Kolloquien der Kommission zur Erforschung der Kultur des Spätmittelalters, 1978 bis 1981*, ed. Bernd Moeller et al. (Göttingen, 1983), 70–83.

theology of piety).[20] The adherents of this movement prioritized matters of practical pastoral concern over abstruse scholastic investigations. There was a flourishing of literary genres that supported lay piety and pastoral care, such as guides for penitence, or treatises on the "discernment of spirits," which provided advice on how to evaluate visions and revelations.[21] Supported by the patronage of Austrian nobility, this movement found particular expression at the University of Vienna, where Meyer's idol, Johannes Nider, was trained.[22] A sizeable faction of fifteenth-century university scholars belonging to this "Vienna School" put their knowledge at the service of lay devotion, providing translations for engaged nobles and handbooks for less educated confessors and clerics.

The focus on university learning in the service of practical piety made theologians of the Vienna School natural allies of the religious reforms which advocated for spiritual renewal through devout observance. I have already mentioned Johannes Nider, a prominent Observant Dominican friar who was educated at the University of Vienna. The Vienna School, in the person of university theologian and ducal confessor Nikolaus of Dinkelsbühl, also fostered the contemporary Benedictine reform movement which spread from the nearby Melk Abbey.[23] Reformers from different religious orders exchanged ideas and texts with each other and with university theologians, as is evident from the patterns of ownership and transmission of the texts they wrote.[24] Laypeople, university

20. Berndt Hamm, "Was ist Frömmigkeitstheologie? Überlegungen zum 14. bis 16. Jahrhundert," in *Praxis pietatis: Beiträge zu Theologie und Frömmigkeit in der frühen Neuzeit*, ed. Hans-Jörg Nieden and Marcel Nieden (Stuttgart, 1999), 9–45.

21. Meyer incorporates a passage drawing on this genre into **3.3**. See that section for relevant scholarship in English.

22. For Meyer's praise of Nider, see **4.18–22**. For the Vienna School of pastoral theology, see William J. Courtenay, "From Dinkelsbühl's *Questiones Communes* to the Vienna Group Commentary: The Vienna 'School', 1415-1425," in *Nicholas of Dinkelsbühl and the Sentences at Vienna in the Early Fifteenth Century*, ed. Monica Brinzei (Turnhout, 2015), 267–316; Klaus Wolf, *Hof – Universität – Laien: Literatur- und sprachgeschichtliche Untersuchungen zum deutschen Schrifttum der Wiener Schule des Spätmittelalters* (Wiesbaden, 2006); Ernst Haberkern, *Die "Wiener Schule" der Pastoraltheologie im 14. und 15. Jahrhundert: Entstehung, Konstitutionen, literarische Wirkung* (Göppingen, 2003).

23. For a study in English that deals with Melk in the broader context of fifteenth-century reform, see James D. Mixson, "Contesting Authority and Community: Models and Practices of Monastic Reform in Late Medieval Central Europe," *Austrian History Yearbook* 41 (2010): 30–47.

24. For example, numerous abbeys associated with the Melk reform movement owned copies of the Observant Dominican Johannes Nider's vernacular sermon cycle *The Twenty-Four Golden Harps*; see Margit Brand, *Studien zu Johannes Niders deutschen Schriften* (Rome, 1998), 110–111. Thomas Peuntner's *Büchlein von der Liebhabung Gottes*, which was strongly

scholars, and religious reformers thus supported each other in composing, copying, and distributing pious literature.

Less concerned with practical matters, the humanist movement strove for the recovery of ancient Greek and Roman texts and held up both the ethics and the rhetorical style of these texts as models for the (late medieval) present. It is a common misconception that humanism was incompatible with Christian culture and the Catholic church, because it advocated a return to a culture, literature, and ethics that predated Christianity and diverted focus away from God towards the human. In fact, many religious reformers saw the humanist ideal of a return to the Roman "Golden Age" as eminently compatible with the return to their order's own "Golden Age."[25] Not all humanists were religious reformers and not all Observants were humanists, but the interaction between these two movements – even in cases of opposition – was culturally fruitful.[26] The Observant reform was thus not an isolated phenomenon pursued by marginal religious fanatics; rather, it was an integral part of a vast cultural movement of renewal, education, and faith, which was subject to the pressures and profits of individual conviction and political manoeuvring.

The Observant Reform

Meyer belonged to the group of friars that Hillenbrand identified as the "third generation" of Dominican Observant reformers, who shepherded the movement to its heyday. The *Book of the Reformation,* finished in 1468 with additions up to 1477, covers a significant portion of the movement's history, at least for southern Germany, but it stops just short of the greatest Observant

associated with Melk Benedictine reform circles, was also widely received in Observant Dominican convents, but not among Dominican friars; see Thomas Peuntner, *Büchlein von der Liebhabung Gottes,* ed. Bernhard Schnell (Munich, 1984), 248.

25. Probably the most famous humanist monk was Johannes Trithemius, who belonged to the German reforming Benedictine network known as the Bursfelde Congregation. See Noel L. Brann, *The Abbot Trithemius (1462–1516): The Renaissance of Monastic Humanism* (Leiden, 1981). For more on German humanists, religion, and reform, see David J. Collins, *Reforming Saints: Saints' Lives and Their Authors in Germany, 1470–1530* (Oxford, 2008); Franz Posset, *Renaissance Monks: Monastic Humanism in Six Biographical Sketches* (Leiden, 2005).

26. Anne Huijbers shows humanist influence among both Observant and Conventual Dominicans with a focus on history writing in Italy. See Anne Huijbers, *Zealots for Souls: Dominican Narratives of Self-Understanding during Observant Reforms, c. 1388–1517* (Berlin, 2018), 283–321.

triumphs. Even near the beginning of the account, however, Meyer's narrative covers only a small strand of the Observant movement's development. So that readers can more easily locate within the chronicle's timeline the persons and places that Meyer mentions, the appendix to this volume includes a historical table with the names and dates of the Dominican masters general and provincial priors of Teutonia from the beginning of the Observant movement to 1500, as well as a table with the dates of the reforms in Teutonia during that time.

Of the mendicant orders, the Franciscans were the first to embark on an Observant reform, although it began fairly quietly with the foundation of a hermitage outside Foligno in 1368. Between 1390 and 1400, reform either spread to or arose independently among Franciscan communities in France and Spain,[27] but the Franciscan Observance did not reach German-speaking regions until the reform of the Heidelberg friary in 1426.[28] In contrast, southern Germany was the region that witnessed both the earliest establishment and, in the long term, the greatest success of Observant reform within the Dominican order.[29] The Dominican Observance began in 1389 when Master General Raymond of Capua appointed Conrad of Prussia (de Grossis) prior of the Colmar friary. Conrad had apparently caused an uproar at the 1388 general chapter in Vienna, earning the support of the master general for his reform project. Raymond's letters regarding the establishment of the Colmar friary as a haven of observance survive,[30] but the acts of the Vienna general chapter do not, making Meyer's account in this chronicle our best source of information for the spectacular beginning of the Dominican Observance (see **4.3**).

Although the movement was begun by friars, Dominican nuns also played a formative role in the Observance, despite barriers to their mobility and communication. Schönensteinbach, founded in 1397, was not the first Observant women's convent of the Dominican order; that honour goes to Corpus Domini in Venice, founded in 1394 by Conrad of Prussia's Italian counterpart, Giovanni

27. Duncan B. Nimmo, "The Franciscan Regular Observance: The Culmination of Medieval Franciscan Reform," in *Reformbemühungen und Observanzbestrebungen im spätmittelalterlichen Ordenswesen*, ed. Kaspar Elm (Berlin, 1989), 189–205, at 194–195.

28. Paul L. Nyhus, *The Franciscans in South Germany, 1400–1530: Reform and Revolution* (Philadelphia, 1975), 12.

29. Claire Taylor Jones, *Ruling the Spirit: Women, Liturgy, and Dominican Reform in Late Medieval Germany* (Philadelphia, 2018), 88–89.

30. See Raymond of Capua, *Opuscula et litterae* (Rome, 1899), 117–119; Daniel-Antonin Mortier, *Histoire des maîtres généraux de l'ordre des Frères prêcheurs*, 8 vols (Paris, 1902–1922), 3: 528–530.

Dominici.[31] Yet while the Observant friars of different provinces interacted periodically at the general chapters, and in the 1440s even began to hold separate Observant summits,[32] the women's Observant movement remained largely regional. This was due in part to language barriers, but mainly to the strictures of enclosure, which required nuns to remain "enclosed" within their convents and limited their contact with the outside world. The Dominican Constitutions for sisters made no provision for a legislative body of assembled representatives analogous to the general chapters of the friars. Thus, Italian Observant nuns, for example, could influence their German sisters only through the networks of the friars who oversaw them.

Differing regional circumstances also influenced women's experience and pursuit of the Observant reform. Southern Germany in particular was set apart by its population of Dominican women. The Dominican province of Teutonia, encompassing the southern German-speaking regions from Alsace to Austria, was unique among Dominican territories for its enormous proportion of women's convents in relation to the number of friaries. When the northern German province of Saxonia separated from Teutonia in 1303, Teutonia included forty-seven friaries and sixty-five convents, whereas Saxonia had forty-five friaries and nine convents.[33] The unusually large number of women Dominicans in Teutonia raises the question of whether they had a direct impact on the progress and success of the reform there. Although the support of local nobility and city

31. Raymond of Capua appointed Conrad prior of Colmar and Giovanni Dominici lector of San Zanipolo in Venice, in which capacities they were responsible for reforming the first friaries and convents in their respective provinces. See Bartolomea Riccoboni, *Life and Death in a Venetian Convent: The Chronicle and Necrology of Corpus Domini, 1395–1436*, trans. Daniel Ethan Bornstein (Chicago, 2000), 4–5; Nirit Ben-Aryeh Debby, "The Preacher's Agenda: A Dominican versus the Italian Renaissance," *The European Legacy* 20 (2015): 462–476, at 464. For women in the Italian Observance, see also Sylvie Duval, "The Observance's Women: New Models of Sanctity and Religious Discipline for the Female Dominican Observance Movement during the Fifteenth Century," in *Religious Orders and Religious Identity Formation, ca. 1420–1620*, ed. Bert Roest and Johanneke Uphoff (Leiden, 2016), 13–31; Duval, *Comme des anges sur terre: Les moniales dominicaines et les débuts de la réforme observante, 1385–1461* (Rome, 2015); Tamar Herzig, *Savonarola's Women: Visions and Reform in Renaissance Italy* (Chicago, 2008).

32. See Claudia Engler, *Regelbuch und Observanz: Der Codex A 53 der Burgerbibliothek Bern als Reformprogramm des Johannes Meyer für die Berner Dominikanerinnen* (Berlin, 2017), 268.

33. Paulus von Loe, *Statistisches über die Ordensprovinz Teutonia* (Leipzig, 1907), 7; Paulus von Loe, *Statistisches über die Ordensprovinz Saxonia* (Leipzig, 1910), 11–12. By 1500, a further nine friaries were either founded or transferred to Teutonia, some of which did not last. See the table in the appendix.

councils played a crucial role in the Observant success in Teutonia, Meyer's chronicle certainly shows the degree to which Dominican nuns actively participated in and promoted the movement.[34]

Despite the early support of prominent nobility, such as the duchess of Further Austria, Catherine of Burgundy, the Dominican Observance grew slowly at first, proceeding in fits and starts.[35] The master general of the order, Raymond of Capua, demanded only one reformed friary per province, a fairly modest measure. Conrad of Prussia, however, did not rest with Colmar but strove to spread the Observance to other friaries in Teutonia. He managed to reform the Nuremberg friary in 1396, but this success was overshadowed by a series of failures. Before 1400, six convents and one friary foiled attempts to introduce the Observance.[36] (Meyer passes over these events in silence.) After these early failures, the Observance stagnated until a second generation of reformers flourished after the election of Bartholomew Texery as master general in 1426 and Nicolaus Notel as provincial prior of Teutonia in 1428. These two men supported Johannes Nider in the back-to-back reforms of what would become the two most important Observant communities: the convent of St Catherine in Nuremberg (1428) and the Basel friary (1429), which was to become Johannes Meyer's chosen home.[37]

Under this leadership, the Dominican order in the 1430s witnessed a wave of Observant reforms, which fell off sharply in the 1440s. The success of the move-

34. Numerous studies have demonstrated the important role of Dominican nuns in both propagating and shaping the southern German Observance. Stefanie Monika Neidhardt, *Autonomie im Gehorsam: Die dominikanische Observanz in Selbstzeugnissen geistlicher Frauen des Spätmittelalters* (Berlin, 2017); Heike Uffmann, *Wie in einem Rosengarten: Monastische Reformen des späten Mittelalters in den Vorstellungen von Klosterfrauen* (Bielefeld, 2008); Anne Winston-Allen, *Convent Chronicles: Women Writing about Women and Reform in the Late Middle Ages* (University Park, 2004).

35. For thorough accounts of the Observant reform in Teutonia, see Engler, *Regelbuch*; Bernhard Neidiger, "Die Observanzbewegungen der Bettelorden in Südwestdeutschland," *Rottenburger Jahrbuch für Kirchengeschichte* 11 (1992): 175–196; Eugen Hillenbrand, "Die Observantenbewegung in der deutschen Ordensprovinz der Dominikaner," in *Reformbemühungen und Observanzbestrebungen im spätmittelalterlichen Ordenswesen*, ed. Kaspar Elm (Berlin, 1989), 219–271; Annette Barthelmé, *La réforme dominicaine au XVe siècle en Alsace et dans l'ensemble de la province de Teutonie* (Strasbourg, 1931).

36. Engler, *Regelbuch*, 231.

37. The timing of the Basel friary's reform reveals the interrelationship of reform movements within the religious orders and throughout the church at large. The Dominican order reformed the Basel friary in anticipation of the council held in Basel from 1431 to 1449. See Dieter Mertens, "Reformkonzilien und Ordensreform im 15. Jahrhundert," in *Reformbemühungen und Observanzbestrebungen im spätmittelalterlichen Ordenswesen*, ed. Kaspar Elm (Berlin, 1989), 431–457.

ment, especially in Italy, gave rise to separatist sentiment: the Italian Observants did not wish to be subject to moral inferiors who happened to be their institutional superiors within the Dominican order.[38] The German Observants, by contrast, swore continued loyalty and submission to the master general and general chapter, but Italian politics had repercussions for the entire order. Once the Italians succeeded in gaining papal approval for a second Observant apparatus of governance, internal to the order and parallel to the pre-existing hierarchy, other provinces with strong Observant contingents followed suit. The independent Observant Congregation of Lombardy was set up by papal intervention in 1459, followed shortly by the deposition of Master General Martial Auribelli in 1462. His successor, Conrad of Asti, lost no time in promoting the Observance. The Congregation of Holland was formed in 1464 and the Congregation of Teutonia confirmed in 1465.[39] By this time, the third wave of reforms was well underway. Master General Conrad of Asti and the sympathetic provincial prior Peter Wellen had entrusted the rapid reform of German convents to three capable men associated with the Basel friary: Heinrich Schretz, Johannes Hohenloch, and Johannes Meyer.[40] By 1475, through the efforts of these three friars and the support of enthusiastic lords and city councils, enough German friaries had either been reformed or founded that the Observants had the majority in the province and elected their candidate, Jakob of Stubach, as the provincial prior of Teutonia. Counting conservatively, by 1500 there were fifty-three friaries in Teutonia, thirty-three of which were Observant.[41] Understandably, but lamentably, Meyer's account of the Observant movement in the *Book of the Reformation* peters out between 1468 and 1477, which is around the time when his own direct involvement in the reforms intensified.

38. For the formation of the Observant Congregation of Lombardy, see Raymond Creytens and A. d'Amato, "Les actes capitulaires de la congrégation dominicaine de Lombardie (1482–1531)," *AFP* 31 (1961): 213–306, at 234–238.

39. Mortier, *Histoire des maitres généraux*, 4: 437–454; Petrus Franciscus Wolfs, "Dominikanische Observanzbestrebungen: Die *Congregatio Hollandiae*," in *Reformbemühungen und Observanzbestrebungen im spätmittelalterlichen Ordenswesen*, ed. Kaspar Elm (Berlin, 1989), 273–292; Gabriel M. Löhr, *Die Teutonia im 15. Jahrhundert: Studien und Texte vornehmlich zur Geschichte ihrer Reform* (Leipzig, 1924), 94–97.

40. Engler, *Regelbuch*, 294–295.

41. Claudia Heimann, "Der Umfang der Dominikanerprovinz Teutonia im späteren Mittelalter," *AFP* 75 (2005): 233–257. It is far more difficult to determine the number of Dominican convents, because many communities following the Constitutions for Dominican Sisters were not officially incorporated into the order, but were under the jurisdiction of their local bishop. For German Dominicans at the end of the Middle Ages, see also Bernward Springer, *Die deutschen Dominikaner in Widerstand und Anpassung während der Reformationszeit* (Berlin, 1999), 11–45.

Friar Johannes Meyer

Johannes Meyer was born in Zurich in 1422 and entered the Dominican friary there in 1432.[42] Ten years later, he transferred from his unreformed home community to the friary in Basel, a prominent centre of the Observance. Evidently destined for the care of souls (and possibly prevented by poor health), he did not receive formal higher education. Instead, after his ordination as a priest, he spent almost his entire career as a confessor to Observant women's communities. Meyer did compose works in Latin, the most important of which are the *Chronica brevis ordinis praedicatorum* (Short Chronicle of the Dominican Order) and his *Liber de illustribus viris* (Book of Illustrious Men).[43] But the bulk of his literary output was devoted to providing Dominican nuns with access to historical sources, as well as to the rules, ordinances, papal privileges, and other normative documents that informed the Observant way of life.

Although Meyer was likely already pursuing archival history while training at Basel, his life's work truly began with his first assignment in 1454 as confessor to the convent of St Michael in Bern. The community had been reformed fifteen years earlier, but he apparently discovered a shocking lack of textual resources for the women's spiritual – and practical – governance.[44] During his first year in Bern, Meyer adapted the *Book of Duties* composed by Humbert of Romans (d. 1277), translating it into German and modifying it to apply directly to the par-

42. Sarah DeMaris's Introduction to her edition of Meyer's *Book of Duties* contains a thorough account of his life and works: see *Das Amptbuch*, ed. Sarah Glenn DeMaris (Rome, 2015), 1–145. See also Werner Fechter, "Meyer, Johannes OP," *VL*² 6: 474–489 and Wolfram Schneider-Lastin, "Meyer, Johannes [Nachtr.]," *VL*² 11: 1003–1004.

43. Although each of these works survives in only one manuscript, this sparsity is no indication of meagre influence. Anne Huijbers has shown that Meyer served as an important source for sixteenth-century Dominican historians: see Huijbers, *Zealots*, 166–167, and Anne Huijbers, "*De viris illustribus ordinis praedicatorum*: A 'Classical' Genre in Dominican Hands," *Franciscan Studies* 71 (2013): 297–324.

44. The dearth of new spiritual literature for Observant women almost sixty years after the foundation of Schönensteinbach is surprising. Regina Schiewer has commented that the Observant Dominican friars were very slow to respond to the textual needs of their sisters and argues that the explosive fifteenth-century transmission of earlier German Dominican literature resulted from women taking matters into their own hands. See Regina D. Schiewer, "Sermons for Nuns of the Dominican Observance Movement," in *Medieval Monastic Preaching*, ed. Carolyn Muessig (Leiden, 1998), 75–92, at 90. For the *loci classici* on Observant transmission of fourteenth-century devotional literature, see the essays collected in Werner Williams-Krapp, *Geistliche Literatur des späten Mittelalters: Kleine Schriften* (Tübingen, 2012).

ticular situation of Observant Dominican nuns. Claudia Engler has argued persuasively that Meyer was also behind the compilation of a manuscript (Bern, Burgerbibliothek, Cod. A 53) containing German translations of the Augustinian Rule,[45] the Constitutions for Dominican Sisters, a partial commentary on the Rule, and numerous documents and ordinances from popes and masters general concerning women Observants. Meyer thus translated and made available both legally binding documents (the Rule and Constitutions etc) and a non-obligatory treatise on governance (the *Book of Duties*). These early works on regulations and practice can to some extent be seen as forerunners of his later writing. The chronicles do not represent a departure from the early regulatory treatises but an expansion into other genres that also provide guidance for religious life.

Meyer already began to explore these other genres while still in Bern. In addition to the *Buch der Ersetzung*, or the *Supplement* (an eclectic compilation of historical material and edifying literature), Meyer's four years there also saw his first German-language historical works. He wrote a *vita* (life narrative) of the mystic Elsbeth Stagel to append to his edition of the Töss convent sisterbook.[46] He also lightly edited the St Katherinental sisterbook, added a new *vita* to the Oetenbach sisterbook, and composed, in collaboration with Prioress Anna of Sissach, a chronicle of the Bern convent of St Michael.

These latter activities are important in our context as a prelude to the *Book of the Reformation*, which draws heavily on the genre of the sisterbook, especially in the books concerning Schönensteinbach. In 1458, Meyer was transferred to Schönensteinbach, where he served as confessor until 1465. Much of the *Book of the Reformation* must have been completed during this period. As confessor at Schönensteinbach, he had direct access not only to documents but also, so he tells us, to the oral history that informed his new project. Although the period Meyer spent at Schönensteinbach was one of peace and stability, many of the tales of the exile and diaspora of the nuns (**2.14–22**) must be second-hand accounts from women who had experienced these trials directly – excepting the account in book 2, chapter 20 of a group's return from Basel in 1446, at which events Meyer could well have been personally present. Meyer did not complete the *Book of the Reformation* until 1468, during his tenure as confessor at the convent of Sylo in Sélestat. This delay gave him the opportunity to include some of the most vibrant accounts, for example, the 1465 Freiburg triple reform (**5.60–**

45. Unlike the Benedictine and the Franciscan orders, the Dominican order did not have its own Rule. Dominicans lived according to the Augustinian Rule, supplemented by constitutions. See Jones, *Ruling the Spirit*, 13–20.

46. See below on the genre of sisterbooks.

66), which he himself orchestrated. The mix of documentary record, oral transmission, and first-hand account is characteristic of the sisterbook genre, with which Meyer had become familiar in Bern.

Meyer did not stop writing after 1468 but rather moved on to other projects. After breaking off work on the *Book of the Reformation,* he composed three more German-language historical works in quick succession. The first of these is the *Lives of the Brethren,* which recounts the lives of the Dominican masters general from Jordan of Saxony (r. 1222–1237) to John of Vercelli (r. 1264–1283), along with other notable contemporary friars. The companion works to this are his *Papal Chronicle,* which recounts papal history from Innocent III (d. 1216) through Paul II (d. 1471), and an *Imperial Chronicle* of the Holy Roman Empire from Frederick Barbarossa (d. 1190) to Frederick III (d. 1493, and still reigning at the time of Meyer's composition).[47] As Sarah DeMaris notes, these texts are important since "together they present a history of the world from the Dominican perspective."[48] Readers of the *Book of the Reformation* will immediately grasp the central importance of papal and imperial politics to the reform movement, and these works communicated to Dominican nuns the ways in which Dominican history was embedded within larger ecclesial and secular histories.

As I mentioned above, the 1470s were a period of intense reforming activity for Meyer. He served stints as confessor at the Observant convents of Liebenau, St Mary Magdalene in Freiburg, and Hasenpfuhl, and he was in the party that reformed the Frankfurt friary in 1474. Meyer then facilitated the sweeping Württemberg reforms of the late 1470s in cooperation with the regional counts, who were determined to reform every convent in their territory.[49] Meyer spent the last three years of his life as confessor at the convent of Adelhausen in Freiburg im Breisgau, where he died in 1485. Even in old age, he did not stop writing, and rough drafts of two further German-language chronicles and an alphabetical reorganization and abbreviation of the Adelhausen sisterbook survive.[50] Meyer ended

47. Christian Seebald's habilitation thesis provides an edition and study of these two chronicles. Christian Seebald, "Reform als Textstrategie: Untersuchungen zum literarischen Oeuvre des Johannes Meyer OP" (habilitation thesis, University of Cologne, 2017). See also Christian Seebald, "Ein Basler Codex mit Schriften des Johannes Meyer: Zugleich ein Beitrag zur Überlieferungs- und Textgeschichte der 'Vitas fratrum,' der 'Pabst-' und der 'Kaiserchronik,'" *ZfdA* 143 (2014): 202–219.

48. DeMaris, Introduction to *Das Amptbuch,* 15.

49. Bernhard Neidiger, *Das Dominikanerkloster Stuttgart, die Kanoniker vom gemeinsamen Leben in Urach und die Gründung der Universität Tübingen: Konkurrierende Reformansätze in der württembergischen Kirchenpolitik am Ausgang des Mittelalters* (Stuttgart, 1993).

50. These drafts are preserved in MS Freiburg im Breisgau, Stadtarchiv, B1 (H) 107.

his life as he had spent the previous thirty years, providing spiritual care for Observant women while combing their archives and writing of their past.[51]

Dominican Structures of Governance

I have repeatedly noted that the support of regional political powers was indispensable to the Observant movement, which could not have carried out its work without the material assistance of city councils or regional lords like the counts of Württemberg just mentioned. In addition to being networked with these secular authorities, the Observants had to operate within the governmental structures of their own order. The Dominican order was led by a master general, who was elected for life, and a representative body with rotating membership. The term "general chapter" may be applied both to the group of people itself and to its meetings. The membership of this body rotated on a three-meeting cycle: two consecutive meetings were attended by elected representatives called definitors, and the provincial priors attended every third.

The order was divided into geographical territories called provinces, each of which was overseen by a provincial prior and a provincial chapter. The provinces were further subdivided into "nations" or vicariates overseen by a regional vicar, who was not elected but appointed by the provincial prior. In the fourteenth and fifteenth centuries, the province of Teutonia had four vicariates: Brabantia (encompassing the Rhineland up to and including Cologne), Alsatia (Alsace and Switzerland), Suevia (Swabia and Franconia), and Bavaria (which included Austria). The vicar could in turn delegate "visitators," whose duty was to visit friaries and convents and to correct deviations or transgressions in lifestyle and adherence to the Dominican governing documents (the Rule, Constitutions, ordinances, etc.). Each friary elected a conventual prior, who oversaw not only his friary but also the smaller local outposts called *termini*. He would also often either be appointed or serve as de facto vicar over the women's convents within his friary's *terminus* district.

Women's convents also elected their own prioress, who, like her male counterpart in the friaries, appointed others to the remaining convent offices. The most important among these were the subprioress, who governed internal convent affairs, and the bursaress, who oversaw the convent's financial matters. This

51. Claire Taylor Jones, "Writing History to Make History: Johannes Meyer's Chronicles of Reform," in *Medieval Cantors and Their Craft: Music, Liturgy and the Shaping of History*, ed. Katie Ann-Marie Bugyis, A.B. Kraebel, and Margot E. Fassler (York, 2017), 340–356.

latter office seems to have been considered excellent training for the post of prioress, and we shall see many former bursaresses sent to become reform prioresses in other convents. Women's convents also often had male bursars (also called procurators or provosts), who assisted the enclosed nuns in negotiating external financial matters. Finally, nuns required confessors to provide them with Mass and confession. Governance thus followed a clear hierarchy, with the master general at the top, supported by (in descending order of authority) provincial priors, national vicars, visitators, conventual priors, confessors, and prioresses.

The Observance threw provincial governance into disarray, as reformed Observant individuals and communities protested being placed under the oversight of unreformed friars whom the Observants judged to be their moral inferiors. The reformers often dealt with this conflict rashly by eschewing, sidestepping, or outright violating the order's democratic mechanisms. From the very beginning of the movement, Observant reformers would forgo elections and impose officers, as we saw with Master General Raymond of Capua's appointment of Conrad of Prussia as prior of Colmar. As the Observant congregations developed, the office of vicar proved a ground for experimentation. In addition to the vicars of the "nations," the provincial prior could appoint a special "reform" vicar to oversee only the Observant communities of the province, as was done in the case of Johannes Nider. Yet the relationships of subordination and authority between these types of vicar remained contentious. This disruption was exacerbated on the local level by the structures of authority over women's convents. Normally, the prior of the nearest friary was responsible for a convent's spiritual and material care, but this arrangement was clearly unacceptable in the case of Observant convents within the *terminus* district of unreformed friaries. The Observants would use the posts of vicar and confessor to remove such convents from the normal structures of authority. Meyer himself, for example, spent many years as confessor to the women's convents in Freiburg while technically remaining a member of the Basel friary, because the Freiburg friary was unreformed. These situations could erupt into violent conflicts, such as the protracted battle between the Observant vicar Heinrich Schretz and the Strasbourg prior Johannes Wolfhard over the convent of St Agnes in Strasbourg (see **5.69** and following chapters). Although a grasp of Dominican governance structures is almost a precondition for understanding some of the events that Meyer relates, the *Book of the Reformation* often vibrantly portrays the negotiations of authority and power that the Observant reformers forced upon their order.

How to Reform a Convent

As fraught as such conflicts of authority were, the consent of the various officials within the Dominican order was not the only approval required for the successful introduction of the Observance to a convent. Respecting broader religious structures, the Observants required the official permission of the pope and they also often sought the blessing of the regional bishop. Yet even with papal approbation in hand, it proved impossible for the Observants to reform a convent without the support of the local secular government, whether that be the city council or the regional lord.[52] A vast apparatus of religious and secular authority needed to work in concert for successful reform.

Meyer's description of the process leading to the triple reform of the Freiburg convents in 1465 provides a fairly good summary of the individuals and hierarchies whose interests and support needed to be coordinated (**5.60–62**). Many reforms were undertaken at the request of the city council or the regional lords, so the Freiburg reforms are unusual in that Meyer claims that the first inspiration was his own, very possibly from reading Anna of Munzingen's sisterbook.[53] Nevertheless, his first action was to approach the regional secular authorities, namely, Duke Sigismund of Austria (1427–1496) and his bailiff, Lord Thüring of Hallwyl (d. 1469). Meyer also enlisted the support of the bishops of both Constance and Basel, thereby uniting the secular and religious regional authorities external to the Dominican order. Especially in a city where the friary was not reformed, it would have been impossible to reform the convent without the consent and the resources of these secular and religious lords.

With the support and financial backing of these local powers, Meyer could begin to assemble the permissions that were bureaucratically necessary. Each stage of the process was a carefully orchestrated demonstration of the support already given, calculated to make it difficult to refuse. First, the duke, the mayor, and both bishops wrote letters to the Dominican master general, as did the prior of the Basel friary. The prior of Gebweiler then brought these messages to the

52. The convent of St Mary in Rothenburg ob der Tauber provides a typical case of Observant failure in the face of political conflict between the city council and the regional nobility, both of which were trying to use the convent as a pawn in their power struggle. Engler, *Regelbuch*, 233–236.

53. When Meyer first introduces the Adelhausen convent in Freiburg, he mentions Anna of Munzingen's fourteenth-century work. In the following chapter, he recounts that he was contemplating "the worthy convent of Adelhausen and its former holiness" when inspired to restore it to religious life (**5.61**). Meyer drew on this genre of the sisterbook for the *Book of the Reformation*, as I discuss further below.

master general in Paris, thereby signalling the support of two relatively close friaries, as well as the regional lords. With the master general's blessing, the Observants then approached the provincial prior, enlisting a representative of yet another local house to demonstrate support, namely, a lay brother from Schönensteinbach. This man was likely sent in order to affirm Schönensteinbach's willingness to provide a reform contingent from within their ranks (which they did: see **5.65**). After the provincial approved, the well-travelled prior of Gebweiler then took the request to Rome and returned with the permission of the papal curia. Each of these journeys was expensive and, given that Observant Dominicans were not supposed to have private resources, Meyer also had to raise funds and duly records who donated the money to fund the messengers.

Even with the permission of these three individuals (the master general, the provincial prior, and the pope), the Observants still needed the consent of two groups and the material support of three more: the general chapter, the Freiburg nuns, and the three Observant convents who would assist in their reform. Rather than delegating one of the Observant friars who was already slated to attend the general chapter, the reforming initiative had Duke Sigismund of Austria send a secular messenger to press the affair. In order to cow the women, Johannes Meyer orchestrated an intimidating show of force. He visited each convent several times, accompanied by six bodyguards and a changing kaleidoscope of city notables, including "Freiburg city council members, doctors, teachers, and masters of the university in Freiburg, and even the two priors and some of the fathers of the Carthusian and Augustinian communities, which are reformed there" (**5.66**). This company of thirty or forty men presented a united front as both Johannes Meyer and Thüring of Hallwyl preached the virtues and rewards of reform. Meanwhile, the Freiburg city council and the bailiff Thüring of Hallwyl wrote to the convents of St Mary Magdalene in Basel and St Catherine in Colmar to request reforming contingents. These convents would need not only to select and part with capable sisters but also to furnish these reformers with a set of liturgical books they could use to perform the Divine Office until their new convent had acquired or corrected its own.[54] By the time the people of Freiburg turned

54. Gisela Muschiol, "Migrating Nuns - Migrating Liturgy: The Context of Reform in Female Convents of the Late Middle Ages," in *Liturgy in Migration: From the Upper Room to Cyberspace*, ed. Teresa Berger (Collegeville, 2012), 83–100; Julie Hotchin, "Reformatrices and Their Books: Religious Women and Reading Networks in Fifteenth-Century Germany," in *Communities of Learning: Networks and the Shaping of Intellectual Identity in Europe, 1100–1500* (Turnhout, 2011), 251–291; Willing, *Bibliothek*, lxxv–lxxxi; Karin Schneider, "Beziehungen zwischen den Dominikanerinnenklöstern Nürnberg und Altenhohenau im ausgehenden

out to welcome the reforming nuns,[55] hundreds of people had been involved, enormous expenses incurred, and vast distances travelled in the service of the reform.

Meyer's account of the process from inspiration to successful reform in Freiburg is unusually thorough but likely usual in most other respects. The dizzying array of permissions and support that Meyer describes acquiring from the secular government (the duke, his bailiff, and the city council), the religious lords (the bishops of Constance and Basel), the local Observant communities (Gebweiler, Basel, Schönensteinbach, St Mary Magdalene, and St Catherine), the order's authorities (the master general, the provincial prior, and the general chapter), and finally from the pope, would have been necessary for each and every reform. The appearance of men associated with the University of Freiburg seems a rarer feature, but in fact, in places where there were universities, they were often engaged in reform politics.[56] One very important group does not appear in Meyer's account of the Freiburg reforms, namely, the families of the nuns in the convents.[57] In the *Book of the Reformation*, Meyer primarily concentrates on the confessors and nuns directly involved in the final stage of a reform and mentions secular lords only very briefly to thank them for support or to chastise them for impeding. But before every reform mentioned in this chronicle, a vast bureaucratic apparatus involving people from numer-

---

Mittelalter," in *Würzburger Prosastudien II: Untersuchungen zur Literatur und Sprache des Mittelalters*, ed. Peter Kesting (Munich, 1975), 211–218.

55. See my analysis of enclosure ceremonies in Jones, *Ruling the Spirit*, 134–142.

56. I have already mentioned the reformist reputation of the University of Vienna, and the University of Basel played a significant role in the reform council that took place in that city. The foundation of the University of Stuttgart was also bound up with the reforming energies of Count Eberhard V of Württemberg (1445–1496). When the Dominicans founded a new Observant friary in Heidelberg, they instituted a *studium generale*, which they were able to have incorporated into the University of Heidelberg. Gabriel M. Löhr, "Die Dominikaner an der Universität Heidelberg," *AFP* 21 (1951): 272–293, esp. 272–274.

57. Freiburg does seem to have been fairly unusual with regard to the low personal investment of the city council families in the city's Dominican convents. See Madlen Doerr, "Klarissen und Dominikanerinnen in Freiburg im 15. Jahrhundert: Sozialstruktur und Reform" (PhD diss., Universität Freiburg, 2012), 247–255. Sylvie Duval argues from the Italian context that the Observance's stricter version of enclosure was feasible only with the consent of the nuns' family members outside the convent. Sylvie Duval, "*Mulieres religiosae* and *sorores clausae*: The Dominican Observant Movement and the Diffusion of Strict Enclosure in Italy from the Thirteenth to the Sixteenth Century," in *Mulieres religiosae: Shaping Female Spiritual Authority in the Medieval and Early Modern Periods*, ed. Veerle Fraeters and Imke de Gier (Turnhout, 2014), 193–218.

ous social classes and areas of authority needed to grind through multiple stages of approval at significant cost before the reforming party was even selected.

Meyer's Chronicle of the Dominican Reform

This summary of reform procedure gives the impression – often fairly correct – that the nuns had little choice concerning whether their community would be reformed or not. Nevertheless, the *Book of the Reformation* frequently does provide enough information for us to read between the lines or against the grain to locate spheres of female agency, choice, or capacity. Meyer treats the virtues, devotions, and reforming efforts of the Dominican women who spearheaded the Observant reform, both because women's narratives were of great interest to his intended female audience and in order to provide them with role models for their own reformed life. Meyer's treatment of individual women within the narrative, and even his choice of genre for the work, celebrate women's literary abilities and encourage his female readership to pursue educational or literary ambitions, provided they remain under the aegis of the Observance.[58]

Contemporary historians could stand to learn from Meyer's sensitive treatment of women's literacy and intellectual capabilities. Early twentieth-century scholarship on medieval nuns often tied assumptions about women's literacy to the narrative of fourteenth-century decline that I described and challenged above. With regard to the Dominican order, it was assumed that early Dominican nuns knew Latin well but that their level of education dropped precipitously during the catastrophic fourteenth century and never recovered.[59] The assumption that late medieval Dominican nuns knew little or no Latin was so tenacious that it was argued, for example, that Johannes Nider's Latin visitation letters (i.e., follow-

58. Anne Winston-Allen and Meri Heinonen have also pointed out that Meyer generally presents a positive view both of women's own talents and capacities and of collaboration between friars and nuns. Anne Winston-Allen, "Rewriting Women's History: Medieval Nuns' *Vitae* by Johannes Meyer," in *Medieval German Voices in the 21st Century: The Paradigmatic Function of Medieval German Studies for German Studies*, ed. Albrecht Classen (Amsterdam, 2000), 145–154; Meri Heinonen, "Between Friars and Nuns: The Relationships of Religious Men and Women in Johannes Meyer's *Buch der Reformacio Predigerordens*," *Oxford German Studies* 42 (2013): 237–258.

59. Peter Ochsenbein, "Latein und Deutsch im Alltag oberrheinischer Dominikanerinnenklöster des Spätmittelalters," in *Latein und Volkssprache im deutschen Mittelalter, 1100–1500*, ed. Nikolaus Henkel and Nigel F. Palmer (Tübingen, 1992), 42–51.

ups to convent inspections) were meant not for the prioress but for the convent's confessors.[60]

Recent scholarship has repaired this view, on the one hand by recovering more evidence of women's Latin literacy, and on the other by taking a more nuanced view of what constitutes literacy.[61] It is clear to anyone who has learned or taught a foreign language that the answer to the question of how much Latin a medieval nun knew must be different for each individual nun. Furthermore, contemporary foreign language pedagogy recognizes reading comprehension, aural comprehension, written expression, and oral expression as distinct skills that can be developed to different degrees and should be eval-

60. Carl Pfaff, "Bild und Exempel: Die observante Dominikanerin in der Sicht des Johannes Meyer OP," in *Personen der Geschichte, Geschichte der Personen: Studien zur Kreuzzugs-, Sozial- und Bildungsgeschichte*, ed. Christian Hesse et al. (Basel, 2003), 221–235, at 223. Marie-Luise Ehrenschwendtner celebrates Dominican women's German literacy but perpetuates the dim view of their Latin literacy; see Marie-Luise Ehrenschwendtner, "*Puellae litteratae*: The Use of the Vernacular in the Dominican Convents of Southern Germany," in *Medieval Women in Their Communities*, ed. Diane Watt (Toronto, 1997), 49–71, and "A Library Collected by and for the Use of Nuns: St. Catherine's Convent, Nuremberg," in *Women and the Book: Assessing the Evidence*, ed. Jane H.M. Taylor and Lesley Smith (London, 1997), 123–132. For a counterargument, see Eva Schlotheuber, "Bücher und Bildung in den Frauengemeinschaften der Bettelorden," in *Nonnen, Kanonissen und Mystikerinnen: Religiöse Frauengemeinschaften in Süddeutschland*, ed. Eva Schlotheuber, Helmut Flachenecker, and Ingrid Gardill (Göttingen, 2008), 241–262. The evidence for women's literacy in the northern Dominican province of Saxonia is quite different from that of southern German Dominican nuns. There were fewer convents overall in Saxonia, and the surviving manuscripts reveal continued creative expression in Latin without an analogous blossoming of German literature. See Jeffrey F. Hamburger et al., *Liturgical Life and Latin Learning at Paradies bei Soest, 1300–1425: Inscription and Illumination in the Choir Books of a North German Dominican Convent*, 2 vols (Münster, 2017); Jeffrey F. Hamburger and Eva Schlotheuber, "Books in Women's Hands: Liturgy, Learning and the Libraries of Dominican Nuns in Westphalia," in *Entre stabilité et itinérance: Livres et culture des ordres mendiants XIIIe–XVe siècle*, ed. Nicole Bériou, Martin Morard, and Donatella Nebbiai (Turnhout, 2014), 129–157.

61. For my own view on this matter, see Jones, *Ruling the Spirit*, 5–8 and 73–76; Claire Taylor Jones, "Rekindling the Light of Faith: Hymn Translation and Spiritual Renewal in the Fifteenth-Century Observant Reform," *Journal of Medieval and Early Modern Studies* 42 (2012): 567–596. For a collection of studies that covers a broad temporal and geographical range within the European Latin Middle Ages, see the three volumes of conference proceedings edited by Virgina Blanton, Veronica O'Mara, and Patricia Stoop: *Nuns' Literacies in Medieval Europe: The Hull Dialogue* (Turnhout, 2013); *Nuns' Literacies in Medieval Europe: The Kansas City Dialogue* (Turnhout, 2015); *Nuns' Literacies in Medieval Europe: The Antwerp Dialogue* (Turnhout, 2017).

uated separately.[62] For medieval nuns, musical literacy would also have been an important aspect of their daily engagement with the Latin language, which they most often encountered in liturgical contexts.[63] Research into the linguistic competencies of women in the past must take this differentiated view of language learning into account in order to understand the full spectrum of medieval literacies.

In his accounts of Observant women, Meyer provides just such a differentiated view of skills, literacies, and intellectual competencies that reflects the innate abilities as well as the education levels of the women he commemorates. Although none of the women in the *Book of the Reformation* speak Latin or write original texts in it,[64] several understand it, translate it, and copy it accurately. In most cases, Meyer associates these abilities directly with liturgical practice. Katharina Langmantel, for example, both understands and sings Latin well (**3.29**); Clara of Ostren is responsible for correcting liturgical books (**3.10**); and Lukardis of Ingen (**2.11** and **3.26**) and Magdalena Franckengrüner (**5.44**) are celebrated as gifted copyists of beautiful and accurate choir books.[65] Meyer treats oral production (i.e., singing the liturgy) and written production (i.e., copying and correcting accurate choir books) as distinct skills that reflect Latin language ability and support the liturgical life of the convent in different ways.

62. The Common European Framework of Reference includes spoken interaction as a fifth skill related to but not identical with spoken production. I thank Ann Marie Rasmussen for encouraging me to make the connection to contemporary language pedagogy explicit.

63. Katherine Zieman, "Reading, Singing and Understanding: Constructions of the Literacy of Women Religious in Late Medieval England," in *Learning and Literacy in Medieval England and Abroad,* ed. Sarah Rees Jones (Turnhout, 2003), 97–120; Anne Bagnall Yardley, "The Musical Education of Young Girls in Medieval English Nunneries," in *Young Choristers 650–1700,* ed. Susan Boynton and Eric Rice (Woodbridge, 2008), 49–67.

64. This omission does not indicate that Meyer thought women were inherently incapable of written and oral production in Latin. In other works he praises women who composed histories and letters in Latin and apparently used that language to communicate orally with Dominican friars from foreign countries; however, his relegation of these women to the past accords with the narrative of educational decline. See Jones, "Writing History," 354–355.

65. For more on Dominican women as scribes and illuminators, see Anne Winston-Allen, "Outside the Mainstream: Women as Readers, Scribes, and Illustrators of Books in Convents of the German-Speaking Regions," in *Nuns' Literacies in Medieval Europe: The Kansas City Dialogue,* ed. Virginia Blanton, Veronica O'Mara, and Patricia Stoop (Turnhout, 2015), 191–206; Anne Winston-Allen, "Networking in Medieval Strasbourg: Cross-Order Collaboration in Book Illustration among Women's Reformed Convents," in *Schreiben und Lesen in der Stadt,* ed. Mossman, Palmer, and Heinzer, 197–212; Cynthia J. Cyrus, *The Scribes for Women's Convents in Late Medieval Germany* (Toronto, 2009).

However, Meyer does not always associate Latin ability explicitly with the liturgy, and acknowledges ways in which even illiterate women support and participate in Latin-literate culture. He credits Lukardis of Ingen with understanding the art of grammar and remarks that she can translate Latin elegantly into German (**3.26**), as can Claranna of Hohenburg (**3.5**). It is unclear precisely what kinds of texts Lukardis and Claranna read and translated, but liturgical texts would not have been the only Latin literature available. Indeed, Magdalena Bechrer, although herself Latin-illiterate, commissioned Latin books for the confessors' library at her own expense (**3.39**) so that the confessors would have more preaching material. Whether or not the confessors lent their Latin texts to the sisters, they did discuss these texts with them, as is evident from Meyer's extensive praise for the fully illiterate lay sister Elisabeth Griss. Despite her lack of formal education, Elisabeth had an extraordinary memory and an incisive intelligence: as the confessor Heinrich Fabri attests, "she had such an enlightened reason that she surpassed many great schoolmen in understanding" (**3.34**). Each of these cases represents a concern with transmitting Latin culture to the Latin-illiterate sisters, whether mediated by confessors or by Latin-literate sisters. These examples demonstrate the variety of forms that participation in Latin literature and culture could take. Direct engagement with Latin primary texts was only one way to participate in Latin textual culture, which was also supported by female patronage and accessed through translation and discussion.

From translation to copying to commission to conversation, Meyer's account of women's engagement with Latin-language texts and culture encompasses a broad range of activities. Notably, literacy – in the sense of the ability to read written literary texts in the language in question – is one of the skills he attributes to women, but the forms of engagement with Latin culture are numerous and differentiated. Meyer seems to distinguish liturgical Latin from other Latin literature and to treat access to these corpora as distinct skills. Furthermore, knowledge of Latin (or for that matter even German literacy) is not a prerequisite for intelligent, high-level engagement with Latin literature and philosophy. Modern readers would do well to learn from Meyer's expansive treatment of the skills and competencies of medieval women.

Indeed, the very genre Meyer chose for this project – the sisterbook – is a genre of women's writing. Produced within, for, and about various southern German Dominican convents in the fourteenth century, a sisterbook is a collection of exemplary life narratives of sisters who lived in a given convent, prefaced by that convent's foundation history.[66] Meyer was deeply familiar with the genre,

66. Gertrud Jaron Lewis, *By Women, for Women, about Women: The Sister-Books of Fourteenth-Century Germany* (Toronto, 1996).

having edited several of them before embarking on this work.[67] The *Book of the Reformation* follows the structure of a sisterbook, but doubles each part of the characteristic two-part structure: the foundation history is split into two books, one concerning the earliest foundation of Schönensteinbach, the other treating its transfer to the Dominican order and the foundation of the Observant women's community. The collection of *vitae* is similarly doubled into one book praising the lives of the first generation of Observant Dominican sisters, the other commemorating the Dominican friars who supported the community and are for the most part buried there. The doubled sisterbook structure then explodes in the sprawling book 5, which opens the convent of Schönensteinbach onto the whole community of all reformed Dominican convents in southern Germany. From this more expansive notion of community, Meyer continually switches to a more personal level, including praise for individual exemplary women. His sensitivity to the interests and activities of the nuns makes the *Book of the Reformation* a work of women's history in three senses: it is a history written *for* women in a language they could easily access and one that attends to their concerns and needs; it is, to a great extent, *about* women and their role in fostering the reform; and it is written in a genre developed *by* women a century earlier to record their own histories.[68]

Meyer was himself a zealous reformer, and his account is coloured by his own investment and personal involvement in returning the Dominican order to the ideals of poverty, piety, and enclosure. This tangible passion has made Meyer one of those historical figures whom scholars either love or hate, but whatever the reaction to his authorial personality, all acknowledge an immense debt to his archival labour and his preservation of oral history. Many of the letters and accounts that he reproduces in this chronicle are otherwise lost, making it an invaluable historical resource, albeit a polemical one that should be approached

67. Sarah Glenn DeMaris, "Anna Muntprat's Legacy for the Zoffingen Sisters: A Second Copy of the Unterlinden *Schwesternbuch*," *ZfdA* 144 (2015): 359–378, at 375–376; Jones, *Ruling the Spirit*, 60–62; Ruth Meyer, *Das "St. Katharinentaler Schwesternbuch": Untersuchung, Edition, Kommentar* (Tübingen, 1995), 66–68.

68. Gertrud Jaron Lewis articulates this triple indebtedness to women: see Lewis, *By Women*, 56. The earlier sisterbooks have the advantage over Meyer's text that they were also composed by women. That said, the manuscript transmission of the *Book of the Reformation* reveals heavy editing by female hands: a study of women's authorial agency in redacting Meyer's text would be richly rewarding. For a list of the excerpts selected by the St Gallen nuns for the Inzigkofen manuscript, see Werner Fechter, *Deutsche Handschriften des 15. und 16. Jahrhunderts aus der Bibliothek des ehemaligen Augustinerchorfrauenstifts Inzigkofen* (Sigmaringen, 1997), 119.

cautiously. Meyer's account of Schönensteinbach and the spread of reform from behind its walls is not an objective record of historical realities but a heavily biased attempt to inspire and persuade his readers to join him in reforming the Dominican order to the Observance.

Although Meyer's open investment in his story may sometimes seem alienating to readers accustomed to modern academic history writing, his practice of historiography is more familiar than it may seem at first glance. Historians today pursue a dual ideal of coherence and objective accuracy, striving to reconstruct an orderly representation and plausible explanation of what happened in the past by drawing on surviving archival sources, narrative accounts, and archaeological and material evidence. In academic historiography – less so in popular histories – historians are expected to provide the reader with enough information on these sources that the reader could locate and examine them, and draw her own conclusions, in a process conceptually similar to the ideal reproducibility of scientific experiments. Nevertheless, certain constraints limit historians' ability to achieve comprehensive accuracy. Leaving aside the problem of lost or destroyed evidence, historians must interpret their sources and then present their conclusions in a logical account. The first task is influenced by each historian's own particular perspective and goals; the second is subject to the requirements of logical or narrative intelligibility.[69] That is to say, historians aim to provide a complete and accurate representation of the past, but due to the limitations of explanatory coherence they must select which evidence to include. In making these selections, each historian is guided by her own outlook and goals.

There are two major differences between the practice of writing history in Meyer's time and in our own. First, in the fifteenth century, no systematic practice of citation had yet been developed either for primary sources or for prior works of historical scholarship. Like modern historians, Meyer compiled the work of earlier chroniclers, dug through archives for original documents, and recorded oral accounts, although in keeping with the practice of his era he generally did not provide references identifying these sources.[70] Second, in Meyer's time, the purpose of history writing was expressly didactic and political, whereas since at least the nineteenth century most historians have striven to produce an objective representation of the past for its own sake. Meyer did not write about the past for its own sake but followed the practice of his predecessors and con-

69. Hayden White, *Metahistory: The Historical Imagination in Nineteenth-Century Europe* (Baltimore, 1973); Paul Ricoeur, *Time and Narrative*, trans. Kathleen Blamey and David Pellauer, 3 vols (Chicago, 1990), 3: 99–274.

70. Huijbers, *Zealots*, 35–59.

temporaries in writing history in order to shape a certain future. For example, Meyer explicitly articulates his principles of selection in terms of his political purpose, explaining that he omitted not only evidence that seemed apocryphal but also anything that would not serve the edification of his readers and the promotion of the Observant reform (**3.3**). Meyer's failure to provide citations and his explicitly propagandistic purpose set his historiographical practice apart from today's standards.

Yet the difference between the cold objectivity aimed at by modern historians and Meyer's politically invested chronicle is not as great as it might at first appear. On the one hand, fifteenth-century humanists had already begun to claim objectivity for their histories.[71] On the other, historians today increasingly articulate their work in terms of their political commitments. Acknowledging that no history writing is free from its author's own worldview and that historical distance does not insulate a narrative from current politics, scholars have called for histories that attend to particular aspects of the medieval world in order to create a more pluralistic and equitable future for our own time.[72] To be sure, Meyer's practice of citation does not meet current disciplinary standards, and his reform politics would be dubious today; nevertheless, he provides enough information to support critical reflection on the role of history writing in political movements. Grounded in Meyer's own dual role as historian and reformer, such considerations continue to be profoundly relevant to our own contemporary practice and the relationship between history writing and activism.

As well, betraying a situation that many scholars will find familiar, some of Meyer's accounts are incomplete, not because he censored them but because he had limited access to information. The reforms of the Alsatian convents are the most colourfully narrated, because Meyer either experienced them first-hand or had reliable second-hand information from people directly involved. In contrast, Meyer is often quite ill-informed about events further away.[73] His account of the Tulln reform, for example, consists almost solely of a letter written by the prioress of the convent of St Catherine in Nuremberg to the community of Schö-

71. Renaissance historians nevertheless knew full well that this claim itself was propagandistic rhetoric: see Margaret Meserve, *Empires of Islam in Renaissance Historical Thought* (Cambridge, MA, 2008), 8–9.

72. See, for example, Geraldine Heng, *The Invention of Race in the European Middle Ages* (Cambridge, 2018); Judith M. Bennett, *History Matters: Patriarchy and the Challenge of Feminism* (Philadelphia, 2006); Kathleen Biddick, *The Shock of Medievalism* (Durham, 1998).

73. Claudia Heimann, "Beobachtungen zur Arbeitsweise von Johannes Meyer OP anhand seiner Aussagen über die Reform der Dominikanerkonvente der Teutonia, besonders der Natio Austriae," *AFP* 72 (2002): 187–220.

nensteinbach. She informs them that some of the Schönensteinbach sisters who had reformed St Catherine's have now been sent further east to reform the Tulln convent (**5.41**). Later additions to the text deal with reforms up to 1477, but the information is extremely uneven, since Meyer had stopped actively working on the *Book of the Reformation*. In the prologue to book 5, Meyer acknowledges his limited access to sources and his lack of time to devote to research. His solution to these problems is to beg his reader for help: "I desire of each God-fearing person who hears this book read, that she expand and add what is proper and right" (**5.1**). Meyer knew that his work was incomplete, and he intended others to continue the task. Whether directly inspired by Meyer's call or responding independently to an evident need, many Observant women did record the events in which they were directly involved, and these female-authored chronicles also deserve continued attention.[74]

In today's world of quick air travel and manuscript digitization, scholars can obtain access to sources with a facility that was unimaginable to Meyer. Even though much has been irretrievably lost over the past five centuries, an astounding amount of evidence concerning the lives, activities, goals, talents, and achievements of late medieval religious women still survives. Although scholarship on these women has increasingly gained steam and garnered respect, much remains to be done. The *Book of the Reformation* offers us a sprawling account – albeit one that is biased and incomplete – of the role of women in an important historical movement and models a more inclusive way of acknowledging and appreciating the values and capacities of historical women. I have translated this chronicle in the hope that Meyer's plea to continue his work will encourage today's readers in turn to understand, celebrate, record, and inspire women as historical actors.

The Surviving Manuscripts

Currently, the only print edition of the *Book of the Reformation* is Benedict Maria Reichert's 1908 diplomatic edition of the manuscript at St Gallen, Stiftsbibliothek, cod. 1916.[75] I will not enumerate the problems with this edition here, but

74. See, for example, Sigrid Hirbodian and Petra Kurz (eds), *Die Chronik der Magdalena Kremerin im interdisziplinären Dialog* (Ostfildern, 2016); Neidhardt, *Autonomie im Gehorsam*; Winston-Allen, *Convent Chronicles*; Uffmann, *Wie in einem Rosengarten*.

75. Johannes Meyer, *Buch der Reformacio Predigerordens*, ed. Benedict Maria Reichert, 2 vols (Leipzig, 1908–1909).

I have chosen to translate directly from a different source manuscript, namely Strasbourg, Bibliothèque Nationale et Universitaire, MS 2934, which is both the oldest manuscript and (as discussed below) probably contains the closest text to Meyer's original. This manuscript will also serve as the primary basis for a planned critical edition of the *Book of the Reformation*. By focusing on this manuscript, I am preparing my translation for future compatibility with a new edition that will meet current critical standards.

In addition to the St Gallen and Strasbourg manuscripts, two further manuscripts containing the bulk of Meyer's *Book of the Reformation* survive: Munich, Bayerische Staatsbibliothek, Cgm 8081 and Tübingen, Universitätsbibliothek, Hs. Md 456. I have also identified brief excerpts in Karlsruhe, Badische Landesbibliothek, St Peter pap. 9, fols 282r–284v.[76] All manuscripts have been digitized and are freely available from the websites of the respective libraries.[77] The relationship among the first four manuscripts was well established by Werner Fechter.[78] Three of them represent a direct line of derivation, and there is even external evidence regarding the conditions of their transcription. Cgm 8081 belonged to the Dominican convent of St Catherine in Nuremberg, whose shelf mark (N XXI) survives on folio 11r.[79] When the sisters of St Catherine's in St Gallen turned to the Nuremberg sisters for assistance in their self-reform, this manuscript among others was sent to them to copy for their own collection of edifying literature.[80] The copy they made survives in St Gallen as cod. 1916, which provided the basis for Reichert's 1908 edition. The sisters of St Gallen copied the text a second time, albeit in a heavily edited form, to produce the

76. In the order in which the excerpts appear in the manuscript, they are selections and abbreviations of passages from **5.47**, **3.11**, **3.14**, **3.35**, **3.10**, and **2.25**. The published catalogue description includes these excerpts as a series of "Contemplations for Attaining Perfection" (*Betrachtungen zur Erlangung der Vollkommenheit*) and names the nuns to whom the devotional exercises are attributed, but does not identify Meyer's *Book of the Reformation* as the source text. See Klaus Niebler, *Die Handschriften von St. Peter im Schwarzwald*, vol. 1: *Die Papierhandschriften*, Die Handschriften der Badischen Landesbibliothek in Karlsruhe 10.1 (Wiesbaden, 1969), 14–20, at 19.

77. The links to the first four are available at www.handschriftencensus.de/werke/2395 and the Karlsruhe excerpts may be found at digital.blb-karlsruhe.de/id/76388 or via www.handschriftencensus.de/5084 (accessed 29 November 2018).

78. Werner Fechter, "Die Nürnberger Handschrift von Johannes Meyers *Buch der Reformacio Predigerordens*," *ZfdA* 110 (1981): 57–69.

79. It appears under this signature in the surviving library catalogue from St Catherine's in Nuremberg. See Willing, *Bibliothek*, 782–783.

80. See *Das "Konventsbuch" und das "Schwesternbuch" aus St. Katharina in St. Gallen: Kritische Edition und Kommentar*, ed. Antje Willing (Berlin, 2016), 169.

Tübingen manuscript Md 456, which they sent as a gift to the Augustinian canonesses of Inzigkofen.[81] These two convents were bound not only by a prayer partnership, but also through a familial connection: Elisabeth Muntprat, the scribe of Md 456 had a biological sister, Veronika, among the Inzigkofen canonesses.[82] Each of these three manuscripts includes scribal interventions and editorial changes that reveal the intentions and interests of the female readers and redactors.

The outlier, Strasbourg MS 2934, is the oldest of the four surviving manuscripts, and there are several indications that it contains the text closest to Meyer's "original" chronicle. Aside from the organizational changes I explain below, MS 2934 retains several sections narrated in the first person singular, although a contemporary hand attempted to turn *ich* and *mir* ("I" and "me") into *er* and *ihm* ("he" and "him") by writing over the words. Furthermore, several portions of the manuscript bear Meyer's autograph hand, including the lists at the beginning, the general prologue, and the additions covering the years 1468 to 1477. Fechter suggests that Meyer reviewed and corrected this manuscript in 1478 when he was sent to Strasbourg and Sélestat to select sisters for the reforms of Weiler near Esslingen and Kirchheim unter Teck.[83] MS 2934 was copied in and belonged to the Strasbourg convent of St Nicholas-in-Undis.[84] Supplementing Meyer's chronicle, it also includes additional information regarding the dissolution of the Strasbourg convent of St Agnes and the subsequent reform of St Margaret through the transfer of the St Agnes community. This lively and detailed account, unique to this manuscript, was most likely written by a Strasbourg nun close to the events.[85] For these reasons, I have chosen to rely on this manuscript, although I have also referred to Cgm 8081 (the oldest manuscript of the other strand) for clarification and occasionally for extra information. Since the extra information from Cgm 8081 is usually very limited (e.g., a person's first name or a specific

81. See *Das "Konventsbuch" und das "Schwesternbuch"*, ed. Willing, 190.

82. Simone Mengis, *Schreibende Frauen um 1500: Scriptorium und Bibliothek des Dominikanerinnenklosters St. Katharina St. Gallen* (Berlin, 2013), 218. For more on the Inzigkofen library, see Fechter, *Deutsche Handschriften des 15. und 16. Jahrhunderts.*

83. Fechter, "Nürnberger Handschrift," 59.

84. The medieval library signature (N LXII) and ownership mark for the convent of St Nicholas-in-Undis survives on the last folio, 263v. Large portions of MS 2934 were copied by a hand whose work is also visible in other manuscripts that were demonstrably produced in that convent. Balázs J. Nemes, "Der 'entstellte' Eckhart: Eckhart-Handschriften im Straßburger Dominikanerinnenkloster St Nikolaus in undis," in *Schreiben und Lesen in der Stadt*, ed. Mossman, Palmer, and Heinzer, 39–98, at 60–61.

85. See **5.82–83**, which describe the abandonment of St Agnes and the reform of St Margaret.

number of days), I have included it silently except in cases of greater divergence (e.g., in **5.19** where a section has been crossed out in MS 2934 but survives in Cgm 8081).

The choice to privilege the Strasbourg manuscript results in two significant divergences from the Reichert edition in the organization of the material. First, Cgm 8081 initially left out some chapters concerning the reform of the friaries, then included them later, indicating their proper chronological place by inserting marginal annotations. Rather than restoring the original chapter order, cod. 1916 (and consequently Reichert's edition) incorporated these annotations into the text as one-line remarks which fail to indicate that a full chapter follows later in the text.[86] Following MS 2934 I have included the chapters on the friaries in chronological order, integrated with the information about the reform of the women's convents. Second, the conclusion of the text has the curious problem that Meyer provided a moralizing summary at the end of book 5, while also inviting continuations should additional convents be reformed, and providing several such himself. In MS 2934, Meyer solved the problem by appending "A Short Prologue" that introduces the additions. Cgm 8081 solved the problem by transferring the moralizing conclusion to the end of book 4, leaving book 5 open for continuation, but nevertheless still included the "Short Prologue." In order to convey to my readers a sense of textual openness, I have opted for a third solution: I have moved the additional chapters back to just before the conclusion, leaving Meyer's edifying admonitions at the end of book 5, but closing the translation overall with the "Short Prologue."

I have not set out to provide a critical edition, and accordingly I have not attempted to include exhaustive annotations. As Anne Huijbers has shown, Meyer followed the historiographical practice of his time, which was heavily compilatory and rarely acknowledged sources.[87] Identifying all of Meyer's sources is beyond the scope of the present translation, although I have made an attempt. I have drawn information from the footnotes in Reichert's edition and have supplied additional information about the individuals, events, and phenomena to

86. For example, Cgm 8081, fol. 211v has a marginal note just before the chapter on the Tulln reform that reads, "Anno Domini 1434, the friary in Vienna was reformed. This convent [i.e., this chapter] belongs before [the chapter on] the sisters in Tulln." In cod. 1916, p. 574, this note appears incorporated into the text at the end of the preceding chapter as "Anno Domini 1434, the friary in Vienna was reformed," but the full chapter on the Vienna friary does not appear until p. 721/fol. 361r. Note that cod. 1916 has, though inconsistently, both foliation (i.e., numbers only on the recto, or front side, of each leaf) – the standard practice in manuscripts – and pagination (i.e., successive numbers on both the front and back of each leaf).

87. See Huijbers, *Zealots*, 35–59.

which Meyer refers. These references are also not exhaustive but are thorough enough to provide a solid background and to indicate first steps towards further research by interested readers.

Notes on the Translation

The decisions I have made in laying out the translation are intended to facilitate easy reference either to Strasbourg MS 2934 or to an eventual critical edition. I have used the chapter headings and the chapter numbering from the Strasbourg manuscript, including the omission of a chapter 9 from book 4 and a chapter 39 from book 5. From chapter 83 of book 5 onwards the manuscript includes chapter headings, but no numbers. I have supplied numbers for these final chapters. Next to each chapter heading there is a folio number indicating where that chapter begins in Strasbourg MS 2934, so that readers interested in the original German may easily find the corresponding passages.

Although I initially considered maintaining much of Meyer's phrasing in order to produce an archaizing style, I decided that a style smoothly readable for contemporary English-speaking audiences would in fact be more faithful to Meyer's work. His writing is often quite conversational, with oral elements thrown in ("Now listen, dear children!"), yet other passages contain mere lists, copies of formal and informal letters, or moralizing lectures. I have attempted to reflect the varying tone of Meyer's chronicle while staying as close to his text as possible, although readability has demanded eliminating most of Meyer's connectors (e.g., the frequent repetition of "And so it happened that ...").

I have kept proper names in the original German with standardized spelling, except in cases where the English equivalent of a notable person's name is commonly used in English-language scholarship. I have removed the feminine *-in* ending from women's last names and have attempted to use the modern or most common spelling of all family names. Much of the narrative takes place in Alsace, which – now French – was German-speaking throughout the Middle Ages. I have kept the Alsatian place names in their German version, but to the extent that I have been able to identify them, I have provided the modern French versions in a table (see the appendix); the two maps provided (see pp. viii–x) will supply the reader with further context.

Meyer uses a fair amount of idiosyncratic language and has some stylistic quirks that have proven difficult to render. For example, he puns on proper names and place names so often that I considered translating *Steinbach* as "Stonybrook" throughout the entire work in order to make his wordplay more transparent. In translating the various titles of convent office holders, I have relied on Sarah DeMaris's translation of Meyer's *Book of Duties*. Every translator of a medieval religious work is forced to make a choice about the word "convent," which medieval writers used indiscriminately to signify religious communities of either sex (the people, not the buildings). In keeping with modern English lay usage, I have used "convent" for women's houses (i.e., *Frauenkloster*), "friary" for men's houses, and often "community" for Meyer's *Convent*. The Friars Preachers were not yet called Dominicans in Meyer's day, but I have chosen to use the latter term, especially since English has no simple equivalent for the single German word *Predigerbruder*. I have retained "Order of Preachers" where it does not seem too unwieldy but have mostly used "Dominicans" and "Dominican order."

I have chosen to translate the terms for bodily (*leibliche*) family with "birth mother" but "biological" father, sister, or brother. Meyer also uses "father" as a term of respect for fellow Dominicans, and "brother" both as a term of religious affection and as the technical term "friar." I have tried to be sensitive to Meyer's tone in choosing translations. Meyer does use the term "monk," but almost never in reference to actual monks (e.g., Benedictines) as opposed to friars (e.g., Dominicans or Augustinian canons). For Meyer, "monk" is a derogatory term applied to bad friars, and when it appears in my translation it should usually be understood as such and not as an indication of religious order.

Finally, two terms that signify aspects of Observant practice differ dramatically from their modern usage and have proven difficult to translate. *Gemein* does not mean "community," but instead designates the practice of holding property in common, which was considered a fundamental prerequisite of harmonious communal life. This usage is not unique to Meyer but is also found in other German-language documents pertaining to Observant Dominican practices.[88] Similarly, *Geistlichkeit* does not refer collectively to clergy or religious persons, but instead is Meyer's umbrella term for both the concrete practices and the devotional attitude proper to life under the Observance. I have usually translated this as "the religious life" and occasionally as "spirituality," according to whether the immediate context stresses the Rule, Constitutions, and ordinances, or contemplative devotion. However, the law feeds the spirit and, for Meyer, strict adherence to the order fosters spiritual fulfilment.

88. Neidiger treats the term *Gemein* as encompassing not just the "prohibition against private property, but also the Divine Office, listening to table readings and sermons, common prayer, [and] working in the scriptorium or the textiles workshop." These other practices were certainly essential practices of communal life, but common property grounded and supported all the others. See Neidiger, "Standesgemäßes Leben oder frommes Gebet?," 207.

The Book of the Reformation of the Order of Preachers

Prologue

Here begins the prologue to the Book of the Reformation of the Dominican convents, of friars as also of sisters, in German lands. [fol. 11r]

To all souls who love God and who bear grace, devotion, and love for the holy religious life of the laudable, worthy Order of Preachers, greetings in God, and may you, through truly righteous and religious living, attain eternal life. Beloved in God, this book is called the Book of the Reformation and was written for the glory of God and out of the love we bear for your salvation.

It is divided into five parts and each part or book has a certain number of chapters. The first book concerns how Schönensteinbach was first founded and tells of its rise and fall before it came into Dominican hands. The second book recounts how Schönensteinbach became a convent under the Order of Preachers, in order to keep the holy Observance for all eternity. It was placed within such enclosure that no one would be seen again, and the pope and the order confirmed this.[1] This book tells also of the accidents that befell the convent and how its enclosure and its religious life were nevertheless so laudably maintained. The third book tells of the blessed lives of certain sisters from that convent and of the wonders God worked in them. The fourth book is similar, and tells of the worthy and blessed fathers who were primarily responsible for beginning to reform the order, especially in German lands, and of those who fostered and promoted

1. The Observant reform advocated an especially strict form of enclosure, such that not only were nuns forbidden from leaving the convent and outsiders from entering, but also special grilles and screens were installed in the speaking parlours so that when the nuns were communicating with people on the outside they would be able to hear each other but not see each other. See Sylvie Duval, "*Mulieres religiosae* and *sorores clausae*: The Dominican Observant Movement and the Diffusion of Strict Enclosure in Italy from the Thirteenth to the Sixteenth Century," in *Mulieres religiosae: Shaping Female Spiritual Authority in the Medieval and Early Modern Periods*, ed. Veerle Fraeters and Imke de Gier (Turnhout, 2014), 193–218; Heike Uffmann, "Inside and Outside the Convent Walls: The Norm and Practice of Enclosure in the Reformed Nunneries of Late Medieval Germany," *The Medieval History Journal* 4 (2001): 83–108.

the nascent Observance. The fifth book is general, and recounts from the beginning how the reform of the Order began, how many convents in the province of Teutonia were slowly reformed, and what happened during that time. It also concerns the graces of the reformers, and their labour, and the wisdom and patience they needed in advancing the reform and the religious life so greatly.

These books have been compiled through hard work, organized and composed by several persons who with special zeal have read many bulls and letters and other records that deal with the reform of the order, or who have recorded it according to the witness of worthy persons. Many experienced such things first-hand and suffered much for it. For this reason, they ask that you who hear or read this book pray to God for them. This was completed in 1468 on the vigil of St Catherine, virgin and martyr [24 November].

Note: if it so happens that more convents are reformed hereafter, this information should also be carefully recorded in the appropriate order. Space has been left for this purpose.

Book One

This little book shows how the reform or enclosure of the reformed convents of the Order of Preachers arose, where it first began, and how it was confirmed by the See of Rome. It also tells of the freedoms and privileges that were given to these convents, both by the pope and by the master general of the order.[1]

1.1 *Concerning the beginning of the convent of St Bridget in Schönensteinbach, which was the origin and mother of the reformed convents* [fol. 12r]

In the name of our Lord Jesus Christ and his dear mother Mary and our holy father Saint Dominic and the worthy lady Saint Bridget,[2] I begin by writing of the foundation of the convent in Schönensteinbach and how it was occupied and restored by worthy fathers and devout sisters of our holy father Saint Dominic of the Order of Preachers.

You should know that this convent in Schönensteinbach was a worthy cloister of old and it initially arose in this way. In the year 1138 after the birth of our Lord Jesus Christ, the illustrious prince Conrad of Saxony from Swabia, the brother of Duke Hermann, became king of the Romans and ruled the Holy Roman Empire worthily for fifteen years.[3] During the reign of this king lived many blessed people and great teachers of holy Christianity, in particular the

1. Jean-Charles Winnlen's dissertation provides further detail and corroborating sources for much of the material in books 1 and 2 of the *Book of the Reformation.* See Jean-Charles Winnlen, "Schönensteinbach: Une communauté religieuse féminine, 1138–1792" (PhD diss., Université de Franche-Comté, 1992).

2. Bridget of Sweden will be the patron saint of Schönensteinbach when it is refounded as an Observant Dominican convent; see **2.5**.

3. Conrad III (r. 1138–1152) was the first of the Staufer emperors. He had no connection to Saxony, but Meyer's confusion may have arisen because Conrad was initially elected in 1127 as anti-king to Lothar III, who was the duke of Saxony. Hermann of Stahleck (d. 1156), count palatine of the Rhine, was his brother-in-law (he had married Conrad's sister Gertrude). The title "king of the Romans" was given to the man chosen by the elector princes as head of the Holy Roman Empire. Only after the pope confirmed the election and crowned the candidate did he receive the title of emperor.

noble and sweet Saint Bernard[4] and the teacher Richard of St Victor,[5] among other dear servants of God in both the religious and secular state.

At this time there lived in Alsace a noble, god-fearing knight named Lord Notker of Wittenheim, the first founder of the convent of Schönensteinbach. He was a devout Christian who ruled his subjects according to his beliefs. His wife was named Lady Benedicta. Just as our dear Lord said, "Every good tree bringeth forth good fruit,"[6] so it happened that, by the mild beneficence of God, these two noble and good people were given good fruit. From them were born the two noble maidens who provided the first occasion and impetus for the worthy convent of Schönensteinbach.

When the two blessed noble maidens reached adulthood and saw so many Christian virtues in their father and mother, they took such a good model from their parents that they freely bade this false world farewell. With mind, soul, and body, and in chaste purity, they gave themselves to God as a living sacrifice into the spiritual life of an approved order. They both became religious women in the convent called Kleinlützel, which the great and noble Udalhard of Pfirt[7] and his wife Lady Adelheid had founded. In this convent were many devout nuns of noble birth, but the two dear sisters, the daughters of the worthy noble knight Notker, stood out among them. They held themselves to a religious way of life, demonstrating that they had wedded themselves to Christ Jesus, the eternal spouse of all pure hearts.

1.2 *How St Margaret's Chapel was founded long before the foundation of the convent of Schönensteinbach and how it came into the possession of the knight Notker* [fol. 13r]

Not far from the castle at the edge of the village of Wittenheim, this aforenamed devout knight Notker of Wittenheim owned a lovely chapel, consecrated

4. Bernard of Clairvaux (d. 1153) was a prominent Cistercian reformer and spiritual leader.

5. Richard of St Victor (d. 1173) was a canon at St Victor in Paris and a prolific mystical theologian.

6. Matthew 7:17.

7. The count of Pfirt in 1138 was named Friedrich. This is Udalhard II of Saugern and his wife Adelheid, who also endowed Frienisberg as a daughter house of Lützel. Their daughter Agnes married a Ludwig of Pfirt. See Auguste Quiquerez, *Histoire des comtes de Ferrette* (Montbéliard, 1863), 18–19; Emil A. Erdin, "Frienisberg," in *Die Zisterzienser und Zisterzienserinnen, die reformierten Bernhardinerinnen, die Trappisten und Trappistinnen und die Wilhelmiten in der Schweiz*, ed. Cécile Sommer-Ramer and Patrick Braun, Helvetia Sacra 3.3 (Bern, 1982), 128–141.

in honour of Saint Margaret, the holy martyr and virgin. This chapel was entrusted to his care by divine order and because he had inherited it from his ancestors. It had been founded long before his time by a baron named Ulrich of Ofhus.[8] This baron was very rich and donated a lot of property to this chapel, including a tithe of his free personal property. Since this tithe of land was not large enough for the chapel to have its own priest, it was arranged that the parish priest of Wittenheim should receive this chapel's tithe and that he should ensure that three masses were sung in the chapel each week.

When this Baron Ulrich of Ofhus, founder of the chapel, was dying, he commanded one of his friends, Constantinus, to give the tithe of St Margaret's Chapel to the parish priest for reading Mass there. After much time had passed, the responsibility for overseeing the chapel and its tithe fell through divine order and the law of inheritance to the devout lord and knight Notker of Wittenheim, father of the two blessed nuns. He worked hard to ensure that the chapel continued to be honoured with worship services. To this end, he appointed a priest of good will named Walter, who cared for the chapel well, reading Mass there as well as fulfilling the pastoral duties in the parish church of Wittenheim.

1.3 *How Lord Notker's daughters asked their father to turn St Margaret's Chapel into a convent estate and how he offered them the barn at Steinbach instead* [fol. 13v]

At that time, the young count of Pfirt was harassing the nuns of the Kleinlützel convent and disturbing them with hunting dogs, horses, hunters, and other irreligious business, such that the dear children of God could not pursue their religious way of life in as orderly and peaceful a manner as they would have liked. For this reason, they complained to their friends and laid out the cause preventing them from fulfilling their spiritual state in peace and quiet. The nuns begged for someone to advise or help them to find a good and safe place for a convent where they could better serve God through religious life in peace and separation from the world.

The two blessed sisters, daughters of the knight Notker, thought of the gracious chapel of St Margaret in Wittenheim, which was under the care of their father. They described to him how they could not live a truly spiritual life in their convent in Kleinlützel because of the misbehaviour of the young count and his company. They asked him if they could have the chapel of St Margaret in Wit-

8. Seraphin Dietler identified Ofhus as a variation of Hus, which would make this Ulrich the ancestor of Dietrich of Hus (see **1.13** and **1.16**) and Hans Ulrich of Hus (see **1.22–23**) and explain their later interest and interference in Schönensteinbach. See Seraphin Dietler, *Chronik des Klosters Schönensteinbach*, ed. Joseph von Schlumberger (Gebweiler, 1897), 9.

tenheim as a place where they might serve the Lord God in right and true religious life.

At this the father thought, "No, that's not for them," and told them that he had another large and wide estate not far from the chapel, about three horse rides away. There was also a barn near the creek named Steinbach [Stonybrook][9] that was his own freehold property. They could go and live there if they wanted. Maybe their father said this because he did not want to advise them to live anywhere near a castle, town, or village, especially since they would be better able to serve the Lord God away from the world and from people, in the woods, in the wilderness, and in solitude, in all spiritual devotion without distraction.

1.4 *How the blessed maidens, Lord Notker's daughters, came with the other nuns from Kleinlützel to the barn at Schönensteinbach in the woods* [fol. 14v]

When these two sisters heard their father's offer, they deftly began to prepare themselves, as did the other nuns. They put everything they owned onto wagons and had themselves driven to Steinbach where the convent of Schönensteinbach now stands. At the time, there were no buildings on the estate there aside from the one barn. The nuns moved in and saw that it was a wild wasteland in the middle of the woods, for around the barn on the creek lay much empty land. The daughters informed their father that they had come to his estate at Steinbach in the woods and were living in the barn.

When Lord Notker heard this, he became very upset. He hadn't thought that his daughters and the other women would actually leave their cloister in Kleinlützel to go to such a desolate place, off in the woods and far from people. But when he realized that the nuns, whether in their simplicity or their ardour, had gone to such a place on his recommendation, he spoke of it with his friends and relatives, and called upon his personal priest, an honourable man named Rudiger, among other worthy people. Once Rudiger had seen them and listened to the knight and his friends on the one side and to the knight's daughters and the nuns on the other, he gave his will and blessing that the women should live where they were. He noted the many virtues and the honourable life of the women, who were living in such deprivation and poverty on an estate in the middle of the wild woods near Steinbach.

Notker then called together all those with an interest in his inheritance and laid the matter before them, explaining the uprightness of the women,

9. Meyer refers to the location and the convent loosely as either Steinbach (Stonybrook) or Schönensteinbach (Lovely Stonybrook). I have followed his usage rather than regularizing it.

their misery and poverty, and how they lived in such a place. He was considering giving them the estate and what belonged to it, so that they could build a cloister there. When his friends and family heard this, they all assented to his decision and praised the knight for wanting to undertake such a godly matter. And so the estate and everything that belonged to it, with the blessing and affirmation of all the knight's inheritors, was given to the nuns in perpetuity for a convent.

1.5 *How the nuns began to build the cloister at Schönensteinbach with the help of Lord Notker and how for a long time the abbey of Großlützel provided them with spiritual care* [fol. 15v]

Once this blessed knight and friend of God, Notker, had given such honourable alms to the servants of Jesus Christ for a perpetual convent, then with the help of this same knight and of other honourable people they began to build a living space in which they could dwell in accordance with the practices and customs of vowed religious. In those days lived the noble teacher Bernard. Around this time, many convents of his order were founded, which is called the Grey Order or *ordo cisterciensis*. The brothers and sisters of all these convents maintained this order in full observance of the Rule of St Benedict in a truly praiseworthy and devout manner.

There was a venerable monastery of this order of dear devout brothers called Cistercians, and the name of the monastery was Großlützel.[10] Not far from there lay the convent called Kleinlützel. It so happened that the abbot of Großlützel personally came to the newly founded convent of Schönensteinbach and received the sisters into his spiritual care and direction, and promised to help counsel them with words and deeds. He assigned them a spiritual father and priest who would preside over them in spiritual and sacramental matters.

The reputation of the convent of Schönensteinbach was so refined, and the good standing and the religious life of the sisters spread so widely, that many dear women came into this convent and order and brought a great deal of worldly wealth into the convent with them. The bursar and the cellarer appropriated this for Großlützel, and this caused some grief.

Not long after the sweet and holy teacher Saint Bernard, who had been a special light and support for his order, had departed from this life into eternal blessedness in the year 1153, the abbot and community of Großlützel rejected the sisters of Schönensteinbach and cut them off and told them that they were

10. For information on this monastery, see André Chèvre, *Lucelle: Histoire d'une ancienne abbaye cistercienne* (Delémont, 1973).

banned from the Cistercian general chapter.[11] And so the sisters were abandoned by the order so that they were no longer provided for in sacramentary, Christian, and spiritual matters. The sisters were thus in no small distress, sadness, and pain because of this harsh and worrisome abandonment.

1.6 *How, after the abbot and the brothers of Großlützel rejected the sisters of Schönensteinbach and refused to care for them, Lord Notker went to the bishop and the pope for help* [fol. 16r]

The noble knight heard about this piteous affair and how his two daughters and the other sisters had been so sorely abandoned, and this troubled him greatly. The true and righteous faithfulness and love of this dear blessed father Notker shone forth, and he took up the cause of these children of God with great zeal and earnestness. At great cost and inconvenience, he rode to Basel and laid before the bishop the case of the abandonment of the Schönensteinbach sisters. He requested help and aid from his holiness so that the sisters of Schönensteinbach might be provided with spiritual and Christian care.

Now this same bishop of Basel was a very holy man, whose name was Ortlieb.[12] When he heard from the knight about the blessed lives of the Schönensteinbach sisters and how they had been abandoned, this bishop also took counsel. The two of them decided together to send the matter on to the pope. And so the blessed bishop acted as a faithful shepherd and wrote to the pope eagerly and humbly about the affair and the misery of the sisters and how they had been abandoned by the Grey Order and how they had not been taken on by another confirmed order and that no one was caring for them consistently and that His Holiness would handle all of this as best he could for God's honour and the salvation of the sisters.

11. The institutional structures of the early Cistercian order are notoriously difficult to reconstruct, especially with regard to the official status of women's communities. Constance Berman argues that Cistercian general chapters began only after Bernard's death, which would make it unlikely that Schönensteinbach was formally incorporated and then rejected. Whether or not Berman's timeline is correct, the relationships between early Cistercian women's and men's communities were often experimental and flexible, and it would probably have been fairly easy for Großlützel to discontinue their oversight of Schönensteinbach. For context, see Martha G. Newman, "Foundation and Twelfth Century," in *The Cambridge Companion to the Cistercian Order*, ed. Mette Birkedal Bruun (Cambridge, 2012), 25–37; Constance H. Berman, "Were There Twelfth-Century Cistercian Nuns?," *Church History* 68 (1999): 824–864; Constance H. Berman, *The White Nuns: Cistercian Abbeys for Women in Medieval France* (Philadelphia, 2018), 3–17.

12. Ortlieb of Froburg (r. 1138–1164).

And so the faithful Lord Notker took this great task upon himself out of great love and rode personally to the pope. There he obtained from him what was needed for the convent – namely, that the bishop of Basel could assume oversight and, with papal authority, arrange for this convent of Schönensteinbach to be entrusted in all spiritual affairs to a monastery of holy brothers within the diocese of Basel who belonged to a confirmed order. The pope granted this, among other things, to the noble servant of God Notker, who brought the papal letters to the honourable bishop of Basel. In those days, the pope was Adrian, the third of his name, a born Englishman.[13]

1.7 *How the bishop of Basel, by papal authority, entrusted the convent of Schönensteinbach to the provost of Marbach, an Augustinian canonry* [fol. 17r]

When this news reached the bishop of Basel, he behaved as befits a wise man. Even though the matter had been entrusted to him, and by papal authority he could make decisions alone, he nevertheless took the counsel of wise men and thought to call a synod of all the priests in his entire diocese. So the bishop called a great common synod, attended by all the prelates and priests who belonged to the diocese of Basel. The knight was called there before the bishop and the whole priesthood. In the presence of all assembled, he gave the bishop the bulls and letters which the pope had written about the convent of Schönensteinbach. After these had been read before the priests and laypeople, the bishop requested counsel from the whole assembly. The matter was placed under the advisement of four canons of the cathedral chapter in Basel and four of the noblest knights of the land of Alsace, who formed a council to take up the case.

These men concluded that they could find no better way to provide honourably for the nuns than through those in Marbach, who flourished in honour and religious life.[14] The worthy father Ortlieb and the entire synod received this advice, approved it, and earnestly commanded the dear blessed provost of Marbach, named Hetzelin, to take the sisters under his protection and governance. After much pleading, this provost and his community agreed for the convent of

13. Adrian IV (r. 1154–1159) is the only Englishman ever to have been pope.

14. Marbach was a community of Canons Regular, or Augustinian canons. Like the Dominicans, this order followed the Augustinian Rule but had a different set of constitutions. For the history of the Augustinian order, see Frances Andrews, *The Other Friars: Carmelite, Augustinian, Sack, and Pied Friars in the Middle Ages* (Woodbridge, 2006), 71–171. Fiona Griffiths has shown that the Augustinian community at Marbach specialized in serving women's communities in the region. Fiona J. Griffiths, "Brides and *Dominae*: Abelard's *Cura monialium* at the Augustinian Monastery of Marbach," *Viator* 34 (2003): 57–88; Francois Auguste Goehlinger, *Histoire de l'abbaye de Marbach* (Colmar, 1954), 91.

Schönensteinbach to be placed under the ministry and care of the provost of the Augustinians of Marbach, who are called *canonici regulares* or professed canons. But they would not assume responsibility for the women's material goods, nor would they have power over them.

At this time, the Roman emperor was the duke of Swabia named Frederick I, who ruled the Roman Empire for thirty-seven years.[15] He came into conflict with Pope Alexander III[16] and declared that a cardinal named Octavian should be made pope at his command. He was named Pope Victor by those who followed him, and for a time there was a schism in Christendom.[17] Pope Alexander, however, remained in the office in the end. This Victor, who believed he was pope, immediately sent the provost of Marbach a bull, which contained among other things the following: "My dear son Provost Hetzelin and the whole chapter of Marbach, we encourage and order you, as our worthy brother Ortlieb the bishop of Basel has commanded, to preside well over the sisters of Schönensteinbach so that they might continue their spiritual life and fulfil a worthy sacrifice to God. May their good and blessed life here lead to the reward of eternal life. Pray to God for peace in Christendom."[18]

1.8 *How the sisters of Schönensteinbach had to give up the Rule of St Benedict and obediently bind themselves to the Augustinian Rule under the provost of Marbach according to the customs of the order* Ordo canonicorum regularium [fol. 18r]

Now that both the papal See and the bishop of Basel had entrusted the sisters of Schönensteinbach to the provost and chapter of Marbach for spiritual and sacramental care, the worthy knight Notker led his daughter, the first *magistra* in Schönensteinbach, to Marbach to see the provost. The worthy *magistra* took with her three sisters and led them before her superior, the provost Hetzelin, at the friary of Marbach, which was two miles from Schönensteinbach. There, at the altar dedicated to all saints, they professed their obedience and bound themselves to their order, placing themselves under the authority of the provost according to the customs of his order. Nevertheless, the canons of Marbach were to oversee the sisters only in spiritual and sacramental matters and other such things required by the order. They were to have

15. Frederick I Barbarossa, Holy Roman emperor (r. 1155–1190).

16. Alexander III (r. 1159–1181).

17. Antipope Victor IV (r. 1159–1164). For more on this schism see John B. Freed, *Frederick Barbarossa: The Prince and the Myth* (New Haven, 2016), 250–275.

18. The convents in this region seem to have sided with the imperial party and recognized Victor's authority. See Fiona J. Griffiths, *The Garden of Delights: Reform and Renaissance for Women in the Twelfth Century* (Philadelphia, 2007), 57–59.

nothing to do with the sisters' property, for the strict and noble knight Notker, who was present, knew well how the sisters previously had lost property to Großlützel.

Once this was accomplished, the worthy mother with her three sisters went back to Schönensteinbach. When all the sisters heard from their spiritual mother how the provost and chapter had received them, they requested that this provost come to Schönensteinbach, where they bound themselves to him with oaths worthy of a saint.

1.9 *Of the time in which the cloister of Schönensteinbach with the chapel was built up into an Augustinian convent* [fol. 18v]

When the *magistra* and the community of Schönensteinbach had bound themselves to the provost of Marbach with oaths of obedience according to the Augustinian Rule for canonesses, the worthy Lord Heinrich, a regular canon of that order, was appointed their prior and father. The dear sisters began to live with devotion according to the religious customs of that order which in Latin is called *Ordo canonicorum regularium*. And so they built a proper little minster according to the customs of this order, with two side chapels and aisles, and two stone towers on either side of the minster. They built the cloister according to the requirements of the order's religious life and law.[19]

In these times, when the convent was built, the noble prince Lord Frederick I, duke of Swabia, was the Roman emperor.[20] He was a good Christian man and ruled the empire for thirty-seven years. He conquered the city of Milan, where the holy three kings lay buried. These he took, and gave them to the bishop of Cologne, named Reinald, who had them brought to Cologne.[21]

Also in these days, there were seen three suns and three moons. The *Decretum* was written by the worthy teacher Gratian, who writes about Christian law.[22] That useful and noble book called the *Sentences* was written by the worthy mas-

19. Meyer's insistence on the fact that the church met the Augustinian order's regulations is noteworthy, since he will later recount how Schönensteinbach's reforming Observant confessor, Thomas of Prussia, found the two stone towers too showy and died while personally helping to tear one down. See **4.16**.

20. Frederick Barbarossa is important to Alsace because he made his favourite residence, Hagenau, a city in 1164.

21. Reinald of Dassel, archbishop of Cologne (r. 1159–1167). Barbarossa's extended conflicts with Milan and his forcible translation of the relics of the Three Magi to Cologne in 1164 are described in Freed, *Barbarossa*, 276–294.

22. The precise date of the *Decretum* is disputed, but it is the foundational text of medieval canon law.

ter Peter Lombard, bishop of Paris.[23] The worthy teacher Peter Comestor,[24] who wrote the *Historia scholastica*, was still living, as well as Lord Theobald, archbishop of Canterbury, a blessed man and useful in all things.[25] Also living was the abbot Joachim,[26] who wrote many good books and foretold future things. In particular, he predicted that the Dominican and Franciscan orders would come into the world and that they would be good and holy men. At this time there lived in Saxony a holy nun named Elisabeth,[27] who received many intimate revelations from God and his dear mother. Among other things, she wrote the book called the *Liber viarum dei* [The Book of the Ways of God]. The holy beloved Saint Bernard maintained a close written correspondence with her while he still lived, and she with him. Many other friends of God lived then in great holiness.

I have written about this not because it was necessary for this book, but rather so that one might note the greatness of that age during which this praiseworthy convent was founded and built by the aforesaid lords and friends of God, so that it shall receive a special honour and worthiness.

1.10 *How the first sisters were esteemed and honoured for their blessed life and how their chapel was dedicated in honour of the Mother of God and the martyrdom of Christ* [fol. 19v]

It must be noted that our dear worthy father and founder Notker and the devout nobility of the region were not the only ones who held this blessed convent of Schönensteinbach and its dear sisters in high esteem. They were also held in honour and friendship by the papal See and by many other high prelates, especially the bishops of Basel and Strasbourg, and by the emperor and other great lords and princes, as we shall see later in this book.

When the minster and the cloister had been partially built, the worthy bishop of Basel sent his auxiliary bishop to Schönensteinbach to consecrate

23. Peter Lombard (r. 1159–1160). His *Sentences* remained a basic university theology textbook into the sixteenth century.

24. Peter Comestor (second half of the twelfth century) organized biblical history and interpretation into a more manageable and appealing narrative form in the *Historia scholastica*.

25. Theobald of Bec, archbishop of Canterbury (r. 1139–1161), seems a strange companion to the three giants of twelfth-century intellectual achievement just mentioned.

26. Joachim of Fiore (d. 1202) was famous for his prophetic interpretations of the Book of Revelation.

27. Elisabeth of Schönau (1129–1164) was a Benedictine nun and renowned visionary. The book Meyer mentions has been translated into English in Elisabeth of Schönau, *The Complete Works*, trans. Anne L. Clark (New York, 2000).

the church and the cloister. The convent was dedicated in honour of the worthy Virgin Mary and the altar in the middle of the church in honour of the Holy Cross and the martyrdom of Christ. The anniversary was to be celebrated each year on the Sunday after the octave of St John the Baptist [1 July][28] and a large indulgence was granted for it, as well as for other holidays. The dear servants of God also ensured that important relics would reside there. But although the first sisters observed a blessed and holy life in the religious practice of their order, they were so poor in material goods that one may well believe that they maintained virtue both inwardly and outwardly longer and better because of this poverty.

1.11 *How Notker the knight donated St Margaret's Chapel to the convent of Schönensteinbach and how the blessed Ortlieb, bishop of Basel, confirmed it* [fol. 20r]

The noble Notker recognized the blessed life and great poverty of these dear sisters, and so he took counsel with Lord Walter, who was the parish priest in Wittenheim and also held holy Mass in the chapel of St Margaret there, as was mentioned earlier. The knight Notker made known that he wanted to give his rights over this same chapel and its properties to the poor sisters of Schönensteinbach, should the priest also wish to give his rights over the chapel to these good children. This pleased the priest, as well as others, who greatly praised them for giving the servants of God such honourable alms for the sake of their salvation. And so it happened that when the blessed father Ortlieb, bishop of Basel, called a synod of his priests, Lord Notker the knight and Lord Walter the parish priest of Wittenheim came as well. They asked him to take the chapel with its rents and other properties and write them over to the poor sisters of Schönensteinbach by his episcopal authority. With the blessing and counsel of all those present, Bishop Ortlieb gave the chapel and its properties to the convent in the hands of the prior Friar Heinrich, so that the convent might own them in perpetuity and so that the friars would provide Mass and Divine Office for the convent within the chapel. This bishop strictly ordered that no one hinder or trouble the servants of God in this matter. As proof and true testimony of these things, the following witnesses were recorded: Egilfus, abbot of the Benedictine abbey of Murbach; Lord Dieter, the archpriest; Lord Burckhard, the deacon; Count Ludwig of Pfirt;[29] and many

28. The birth of John the Baptist was commemorated on 24 June and, as a major feast, it continued over eight days (hence the term octave) until 1 July. The anniversary of the convent's dedication would be celebrated on the first Sunday after 1 July.

29. Ludwig I of Pfirt (r. 1161–1180). It is possible that this is the same count of Pfirt who in his youth harrassed the nuns of Kleinlützel; see **1.3**.

other notable persons. This occurred in the year 1161 in the times of the honourable lord, the Roman emperor Frederick I.

This aforementioned blessed father Ortlieb was a special friend to the convent Schönensteinbach and a great lover of all God's children. He was considered the holiest bishop who ever reigned in Basel since the time of St Pantalus, the first bishop there, who received the martyr's crown in Cologne along with the eleven thousand virgins.[30] This holy bishop Ortlieb acquired for his diocese and the surrounding region the miraculous blood of Christ and had it enclosed in a precious cross. On the day that it came to Basel, the thirteenth of the calends of July on the Feast of Saints Gervasius and Protasius [19 June], he declared an annual holiday throughout the diocese in honour of the worthy blood of Jesus Christ. How all this came to pass with the blood of Christ and how it came to Basel through this holy bishop is all recorded in Basel in the cathedral chapter and is read in the lections for Matins on this feast, which is called *Festum sanguinis Christi* [the Feast of Christ's Blood]. Take note, dear sisters, of what a blessed friend our Lord gave this convent.

1.12 *How Count Hermann of Froburg gave the fields that surrounded Schönensteinbach to the convent and how Saint Dominic was born in these times* [fol. 21r]

We have seen the favour and love of the worthy bishop of Basel for the convent of Schönensteinbach and the privileges he granted, particularly regarding collecting the rents of the chapel of St Margaret. The worthy Lord Leuthold,[31] bishop of Basel, did the same and confirmed all the favours and privileges that his predecessor had granted to the convent, and Pope Celestine III[32] granted the chapel and all its properties to the convent by papal bull.

During these times the convent had many good friends, especially the noble Count Hermann of Froburg,[33] who held many fields in fief from the bishop of Strasbourg.[34] The count released these properties, which lay in the parish of Wittenheim between Steinbach and the village of Wulferheim, over into the hands

30. Elisabeth of Schönau consulted on excavations made in Cologne and in her *Book of Revelations* first brought the legendary Pantalus into connection with Saint Ursula and her eleven thousand martyred companions. See Mary Marshall Campbell, "Sanctity and Identity: The Authentication of the Ursuline Relics and Legal Discourse in Elisabeth of Schönau's *Liber revelationum*," *Journal of Medieval Religious Cultures* 38 (2012): 159–192.

31. Leuthold I of Rotheln, bishop of Basel (r. 1192–1213).

32. Pope Celestine III (r. 1191–1198).

33. Hermann of Froburg (d. 1211/13).

34. Probably Rudolf of Rothweil (r. 1162–1179), if the 1170 date suggested by the birth of Dominic and the death of Thomas of Canterbury is accurate.

of the bishop on condition that they be given to the chapel of Schönensteinbach. This bishop agreed and gave these fields to the convent and the church in perpetuity. This count accomplished many other virtuous and good deeds on behalf of the convent.

Many other good friends of God also lived in Christendom. At that time our holy father Saint Dominic was born into this world and the holy bishop Saint Thomas of Canterbury was martyred.[35]

1.13 *How the church in Wittenheim was given to the convent of Schönensteinbach by the bishop of Strasbourg* [fol. 21v]

In those days, there was in Strasbourg a worthy bishop named Lord Conrad,[36] who was an especially good friend to the sisters and brothers of the convent of Schönensteinbach because of their blessed way of life. Up until that time, the parish church of Wittenheim had always belonged to the bishops of Strasbourg, who had the power to confer it. It so happened in the time of Bishop Conrad that the church of Wittenheim was held by a count who surrendered the rights and inheritances of all his fiefdoms into the hands of this bishop, thinking that he would like to give these things to the convent in order to counteract their poverty. So the bishop brought the matter before his chapter in Strasbourg, how the church in Wittenheim had again fallen to him and how he wanted to give it to the poor convent. This pleased all of them and they gave their blessing.

There was a knight residing in Ruffach named Lord Dietrich of Hus. He also claimed rights to the church, although many denied his claim. Nevertheless, the worthy bishop paid him eighty pounds for his rights, which he accepted. Since the church lay in the diocese of Basel, the bishop of Strasbourg requested the permission and counsel of the bishop in Basel. And so Bishop Conrad gave the church in Wittenheim to the convent along with the chapel in Küngersheim, so that they would commemorate him and his family annually, giving donations and alms on the anniversary of his death. He died in 1203 on the Feast of Saints Simon and Jude [October 28].

The church was given to the convent with the intention that the prior with his priests, or another priest of the convent, should sing there and provide spiritual care. It became the practice that each prior of Steinbach with his priests would oversee the churches of Wittenheim and Küngersheim. Usually there were many priests and friars who presided faithfully over the convent in spiritual and

35. In 1170 Dominic of Caleruega was born and Thomas Becket, bishop of Canterbury, was assassinated.

36. Conrad II of Hüneburg, prince-bishop of Strasbourg (r. 1190–1202).

material affairs. One can still see that their old necrologies list almost as many friars as sisters.[37]

1.14 *How Pope Innocent III allocated the church in Wittenheim with its chapels to the church in Schönensteinbach and about the devout life of these same sisters* [fol. 22v]

At this point, it must be noted that the tithes of the church in Küngersheim and of St Margaret in Wittenheim belonged to the church of Schönensteinbach and were administered through that convent. The papal See also confirmed this and incorporated them. In particular, the holy father Pope Innocent III[38] wrote a bull that no one should trouble the sisters in this task, by papal command and the wrath of God and of Saints Peter and Paul. This was the blessed pope to whom the holy father Saint Dominic came to petition for confirmation of the Order of Preachers, which he did shortly thereafter.

These were the renowned times in which God could be received in the peaceful and devout lives of so many good children, who turned zealously towards divine love and praise and maintained spiritual conduct by following their order and all the virtues of religious life. Therefore, the Lord God was especially pleased, as well as his mother and all the citizens of heaven who desired to live among them. We read this especially of Saint Adelphus the holy bishop,[39] who also became their patron saint, as is written of him in their books.

1.15 *How Schönensteinbach had a conflict with various people, and how at that time the Order of Preachers blossomed so greatly and grew in life and teaching* [fol. 23r]

For many years after the first foundation of Schönensteinbach, they observed such a devout and religious way of life that the community grew in members and in material assets. This also meant an increase in duties in order to manage their property well. Because of this care and worldly toil, the sisters could not serve God with free hearts as they had done before in poverty. And so the devotion of their early religious life began to wane and the sisters exalted themselves.

In 1238, this convent engaged in a massive conflict with the noble lords called von Warzenstelzen and fought for a long time over the offerings and the grain tax from Küngersheim. Finally, Pope Gregory IX[40] entrusted the affair to certain prelates to make peace. After a long time, the worthy lord Berthold,

37. A necrology was the record a community kept of their deceased members and the date on which they were to be commemorated each year.

38. Pope Innocent III (r. 1198–1216).

39. Saint Adelphus, bishop of Metz (fifth century), was honoured in Schönensteinbach, but Meyer is referring here to Adolf of Tecklenburg, bishop of Osnabrück (r. 1216–1224).

40. Pope Gregory IX (1227–1241).

bishop of Basel,[41] with the abbot of Altorf and the schoolmaster of the canonry in Strasbourg brought this matter to a good end. The offering fell to St Adelphus[42] and the grain tax to the convent, so that the convent would commemorate the aforesaid noble lords annually, maintain the chapel building, and provide it with lights and Mass. If they did not comply, the abbot and prior of Marbach were to present themselves in the city of Basel when summoned and remain there until the neglect was rectified. But the nobles were to surrender all their rights to the estate.

In these days, the holy father Saint Dominic, founder of the Order of Preachers, parted from this world and was received into the ranks of holy confessors by the aforementioned pope.[43] This same order grew greatly in convents and membership, in religious life, and in doctrine and learning. The friary of our dear fathers in Basel was first founded in 1233, and for many years they lived in great holiness. In the year prior, the convent called Unterlinden in Colmar had been founded for Dominican sisters.

In 1246, the community of Wittenheim requested that the convent of Steinbach provide enough oil every year that the holy sacrament would not stand in the dark. In return, they gave the convent the pastureland called Benzelshurst. Count Ludwig of Froburg[44] confirmed this, with the bishops of Basel and of Strasbourg and Count Rudolf of Habsburg[45] appending their seals.

1.16 *How trouble befell Schönensteinbach and how it declined both spiritually and temporally and how they took a noble man as custodian or advocate* [fol. 23v]

As the Dominican order increased in spirituality, the Canons Regular declined, especially in the convents of Marbach, Schönensteinbach, Goldbach, and Schwartzenthann.[46] And as Schönensteinbach lost spiritual goods, so they lost temporal goods as well, for at this time two brothers named Friedrich and Burckhard of Masmünster started a conflict with them over the estate and properties in Waltwiler. Pope Alexander IV[47] entrusted the matter to the deacon of St

41. Berthold II of Pfirt, bishop of Basel (r. 1248–1262).

42. Meyer does not mean the bishop saint himself but rather a chapel in the village of Küngersheim (see **2.21**) that had been dedicated to him.

43. Dominic died in 1221 and was canonized in 1234.

44. Ludwig III of Froburg (d. 1256/1259).

45. Rudolf became count of Habsburg around 1240 and was elected king of the Romans (i.e., of Germany) in 1273.

46. For the Canons Regular (Augustinians) and for Marbach's relationship to Schönensteinbach, see **1.7**.

47. Pope Alexander IV (r. 1254–1261).

Martin in Colmar. In the end, the convent retained barely a third [of its property] and the knights made off with two thirds, but the great cost and the troubles they had and how much property they lost is impossible to describe.

It also happened that the abbess and the women of Eschau in the diocese of Strasbourg claimed the chapel of St Margaret in Wittenheim with all its properties and thus at great cost to the convent of Steinbach. The pope entrusted the matter to the schoolmaster of Hagenau, who concluded that the convent would retain only the chapel of St Margaret with its rights. From these affairs and many others, the convent shrank considerably in spiritual and temporal matters.

And so during Easter Week of 1280 [14–21 April] when the convent performed a general audit, they were so poor that they could not have given anyone even bread, salt, or vegetables, and they had no livestock except for five young colts. Moreover, they owed forty-five marks to a Jew named Salman and needed to pay by Christmas. Over and above this debt, they also owed a lot of grain and money. The whole community begged Lord Dietrich of Hus to oversee the convent's temporal affairs and to be a custodian, which he did zealously.

1.17 *That it displeased the good devout sisters that the religious life had so diminished and how one Hedwig left the convent for the Dominican order* [fol. 24v]

That the convent of Schönensteinbach was doing so poorly in spiritual and temporal affairs displeased many of the old sisters who had been there since childhood. They thought that the convent could not be restored to its first spiritual foundation and desired to serve God in a stricter life. There was in particular a sister named Hedwig, who witnessed the destruction of the religious life in her convent and saw that the Dominicans flourished in all the virtues. She requested to transfer into this order, and so she left her order and her sisters and joined the holy sisters in Unterlinden at Colmar, where she led a holy life. This is written in the Latin book of the lives of the holy sisters of Unterlinden.[48]

48. This work survives, both in the original Latin version written by Katharina of Gebersweiler in the early fourteenth century and in a German translation and redaction by Elisabeth Kempf in the late fifteenth, after Meyer composed the *Book of the Reformation*. The Latin text is edited in Jeanne Ancelet-Hustache (ed.), "Les *vitae sororum* d'Unterlinden: Édition critique du manuscrit 508 de la bibliothèque de Colmar," *Archives d'histoire doctrinale et littéraire du Moyen Âge* 5 (1930): 317–513. For more about Elisabeth Kempf's translation, see Sarah Glenn DeMaris, "Anna Muntprat's Legacy for the Zoffingen Sisters: A Second Copy of the Unterlinden *Schwesternbuch*," *ZfdA* 144 (2015): 359–378.

1.18 *About the bad habits that were so ingrained that the religious life and common weal were barely respected* [fol. 25r]

We may well believe that the blessed dear mother and founder, Mother Kunigund of Wittenheim, the first *magistra* in this convent of Schönensteinbach, and Sister Kunigund of Wittenheim, her biological sister, led a blessed and spiritual life with their first sisters, since their successors were so blessed. Just as Christ, the mouth of wisdom, says, "Arbor bona bonos fructus facit," Matthew 7:[49] a good tree gives good and enduring fruit. This may be seen in Lord Notker and his daughters and the many spiritual children who were born from the stem of this tree. In the records of other convents, I find that the following sisters lived a holy life in convents of the Dominican order alone: Sister Gisela of Wittenheim and her sister Kunigund, and Sister Elisabeth of Wittenheim. I do not mention those who entered other orders. See how much good fruit these good trees brought forth!

But, as is written above, the religious life in Schönensteinbach had greatly diminished and its material welfare decreased accordingly. For this reason, there were no longer many priests or friars in the convent who could perform the Divine Office and preside over the sisters' spiritual lives. And so the church in Wittenheim was given to secular priests and the sisters suffered much trouble and harm from this. A priest named Trutman, parish priest of Wittenheim, especially troubled them over the offerings of the chapel of St Adelphus and hounded them with the ecclesial court in Basel. By 1320, the sisters no longer heeded their common good and many were using their own property more to see and be seen than to seek the common good of the convent. The greatest offering of St Adelphus, due yearly on his feast day [29 August], was taken by the priests and sisters and divided among themselves, thereby depriving the community of it and lending private property a grand figure.

At this time, the noble lord Count Ulrich of Pfirt, who had been lord over this land, died and left a daughter who was married to Duke Albert of Austria, bringing the region of Pfirt under the rule of Austria.[50]

1.19 *On the wantonness and misbehaviour that took place in the irreligious life of Schönensteinbach* [fol. 25v]

The convent declined so much that not only was there little religiosity left but the women also practised a wanton life. The abbot of Marbach, who oversaw

49. Matthew 7:17.

50. Count Ulrich III's daughter, Johanna of Pfirt (d. 1351), married the Habsburg Duke Albert (Albrecht) II of Austria (d. 1358), who gained control of the region when Ulrich died in 1324. Their great-grandchildren by their son Leopold will feature in book 5 as important supporters of the Observant reform.

the convent's spiritual matters, paid little mind to them. Earlier many blessed priests and brothers had been with the convent to care for their spiritual and temporal affairs, but now they had to confess to fathers who were not of their order. This being the case, they sought the freedom of their own will and found confessors who suited their lifestyle, let them live in disorder, and did not advise them in the religious practices of their order. The carelessness and laissez-faire attitude among the confessors, the superiors, and the sisters themselves became so great that it resulted in serious misbehaviour in the convent. When the confessors were supposed to ride to the convent for important feasts, they organized a hunt and brought rabbits and venison to the sisters. Some nuns also engaged in such unspiritual and unheard-of wilfulness that they had a May bath[51] built underneath the great oak trees in the courtyard of the convent and bathed in the tub under the trees. You can judge for yourself whether the beauty of Schönensteinbach's religious life had not been sullied.

For this reason, their material goods also ran out. The regional lords barely valued the convent. Few were present in God's house, certainly no wise and God-fearing people. The convent became dilapidated from neglect. Few had respect and devotion for such a life, and the convent therefore approached its demise.

In those days lived the holy noble woman Saint Bridget,[52] who received great revelations from God and his dear mother and other saints, about which she wrote great and beautiful books.

1.20 *How the convent of Schönensteinbach was damaged, destroyed, and burned by the English and how the sisters died out and the convent faded away and how Saint Bridget died* [fol. 26v]

With the situation in Schönensteinbach thus, a great plague came over the land of Alsace and brought great harm to the convent. In 1365, twelve thousand men, of whom six thousand were armed, came for the first time from England. They passed through Saverne and, having wrought great damage, afterwards went from there back out of the land towards Mumpelgart. The emperor pursued the English and wrought even greater havoc than before.[53] Schönenstein-

51. A bath with aromatic spring herbs, popular as entertainment in the fifteenth and sixteenth centuries.

52. Bridget of Sweden (1303–1373) was canonized in 1391. When Schönensteinbach is rededicated as a Dominican convent, it will be consecrated in her honour.

53. This refers to the invasion of Alsace by the brigand Arnold of Cervole (d. 1366) with English mercenaries left unemployed during a lull in the Hundred Years War. The pursuing emperor is Charles IV (king of the Romans 1346–1378, Holy Roman emperor from 1355).

bach [Lovely Stonybrook] was so thoroughly destroyed and razed of all its beauty that it could no longer rightly be called such, but rather "Hard Gravel Stonybrook." I have not been able to find a record of where the convent's property ended up nor whither the disgraceful nuns fled. Nevertheless, we may surmise (and the elderly still say) that the convent was miserably dissolved and disbanded, losing its property and inhabitants, so that the Divine Office was seldom held there. Lords, cities, and villages appropriated the convent's holdings.

Once this furious storm had passed and the land returned to peace and the sisters came back to the poor cloister, I do not find that any improvement followed. For this reason, the Lord God sent a plague among them so that few of the sisters remained alive. Nor do I find that these surviving sisters improved their lives.

In those times, there was a Sister Agnes zu Rhein, a *magistra* in Schönensteinbach. Although there were not many sisters in the convent and their needs were not as great as they had once been, the convent still could not recover. So this *magistra* and the sisters sold a great part of the convent's property and rents, especially what lay in Wulferheim and the village of Rotenschuren and other places, to Lord Burckhard of Laubgassen in 1369.[54]

The convent had already greatly declined when the English returned to this land with an innumerable force. Those on horseback numbered nearly fifty thousand, not counting the foot soldiers. They came again through Saverne, occupied the land between the mountains and the Rhine, and stayed in Andlau for nearly ten weeks, doing great harm. There was massive murdering, burning, robbing, and stealing. The moveable property of Schönensteinbach was plundered along with the property of the lords of Marbach, the relics, the letters, and such things. The sisters were destroyed and scattered as sheep without shepherds, and the convent was burned by the enemy in 1375. After this great destruction, the English marched past Basel into Switzerland and came to a Cistercian convent called Fraubrunnen. The citizens of Bern came out to meet the enemy and killed the king of England's son and many with him.[55]

54. Burckhard of Laubgassen fell in the battle of Sempach (1386) on the side of Duke Leopold III of Austria against the Swiss Confederacy. See Aegidius Tschudi, *Chronicon Helveticum*, ed. Johann Rudolf Iselin, 2 vols (Basel, 1734–1736), 1: 528.

55. This conflict, known as the Gugler War, occurred during a lull in French fighting, but was led and motivated by Enguerrand de Coucy, a son-in-law of King Edward III and related to the Habsburgs through his mother. He took advantage of the unemployed mercenaries and hired them to march against his Habsburg relatives and stake his own claims to the region. He was not in fact killed in this conflict but died in Turkish captivity in 1397. For a classic, albeit unscholarly account, see Barbara W. Tuchman, *A Distant Mirror: The Calamitous Fourteenth Century* (New York, 1978), 271–280.

After peace was restored, the sisters of Schönensteinbach were not able to restore their convent and none wanted to devote herself to the order. And so they died out except for five old and sick sisters, of whom four also soon died, leaving one old, weak, and frail sister. One day, she was wandering inattentively about the cloister, which was mostly in ruins, and her servant was not watching out for her. She fell in the brook that ran through the convent and drowned. Thus the convent passed fully away. About two years before this, the holy woman Saint Bridget had died in Rome in 1373.

1.21 *How all the moveable property was pillaged from the destroyed convent of Schönensteinbach and the cloister stood wild and deserted* [fol. 27v]

After the convent of Schönensteinbach had lost its community, it lay deserted for a long time. The abbot and canons of Marbach thought they might place some of their canons and brothers there and petitioned the bishop of Basel for Schönensteinbach to be a men's convent henceforth. But it did not come to pass, since the community of Marbach had also deteriorated and did not have enough people to occupy the grounds effectively. The buildings of Schönensteinbach were in ruins, and the following years brought immense inflation, mass death, and hard times. Under these pressures, the canons of Marbach seized the moveable goods from Steinbach – the precious reliquary of the holy bishop Saint Adelphus and the other holy relics, as well as letters, books, and other things – and left the convent a wasteland, entirely bare of all its possessions, such that no human habitation could be made there, nor the Divine Office or Mass celebrated. The convent disintegrated and was grown over with bushes, thorns, and weeds of all kinds in the courtyard, in the choir, and high up into the church. It was so nasty with worms and adders and snakes and other unclean things that it was a pitiable affair. One could see the old walls of the convent rising miserably above the wild wood, while the wild animals made their nests in the choir. And so it stood for many years.

In those days, both the male and female branches of the Dominicans and Franciscans had also declined from their early observance such that they did not live with the gravity that had reigned in Saint Dominic's time. For this reason, numerous convents of brothers and sisters of these orders all over Christendom needed to be reformed to the religious life – and still need to be reformed.

1.22 *How the property and rents of the convent of Schönensteinbach were confiscated* [fol. 28v]

In those days, the properties, fields, rents, and incomes of the convent were transferred and stolen. Lords, cities, and villages seized the property of the convent for themselves, and the convent's estate was dissolved. In particular, there was a knight named Hans Ulrich of Hus who, in defiance of God and right, arrogated the convent's property to his own person. He thought it had fallen to him by inheritance, since his parents had been the convent's advocates.[56] For this reason, he appropriated the property closest to Steinbach and that of the church in Wittenheim as well as the offerings of Saint Adelphus. When the canons of Marbach realized that this knight was receiving so much property from the abandoned convent, they appealed to the bishop of Basel. This caused a great disagreement between the friary of Marbach and the said knight, since each party thought they were in the right. The bishop, Lord Imer,[57] commanded that neither the knight nor anyone else should receive the property of Schönensteinbach's church nor any of the other goods. Nevertheless, the knight of Hus did not give up his claim right away.

This happened in 1388. In the following year Saint Bridget was canonized by Pope Boniface IX.[58]

1.23 *How a monk of the Premonstratensian order wanted to rebuild the convent of Schönensteinbach but could not, so the Dominicans were asked to make it a convent of sisters who would observe the order* [fol. 29r]

After the death of the aforementioned bishop of Basel, Lord Frederick the bishop of Strasbourg[59] assumed responsibility for the diocese of Basel. He had a chaplain named Andreas of Zweibrücken who was a monk of the Premonstratensian community of Wedigesheim in the diocese of Trier. This Andreas thought to restore the convent of Steinbach to its original properties and possessions. When the abbot of Marbach learned this, he thought he could defeat the knight of Hus and the other nobles in the matter of these properties. So the abbot and his community sent letters and messengers to the bishop, urging him to install Andreas as prior over the convent of Steinbach and as parish priest over the

56. He was probably a descendant of Dietrich of Hus, who accepted the convent's advocacy in 1280 (**1.16**).

57. Imer of Ramstein, bishop of Basel (r. 1382–1391).

58. In fact, it was in 1391 that Pope Boniface IX (r. 1389–1404) canonized Bridget of Sweden.

59. Frederick (Friedrich) II of Blankenheim, bishop of Strasbourg (r. 1375–1393) and (as Frederick III) bishop of Utrecht (r. 1393–1423).

other churches and chapels that belonged to it, and that Andreas should restore the convent and govern its churches. This happened in 1391.

Andreas tried for almost six years and met only obstacles regarding alms and the properties of the convent. He acquired letters with strong commands and pronouncements, but he could not accomplish what he had hoped to do. He could do no more than rebuild the roof over the choir and a house with a small room and a chamber. When some good people saw that he could accomplish nothing useful, they asked some blessed friars of the Order of Preachers to take the convent into their hands and restore it for sisters of their order to keep the order's law. To this end, they offered help, advice, and donations in good faith before the pope and wherever else it might be necessary. Alone in German lands, Friar Conrad of Prussia maintained observance of the Dominican order with his brothers in the convents of Colmar and Nuremberg, where he was prior. He took on this task and founded a noble and religious enclosed Dominican convent there to uphold the order in full spiritual devotion, as is described hereafter in the second book.

It tells also how much profit and fruit came from this restored Schönensteinbach, from which so many convents were reformed. It also describes certain gracious and devout sisters of this same convent.

Here ends the first part of this book and begins the second book or second part.

Book Two

2.1 *How our dear Lord showed his grace so richly by restoring the destroyed convent of Steinbach: the first chapter or the prologue* [fol. 29v]

Apparuit gracia dei salvatoris nostri etc.[1] The grace of God our preserver has appeared to us and been revealed as a lesson that we should repudiate all harshness and worldly desire and live moderately, justly, and mildly in this world. Since the grace of our Lord Jesus Christ has been shown to us so mercifully, we are obligated to protect ourselves from hateful unkindness and evil sensuality. We must live mildly in prudent moderation and in justice here in the religious space of the cloister, to which God by his grace has called us from the world, in order to faithfully serve him alone. Yet we should not imagine that the Lord has bestowed his grace because of the just works we have done. Rather, as Saint Paul says of the great kindness of his unfathomable mercy, he has sustained us poor people and kindly called us to him. We must recognize that he does not need to speak to us, as he does in the gospel of Matthew, saying: "Why do you not know my voice?"[2] But he says this particularly so that we will respond: "I want to hear what the Lord speaks in me."[3] That is: "I should acknowledge the grace that God the Lord daily bestows so plentifully upon me in the holy place of this cloister through the sacraments of holy confession and the holy Eucharist and other Christian things such as preaching, reading in the refectory, admonishments, and teaching. Furthermore, I should lift up in praise the inner inspiration, good thoughts, and innumerable other blessings that God bestows on me and let them serve only good. I should not receive in vain the grace of God that I so richly have, and futilely waste it, lest I be thrown out like the useless servant. Rather, I want the Lord to speak to me as to the faithful servant, saying, 'Oh, good and faithful servant, because thou hast been faithful, enter thou into the joy of thy Lord.'"[4]

1. Titus 2:11.
2. John 8:43.
3. Psalms 84:9.
4. Matthew 25:21–23.

Hereafter, the second book describes how this convent of Schönensteinbach was restored to a glorious state of spiritual observance and perfect enclosure according to the practice of the full observance of the holy Dominican order.

2.2 *How the holy father Friar Conrad of Prussia found many willing sisters who had been scattered in Dominican convents and wanted to maintain their order* [fol. 30v]

There was a good and blessed father named Friar Conrad of Prussia, a great lover of souls. He wanted to establish and raise a convent, in which the sisters would follow the entire observance of the order according to the perfection of the Rule, as in the time of Saint Dominic, and who would maintain the best and most secure enclosure. He greatly desired this, and since he was a very gifted preacher and travelled the lands to preach, he found many willing dear sisters in convents all over who wanted to uphold the order with such observance as Saint Dominic had ordained. They also wished to be enclosed, such that not only would no one come into the convent any more, but also they could not be seen by anyone outside. They wanted to live in voluntary poverty without property in chaste purity and humble obedience. When the worthy father Friar Conrad of Prussia discovered this, he thought over how he might bring together these willing sisters, these children of God, from their convents into a single cloister where they might fulfil their holy intention to observe the holy Dominican order.

In those days, many holy persons were earnestly inspired and understood through special signs how the convent of Schönensteinbach, which had been completely destroyed, might be rebuilt and replanted in honour of God. When Father Conrad heard this, he travelled to the destroyed convent to inspect it. He was immediately enflamed with love of the cloister to the honour of God and he liked both the estate and the location of the convent. He thought it would be an excellent place for a true religious life, since the grounds were isolated in the woods far from people. He decided to willingly devote himself to this and take on the work of requesting from the pope and other prelates, princes, and lords their will, blessing, permission, and privilege to rebuild Schönensteinbach as an enclosed convent of Dominican sisters, upholding full observance of the order. He received all of this fully from religious and secular prelates, and Schönensteinbach became an honourable convent of Observant Dominican women.

2.3 *How the crumbling cloister of Schönensteinbach was given to Friar Conrad and his brothers to make into an Observant women's convent* [fol. 31v]

The worthy father Conrad put the matter to the illustrious prince Duke Leopold of Austria, who was lord of those lands where the convent of Steinbach lay, and to his wife Lady Catherine of Burgundy.[5] He told them both that they should re-establish the convent for the glory of God and the salvation of their souls, and as comfort for the souls of their ancestors and descendants. This pleased the noble prince and his wife, and they zealously assisted in the foundation and rebuilding of the convent for Dominican friars and sisters to uphold the order with full observance in perpetuity.

Now Conrad considered how he could begin in good order so that his project would see good and peaceful progress and come to a blessed and fortunate end. He sought the advice of wise people and found in old letters that the convent of Schönensteinbach had been incorporated and assigned to the Order of Canons Regular.[6] In particular, this convent's spiritual affairs had been entrusted to a community of that order named Marbach, and its material affairs to the lord of the land, which had fallen to the duke of Austria. These canons had the power to restore the convent for the glory and in the service of God.

A worthy bishop noted these matters and came with many other good friends of God to the Dominican fathers of the Observance to offer them the convent of Schönensteinbach, on the condition that they reform it. If the order were observed there in perpetuity, they would render aid before the pope. But when the fathers of the Dominican order heard that the convent had earlier been under the canons of Marbach, they sent a worthy father named Friar Dietrich of Wald and with him a Friar Johannes of Baden to the abbot of Marbach. These two told the abbot and friars of Marbach that if they no longer wanted or were able to restore the convent of Schönensteinbach, they should give their permission and blessing for someone else to bring the convent back into God's service. The abbot and friars said they wished to think it over, but they never gave the Dominicans an answer. The noble prince Duke Leopold then sent a knight named Johannes of Masmünster to the abbot of Marbach, demanding that he present the rights that he and his canonry had over the convent of Schönensteinbach. The canons of Marbach sent a canon from their own community to the duke, but this messenger could

5. Catherine of Burgundy (1378–1425) married Leopold IV, the duke of Austria (r. 1392–1411), in 1387/93 and received the county of Pfirt as her morning gift. The morning gift was a substantial amount of property or money that the husband gave to his bride on the morning after their wedding and was intended to support her in widowhood if he were to die first. Both during her marriage and after Leopold's death, Catherine's primary residence was the Habsburg estate in Ensisheim, not far from Schönensteinbach and within the county that had been her morning gift.

6. The Canons Regular were also known as the Augustinians. For a note on the history of the Augustinian order and for Marbach in particular, see **1.7**.

not produce any reasonable documentation that the abbot and the community of Marbach had rights over the destroyed convent of Steinbach.

2.4 *How Schönensteinbach was given to the Dominicans, signed over, and confirmed as a religious convent of Dominican women* [fol. 33r]

In those days, there was a priest of the White Order (called *Ordo Premonstratensis*) in Schönensteinbach, Friar Andreas of Zweibrücken. Andreas had received the poor, dilapidated convent from the abbot of Marbach, in order to occupy, restore, and rebuild it. Frederick, the bishop of Strasbourg, and custodian and administrator of the diocese of Basel,[7] had confirmed and approved that this Andreas should be prior of Steinbach and restore it. Andreas had been there for six years, but he and others saw that he would not be able to finish, so he relinquished the convent to the Observant Dominican fathers with the good will, blessing, and knowledge of the prince, Duke Leopold of Austria.

The matter between Andreas and the Dominicans was brought before Ulrich, the bishop of Brixen and chancellor to Duke Leopold,[8] to order the affair so that it would be permanent. This bishop declared that Steinbach and all its possessions should be given in perpetuity to Dominicans who would uphold the order,[9] with the stipulation that these Dominicans and their successors give Friar Andreas sixty Rhenish florins and twenty quartals of wheat[10] annually for the rest of his life and render assurance and guarantee of this. Thus the order gave Friar Andreas this sum for many years up until his death.

2.5 *How the pope gave Schönensteinbach to Raymond, master of the order, and how Raymond received it and then entrusted it to the blessed Friar Conrad of Prussia with complete authority* [fol. 33v]

So that the restoration of Schönensteinbach would proceed according to regulations, the worthy father Conrad of Prussia asked the duke of Austria to

7. Frederick (Friedrich) of Blankenheim, bishop of Strasbourg; see **1.23**.

8. Ulrich Prustl (r. 1396–1417) was made bishop of Brixen through Duke Leopold IV's influence.

9. Meyer's understanding of "upholding" or "keeping" the order involves a complex relationship between strict regulations and virtuous behaviour. For Meyer, the Dominican order is defined by the Augustinian Rule and the Dominican Constitutions. These in turn are embodied by the friars and nuns who follow the "form of life" laid down in these documents. Because of his reforming programme, the phrase "upholding" or "keeping the order" also has a sense of preservation. Those who "uphold" or "keep" the order protect it against dissolution by living strictly according to its statutes.

10. A quartal was a measure of volume; like most units of measure prior to modern reforms, it varied from region to region.

zealously petition and earnestly write to the pope that he give his blessing and will for Schönensteinbach to be an enclosed convent of Dominican sisters keeping the order. The duke, along with many other notable and blessed persons, petitioned the pope for this. When the pope,[11] who was a great lover of the religious life, heard this, he was glad in his heart and gave all the blessing, permission, will, and papal privilege they desired. He commanded the master general and the Dominican friars to grant the convent all the same privileges and papal honours as other convents under Dominican care. He released a good and certain bull concerning this, and informed the abbot of Murbach[12] by papal authority that he had considered all things thoroughly and decided to incorporate the convent into the Dominican order by papal authority and to transfer it honourably with public ceremonial dignity. This all was done, and the same facilitator who carried out the papal commands zealously saw to this matter in person.

Not long before, this same holy pope had blessed and canonized the worthy and holy woman Saint Bridget. He wrote in the bull of incorporation: "We want this convent henceforth in perpetuity to be called St Bridget's Convent[13] at Steinbach and the prioress and sisters should be under the care and protection of the Dominicans." This happened in 1397 on Pentecost [10 June], while the Dominican general chapter was being held in Frankfurt, in German lands. The papal orders and bulls were brought there before the worthy master general of the order, the blessed Raymond, who was a very holy man. After presenting this to the fathers of the order, he wrote to Father Conrad of Prussia in these words:

> Dear Conrad,
> At the request of Duke Leopold of Austria, our holy father Pope Boniface IX has entrusted to me the convent Schönensteinbach in the diocese of Basel, which used to be a convent of Augustinian sisters. The pope has given

11. Pope Boniface IX (r. 1389–1404).

12. There is some confusion about which convent oversaw Schönensteinbach before the Dominicans received it. In **2.4**, the manuscripts actually state that Andreas of Zweibrücken had received permission from the abbot of Marburg, which conflicts with the account in **1.23**. It would seem likely that "Murbach" is also a confusion for "Marbach," but **2.7** explicitly calls the abbot in question a Benedictine and provides the name Wilhelm, which fits with the known succession of Murbach abbots. Since Murbach Abbey exercised considerable political power in the region, it is more likely that the abbot was not involved as a spiritual advisor but rather was enlisted for political support, as Duke Leopold IV and Catherine of Burgundy were.

13. This dedication explains Meyer's asides locating Bridget of Sweden's life and canonization historically in the earlier chapters. Because of her visions and her efforts to found her own reform order (the Bridgettines), Bridget was associated with reform and thus an appropriate patron saint for an Observant convent.

> it the name of St Bridget and commanded that sisters of our order should reside there, maintaining observance and enclosure according to the customs of the Venetian convent of Corpus Christi.[14] For this reason, dear brother, I commend to your faithfulness and piety the spiritual and temporal care of St Bridget's convent in Schönensteinbach. You have as much authority as I would have were I there. You may receive and admit from other convents willing sisters who wish to uphold the Observance and join this convent. Since at the moment there is no community there, I grant you the authority given me by the pope to select and confirm a prioress and entrust the convent and sisters to her. By the power of the Holy Spirit and holy obedience and under threat of excommunication, I forbid all friars and sisters from hindering you or withholding their help. Although it would be good and even necessary for you to be at the convent at all times, you cannot do this because you must preach the divine word everywhere. You may therefore grant full authority to Friar Dietrich of Wald or another capable friar of our order.

This convent has also received great privileges from the princes of the land, especially the Roman emperor Frederick[15] and other dukes of Austria, from whom they have many reliable bulls.

2.6 *How, from among all his dear, willing spiritual daughters, the worthy father Friar Conrad of Prussia chose only thirteen sisters to found the convent Schönensteinbach* [fol. 35r]

When the blessed father Friar Conrad of Prussia had had enough of Schönensteinbach built so that one could live there and that the cloister might have a more secure enclosure, he chose from among all his dear spiritual children (of whom he had many) only thirteen in the honour and memory of our dear Lord and his holy twelve apostles. He did not want to accept any more to begin the community, although he had found many more Dominican sisters and other blessed servants of God, who wished to participate in such a blessed enterprise. He recognized that by religious law one superior with twelve subordinates con-

14. Conrad of Prussia's Italian counterpart, Giovanni Dominici, had founded Corpus Christi in Venice as an Observant convent in 1394. See Bartolomea Riccoboni, *Life and Death in a Venetian Convent: The Chronicle and Necrology of Corpus Domini, 1395–1436*, trans. Daniel Ethan Bornstein (Chicago, 2000), 4–5.

15. Frederick III (r. 1452–1493) was the last emperor to be crowned in Rome and the first from the Habsburg line.

stituted a whole convent and no fewer,[16] but he did not wish to burden the fledgling community with too many persons nor too few. These thirteen persons were nine Dominican sisters and four secular persons. Five sisters were from the convent called St Katharinental in Diessenhofen, two sisters were from [the convent of] St John the Baptist called Unterlinden, one sister was from St Catherine's in Colmar, and one was from the convent in Schlettstadt called Sylo. Of the four secular people, one was to be a veiled choir sister and the other three would be lay sisters, so that there would be ten veiled choir sisters and three lay sisters.

2.7 *How it was proclaimed throughout the land how and when the convent would be inaugurated, and the names of the first blessed mothers through whom this was accomplished* [fol. 36r]

Now our holy father Pope Boniface IX commanded the noble lord abbot of Murbach, Wilhelm of the Order of St Benedict,[17] to transfer the convent to the Dominicans, publicly and with ceremonial dignity, so that the convent might henceforth be a convent of Dominican nuns in perpetual enclosure under the authority of the master general of the order, and of the provincial prior of Teutonia, and of the friars, according to the custom of the order. And so the abbot of Murbach had it proclaimed throughout the land and preached everywhere, that Schönensteinbach would be given to the Dominican order. It was determined that all persons joining the community should be present on St Martin's Day [11 November]. The thirteen sisters were brought together in Ensheim. Those coming from Diessenhofen spent about six weeks in the convent of Klingental in Basel, attending choir and refectory with the sisters there. There was a secular maiden in the convent of Klingental who developed such zeal and devotion to the life that these five sisters had chosen that she left Basel with them for Ensheim, the city which lies about a half mile from Schönensteinbach. The other persons were also led to Ensheim and assembled there.

The names of the sisters were as follows: Five came from Diessenhofen and were called Sister Claranna of Hohenburg, Sister Adelheid of Hattingen, Sister Elisabeth Goldschmidt, Sister Elisabeth Meringer, and Sister Magdalena Betminger. The two sisters from Unterlinden were named Sister Margaretha of Masmünster and Sister Beatrix Voigt, a lay sister. From St Catherine's in Colmar came Sister Clara of Ostren. From Sylo came Sister Adelheid Lutzmann. Gertrud

16. Distinctio 2, chapter 1 of the Constitutions for Dominican friars forbade approving a new community with fewer than twelve members. See "Liber Constitutionum Ordinis Fratrum Praedicatorum," *Analecta Sacri Ordinis Fratrum Praedicatorum* 3 (1897): 98.

17. Wilhelm of Wasselnheim (r. 1393–1428). See **2.5** for a note about Murbach Abbey.

of Eelswerd, Susanna of Masmünster, and her maidservant Katharina of Sulz were also led there. I have recorded here the names of these thirteen devout mothers[18] because they were the holy foundation, cornerstone, and precious and noble living rock not only of the worthy convent of Steinbach but also of all reformed Dominican convents in German lands. In confirmed divine texts, one also reads the names of distinguished holy fathers worthily commemorated in this way.

2.8 *How on St Martin's Day the thirteen sisters and mothers were led in dignity to Schönensteinbach in order to begin and replant the holy Observance there* [fol. 37r]

Early on St Martin's Day [11 November] in 1397, a great company of lords gathered, along with so many common folk, both men and women, that it was a wonder to see. There were not only many Dominican friars but also many religious people and worthy priests, who would devoutly perform the Divine Office in Schönensteinbach that day. In addition, the high-born princess Lady Catherine came, daughter of the illustrious prince Duke Philip of Burgundy[19] and wife to Duke Leopold of Austria. She had proven especially zealous and earnest to refound Schönensteinbach as an enclosed Dominican convent. Through her retinue, this worthy princess provided at great cost everything needed with regard to material things, such as food, drink, and the like.

The dear, devout servants of God were led out of the city of Ensheim, and as they approached the convent Schönensteinbach both the secular priests and those in orders came to meet them with the reliquary, burning candles, and devout song, and received them honourably in a beautiful and devout procession. A great crowd followed them with solemnity and spiritual joy, leading the holy mothers with their songs and prayers into the church. When silence fell, the priests went to the altar. The blessed father, the founder of this religious movement himself, sang Mass and, with great devotion, presented the word of God to these loving and desirous hearts. The noble princess Lady Catherine of Burgundy, along with other honourable persons of the nobility, diligently attended the dear mothers with faithful hearts. There were so many people, noble and common, in the courtyard that they could not all fit into the church. A pushing and shoving mob formed around the convent, since they had such a great desire to see this holy beginning.

18. Margaretha of Klingental is not named here, but she was the enthusiastic secular maiden from Basel mentioned in the previous paragraph, and the thirteenth of the founding nuns. She is recorded as one of the first thirteen in the chapter dedicated to her life. See **3.31**.

19. Philip the Bold, duke of Burgundy (r. 1363–1404).

During Mass after the Agnus Dei, the dear sisters, who now all wore the order's habit, received the holy sacrament. After the offertory, the blessed father Conrad invested the four secular persons with the order's habit in such ceremonial dignity as is the custom of the order.

2.9 *How the dear thirteen mothers were enclosed with desirous hearts in the convent Schönensteinbach, never to see anyone again*[20] *and to uphold the holy Observance* [fol. 38r]

Once the papal bulls and episcopal letters and also the letters from the master general and all the other bulls and letters had been read and everything else publicly announced and spoken according to regulation, the blessed father Conrad chose Sister Claranna of Hohenburg as the prioress of the convent of Steinbach and requested her obedience, which she humbly demonstrated. He then confirmed her and gave her plenary power. The pope had specially authorized Father Conrad to select and confirm the first prioress and to enclose the sisters and teach them so that they and their successors might eternally maintain enclosure and live according to the form of the first saints of the order. The servant of God fulfilled this in all faith and entrusted the prioress to her sisters and the sisters to their prioress, giving them all his priestly blessing. The new prioress stood up with her sisters and came before the noble princess, the duchess of Austria, and bowed to thank her for the faith and grace that she and her husband Duke Leopold had so generously shown.

Now, the worthy father Friar Conrad would have liked to give the sisters something similar, each just like the other. He had little images of the Passion of our Lord, but they were all different: one showed him being flogged, one crowned, one like this, the other like that. In a miraculous sign, our dear Lord transformed all the images so that they all showed an identical scene of the Crucifixion with Mary and John standing under the

20. This form of strict enclosure required that contact with the outside world be conducted through a device like a revolving door or through a spiked grate or grille, both of which prevented physical contact and sight. It was probably the single most controversial measure of Observant reform, but a sister from the Strasbourg convent of St Nicholas-in-Undis will explain its importance in **5.74**. See also Heike Uffmann, "Inside and Outside the Convent Walls: The Norm and Practice of Enclosure in the Reformed Nunneries of Late Medieval Germany," *The Medieval History Journal* 4 (2001): 83–108; Marie-Luise Ehrenschwendtner, "Creating the Sacred Space Within: Enclosure as a Defining Feature in the Convent Life of Medieval Dominican Sisters (13th–15th c.)," *Viator* 41 (2010): 301–316.

cross.[21] This blessed man gave each sister an image of the crucified Christ. They took their crucifixes, blessed this father and the duchess, and acknowledged the crowd. They then took leave of the world and all that is in it, and went willingly into the convent. Father Conrad closed it with the most secure lock with which one could enclose a religious cloister, in the name of God the Father, the Son, and the Holy Spirit, our dear Lady, Saint Dominic, and Saint Bridget.

After midday, the noble princess took leave of the sisters at the grille, commended herself to them in prayer, and left with her retinue. The crowd went home, greatly edified and praising God for the great grace he had shown his dear servants, who with joyful and kind-hearted demeanour had renounced the false world and chosen the best part.[22]

2.10 *How the sisters of the reformed convent of Schönensteinbach led such a virtuous life that both religious and secular people favoured them* [fol. 39r]

The dear devout mothers began to live earnestly for God alone and, in keeping with the holy Dominican order, they served God devoutly night and day. With soulful desire, they cleaved to God with manifold virtues. They willingly gave themselves into great poverty and led a strict life. Because they followed the virtues of prudence and moderation in all things, the worthy father Conrad of Prussia stayed with them for a time at the beginning, along with two spiritual and honourable friars of the order as confessors. Friar Dietrich of Wald and Friar Johannes of Witten were noble, wise, brave, and experienced men. Through their life and teaching, they directed the convent of sisters to uphold godly love, sisterly faith, humble serenity, true patience, and right obedience in a clean and pure life, instead of pursuing rash austerity over and above the directives of the order.

21. For the symbolic importance of this image miracle to the foundation of the Observant community at Schönensteinbach, see Thomas Lentes, "Bild, Reform und *cura monialium*: Bildverständnis und Bildgebrauch im Buch der Reformacio Predigerordens des Johannes Meyer (d. 1485)," in *Dominicains et dominicaines en Alsace: XIIIe–XXe s.*, ed. Jean-Luc Eichenlaub (Colmar, 1996), 177–195; Jeffrey Hamburger, *The Visual and the Visionary: Art and Female Spirituality in Late Medieval Germany* (Cambridge, MA, 1998), 428–431; Claire Taylor Jones, *Ruling the Spirit: Women, Liturgy, and Dominican Reform in Late Medieval Germany* (Philadelphia, 2018), 134–135.

22. Luke 10:42. The contrast between the hard-working Martha and the attentive Mary was a medieval commonplace for the "active" religious life of service and the "contemplative" life of enclosure. See Giles Constable, "The Interpretation of Mary and Martha," in *Three Studies in Medieval Religious and Social Thought* (Cambridge, 1995), 1–141.

And so the good reputation of their holy life spread so far abroad that religious and secular prelates, princes and lords, and many of the common folk held them in devotion and favour. In particular, our holy father the pope wanted to grant the convent's church an indulgence so that all who came there at any time would receive forgiveness for all their sins, but the devout sisters were concerned that they might lose their quiet rest and inner devotion through the disturbance of visiting crowds. The archbishop of Besançon and the bishop of Basel demonstrated their faith and love for the sisters through special favours, indulgences, and privileges in letters. In particular, the archbishop of Besançon, Theobald,[23] came personally to the convent to consecrate and confirm it. The worthy father Raymond of Capua also honoured the convent with gifts and privileges, as his successors as master general have also done. The worthy fathers who served as provincial prior of Teutonia, especially Father Giselbert of Utrecht,[24] occasionally told the sisters of the other convents that none of them could be compared to Schönensteinbach. Even the secular lords held the blessed sisters of Schönensteinbach in great esteem, especially the princes of the house of Austria such as Duke Leopold, Duke Frederick, the Roman emperor Frederick III, and his brother Duke Albert of Austria.[25] The last two both favoured this convent, as one sees in their letters. Duke William of Holland[26] also held this convent in special favour and wished to have his death commemorated there. Similarly, Lady Catherine of Burgundy and many other noble and common people had such great devotion to this convent that they offered up themselves and their possessions. Many of them joined this blessed community and committed themselves to the Dominican order to serve God almighty.

2.11 *How honourable and worthy persons came to Schönensteinbach from near and far to serve God in the order and in the Observance* [fol. 40r]

Among the distinguished persons who joined this blessed religious life, some were nuns from different convents, some honourable young maidens from the world, and some honourable widows and wives from near and far. First came the

23. Thibaud of Rougemont, archbishop of Besançon (r. 1405–1429).

24. Giselbert of Utrecht was provincial prior of Teutonia from 1408 to 1426. See *SOPMA*, 2: 43–44.

25. These are the Habsburg dukes of the Leopoldian line, Leopold IV of Austria (Catherine of Burgundy's husband), Frederick IV of Austria (r. 1402–1439, count of Tyrol from 1406), Emperor Frederick III (r. 1452–1493), and his brother Albert VI of Austria (r. 1424–1463).

26. William IV, count of Holland, also William II, duke of Bavaria-Straubing (r. 1404–1417), was married to Catherine of Burgundy's sister, Margaret of Burgundy (d. 1441).

honourable woman Elisabeth, called van Sterre, abbess of the convent of St Servatius in Utrecht in the Netherlands. She gave up the abbacy, came to Alsace (for her a foreign land), and became a submissive and humble sister in Schönensteinbach. From the open convent of St Leodegar in Masmünster, which is a community of canonesses, came two noble, capable women to submit themselves to the sweet yoke of Christ. One was called Sister Dorothea of Ostren and the other Sister Margretha of Baden. They were both such wise and spiritual sisters that afterwards they were sent out to reform other convents. One became prioress of Unterlinden, and the other prioress of St Mary Magdalene an den Steinen in Basel.

Dominican sisters from other convents also came because they wished to uphold their order. For example, the dear sister Anna of Scherenberg came from St Mark's in Würzburg; from St Nicholas-in-Undis in Strasbourg came Sister Clara Folz, who long was a loving and gracious subprioress in Steinbach; from St Walburga's in Münsterlingen by Lake Constance came two beautiful sisters, Elisabeth of Rosenberg and Margretha Schwartz. The latter sister was so full of grace that she became the second prioress of Schönensteinbach. Many other God-fearing and well-suited people came from other convents, from Diessenhofen and from St Catherine's as well as St Margaret's in Augsburg.

Many honest maidens of the world also entered this convent – for example, Sophia of Veld, a zealous subprioress and a great lover of the religious life, and Sister Lukardis, who became the bursar as well as scribe of the mass books, graduals, antiphonals, lectionaries, and other books of the choir. Sister Udela of Utrecht, Sister Mechthildis of Polwig, and many other well-bred maidens became veiled choir sisters in the early years and upheld the order with great zeal.

There were not only well-born yet humble choir sisters; many other worthy people became poor, humble lay sisters there. For example, the noble and blessed Sister Katharina of Bruges in Flanders, Sister Gertrud of Kulenburg, Sister Dorothea of Freudenberg, Sister Margretha of Dieffenbrug, sister of the duke of Cleves,[27] and many other honourable persons, who enriched the convent greatly with their material possessions.

27. Anne Winston-Allen (following Seraphin Dietler) identifies this sister as Margaret of the Marck and Nassau-Dillenburg (d. 1409), sister of Adolf III of the Marck (r. 1391–1393) and the count of Cleves (r. 1368–1394). See Anne Winston-Allen, "Making Manuscripts as Political Engagement by Women in the Fifteenth-Century Observant Reform Movement," *Journal of Medieval Religious Cultures* 42 (2016): 224–247, at 232–234.

2.12 *How the sisters of Schönensteinbach were grievously harried and troubled by the abbot of Marbach* [fol. 41r]

It is characteristic of the evil spirit that, wherever he knows that one serves God in peace, he does what he can through his trickery to trouble such minds so that they stray from their good lives. He cannot do this entirely by himself, so he employs all kinds of tricks. And so it happened that Peter, the abbot of the Augustinian canonry of Marbach, died and left his office vacant around the time that Schönensteinbach was entrusted to the Dominicans by the holy father pope and by Duke Leopold of Austria with the agreement of Abbot Peter. His successor, who was named Nicolaus, claimed that the convent belonged to his order and to his canonry. With his helpers, he began to war against the sisters and wanted to bring the convent, to which he believed he had a right, back under his abbacy. He wanted back the relic of the worthy father Saint Adelphus, which Marbach had given to the convent along with many other relics, letters, and books. When the Dominicans told this abbot and his allies all about the convent, that the transfer had been conducted in an orderly manner according to God and right, and that neither he nor his community had any claim or right, this did not help. On the contrary, the sisters were so greatly and severely pressured that they worried they might have to leave the convent and that their religious life would decline. Furthermore, the enemies of the sisters slandered them so greatly with lies about dishonest things that the convent paid for it noticeably. In addition, the sisters had to assume great costs for sending messages to the pope and many other places about this affair.

Yet after much worry and great cost, everything was settled in the sisters' favour, and the abbot and the Augustinian house of Marbach gave letters and seals to the sisters of Steinbach in which they acknowledged that they had no right or claim to the convent of Schönensteinbach.

2.13 *That the convent of Schönensteinbach should not lack suffering* [fol. 42r]

From the beginning of the convent up until our time, God the Lord generally visited special suffering upon this convent at least once a year, sometimes for longer, sometimes shorter. For this reason, at the beginning of the restoration of the convent, a holy person of our Dominican order saw a sword hanging above the convent in the air as a sign that suffering would never be entirely lacking in Schönensteinbach. Blessed be the one who happily receives suffering with grateful patience from the kind hand of God.

Certain noble and non-noble people greatly troubled this convent and burdened it substantially in numerous ways, such that the convent's worldly possessions considerably diminished in both landed and moveable property. One knight in particular appropriated the convent's properties without right to them, but his ferocity was so great that the dear sisters did not dare stand against him or the persecution by which he did great harm to the convent's holdings. After his death, he sometimes appeared in the plain light of day, circling the convent in a fiery wagon and suffering miserably in excruciating pain. The knight's relatives returned the stolen property to the convent in kind, and afterwards he was seen no more. Another nobleman, who persecuted this convent in many ways and grievously harmed and troubled it, was plagued with St Anthony's fire and died a miserable death.[28] It was believed that he owed this fate to his behaviour towards the convent.

So many other noble people harassed and harmed this convent in so many different ways that it would be too much to record. Therefore, regarding these affairs, Pope Martin V[29] wrote and commanded in a special bull that whatever goods had been unjustly stolen or confiscated from the sisters of Schönensteinbach should be returned to the convent by papal decree.

2.14 *Of the three flights of the sisters of the convent of Schönensteinbach and the great sorrow, suffering, worry, and repeated dispersions it caused* [fol. 43r]

In the year 1415, our loving God granted his children a special gift of suffering. The cause of this suffering arose when Duke Frederick of Austria helped Pope John XXIII escape the council that was being held in Constance.[30] Great suffering and sorrow followed when many marched against the duke in order to claim his land. The sisters of Steinbach, who lived under the lordship of Austria, had to flee their convent to a wealthy city called Mülhausen about a mile distant from their cloister. They were safely enclosed there for fourteen days in the cloister of

28. Ergotism is a deadly form of fungal food poisoning that results in terrible symptoms, including convulsions, gangrene, and psychosis. In the Middle Ages it was called St Anthony's fire after the hospitaller Order of St Anthony, which specialized in treating it.

29. Pope Martin V (r. 1417–1431).

30. The Council of Constance (1414–1418) was working to end the Great Western Schism (1378–1417) and reunite Latin Christendom under a single pope. John XXIII had declared himself willing to abdicate, provided the other two antipopes did likewise, but then fled the council disguised as one of the squires of Duke Frederick IV of Austria, in order to avoid fulfilling this vow. He was captured somewhere in the Breisgau, just east of Schönensteinbach, and held prisoner until the resolution of the Schism. As punishment for aiding the fleeing pope, Duke Frederick was reprimanded by Emperor Sigismund and lost several of his territories in the region. See Phillip H. Stump, "The Council of Constance (1414–1418) and the End of the Schism," in *A Companion to the Great Western Schism (1378–1417)*, ed. Joelle Rollo-Koster and Thomas M. Izbicki (Leiden, 2009), 395–442, at 409–410.

the Hospitallers, where they could sing and read their hours. Once peace had returned, they were honourably led back to their convent of Schönensteinbach.

Thirteen years later, in 1428, the duke of Lorraine warred against the duke of Austria[31] and the land that contains Schönensteinbach. The sisters once again had to leave their convent and their security, and were housed in the city of Ensheim. They spent nine days in watchful enclosure at the manor of the noble family of Andlau. The third exile happened eleven years later in 1439.[32] When those hard and ferocious people, the bandits called the Armagnacs, came into Alsace for the first time, the sisters of Steinbach again left and spent four weeks in the city of Ensheim at the same manor of the von Andlau family.

It must be noted, that even though the perils of war forced the sisters to leave the convent so frequently, this was always conducted with great care and zealous caution in order to protect the community as much as possible. The sisters were led there and back in great devotion, veiled, in a procession with the cross and reliquary, calling on God in prayer and the like. Even outside of the convent, they conducted themselves religiously according to the customs of the order and the Observance, communally singing and reading the canonical hours and everything else, just as if they were still in the convent, to the extent that they were able and as circumstances permitted.

2.15 *Concerning the fourth departure of the sisters from the convent of Schönensteinbach, which was the longest and in which they experienced much worry, suffering, and trouble, and many sources of fear and distress* [fol. 44r]

The fourth exile was the longest. Moreover, the sisters were separated and sent far and wide. It started in 1444 on St Bernard's Day [20 August], because the king of France, while he was still dauphin and his father the old king still lived,[33] marched at the request of certain German nobles with a great and enormous army into the German lands through Alsace. There were many thousands of

31. The duke of Lorraine in 1428 was Charles II the Bold (r. 1390–1431). For the year 1428, I have only been able to identify his involvement in a conflict with Metz known as "The War of the Basketful of Apples," in which Duke Frederick IV was not involved.

32. When Charles II of Lorraine died in 1431, he left no male heirs, yet had explicitly disinherited his brother's son, Count Antoine of Vaudémont, six years earlier. Charles's daughter Isabelle (r. 1431–1453) claimed control of Lorraine together with her husband, the forceful Duke René of Anjou (r. 1434–1480), but Count Antoine challenged their claim. The mercenaries who had fought for the Armagnac faction in the French succession war were also hired in this conflict, which is why Meyer identifies the invading force as Armagnacs.

33. Louis XI (r. 1461–1483) became dauphin in 1440 and succeeded to the throne at the death of his father, Charles VII (r. 1422–1461).

them, and with the French were those murderous, inhuman, and berserk people, the Armagnacs. The lords of the land thought that this army would help them and the duke of Austria to fight against the Swiss Confederacy, but the greatest harm was done to the duke's people and land.[34] So much evil was committed – murdering, killing, burning, displacing of the populace, violating of priests and women – that if all this should be written it would make a heavy book.

So the sisters of Steinbach went to the city of Ensheim to the manor of the Lützels, who had a consecrated chapel. They were enclosed there for four weeks and carried on as if they were in their own convent. At this time, there was so much positive talk and so many faithful promises to the people of Ensheim, that they believed they could let the invading foreigners into their city without any harm or concern. As it happened, they let the foreigners into the city, but the latter did not keep their faith, and the unholy ruffians worked great mischief. With ill intent, they wished to see the sisters, and repeatedly stormed their enclosed manor and had to be driven off, causing distress and worry on the part of the defenders.

Since this was such a problem, some of the nobles who were good friends of the sisters were convinced by the lord dauphin (who is now king of France) that the sisters could be transported via the Rhine to a secure location safe from the evil mob. So the sisters, with strong and secure aid and accompaniment, travelled to another city called Neuenburg am Rhein in the diocese of Constance. As safe as the sisters' escort was, about four hundred of the evil youths rode after them, all with bared teeth and burning eyes. But by divine grace and with the help of good people, the sisters made it safely to Neuenburg and were lodged in the house of a noble widow. They were there for a long time and suffered much worry, pain, toil, poverty, and lack.

2.16 *How twenty-one sisters went from Neuenburg to Basel* [fol. 45r]

The sisters had been together for a long time, watchfully enclosed in this house in great poverty, and their confessors and servants suffered with them. The wise and worthy father Friar Conrad Schlatter, prior of the Dominican friary in Basel,[35] who also had great faith and love for the sisters and was their vicar, real-

34. This event was a side effect of a conflict known as the Old Zurich War, which began when Zurich occupied a county that was left without successors. In 1443, the Old Swiss Confederacy invaded Zurich, which was in alliance with the king of Germany, the future Holy Roman emperor Frederick III (r. 1440–1493, emperor from 1452). He turned to Charles VII of France for help, who took the opportunity to send out of France his restless son Louis and the bands of mercenaries lying idle during a truce period of the Hundred Years' War. See Alois Niederstätter, *Der alte Zürichkrieg: Studien zum österreichisch-eidgenössischen Konflikt sowie zur Politik König Friedrichs III. in den Jahren 1440 bis 1446* (Vienna, 1995).

35. See *DDS*, 249–252; *SOPMA*, 1: 287–288.

ized that the war in that region would not end quickly. He saw that so many sisters with such a retinue in such a small place with such great want could not long remain enclosed together like that. So he considered how he could bring them to the great city of Basel.

With many good and honourable people, he went before the city council of Basel and, with difficulty, arranged for the city to let in twenty-one sisters. These were escorted to Basel from the city of Neuenburg, three miles distant, in 1445 on St Vincent's Day [22 January]. They behaved in a very religious manner and kept themselves enclosed. The house or manor had been fitted with a wheel through which they could pass items and speak with those outside through a wall, just as if through a locked speaking window.[36] Inside, they acted as if they were in a convent. Their confessor stayed with the other sisters in Neuenburg, who also lived very religiously, to provide them with confession and the sacrament and Mass and other necessary things, and so the prior of Basel appointed two honourable, tried and true spiritual fathers as confessors for the sisters in the Basel house. The sisters thus had a mass every day, confession and sacrament every week, and sermons and other spiritual needs. The friary also supported the sisters materially, even though they were there for a year and four months, and the city folk of Basel also treated them well.

The other sisters who remained in Neuenburg, the duke of Austria's city, wrote a letter to the mayor and the Basel city council, in which they thanked him profusely for taking in their sisters. They pitifully bewailed their own misery and asked for further help from him. The letter is signed "the prioress and community of Schönensteinbach, unfortunately now of Neuenburg."

2.17 *How fourteen sisters sailed down the Rhine from Neuenburg to be accommodated in various convents until there was peace* [fol. 45v]

The sisters had been in Neuenburg for a while because of the unrest and were still unable to return to their convent of Steinbach. They were beginning to suffer severe lack, so they called upon Duke Albert of Austria,[37] who told them to ask his advisors for money and wine. Yet the poor sisters received nothing, for the advisors claimed they had nothing to give. So the duke told the sisters that he had arranged for the Dominican convent of St Agnes in Freiburg im Breisgau to shelter them for a time. In exchange, he would forgive them the hundred florins they owed him in taxes. The sisters of St Agnes responded that the exiled sisters

36. The wheel or turn was a common feature of strict convent architecture. See Uffmann, "Inside and Outside," 94.

37. Albert (Albrecht) VI, duke of Austria (r. 1424–1463, archduke from 1453) was the brother of Emperor Frederick III, and held authority over Further Austria, including Alsace.

need not leave Neuenburg; they would rather pay the duke the hundred florins, which they soon did. They threatened to throw bricks at the nuns from Steinbach, if they came. They said this because they were worried about the blessedness of the Steinbach sisters; they feared that they would be drawn into the religious life of the Observance.

Time passed and the sisters had still been long together. Finally, fourteen of them left Neuenburg for Strasbourg on the advice of good friends and with permission of the master general, Father Bartholomew Texery.[38] He had recommended this to Father Conrad Schlatter at the advice of the provincial, Nicolaus Notel, and with the blessing and permission of Duke Albert. The mayor and the city council of Neuenburg gave these fourteen sisters a letter of introduction that read thus:

> We, the mayor and city council of Neuenburg, proclaim to all through this letter that these professed nuns were driven from Schönensteinbach by foreigners, the Armagnacs, and came to us in our city. These same sisters have behaved so honourably and in such a religious manner that we have seen nothing but honesty and piety from them, which we document with this letter. We hereby close this writ with the special seal of our city.

Once the fourteen sisters and their confessor, Father Heinrich,[39] along with five servants and six horses, had arrived in Strasbourg, our dear sisters in St Nicholas-in-Undis received one of the fourteen sisters to house her in their convent for a year. This sister had been born in Strasbourg. The confessor Heinrich then rode on to Pforzheim with the thirteen sisters and their servants. There they were all received in an exceedingly loving, virtuous, and kindly way by the sisters of our order, who had only been reformed for less than two years. They kept all of the sisters with them in the convent for fourteen days until Holy Week and Eastertide [28 March] arrived.

2.18 *How sixteen sisters were sent far and wide into foreign Dominican convents where they could stay until peace was restored* [fol. 47r]

The sisters of Pforzheim kept two of the sisters from Schönensteinbach, one veiled choir sister and one lay sister. Of the remaining eleven, six left for Nurem-

38. See Daniel-Antonin Mortier, *Histoire des maîtres généraux de l'ordre des Frères Prêcheurs*, 8 vols (Paris, 1903–1920), 4: 141–335.

39. Heinrich Fabri appears repeatedly in book 3 as an interlocutor of the Schönensteinbach sisters. See also *SOPMA*, 2: 195.

berg and stayed for more than a year in the religious convent of St Catherine. Seventeen years earlier, ten sisters from Schönensteinbach had reformed that convent. Now these six sisters, most of whom had been born in Nuremberg, remained in St Catherine's with the blessing, good will, and permission of the city council. The other five sisters went to St Catherine's in Augsburg. Although the latter convent had not been reformed to the Observance, they did respectably maintain enclosure. These sisters were for the most part born in Augsburg and many of them had entered the order there. And so these five sisters remained in this convent for a year and four months but did not go to choir with the other sisters, as did those who stayed in reformed convents. The Augsburg exiles kept to themselves and lived according to the customs of the Observance. As irritated as the sisters of this convent at first were to receive these five sisters, they came to love and honour them when they saw their virtuous ways. For this reason, they still maintain favour and a special friendship with the convent of Steinbach to this day, which they have shown in the many good deeds that the Augsburg sisters have done for Schönensteinbach.

In the same week that these fourteen sisters left Neuenburg together and departed for various convents, as I have said, two sisters went to Swabia to St Katharinental in Diessenhofen on the Rhine and found their own special place in this convent. Because the Diessenhofen sisters saw their serious yet lovely life, they treated them with respect, love, and honour, even though this convent was not reformed, nor did the sisters trouble themselves much with spiritual matters. One of the two exiled sisters had entered the order in this convent but had left long after her profession to take up the holy Observance in Schönensteinbach.

2.19 *How some sisters returned to Schönensteinbach before it was time and were driven away again, and how the confessor and some of the servants were captured and all of the convent's livestock taken* [fol. 47v]

No more than seven sisters remained enclosed in Neuenburg in the same house as before. The prior of Basel appointed a confessor for them and the sisters remained where they were until a part of the foreign mob left the land.

Of the six sisters who were in St Catherine's in Nuremberg, after they had been there for five months, two of them left for the reformed convent of Tulln in Austria with the permission of the provincial, Nicolaus Notel.

Now, the sisters who had been dispersed all over conducted themselves so honestly, wherever they were, and maintained the religious life, whether in a reformed or unreformed convent, or enclosed in a house or manor, that many were edified by their example and came to love, favour, and value them greatly. Yet the sisters had a great desire and longing to return to their convent of Steinbach. Since a great part of the harmful mob had departed, the sisters who had remained in Neuenburg (only three miles away from Steinbach) went home to their own convent on the day after St John the Baptist's Day [25 June] in 1445. Since there still was no peace agreement, they could remain for no more than fourteen days and went to the city of Ensheim, where they had stayed in the first exile, a half mile away from the convent. On the eve of Our Lady's Assumption [14 August], these sisters returned from Ensheim to their convent in Schönensteinbach. Before they had been there a full four weeks, the enemy returned and stole thirty-three cows from the convent, and the sisters fled back to the city of Ensheim.

On the Exaltation of the Cross [14 September], their old confessor Heinrich left the city of Ensheim for Schönensteinbach in order to see the convent and the servants who lived near it. The enemy came and stole thirteen horses from the convent and captured the old confessor, along with a lay brother and three servants. They later let the confessor and the lay brother go, but they took the three servants with them, never to be seen in German lands again. Many think that these evil people actually killed the three servants, as they miserably and deplorably killed so many others in these lands.

The sisters remained in the city of Ensheim until the eve of the Feast of St Martin [10 November]. They returned to Schönensteinbach, even though peace had not yet come, but they remained in the convent and were not driven away again.

2.20 *How the sisters who were in Basel went back home to their convent of Schönensteinbach* [fol. 49r]

When the vicious and harmful foreigners left the country, many of the sisters returned to Schönensteinbach from all the places to which they had been dispersed, because of the great longing they had for their convent, even though the war was not yet finished between the lords of Austria and the Swiss Confederacy. Once the sisters who had remained in Neuenburg came back to Schönensteinbach prematurely, the other sisters also returned. In 1446, the sisters who had been in St Nicholas-in-Undis in Strasbourg returned to the convent on the day of our dear Lady during Lent [25 March]. All of the sisters who had been in Basel returned on May Day [1 May].

When the time came for them to leave Basel, they were honourably escorted by noble and patrician women of the city of Basel. They walked in a line from the house where they had been enclosed for a year and four months to the Dominican church with one of their confessors carrying a cross before them. Once the sisters had come into the church, the friars sang an admirable morning mass and the prior gave a beautiful sermon for the benefit of the sisters. Afterwards, they were led to the Rhine, where they got into a ship and sailed away in God's name. When they left the ship to continue over land home to their convent, the sisters of the Klingental convent in Basel had arranged for food and drink to be available for these pilgrims in a village. They came home with fortune's favour and were lovingly and well received by their sisters.

After this, on the Feast of the Trinity [23 May], there was a great assembly of princes and lords in Constance, where the lords of Austria and the Swiss Confederacy signed a full peace treaty.[40]

2.21 *How the sisters from Nuremberg and Pforzheim returned home to Schönensteinbach* [fol. 49v]

Once this peace was concluded, the two sisters who had been in Diessenhofen returned to Steinbach on St Procopius's Day [4 July] under a very watchful escort of honourable people. On the day before the Feast of the Assumption [14 August], the sisters who had been in St Catherine's in Nuremberg and those who had been in Pforzheim returned. An old and honest father, Friar Diebold from the Basel community, had been sent to Nuremberg to accompany the sisters from there back to Steinbach. He brought them from Nuremberg with a careful escort to Pforzheim, where the sisters of Pforzheim received the pilgrims from Steinbach into their convent very kindly. Afterwards, they took the two sisters who had stayed in the meantime in Pforzheim and went home. On the way, they were shown much love and honour by the people of the cities through which they travelled, as well as in Strasbourg and by the abbess and women of Andlau, and by the Dominican fathers in Colmar and the mothers and sisters of both of the Colmar convents, Unterlinden and St Catherine's.

Before they entered the convent, they came to the chapel of St Adelphus in the village of Küngersheim. There the sisters sang a mass for their dear patron and father Saint Adelphus. Afterwards, they went to the convent and were honourably received by their dear sisters singing the Te Deum in joy.

2.22 *How the sisters from Augsburg and from Austria came home to Schönensteinbach* [fol. 50r]

On the day after the Feast of St Adelphus [30 August], the sisters who had been in St Catherine's in Augsburg came home. Although five had gone there,

40. This treaty represents the conclusion of the Old Zurich War, the first effects of which on Schönensteinbach are described in **2.15**. A preliminary peace treaty was signed at this meeting but the conflict was not fully resolved until 1450.

only four returned to Steinbach. The oldest of them, who had been born in Augsburg and there entered the order in St Catherine's, had died there as well. Despite being in an unreformed convent for so long, these sisters had still received our dear Lord every other week and had a special Dominican friar as a confessor. These sisters went through Diessenhofen, where they stayed overnight, and the community there received them virtuously. Afterwards, they went through Basel, and home to the convent of Steinbach, and were worthily and lovingly received by the whole community with the song of praise, the Te Deum, as the others had also been received. And so all the aforesaid sisters came home to their convent after two years. Even though some could have stayed in the other convents where they were welcome, they were determined not to be anywhere other than in Schönensteinbach, their convent in the woods.

Now, the two sisters who were in Tulln in Austria also wished to come home to Steinbach. Since they were so far away and were welcome in the Tulln community, they were advised against daring to travel such a long distance. But there was nothing for it: they wanted to go home to the woods of Steinbach. After they had been in Tulln for almost four years, they came back to their gracious little wooded convent on St Urban's Day [25 May] in 1449.

It is a great miracle of God that so many religious women dispersed so far and wide into foreign lands, travelling hither and thither through so many countries with such great caution and religiosity. God the Lord sheltered and fed them and in a fatherly manner provided them with all necessities. Many people were improved by their example, as is clearly recorded by the worthy, wise, and devout father Friar Johannes of Mainz in the little book he wrote fifteen years ago about the convent of Schönensteinbach.[41]

2.23 *On the fifth exile from Schönensteinbach and the great care taken* [fol. 51r]

In 1468, the Swiss and their confederates, fighting against Sigismund of Austria,[42] invaded Sundgau and Upper Alsace. That summer they did considerable damage by fire and many villages belonging to these lords were burnt, including the villages closest to Schönensteinbach.[43] For this reason, the sisters of Schönensteinbach left their convent with everything they had and went to the city of

41. This work has been lost, but his chronicle of the Basel friary, among other works, survives. See Anne Huijbers, "Observant Memory and Propaganda in Johannes of Mainz's *Vita fratrum predicatorum conventus Basiliensis* (1442–1444)," *Church History* 87 (2018): 718–739; *SOPMA*, 2: 480–481.

42. Sigismund, duke, then archduke of Austria (r. 1439–1490, archduke from 1477).

43. For a brief treatment of this conflict, see Tom Scott, *The Swiss and Their Neighbours, 1460–1560: Between Accommodation and Aggression* (Oxford, 2017), 19–22.

Gebweiler to the manor of a nobleman named Hans of Wettelzen. They were enclosed there during the summer for almost fifteen weeks, just as it was described before how they remained enclosed during all their exiles. Dominican fathers and friars honourably conducted them from Schönensteinbach with songs and readings. Respectable men and women accompanied them into the city of Gebweiler and led them to the Dominican church, which was on their way. Once they had sung, read, and prayed what had been arranged for this journey, they were brought into the said manor, in which they remained enclosed for fifteen weeks until God restored peace and they returned home.

In the meantime, the friars of the community in Gebweiler tended to them virtuously with masses, sermons, and temporal service as well. During this time, two priests from the friary in Gebweiler stayed in the abandoned Schönensteinbach. Since their labourers did not dare to roam outside, the friars from Gebweiler went to Schönensteinbach, harvested the convent's hay and grain with great labour, and demonstrated their faithfulness in many other ways.

2.24 *How they were escorted back to Schönensteinbach in devout honour and, by fortune, spent a short time in Engelport* [fol. 51v]

When they were supposed to return to their convent, they prepared themselves carefully for the journey in a brave and pious demeanour. They walked in an orderly procession from the Dominican church, where they heard Mass, to the convent of Engelport. The sisters of Engelport worthily received the sisters of Schönensteinbach with great love and devotion, for the convent of Engelport was but a stone's throw off their path. When they had sung and prayed in the choir, they went to table, since the Engelport sisters had prepared a meal for them. Many wagons and carts were loaded up with the sisters' personal items and moveable goods – namely, relics, books, and whatever belongs to a convent. The sisters themselves were just preparing to leave for their own cloister, which was only a mile away from Gebweiler, when they received a message that they should not return home, since enemies again were in the field.

When they received this message from the duke of Austria's servicemen, they became very frightened. All the wagons and carts turned around and those from Schönensteinbach stayed with the dear children of Engelport for five days, going to choir and refectory with them. They were amply provided with poverty and lack, especially regarding places to sleep at night, since the bedding of the Schönensteinbach women was packed up with their other belongings. The sisters of Engelport had a poorly constructed cloister and very little stocked up. Between the two communities, there was a huge number of sisters, and although the sisters of Engelport would have liked to serve their guests respectably, they didn't even have enough for three sisters together to share a single straw mattress. Nevertheless, they all stayed together under one roof – some lying on boards – but all this could be disregarded, for they were together with their dear faithful sisters, with whom they shared the holy sacrament on the Feast of Our Lady's Nativity [8 September].

When they heard that the foreign mob had left, they departed gratefully from their sisters in Engelport and once again were honourably escorted home by their fathers and brothers and other estimable people. In the city of Sulz, through which they passed, priests and laity devoutly received them with songs and readings in the parish church. Finally, they entered their convent with great joy, singing the Te Deum and other songs for their dear patrons.

I have written this expressly so that the sisters whose communities lie in the countryside, especially those in reformed convents, know better how to conduct themselves when they must leave for such reasons. They should know how to remain unseen in enclosure and how to travel together according to the order, covered and veiled and with honest escorts. Do just as these dear blessed sisters often did. Give the world no annoyance but rather great edification. I have also written this so that the sisters who reside in cities are grateful to God and their city folk and are that much more eager to serve God the Lord through religious living, so that after this exile we may attain eternal peace in the heavenly convent. Amen.

2.25 *The close of the second book, with a brotherly and faithful admonition* [fol. 57r]

Once the sisters had gathered back in their convent from all the places to which they had been dispersed,[44] they began again to serve God the Lord by upholding our holy order. They organized the duties anew and immediately appointed honourable persons of the order. While the sisters had been outside, virtuous people who noted their good life had given them sizeable donations, which they brought back to Steinbach to alleviate their poverty.

Now, my dearest sisters and children, since God has gathered us from many countries, peoples, and languages, we should zealously strive to live in God and maintain our religious life and good reputation in praise of Lord Jesus. We achieve this when we wisely observe the following points and articles:

First, the superiors, who should be called shepherds, may not be neglectful, lazy, and careless. For if one lets the smallest things go, the more important prin-

44. This chapter picks up from the end of chapter 22, since the events of 1468 took place after Meyer completed the work. Chapters 23 and 24 were added later, and there are several additional blank pages before the beginning of chapter 25.

ciples will follow after. Doubtless, as the Lord Christ says in the holy Gospels, while people sleep the enemy comes and sows weeds.[45]

Second, those who are responsible for punishment must take care that they never act harshly and impose unreasonable, cruel, and rash punishments. They must always let the spirit of kindness influence them.

Third, we must not fight among ourselves or be hateful, argumentative, or divisive. This would be a sign of the greatest evil, since the Lord Christ says that every kingdom divided against itself shall fall.[46]

Fourth, one must ensure that the Divine Office is zealously performed, neither shortened nor abbreviated.

Fifth, we must guard against idleness, since, as the Constitutions say concerning the work of the sisters, idleness causes much evil.[47] Idleness often incites gossip, sometimes causes severe factions or antipathy towards the Rule or the order, world-weariness, and occasionally extraordinary enmity and malice.

Sixth, we must show greater zeal, seriousness, devotion, and interiority several days before and after receiving the holy sacrament.

Seventh, irreligious misbehaviour in gesture must be avoided. These wandering eyes, these eavesdropping ears, this loquacious tongue, showing the teeth when breaking out in laughter, holding the head upright, and gesturing wildly with the hands in speech – what else do you think these things signify but a careless and lukewarm spirit?

Eighth, one must also ensure that the elders are not a bad example for the young, but rather present a good and gracious image in word and deed. Furthermore, the young must act with due deference to the elders.

May God the Lord grant that we remain here together in his holy name. May we live blessedly and well in his divine service, so that after this exile we may never be separated from him but receive eternal life. May God the Father, the Son, and the Holy Spirit grant us this. Amen.

45. Matthew 13:25.

46. Matthew 12:25.

47. Chapter 27 of the women's Constitutions, "On Work," begins: "Since idleness is inimical to the soul and a mother and nursemaid to the vices, none shall be idle." See "Liber Constitutionum Sororum Ordinis Praedicatorum," *Analecta Sacri Ordinis Fratrum Praedicatorum* 3 (1897): 337–348, at 346.

Book Three

Here begins the prologue to the third book, containing the third section of this work's material. It recounts the holy and devout lives of the first sisters of the convent of Schönensteinbach as well as several miracles that occurred there. [fol. 58v]

Generacio preterit et generacio venit, terra autem in eternum stat.[1] These words are spoken by the Holy Spirit and written in the Books of Wisdom. According to their sense, these words in German are: As each generation after the other declines, dulls, and dies, so each generation after the other comes, rises, declines again, and passes away, one after the other. So many noble generations of blessed fathers, mothers, and sisters, who worked and fulfilled so many holy images of spirituality, gracious examples of virtue, great devotion, and holy life in Schönensteinbach have passed away and died out. The greater portion of this has unfortunately passed and faded away, but a little has been recorded about some of the blessed sisters of this convent and their virtues. As much of this as we know, it must have been very different, for they hid the virtues of their lives from the people, just as our dear Lord says in the Gospel: "Do not work your justice before the people so that it might be seen, lest you win no reward from your father in heaven."[2]

Although the blessed lives of our dear mothers are so lost that we will never fully know or grasp them in this world, I have nevertheless made this book in praise of God, to the honour of this convent of Schönensteinbach, and for the use and spiritual delight of all sisters of the holy Observance in the Dominican order. In it I have written the lives of some of the devout and blessed sisters of this convent as an example for us who follow after, so that we may eternally remember the spiritual nobility and dignity of the great, holy generation that has passed away.

As the Holy Spirit says in my epigraph, one generation passes away and the other comes, but the earth, that is, the convent, stands eternal in its spirituality. Yea, the inhabitants of this world, that is, the convent, will rejoice in future honour with their eternal reward.

1. Ecclesiastes 1:4.
2. Matthew 6:1.

3.1 *How forgetfulness and imprudent humility have suppressed much concerning the virtuous lives of the first devout mothers and blessed sisters of the convent of Schönensteinbach* [fol. 59v]

Schönensteinbach increased richly and flourished in spiritual and temporal wealth, especially in good and blessed persons, who served God with great zeal by faithfully upholding the order and maintaining virtue. This short time that is lent to us for the sake of our salvation was fruitfully and usefully employed by these sisters in praise of God and for the eternal health of their souls. In those days, the sisters practised an inward turn towards God, which they sustained in soul, mind, and heart. This is impossible for us to describe, for in those days the sisters kept to themselves what they did with God and God with them, unless on occasion a sister sought reassurance from her confessor, revealing something in strictest secrecy, or perhaps confided in an old and trustworthy sister. In this way, many remarkable graces and miracles, which the almighty God works in many ways even now, were lost and forgotten to this convent. Many sisters suppressed much of this out of imprudent humility. For this reason, no one can describe all of God's graces that have happened there from the first beginning up until this time.

Because the evil spirit is jealous of the soul's blessedness, he inflicted much stress and concern on the sisters with all kinds of temptations, troubling them sorely and frightening them in many ways, visibly and invisibly. Once the evil spirit came to a sister to trouble her. She said to the evil spirit, "Why do you inflict so much pain on us?" The evil spirit answered, saying, "In my wrath, I am jealous that no soul has ever become mine nor been damned in this place."

They cultivated great love of God and for his service – that is, holy Mass, the canonical hours, and other common prayers – such that the choir and consecrated holy places were seldom found without sisters present. This was especially true on holy feast days, unless obedience or great need required otherwise. Even in common – in the refectory, the workroom, the dormitory, and such places where the sisters are generally required to assemble in silence with the community – in those places where this was required of them, there could be no disturbance or gossip, no wasted time or irreligious behaviour.

3.2 *A little commemoration of the first blessed sisters of the convent of Schönensteinbach and the icon of Our Dear Lady across the Brook* [fol. 60v]

Despite trial and tribulation, the children of God gained many good people, who came from the Netherlands and other places and cities, into the wilderness of the woods at Steinbach. They were hardily strengthened in spirit, for many of them were tender and noble, yet willingly gave up the pleasures, luxuries, and honour of the ephemeral world with free minds and hearts desirous for the love of our dear Lord, whom they followed in voluntary poverty with pure souls and great zeal. The Lord Jesus desired to live with these children of men by his favours, as did the highly praised Virgin Mary and the other dear angels and saints. They bestowed many beautiful miracles, which have been erased from human memory. Nevertheless, some of these examples, which reliable sources related to me, are written in this book.

It happened in those days that someone over a hundred miles away sent a devout sister in the convent of Steinbach a small ivory icon of our dear Lady with the baby Jesus as a token of especially great love. She devoutly received the image, washed it, and placed it in the sun in a window of the refectory, so that it became lovely and white. Now listen: A bird came flying to the refectory window, snapped up the icon, and flew quickly out the window and over the brook in the garden. The sister became very upset and cried, "Oh no, a bird has stolen our dear Lady from me!" The sisters went into the garden and looked for the gracious icon in the water of the brook and in the grass, but they did not find it. Then one sister saw that in one place a great number of birds were sitting and singing as if they had a special treat at hand. The sister said to herself, "I should go check out those birds and see what they're up to." When she got there, she found the icon of our dear Lady lying underneath the birds. Afterwards, they secured the image in a shrine and adorned it with relics and decorations. In the convent, this icon is called "Our Dear Lady across the Brook," and some occasionally call upon it in their troubles through prayer. Recently, a great sign was given: a sister had such an illness in one foot that she could hardly step on it. She earnestly appealed to this icon of our dear Lady and promised to pray something for her. Immediately she became well and felt no more pain. Even though this gracious icon is barely as long as a bone of the little finger, the mother of grace wishes us to honour, praise, and dignify her in this little image.

3.3 *An admonitory warning about how to recognize whether a good person's holiness is genuine and whether their visions are true* [fol. 61v]

This third book treats the virtues and the good blessed lives of certain persons and sisters of the convent of Schönensteinbach who lived there in great devotion. Since the Dominican order took on the convent in order to uphold the Observance there, by the grace of God, the Observant life has been praiseworthily maintained from the first beginning up until the time of this book's composition, that is, for seventy-two years. Indeed, the religious life of the holy Observance is still devoutly pursued even today. So that we will not lose the gracious and blessed lives of our departed sisters who lived in Schönensteinbach so devoutly and virtuously, I went out with the dear lady Ruth as she went into the beautiful field of the rich man Boas.[3] As one reads of her in Scripture, she saw that the servants of this lord were cutting down this lovely field and carrying off great sheaves. She then came into the cut field and industriously gathered up the little grains and ears of wheat that had fallen from the hands of the reapers. When the lord of the field saw that this dear lady Ruth was so zealous in this great labour, gathering and picking up the loose grains, he went to his servants and forbade them from shooing off the poor women gathering the fallen grains. Rather, he ordered them to throw parts of their sheaves to her.

Just so have I gone out into the beautiful, wide, and broad field of the Observant religious life in this gracious convent of Schönensteinbach, and have tried to reap the good images and holy examples of the virtuous life of the blessed departed sisters. I wanted to make it into a great and lovely sheaf, but I find that the servants of the most worthy heavenly Lord have reaped and harvested this spiritual field quite thoroughly. They have gathered many lovely sheaves of holy souls into the heavenly barn of eternal blessedness, along with the holy lives and blessed virtues that they practised here on earth. Unfortunately, these have disappeared, so we no longer know much about the blessed sisters, especially those who died early on in the beginning of the Observance. Nevertheless, I have gone after the heavenly reapers, the dear holy angels, who have taken before God the lofty graces and virtues in the souls of these holy sisters. I have looked for anything left here that I might industriously gather in. And if I cannot find enough to make whole sheaves of lofty things, at least I have gathered together broadly useful and edifying material, which truly I found with the blessed lady Ruth. I have done this so that these things will not fade away with the others and pass from our minds into forgottenness, but rather remain as eternal betterment for the lives of all who come after, following virtue and religious life and joyfully maintaining the holy observance of our order with willing heart and devout zeal.

For this reason, I have asked our elders about the graces and virtues that our ancestors received from God. Some of what they heard from their elders and some of what they saw and experienced themselves, they have faithfully told me. In fact, I have left out many things, for some of them were half forgotten or doubtful. In particular, I wrote very little about dream visions and revelations, which I have left out for two reasons. First, it seems to me that it is not as fruitful and profitable for people to hear about such revelations, dreams, and apparitions as it is to hear about virtues like divine love, humility, patience, poverty, serenity, peacefulness, obedience, purity, mildness, devotion, prudence, and other such virtues. Second, it is unsafe to ponder, write, and recount such revelations, for

3. Ruth 2:1–17.

we read that many are sorely deceived in such matters. As Saint Paul says, the evil angel appears in the form of a good angel.[4] Therefore, before I begin to recount the lives of these holy sisters, I leave you with a useful lesson.

One must carefully observe and test a person who has revelations and visions by the following seven criteria, according to the teaching of the holy fathers:[5]

The first criterion is whether the person is truly humble. This humility may be recognized through the following: first, if she[6] lives under the obedience and direction of an experienced, virtuous, and spiritual father, approved by the holy church; second, if she does not arrogate anything to herself, nor praise herself in any way, nor insult anyone, nor desire any human fame; third, if she does not hide her visions, but reveals them and humbly submits them to the consideration and judgement of the prudent, and does not believe the justice or injustice of them except according to the consideration of the wise and experienced.

The second criterion is whether the heart and mind of such a person when she receives such revelations is completely filled and sweetly enflamed with the fire of divine and brotherly love. This may be noted by the following: first, by her

4. 2 Corinthians 11:14.

5. Much research has been dedicated to the late medieval literature on the "discernment of spirits." For the German Dominican Observant context, see Werner Williams-Krapp and Ulla Williams, "Die Dominikaner im Kampf gegen weibliche Irrtümer: Eberhard Mardachs 'Sendbrief von wahrer Andacht' mit einer Textedition," in *Deutsch-böhmische Literaturbeziehungen: Germano-Bohemica; Festschrift für Václav Bok zum 65. Geburtstag*, ed. Hans-Joachim Behr et al. (Hamburg, 2004), 427–446; Werner Williams-Krapp and Ulla Williams, "Eine Warnung an alle, *dy sych etwaz duncken*: Der 'Sendbrief vom Betrug teuflischer Erscheinungen' (mit einer Edition)," in *Forschungen zur deutschen Literatur des späten Mittelalters*, ed. Horst Brunner and Werner Williams-Krapp (Tübingen, 2003), 167–189. For studies in English, see Rosalynn Voaden, *God's Words, Women's Voices: The Discernment of Spirits in the Writing of Late-Medieval Women Visionaries* (Suffolk, 1999); Dyan Elliott, *Proving Woman: Female Spirituality and Inquisitional Culture in the Later Middle Ages* (Princeton, 2004); Nancy Caciola, *Discerning Spirits: Divine and Demonic Possession in the Middle Ages* (Ithaca, 2003); Moshe Sluhovsky, *Believe Not Every Spirit: Possession, Mysticism, and Discernment in Early Modern Catholicism* (Chicago, 2007); Wendy Love Anderson, *The Discernment of Spirits: Assessing Visions and Visionaries in the Late Middle Ages* (Tübingen, 2011); Nancy Caciola and Moshe Sluhovsky, "Spiritual Physiologies: The Discernment of Spirits in Medieval and Early Modern Europe," *Preternature* 1 (2012): 1–48.

6. Throughout this section Meyer uses *Person* (a feminine noun) and *Mensch* (a masculine noun) interchangeably and switches back and forth between the masculine and feminine pronouns *sie* and *er*, depending on the grammatical gender of the most recently used noun. Therefore, it does not necessarily follow that women are the only ones susceptible to such visions, but in keeping with his gendered audience, I have chosen to use "she" throughout.

manners and gestures when she discloses her revelation and reveals the interior of her mind and heart, since usually in such people what is hidden within is shown externally in the limbs of the body; second, if her devotion to or respect for Christian matters continues to grow, such as the articles of the faith, the Roman church, and her superiors; third, that she is increasingly enflamed for the salvation of the souls of believers as of all people; fourth, if she admits these things in holy obedience fully and without contradiction or complaining and surrenders as much as she has.

The third criterion is whether such a person's reason and understanding begins to experience an inpouring of supernatural comprehension of the light of truth, whether in bodily or spiritual visions, for such inspirations of truth cannot be poured in by the evil spirit, as Saint Thomas says.[7] This may be noted thus: first, if the person is clearly shown the truth of the matter; second, if she can grasp the true symbolism of these revelations, visions, and words; third, if she is able to report such things as gracefully as they are in themselves, neither more nor less.

The fourth criterion is if the person always says true things that are honourable and pertain to good habits. It is certainly true that this mark could also be from the evil spirit, who sometimes says true and honourable things. But in the end, he tricks those who believe him, which the Holy Spirit does not do. Therefore, this criterion may be judged hereby: first, if such a person is not possessed by the evil spirit; second, if she is not mentally ill; third, if she does not speak or witness against obvious truth; fourth, if she loves all the good practices which are upheld by holy Christianity and which she should have in herself and follow according to her station.

The fifth criterion is if good and holy beneficial things result from such revelations and if this good persists for a long time. For no evil tree can produce good fruit, nor any good tree evil fruit that lasts. This criterion may be noted thus: first, if the person's mind and understanding is illuminated by such appearances and visions; second, if her conscience and life are improved by it; third, if sinful people are thereby converted to a good life; fourth, if some open disobedience, contrariness, or pride, jealousy, and discord are laid low and dissolved, and if this lasts. This is a quite certain and good sign that it is not from the enemy, but rather from the Holy Spirit.

7. This is a very watered-down version of Thomas Aquinas's nuanced position on angels and demons, and their influence on the human intellect. It is possible, even likely, that Meyer is receiving Aquinas mediated by a later treatise on the discernment of spirits. For Aquinas's discussion, see his *Quaestiones disputatae de malo,* question 16, article 12; I thank Thérèse Cory for this reference.

The sixth criterion is if the person ends her life in virtue with a praiseworthy death and this may be noted thus: first, if the person has not fallen into noticeable error before her death; second, if she does not meet a sudden death unprepared; third, if she does not pass without the sacraments; fourth, if she is not murdered by the evil spirit, since it has often happened that, in the end, he ill rewards those whom he tricks.

The seventh criterion is if God honours such a person after her death with miracles. For whoever is deceived up to her end by the evil spirit with visions and revelations is not worthy of being honoured by God with miracles after death. Only those who in this world have been shrines of the Holy Spirit's grace and whose revelations come from God, such as the holy prophets and the holy virgins, Saint Bridget and Saint Catherine of Siena,[8] and certain other friends of God, who displayed all of these signs. Therefore, it may be believed all the more certainly that the revelations that they had came from the good spirit of God and not from the evil spirit.

For this reason, these criteria must be carefully observed in persons who are burdened with such visions and revelations, so that one may better be able to distinguish the certain from the uncertain.

3.4 *Of Sister Claranna of Hohenburg, one of the first of the convent of Schönensteinbach, and how she began to favour the two great lords of heaven and special kin of Christ, Saint John the Baptist and Saint John the Evangelist* [fol. 65v]

Because of forgetfulness and the passage of time, it is no longer possible for me, or any of us, to know how many blessed dear sisters, who served God the Lord in manifold virtue and great devotion, were in the convent of Schönensteinbach. Nevertheless, we still remember this much and we will faithfully describe the things that God truly worked through certain dear blessed

8. Bridget of Sweden (1303–1373) and Catherine of Siena (1347–1380) were both visionaries who advocated for church reform. Catherine was canonized in 1461 – for Meyer, quite recently. Dominican Master General Raymond of Capua's account of her life was highly influential in German Observant circles. For an example of its influence, see **3.42**; see also Thomas Brakmann, "The Transmission of the Upper German Life of Catherine of Siena," in *Catherine of Siena: The Creation of a Cult*, ed. Jeffrey F. Hamburger and Gabriela Signori (Turnhout, 2013), 83–107. Editions of the Latin work and the medieval German translation can be found in Raymond of Capua, *Die* Legenda Maior (Vita Catharinae Senensis) *des Raimund von Capua: Edition nach der Nürnberger Handschrift Cent. IV, 75, Übersetzung und Kommentar*, ed. Jörg Jungmayr, 2 vols (Berlin, 2004) and Thomas Brakmann, *Ein geistlicher Rosengarten: Die Vita der heiligen Katharina von Siena zwischen Ordensreform und Laienfrömmigkeit im 15. Jahrhundert; Untersuchung und Edition* (Frankfurt, 2011).

sisters of this convent in Steinbach for the devotion and edification of our successors.

First, we should hear about our dear mother Sister Claranna of Hohenburg, the very first prioress of the convent of Schönensteinbach after it had come into Dominican hands and the spiritual life of the Observance had begun. This blessed sister Claranna of Hohenburg was of good and noble birth, and as a child had been placed in the Dominican order in the convent called St Katharinental near Diessenhofen in the diocese of Constance. She developed great love and devotion for the worthy, holy Saint John the Evangelist. At that time and even before, it was a womanly habit of that convent that some of the sisters loved Saint John the Baptist, and some Saint John the Evangelist, with such unrespectable devotion that many sisters who were devoted to one Saint John would sometimes insult the other Saint John. For this reason, one group called themselves the "Baptists" and the other the "Evangelists." There was extraordinary discord between them, to such an extent that the two parties warred against each other for the sake of the two Saint Johns.[9]

So it happened that on the Feast of St John the Baptist [24 June] this sister Claranna went into the cloister, where an image of him was painted, and exclaimed, "Look how this lumberjack stands here!" By this, she intended to elevate and promote her own Saint John the Evangelist. But God, who wishes to be honoured in all his saints, gave her and the others to understand that such things are not pleasing to him. She was invisibly struck down to the ground and lay there for a long time with eyes wide open, neither seeing nor speaking nor responding at all. However much the other sisters yelled and whatever they did, she remained stiff as a board. When she regained consciousness and saw how violently she had been punished and admonished by God, she began to love Saint John the Baptist just as much as Saint John the Evangelist.

From this, all sisters should take a good lesson: not only should they behave devoutly and honourably towards all the saints in eternal life, but they should also learn to treat all the friends of God on earth with equal love and honour without disdain. In particular, they should hold both of the convent's confessors in the same esteem. If ever someone should be more inclined to one of the confessors for a respectable, just, good, and godly reason, she should behave with such prudence and care that no one knows it but God, and that even the confessor in

9. Diessenhofen was not the only convent that struggled to balance devotion to the two Saint Johns. See Hans-Jochen Schiewer, "Die beiden Sankt Johannsen, ein dominikanischer Johannes-Libellus und das literarische Leben im Bodenseeraum um 1300," *Oxford German Studies* 22 (1993): 21–54.

question may not notice it in any way. Equal treatment should be given to both confessors in all things to the extent that this is possible, such that one is not preferred nor the other scorned, unless there is by chance some respectable reason that it must be otherwise.

3.5 *Concerning the blessed life and death of this sister Claranna, the first prioress in Schönensteinbach* [fol. 66v]

After the worthy father Conrad of Prussia had established Schönensteinbach as an enclosed religious convent of Dominican nuns, and had preached throughout the land, seeking good and suitable people who desired a gracious and good beginning, he found this noble creature, who offered herself with heartfelt devotion as the first prioress and mother in Schönensteinbach. She performed this office with great zeal, earnestness, and humility, and said, "I should more justly lie under the feet of all the sisters than occupy such an office." Although the office was unpleasant to her because of her humility, she nevertheless had particular zeal that the Divine Office be devoutly performed, that enclosure be maintained completely and according to the order as it had begun, and that the holy observance of religious life increase and devoutly grow and flourish. She understood holy Scripture so well that she could translate difficult Latin texts into orderly German. She was also talented and gifted at many other good things. She was pleasing to God, so he honoured her as he does his chosen by sending her an illness that made her lame in her hands and feet for twelve years before her death. She suffered this illness with great patience. When she wanted to hear Mass, the sisters put her in a chair with four wheels and pushed her to the choir door then helped her into the choir. When she had received the holy sacrament or heard Mass and the service concluded, the sisters helped her back to her rest. After she had led a blessed and devout life in Schönensteinbach for twenty-nine years, she found a blessed end in 1426.

3.6 *Concerning the virtuous life and gracious death of Sister Elisabeth Meringer, a dear devout mother and prioress of the convent of Schönensteinbach* [fol. 67v]

Among all the sisters of the convent of Schönensteinbach, none is so brilliantly remembered as Elisabeth Meringer. She was a faithful dear mother, who exercised the office of prioress honourably, fruitfully, and well for nearly thirty years with grace, efficiency, zeal, and virtue, to the satisfaction of all the sisters. She had an honourable, modest, quiet, and kind manner, a faithful heart, and zealously observed silence. She did not like noise, and whenever she heard people speaking or walking loudly or banging things about, she said, "Sisters, remember that you are religious people." Often when ten or twenty sisters knelt before their beds before prime or after compline, there was great stillness, and similarly also in the choir. She rarely went to the wheel[10] before lunch or after compline. She was an inwardly contemplative, devout person. This prioress was a mirror of virtue, a model of religious life, a clear pillar of blessedness, and a praiseworthy and well-ornamented vessel of divine grace.

This sister Elisabeth was among the first thirteen mothers who helped to found the convent of Schönensteinbach, which our blessed father Conrad of Prussia converted to such a blessed life. When she came from her convent of Diessenhofen, where she had long been in the order, she was thirty-two years old. She lived for forty-five years with a devout and holy life in the Observance of the convent of Steinbach until her death, when, full of virtue, she departed this world for eternal peace. So that her edifying life does not wholly pass from us, especially since she acted as prioress, we should record a little of the much there is to say.

She fulfilled the office of prioress profitably, and comforted her sisters through her good religious life and her admonitory teaching and instruction. She demonstrated great zeal and seriousness that the sisters devoutly uphold the holy observance of the order in all things, both great and small. She was especially concerned that they prepare themselves with desirous and inward devotion for the holy worthy sacrament, and accordingly that they dispose themselves in an orderly manner for holy confession, and above all that they protect themselves from all that goes against God, the order, and virtuous religious life.

One time she secretly had some silver and golden thread and did not know what to use it for. At that time, the sisters wanted to move our dear Lady's childbed to a more appropriate place.[11] Although they had little decoration for it, the sacristan collected it for our dear Lady. At night while she slept, our dear Lady spoke to her, "Tell Sister Els Meringer to make me a border hem with the silver thread she has." When the sacristan mentioned this and asked Elisabeth about the silver thread, she was surprised, saying, "Who told you this?" Still, the worthy prioress made a lovely border, which is still used on our dear Lady's childbed.

She also did not allow any injustice, discord, or inequality, as far as she could prevent it. Instead, the sisters had to show peace, love, and kindness to each other. There would be much to say about the great order and religiosity to which she held all sisters in outer manners, in walking, in standing, in dress, and in all behaviour, for she was so gifted with grace that this cannot be easily described. She

10. For a description of and note on this feature of convent architecture, see **2.16**.

11. Schönensteinbach likely owned a small statue or figurine of Mary with the infant Jesus in a bed. These common figures represented Mary's lying-in (the confinement and rest period after giving birth). See Lothar Schultes, "Die Madonna im Wochenbett im Stift St. Florian," *Jahrbuch des Oberösterreichischen Musealvereins* 156 (2011): 49–73.

could be strict when it was right and necessary to rule the sisters in motherly honour and fear, but at times she offered such tender love that the sisters also had to hold her in virtuous, childlike love. After she had laudably practised so many virtues during her life, she departed from this world in 1442.

After her death, another sister was given her bed. This sister erected a tall private altar by her bedside with holy images and all sorts of things. This blessed sister Els Meringer appeared to her and said, "I decorated this bedstead with great poverty and you have erected such a construction with clutter." With these words, she took the sister by the arm and pulled her so hard that she had finger marks on her arm for a long time. With the other hand, Els reached for the altar and threw everything down with a great crash. Thus, even after her death she showed that religious people should hold in honour the holy poverty that she had so loved during her life.

3.7 *Concerning the pure, innocent life of Sister Elisabeth Goldschmidt* [fol. 69r]

In this same convent of Steinbach there was also a blessed devout sister named Elisabeth Goldschmidt, one of the first thirteen who helped institute the religious life. She had previously been in the order for a long time in Diessenhofen, and when she was thirty-four years old she gave herself to the beginning of the holy Observance in the convent of Steinbach and led a blessed, virtuous life there for forty-eight years. She especially had great love for and devotion to the high virtue of holy obedience, and no obedience was too much or too hard for her that she would refuse to fulfil it with devout zeal. She never talked back but rather, out of the great love she had for God, she said with Saint Paul, "I can do all things through him who strengthens me."[12]

She had great devotion to the holy humanity of our dear Lord Jesus Christ and especially to his holy suffering and death.[13] She was often seen in great devotion and grace during holy Mass. She had a pure and innocent mind and knew little of the worldly or sinful things that often follow the snake, such as pride, vainglory, and such. For this reason, her confession and her faults in chapter[14] were

12. Philippians 4:13.

13. For women's devotion to Christ's humanity, see Caroline Walker Bynum, "'...And Woman His Humanity': Female Imagery in the Religious Writing of the Later Middle Ages," in *Fragmentation and Redemption: Essays on Gender and the Human Body in Medieval Religion* (New York, 1991), 151–179.

14. The "chapter of faults" was a weekly meeting in which friars or sisters exposed their own shortcomings and the faults of others and received discipline from the prior or prioress. The provincial and general chapter also had a chapter of faults component, and it is in this context that Conrad of Prussia made his successful bid for reform at the Vienna general chapter in 1388 (see **4.3**).

very simple, just as her whole life was simple, straight, and upright, as her fellow sisters noted well. Once a confessor asked her why she only ever said one thing. She answered, "Dear father, I know nothing new to say." She was a loving, merciful, compassionate, and virtuous person, and demonstrated this very kindly to all sisters. In particular, while she was the infirmarian, she served the sick with such great love in the things they needed that the dear sisters were greatly comforted. If a sister came to the infirmary in frailty, she received her in a friendly manner, embraced her kindly, and said, "My very dear sister, we will treat you kindly and you will receive what you need for food and drink, so that you quickly regain your strength and become well, so that you may long serve our dear Lord." She was very comforting to them in word and deed.

Once, something or other had been digging around in the orchard and she found a skull. She brought it to the brook, washed it, and carried it with devotion and prayer into the charnel house. That night an honourable old nun came to her and said, "God thank you, dear sister, for treating my unconsecrated skull so faithfully. Know that I was one of the old sisters who were here before you and your order."

3.8 *How the blessed devout sister Elisabeth Goldschmidt found a holy end and was buried in the Dominican friary in Basel* [fol. 70r]

While they were trying to reform St Catherine's in Nuremberg completely, the Nuremberg city council wanted those in Schönensteinbach to send sisters to their convent who would be fit to begin such a great and holy good work. In particular, they wanted them to offer up and send one of the first thirteen sisters who had helped begin the Observance, in order to reform the Nuremberg convent in an orderly manner. Thus, the blessed sister Elisabeth was chosen for this holy work with many other dear sisters. According to her good habit, she assumed this obedience humbly, as hard as it was to leave her convent of Steinbach. When the other sisters who had been chosen with her also humbly took up this obedience, knowing nothing other than that they were to leave in the morning, the dear mother, Sister Elisabeth, became so sick that she could not move from her place without help. And so she stayed in her convent of Steinbach. How she reconciled this with God is between her and our Lord.

After she had long served God the Lord with manifold virtue into her old age, it so happened that the unrest in the country forced the sisters to leave Steinbach. While the sisters were enclosed together in a house, the blessed old mother became sick, suffered her pains with patience, and found a blessed and reasonable end, just as her life had been. Since the fighting prevented them from returning her to Steinbach for burial, they sent her dead body to the Dominicans in Basel. In 1445, she was buried in the friary's cloister in the presence of several friars.

In these same four weeks during which this sister passed from this world, a young priest of our order named Friar Johannes died among the sisters in Neuenburg. The Dominican fathers in Colmar had lent him to the sisters as their confessor and to help accompany them in their exile. He was also sent to the Dominicans in Basel for burial. At this time, a lay sister named Adelheid Voigt also died and was also buried next to the blessed mother Elisabeth Goldschmidt.

3.9 *Concerning the noble, blessed, devout Sister Clara of Ostren, who founded the religious life in the convent of Schönensteinbach* [fol. 71r]

Sister Clara of Ostren was a blessed person and gifted by God with many graces. She was of noble birth, but nobler still in virtue and in her spiritual, blessed, and good life. Before Sister Clara entered the order, she lived in her home city of Masmünster with those who call themselves "the free women,"[15] where she could have many luxuries and worldly honour, joy, and worldly pleasure from her friends. Yet she gave herself into the Dominican order in a poor convent in the city of Colmar called St Catherine's, which at the time was still largely unbuilt. They did live in poverty there, but at the time, there were no Dominican convents anywhere in these lands that practised true Observance as it now exists there and in many other convents by the grace of God.

When she heard that the dear, blessed, worthy father Conrad of Prussia wanted to rebuild the destroyed convent of Steinbach with papal privilege and make it an enclosed convent of Dominican sisters, she could hardly wait to be among them. God granted her desire and she became a special cornerstone of this first spiritual life in Schönensteinbach, for she was one of the first thirteen sisters. She served them blessedly for fifty years and was the last of the original thirteen mothers to depart from this world.

3.10 *How the prayers of this sister were so powerful that she asked our dear Lady for a good voice and became chantress for thirty years* [fol. 71v]

In the beginning, this blessed sister Clara was given the office of turnkeeper to watch the wheel[16] and correspond with the people outside, for she was a stead-

15. St Leodegar in Masmünster was a community of secular canonesses. These women did not take religious vows and could leave. They did not necessarily even pursue a particularly devout lifestyle, as the story of Clara's sister Dorothea of Ostren demonstrates (see **3.13**).

16. The turnkeeper supervised contact and exchange with the outside world. For a note on the turn or wheel, see **2.16**. For Meyer's explanation of this officer's duties, see Johannes Meyer, *Das Amptbuch*, ed. Sarah Glenn DeMaris (Rome, 2015), 408–425.

fast, religious, and God-fearing sister. People were greatly improved by her speech and words, which she kept short and good. She humbly assumed this duty of obedience, even though it was very hard and disagreeable for her. Her heart and mind were more set on the choir and praising God by singing and reading than on the burden of speaking at the wheel with the people outside. Yet she recognized that this could not be, because she did not have a voice for singing. Still, since this office was so hard on her and her desire for singing the canonical hours in the choir so great, she approached our dear Lady with great earnestness and devout prayer and reminded her of three things. First, she reminded her that God the heavenly everlasting father of eternity had chosen her as a mother for his son. Second, she reminded her of the joyful voice with which the archangel Saint Gabriel greeted her when she received the eternal fatherly word. Third, she reminded her of the jubilant voice with which her only begotten son, our dear Lord Jesus Christ, joyfully appeared to her on Easter with transfigured body, greeted her with a sweet voice and kind comfort, and told her that all pain had been taken from him and no pain would ever touch him again. Now, Clara's prayer was so powerful before the worthy queen of heaven that she received a good voice. She was made first chantress and fulfilled this office for many years zealously and laudably in great devotion and faithfulness. And so she was relieved of the duty by the wheel.

She was especially zealous in teaching the young sisters to sing, and everything that it is necessary to know and be able to do for the Divine Office in order to be useful in the choir, and to praise and honour the Lord God in an orderly manner, as is proper. She had special zeal for the vigils in the workroom, for common prayer, and for the prayers assigned by the prioress, and she lovingly led the young sisters in these things with all virtue. Even after serving as first chantress for more than thirty years, she had great ardour for the Divine Office and the choir, for everything pertaining to these duties, and for the careful correction of all the books.

3.11 *How she taught the young sisters with such faith and love and how she interpreted singing the notes so graciously for them* [fol. 72v]

When this dear sister Clara taught the young sisters to sing, she interpreted the notes for them so graciously, telling them what each note meant, that the sisters she had taught could recount it to me very well more than seventeen years after her death.

The first note, she said to her children, is called *ut* and signifies humility. It tells of how God the Lord humbled himself, descended from the fatherly heart into the pure and chaste body of the worthy Virgin Mary, and from her took on human nature, as well as how he humbled himself and knelt before the feet of his disciples to wash and kiss them. She said many similar things by which her students, the young sisters, learned the lowest note, *ut*, and by which she admonished them in the deep virtue of holy humility.

The second note is *re* and signifies holy obedience. This virtue, she said, God holds in the highest esteem. He was obedient to the worthy, pure Virgin Mary, his dear mother, and to the holy Saint Joseph up until the time when he fulfilled the will of his heavenly father unto death on the cross. She said many other similar things.

The third note is called *mi* and signifies the worthiest holy virtue called charity, that is, divine love. This virtue made the son of God, our Lord Jesus Christ, sacrifice himself in humility and obedience and willingly suffer bitter death for us, and she said beautiful things about this.

The fourth note is *fa* and signifies patience. The Lord Jesus was so patient that he never showed any impatience when he was roughly bound to the pillar and cruelly beaten with sticks and whips. He also showed no indignation at the mockery of the bitter crown, nor spoke a word against those who tortured him with such heavy martyrdom, nor at the verdict of the trial. He assumed with great patience the unjust judgement of the cross for the sake of our salvation. She said such beautiful things about the patience of our dear Lord and how one should practise patience in praise of God.

The fifth note is *sol* and signifies serenity. Here remember how the Lord Jesus was fully stripped before the cross and abandoned by all his dear friends so that, out of human frailty, he called out to God, his heavenly father, "My God, my God, why have you forsaken me?" Yet he gave himself willingly and serenely into the bitter death of the cross for our sake.

The sixth note is *la* and signifies prudence. In this, we may see or understand the resurrection of our dear Lord and his joyful ascension. Here each person should swing up above all earthly things to God the Lord in eternity and should render praise, grace, and thanks to God the most worthy holy Trinity for all the good that has ever happened to the human race.

This blessed mother taught the young sisters such and similar things, which had a very fruitful effect on them.

3.12 *How this blessed sister Clara earned great things from God and his worthy mother through her devout and ardent prayer* [fol. 73v]

She held the holy life and the worthy, precious suffering and death of our dear Lord Jesus Christ in especially great favour and devotion and ordered all of her doings hereby. Every night after compline, she prayed five Pater Nosters and Ave

Marias in the choir before the holy sacrament with arms outspread, just as Christ hung on the cross. Some say that she prayed for God the Lord to protect all people from harmful pestilence, trouble, and suffering. Her prayer was powerful and pleasing to God, who was responsive to her, as one sees in this example.

During this sister's time, there was a lay brother at the estate of Steinbach, who zealously showed great faithfulness through hard work for the convent. God struck him with the great suffering, trouble, and sorrow of being put in prison. When this dear blessed sister heard this, it aroused great compassion in her. In devout and serious prayer, she brought him before our dear Lord and the worthy Mary, mother of God, that they might aid him. And so it happened that the praiseworthy queen of heaven, Mary, came to this brother, the door of the prison was miraculously opened, and the pure Virgin Mary told him to leave without fear. He came back to his convent of Steinbach and recounted what had happened to him and how he had been told that Sister Clara of Ostren had prayed to our dear Lady for this on his behalf.

3.13 *How this devout and good sister Clara converted her biological sister from sin to a religious life through her heartfelt and ardent prayer* [fol. 74r]

She had a biological sister named Dorothea of Ostren, who lived in Masmünster with those who called themselves the "free choir sisters."[17] She was a child of the world and seldom came to Steinbach to visit her sister Clara, because she did not like being lectured about spiritual things. Nevertheless, when God willed it, it happened that some noble persons wanted to go to Schönensteinbach to visit the sisters out of devotion. These noble people came first to this Lady Dorothea and told her, "We want to go to Steinbach and you must come with us to hear your sister." She was unwilling and said, "I can't go. My sister and the other women there can't do anything but talk about God and about the religious life, how you should spurn the honour and joy of the world, and such stuff. I feel uncomfortable there and don't like hearing that. I can't go with you." Yet as staunchly as she resisted the trip, she had to go with them.

When she came to Steinbach, the blessed Sister Clara said to her biological sister Dorothea, "Sister, it's time for you to improve yourself and come into the convent with me to become a true religious person." Her sister received this with disgust and disrespect and responded immediately, "Sister, coming to you in this

17. This is the same community of secular canonesses, St Leodegar in Masmünster, to which Clara herself had belonged before entering the Dominican convent of St Catherine in Colmar; see **3.9**.

convent is not at all in my heart. I can do six kinds of courtly dance and I want to learn a seventh."

When the blessed Sister Clara heard this, it shot through her heart. When she saw how the tether of the world and the evil spirit so distressingly harnessed her sister, she exclaimed, "Oh, dear sister, wait here." She stood up, left her at the speaking window, went into the choir, and knelt before the holy sacrament. In great devotion and serious prayer, she came before God on behalf of her sister, whose soul was in such a dire state. After her prayer, Clara returned and said, "My dear sister, how does it stand now?" Dorothea answered with ardent and desiring heart that God the Holy Spirit had just enflamed her. She said, "Sister, I must come into the convent! Even if it's just an idle passion, I must enter." So she entered the order in that convent of Steinbach when she was twenty-three years old and surrendered herself willingly and joyfully into enclosure and poverty to serve God the Lord with great zeal in a fully religious life.

By this, one may see how powerful Clara's prayer was before God. Master Johannes Nider also describes such a miracle in the ninth chapter of the *Formicarius*.[18] The blessed sister Colette, of the order of Poor Clares, through her prayer also got a worldly and frivolous youth to leave the world and become a good friar in a reformed Franciscan convent. In his book, this teacher writes that a great miracle occurred, as if a dead person had risen to bodily life through this blessed virgin. We may similarly regard the extraordinary miracle that God the Lord worked in Sister Dorothea through the blessed, chaste, devout prayer of this pure Sister Clara. Many of the dear sisters of the convent of Steinbach have recounted how God heard her whenever Sister Clara prayed to him earnestly, and how God often granted her much joy, even in great suffering. Every year, she prayed a psalter for her own failures and those of all her sisters.

3.14 *How this good sister Clara spoke edifying words, especially to the young sisters* [fol. 75v]

Dear Sister Clara had such a loving heart that she found the best in everything. Whatever she saw or heard, she could find something good in it. She was particularly loving and comforting to the new and young sisters. So that they would uphold the order and spiritual life in greater love, favour, and devotion, she often told them beautiful things. For example, she told them the spiritual meaning of each thing the sisters wore. The wimple signifies the cloth with which our dear Lord's clear eyes were bound. The veil signifies the cloth in which the worthy mother and virgin Mary wrapped him when he stood naked before the

18. Nider writes of Colette of Corbie in the *Formicarius*, book 4, chapter 9.

cross. The cloth which the sisters bind over the veil, which they call a *peffe*, signifies the thorny crown, she said, which was pressed into the holy head of our Lord Jesus. The second veil signifies the tombstone, the undertunic signifies the white robe that Herod gave him in mockery. The belt we wear above it signifies the rope with which he was bound to the pillar. The tunic over that signifies the robe in which the Lord was crowned. The sleeves, which are attached to the tunic on the back by the shoulders, signify that we should have angelic life when we joyfully depart with the holy angels after this life into eternal life. The scapular signifies the white cloth in which the Lord was wrapped when he was carried to the tomb. The black cappa signifies the burial shroud that was laid on our dear Lord's corpse when they carried him to the tomb. She explained such things and much else to her students and other young sisters, thereby teaching them to orient their lives around virtue and devotion.

She also sometimes told them to learn from these things, saying, "Every day, I lock myself up with three locks. The first lock is the pure, clean, maidenly heart of the noble Virgin Mary against all temptation of the evil spirit. The second lock is the kind heart of our dear Lord Jesus Christ against all temptation of the body, for his holy heart was between his body and the cross. The third lock is the holy tomb. There I hide with our Lord from the world and from all harmful creatures." She also had great devotion and recourse to the six sorrowful eyes. Two belonged to the Lord Jesus, as he hung on the cross and sorrowfully watched his sad, grieving mother. Two were his dear mother's, as she stood under the cross and looked with great sorrow upon her dear, martyred child in frightening, deathly misery. Two were Saint John's, as he stood under the cross with the Lord's mother and witnessed their painful, heart-wrenching suffering.

3.15 *On her good works and her spiritual and edifying habits* [fol. 76v]

This blessed servant of our dear Lord was a sister to voluntary poverty and protected herself from unnecessary superfluity. She received whatever necessities were given to her so humbly and thankfully that she raised her hands and eyes to heaven, then bowed and said, "Benedictus Deus in donis suis."[19] When she found wool or linen scraps or bits of thread lying on the ground, she picked them up and, with permission, improved her clothes with them. When the sisters did favours or services for her that from age or frailty she could not do herself, she was so thankful that she would not let such a sister leave without specially thanking and praying for her. For this reason, the sisters liked to serve her.

19. "Blessed is God in his gifts." This was the opening of a prayer of thanks said after a meal. See *Ordinarium juxta ritum Sacri Ordinis Fratrum Praedicatorum* (Rome, 1921), 133.

She was also very humble and did not show her high birth in either words or deeds, nor could anyone tell from her clothes or her behaviour. Her words were short, straight, and firm, as were her confessions. Whenever she thought that she had hurt someone, she would not sleep before reconciling herself with her. She knelt humbly before them, young and old alike, and asked forgiveness. She told the young sisters, "Our dear father, the blessed Friar Conrad of Prussia, our first vicar, taught us such things."

She had the habit, also done out of obedience, of gathering up the herbs from the garden, drying them, and making them into powder. When she had filled a little satchel, she laid this satchel with the powder on the altar and prostrated herself before the holy sacrament with devout prayers. She then took the satchel and gave it to whichever sister desired it with great love. The powder was so good for the sisters that they took little other medicine. Clara herself never took any medicine, even though in her old age the sisters wished to help her back to strength. She only let them give her the first and last medicine, since God the Lord was her only physician. Although she never had blood let, she never became sick, and though she never took medicine, she still lived for seventy-three years.

3.16 *On the holy, devout end of Sister Clara of Ostren* [fol. 77v]

When she reached a good age with healthy body, her physical strength sharply declined over a period of two months. Nevertheless, she never missed Mass so long as she could walk or could be helped into the choir. Every Sunday she received the holy sacrament in the choir at the Jesus window.[20] In this, she was especially devout.

On Christmas Day, she heard the third Mass, received the holy sacrament, and afterwards lay down in a bed in the sickroom. Since God the Lord was so deeply rooted in her heart, soul, and mind, she could orient all things to her devotion, as sick as she was. She made the sickroom in which she lay into the stable in Bethlehem. In a corner of the room across from her, she placed the pure Virgin Mary, the worthy new mother, with her dear child Jesus and the dear Saint Joseph next to her in the corner. The floor of the room on the other side and the three windows were the three roads by which the worthy holy Three Kings arrived. The door of the room was the path by which the shepherds and the common folk came.

Now, the sister who cared for her was especially close and dear to her. She knew much about her, as we learned after their deaths from certain writings that

20. The Jesus window was a small opening in the wall between the nun's choir and the rest of the church. It was locked from both sides and only opened for the priest to pass the Eucharist through. See Uffmann, "Inside and Outside," 93.

were found after this sister who was caring for Clara died. This sister recounted that while Clara lay sick in Bethlehem by the crib of the Lord Jesus, the other sisters began to say to each other, "We should go to Bethlehem." After the third day of Christmas, whoever visited Clara had to sing or say something good to her. During these holy days, she did more than I can say for the holy birth of Christ and his holy mother at her lying-in. On the gracious Feast of the Circumcision [1 January], she suffered compassion with the loving child and with his blessed, pure mother and exclaimed several times that day, "Oh, the mild and sorrowful heart of Mary!" In this way, she prepared herself for the Feast of the Three Kings [6 January].

On that feast, she was so introspective that her caretaker did not dare speak with her much until early in the morning. Then her caretaker heard a great racket outside the convent on the street, as if there were wagons and carts. She said, "Sister Clara, listen. What is that?" She answered, "The lords from the Orient have received a message from the angel that they must not return to Herod. They are going straight home."[21] Afterwards, she received the baptism of Christ and then her strength declined sharply. Whichever sister came to her, Clara gave her some good word of advice. In this way, she prepared herself for death, which she approached willingly, saying to the sisters, "Dear children, do not deter me. It is time that I depart from here. God help me get to heaven, so that I may pray for you. I will never forget you." At a praiseworthy age and after a good life, Clara met a blessed end and departed from this world in the year of our Lord 1447.

3.17 *Of the life and virtues of the mild Sister Sophia of Veld* [fol. 78v]

Among the other blessed sisters, of whom there was an enormous number living in the convent Schönensteinbach in great devotion and spirituality and serving God zealously and faithfully, the gracious Sister Sophia of Veld was not the least. This blessed, devout, and dear Sister Sophia was born in the Netherlands as the daughter of a noble knight. From childhood on, she had a good, blessed life and a contemplative and devout mind, such that she especially loved to pray. While she was still in the world, she gave great aid to the poor and comforted them as she could, for she had a very compassionate, kind, and merciful heart. She could truly say what is written in Job, "From my infancy mercy grew up with me."[22] Since she wished to flee the world, she entered a community of sis-

21. Matthew 2:12.
22. Job 31:18.

ters called beguines[23] (of which there are many in Brabant in the Netherlands, who support themselves by the work of their hands), since at that time there were very few convents of the confirmed orders where the religious life of the Observance truly reigned. This sister Sophia had a blessed relative in this community, who raised her zealously in God to live a virtuous life. The good and holy reputation of the convent Schönensteinbach had travelled far and wide through many lands, and word spread that the convent had been founded and the good word of religious life was growing laudably in words and deeds. Then God the Lord wished to adorn the spiritual garden he had newly begun to plant by sowing this noble blossom, the violet, from the field[24] of this unfaithful world.

Sophia proved worthy of her name through her spirituality and manifold virtues, above all mercy and compassion. She was a comfort to all sisters who came to her in sorrow. She instructed the sisters about temptation especially well and profitably. She was zealous in everything concerning the order and religious life. She had such great desire for God that one heard it in her words and saw it in her eyes when she spoke of him. She had such a great love of obedience and for the holy worthy sacrament and for all good things, that one could not easily record all of it. She wasted little time and did not spend it idly.

3.18 *Of the mild constancy and holy devotion of Sister Sophia of Veld* [fol. 79v]

When the convent of Schönensteinbach was founded in spirituality, this blessed sister Sophia of Veld came to the convent in the very first year from the far-off Netherlands. She showed such great virtue in religious life that she was burdened with the duty of serving as subprioress, which she performed with devout zeal for many years, often even with a weak body. However sick she was, she never withdrew from the community if she could help it. The Lord showed

23. Beguines were pious laywomen who lived in all-female communities of varying size and devoted themselves to handiwork (often textiles) and public service (care for the poor and sick). In the Netherlands, they formed large communities that rivalled the size of convents, but they did not take solemn vows nor observe enclosure. See Walter Simons, *Cities of Ladies: Beguine Communities in the Medieval Low Countries, 1200–1565* (Philadelphia, 2003). Meyer's positive disposition towards the beguines is noteworthy, since Observant Dominicans could be violently opposed to their way of life. Meyer seems to follow Johannes Nider in his esteem for "religious laypeople." See John Van Engen, "Friar Johannes Nyder on Laypeople Living as Religious in the World," in *Vita religiosa im Mittelalter*, ed. Franz J. Felten and Nikolas Jaspert (Berlin, 1999), 583–615. For a negative extreme, see Sabine von Heusinger, *Johannes Mulberg OP (d. 1414): Ein Leben im Spannungsfeld von Dominikanerobservanz und Beginenstreit* (Berlin, 2000).

24. Meyer is punning on Sophia's name: *Veld* means field.

her such kindness with his manifold graces, which followed her from a far land into the wilderness of the woods of Steinbach. But I leave all of that unrecorded and commend it to divine grace – for example, how greatly she helped the poor souls in purgatory through her prayers and other good works, such that many souls often came to her to ask her for help and the sisters frequently heard her speaking with the souls and the souls with her. One good sister saw three times that when Sister Sophia left the choir after Matins and took holy water, she was surrounded by many souls who raised their hands to her, and when she sprinkled the holy water on them they bowed. She gave such great aid to the dear souls and the poor sinners that she could well be called a mother to them all. Once, she knew about the death of some people outside the convent a long time before people within the convent were informed, proving that the state of many souls was known to her.

For a long time, she was very sick from a fever, which she suffered with great patience on behalf of the soul of a sister of her convent who had asked her for help because she was in great pain. With her kind heart, Sophia took immeasurably great prayers and discipline upon herself, as well as this severe illness until her end. Thus her soul was released from its pain.

3.19 *On her blessed end and how she visibly appeared after her death* [fol. 80r]

Before her death, Sophia suffered such a harsh illness that it cannot be described, but nevertheless she displayed great patience. Whenever her illness was most severe, she said, "If it were now God's will, I would gladly remain in this agony till Judgement Day in his praise." Three days before her death, she showed no sign of life, but it was obvious that she neither slept nor had passed away. When she awoke, she requested the holy sacrament and one could see that she knew the hour of her death. When the sisters watching her spoke to each other after compline or at another forbidden time, she said, "Sister, had you seen the great pains I have seen that one must suffer for this, you would not be speaking so lightly." As death neared and she was about to die, she said, "Dear sisters, do you not see the beautiful virgin? Stand aside! Stand aside and let her approach!" She bowed her head and soon after departed, leaving behind her mortal body. And so, we trust, she achieved eternal peace in the year of Christ 1435. Since she loved the holy eleven thousand virgins and had served them so zealously, and prayed eleven thousand Pater Nosters to them so often during her life, these holy maidens, along with other saints, led her at her end to eternal life, as this following example shows:

In the time of this blessed sister Sophia, when their vicar Master Johannes Nider was prior in Basel and that friary was being reformed, he sent one of his brothers, Friar Augustinus, to Steinbach to help our confessor sing Mass and perform similar things. Since he was such a dear devout friar, Sophia chose him, after his desire, as a spiritual son. They promised each other to pray to God on the other's behalf, since they were both from the same home country. When Sophia departed this world, a letter was sent to Friar Augustinus, who was currently in Bern, that she was dead. When he read the letter and wept, she appeared to him, beautiful and joyful, yet the friar was frightened. She spoke to him, "Brother, do not be afraid. I am your sister, Sophia of Schönensteinbach. You should not weep for me, for I shall have eternal life." Then the friar heard something else with her and asked who was there. She said, "It is two blessed brothers of our order who also have departed, and several maidens from the host of the eleven thousand virgins who will lead us into eternal life."

May God Almighty grant us the same. Amen.

3.20 *Of the devout sister Margretha Schalffing and how she held the holy sacrament in such great favour* [fol. 81r]

At the time when the blessed father Conrad of Prussia restored Schönensteinbach, there lived in the city of Constance a wealthy maiden named Margretha Schalffing, who behaved according to the ways of the world. She wore clothes with gold, silk, and pearls and behaved quite merrily in other aspects of her life. God brought it to pass that the blessed father Conrad of Prussia converted this young, worldly, frivolous woman from the world and all its luxury, when she was twenty years old. She remained steadfast in God until her end. As before she had lived in the eyes of the world, she wished henceforth to live for God.

When this father Conrad, who was a great itinerant preacher, was speaking in Constance, this woman developed an earnest desire to leave the world and join the blessed community of the convent of Steinbach. Her friends made her agree to wait four years, but she remained so steadfast in her good intention that God helped her enter the order with her daughter four years after the foundation of this convent. She led a devout, spiritual, blessed life for nearly thirty years, and appeared as a vessel of grace and manifold virtue among all the sisters.

This sister enjoyed such great, lofty, and devout contemplation that she was often rapt from herself, even in the choir. Once, they had to carry her out to her bed, and she remained long in that state before she could return to herself. Sometimes, such interiority came upon her at table that she was rapt from herself, so they left her there until she came to.

She had unspeakably great favour and devotion to receiving the holy worthy sacrament, yes, even just to seeing it. When the holy sacrament stood on the altar in the monstrance during the octave of the Feast of Corpus Christi,[25] God knows best the heartfelt inner desire and devotion she had. When the priest removed it from the monstrance on the octave, she showed such gracious, devout desire that the other sisters were also ignited in devotion. She followed after the priest carrying the sacrament out of the choir and clasped her hands together so tightly, as if she were saying, "Woe, they are removing from our sight this high jewel, this precious treasure, the only heartfelt love of my soul." With the permission of the prioress, she fasted that day until after compline, so that she might attend the washing of the priest's fingers, with which he had touched the holy worthy sacrament that she received with great desire and devotion.

Each devout heart should consider the fiery love and hot desire that this devout heart had for the worthy sacrament and the readiness with which she prepared herself for it weekly and how she behaved so devoutly even for the washing.

Sister Sophia of Veld, the devout subprioress, sometimes saw in the choir, that when the blessed sister Margretha was at her devotion, a lovely child was with her. We believe it was none other than the beloved Lord Jesus.

3.21 *On the blessed life and death of Sister Margretha Schalffing and how she appeared after her death to a good sister* [fol. 82v]

This gracious, blessed sister held humble obedience in especially great favour. If her superiors ordered her to do anything that needed to be done in the convent, she inclined to it with a good heart. She was the infirmarian for a long time, and whenever the prioress sent a sister to the infirmary, Margretha received her and welcomed her lovingly and kindly. She served the sick with such great zeal and virtue, that the sick sisters had great comfort from her. Whatever she was ordered to do in obedience, she performed with special devotion and a great zeal, which she also had for the holy canonical hours. She also was especially diligent at keeping the laws of silence, most of all at the forbidden times and places. After she completed her blessed life, God the Lord wanted to reward the faithful work and great love that she had shown him and done on his behalf. She enjoyed a reasonable and gracious end on St Andrew's Day [30 November] 1432. Not long after her death, one morning before prime, a blessed and devout sister was kneeling before her bed at prayer. She saw a lovely white glow floating above the bed, which sang with a sweet and gracious voice these words: "Modo reddo tibi

25. Corpus Christi is a moveable feast on the Thursday after Trinity Sunday, eight weeks after Easter. "Octave" can refer either to the day one week after a major feast or the entire intervening week. It is used in both ways in this passage.

creatori animam meam,"[26] which in German is "Now at last, I return my soul to you, my creator." We truly believe it was the pure soul of this blessed sister Margretha, for upon a blessed life follows a holy and good death, yea, even eternal life. May God the Lord grant us this. Amen.

3.22 *Of the contemplative, holy, and devout life of Sister Clara Folz, who was a blessed, dear mother in the office of subprioress* [fol. 83r]

In the days when the first blessed mothers in Schönensteinbach were all still alive in devotion and holiness, and before any other convent in the province besides Steinbach had been reformed to the Observance, there was a devout and blessed sister in St Nicholas-in-Undis in Strasbourg, called Sister Clara Folz. She had great determination and zeal to be pleasing in the eyes of God, to live in a wholly spiritual place according to the dearest will of God, and to love him with all the powers of her heart. For this reason, the Lord, who does not scorn but rather hears the desires of his devout, gave this sister the grace to earnestly petition for admittance to the community of his children in Schönensteinbach. There might her loving heart do everything it desired. By the grace of God, she was received there and led such a devout, loving, and blessed life that it was greatly to be admired.

Since she had a good heart that God had so richly bestowed with grace, she was made subprioress. Even though she was often so sick that she walked with a cane, she fulfilled the office of her obedience in all zeal.

She held the kind, mild, tender heart of our dear Lord and the sweet name of Jesus in special favour and devotion. The powerful Lord worked great things and gracious miracles through her, all of which have been forgotten and suppressed, just as the graces and virtues of other blessed sisters who died many years ago have disappeared.

In her holy contemplation and prayer, she was often rapt from herself and lifted up into God such that she remained unaware of herself for two or three hours. She often prayed in the choir with a young sister, even while she was subprioress, since she could not stop it. Whenever she noticed that she was becoming rapt into God in her devotion wherever she was kneeling or sitting, she said to the young sister, "Stay close and pray or contemplate God, and if any sister comes to ask permission, turn them away from me."

26. From a responsory of the Office for the Dead, "Antequam nascerer."

3.23 *On her death and how her heart was found fresh fifteen years after her death* [fol. 84r]

Whenever the sisters spoke of divine things among themselves, they saw the joy of this sister's heart in her gracious expression and demeanour, especially when the sweet name of Jesus was mentioned. The fullness of her heart shone, richly bedecked with the dew of divine grace through her many holy and virtuous works.

When she had served God many years through spirituality and sweet demeanour in a pleasing and blessed life, the Lord to whom she had given her heart took her from this world and she departed in the first week of Advent [1–6 December] 1421. Fifteen years after her death, they opened up her grave in order to bury another sister in it. Her body was decayed, but her heart, which had been full of devotion and grace, lay completely fresh within her bones. Out of humility, or small-mindedness, or maybe carelessness or imprudence, the senior confessor threw this noble treasure back into the earth of the grave. Afterwards, when learned men heard of it, they ordered that the heart be examined the next time the grave was opened up. Many years later when another sister was to be placed in the same grave, they went to look for the heart, but it could no longer be found. The first failure and the imprudent humility – or better, inattention – had been too disorderly.

More of this sister's virtues have been suppressed and forgotten than one can say. Her holiness was so great that the old sisters who knew her say it is a certain truth that she was a holy person in whom God worked his gracious miracles in many ways.

3.24 *Of the devout and blessed sisters, Sister Dorothea of Ostren and Sister Margret Ursula of Masmünster* [fol. 84v]

There was a holy sister in this same convent of Steinbach called Dorothea of Ostren,[27] noble of birth yet much nobler in virtue. She came into this convent through the devout prayers of her biological sister Clara of Ostren, as you read previously. When she was twenty-three years old and a fresh and merry person, she gave herself joyfully into enclosure and poverty. She had been a secular canoness in Masmünster, but when she surrendered herself to the Observance of the holy Dominican order, she began very zealously to serve God the Lord with a virtuous life. In the choir, she exercised herself especially faithfully in the holy canonical hours, to which she was well suited. She had the voice, knowledge, and desire to become chantress, which office she fulfilled with great zeal. For a while,

27. *DDS*, 605–606.

God the Lord directed her tenderly and she was so happy that she said, "The evil spirit has not yet realized that I have come into the convent." Some time after this, she thought the enemy had learned of her and she perceived this well, but she took refuge in God and manfully resisted the enemy with divine aid. She performed good works and led a virtuous religious life, so that the sisters took a good example and much edification from her.

Since she had proven her conduct, she was chosen as one of the thirteen good and useful children to reform the convent of Unterlinden. At the command of the master general of the order and the provincial, she was sent from Steinbach in 1419 to begin the spiritual life. Sister Dorothea laid the cornerstone of spirituality in the convent of Unterlinden so deeply and so firmly that, in obedience, she later had to produce such fruit once more. She was again sent with thirteen others from Unterlinden to Basel in order to begin the holy Observance in St Mary Magdalene an den Steinen, where she became the first mother of the religious life and their prioress. She wore the yoke of the Lord with patience and humility and fulfilled this duty of obedience with great zeal until God the Lord relieved her of it with a blessed end, which she found in that community in 1425.

After her, Sister Greta Ursula of Masmünster became mother and prioress there, who in her innocent days had come into the order in Steinbach as a child of four years.[28] She had lived so virtuously there that she helped to begin the holy Observance in Unterlinden and afterwards in St Mary Magdalene in Basel, where she became the second prioress. She fulfilled this office with such loving virtue that she was very pleasing and dear to the sisters. Even though she wished to return to Steinbach, where she had learned her loving demeanour, in 1448 God the Lord took her to his grace from the Basel convent of St Mary Magdalene an den Steinen after a long, severe illness.

3.25 *Of the beautiful, gracious, devout Sister Lukardis, who was a bursar* [fol. 85v]

There was also a holy sister in the convent of Steinbach named Lukardis of Ingen, an especially diligent, blessed sister from the Netherlands, whom God had endowed with many graces. When the Lord wished to make his Schönensteinbach yet lovelier and more graceful, he drew this handsome, noble pearl from the great and beautiful city of Utrecht in the Netherlands and placed it in his Schönensteinbach, where it kept its white and virginal purity while drawing yet more lovely adornments to itself. She was truly an ornament to the convent.

28. It is possible that she is the daughter of Johannes and Susanna of Masmünster, who became a lay brother and a lay sister at the same time. See **3.31** and **4.11**; see also *DDS*, 606.

Physically, she was a tall, beautiful, and noble person, lovely in all her limbs and handsome of face, so that one well might say, "God has forgotten nothing in this lovely image." She was mild, gentle, and kind, quiet yet also firm, of gracious and noble manner, and very faithful. She was also quite wise, reasonable, and very skilful, and used all of this commendably to the honour of God and for the common good of the convent in spiritual and temporal affairs. Despite all this, she was completely humble.

She was also virtuous and deeply compassionate with poor people, which pilgrims and the destitute appreciated while she was bursar, for she helped them and did them much good. She was so kind that she seldom withheld anything desired of her. If she did not have something at the time, she said, "Oh, wait for me a bit," and did everything she could to acquire it. She usually gave the sisters more than they requested. If a sister asked for a sheet of paper or a needle, she gave them five or ten. Moreover, whenever she noticed that something would be useful or opportune, and if she thought the sister did not dare ask her out of fear, she would secretly put the thing that she needed in her bed. She paid careful attention to all the things the sisters needed, whether food, clothing, or other items. She faithfully and efficiently met every need, so that the sisters had no cause for impatience.

3.26 *Of the outer bodily and inner spiritual graces and beautiful gifts of this sister* [fol. 86v]

This blessed sister Lukardis, although she lived the life of Martha for many years as bursar, was nevertheless so devout that she never neglected the contemplative life of Saint Mary Magdalene.[29] For this reason, she diligently strove never to speak unnecessarily and one seldom heard her break her silence. Only a very important matter could make her go to the wheel after compline or before sext. She was quiet, withdrawn, and silent, but she could sometimes charm with very few words, and it was good to be with her. She was wholly peaceful and submissive, especially to the sick. She tended one sick sister with great faithfulness for nearly fifteen years, day and night. She treated her as a mother treats her child, lifting her and laying her down and everything that was necessary for washing and such, since the sick sister could not control her body from the illness and was very heavy. During these years, Sister Lukardis suffered many a miserable night with this sick sister.

I cannot describe all her fasting, vigils, prayer, kneeling, prostrations, other devotions, and good holy exercises, or how she often, in particular every Friday,

29. Luke 10:38–42. The Mary in this passage later became conflated with Mary Magdalene, hence Meyer's mention of her here. For a note about Mary and Martha, see **2.9**.

flagellated and disciplined herself in honour of the suffering of Christ. She managed her time profitably and well and was never idle. She busied herself with reading and prayer or with the sick sisters or the bursar's duties or with writing, in which she was a great master. We see this in the large and beautiful, useful choir books that she prepared, copied, notated, and completed so well to the comfort of the convent. When they see the missal she copied for sung Mass, some friars and many priests have been amazed that a woman could write in such a good, straight, and uncorrupted script and carry it out so orderly and evenly.

She was a refined, clever, and skilful person in many kinds of work, and understood the art of grammar and translating Latin into German. She was richly endowed by God with much inner and outer grace.

3.27 *On the blessed death of Sister Lukardis* [fol. 87v]

Into her old age, indeed until her death, she diligently practised holy obedience in spiritual and temporal matters. Whatever she had to do for external affairs, especially regarding the bursary, she did quietly and privately. At the speaking window, she spoke straightforward and friendly words briefly and reasonably. She and the gracious, blessed mother Sister Elisabeth Meringer, the worthy prioress who lived during the time Lukardis was bursar, made many good friends for the convent through their virtue, fulfilling their duties in all diligence. Spiritually and materially, they both sought the best for the convent in all faithfulness and in great peace and unanimity. When this blessed sister Lukardis reached her final illness, she departed with a blessed end in 1438 on the Feast of Mary Magdalene [22 July], who had been especially dear to her. After her holy death, a hair shirt and whip were found in her straw mattress. They were bloody, which proves her love, seriousness, and devotion to God and the secret virtue she held in her soul and heart to treat her chaste, pure body so harshly with strict severity.

3.28 *Of the virtuous, blessed, gracious life of Sister Katharina Langmantel, who was prioress for many years* [fol. 88r]

In the city of Augsburg there was a rich and powerful man named Langmantel who had more than twenty-six children. Among them were four daughters who became Dominican nuns and one of these four was named Katharina. When she was six years old, her father gave her to the convent of St Catherine in Augsburg as a sacrifice to God and Saint Dominic. She grew in virtue and religious habits, in reason and wisdom, so the convent entrusted her with great responsibility. She led a blessed life, was careful in her words and deeds, and behaved religiously, but she still wished to enter a more certain state of religious life in the convent of Steinbach. For many years she petitioned to be transferred, but her request was hindered by the influence of her friends. Finally, after she had been prioress and bursar in St Catherine's for almost twenty years, during which she always remained firm in her good intention, her friends and her convent sisters, who loved her, let her go to Steinbach according to her desire, yet not without weeping greatly, for they hated to lose her.

When she arrived at Steinbach, she behaved graciously, appearing among the sisters as a mirror of the religious life. So the sisters elected her to be the prioress and a spiritual mother to them all. She was gracious and of a good, sweet spirit and few words. She was hardly ever seen breaking her silence, and when she spoke her words were kind and edifying. Wherever she saw silence broken, she rebuked with a kind expression, placing a finger to her lips and saying, "*Silencium.*"

She was so honourable that after she had been at Steinbach only a short time and had not yet become prioress, sisters doing something inappropriate at forbidden times and places feared her from afar. When she was at her bed and heard chatting in the dormitory, she cleared her throat a little and all were immediately silent. If someone lacked something, she would go to them and say, "Dear child, do you want anything, can I do or get anything for you?" She never spoke any unnecessary words to anyone, but was brief, quiet, and friendly.

3.29 *Of her devout, contemplative, interior life* [fol. 89r]

When this blessed Sister Katharina came from her convent in Augsburg to Steinbach, she had to give a full confession of her whole life, as is the custom for sisters who come from unreformed convents into the holy Observance. She completed this in under an hour. Her weekly confession was also very short and so gracious that the confessors claimed to receive grace from her. She was especially zealous and devoted to receiving the holy sacrament, such that the senior confessor, Father Heinrich Fabri, said, "She is so righteous in God that I would give her the holy sacrament every day if it were customary." She adapted fully to the practice of common property. Her outward purity was a sign of her pure soul. She always was as white and pure on workdays as if it were a holiday. She was a wholly angelic person, and even though she was kind, loving, and friendly, she also had the grace of being forthright and candid when it was called for.

She was a very wise, intelligent woman, skilled in singing and understanding Latin, but above all a contemplative and devout person. She wept over the suffering of Christ daily. She held holy Mass in such devotion and favour that she often cried during Low Mass so that tears ran down her cheeks. She was also so devoted to the divine word that she cried at almost every sermon, however simple the sermon was. She was so quiet that if you did not see her, you could not hear her coming.

For the sake of brevity, I will leave out how the souls of certain dear departed sisters of Steinbach appeared to this blessed mother in joy and glory. She had such an elevated temperament for contemplating heavenly and divine things that she often neither heard nor saw what was happening in front of her. While she was prioress, she would often stand with her eyes on heaven and not notice three or four sisters standing before her, asking permission and plucking at her sleeves, so that the subprioress mostly had to give permissions.

Her heart was jubilant when she sang in the choir and she sat at table with an inner, devout spirit.

3.30 *Of her blessed end and what was seen then* [fol. 89v]

When this dear mother Katharina Langmantel had brought her blessed life to an old age, she lay sick in bed for nine days. In these days, she received the holy worthy sacrament six times, for she was so sick they thought her departure was nigh. Yet whenever they gave her our dear Lord, she became so fresh that the weeping sisters rejoiced and thought she might recover. Yet after nine days, she departed with a blessed end in the year 1442 amidst great sorrow and weeping among the sisters, for it is to be feared that such a one is not soon found again. She lay with great patience and devotion in her illness.

In the days of her sickness, our worthy father provincial, Friar Nicolaus Notel from Gmünd, was at the convent of Steinbach. He had known her good, blessed life for many years in Augsburg and in Steinbach. He had taken her full confession and helped her from her convent in Augsburg to Steinbach into the Observance. Many years earlier, they had both promised in godly faith and all good to be faithful to each other's souls before God. For this reason, they were very dear to each other in God and he strongly desired to come to her deathbed before she died. When they told her this, she said, "I don't want that. No one should do anything new or special for me. He is dear to me in God, who will reward us both for it. But tell him that my dearest love has invited me into his presence, for whom I long and before whom we shall be true to one another." When she departed, two sisters saw a sparkling, snow-white dove fly over them from the window of the room where she lay and up so high that they could no longer see it. Their confessor was walking across the courtyard into the church and heard a buzzing noise. He looked up and thought he saw a great swarm of bees stream out of the roof of the infirmary and fly up so high that he could no longer see them. By all this, we may note that she was a dear friend of God.

3.31 *Of Sister Margaretha from Klingental and her devotion to the holy sacrament and the suffering of Christ* [fol. 90v]

In the beginning, the worthy convent of Schönensteinbach was not only ornamented by wise, blessed, and learned fathers and confessors and by the veiled choir sisters. The holy devotion of the unlearned lay sisters within and the *conversi*, or lay brothers, in the outer court also so graced this convent that we may well say with Saint Augustine, "the simple, unlearned people seize the kingdom of God by force."[30]

The first among these was Sister Margaretha from Klingental, a mirror of the religious life. This sister was among the first thirteen who helped to refound the convent of Steinbach, making it graciously flow with virtue and the blessed religious life. She had been a secular servant in the convent of Klingental in Klein-Basel. When the five sisters from Diessenhofen stayed for several weeks in Klingental while waiting for the proper time to go to Steinbach and start the holy Observance, this blessed, devout maiden from the convent of Klingental gained more divine favour than any of the other seventy women in the convent. In accord with her desire, she was permitted to enter the convent of Steinbach with these very first sisters. She was invested as the first lay sister and received the holy order on the very day of their entry from the hands of the blessed priest of God, Father Conrad of Prussia, together with Susanna of Masmünster, who had been the wife of a knight. This knight was a lay brother in the outer court until his death.

This sister Margaretha, about whom we are speaking now, was an exceptionally humble, quiet, silent, and merciful person and had especially great grace, love, and devotion to the holy worthy suffering, life, and bitter death of our dear Lord Jesus Christ and also to the holy sacrament. In great desire, she very often spoke of these with the sisters, sweetly and devoutly in an admonitory tone, so that the sisters were also enflamed in grace and devotion for the holy, precious, and beneficent suffering of our dear Lord.

3.32 *Of her blessed, gracious departure and death* [fol. 91v]

She was such a virtuous and peaceful person that it is doubtful if she ever troubled or upset another sister. She observed the required silence so diligently

30. Augustine exclaims this in book 8, chapter 8 of the *Confessions* just prior to his famous conversion scene in the garden. Meyer and his audience need not have known the *Confessions*, however, since this passage is included in the Matins readings for the Sunday within the octave of Augustine, i.e., the Sunday following his feast day. See Anne-Élisabeth Urfels-Capot, *Le Sanctoral du lectionnaire de l'office dominicain (1254–1256): Édition et étude d'après le ms. Rome, Sainte-Sabine XIV L1* (Paris, 2007), 333.

that one heard little from her but "yes" and "no" or other short words, unless she was speaking of good, divine things. She also kept such speech short, lest her mouth run to other things. If she had spoken with someone for the length of a Pater Noster, she considered it breaking silence. At forbidden times and places, she said nothing but "yes" and "no." No sister was too highborn or old or young – if she caught anyone speaking at a forbidden time or place, she would lay her finger to her mouth and signal that the law of silence should not be trespassed. Whenever sisters saw her, they were afraid she had seen their levity.

She was a small, thin figure and had special zeal for the Divine Office. When she had upheld the order diligently and served God in a religious life in this convent of Steinbach for forty-two years, she lay on her deathbed, but the convent did not foresee the hour of her death. Only three sisters were with her. This blessed Sister Margaretha began to pray, greeted our dear Lady, and then smiled kindly. One of the sisters said to her, "Dear sister, why did you laugh?" She answered, "Our dear Lady has been here and promised me eternal life." Quite soon after, she departed and in that place there was a lovely odour. By this, we may know that her death was precious in the eyes of God. Her passing occurred in 1439 on St Gall's Day [16 October].

3.33 *Of the noble, gracious Sister Katharina from Bruges in Flanders* [fol. 92r]

In the first years that Steinbach began the spiritual life of holy Observance, the good reputation of its name flew far and wide into distant lands. In the worthy city of Bruges in the land of Flanders there was an honourable, noble maiden called Katharina, who decided she would like to be the servant of these nuns and to please God through service performed for his dear children. In the very first year, she obtained entrance into the convent, first of all people after the original thirteen mothers. When this honourable person arrived, she wanted nothing other than to be a lay sister and showed such great faithfulness and humility in her work that it was a wonder. For more than seven years, she organized the kitchen and washed all of the sisters' undergarments single-handedly, unless a sister was assigned to help her. She took care of duties in the garden and rang Matins every night, as well as prime. Whatever disgusting work was to be done in the convent, she applied herself to it and, as much as she could, hid and suppressed the nobility of her birth so that no one knew or noticed it. She did the same with her blessed life, and for that reason there is less for us to know.

Her prayer was strong before God and his worthy mother, whom she held dear in particular devotion. One time there was a great war in these lands, and a concern arose that the sisters might have to flee the convent. When this sister Katharina heard this, she was troubled and went after Matins to her devout prayer, calling urgently on God and his worthy mother to protect the convent so they would not have to leave the cloister. She was rapt in her devout prayer and saw our dear Lady descending to the altar, honourably surrounded by many holy angels. She knelt before the worthy holy sacrament, which stood on the altar there, and prayed for the convent and for peace in the land. The next morning, news of a good peace arrived.

When, for the sake of his love, she had faithfully served God the Lord and his children in that convent with great devotion for twenty-six years, she departed this exile in 1424.

3.34 *On the devout Sister Elisabeth Griss and how she grew so quickly in her youth* [fol. 93r]

In the Alsatian village of Hartmannsweiler near Gebweiler, there was a young widow named Anna Griss who had a ten-year-old daughter named Elisabeth. This woman, when she saw how beautifully Schönensteinbach had developed, gained such great love and favour for the religious life of the persons in this convent that she wished to sacrifice her child (this same daughter) to God the Lord in this convent as an eternal service to God and the nuns. Thus the child was received as a lay sister, and although she was heavily burdened in the church and elsewhere with many kinds of work, she always had a gracious, contemplative, devout heart. Hardly a mass occurred during which she was not seen thoroughly sighing and weeping, especially when she received the holy worthy sacrament. She showed such desire, devotion, and love for God and the holy sacrament that it would be impossible for me to write of it. She could not hide her fullness of heart at these times, nor keep it secret, as she would have liked.

This dear sister was richly endowed by God both naturally and by grace, and had such a sharp mind that she possessed remarkable insight into divine things. Her father and confessor, Friar Heinrich, told certain sisters that she had such an enlightened reason that she surpassed many great schoolmen in understanding. She could not read, but loved to hear the divine word read and preached and could repeat what she had heard many years later as if it had been that same day.

3.35 *Of the great, devout prayer of this blessed Sister Elisabeth* [fol. 94r]

During her life, she completed such unspeakably lengthy prayers that many might not believe it, even if it were recorded. Although she held many saints in special love and devotion, she held the great saint and father Saint Anthony in particularly special favour and zealously honoured him above all others. Over the course of her life, she prayed in his honour twenty-five thousand Pater Nosters as a spiritual cloak and twenty-eight thousand Ave Marias for the lining; one thousand times Te Deum as a necklace, and one thousand times the antiphon "Confessor Domini" to embroider it.[31] In her devotion, she also made for him a lovely, ornamented choir frock, which she completed with thirty thousand Te Deums, which she prayed in praise of God and in honour of all the holy hours the holy father Saint Anthony lived on earth for God's sake, saying a verse for each hour. Saint Anthony lived to be 105 years old, but after that number of years, there were more verses left in the prayer Te Deum than there were hours of the holy father Saint Anthony's life. From this extra, she made him a lovely golden crown with many noble, precious stones and pearls and other ornaments.

She had a devout orderliness and intention in her prayers, which I must leave out for the sake of brevity. I will only record one prayer to represent the aforementioned: several times she prayed for Saint Anthony forty-three thousand Te Deums, thirty-six thousand Pater Nosters, fifty-nine thousand antiphons on the Holy Cross ("O crux admirabilis"), ten thousand times the responsory "Sancte Antoni" with the verse "O Sancte Antoni," and the antiphon "Confessor Domini" twenty-eight thousand times, thirty-five thousand times "Nunc dimittis," twenty-five thousand times the psalm "Ecce nunc benedicite" with "Gloria patri," nine thousand times "Gloria in excelsis," and many more prayers that I am leaving out. In Christ's honour and to increase Saint Anthony's joy, she also prayed eighty thousand Pater Nosters for the derision undergone by our dear Lord Jesus Christ in his suffering for our sake. She also especially loved Saint Ursula and the holy eleven thousand maidens, for whom she prayed eleven thousand Pater Nosters, and for the nine choirs of holy angels nine thousand times the Te Deum. She gave herself much hard work with this, perfecting her obedience with devotion.

Here each good sister should note how little time this sister left unused, even though her heart, mind, and senses were so burdened with the prayers of the canonical hours and the office of the dead, beyond which she was burdened with many outer works of obedience.

3.36 *Of this blessed sister Elisabeth's inner, devout, fiery desire for heavenly joy in the fatherland of eternal life* [fol. 95r]

She was also a mild, compassionate sister to all poor, sick persons both inside and outside of the convent. She had special grace and love for the worthy holy suffering of our dear Lord and for his holy sacrament, and especially for the pure, worthy mother of God, the queen of eternity, to whom she prayed such great prayers that I cannot write about them. She also prayed to her apostle Saint James

31. For this kind of "counted prayer" see Arnold Angenendt et al., "Gezählte Frömmigkeit," *Frühmittelalterliche Studien* 29 (1995): 1–71.

the Great and to Saint Barbara, whom she loved because of the holy sacrament.[32] She so greatly desired the heavenly joy of eternal life, to arrive there quickly, and to enjoy eternal praise of God and divine vision with all chosen angels and saints. For this reason, every year she bought the rights of citizenship from those in heaven by praying to each saint, for whom she knew how to say a special prayer. For each saint whom the order customarily honours with nine lections,[33] she performed a special prayer with prostration. We may see that her prayers were ardent, devout, and pleasing to God by this sign: once, on the eve of the Feast of St Catherine [24 November], she prayed very devoutly in the choir, and another sister saw a lovely, bright lamp burning near her head.

In her youth, this dear blessed Sister Elisabeth inflicted great discipline upon herself and secretly practised such great abstinence that she later regretted it. When she was too young, she fasted secretly so much that it made her ill. When they thought she ate with the younger sisters, she stayed away from table so that no one knew. She reaped much regret and pain from this childish devotional folly. When she neared forty years of age, she could hardly fast any more and this was a great sorrow to her.

Remember that you must attend to the young and new brothers and sisters who aspire to too much, when they first begin, through irresponsible fasting, vigils, and other hardships. You should direct them in true humility, obedience, patience, and other virtues lest they be corrupted and become useless to the order. For we know that no one is pleasing in God's eyes through fasting, vigils, and great severity without true humility, patience, obedience, meekness, peacefulness, and other such virtues. Yea, we have often seen that such people, who practise their severe exercises secretly without the advice or knowledge of their superiors or a sensible confessor, very often become more sensitive, troublesome, insufferable, and unbearable than those who adapt themselves to the common exercises according to the order's written law. For this reason, you must be most diligent that young religious people are trained in orderly discipline and true prudence, so that they do not turn towards themselves and away from virtue by overusing good outer practices. They must not scorn the good practices and the holy works and let too much slide, but they also should not overextend themselves unwisely, ruining the Lord's draught horse and making useless people of themselves.

32. Saint Barbara protected her devotees against suddenly dying without receiving the sacrament and last rites.

33. The Dominican liturgy prescribes either three lections (readings) or nine lections for Matins. More important saints and feasts are honoured with the greater number of lections.

3.37 *How this blessed sister Elisabeth found such a holy end* [fol. 96r]

Two years before her death, this sister Elisabeth suffered a great illness and sore inner temptations, some of which concerned strange matters she knew about. She had to suffer them without comfort. She became as ugly as she had been beautiful and was declared leprous. She was constantly worried that she would be ostracized and left alone. Nevertheless, she had the lofty grace that she bore all her suffering, illness, scorn, and the manifold severe temptations well and entrusted everything devoutly to God. Well may she say with Saint Paul, "*Bonum certamen certavi*, I have fought a good fight and triumphed. I have completed the course of my life and placed my faith wholly in the Lord."[34] While she lay on her deathbed on the eve of the Feast of St Barbara [3 December], the night before she departed, a sister said to her, "Dear Sister Elsie, if Saint Barbara were to receive you tomorrow, how would you like that?" She said, "That would be my greatest joy if God released me from this exile. Know that I have suffered so much in this world that it could not be written in the largest missal in this convent. May God will that I have suffered justly." The next morning, on the Feast of St Barbara [4 December], while the convent was at table, she asked a sister to read to her from the life of Christ and wanted to receive the holy sacrament. They gave it to her, but since she spoke so energetically and said the Confiteor so loudly before receiving the holy sacrament, the sisters did not expect death to arrive. Before the priest and the sisters who followed him had gone a stone's throw from the infirmary, the sick sister said to the sister standing closest, "The great Anthony is here!" She bowed her head and, with that, departed before the worthy Father Heinrich, who had given her the holy sacrament, made it out of the sisters' choir. We believe and hope to God that she had an easy journey, for a holy, good end follows well on a good, blessed, spiritual life.

After her death, she appeared to a sister and said, "Since I honoured the holy sacrament during my life and had it by me in my death, the evil spirits have no power over me, nor do they frighten me." She also appeared to a sister holding vigils and looked completely red. The sister was afraid and thought she suffered the pain of purgatorial fire. The dead sister said, "No, I did not go to purgatory, nor do I feel any pain. That I appear so red to you signifies my longing and great desire to see the clear vision of God. Lacking this for a time has been set as my purgatory and my pain." Note how pure one's soul must be to eternally contemplate the spotless, clear mirror of the divine, holy, worthiest Trinity. This blessed sister departed on St Barbara's Day [4 December] 1443.

34. 2 Timothy 4:7. This scriptural passage is read on the Commemoration of St Paul (30 June).

3.38 *Of Sister Anna Griss, the dear, old, faithful mother of the servants* [fol. 97r]

As I noted before, the birth mother of this Sister Elisabeth, whom we commemorated above, was named Anna. As is recounted above, she had sacrificed her child to the Lord God so that this child might live out its days serving this convent within enclosure. She also gave herself and her own person to God and this convent to serve outside in the court. She served this convent faithfully for more than forty years, from which the convent benefited greatly. She was the mistress and mother of the servants in their external quarters and suffered immeasurable scorn and trouble from them, because she taught, directed, and punished the servants for the sake of usefulness to the convent. Even though she led a life of labour with Saint Martha[35] – directing the servants' work, caring for them as a mother and feeding them, organizing the convent's possessions, diligently admonishing the servants to fulfil their service to God and the convent faithfully, and other things that she performed in outer practices – she did not forget her soul. Rather, in addition to her other good works, she confessed quite often and many times a year to the senior confessor, Father Heinrich, even if she had not become impatient with the servants in the interim or fallen into any other offence or sin that needed to be confessed and absolved.

For such work, she also called on some of the maidservants of the cellaress and the convent. When she had reached a good age and had suffered much in such faithful work among the convent servants, she petitioned the prioress and the sisters to be admitted to the cloister as a lay sister for the sake of God. She was granted this, as loath as they were to lose her from the outer court. And so she sacrificed her soul, body, and property to God and the convent for a second time and, before her death, lived within the order for seven years. From that moment forth, she was very quiet and a peaceful, devout, humble sister, who worked much and prayed often into her old age. When she lay at her death, she received the holy sacrament with good sense and Christian devotion from me in the first week that I was confessor there. When I encouraged her to have faith in God and not to fear nor be scared of death, she answered, "I have never lived a day as joyously as I delight in the day of my death." And thus she departed from this world in 1458, at a ripe old age.

3.39 *On the good, virtuous life of the devout sister Magdalena Bechrer* [fol. 98r]

We had a lay sister named Sister Magdalena Bechrer, who was born in Nuremberg as the daughter of very wealthy, rich, honourable people. She was a good thirty-six years old before she came into the order in this convent. In her youth, she had diligently protected herself from sins and loved God with all her

35. Luke 10:38–42. See **2.9**.

heart. When she was fourteen years old, a noble man asked her father to give his daughter to him in marriage, but she would not assent. Rather, she desired God to preserve her maidenly purity unblemished until her end and took up a harsh and strict life. She put on a hair shirt and treated herself so excessively severely that she became very mentally ill and was so uncompliant that she almost gave up the severity of her life. But the merciful God, who wishes for all people to be steadfast and blessed, helped her from this error onto the right path through a distinguished, wise, spiritual, experienced Dominican friar named Conrad from the friary in Nuremberg, who became her confessor. He directed her towards virtue and she became a very humble, compassionate person. She gained the confidence of a very holy woman, who was known in Nuremberg as the Blessed Miss Nagler and through whom God had worked many miracles. This maiden Magdalena was led by her confessor and this blessed woman to become a virtuous person, following the example of the highly praised Saint Elisabeth, the landgravine of Hessen.[36] She served the poor in the hospitals and leper houses personally and through her property. So that the virtue of humility would be more deeply rooted in her, and on the advice of her confessor, she served her maidservants. For the sake of brevity, I will leave out how she cared for the poor, sick, miserable, and stricken people in such a motherly manner, washing, lifting, and laying them down, and other such things.

After all of this, God called her to a poor, withdrawn life and asked her to give up not only her temporal goods but also her free will and to submit to the obedience of a true religious life. With the advice of her confessor, the aforementioned Dominican, Friar Conrad Spielberger, she came to Schönensteinbach and became a humble lay sister. She could have entered as a veiled choir sister because of her honourable status, but she would only be a lay sister or go home. At her own cost, she commissioned many good, useful Latin books in the confessors' library in Schönensteinbach for the comfort of the sisters, so that one could preach from the books. After she had joyfully served our dear Lord in the convent for twenty-five years, she departed this world, as we believe, for eternal peace in 1446 on the eve of the Feast of St Gall [15 October].

3.40 *On the great patience and religious life of Sister Adelheid Voigt* [fol. 99r]

In the convent of Schönensteinbach there was another lay sister named Adelheid Voigt. She was from Bern in the Üechtland and, in the world, had been the

36. Elisabeth of Hungary (d. 1231) was actually landgravine of Thuringia, but the church housing her relics is in Marburg, which is in Hessen.

maid of a well-born noblewoman. From youth, she had been very contemplative and devout towards God. She was a tall, handsome, strong person. Through a dear, blessed Dominican friar, God helped her to enter the convent of Schönensteinbach, where she became a lay sister, even though she could read German and Latin and could write. She diligently maintained the holy observance of the order, especially the law of silence, for no sister ever noticed her breaking silence, whether in or outside the kitchen. She kept the kitchen for twelve years or so, and was the best cook the convent ever had.

Whenever she was in the kitchen, her heart was with God and in the choir. Every day she prayed the Little Office of the Virgin just as it is read in the choir and at least one Office for the Dead. She also prayed much otherwise, even though she was very burdened with work. As far as she could, she never missed hearing one mass a day. After many years, God imposed such a great illness on her that she could not do her work in the kitchen. Since the illness did not manifest outwardly, they thought she was faking and ordered her to perform the work of her obedience. When she did not and could not do this, they thought she was resisting out of frivolity and disobedience, and locked her up like an insubordinate sister. She suffered this patiently and silently until, after a few days, the illness broke out visibly. Both her legs swelled considerably, she had dropsy in her feet, and she suffered great pain. She often went to the canonical hours and to Mass or wherever the community was, in the refectory or at table or in the workroom, hobbling very painfully on two crutches – yet seldom was she seen idle.

3.41 *On the blessed death of this sister Adelheid and how she was buried in Basel* [fol. 99v]

This sister Adelheid held holy Mass in especially great favour and devotion and had knelt through many on her sick knees. She did not have particularly friendly manners and some of the sisters did not like her much. She did this on purpose, so that she would have fewer attachments and relationships and be less hindered in better things. When her pain and trouble befell her, she could face it easily in silence. She was wholly candid and upright and had a clear conscience, according to her confessor.

When she had been in the convent for fifteen years, a great disruption arose in the land because of war and the sisters had to leave the convent. This sister Adelheid said, "I will not live out this year and I will never see this cloister again." And so it happened. She died in Neuenburg among her sisters and her body was transported from Neuenburg to Basel and buried there in the cloister of the dear Dominican fathers on Christmas Eve in 1444.

One sister was so deaf and senile, that when the illness struck her, she lost her senses and reason so completely, that they worried she might do herself physical harm. On the day after Adelheid's passing, three sisters lay in a small room and did not know that the sick sister had lost her senses again. The dead sister Adelheid came to them three times that night and woke the three sisters up to go help the sick sister. She was found in a place where, if they had not come to her aid that night, the poor sister would have lost her life. God the Lord provided through the good spirit of Sister Adelheid.

How she had revelations during her life, as her confessor has said of her, and how she appeared to a confessor after her death and what she said to him – all this I commend to eternal wisdom. Her confessor said that she wanted no husband in the world. Even though she had many suitors, she wanted God alone, to whom she had promised her purity and for whom she kept it until her death. She died a pure virgin in body and soul.

3.42 *In memory of the blessed sister Katharina Holtzhauser* [fol. 100v]

There was yet another blessed lay sister in this convent named Sister Katharina Holtzhauser. She was a widow and already at an advanced age when she entered the convent. She had a son who was a very blessed priest of the Order of Preachers in the Dominican community of Nuremberg. This widow Katharina also wished to lead a spiritual life within the Dominican order, but there was not yet any convent in all these lands where the Observance was upheld – except for Schönensteinbach alone, which was just starting.[37] She did not dare enter any convent, since she worried that she would not be able to do enough for God and the order. For she saw well, that all the women's convents sorely needed to be reformed to the religious life and enclosed. Therefore, she lived as a religious woman in the world and was a mild, generous woman to poor people, giving such great alms and being such a comfort to the poor that she was justly called "mother of the poor."

She had with her a blessed maiden, whom she had raised and who was also named Katharina. She helped her in all her good works. The Dominicans in Nuremberg told them so much good about the holy virgin Saint Catherine of Siena of the order of Penitents of St Dominic and about her holy confessor Master Raymond, who had been master general of the whole order and who lay buried in the choir of the Dominican church in Nuremberg.[38] These two women

37. The Nuremberg friary was reformed the year before Schönensteinbach was founded, meaning that Katharina's son was newly Observant.

38. For Catherine of Siena's significance to the Nuremberg Observants, see the note in **3.3**.

strongly began to desire to assume the Dominican third order, and so they did.[39] They were vilified and driven out of the city of Nuremberg, for this was unusual and unheard of to many people. So they moved to another little town named Neukirch and there they served God.

Afterwards, once Steinbach had grown well, the elder Katharina applied to be received as a lay sister there. She was accepted and came to the convent in the same year that Unterlinden was reformed by Schönensteinbach.[40] There, she lived a spiritual, devout, earnest life and was very quiet. She had great pain from bladder stones but suffered the illness patiently in solitude. She prayed often and was seldom ever idle. She also copied very good, useful books on excellent subjects.

3.43 *On the solemn end of this good sister* [fol. 101r]

When this sister Katharina had led a virtuous, serious life in Steinbach for twenty years and had suffered much, our dear Lord took her from this world with a very strange, miraculous end, such that the sisters could not know how she died. Three days before her death she lay so still that she gave no outer sign. On the Feast of St Vincent the Holy Martyr [22 January], when Matins was rung, the sisters found no life in her. They dressed her in burial garb and laid her on the bier. Once the convent had prayed the psalter up till the fifth nocturn, at the psalm "Salvum me fac Deus,"[41] she twitched on the bier, stirred, and made a noise. How the Lord took her to him, or what this miracle means, we do not know, for the secret judgements of God are hidden to us. Yet we trust that her good life was followed by an even better end and we take an example from her.

After her death, the sisters asked the senior confessor, Father Heinrich Fabri, how it happened that this sister was so greatly honoured in Nuremberg and had such great wisdom but was not as respected in the convent and found such a startling end. The confessor answered: "While she was still in Nuremberg, a poor person came to her on a cold winter night and asked her for alms for God's sake. Contrary to her custom, she denied alms to this poor person with dismissive words, for she had much to do at the moment and was burdened with all sorts of

39. The first order consists of the friars, the second of the nuns, and the third order is for pious laypeople. For the increasing regulation of lay religious life under the Observants, see Alison More, "Institutionalizing Penitential Life in Later Medieval and Early Modern Europe: Third Orders, Rules, and Canonical Legitimacy," *Church History* 83 (2014): 297–323; Alison More, *Fictive Orders and Feminine Religious Identities, 1200-1600* (Oxford, 2018), ch. 3.

40. This happened in 1419.

41. Psalm 68/69.

business. She immediately regretted it and looked after the poor person, but he was gone. That night, a voice spoke sternly to her, 'Katharina, since you have left me uncomforted on this cold night, this shall be your penance: you will remain in misery and scorn until your death and your end will appear to be merciless. This is my grace, that you atone in misery in this world.'"

3.44 *On the virtuous, religious, and physically beautiful sister Margaretha Scheller and how she fought so faithfully and zealously for the sake of her virginal purity and triumphed with the help of God* [fol. 102r]

In this same convent of Steinbach there was a young lay sister named Margaretha Scheller of Thann, a noble, tall, pretty person, joyous and willingly obedient. When she was a lovely maiden in the world, her father promised her to a man in marriage. As the priest held both their hands in his and was about to give them to each other, she tore away and fled from there in all haste. She ran so quickly that no one could catch her, even though a great many people were present. She came into an empty courtyard and found a locked door. She kicked it open with a single blow and hid herself in an old cellar, where she remained until she was better able to protect herself. She cut off her own beautiful hair and promised God and his mother to protect her purity.

This tale reached an honourable knight, Wilhelm of Masmünster, who was a special friend to the sisters of Schönensteinbach. He sent for this maiden, and when he saw her decorous beauty he was moved to compassion and kept her with him as his child, so that she might remain in her good intention and keep her purity for God. Her biological father and her family, in their evil perfidy, had placed lookouts for her everywhere. This pious knight had a young priest in his retinue, who was so harmfully captivated by the beauty of this maiden that his mind and heart were enflamed with unseemly desire for her. She suffered so much distress and worry from him in numerous ways that it is impossible to recount all of it. The harassment she suffered from the priest was worse than all the worry and pain she had undergone before, and her honour was not safe. After a great struggle, in which she triumphed for the sake of virginal purity, God helped her into the convent of Steinbach through the knight.

3.45 *Of the great patience in suffering and of the gracious end of this blessed sister* [fol. 102v]

When this sister Margaretha entered the convent of Steinbach, she behaved in such a religious manner and so lovingly that all sisters universally liked her. She fulfilled her obedience so eagerly that it seemed as though she flew to her work. Seldom was some task too much for her and occasionally one had to prevent her from working, yet she was a tender person. In all communal work, she was among the first there, and whatever work she was doing, it seemed to her as though God was always present. When she prepared food for the sisters, she beat her breast and her eyes teared up and she said, "Oh, see how our dear Lord sits with his dear disciples," and it was a great joy to her to be Martha.[42] The convent has not had many like her in the kitchen since.

Otherwise, she kept the convent clean and tidy. She was particularly virtuous, humble, and avid for everything that pertained to God. Her whole life was of such purity that the confessor who heard her full confession testified that he could not find that she had ever angered God with a mortal sin in her whole life. God gave her what he customarily gives his dear friends – suffering and pain. Her head burst and she suffered such great pain that it is impossible to describe. When they ripped her hood off, her skin and hair completely came off, so wide was her head. Yet in all her suffering never an impatient word was heard; she only praised God. For a whole year before her death, she suffered illness with great patience. On the eve of St Valentine's Day [13 February], when she lay at her end, she said to the sister who watched her, "Sister, a huge, horrible toad has just crawled in the door. Quick, pour consecrated water on it!" Then she smiled kindly and said, "It's gone!" A while later, she again had her pour consecrated water there, and then became very ill. Nevertheless, the convent lay down to sleep and rest a while, so five sisters were appointed to remain and lie by her. When it had struck eight o'clock, she said to the servant, "Jesus is here! Jesus is here!" and with those words, she departed so quickly that the sisters who were sitting by the window could not come in time. When the convent arrived, she was lying in a way that was a pleasure for all the sisters to see, just like a loving soul who has fallen asleep on her beloved. She departed in 1442 in the bloom of her youth, when her soul was pleasing to God.

42. Luke 10:38–42. On Mary and Martha, see the note in **2.9**.

Book Four

Here begins the prologue of the fourth book of the reformation of the Order of Preachers and of the virtues of the fathers who started it. [fol. 107v]

Mementote filii patrum.[1] Remember, dear children, your worthy fathers and the great good deeds they have done. Thus spoke a saint to his people, as we read in Maccabees. Therefore, this fourth book recounts what is especially good and useful to know about our blessed fathers who, by the grace of God, invented the method and form of the reformation of the order. With great effort, they undertook and began this great, holy, good work, especially in German lands, first in Colmar and Nuremberg. They and their next successors managed the newly restored religious life diligently. This book treats their holy lives and the manifold graces they received from God.

Nevertheless, it must be known that there were many more blessed fathers not recorded here, who wanted the holy observance with such heartfelt desire that it was restored. They worked with ardent zeal and diverse, indescribable labour towards the religious life of the Observance, for which they suffered much. Finally, they brought their holy, spiritual, devout life with much virtue to a good, blessed end with which they followed eternal life. May the Lord Jesus grant us the same for their holy prayer and merits. Amen.

4.1 *This fourth book tells how before the beginning of the reform and the restoration of observance, many blessed fathers and brothers were spread throughout the order, how they finally began the holy observance in various men's houses, and how they behaved.* [fol. 108r]

In the times when Friar Elias of Toulouse,[2] a master of holy Scripture and a wise and learned man, was master general, the Dominican order had fallen very far from its first holy beginning. The brothers and sisters did not behave according to

1. 1 Maccabees 2:51.

2. On Master General Elias Raymond of Toulouse (r. 1367–1380), see Mortier, *Histoire des maîtres généraux*, 3: 385–490.

the direction of the Rule and Constitutions in religious life as had been the case in the old days of the first fathers and their blessed successors. The brothers and sisters in the convents did not fully maintain observance of the religious life according to the written law of the order, as the text of the holy Rule of St Augustine and the Constitutions of the brothers and sisters of the holy Order of Preachers instruct. Nevertheless, here and there in German and Italian lands, in Lombardy, France, and Sicily, and in the other provinces of the order, certain good friends of God and devout, dear, holy fathers of the order upheld the order's religious life, each as best he could. For this, they suffered scorn, humiliation, and oppression from those who had neither such a life nor the grace for it. Although the number of these blessed brothers was not so great as the number of fathers who lived blessedly in the old days at the beginning of the order, at that time there were some living among the imperfect brothers who surpassed the first fathers in grace and way of life.

4.2 *The names of certain blessed friars who loved the renewal and reform of the ancient observance* [fol. 108v]

The aforesaid master general ruled the order at the time when one counted from the birth of our Lord 1370 years. He was unable to force the people of the order to direct their lives by the order's law, because the evil customs were too ingrained, having gained the upper hand long before he became master general. The holy old observance was disrupted. Unfortunately, many brothers and sisters were living quite freely according to their whims and few still heeded and sought out the religious life of their blessed, ancient predecessors. Nevertheless, although they were very few compared to the others, some blessed brothers living then desired from their hearts that throughout the order one might live spiritually in true observance, as they had lived in the time of Saint Dominic and his successor, the blessed Jordan.[3] Yet it could not be, for the damage was so great, the weeds and rats had overrun the noble meadow, the wilful were too headstrong and unbreakable. What else was this but a great burden and a cross for the spirits of the willing fathers and friends of God?

Here are the names of some of these friends of God who lived in the order at this time: Friar Raymond of Capua,[4] of the province of Sicily, in whom God worked great miracles. He especially desired the restoration of the order. He was a lover of good people and he sought them out as friends. God recommended to him an exceptionally good person named Catherine of Siena,[5] whom he took as

3. Jordan of Saxony, second master general of the Dominican order (r. 1222–1237).
4. Raymond of Capua, master general of the Dominican order (r. 1380–1399).
5. See the note on Catherine of Siena in **3.3**.

his spiritual mother. He was her confessor and at her advice and instigation, he did many good works for the salvation of his neighbour. He was a high master of holy Scripture and his wisdom and holiness made him beloved of and close to Pope Gregory XI and afterwards Pope Urban VI and Pope Boniface IX.[6] After the aforementioned master general, God in his merciful grace made this Friar Raymond master. What he did, and in particular how he reformed several communities in German lands and returned the convent of Schönensteinbach to the religious life of the Observance, will be recounted later.

Friar Bartholomew,[7] a master of holy Scripture and lover of religious life: He was also a special friend of the said Raymond and Catherine of Siena. He later became provincial prior over the Roman province.

Friar John Dominici,[8] a blessed man, who especially desired the order to uphold the Rule and the Constitution: When the aforesaid blessed Master Raymond became master general, John supplied him with much helpful advice so that many convents and communities were zealously reformed to Observant religion. Although while in Venice, where he had been before Master Raymond began to reform any convents, he had previously observed the order in life and deed, especially its poverty, afterwards he founded a new community through papal authority.[9] With the help and good will of Raymond, the master general, he was the first to uphold the order in Italian lands with many blessed brothers in full perfection of the Rule and Constitution as one lived at the beginning of the order. He greatly advanced the holy Observance in Italy.

The blessed life of this father John and his blessed brothers spread far and wide and greatly pleased the high prelates, both secular and religious, who took it as a model. He was forced against his will to become a cardinal of the Roman church. He was an intimate, special friend of the emperor Sigismund.[10] While the papal schism split Christendom, he and this Roman king Sigismund worked together to reunify Christendom and restore peace. When he became cardinal, he did not cease to observe holy poverty, which he much loved. For this reason, whatever he gained through the dignity of his office, or indeed at all, he did not

6. Popes Gregory XI (r. 1370–1378), Urban VI (r. 1378–1389), and Boniface IX (r. 1389–1404).

7. Bartholomew Dominici of Siena, Roman provincial prior (r. 1388–1398). See *SOPMA*, 1: 148–149.

8. Giovanni Dominici (d. 1419), Conrad of Prussia's Italian counterpart, who spearheaded the Italian Observance. See *SOPMA*, 2: 406–413.

9. Giovanni Dominici founded the Observant friary in Fiesole in 1406.

10. Sigismund of Luxembourg, king of the Romans (r. 1411–1437) and Holy Roman emperor (from 1433).

keep. He asked to be indulged in three things: first, that he not have to wear such courtly clothes as is the custom of cardinals; second, that he be allowed to pray the hours as a Dominican friar; and third, that he be allowed to travel and preach the word of God.

Friar Elias of Languedoc:[11] He greatly loved the Observance and his holy company of twenty-four friars. They were all holy friends of God who worked miracles. When they realized that our holy father Saint Dominic had founded the Order of Preachers expressly to preach the divine word, they so zealously pursued this that they readily achieved the salvation of souls. Pope Gregory XI sent them all to preach in Armenia, Tartary, and the Land of the Rising Sun. The pope gave each friar a bible, a breviary, and many other books, with which they accomplished great profit for Christianity.

Friar Vincent Ferrer of Valencia,[12] a highly educated holy master of theology: He had extremely deep love for the religious life of observance, which he himself upheld in his own person according to the Rule and Constitutions of the order. He also expected his dear companions and other willing brothers to love the Observance. He also wrote a very good and useful book for friars concerning how they should uphold the order not only in larger matters (in obedient life, without property, remaining clean and pure) but also in everyday matters such as silence, going quickly and without hesitation when the bell is rung, and not wearing clothes other than what is stipulated in the Constitutions: poor-quality cloth, the cappa shorter than the tunic, and a wide scapular.[13] He wrote many other things in this book, providing delightful regulations and instructions for diligently maintaining observance and the order according to the foundation of Saint Dominic. This master Vincent was such an exceptionally good person in life and teaching that Friar Johannes Nider writes of him in book 2, chapter 1 of the *Formicarius* that he surpassed his fathers, Saints Dominic, Peter, and Thomas. He was canonized by Pope Calixtus III,[14] who ordered that he be honoured throughout Christendom as a high, worthy, holy teacher of the world.

11. Master General Elias Raymond of Toulouse appointed Elias Petit of Languedoc vicar general of missionary friars in 1374. See Mortier, *Histoire des maîtres généraux*, 3: 444.

12. Vincent Ferrer died in 1419 and was canonized in 1455. The book is his *Treatise on the Spiritual Life*. See *SOPMA*, 4: 458–474; Laura Ackerman Smoller, *The Saint and the Chopped-Up Baby: The Cult of Vincent Ferrer in Medieval and Early Modern Europe* (Ithaca, 2014).

13. These requirements are spelled out in distinction 1, chapter 10 of the 1256 Constitutions for Dominican Friars. See "Liber Constitutionum Ordinis Fratrum Praedicatorum," *Analecta Sacri Ordinis Fratrum Praedicatorum* 3 (1897): 26–60, 98–122, 162–181, at 49.

14. Pope Calixtus III (r. 1455–1458).

Friar Raphael of Cardona, a worthy, learned master of theology: I have read of the love he had for the Observance in an open letter he wrote with his own hand. In it, he admonishes a friar to consume his life in observance for God and to spend the rest of his life in a reformed convent according to the will of God and Saint Dominic. He was a companion and disciple of Saint Vincent, as were Friar Godfrey and Friar Peter, both companions of Saint Vincent who had great love for the order. They were so perfect that they greatly benefited holy Christendom through their lives, through teaching holy Scripture and proclaiming the divine word. God the Lord worked great miracles through their holy merits and they performed great signs and wonders during their lives and after death. The names of these three fathers are written in the Legend of St Vincent.[15]

Friar Manfred of Vercelli,[16] a learned, holy man, who only associated in the order with God-fearing friars who were of good and clear conscience and willingly upheld the order. Saint Vincent held him dear. Now this friar so greatly loved upholding the order that he not only helped and advised in the reform of many convents, he also instructed and taught the brothers and sisters of the third order *de Penitencia Beati Dominici*, that is, of the Penitence of St Dominic, to behave perfectly according to the form of their Rule.[17] He had many good and blessed children of the third order in Italian lands. He was a talented itinerant preacher and hundreds of people would follow him over hill and vale. This father Manfred lived to see not only the beginning of the Observance, which he had long and ardently desired, but also the Observant reform of several convents and communities in German and Italian lands. The communities in Colmar, Nuremberg, Bern, and Basel were reformed, as well as many in Italian lands whose names I do not know, but especially the community of Bologna, where our holy father Saint Dominic lies buried, and both friaries in Rome. He lived and died in the one called Santa Maria sopra Minerva,[18] not without signs that God the Lord worked graciously in him.

15. Raphael of Cardona may have been Johannes Nider's direct source of information on Vincent Ferrer for the *Formicarius*. Smoller, *The Cult of Vincent Ferrer*, 167.

16. Although Manfred was a popular apocalyptic preacher, little is known about him. He first appears in records in 1417 and apparently died sometime after 1431. See Raymond Creytens, "Manfred de Verceil et son traité contre les fraticelles," *AFP* 11 (1941): 173–208; *SOPMA*, 3: 101–102.

17. For the origins of the Dominican third order, see Maiju Lehmijoki-Gardner, "Writing Religious Rules as an Interactive Process: Dominican Penitent Women and the Making of Their *Regula*," *Speculum* 79 (2004): 660–687.

18. Meyer actually calls this friary "Santa Maria in Minora," an alternative name which distinguished it from the papal basilica of Santa Maria Maggiore. The Bologna friary was reformed in 1426, roughly around the same time as Bern (1419) and Basel (1429). Both Santa Maria sopra Minerva and the other Roman friary, Santa Sabina, joined the Observant Congregation of Lombardy but not until decades later, likely long after Manfred of Vercelli had died.

At that time, many more holy friars living everywhere in the order would gladly have seen some convents in which only brothers and sisters who wished to maintain observance could be. Many were considering how the children and friends of God distantly separated from one another could be brought together in special communities where they could uphold the order according to the Rule and Constitutions. In German lands, there were also many notably learned fathers who shared this opinion. Among them in particular was Friar Conrad, called von Grossis, born in Prussia, a holy man and the first father and founder of the reformed convents of brothers and sisters in German lands.

4.3 *How the blessed Raymond was elected master general, how Friar Conrad of Prussia began to reform the friary in Colmar, and how the pope confirmed this* [fol. 112r]

In 1378, during the generalate of the aforesaid Elias, while he was master general of the order, Urban VI was elected pope in Rome. Some of the cardinals dissented and elected another pope named Clement VII, causing a schism in Christendom that lasted many years.[19] The master general, Elias, held to the pope named Clement and withdrew from the obedience of the true pope in Rome and many friars with him. But many more, the majority of the order, remained under the obedience of Pope Urban.[20] Since the master general did not want to recognize the pope in Rome, sixteen provincial priors assembled with other delegated friars and elected another master general. The beneficence of God granted that the holy father Raymond of Capua was elected master general. He had long been confessor to the blessed Saint Catherine of Siena, as was said before.

Once this worthy father became master general, he deliberated how to rule the order well and reform it to a religious state. He found many willing friars in the order who desired to uphold the order according to the Rule and Constitutions and who wished to congregate together so that no one would divert them from this. So this master took counsel with the aforesaid friars to consider this matter. They decided such a good matter should be submitted to the pope, so the master general faithfully did this. Now at this time, there was a very honourable father named Friar Conrad de Grossis, or of Prussia, who proved very zealous in this affair and more hard-working and diligent than any of the fathers or brothers described above.

19. The Great Western Schism lasted from 1378 to 1417. For more, see Joelle Rollo-Koster and Thomas M. Izbicki (eds), *A Companion to the Great Western Schism (1378–1417)* (Leiden, 2009).

20. The Dominican order split by province into an "Avignonese obedience" and a "Roman obedience," according to the seat of the pope they followed. See William A. Hinnebusch, *The Dominicans: A Short History* (New York, 1975), 62–63.

In 1388,[21] the order held a large general chapter. The fathers were to state their faults before the master general, the provincials, and the definitors, as is usual at general chapters. When it was Father Conrad of Prussia's turn to stand and state his faults in the presence of hundreds of fathers and friars, he laid a great rope around his neck and entered, proclaiming his guilt, crying that he was worthy of death and that one should hang him from the rope around his neck, for up until that time he had not upheld his holy order. He spoke many pitiful, humble words there, and moved many a devout heart. It was then publicly debated and taken under advisement how the blessed Friar Conrad of Prussia and the dear friars who shared his holy intention of upholding the order could be given a friary where they could maintain observance of the order unhindered. The master general, the blessed Raymond, gave the well-intentioned friars of German lands the friary of Colmar and made this father Conrad of Prussia the prior. After this friar and father, together with thirty upstanding, experienced, honourable fathers, entered the Colmar friary in 1389, they began to maintain observance of the order so laudably in life and teaching, that it not only edified the whole land, but also earned praise at the Roman court before the pope and the cardinals. For this reason, Pope Boniface IX gained a great love and affection for this Observance and confirmed it with papal authority. For the sake of brevity, I leave unwritten the great intransigence and scorn these fathers suffered for the sake of their life and teaching from the people who did not share it, the poverty and trouble that befell them, how they remained obediently steadfast through all these things, how blessedly they lived in manifold virtue and observance of the order, and the miracles God worked through them.

4.4 *How Master Raymond commanded all the provincials to select one community in each province where one might maintain observance, and how the pope confirmed this* [fol. 113v]

This blessed life pleased the pope and the master general and they saw that it greatly enhanced the honour of God and of the order and the salvation of souls. With the pope's assent and blessing, the master commanded all provincials throughout the whole order that each should arrange for one friary within his province where at least twelve brothers would go who desired to maintain the observance and the order rigorously. If a provincial found more than twelve friars in his province who desired of free will and just ambition to uphold observance, he should help them realize this good intent. Any provincial who failed in this and did not facilitate such a friary for well-intentioned brothers in his

21. The manuscripts have 1300, but this is clearly an error of scribal omission.

province would be dismissed from his duties as provincial and declared ineligible for this office for ten years.

And so the holy Observance advanced quite laudably in many convents in German and Italian lands, but the friars who did not follow this intent and this life heaped their disfavour upon the Observance and scorned and disdained it. Just as is written in the Book of Exodus that the more the harsh unbelievers of Egypt oppressed and reviled the people of God, the more they rose, increased, and grew, so it was for these blessed friends of God. The more they suffered and were oppressed by false friars, the more they advanced in their patience and grew.

Still, the blessed Pope Boniface IX, before whom this grievance came, confirmed the Observance a second time. He ordered all friars of the Order of Preachers, whether they be prelates or subjects in the present or future, strictly on pain of excommunication never again in any way now and henceforth to act against the Observance or to hinder or divert a friar who wished to submit to the Observance. This pope Boniface wrote such and similar things in a particularly notable bull in the fifth year of his papacy at St Peter's in Rome.[22]

At this time, in 1392, the worthy father Friar Ulrich Theobaldi,[23] who was provincial at the time, held a provincial chapter in Speyer. The blessed Master General Raymond delegated full authority to his close companion, Friar Jakob, a blessed man and a lover of the Observance. He instructed the provincials and the fathers in Speyer to protect the Observance that had begun in Colmar. So this provincial and the fathers wrote a letter ordering all friars, by the constraint of holy obedience, neither to trouble nor to hinder anyone who wished to enter there. Through this, all the fathers of the province took under their protection Friar Conrad of Prussia, prior of Colmar, and his brothers.

The provincial was from the friary of Basel and was a wise and learned father, a master of holy Scripture, and lies buried in that friary. He was the first to set his seal on this letter and signed it with his own hand, by which he confirmed the Observance, administered it, and protected it from all things. Afterwards, Friar Ulrich Wintner of Regensburg,[24] also a master of holy Scripture, laid his seal on this letter. This father had been provincial previously but had been relieved at his own request due to illness. The third father was Friar Peter Engerlin of Augsburg, who had also been provincial and was a praiseworthy man and a master of holy Scripture. He signed as: "I, Friar Peter Engerlin, a proclaimer of holy Scripture, since I do not at present have my own seal, have asked the worthy father

22. See *Bullarium Ordinis FF. Praedicatorum*, 8 vols (Rome, 1729–1740), 2: 315–316.
23. Ulrich Theobaldi (r. 1390–1398). See *DDS*, 243–244; *SOPMA*, 4: 423–424.
24. See *SOPMA*, 4: 424.

Johannes Arnoldi[25] to do this for me." This father Peter Engerlin became provincial again later. The fourth father was Friar Peter Florin, who became provincial shortly thereafter. He also appended his seal willingly. He died in the first year of his provincialate and had himself buried with the Observant friars in Colmar. The fifth was Friar Gottfried of Mengen,[26] vicar over all Swabian convents and definitor to the general chapter. His signature reads: "I, Friar Gottfried of Mengen, swear and proclaim myself a shield and protection." This father lovingly received Observant friars when they came as guests to his friary in Constance and treated them very well. The sixth father was Friar Franz of Retz,[27] a blessed, wise, learned master of holy Scripture and an especially ardent servant of the highly praised, worthy mother of God, Mary. He wrote: "I, Friar Franciscus, swear the same with my own hand." This father was the very first doctor and master to obtain a degree from the University of Vienna. He also wrote long and beautiful books about the Salve Regina.[28]

Many other fathers signed and sealed this document at the chapter in Speyer, promising to support the Observance in German lands and declaring that no one should hinder it on pain of strict penance and penalty.

4.5 *How Raymond, the master general, reformed the friary in Nuremberg to the Observance through Conrad of Prussia and how the convent of St Catherine there was enclosed but not reformed* [fol. 115v]

In 1396, the blessed Master General Raymond reformed the Dominican friary in Nuremberg to the holy Observance with the support and authority of Pope Boniface. First, the worthy father Friar Johannes Mulberg was sent to Nuremberg to serve as the convent's vicar in place of a prior.[29] The blessed father Conrad of Prussia suggested this. Although at first he was not there, when it came time to fill the offices, Conrad was elected the first prior and many good and upright fathers came from Colmar to start the Observance. Nuremberg flourished so greatly that it reformed many other friaries in the German province and in the province of Saxony.

Once this worthy father Conrad of Prussia and his blessed friars were laudably maintaining full observance of the order in the Nuremberg friary and the old friars who did not want to keep it had left, the irreverence and great abandon

25. See *SOPMA*, 2: 377–378.

26. *DDS*, 405.

27. See Klaus Grubmüller, "Franz von Retz," *VL*² 2: 834–837; *SOPMA*, 1: 397–400.

28. For Franz of Retz's lengthy commentary on the Salve Regina, see Johannes Maier, *Studien zur Geschichte der Marienantiphon "Salve Regina"* (Regensburg, 1939), 22.

29. See Sabine von Heusinger, *Johannes Mulberg OP (d. 1414): Ein Leben im Spannungsfeld von Dominikanerobservanz und Beginenstreit* (Berlin, 2000); *SOPMA*, 2: 490–493.

of the Dominican sisters in St Catherine's convent there weighed heavily on the conscience of this prior and his brothers. They believed that the evil spirit had a great advantage there, because there was no proper enclosure. Religious life was seen little there and the sisters had inherited evil habits. However often they were admonished to improve, their irreverence was so ingrained that they did not want to depart from their evil ways and despicable life.

The friars obtained a bull from the pope and, with the help of certain dear fathers and other friends of God and city servants, the prior, Father Conrad, secured the authority to enclose the convent so that the sisters could no longer leave nor anyone go in to them, from which much evil had previously arisen. If they wished to be frivolous and disobedient, he could punish them. So the prior, Friar Conrad, along with certain of his brothers and many good citizens of the city council, came to the sisters of St Catherine's convent and told them what the pope had commanded. In virtuous prudence, the prior earnestly requested the sisters' obedience and exhorted them to enclosure.

When the sisters heard this, they objected. They renounced papal and divine obedience with extravagantly obscene gestures and unruly, unwomanly manners. The prior ordered that such publicly disobedient sisters be seized and bound. He called a friar to lift one sister's feet, and she cried, "I will be bound by no one but this citizen, my cousin." So the man went to do what she had said, but when he bent over her feet, she heaved her feet strongly upward and impudently kicked the honourable man so fiercely that he fell backwards onto the ground. At that, the turbulence and raucousness became so great that the prior, his friars, and the citizens had to leave and abandon their intentions for the moment.

Not long afterwards, the friars and their prior deliberated how to fulfil the command and intention of the pope and bring the sisters to an orderly life. One brother, named Johannes Mülich, said: "We should look into this matter wisely and proceed with caution so that we do not come away with any damage or imprudence. The sisters are outrageous and headstrong, with no conscience or fear of God. They will care very little whether any of us loses his life. It would be to our great harm if we hit or pushed them when they flagrantly laid their hands on us. Hits or punches would be impugned to us as a great error. It seems advisable to me that some friars should hide little sacks of flour under their cappas, and when we see the sisters begin to raise a ruckus and treat us outrageously, they should take out their flour and throw it in the sisters' faces. Then they will be so busy with themselves that we will be certain of our lives."

Now, the sisters strongly resisted obedience and took counsel from worldwise and well-educated clerics who told them that they could do whatever they wished. If they did not hear the papal bull and command, they could not be placed under interdict. So when the blessed prior, his friars, and the citizens gathered once more to go to the convent, the sisters prevented them from entering. But when workers were supposed to come into the convent on the direction and order of the sisters, the prior and his company came in too. When the sisters realized this, two of them took a huge crucifix and tried to beat in the blessed father prior's head. The worthy father inclined his head to the blow and would have received it patiently, but some of the citizens got under it and caught the stroke. Now they were all in the convent, and the friars had their cappas or mantles on. One stood forth and began to read the papal bull and letter. When the sisters heard this, they made a huge commotion and when the brothers and fathers tried to stop them, some sisters fell upon them with great impropriety. The previously mentioned Friar Johannes Mülich cried, "Now! You have cause to defend yourselves from the sisters!" The friars drew out the flour and threw it in the faces of the sisters, so that they could not hurt them. With this proper cause, they repelled the sisters from them, so that they could not hit, nor push, nor do anything untoward.

And so it happened that, through great toil, this convent was enclosed. Afterwards not as much coming and going and impropriety happened as before. Yet we shall see how this convent was reformed to the holy Observance many years later.

4.6 *An exhortation to note the virtues of the blessed fathers, whose labour reformed the friaries, and to imitate their good lives* [fol. 117v]

Attendite ad petram unde excisi estis, et ad cavernam laci de qua praecisi estis. Attendite ad Abraham, patrem vestrum, et ad Zaram, quae genuit vos.[30] Thus spoke the holy spirit to us poor children of God through his prophet, the holy Isaiah. Look unto the great stone and boulder from which you are hewn and to the cavern of the stony lake from which you were cut. Take note of your father Abraham and also Sara, who bore you. These words are written in the book of the prophet Isaiah in the fifty-first chapter, and admonish great zeal and earnest faith upon the brothers and sisters of our holy order, especially those in reformed friaries and in properly enclosed women's convents. We must diligently bear in mind not only how the first foundation of our order was laid, from which we are hewn, formed, and cut, but also Abraham, that is, our holy father Saint Dominic, and Sara, that is the first religious observance, which existed at the origin and beginning of our order in the times of the first holy fathers. In these words, the holy one especially exhorts us to contemplate in our mind's eye all holy religious life and the blessed

30. Isaiah 51:1–2.

fathers, mothers, and sisters, who have ever lived religiously in our order. We especially should commemorate the gracious friars and sisters who through great labour over the past seventy years have reformed and restored the fallen spiritual life in men's and women's convents in many countries, but especially in German lands. We should remember how these brothers and sisters toiled so diligently in such great faith and ardent devotion, if we believe ourselves to be their successors, formed by them and, in particular, by the first fathers and mothers of the convent Schönensteinbach, from whence comes the first origin of all reformed convents of sisters.

4.7 *How, in the image of the holy patriarch Mattathias, the blessed father Conrad of Prussia began to reform the Dominican order in various friaries and convents* [fol. 118v]

We read in the second chapter of Maccabees, that the worthy man Mattathias saw how observance of God's laws had so lamentably declined and so few people still lived according to the written law, and this troubled him greatly. He gathered his sons and certain willing hearts and admonished them to uphold justice and the written laws, saying, "*Mementote, O filii, patrem quae fecerunt.*[31] O dear sons and brothers," he said, "remember the holy fathers and how well they lived in their generations. How it has fallen!" He counted by name many dear fathers, Abraham, Joseph, Phineas, Caleb, David, Daniel, and Elijah,[32] and said, "So, dear brothers, remember from generation to generation." This prophet did and said much else when he restored his sons and helpers.

And thus also did the blessed, devout father Friar Conrad of Prussia. In his youth, he entered the Dominican order and God enlightened him with some reason and wisdom, so that he recognized in his own prudence that the order generally had fallen from its first original religious life. He read the Rule and Constitutions, considered the lives of the friars and sisters, and recognized that these were wholly different and far apart. He read the Life of St Dominic and of the first fathers, how blessedly they lived in great devotion and holy observance throughout the friaries of the whole order. He then considered the lives of the friars and sisters in his own time and saw that they were wholly dissimilar. He could neither see nor find in any community the life of the early institution. When he realized that the holiness of the observance had fallen so far and that the order had so cooled in its members that few still heeded the order, the Rule, and the Con-

31. 1 Maccabees 2:51.
32. 1 Maccabees 2:52–60.

stitutions with any diligence, this blessed brother cried out to God the Lord in his heart with bitter and mournful spirit. In his first youth, he had been a wild and untamed friar, who knew little of the order and paid little attention to it, until God enlightened him through a blessed cardinal.

4.8 *How Father Conrad of Prussia pondered how he and other willing brothers might maintain holy observance in a friary together* [fol. 119r]

Now this father was a gracious man, endowed by God with wisdom and virtue, and an especially gifted preacher of God's word. Once he recognized the state of the order, that it no longer possessed the fire of religious life as in the time of Saint Dominic and his first followers, he thought over what to do. He went to Rome for the sake of his own and his order's blessedness. After being received at the papal court and making his holy desire understood, and after his blessed life and behaviour gained attention, he was made papal penitentiary and became very close and dear to the pope, his cardinals, and other prelates. At one point, he travelled overseas with a cardinal to the Holy Sepulchre in Jerusalem. While there, he petitioned this cardinal to reform the order in some measure to the order's first religious life. This reform should happen by degrees: one friary could be founded in religious practice and some time afterwards, if chance and fortune would have it, yet another friary, for it would be impossible to reform the order all at once with all the friaries and convents together. This was because there were so few well-intentioned souls who desired reform and, unfortunately, many unwilling. This worthy father had thoroughly planned out how he could arrange for some of his brothers to secretly assemble with him in a friary and live together there in full religious life according to the order's law as was done in the first days in conformity with all religious regimen.

4.10[33] *How our three holy fathers Saint Dominic, Saint Peter, and Saint Thomas appeared to the blessed father Friar Conrad of Prussia and commanded him to undertake the reform* [fol. 120r]

"What a blessed man this father Conrad of Prussia was!" This was a common phrase among our elders who saw or knew him or a part of his blessed life. They now have all departed from this world and so the holy life of this father is hidden from us. Yet God worked certain miracles in him, which have truthfully come down to our times.

While this blessed father was thinking over how to bring a friary to a reli-

33. Neither MS 2934 nor Cgm 8081 has a chapter 4.9.

gious state such that others might also follow, one time he was out and about absorbed in this thought and met three fathers of the Dominican order. They had very proper habits on: their scapulars were very wide, the hood small, the cappa shorter than the tunic. The eldest among them told Father Conrad that he should restore the friary in Colmar to the religious state and life and that he and the two with him were dressed as friars of the order should be. Friar Conrad then asked who they were and was given to understand that the first was the founder of the Order of Preachers, Saint Dominic; the second, Saint Peter of Verona, whom he recognized by the wound in his side; and the third was Saint Thomas Aquinas. I cannot describe the gracious vision of our worthy, holy father and all the good teaching and instruction they gave him. The servant of God rejoiced and noted that it was a good, holy task set by God and his dear saints, from which much profit and fruit should come. From this time forth, he strove with even greater serious desire in these holy matters.

4.11 *How an honourable nobleman saw the blessed Friar Conrad's face shining brightly* [fol. 120v]

At the time during which this friend of God, the blessed father Conrad, was working out how Schönensteinbach could be rebuilt as a convent where sisters would uphold the order as in the days of Saint Dominic and maintain the most perfect, secure enclosure as well, he had arranged for construction to begin on the deserted estate. This news reached a good nobleman, who knew the place well and held Father Conrad in special favour. Hearing that he was in Schönensteinbach, he went there himself to advise Conrad in good faith that he should not undertake this work, since none of the necessities for a women's convent were available there. When he arrived, he found the devout priest of God standing over the altar at holy Mass and saw such a great, bright glow streaming from his face that he could not look at him for the brilliance, just as happened to Moses, that great friend of God.[34] Upon seeing this, the man realized that the will of God was for this to proceed and that it was not human but God's doing.

Thanks to God, once this convent was founded, this nobleman's father, a knight named Johannes of Masmünster, became a lay brother there, living on the grounds of the convent Steinbach and leading a blessed life until his end. When he died, he was buried according to his wishes at the feet of all the sisters before

34. When Moses returned from Mount Sinai with the Ten Commandments, his face was shining in a way that made others afraid to approach him. Exodus 34:29–30.

the door of the lay sisters' chapel. This knight's wife and daughter both entered the order in the convent of Schönensteinbach.[35]

4.12 *How the worthy holy prelates were witness to the holiness of Father Conrad of Prussia* [fol. 121r]

In the papal bull and letter from Boniface IX, in which he confirms the reform for the fourth time, he also briefly describes the virtuousness of the blessed father Conrad of Prussia, the first founder of the reformed convents. Among other things, he says of him, "Our dear son Conrad of Prussia is a man of edifying life and laudable reputation, a pillar of his order and a fruitful preacher of the divine word, which he proves through a virtuous life on the example of Saint Dominic." The worthy Master Raymond also wrote a letter to a cardinal, saying among other words, "I have found in our order a man, named Friar Conrad of Prussia, a most worthy person and of the best life and reputation in German lands, who by himself brings greater fruit than all the other religious men of the order." This same worthy master general wrote an open letter from Rome to the council and community of the city of Colmar. This letter, dated "Rome anno domini 1390, on the ninth day of the month of May," says, among other things: "I recommend to you Friar Conrad, whom I have made my vicar over our convents in your city of Colmar. He is a true, righteous follower of Saint Dominic, our holy father."

The wise, devout father Master Johannes Nider, a great, enlightened master of holy Scripture who wrote many beautiful books to the comfort of Christendom, reports the worthiness of this laudable father in the third and fourth parts of the book called *Formicarius*. Among other things, he says of him: "Our father of holy memory, Conrad of Prussia, the first reformer of our order, was the most gracious preacher in German lands and a man worthy of all praise."[36]

See what dignified people gave remarkable testimony regarding this father – and we believe that all three statements about him are true – the head of Christendom and representative of our dear lord Jesus Christ, the head of the holy Dominican order, and a distinguished, enlightened, divine teacher of holy Scripture.

35. Johannes of Masmünster himself had been involved in negotiating with the Augustinian friary of Marbach for the rights to the Schönensteinbach estate (see **2.3**). His wife, Susanna of Masmünster, was among the first thirteen women in Schönensteinbach. The daughter mentioned is probably Margret Ursula (see **3.24**).

36. *Formicarius*, book 3 chapter 1.

4.13 *Of his devout pilgrimage and the manifold graces granted him by God* [fol. 122r]

This worthy father Conrad of Prussia led such a holy life that it was hidden from all people, since he often concealed it from others out of humility. He had an intimate, dear companion, who was also a dear friend of God, named Father Johannes of Witten. He knew about the secret and open graces God gave him and much about his holy life. When he was confessor there, this father often said to some of the first sisters of Schönensteinbach, "If I outlive our worthy father the vicar, Friar Conrad, I will tell you great wonders about him, which God the Lord has worked through him." But he died fifteen years before Father Conrad.

He had been his companion in many places where God's travels had taken them into such great hardship that many people would hardly believe it if it were written. Conrad had been to Rome nine times and three times to the Holy Sepulchre in Jerusalem. With his companion, this Friar Johannes, he visited all the holy places where our dear Lord lived in his holy humanity, in particular the place Calvary, where the Lord Christ was hung on the cross for our sake. There he knelt down in heartfelt devotion and bowed his head into the hole where the holy cross had stood. He went from one holy place to another where our dear Lord had performed his miraculous works, his suffering, and his martyrdom, completing the journey in great devotion. When he came to the Jordan to the spot where our Preserver was baptized by Saint John, he had himself baptized with great devotion by his companion, the father mentioned above. Afterwards, he went to many other holy places, especially to Mount Sinai to the convent and grave of the highly praised noble virgin Saint Catherine.[37] This father Conrad always had with him the necessary things for holy Mass – altar stone, chalice, missal, and vestments, and other things so that he might say Mass when he desired – yea, even in the wilderness. God often sent great things to him and holy angels appeared visibly to him during holy Mass. I do not have the will to write further about these nor also about the numerous other miracles, revelations, and graces which God the Lord richly sent him to experience.

4.14 *On the great suffering he encountered because of a blessed sister, who was being forced out of the order* [fol. 123r]

This father Conrad suffered great contempt and harsh scorn for a good, blessed cause. Namely, when he wished to reform any convents, draw wanton

37. The convent of St Catherine on Mount Sinai, where Catherine of Alexandria had supposedly been buried by angels, was a popular pilgrimage destination in the fifteenth century. Another Observant Dominican from Germany, Felix Fabri, turned his pilgrimage there into contemplative material. See Kathryne Beebe, *Pilgrim and Preacher: The Audiences and Observant Spirituality of Friar Felix Fabri (1437/8–1502)* (Oxford, 2014).

people away from sin, or the like, he had to earn it bitterly through cruel suffering, adversity, and worry. Once he had restored Steinbach to a blessed life, shortly thereafter a convent in the Netherlands, Wijk near Utrecht, was founded in the holy Observance with four sisters from Schönensteinbach. A rich and powerful bannerman named von Breitenrot and his wife agreed to leave the world for a religious life in God. The lord became a Carthusian in a community called Monnikhuizen, but the noble, worthy lady his wife became a Dominican sister in the convent of Wijk. After they had sworn obedience and had each been in their convents and orders for several years, the lord allowed the evil spirit and his own depravity to triumph, and in an audacious act of violence, the bannerman gave up the order and went back into the world. Moreover, he wished to have his wife back from her convent, which she, however, did not want. The convent's vicar, the blessed father Conrad of Prussia, discouraged him, and when this raging man saw that he would not, for love or money, get the blessed nun back according to his wishes, he and his people began to ravage the area. This wrought much damage and caused concern. In particular, the city of Wijk where the convent lay was sorely intimidated. Even Father Conrad was evilly mistreated by mobbing and shoving and trampling horses, such that God barely helped him escape with his life.

Since, however, the bishop of Utrecht[38] was a faithful father to the sisters of Wijk, and since his dear subjects and land were gravely harmed by this grim persecutor, it was arranged for the events to be interrupted by a parley and summit over the matter. The lady was to be led to the lord and her will in the matter heard. Many distinguished persons came together, including the Lord Apostate Monk[39] and his retinue, and the lady was escorted out of the convent and led before him. Before the whole assembly, the bishop stood and addressed her, saying, "Dear and worthy lady, you may choose between two alternatives, whichever you best prefer. If you wish to return to your lord, who so tremendously wishes to have you back, and to live by his side in the honour accorded your station and birth, then you should step towards him. If, however, you wish to remain a poor nun, it is up to you whether to return to the convent or not." Before all the people, this blessed, noble creature answered the bishop, saying, "The almighty God forbid that I ever leave the Observance of the holy Dominican order and return to my lord in the world. My lord husband may do what he thinks best, but I will never leave my order for love or money. Above all else, I choose to return to my convent, out of which I have been forced to come." And so she left the assembly

38. Frederick (Friedrich) of Blankenheim, bishop of Utrecht (r. 1393–1423); see **1.23**.
39. Meyer is using this epithet as a facetious title.

and returned to the convent, not without moving many a heart. The faithful shepherd, Father Conrad, took his dear lamb, so endangered by the ravening wolf, and joyously placed her in the sheep pen of the convent.

But when the cursed tyrant perceived this disgrace, he rode out into the country with some of his knights and approached the king of France, who at that time was waging a great war against the king of England.[40] He intended to help him, but the king of France said to him, "You should by rights be a Carthusian, as you have sworn to God and that order in your profession. I believe that if you joined our army, any luck we had had would turn to misfortune because of your ways." He was scornfully dismissed, which did not make him better but only madder and angrier. He joined the king of England to help him fight against the king of France and was soon felled in battle.

4.15 *On the holy end of Friar Conrad of Prussia and how he was buried with honour and devotion* [fol. 124v]

After the great labour which this blessed father Conrad performed, and once he had reached a good age, he dedicated himself to remaining by his dear children in Schönensteinbach, towards whom he had demonstrated inexpressible faithfulness in his good works. He remained there several years until his death, before which he became lame so that he could not walk. Nevertheless, they carried him on a chair into the church every day for Mass. Even though he was sick and lame, he preached and heard confession, especially for laypeople, since he had the authority of the pope. He governed the sisters in religious life and directed them towards virtue, of which he was full. In 1426, on the Sunday in the middle of Lent called *Laetare* [10 March], this blessed father departed the world for eternal peace, as we trust in the mild grace of God. He was worthily buried before the high altar of the sisters' choir in Steinbach. When news of his blessed passing spread through the convents and places where he was known for his good, blessed life, he was honourably and devoutly commemorated with sung masses, readings, and prayer by both secular and religious people who had known his godly way of life. For all this, may God be eternally praised. Amen.

4.16 *On the blessed life and death of Friar Thomas of Prussia, his biological brother* [fol. 125r]

In the same convent of Schönensteinbach, next to the grave of Friar Conrad of Prussia in the choir before the main altar, lies buried the honourable, blessed,

40. This conflict is the episode in the Hundred Years War when Henry V of England (r. 1413–1422) went to war against Charles VI of France (r. 1380–1422).

devout father Friar Thomas of Prussia, who was Friar Conrad's biological brother. Our elders, who knew the two holy fathers, all say that this Friar Thomas surpassed his brother Conrad in devotion, holiness, and knowledge. Even though Father Conrad reaped more fruit and profit in the souls of others, this Father Thomas was very solitary and led a contemplative life with a heart burning with love for God. The honourable father and master Johannes Nider testifies to this in his *Formicarius*, book 4 chapter 12. Among other things, he writes, "Friar Thomas, confessor of the devout sisters in Schönensteinbach in the diocese of Basel, was a man praiseworthy in all things. He led such a guarded, cautious life, that he was a mirror of virtue for others until the end of his life."

After serving as prior and lector for the friars of Colmar, this dear, devout father became confessor of the sisters in Schönensteinbach. The church there had two huge bell towers, one on each side. So that the convent would not be so worldly with two such towers, he had one tower torn down. One day, when he had finished his prayers and contemplations and had said Mass with great devotion, he went to help with the work. When he walked out onto the choir's ceiling, he slipped, fell from that height, and landed on his head in the choir. The sisters quickly came running and found him lying stretched out, both arms wide in the shape of a cross with a hammer in one hand and three nails in the other.[41] His dear brother, Father Conrad, arrived and when he saw him there in such mortal pain, and how the sisters were holding him up in their arms, he fell prostrate with his arms out in crosswise before the holy sacrament. When he had finished his devotion and looked pitifully at his brother, he said "*O frater carissime*, O my dearest brother." After he gave him the holy unction of the final baptism, his blessed soul departed this world for eternal life in the presence and view of all the sisters. By the merciful weal of our Lord, we trust this is so, especially since it was disclosed in revelations that good, blessed people received after his death. He died on the Feast of St Euphemia [16 September] 1416.

4.17 *The great faith, love, and friendship the first three confessors of Schönensteinbach showed for the convent* [fol. 126r]

There is another blessed father buried in Schönensteinbach named Friar Johannes of Witten. He was a very honourable, upright man full of devotion and faithfulness. He took on especially great toil and labour on behalf of this convent, for the sisters were so poor and their dormitory so dilapidated that an army of carpenters could not have rebuilt it. Therefore, in seriousness and great loyalty, he

41. Christ was thought to have been crucified with three nails, one in each hand and one for both feet.

went to work himself personally according to his custom and broke a leg. Afterwards he always limped and walked with a cane. While he was traveling to Basel on behalf of the convent, he became sick and died in the Dominican friary there. According to his wishes, his body was returned to Schönensteinbach, for the community in Basel was not yet reformed. He died an honest, devout death during Lent 1411.

The sisters of Steinbach wrote about these three aforementioned fathers for their eternal memory in their book called a martyrology or calendar:

> Let it be known that our dearest father, the honourable Friar Conrad of Prussia of the Order of Preachers, was the first founder and director of this convent, representing the master general. He acquired prodigious alms for us, performed an astonishing amount of work for this convent, and until his death showed us such great fatherly loyalty that we are greatly indebted to him in faith. Also his brother, Thomas of Prussia, our faithful father, and our dear beloved father Johannes of Witten, who also won considerable alms and toiled greatly for us, as long as he lived. The three aforenamed fathers were the first fathers, vicars, confessors, and visitators of this convent, as long as they lived. To the best of their ability, they always showed us great faithfulness in both spiritual and temporal matters. For these, our dearly beloved fathers, for all their predecessors, and for whoever desires it, we faithfully owe it to them always to celebrate their anniversary as long as this convent stands.

4.18 *Of Friar Johannes, a master of theology, and the grace he naturally received from God* [fol. 127r]

As a blessed memorial for our successors, I must also say a little about a distinguished father. Although he lies buried with the fathers in Nuremberg and not with the sisters in Schönensteinbach, I should still commemorate him with honour in this book, for he was the first vicar of this convent after the blessed father Conrad of Prussia. The name of this worthy father is Friar Johannes Nider, a highly learned master of divine Scripture.[42] The life and teaching, bearing and

42. Meyer cites Nider's *Formicarius* constantly, but these chapters are the first time Meyer writes of the man himself. For treatments of Nider's biography, see Michael D. Bailey, *Battling Demons: Witchcraft, Heresy, and Reform in the Late Middle Ages* (University Park, 2003), 11–28; Werner Tschacher, *Der Formicarius des Johannes Nider von 1437/38: Studien zu den Anfängen der europäischen Hexenverfolgungen im Spätmittelalter* (Aachen, 2000), 31–74; *SOPMA*, 2: 500–515.

habits of this worthy master, Johannes Nider, were so prudent and gracious that they were commonly praised and commended by both secular and religious people; and if this is not true of certain perverted people, that is to his honour. As Seneca says, "*Laus est displicere malis*. Displeasing the wicked is praise."

Yes, this praiseworthy father and master was a true mirror and a right, good model for all convents of the Observance in German lands. His memory is still so vivid throughout the whole Observance that many remember his words, works, and the good manners of his gracious life. There is even a common saying in the reformed convents: "Thus did Master Johannes Nider do. Thus did he teach and command and forbid. Thus did he himself live." And such things. He was so gifted in natural arts and graces that great university masters from our order sought him out. Even after some of them became cardinals and bishops, they said of him that they did not think they had ever seen a person in whom so much grace and virtue and so many good characteristics appeared.

4.19 *How this honourable father Master Johannes Nider bore various kinds of labour* [fol. 127v]

It would not be possible for me to express how the Holy Spirit granted this master extraordinary wisdom. It is a marvel how prudently he behaved in the great affairs that were entrusted to him and what benefit has derived from his works. In particular, he showed remarkable devotion to God in all his trouble at the Council of Constance, and he afterwards had a great deal of trouble in Basel. Because of the unbelieving Bohemians and for other matters, he was often sent on distant and difficult journeys at the command of the Council, in order to negotiate great and important affairs on behalf of holy Christendom. He also had much work and worry in the reformed friaries as the vicar of the Observant communities and also as regent of the University of Vienna, not to mention the office of prior, and preaching and hearing confession, and dealing officially with the people, both secular and religious, who ran after him for his valuable advice. He was constantly troubled with such and similar matters.

These various kinds of external obedient service did not prevent him from writing beautiful books for the comfort of Christianity, nor inhibit his devotion or his sleep noticeably. He sometimes said of himself to his companions, "When I remove my belt at night, I also remove all care from my mind." For this reason, he never opened letters in the evening unless it was an emergency, nor in the morning until after Mass, putting off all external affairs as long as possible. During Matins, one could see how he unified the strength of his spirit and his body in inward contemplation, heartfelt devotion, and prayer to God. Even though he often held lessons in Scripture for the friars at night, preached for the people in the church in the morning, and on top of that, held chapter for the brothers twice a week while he was prior in Nuremberg, he personally maintained the Observant life diligently with regard to food, clothing, and other things. When illness or some other respectable matter deterred him, he told the brothers openly in chapter. Some therefore marvelled at his humility, some at his prudence and meekness. Some were especially awed that, at a single time and place, he could rebuke the wicked so sharply and with appropriate severity, while treating the timid and fearful so kindly and so virtuously.

4.20 *On the many kinds of scorn and suffering this honourable master encountered because of his zealous practices in reforming convents* [fol. 128v]

There would be much to say about his patience throughout the great scorn he suffered for the honour of God and his neighbour's salvation, especially while he was prior of the Observance in Basel. Once, he was entrusted with the enclosure of a convent and directing the sisters onto the path of true religious life. When he set himself to the task out of obedience, they brought him a meal out of the convent, served in beautiful covered dishes as if to show him special honour. But when they were uncovered, there was nothing on the plates but a clapper, such as those that lepers use for begging. When he understood the intention behind this, he thanked God in his heart for this contempt and proved a model and example of patience for his neighbour.

Another time, he was travelling across Germany with a cardinal, the papal legate,[43] in order to reform and enclose another convent. When the sisters heard of the presence of these prelates, they began screaming with severe obstinacy and resisting in word and deed. When the lock was set on the outer doors in order to enclose the convent properly, the sisters within gathered at the doors to read, in their egregious womanly stupidity, the psalm "Deus laudem meam."[44] They behaved outrageously, in particular against Master Johannes Nider, singing in their raging folly the responsory "Revelabunt celi" with the verse "In diem."[45] Through

43. Cardinal Julian Cesarini, who shows up again in **5.42**, was the papal legate to the Council of Basel. See Gerald Christianson, *Cesarini, the Conciliar Cardinal: The Basel Years, 1431–1438* (Sankt Ottilien, 1979).

44. Psalm 108:2. "O God, be not thou silent in my praise: for the mouth of the wicked and the mouth of the deceitful man is opened against me."

45. Chants for Maundy Thursday Matins. Responsory: "The heavens have revealed the iniquity of Judas and the earth will rise up against him and his sin will be shown on the day of God's anger with those who said to the Lord God, go away from us, we do not want knowledge of your ways." Verse: "He will be held until the day of perdition and led to the day of vengeance."

this chant, which they performed with great rudeness, they showed him what they truly felt about him and the religious life.

The worthy Lord Julian, the cardinal legate, entrusted another convent to him for reform. From this, he suffered so much scorn that he sometimes had to travel over the fields in secular garb because he feared for his life and did not dare appear in the open streets.

See how much God's friends, those who belong to eternal life, must suffer. Note also how good things must be bitterly earned through such hardship.

4.21 *Of the beautiful, profitable books that the honourable Master Johannes Nider wrote for the comfort of Christendom and as teaching and instruction for all those who read them* [fol. 129r]

They say that in the days of this blessed father, all Christendom did not see his like in life, knowledge, and wisdom. His enlightened knowledge poured out the salutary balm of good Christian teaching into the beautiful books he wrote for the holy Church. There are many of them, but I will name here only a few of those I know.

The first book he wrote was about the Ten Commandments, in which he read and very clearly summarized a great deal of useful material about holy Scripture and canon law.

In the second book, called *De morali lepra* or *On Leprosy of the Soul,* he describes the seven cardinal sins and their daughters, the distinction between large and small sins, common and exceptional sins, and sins against the sacrament, the ordinances of the Church, and canon law. This book is extremely useful for all preachers to have for directing, teaching, and advising the people.

The third book, called *The Manual,* he compiled from the most distinguished teachers as a comfort and help for all confessors. It explains what a truly contrite will should look like, before and during confession, and contains a lot of profitable material.

The fourth book is called *De timorata consciencia,* or *On the Fearful Conscience.* It is a huge book and talks about good and bad conscience and the stages of conscience.

The fifth book contains lovely sermons for Sundays throughout the whole year, for all feasts, and for every day of Lent, as well as a number of sermons about all sorts of things.[46]

46. Two different collections of German sermons attributed to Nider survive, but here Meyer is referring to his comprehensive Latin collection, which comprises over one hundred sermons. See John Dahmus, "A Medieval Preacher and His Sources: Johannes Nider's Use of Jacobus de Voragine," in *AFP* 58 (1988): 121–176.

The sixth book is called *De secularium religionibus*, or *On the Religious Life of Laypeople*.[47] In this book, he recounts marvellous, strange, and beautiful matters, which are quite useful and good.

The seventh book is called *Contractibus*, or *On Purchase, Mortgage, Rents, and Incomes*. It contains lovely instruction and good distinctions concerning these matters, what is right and what is not.

The eighth book is called *De reformacione*, or *On the Reformation of Monastic Life*. This book is a must for religious people in every order, for it contains so much about the practices of life in confirmed orders and similar good things.

The ninth book concerns the many kinds of heretical unbelief and how heretics are not all the same in their faith.

The tenth book is called *De formicis*, or *On the Characteristics of Ants*. In it, he talks about six characteristics of ants and compares them to several virtues. He writes beautiful exempla of things that happened in his times. I have excerpted a good deal from that book for this one.

The eleventh book is about not eating meat and the twelfth is about preparing for death. The thirteenth book is called *De paupertate perfecta secularia*, or *On the Perfect Poverty of Secular Laypeople*, and is a very beautiful book. The fourteenth book is called *De vera et falsa nobilitate*, or *On True and False Nobility*, and the fifteenth book *De vigore consuetudinis et dispensacione canonica*.[48]

4.22 *On the blessed end of this honourable father Master Johannes Nider* [fol. 130r]

This blessed father worked much good in Holy Christendom and in the Dominican order, especially for his children in Schönensteinbach, whose vicar he was for many years and for whom he had particular love and favour, as may well be seen in the letters he wrote to them.[49] It is also recorded in a book that he showed great faithfulness to this convent. He left Basel, where he had secured the Observance, and moved home to his own friary in Nuremberg. He quickly became sick and called together all the fathers of that friary. First, he recanted anything unrespectable he might have written or preached. Second, he declared before all of them that he did not want to die except in the truth of the Christian

47. See John Van Engen, "Friar Johannes Nyder on Laypeople Living as Religious in the World," in *Vita religiosa im Mittelalter*, ed. Franz J. Felten and Nikolas Jaspert (Berlin, 1999), 583–615.

48. *On the Vigour of Custom and Canonical Dispensation* is another monastic reform treatise. A "dispensation" was official permission to omit some practice normally required by the order.

49. See Wilhelm Oehl, *Deutsche Mystikerbriefe des Mittelalters, 1100–1500* (Darmstadt, 1972), 515; Margit Brand, *Studien zu Johannes Niders deutschen Schriften* (Rome, 1998), 225–235.

faith and asked them to witness to that at the Last Judgement. Third, he admonished them in a fatherly manner to manage the Observance diligently in good faith and to hold each other dear. Then he asked them to read to him from one of the books of Saint Bernard against the struggle of death.

One of the brothers advised him to give full confession. He responded confidently, "I do not need to, for after the full confession I gave when I first entered the order, I have always purified myself diligently in the required confessions before holy Mass." Note from this his great reliance on and trust in God. Afterwards, he devoutly received the final unction. The priest lifted the holy sacrament of our Lord's body to offer it to him, saying, "Do you believe that this is Christ, preserver of the world?" He said, "I believe," and as soon as he had said these words, he departed and went to rest in the Lord. And so he died in the tunic and scapular, lying on a straw mattress, for the brothers refused to grant his request to be laid out on the bare earth. He died on the Feast of St Hippolytus [13 August] in 1428. May God be honoured in all his works. Amen.

4.23 *On Friar Johannes of Mainz, a lector and a faithful confessor to the sisters of the convent Schönensteinbach* [fol. 131r]

Friar Johannes, called Fintzel or Binder,[50] born in the city of Mainz, ardently loved the worthy mother of God, the holy virgin Mary, noble queen of heaven and earth. He was confessor to the sisters in the convent of Schönensteinbach for many years before his death. He is also buried there in the cloister before the chapterhouse of the convent.

When this Johannes was born, at the moment that he was separated from his mother's body, church bells throughout the whole city were ringing for the evening prayer, Ave Maria. The midwife said to the child's mother, "You should note that this child, born during the prayer of the holy Ave Maria, will become a special servant of the revered mother and child-bearer of God, Mary." The words of this woman came true, for he was an especially devout lover and servant of our dear Lady. Afterwards, during the time of the Great Death of the plague, this

50. Johannes of Mainz (d. 1457) was Meyer's contemporary. His unedited *Lives of the Friars in Basel and the Reform of the Said Convent* served as a major source for Meyer's works and is preserved in Basel, Universitätsbibliothek, MS A XI 42. See Anne Huijbers, "Observant Memory and Propaganda in Johannes of Mainz's *Vita Fratrum Predicatorum conventus Basiliensis* (1442–1444)," *Church History* 87 (2018): 718–739; Anne Huijbers, *Zealots for Souls: Dominican Narratives of Self-Understanding during Observant Reforms, c. 1388–1517* (Berlin, 2018), 253–259; *DDS*, 272; Hans Neumann, "Johannes von Mainz," *VL*[2] 4: 675–677.

child's mother was worried and promised the pure mother of God that if she spared the child's life through her holy intercession, he would become her eternal servant.

When he grew up, he began to teach, at first for five years in the temple of the mother of God, that is, the Minster in Mainz.[51] He grew quickly in grace and devotion, love and contemplation for her and prayed the hours of her *cursus*.[52] When he called upon her in his spiritual and temporal troubles, he received her gracious, motherly aid. Even though he lived in dissolution for a time, he was so diligent and talented that he understood the liberal arts remarkably well. Since, however, God the Lord wished to call him away from the world into a religious place to serve him and his dear mother, it so happened that Johannes went to the Council of Basel with the worthy lord bishop of Mainz,[53] whose servant he was. When he saw the virtuous life of the Dominican friars, whose convent had recently been reformed to the holy Observance, he entered the Dominican order in Basel and advanced so greatly in life and knowledge that he became the first Observant lector there.

He was very experienced in natural and divine sciences, a gracious preacher, and an author of beautiful books. Whenever he wrote another book or gave a sermon in German or Latin, he would rarely begin without consulting the worthy mother of God, Mary, whom he loved wholeheartedly from his childhood days until his end.

4.24 *On the numerous great devotions of the honourable lector Friar Johannes of Mainz* [fol. 132r]

When I saw so many virtues shining in this friar, although he hid them, I wished, following the teaching of the natural scientist Seneca, to keep this dear friar in my heart and thus place before my eyes a good man so that I too would live better. For this reason, in my youth I gave a general confession to him and afterwards confessed often to him, through which I, and other friars too, experienced his virtue and became familiar with a part of the grace with which God so

51. This refers to St Maria ad Gradus, which was badly damaged in the siege of Mainz in 1793, and demolished in the early nineteenth century.

52. A *cursus* was a daily prayer cycle that mimicked the monastic communal liturgy in form but was intended for private use. Many different *cursus* with different dedications circulated in the Middle Ages, but those for Mary were the most popular. See Rachel Fulton Brown, *Mary and the Art of Prayer: The Hours of the Virgin in Medieval Christian Life and Thought* (New York, 2018).

53. Dietrich Schenk of Erbach, archbishop of Mainz (r. 1434–1459).

richly endowed him. A common practice that I and others in the community noticed in him was that he would usually wake and rise before Matins of the Little Office of the Virgin and devoutly perform this. After Matins, he would kneel, sometimes crying, sometimes rejoicing, before the altar. He sang holy Mass with great devotion. He withdrew from human contact as much as possible. Reading books and studying were his most common work, as well as commending himself to the divine.

Whenever in his contemplation he regarded the immeasurable greatness of the most worthy mother of God, Mary, he received such great grace from her that he did not know how to respond in heart, soul, and mind, in word or deed to the manifold grace she visited upon her servant. He often felt the same way before Eternal Wisdom when the grace befell him. He concentrated so much on the worthy suffering and death of our dear Lord and his tender, pure mother that it would be impossible for me to describe the graces he won and what happened to him when he sank devoutly into the passion of our Lord and the compassion of his dear mother. Sometimes, when he had time, he gathered up his mind and spirit in devout contemplation of Christ's bitter suffering. He imagined that the spear, nails, and crown of our Lord were on his own limbs and his body trembled from it. Sometimes he saw Christ the Lord hanging on the cross with flowing wounds, and he embraced the cross beneath and was drenched in the rose-coloured blood. If he were in pain, which he often was, it would become that much lighter. If some burden fell to him that was difficult or painful for him, he sensed it in advance and would say to those around him, "Pray God for me, for suffering is coming upon me."

4.25 *On his humility and on the grace with which God endowed him and on his death* [fol. 132v]

This father was such a knowledgeable lector, that we believed there was hardly his like in German lands. Although he was held in great honour for his considerable knowledge, he fled all honour and worthiness in a very marvellous way. In all his life and manners, he showed humility and spent more time with the simple brothers than with the great fathers. He comforted the sad and helped those in temptation, such that sometimes many friars came to him for advice on a single day. He was so devout that, for his own sake and for his neighbour's, he flagellated himself with strict discipline after the example of our holy father Saint Dominic. Sometimes he slept on the bench in his cell at night wearing what he wore during the day. If he could not sleep, he called on the mother of God to bless and sprinkle holy water on him, as she had done for the first holy fathers of the order. Sometimes, in honourable devotion and dignity, he began to call out the sweet name of Jesus over and over again. Before he had called out the name twenty or thirty times, all his useless thoughts disappeared and he found proper sleep. Whenever he heard someone commemorating the holy Trinity, the blood of Christ, the pure virgin birth, or similar things, he made a reverence, secretly if he could not well do it openly. Such and similar things did he perform during his life.

At the end, he was appointed confessor to the sisters of Schönensteinbach, where he stayed until his death. He showed much faithfulness to the children of the convent. When he had been there for ten years, he departed from this world in the first days of March 1457 and was buried in the cloister before the sisters' chapterhouse. Amen.

Book Five

Here begins the prologue of the fifth book or fifth part of this material, which records the reformed convents of Dominican friars and sisters in German lands, including how and when each convent was reformed. [fol. 144r]

The fifth part, which here follows, recounts how certain communities of friars and especially certain convents of sisters in the province of these German lands were reformed. It should be noted that the friaries in Colmar and Nuremberg were the first of all the friaries to introduce the Observant religious life in German lands. The other friaries in German and in Saxon lands were started by and drew their religious practice from these two communities. The same may be said of the worthy convent of Schönensteinbach, since this was the very first of all the Dominican women's convents in these lands to introduce the religious life of the Observance. The other sisters' convents that, by the grace of God, have been reformed in German lands and also in Saxony originally modelled their enclosure on this convent. Therefore, with the help of God, I want to write briefly about these convents, how and when and by whom they were reformed.

But you should know that I have not written this fifth book as an exhaustive account, although I assembled and compiled it with particularly great effort from excerpts of sealed letters, other writings, and books, and also from things I have seen and experienced myself or have heard from trustworthy persons, most of all from those God-fearing people who were present for these affairs and were sorely tried by them. But if I myself were to describe the great suffering and trouble through which these convents were reformed to the religious life, the great resistance with which such a blessed endeavour was commonly met – certain good people feared for their lives, yes, and some risked their lives for the sake of holy obedience and the religious life – the poverty, suffering, and deprivation, the slander, contempt, and disruption, and much more which they met in such matters, the great costs incurred and labour required – at times it occupied not only an entire region, but even the papal court had to intervene – that would be beyond my powers to write.

I have viewed all the letters and writings that recount this. Many of the blessed people who could have said much on this topic have passed away. They have said that just a few years ago it was much more troublesome and arduous to reform convents than it is now in these times, although it still must be hard fought. Given the resistance of people unwilling to pursue the religious life of the Observance, it is much easier to found a convent peacefully and quietly in all religious living for the first time than it is afterwards to reform and restore one that has fallen from its religious ways. This is just like what we read in 3 Kings and in 2 Chronicles about King Solomon's first foundation of the Temple of God in Jerusalem in peaceful devotion.[1] Many years later, when that temple had declined and the worthy, devout Prince Zerubbabel wished to restore it, he and those who helped him in this work encountered great resistance from those evil-intentioned people who were not inclined to the affair and subjected them to great scorn and suffering, as we read in the Book of Ezra.[2] Just so has it often happened in the reform of the convents and may well happen again. This caused an experienced master of holy Scripture, who had helped reform many convents, to comment that sometimes, when a convent was to be enclosed and the spiritual life begun, he felt as though all the powers of hell mobilized to hinder the good work. Great misery and suffering arose from the perverted, hard-hearted people against kind, good-willed, religious persons who greatly increased the crown of their merit through patience and persistence.

It is profitable and good as instruction and as a model for our successors that such things be written, but who could do all this and who possesses the grace for it? For this, my right dear sisters in God, you dear children of our Lord, who are gathered in the religious, reformed convents I describe hereafter – for this, I have written to the best of my poor ability, in God's honour and out of the faithfulness and love I harbour in God for your religious life – for this, I have composed this little book, which recounts how your worthy convents and chapels were reformed through the flowing grace of the Holy Spirit to such a secure state of religious life, that within it you might richly earn your salvation through the mercy of God, the heavenly father. More than to any particular persons, you owe thanks and praise to God for electing you and sequestering you from the unfaithful, sinful world and all its painful bonds, to live for him alone with heart and soul.

Know also, dear children, that I have set the convents in this book in the order in which they were reformed. Sometimes, I have taken artistic licence to put earlier something that happened later and vice versa, but only seldom. If I have

1. 3 Kings 6 and 2 Chronicles 6.
2. Ezra 3:6–13.

written more about some convents than about others – as if God had shown his grace and revealed his miraculous ways more in one than another, and maybe I wrote more for that reason – you should not take umbrage with me, for this happened because I did not know and was not acquainted with such things. In some cases, I have read more of one convent's letters and books recounting their reform than those of another. Or I have heard more about the reform of one convent than of another. And so I desire of each God-fearing person who hears this book read, that she expand and add what is proper and right. Especially if hereafter any convent of our order in German lands is reformed, she should write this at the end, after chapter 90.

I pray to the sweet heart of our dear Lord Jesus Christ that the hearts of all who see or read this be enflamed in his love and inspired to a religious and devout life. May the most worthy Holy Trinity grant us this for the sake of the worthy Virgin Mary. Amen.

5.1 *What fruit, profit, and spiritual good came from the convent of Schönensteinbach, for they reformed many convents* [fol. 146v]

A fructibus eorum cognoscetis eos.[3] Thus spoke our dear Lord in the holy Gospel, "By their fruits and in their fruits you may well know them." Whether one claims to be good or bad, if his works are good and blessed, then without a doubt everything in him is good. Just as the Lord Christ said, *Arbor bona fructus bonos facit.*[4] "A good tree or stem produces good fruit." For a good root cannot do evil, just as little as a bad root can bear good fruit. Thus says the Lord Jesus, "By their fruits you shall know them."

By the holy, good, useful fruits which sprouted and grew from this good stem – that is, the holy persons of the worthy Christian, Dominican convent of Schönensteinbach and the other reformed convents which received their impetus and origin in the holy Observance from them – by the fruits of these women's convents described hereafter, one may know the goodness of the origin and root. Just as the convent of friars in Colmar was the first reformed Dominican friary in German lands, from which the other reformed communities received their model and impetus, so also is Schönensteinbach the very first convent of the Observance among all the Dominican sisters' convents in German lands and a font and mother to the other convents reformed afterwards, which based their form of enclosure and Observance on this convent's model. Note how these convents came to the holy Observance after Schönensteinbach, their worthy mother.

3. Matthew 7:16.
4. Matthew 7:17.

5.2 *How a convent was built in the Netherlands in the diocese of Utrecht and given to the Dominicans, and how sisters from Steinbach were brought there* [fol. 147r]

Since the good reputation of the convent of Schönensteinbach had flowed far and wide throughout the land, devout women from several cities came, desiring to enter the convent and receive the holy order. Many noble citizens, particularly from Utrecht and the surrounding area, wished to enter Steinbach, but with so many people who wanted to join, the convent was overcrowded. And so Lord Friedrich, the bishop of Utrecht,[5] and other blessed, wealthy people founded a women's convent in the city of Wijk in the diocese of Utrecht. They had it designed and constructed to resemble the convent of Schönensteinbach in enclosure and religious life in every measure and form. While the cloister was being built, they requested the pope's permission to make the new convent a community of Dominican nuns just like Schönensteinbach. In the meantime, they instructed many young maidens and some more experienced people in religious behaviour and taught them to sing and read, for they were very good-willed people.

When the convent was completed and consecrated in honour of the holy penitent, Saint Mary Magdalene, the worthy lord and father Humbert, at the time an auxiliary bishop of the aforementioned bishop of Utrecht, was sent to Steinbach with letters of authority together with many honourable men and women. When they arrived in Alsace at the convent of Schönensteinbach, they presented the reason for their long and costly journey. When the blessed father vicar, Friar Conrad of Prussia, and the whole community of the convent heard this, they turned mournfully to God and gave the honourable messengers four blessed, elect sisters to begin the convent of St Mary Magdalene in Wijk with confidence.

Here are the names of these sisters. The first was Sister Elisabeth of Sterre, who had been an honourable abbess in the city of Utrecht in the abbey of St Servatius before she entered the Dominican order in Steinbach. She became the first prioress in Wijk. The second was Sister Magdalena Betminger, who was prioress in Schönensteinbach and later became prioress in Wijk and then prioress in Tiel in the convent called Westeroye. She had been one of the first thirteen blessed mothers who originally founded Steinbach. The third was Sister Margreta Schwetz, who had also been prioress for a time. The fourth was Sister Gertrud of Eelswerd, from the Netherlands. She became the subprioress in Wijk and had also been one of the first thirteen sisters in Schönensteinbach.

5. Frederick of Blankenheim, bishop of Utrecht; see **1.23**.

5.3 *How honourably and with what great devotion this convent was founded in the Observance* [fol. 148r]

These four blessed sisters humbly assumed the holy obedience of this great, good, divine task from Father Conrad and, with saddened hearts, thanked the whole community, which let them leave amidst great, sorrowful, and bitter tears. They were then entrusted with great faith to the honourable lord bishop and the others.

The bishop cared for them in spiritual and temporal affairs. They had commissioned a great ship, in which there was a little room where the sisters hardly saw anyone. There he preached to them daily and gave them the holy sacrament, as he had been commanded. When they came to the convent in the city, they were received very honourably. The noble maidens who had been taught to sing and read according to Dominican law – there were twelve of them – as well as the other worthy persons who wished to enter the convent were publicly invested with the holy habit of the Dominican order. They were enclosed in the name of God, the holy Trinity, the queen of heaven the Virgin Mary, Saint Mary Magdalene, Saint Dominic, and all the angels and saints, and began to maintain enclosure and the holy Observance devoutly just like the convent of Schönensteinbach. So many people entered the convent that there is a great number of them who zealously serve God to this day. People hold them in great love and favour because of their blessed, spiritual, devout life.

5.4 *How another convent of the Observance called Westeroye near the city of Tiel was founded* [fol. 148v]

Once the religious life and the membership of the convent of St Mary Magdalene in Wijk had grown, they could no longer receive into the order all the good, well-suited people who desired it. So another new convent was founded in the same diocese of Utrecht in a city called Tiel and this convent's name is Westeroye. Once this cloister had been outfitted with all the necessaries, the worthy mothers took Sister Magdalena Betminger, who had come to Wijk from Schönensteinbach, and gave her enough specially selected sisters to found a convent properly in holy Observance. The blessed Sister Magdalena was installed as prioress to govern this convent, which remains a religious community of blessed, devout, spiritual sisters to this day.

Behold, noble Schönensteinbach, how far you have flowed out, since only four little grains of wheat have so quickly filled two convents with so many blessed children of God diligently serving their bridegroom, Jesus Christ, the heavenly king. But of the miracles that the eternal God performed and wrought in these children little has come to us, because neither of these convents of sisters is located in the German province, but rather in the province of Saxonia. For this reason, these two convents have been able to send few messages to Steinbach, for they are not under the same provincial and lie very far away, almost a hundred miles from Schönensteinbach. Nevertheless, the Lord of nature has also wrought supernatural things with these blessed children through his grace. This may we see in the following examples.

5.5 *Of the manifold graces which God the Lord did for these sisters of Westeroye* [fol. 149r]

In this aforesaid convent, there was a sister whom God wished to prepare for himself. To this end, he sent her suffering, which he usually does for his dear friends. Among other trials, this sister laboured under doubt and unbelief in the worthy holy sacrament of the body and blood of our dear Lord Jesus Christ. Even though she firmly held to Christian belief about this holy sacrament, her senses fought and struggled mightily against the holy faith. After she long had suffered this troublesome affliction with heart calling out to God, God led her one day before the altar where the holy sacrament stood. With a devout heart, she knelt down and called upon God to help and come to her aid in her difficult anguish and concern. She completed her prayer with a troubled heart. Behold, in front of the shrine in which the holy sacrament lay, she saw a small, beautiful, lovely child come out and say to her, "Look at me. I am both God and man, flesh and blood. Doubt in me no longer." Then the lovely child went back into the shrine and illuminated this sister's heart with grace and firm Christian faith. As is proper, she thanked God the Lord for this all the days of her life.

The Lord Jesus appeared to another young sister in the choir and in the refectory. Sometimes she saw the Lord in the form of a heavenly child, lovingly greeting and presenting himself to each sister in the whole community. Furthermore, when the sisters of this convent died and were prepared and dressed for burial, they appeared so lovely and white of skin that it was unnatural for a dead body. This was interpreted as a sign of their final, honourable resurrection at the Last Judgement.

After this convent, the convent of Unterlinden in Colmar was reformed. The tale of how that happened and what holy sisters lived there has its own book.[6] Therefore I will leave it out, but it should be known that it was reformed in the year of our Lord 1419.

6. Sarah DeMaris suspects that Meyer is referring to Sister Elisabeth Kempf's "House-book" with her German translation of the originally Latin Unterlinden sisterbook. See Sarah Glenn DeMaris, "Anna Muntprat's Legacy for the Zoffingen Sisters: A Second Copy of the Unterlinden *Schwesternbuch*," *ZfdA* 144 (2015): 359–378, at 376 n49.

5.6 *How the Dominican friary in Bern was brought to the holy Observance by the fathers of Nuremberg* [fol. 150r]

Well may we believe that the Lord has wrought much in the blessed sisters of Unterlinden, since they have upheld the order and its observance for forty-four years now, but God alone knows the extent of this grace.

In the same year that Unterlinden was reformed, our Dominican friary in Bern was also reformed by our fathers, the Dominicans of Nuremberg. That was in 1419 under the master general Friar Leonardo Dati of Florence and the provincial prior, Friar Giselbert.[7] Through zealous and earnest petition, the whole city council requested and obtained this Observance of the Bern friars, which was the third reform and Observance among the friaries in German lands. The first prior of this new religious life was Friar Johannes Füller,[8] a simple, plain, upstanding man, who brought the community out of great debt and afterwards suffered much there in Bern. With him came Hermann Schmer,[9] a great preacher of the divine word, who shortly thereafter became prior of this friary, along with Friar Johannes Gerlach[10] and some other friars, who started the Observance there, which still stands.

Praise and honour be to God, the holy worthy Trinity. Amen.

5.7 *How the city council of Basel requested the reform of the convent of St Mary Magdalene an den Steinen in Basel* [fol. 150v]

Since the lives of the brothers and sisters of the Observance were so edifying that secular people found a good example in it, people in some cities wanted the communities of friars and sisters of our order, who did not keep the order nor the Observance, to be drawn to the religious life and reformed. In particular, the wise councilmen of the honourable city of Basel noted the great spirituality and devotion of the sisters of Schönensteinbach and Unterlinden. The city of Basel wanted their city to have a women's convent that resembled Schönensteinbach in its religious life. And so the Basel city council called upon the honourable father Friar Conrad of Prussia for instruction, help, and advice, sending

7. Leonardo Dati, master general (r. 1414–1425) and Giselbert of Utrecht, provincial prior of Teutonia (r. 1408–1426). For Dati, see Mortier, *Histoire des maîtres généraux*, 4: 85–140; *SOPMA*, 3: 73–77.

8. On Johannes Füller, see *DDS*, 315–316.

9. On Hermann Schmer, see *DDS*, 316.

10. It is possible that Johannes Gerlach is identical with the Johannes Mülich whose flour trick saved the reforming friars from the violently resisting sisters of St Catherine's in Nuremberg (**4.5**). See *DDS*, 303 n68.

an earnest letter with these requests to Steinbach, where he was living in great devotion at that time. He encouraged them to write about this to the honourable father the provincial prior in German lands, who was a good advocate for religious affairs. And so the council wrote to the provincial. The contents of this letter are recorded here, so that one may see to a good extent how St Mary Magdalene in Basel was reformed to the Observance. Here are the contents of this letter:

> To the honourable, spiritual father and lord, Friar Giselbert, provincial of the Dominican order in German lands, from Hans Reich of Reichenstein,[11] knight and mayor, and from the city council of Basel. We extend our willing service to Your Worthiness and offer in advance whatever good and honour we may ever perform.
>
> Dear Honourable Lord,
> Since it is evident that throughout holy Christendom, not only here but in all lands and kingdoms, it is unfortunately going poorly for religious belief and many other matters, it is necessary for us and all Christian people to pray and call upon the almighty eternal God with our prayers, fasting, and other good deeds, that he might show his divine grace and mercy by amending our misdeeds and, for the good of holy Christendom, ending the great and difficult trials which arose from heresy and war and have now lasted too long. Since we have noticed and come to understand that such righteous invocations of the eternal God are better received and more pleasing coming from honest religious people than from other sinful humans, we are inclined and would very much like to see especially a women's convent of your order established by us in our city, which would uphold your order as is done in Schönensteinbach, Colmar, Nuremberg, and other places. We believe this would bring great honour to your entire order and would greatly comfort us and ours, if we now and hereafter could eternally enjoy such a thing in the almighty, eternal God. So that this might be done, know that we have ascertained that some of the nuns of St Mary Magdalene here in Basel have a favourable opinion in this and are wholly inclined to let themselves be enclosed in this way and to uphold the order, as we wrote above and as is done in Steinbach and Unterlinden. Some, however, are against this. There-

11. For this Basel official, see the numerous references in Elsanne Gilomen-Schenkel, *Henman Offenburg (1379-1459): Ein Basler Diplomat im Dienste der Stadt, des Konzils und des Reichs* (Basel, 1975).

fore, since you have full authority in your province to arrange such affairs for the best, we zealously and earnestly beseech Your Honour that you strive, for the honour and glory of Christ Jesus and the comfort of those in our city, to bring the good intention of the honourable women in St Mary Magdalene to a fruitful and praiseworthy conclusion, enclosing them as is prescribed. If any one or more of them do not agree to this or do not wish to be enclosed in this manner, let them go to Klingental or another convent of your order and provide for them there, as you judge beneficial and good for each person's situation, just as was previously done in similar matters during the change in Colmar. However we the whole council can and may assist, we shall not cease. Should Your Honour agree to take this matter in hand, which we request of you subserviently and desire with our whole hearts, it seems necessary to us that you come to us in person as soon as possible. We will set ourselves to the matter with you and handle the matter according to your advice in the best and most honourable way. If we can earn this for your merit and the whole order, here with us or anywhere else, in your service, we will always be very willing. We hope and trust that, if the affair should proceed, we will not turn aside, and that so many wealthy persons will enter this convent that they will bring much property with them, which by the grace of God will redound to the honour and profit of your whole order. Please respond with your intention and answer by this messenger.

Dated the Saturday before the Feast of the Holy Trinity [6 June], 1422.

5.8 *How thirteen sisters from Unterlinden in Colmar were sent to Basel to reform St Mary Magdalene* [fol. 152r]

After they had long pressed the issue that the convent of St Mary Magdalene an den Steinen should become like the convent of Schönensteinbach in enclosure and religious life, and had written to the honourable father vicar Friar Conrad of Prussia to this effect, and laid the matter before the sisters of Schönensteinbach, it was decided in the end that sisters from the convent of Unterlinden in Colmar should be selected to reform St Mary Magdalene to the holy Observance. This was particularly appropriate, since the sisters of Steinbach only a few years earlier had sent thirteen upstanding, talented sisters to Unterlinden to begin the Observance there, some of whom could be spared to begin the Observance in St Mary Magdalene. So it happened by the authority of their superiors.

In 1423 thirteen dear sisters from Unterlinden in Colmar were escorted to St Mary Magdalene in Basel to begin the religious life of Observance: Sister Dorothea of Ostren, prioress; Sister Ursula of Masmünster, afterwards prioress there for many years; Sister Mechthildis of Polwig; Sister Anna Reinhold; Sister

Margretha Zorn;[12] Sister Margretha Regenstein; Sister Margretha Christl; Sister Gertrud Kranich; Sister Elisabeth Henig; Sister Truta of Polwig; Sister Margareta of Kenzingen; Sister Susanna of Hatstadt; Sister Elisabeth of Ulm; Sister Elisabeth Thomann. See what a secure, good foundation of religious life was brought to St Mary Magdalene in these thirteen blessed, devout, well-suited children, five of whom had been sent from Steinbach to Unterlinden.

5.9 *How St Mary Magdalene in Basel grew so greatly in spiritual and temporal matters* [fol. 153r]

Since this convent was poor and the sisters had to suffer much, the council of Basel gave the newly begun Observance in St Mary Magdalene a sizeable tithe from the village church in Frick in the diocese of Basel under the condition and on the assurance that they would maintain the Observance eternally, as it was laudably upheld in Steinbach. And so the spiritual life increased so greatly that many notable, rich persons came to the convent with their property and rebuilt it in a suitable and orderly manner. As insignificant as it had been before in both spiritual and temporal matters, it now blossomed in great poverty and became a worthy, distinguished convent spiritually, materially, and in the number of honourable sisters, of whom there were nearly fifty serving God the Lord by diligently upholding the order and strictly maintaining the enclosure of the Observance. What special grace God the Lord granted certain sisters in the forty years since the Observance began, he himself knows best. To him be great, worthy praise and honour now and evermore. Amen.

5.10 *On the gracious virtues of certain sisters of St Mary Magdalene in Basel* [fol. 153v]

I have occasionally heard in confidence from the persons I knew in St Mary Magdalene in Basel about many notable and devout things and divine favours that certain blessed sisters experienced in life and in death. It would serve the devotion and benefit of good-hearted people if such gracious matters were written down, but only some of the many things, and briefly.

About a sister named Gertrud Kranich: When she had to leave Unterlinden out of holy obedience and go with the other sisters to begin the Observance in St

12. Margretha Zorn had originally entered the Dominican order at St Margaret's in Strasbourg but had transferred into the Observance in Unterlinden. See Sigrid Hirbodian, "Dominikanerinnenreform und Familienpolitik: Die Einführung der Observanz im Kontext städtischer Sozialgeschichte," in *Schreiben und Lesen in der Stadt: Literaturbetrieb im spätmittelalterlichen Straßburg*, ed. Stephen Mossman, Nigel F. Palmer, and Felix Heinzer (Berlin, 2012), 1–16, at 10 n40.

Mary Magdalene, she was burdened with the responsibilities of the sacristan's office. Even though this office gave her much to do, she was still very silent and so zealous in turning to God that the Lord worked such great grace in her that she was often rapt into ecstasy in choir or at table. This good sister was adorned with many virtues. She was very devout, silent, humble, and long-suffering, and avoided all temporal pleasures and even those comforts that may be enjoyed without sin, such as speaking affably with the sisters. She withdrew from such things and practised love of her neighbour. She had the daily habit of praying thirty Our Fathers and Ave Marias while prostrate in the form of the cross. She was already used to doing this when she secretly told a sister that while she was saying these prayers she was never troubled by useless thoughts. Since she was such a talented, spiritual sister, she was sent in holy obedience with other blessed sisters to Strasbourg to reform the convent of St Nicholas-in-Undis, where she is buried. Before her death, the Lord prepared her with a chronic illness, in which she was very patient. She suffered an extremely painful putrefaction in one of her breasts. She had this illness for a long time but joined the community in the choir, in the refectory, and in the dormitory as long as she could. Finally, the prioress commanded her to go to the infirmary. She always anticipated her death and often said, "If the Lord wishes, then I am ready." She said this serenely in God's will, for this sickness has the characteristic of usually ending suddenly, as happened to her. Yet she devoutly prepared herself in advance with all the Christian sacraments and while they were transferring her from the chair to the bed, she died in the hands that lifted her.

Another sister also in St Mary Magdalene was called Sister Katharina of Zässingen.[13] She was prioress before her convent was restored to the holy Observance. She so greatly desired her convent to attain the blessed state that Schönensteinbach had and demonstrated her seriousness, for it was a considerable affair to bring the holy matter to blessed progress. Many years after the beginning of this Observance, she again became prioress because of her wisdom and upright life. She also had two nieces who were secular women in the community of St Leodegar in Masmünster, where they call themselves canonesses and are permitted many physical comforts and worldly honour. They left this unsafe place and became humble sisters with her in St Mary Magdalene, where they laudably upheld the observance of this order for many years. This blessed Sister Katharina lived a virtuous life, about which there would be much to write, until her final age. She found a death as gracious and blessed as her life had been. God the Lord be praised eternally.

13. See *DDS*, 605.

Another sister was named Anna zu Rhein.[14] She was of noble birth, as was the above-named Sister Katharina, but much more noble in virtue and religious life. When this dear woman's noble, honourable husband died and left her, she hitched herself under the sweet heart and yoke of Christ to pull the Observance of the holy Dominican order in St Mary Magdalene in Basel. She became a humble lay sister and led a blessed life until her end.

5.11 *Of a good sister named Margareta of Kenzingen and her good youth* [fol. 154v]

There was a particularly distinguished good sister in this same convent named Sister Margareta of Kenzingen, whose exemplary life I will describe here briefly. This dear person and sister was born to rich, honourable people and they raised her well, but she was raised even better by God, the Holy Spirit, who blessed her with his divine grace in his gracious, sweet kindness. When she was old enough, her family gave her in marriage to a rich, God-fearing merchant. From her childhood on, she had been raised in the fear of God and had been required to confess and hear sermons often. When she came to her husband, she was given an upstanding, stern old maid to watch over her, instruct her, and teach her. Since she was under the mastery of this maid, this dear maiden was so submissively obedient to her servant that she would not even go visit her birth mother without the express permission of this maid. Sometimes when she requested permission to go to her mother in her father's house and this maid refused, she was patiently silent and obedient and did not ask again until the maid herself told her to go to her mother. And so she practised the virtue of obedience towards her servant in surrendering her free will while she was still in a secular marital state, but for the sake of the obedience of our dear Lord Jesus Christ, who for our sake was obedient to his heavenly father unto the bitter death of the cross.

Now, her husband was a wise and reasonable man on the Kenzingen town council and kindly indulged whatever good she did, yea, even was pleased by it, for he himself led a good, Christian life. He also had the grace that whenever he sat in the council and they condemned a man to death, he contemplated the suffering of Christ and his innocent death so deeply that he could hardly bring forth an opinion on the matter.

This blessed woman had an orderly marriage with her husband. Since she wished to be pleasing to the Lord Christ, who is betrothed to all pure souls, as long as she lived in marriage she maintained the custom of confessing once a week and purifying her soul and her conscience.

14. As Ennelin ze Rhin in *DDS*, 596 n90.

5.12 *How this sister Margareta of Kenzingen lived in exile and scorn with great patience* [fol. 155v]

This sister Margareta, when she became a widow at the death of her husband, considered what the quickest, surest path to serve God the Lord in a blessed, Christian life would be. She followed the advice of our dear Lord, who says in the holy Gospel, *Si vis perfectus esse, vade*:[15] "If you want to be perfect, sell all you have and give it to the poor and come, follow me." This woman did just that. She placed her only child in a convent of Poor Clares,[16] gave away all her possessions, and went begging for bread in exile for five years, suffering great scorn and misery. She went to the city of Marburg and served the invalids in the hospital there, which was founded by the holy woman Saint Elizabeth.[17] She practised great devotion there in a contemplative and active life. She desired that God grant her the grace of being the most scorned person on earth.

Now God sent her extraordinary suffering and disgrace, as he commonly imposes upon his friends, and she was accused of being a nasty thief who meddled in indecent matters. She was arrested and led before the judge. Since she did not defend herself but, in joyful patience, surrendered herself willingly to death in God the Lord, she was sentenced by the court to be drowned to death. When the crowd of people gathered, God arranged that a distinguished priest from her homeland in the Breisgau was in these lands on business. He saw the blessed woman that was being led to her death, and when he looked at her closely he recognized her and was enormously surprised. He told the judge and the lords what an honourable person she was and what distinguished, blessed people her family, father, mother, and husband had been. When they themselves discovered and ascertained her complete innocence, she was set free.

5.13 *How this sister Margareta came to the great Friend of God from the Oberland, who advised her to enter the Dominican order in Unterlinden* [fol. 156r]

The true, right, and humble do not like ephemeral human praise nor to be lauded by people. According to Saint Gregory, it is a cross for the spirit of the humble when they are publicly praised before the world. For this reason, this dear woman Margareta left this land and considered what she was now to do. It

15. Matthew 19:21.

16. This daughter, Magdalena Beutler, remained in the Clarissan convent of Freiburg im Breisgau and became a well-known mystic in her own right. An account of her life and her visions survives. See Magdalena Beutler, "*Erklärung des Vaterunsers*: A Critical Edition of a Fifteenth-Century Mystical Treatise by Magdalena Beutler of Freiburg," ed. Karen Greenspan (PhD diss., University of Massachusetts, 1984).

17. Elizabeth of Hungary, landgravine of Thuringia (d. 1231).

occurred to her to go to the great Friend of God,[18] who lives in the mountains of the Oberland with his holy companions. She had heard exceedingly good things about this holy man of God – how he had devoutly served God from childhood on and now was quite old and very experienced in all divine matters by the grace of God, the Holy Spirit. All of this was true, for this blessed man of God was one of the five holy men written about in *The Book of the Five Men*. Indeed, he was the most perfect among them, as one finds in this book. This holy man taught the Alphabet of Virtue to that master of holy Scripture from the Dominican order and made a blessed person of him.[19] He was Rulman Merswin's intimate friend and, with advice and assistance, helped him found the religious life of St John on the Grüner Wörth in Strasbourg.[20] God the Lord worked many other great, supernatural, lofty, divine matters through his dear friend, as is recorded extensively in both Latin and German in this same honourable house of God.

With great difficulty, the blessed woman came to this holy man. Through God's special favour, she found him in his residence (otherwise, she might not have found him), laid before him the events of her life, and desired his salutary advice. How should she now better follow the paths of God? What sort of life should she take up that would be most pleasing to God? He then told her about the convent of women in Schönensteinbach. There was another convent in Alsace, namely, Unterlinden in the city of Colmar in the diocese of Basel, which

18. The Strasbourg merchant Rulman Merswin (d. 1382) claimed to have received numerous mystical writings from a hermit living in the wilderness outside the city whom he called only "The Friend of God." It is now generally accepted that this Friend of God was Merswin's invention and the mysticism his own. In the Middle Ages, however, many people, evidently including Meyer, took Merswin at his word. See Christiane Krusenbaum-Verheugen, *Figuren der Referenz: Untersuchungen zu Überlieferung und Komposition der "Gottesfreundliteratur" in der Straßburger Johanniterkomturei zum "Grünen Wörth"* (Francke, 2013).

19. In the *Book of the Master*, Merswin's Friend of God teaches a master of Scripture to pursue mystical contemplation. The second chapter of the work includes a list of virtues that each begin with a letter of the alphabet. The master of Scripture in the story was long assumed to be the Dominican friar Johannes Tauler (ca. 1300–1361), a disciple of Meister Eckhart. It is now considered most likely that the master was also a fictional character invented by Merswin. See Helen Webster, "Tauler and Merswin: Friends in God?" *Oxford German Studies* 36 (2007): 212–226.

20. Rulman Merswin used the wealth he accumulated as a merchant to found a commandery of the religious military order of the Knights of St John, also known as the Hospitallers, on an island called the Grüner Wörth in Strasbourg. See Karl Borchardt, "Hospitallers, Mysticism, and Reform in Late-Medieval Strasburg," in *The Military Orders*, vol. 3: *History and Heritage*, ed. Victor Mallia-Milanes (Burlington, 2008), 73–78.

was also reformed to the religious life of perfect observance fully according to the custom of the Dominican order. He advised her to enter that convent, to live in obedience, and to uphold the order as a humble lay sister.

If anyone is thinking, how can it be that the Friend of God, the man in the Oberland who was Rulman Merswin's intimate friend and companion, was still living at the time of this sister, since there is a written record of him living in all holiness long before this as a wealthy youth in 1350 (a jubilee year in Rome during the time of Pope Clement[21]), you should know that this holy friend of God lived for a very long time in this world and became extremely old. God had foretold this to him and commanded him to accept it. He lived further past a hundred years old than I know to tell.

5.14 *How this blessed sister Margareta was sent from Unterlinden to St Mary Magdalene in Basel with other sisters* [fol. 157v]

After this blessed sister Margareta had been in Unterlinden for several years, she was sent with other sisters in obedience to St Mary Magdalene in Basel to help reform it. When she realized that she had been sent as a good model for the other old sisters in St Mary Magdalene, she thought herself unworthy of this, but persisted in such loving virtue that the sisters were much improved by her life. She was entrusted with the offices of turnkeeper and subbursar and was supposed to help with accounting, record-keeping, and such things, which she was unable to do because of her great contemplativeness. Since she often went into ecstasy, they had to remove her from external offices. It very often happened, from the great passion and devotion that she had for the loving God, that she was rapt, especially at table and whenever she was supposed to receive the holy sacrament. She ate little else on the day she received communion. She was usually in the choir, where they had constructed an enclosed chair for her because of her contemplation. It also often happened that she was rapt while sitting in the workroom or at the spindle.

Beyond this, she did not have any more spiritual practices than other sisters, except for speaking very seldom. In particular, she never came to the wheel or speaking window, even if noble and well-born people requested her, unless she felt it would serve her peace of mind. When she heard an outside person speaking, she could tell by the grace of God what spiritual state he was in and could choose accordingly to talk with him much or little.

Once on Christmas Night, they were holding the great chapter meeting and calling out in a loud voice the gracious words that proclaim our salvation through

21. Pope Clement VI (r. 1342–1352).

the holy birth of the eternal fatherly word, "Jesus Christus, filius dei, in Bethlehem Iude nascitur."[22] She heard this holy proclamation and statement with devotion and grace, contemplating how God became human from such great love for the sake of us poor sinners, and how the highest majesty lowered and humbled himself so deeply. Her contemplation was so full of this enormous divine miracle that in the refectory on this evening she called out in a loud voice, "Jesus Christus, filius Dei!" She then bowed her head and was rapt and stayed sitting like that until Vespers.

Master Johannes Nider commemorates this blessed sister in his *Formicarius*.[23]

When God the Lord wished in his grace to take his dear child from this world, he wanted to prepare her well and gave her a difficult illness. She had St Anthony's fire[24] in one leg and it swelled enormously and the abscesses ran day and night with such a monstrous, insufferable stench that the sisters serving her often became sick from it. However great her discomfort and insufferable pain, she never became impatient nor desired God to lessen it. If he also wanted to inflict it on her other leg, that would have been fine with her. When the sisters lifted her from the bed (she was a very tall woman) and accidentally hit or touched her sick leg and she said "Ow!" she punished herself severely for it, saying to herself, "you poor sinner and evil-smelling sack! Why are you not thinking about the miserable hanging of our dear Lord Jesus Christ on three nails on the holy cross without any comfort?" When God the Lord wished to reward her holy life, she received the holy worthy sacrament, which was also her last meal. She departed with a blessed end in 1428 on the night before Christmas when the great chapter is held.

5.15 *How the convent of Dominican sisters in Nuremberg was reformed and who facilitated this* [fol. 159r]

There would be much else to write about the virtuous lives of the dear sisters in St Mary Magdalene that would serve the edification of good-willed persons. But since I am rushing to tell how other convents were reformed to the Observance, I will leave it out for the sake of brevity. I now intend to write about how

22. "Jesus Christ, Son of God, is born in Bethlehem in Juda."

23. Nider praises Margareta in order to contrast her with her daughter, Magdalena Beutler, whose visions he condemns in the *Formicarius*, book 3, chapter 8. See the note in **5.12** above, and Dyan Elliott, *Proving Woman: Female Spirituality and Inquisitional Culture in the Later Middle Ages* (Princeton, 2004), 197–200.

24. I.e., ergotism, which can express itself in convulsive symptoms, such as those described of the knight in **2.13**, or gangrenous symptoms, such as Margareta suffers here.

and through which persons the worthy convent of St Catherine in Nuremberg was fully reformed to the Observance. So that this will better be understood and noted, I set here the letter Master Johannes Nider wrote to the sisters of Schönensteinbach:

> Our humble prayer and all good in Christ Jesus, to the most honourable of all dear women and sisters, for you and we also should diligently, with body and soul, seek the health and salvation of souls, in particular of those in our order. We are encouraged in this by our name, for we are called Preachers and Preacheresses, to which we are driven by the love of him who suffered the death of the cross for everyone's sake. Therefore, dear children, we are writing to you now more urgently than we ever have before on behalf of our convent of sisters of St Catherine here in our city, who have up until now led a life in which you would not wish to die. For this reason, about twenty years ago, we separated ourselves from them as if they did not belong to us.[25]
>
> Now the almighty God has illuminated some of their hearts and they desire to be reformed to what they are obligated to observe. Without their knowledge or request, the merciful God has also admonished the hearts of the entire city council here that they should want the aforementioned convent of St Catherine to begin a pure reform according to your rule and customs. They have requested this of the worthy master general who has joyously promised to complete this to the best of his ability. Even though we did not begin this affair, nor bring it to the citizens, we are well pleased by the fact that we will have the said convent under our care and protection again.
>
> I, the prior, am their vicar. A master of arts, a learned and devout man of our community, has become their confessor. We are now providing them with singing and reading as our children. The council is earnestly rendering material aid in all things and the entire city is rejoicing as for a new light of future good.
>
> If this holy beginning should see loving progress, it is necessary most of all for sisters to come who know and can teach observance of the order according to your practice, who can occupy the offices and do the things that you now do. For without a group of such sisters, that which now has started so well will be defeated. Since we trust you above all other convents, we beseech you as earnestly as we ever could, for God's honour, which we purely seek, that you send us a group of talented women, so that we may lay a good foundation.

25. This estrangement followed the spectacularly failed reform attempt described in 4.5.

So that you will be kind and willing in this, your divine love should kindly incline you to consider eight things. First, augmenting your divine honour. How could you serve God better than by teaching and coaxing the ignorant sisters, who now are in the convent of St Catherine, away from many sins? If you do not help them, we fear that you will be responsible for these sins and all the dishonour that could be done to God by all the successors who enter a disordered convent.

Second, our holy father Saint Dominic's intention and order, for he organized sisters and friars as best he could so that they would not be piled on top of one another but would be spread out in many convents, drawing them into God's service. He gave an example of this: just as seeds lying close together tend to rot, but when they are sown far apart and cast here and there, they bring much fruit.

Third, the great benefit for the many secular people around us, whom we may convert, as well as the many other convents in the area. Here, you should reflect on whether you fear that your material wealth will be reduced because of our convent. If this is the reason you do not want to support such a good project, it would be a sure sign that you are privileging your temporal well-being and rejecting God's honour. Therefore, seek first the kingdom of God[26] and the temporal matters will often follow. As is to be expected, here by us one can always find pure hearts, rich in goods, who would rather be in your convent far from their friends and family than here in our city near them.

Fourth, the great deterioration of holy Christendom. All the laypeople are now crying out, saying that the Hussite heresy has arisen because the clergy, monks, and nuns are not reformed. For this reason, our citizens are now seriously doing all they can for the aforementioned reform. They are currently building walls for the said convent and, following our instruction, enclosing it even more strictly than specified in your statutes. They are now sending you their own messenger at their own cost. I know someone who, for God's sake, wants to invest nine hundred florins to provide the convent with a perpetual income. If you now refuse to send responsible persons to help that which God is leading, then without a doubt you are a cause of the sickness afflicting the Christian faith. First the laypeople say that nothing good comes from monks and nuns, and next the Hussites will corrupt them to the core, and you would have to fear the proclamation of a command that would not be profitable for your convent's property and persons.

26. Matthew 6:33.

Fifth, the favours I have done for you and will continue to do if you wish. Furthermore, the incomes of the sisters you send to us will remain with your convent, as well as all the books of those who come here – that is, after their deaths. While they live, they should use them, as the master general wishes.[27] Until now, I have taught you what it is to receive. It is now godly to give persons up for a time. We believe that God specially ordained the expansion of your membership, so far away, expressly so that now you may help the city from which so much profit has flowed to you.

Sixth, the great eternal reward you may gain from it. You should know that it is more meritorious to restore an old convent to propriety than to found a new one. You will be the founders, the impetus, and the beneficiaries of all the good that will eternally come from St Catherine's. This is also the reason why I, Friar Johannes Nider, and the prior of Bern[28] are risking our own skins for reasons you well know.

Seventh, the honour of our community of Dominicans here and the humblest prayers of us all, to whom you are in many ways indebted. Know also, if you do not send your sisters here as is written above, you will give us a reputation that would be very harmful to us, as Friar Conrad Spielberger will tell you. In this regard, you are obligated to protect us because of the service we have done for you and will continue to do.

Eighth, the great uproar here in the whole city of Nuremberg which will result if you do not hear us. All the people within and without now know that such a holy thing has been started in the convent. If you do not send us responsible women, this project will become a mockery, and furthermore, so much divine work will be hindered, which it is not appropriate for us to reveal or write about.

So, consider the honour of God, the intention and order of our holy father Saint Dominic, the piety of the devout, the furtherance of Christendom, your spiritual profit, gratitude in reception of gifts, prevention of great

27. Reforming parties commonly brought with them a set of liturgical and devotional books, as well as books owned privately by the reforming sisters. See Gisela Muschiol, "Migrating Nuns – Migrating Liturgy: The Context of Reform in Female Convents of the Late Middle Ages," in *Liturgy in Migration: From the Upper Room to Cyberspace*, ed. Teresa Berger (Collegeville, MN, 2012), 83–100. For the specific books sent from Schönensteinbach to St Catherine's in Nuremberg (which were never actually sent back), see Antje Willing (ed.), *Die Bibliothek des Klosters St. Katharina zu Nürnberg: Synoptische Darstellung der Bücherverzeichnisse* (Berlin, 2012), lxxii–lxxv.

28. This prior is probably Hermann Schmer/Schiner, who also helped Master General Bartholomew Texery to reform the Basel friary shortly hereafter. See *DDS*, 316.

turmoil, our poor prayer, and the will of our superiors who do not wish to command you roughly in this. For they, and we also, trust that you are good and will send us such women and sisters as those written above have desired and requested. We all have entrusted this orally to Friar Conrad Spielberger, whom you should believe in this matter as you would us. Nuremberg 1428.

5.16 *How ten sisters from Schönensteinbach were brought to Nuremberg to reform St Catherine's convent there* [fol. 162r]

In this copy of the letters that were sent to Schönensteinbach from Nuremberg with regard to the reform of St Catherine's convent, one can see the great seriousness and zeal applied in the matter. The highest master of the Dominican order and the provincial prior of Teutonia,[29] who wanted to restore the order's religious life through the authority of their offices, invested such great effort in this that they personally came and had to deal with much strife, even though the city council stood by them.

These prelates, with the blessing and aid of the Nuremberg city council, prepared the convent of St Catherine for the Observance. They sent a messenger to Schönensteinbach, a wise and spiritual father named Friar Conrad Spielberger, who laid everything before them as the master and the provincial had instructed him. The city council sent a similar message. And so ten dear sisters were chosen to assume this great task. Two wagons were prepared, which the city of Nuremberg arranged. They placed the dear, obedient children within, and drove off with them on St Cecilia's Day [22 November] 1428. They travelled with the senior confessor, Father Heinrich Fabri, as well as a lay brother from the Steinbach estate and certain other honourable people, who worthily escorted them to Nuremberg.

But when the sisters from Schönensteinbach arrived in Nuremberg and were supposed to enter the convent to begin the Observance and teach the other sisters the customs of the order as the master general and the city council of Nuremberg had so earnestly requested of them, sending costly and expensive messages to them in the dead of winter, and even with great effort barely getting them to set out – Listen to this! – the hostile, evil spirits, who are so massively jealous of all good works and of our soul's salvation, bestirred themselves. The old sisters in the convent piteously complained to certain laypeople who were their friends. This produced such a great tumult in the city that they feared a violent uprising. In particular, a powerful, hostile person influenced the city

29. Master General Bartholomew Texery (r. 1426–1449) and Provincial Prior Nicolaus Notel (r. 1426–1446).

council to withdraw the city's support from Master General Bartholomew and the worthy provincial.

5.17 *The names of the sisters from Steinbach who reformed this convent* [fol. 162v]

Because of this great resistance, they put the poor, patient sisters from Steinbach in the house of a patrician woman in the city, where they remained for many[30] days in great sadness. Their confessor was very distressed that everything was not running as smoothly as he had hoped. When the city council dealt with the matter by properly arranging for the foreign sisters to be escorted back home with honour, the blessed father master general was filled with the counsel of the Holy Spirit and went to the convent of St Catherine. He secretly called for the sisters of Steinbach to be led to the convent and ordered the convent to be opened. He spoke so graciously with both contingents of sisters that they agreed with his words and let him staff the offices according to the Observance and reform the convent completely so that they would maintain the Observance eternally.[31] The city council was then informed that the matter had been settled, and was very pleased. Those who had slandered this affair were humbled and shamed, the meek strengthened, the good-willed made happy, and God's praise and honour increased.

These are the names of the dear sisters from Schönensteinbach, who were sent to Nuremberg to enter the convent of St Catherine. The first: Sister Gertrud Gewichtmacher, the first prioress of this Observance who is still prioress there after forty years.[32] When she first arrived in the office of prioress, she found more than thirty sisters already in the convent and treated them so well that very few of them left for other convents, as is recounted hereafter. This convent now has so many persons that more than seventy sisters are there who hold themselves to the religious life in an orderly manner, even though they have since reformed four other convents to the Observance (Tulln, Pforzheim,

30. An interlinear annotation in Cgm 8081 specifies this as eight days.

31. An independent account of this event, recorded by a nun of St Catherine's, does not represent the reform as having been as contentious as Meyer claims here. Otherwise, it confirms Meyer's account, including the names of the ten sisters from Schönensteinbach, and provides additional details, such as the names of the sisters previously residing in St Catherine's, a complete record of the offices assigned to the reforming sisters, and an account of the finances involved in the transition. See Theodor von Kern, "Die Reformation des Katharinenklosters zu Nürnberg im Jahre 1428," *Jahresbericht des historischen Vereins für Mittelfranken* 31 (1863): 1–20.

32. The scribe initially wrote thirty-eight, which has been partially crossed out and corrected to forty.

Holy Sepulchre in Bamberg, and Altenhohenau in Bavaria, as will be recounted hereafter).[33]

The second sister was named Katharina of Mühlheim. She later became the first prioress of the Observance at the convent in Tulln. Many years later when she reached a good age, she was sent by our vicar, Father Innocent of Vienna, with other sisters to the province of Bohemia to reform a convent in 1466.[34]

The third sister was Ursula Tott, later the first prioress of the Observance in the convent of Our Dear Lady in Pforzheim. The fourth was Elisabeth Karl, the second prioress of this great house of God in Pforzheim. The fifth was Sister Anna Burgrave, subprioress. Sister Margaretha Kartheuser, chantress.[35] Sister Margaretha Vornan, Sister Ursula Wolsack, Sister Margaretha Imhof. The tenth sister was named Agnes Taffer. She was a lay sister, but the other nine sisters were all veiled sisters in the choir, talented, spiritual, and dear children, who have filled this land with the good reputation of their blessed, devout lives. Praise and honour be to you, Lord Jesus Christ, for your holy, divine work, which you have completed so graciously in your eternal wisdom.

5.18 *What the reason was that the council of Nuremberg requested the reform of St Catherine's* [fol. 164r]

Here it should briefly be noted how it was caused and came to pass that this convent of St Catherine in Nuremberg joined the holy Observance. When the good, praiseworthy reputation of the religious life of the dear, devout children in Steinbach had spread through many lands, many notable, good persons had gone there from faraway cities with their wealth to assume the Dominican order and its religious life there and to serve God the Lord devoutly. There was a dis-

33. A scribe has also updated this passage in Cgm 8081, raising the number of reformed convents to five and adding Medingen to the list in a marginal annotation. This manuscript also includes the information that Tulln is in Austria and Pforzheim in Swabia.

34. Katharina of Mühlheim was sent from Tulln to reform Marienzelle in Brno in modern Czechia, making her a much more widely travelled reformer than Johannes Meyer himself. See Anne Winston-Allen, *Convent Chronicles: Women Writing about Women and Reform in the Late Middle Ages* (University Park, 2004), 104–106.

35. For Margaretha Kartheuser's activity as a scribe, see Anne Winston-Allen, "'Es [ist] nit wol zu gelobind, daz ain frowen bild so wol kan arbaiten': Artistic Production and Exchange in Women's Convents of the Observant Reform," in *Frauen – Kloster – Kunst: Neue Forschungen zur Kulturgeschichte des Mittelalters*, ed. Jeffrey Hamburger et al. (Turnhout, 2007), 187–195, at 193–94; Christine Sauer, "Zwischen Kloster und Welt: Illuminierte Handschriften aus dem Dominikanerinnenkonvent St. Katharina in Nürnberg," in *Frauen – Kloster – Kunst*, 113–129, at 122–129.

tinguished citizen in the city of Nuremberg, who had a dear wife named Kunigund. She held the religious life in special favour, particularly that of the sisters in Schönensteinbach. Her husband recognized quite well that she was inclined with a good will to a religious life. When God wished to take this citizen from the world and he lay on his deathbed, he asked her to come to him and said, "Since I see the good will that you have towards God and towards religious life, I will leave you all my property so that you can become a nun with the blessed children of Steinbach. But if you wish to go into another and not that convent, I will dispose of my property in a different way." Since the dear woman so greatly loved this convent, she was very willing and, shortly after his death, requested entrance there for herself and her maid Cecilia for the sake of God. The sisters agreed, but when she prepared herself to travel so far from the city and region with her property, the council objected to such a woman travelling so far from them, since many women had already left the city for Steinbach with great wealth. Kunigund claimed that she sought nothing more than God and the religious life, and she wished to become a nun in a community that upheld the order according to its Rule and Constitutions. She told the city council that if they, through petitioning the Dominican superiors, could achieve that the convent of St Catherine in that city be reformed and brought to the perfection of those in Schönensteinbach, she would stay there. And so the honourable city undertook to write to the honourable fathers and prelates, the master general, and the others, for the reform of this convent. This reform occurred and was initiated completely by those from Steinbach, as is written above. But it is not possible to write about all the great trouble that it caused.

5.19 *How the blessed first prioress of this Observance in St Catherine's in Nuremberg behaved so virtuously* [fol. 165r]

When this blessed father the master general, named Friar Bartholomew Texery, had placed these ten sisters from Steinbach in the convent of St Catherine and had appointed the officers in an orderly manner, he ordered that all the sisters who had been in the convent before should remain there and test themselves prudently, as much as they could and would. He set a decent time frame, so that they could try it out thoroughly. Whoever did not want to stay after this date would be placed in another convent of our order. He gave the prioress the authority to allow all the sisters who had been in the convent before to live according to their custom – to eat meat and not fast much, to lie on beds, to wear the shirts and clothing they were accustomed to, and the like – unless our Lord was so dear to a sister that she wished to do the things of the order of her free will and uncoerced.[36] Nevertheless, they should show humble obedience and especially observe the common life and live without property. They were all to observe enclosure.

And so the prudent, devout, dear mother prioress behaved so virtuously and lovingly, that all the sisters stayed in the convent, all thirty of them. When the probationary period had passed, the honourable prioress knelt before each sister and embraced her and asked her virtuously and in a motherly fashion – each sister individually, as zealously as she could possibly beg – that no sister leave, but rather stay in the Observance for the sake of God and the salvation of their souls. She tried to be loving and kind in motherly faithfulness, for she did not want any sister to do something that she would not do of free will, but only to love God and keep the common life and enclosure with them. Whatever else they were supposed to do and observe for the order, she would do and observe according to the order's law with her sisters who had come with her from Steinbach, with those who would enter the order afterwards, and with the other convents who would receive the holy Observance from Steinbach.

It so happened that all the sisters stayed, except for a small number. They did not want to submit, so some went to a convent called Frauenaurach. One died very soon afterwards and another sister also did not live long. Two of these sisters[37] were seized by great regret and very earnestly desired to be received back into this blessed life for God, but they were refused. They demonstrated great sincerity, saying to Master Johannes Nider, "Father, help us back into the devout religious life. Otherwise, we will climb in over the walls!" When the honourable father Master Johannes Nider, who was the vicar of this convent, understood that these sisters were serious, he helped them to be received back in.[38] They proved afterwards by their good, virtuous life that their desire and request had been on true grounds. The same was demonstrated by all the sisters who remained there. Our dear Lord was soon so dear to them that they laid off worldly clothes, and more and more began to follow the other sisters, who provided a good example for them. They did of free will the things that should be observed

36. MS 2934 has this passage scratched out so thoroughly with red ink that it is illegible and a sentence fragment is added in the margin. What remains is: "He gave the prioress the authority to allow all the sisters who had been in the convent before to eat meat and be lax in such things at times." Perhaps the extensive description of this lascivious behaviour was deemed too tempting.

37. In Cgm 8081 a second hand has altered this entire passage to make it singular.

38. Cgm 8081 adds the marginal annotation "that same day before nightfall, around the time of compline."

according to the custom of the order and began to live like the other sisters. They became so perfect that some of these old sisters were later sent out with others to reform the convents of Tulln in Austria and Pforzheim in Swabia, and in these convents taught the Observance to other sisters who did not know how to follow the order's law.

After the convent of St Catherine in Nuremberg was first reformed, for a long time the dear sisters were sorely troubled day and night by monstrous ghosts. Someone had to hold watch with the holy sacrament to protect the sisters, who suffered great disturbance and worry from the tumult of the enemy. There was throwing, hitting, and knocking, and sometimes he showed himself openly in various shapes. Their vicar, Master Johannes Nider, thought they should not believe that it was the evil spirit, but rather large rats and cats. One night before Matins, a sister got up who earlier had been fully opposed to the Observance and especially disrespectful and disobedient, but afterwards submitted willingly once the convent was enclosed. The evil spirit seized this sister, and tortured and crushed her so extraordinarily badly that they thought she would die that very day. Afterwards, the evil spirit troubled the whole convent day and night, such that someone had to stand watch in the cloister at night. The poor female sex was so disheartened and frightened that their vicar himself did not know what he should do for the sisters. Some sisters said, "Look and take note. When we used to walk the wide path, such things never happened to us." But the dear fathers urged patience and that they should place firm trust in God and call upon him longingly for aid. And so the evil spirit, who set out to destroy this Observance and cast off the religious life, lost greatly in this matter. Many obstinate sisters, who had not been wholly convinced by the kindness and prayers of those who started the convent to assume the religious life, gave a full life confession out of fear and terror. They laid off their old clothes and began to wear what the others did, taking on a wholly new religious life. When the evil spirit saw this, he completely left them by the grace of God. Such things were never heard or seen again.

Every person can see from this miracle how praiseworthy, good, and fruitful it is to reform convents. Thine be the praise and honour for all thy grace Lord Jesus Christ, from whom all good comes. Amen.

5.20 *How the community of friars in Basel was reformed, and the worry and labour that went into it* [fol. 167r]

In 1429, the friary of our dear fathers in Basel was reformed to the religious life of the holy Observance. They negotiated at length and invested a lot of time in it, as well as financial resources, an unbelievable amount of labour, harsh adversity, and all kinds of trouble, before it ever got to the point that the Observance was begun there. There were many good-willed people who would happily have seen this work carried out, but there were also many against it. In particular, very few friars were willing to adopt the religious life. Nevertheless, the wise city council of Basel wrote to the blessed father Bartholomew Texery, who at the time was master general, asking him to reform the community of friars in their city to the religious life by the authority of his office and for the honour of God. This worthy master acquiesced to the council of Basel, since he was very willing, especially if they would help him in such a good work.

For this reason, the master general commanded the provincial of Teutonia, Father Nicolaus Notel of Gmünd, to go to Basel personally and pursue the matter until he could come himself. Once these two prelates, the master and the provincial were handling the matter of the reform with the city council and had sent for the honourable father Master Johannes Nider and other spiritual fathers and brothers from Nuremberg to begin the religious life of the Observance in Basel – Behold! – the devilish tumult of hell's power bestirred itself and turned the friars against the religious life. Even the sisters of the convent of Klingental resisted strongly, and their friends among the laity, both powerful and common, were so obstreperous and obnoxious that the whole city of Basel feared substantial damage and horrible disagreement.[39] The master general had to retreat, and those in the city withdrew the request and support that they had given him before. The friars who had been sent from Nuremberg had to return. The resistance and the disobedience of these friars and sisters were so great that this reform alone would make a fat book.

5.21 *How Pope Martin wrote from Rome and ordered that the friary in Basel be reformed* [fol. 168r]

Now the blessed father, the master general, thought it better not to let the matter drop after the disobedience of the brothers and sisters in these two aforesaid convents. Rather, the friary had to be reformed. Many members of the council also wished to see this happen, although, as was said before, many were also against it. Indeed, many great, noble, and powerful people engaged themselves in preventing it, so that news of it spread far and wide and caused great suffering. This is how it reached our holy father Pope Martin V. He wrote a global papal bull to all the patriarchs and archbishops, to all dukes, princes, and counts, to all the prelates both religious and secular, that they should not hinder the Dominican

39. Klingental was populated with nuns who had already resisted reform once, since the unwilling sisters of St Mary Magdalene had been sent to Klingental; see **5.7**.

master general, but rather assist in the reform of the friars and sisters of his order. This Pope Martin also earnestly wrote a special bull and papal letter to the city of Basel. Among other things, he said:

> We have been given to understand that our dear son, Bartholomew, master general of the Dominican order, has reformed some convents in several lands and returned them to the religious life with diligent gravity. For this reason, we have often rejoiced in God, who has granted this master general much grace. Now, however, we understand that when he attempted to reform the friary in Basel, these friars, in their perverted mental state, resisted their superior, the master general. They even drove out the honourable men and friars who were chosen to reform them. Since it is just that the disobedience and evil audacity of these friars be punished, through this papal writ we admonish you in the Lord and command you by the authority of holy obedience to offer neither aid nor counsel to the friars who stood in defiance. Instead, you must give counsel and aid to the master general and those who have been appointed to reform, so that, through his wisdom and religiosity, he might reform them according to the order's Constitutions. Also, if any brother or sister proves disobedient to the master general and his ordinances or resists the institution of religious observance, they should be punished through your secular authority with imprisonment or some other penalty, as requested of you by the master general or any whom he appoints. May your devotion place this reform above other matters. Dated in Rome before the holy apostles on the Ides of November [13 November] in the tenth year of our pontificate [1427].[40]

5.22 *How Pope Martin wrote to the bishops of Basel, Constance, and Strasbourg and to the margrave of Rötteln to insist on the reform of the Basel friary* [fol. 169r]

This pope Martin was so intent that he wrote about this matter to three bishops, each individually – the bishop of Basel, the bishop of Constance, and the bishop of Strasbourg[41] – in the way that is recorded here:

> To my honourable brother, the bishop of Basel/of Constance/of Strasbourg: Honourable brother, know that we always are inclined with a good will to

40. It makes little sense for Pope Martin V to have written letters about the same matter exactly one year apart. More likely this letter was written in 1428, like the letters in the following chapter, and the date here is a scribal error.

41. Johann of Fleckenstein, bishop of Basel (r. 1423–1436); Otto III of Hachberg, bishop of Constance (r. 1410–1434); Wilhelm II of Diest, bishop of Strasbourg (r. 1393–1439).

> reform all religious persons. Nevertheless, we should now be especially diligent and cautious in reforming the Order of Preachers according to the religious practices laid forth by our dear son, Bartholomew, master general of this order. We know that he is inclined to reform simply for the honour of God and for the growth of his order's religious life. Therefore, we ask you in brotherly love to provide help and counsel, and to stand by this master general, or whomever he has selected to complete the work of the reform and to institute observance of religious life among the friars and sisters of that order. They will encounter the audacious temerity of these persons, especially the friars of the Basel community, their adherents, and the enclave of people who strengthen and manipulate the insolence of their obnoxious disobedience. If you grant your faithful help and support to such a good work, you render a pleasing service to God, which is also especially agreeable to us.
>
> Dated in Rome before the holy apostles and sealed with the piscatory ring on November 13, year 11 [1428].

The same pope also wrote to the margrave of Rötteln, whose land lies nearest to the city of Basel, in approximately these words:

> Dear son, we have been given to understand that the friars of the Dominican order in the city of Basel will neither tolerate nor suffer the introduction of the observance of religious life in their convent by my dear son Bartholomew, master general of that order. When they should have received those who were appointed and sent to reform them in humble and childlike devotion, they drove them out with scorn and insolence and even with weapons, through the help of certain laypeople and nobles. God himself is scorned in such actions, the order is weakened, and we are saddened that the friars, with the support of the laity, have offered such resistance to the master who is their head and superior.
>
> Now we know that this same master is a man of great perfection and spirituality, of burning sincerity and great wisdom. From his ordinances, which God reveals to him, we expect nothing but good, salvific fruit. Therefore, we petition your nobility and request that you support this master general, or those he has appointed to begin the religious observance in the convents of friars and sisters of his order, with help and counsel for our sake, for the honour of the papal See, and for love of the religious life. We also ask that you admonish the laypeople who help the friars and sisters in their insolent resistance, and if it is necessary, that you chastise them, so that they desist from this dishonourable and unkind partnership, through which they anger God, the Christian church, and the order. In these matters, we desire

that your devotion, our will, and our wishes be enough for you. In this you do God a service and a favour for us, and you yield profit and salvation for the order and happy blessedness for yourself.

5.23 *How after great worrisome labour the observance of religious life was begun in Basel* [fol. 170r]

After much worry, expense, and labour had been put into this matter – more than I can say – and many messengers had been to Rome and other places, the blessed master general remained firm in his wish to have this community reformed, despite the requests of the citizens of Basel and other people that he leave it unreformed for the sake of peace. Indeed, such great, severe trouble had gone into it and so much greater misery was expected, that the master answered, "I will die for it, or I will have religious life and observance of the order in this friary." Since the master general did not dare stay in Basel, he directed the affair from Nuremberg, Bern, or wherever else he was. He relieved the prior and sent him to the community of Hagenau, where he was from, and ordered the remaining friars to uphold the Observance. The friars demonstrated their unwillingness to obey, so the master general placed them under interdict. They appealed, challenging the authority of the master.

Yet after many messages from the city of Basel, some good, noble citizens of the Basel city council rode with more than thirty horses to Bern, where the master general was at the time. After much discussion, it was decided that the holy Observance should be introduced in Basel. Four friars also came, who, it is said, had mounted particular resistance against the work of the Observance. These four friars, one of whom had been prior in Basel and another a master of holy Scripture, came before the master general. They asked him to forgive their disobedience and lift the interdict. The blessed master punished the ferocious hardness of their hearts and the audacity of their disobedient resistance, since they had caused such great worry and vexing scandal and had greatly saddened and angered him and God. He said such things to them before all who were present, and the four brothers prostrated themselves before the master general. He decided to release them from the interdict, but as he began to speak the absolution formula, he remembered what he had suffered in this affair, and his heart was so moved that he was struck by a fit of tears and could not say a word. Another father had to absolve the friars in his place.

After all these things, they again sent for fathers and friars from Nuremberg to start the Observance in Basel. They taught the friars there the religious life of the order and presented a good example of virtuous living. For this holy work, thirteen very honourable men were chosen in honour of the Lord Jesus Christ and his holy apostles. Their names are recorded here:

The first, Friar Johannes Nider, master of holy Scripture, former prior of the convent in Nuremberg. He became the first prior of the Observance in Basel. The second, Nicolaus Cipriani, first subprior there and afterwards prior in Colmar. The third friar, Ulrich Sellatoris, afterwards prior in Pforzheim. The fourth friar, Bitzmann, afterwards prior in Colmar. The fifth friar, Conrad Herbst, later a master of holy Scripture.[42] The sixth friar, Johannes Bollander, the first bursar of the Observance in Basel. The seventh friar, Gerhard Hel, afterwards confessor at St Mary Magdalene in Basel.[43] The eighth friar, Marcus of Athis. The ninth friar, Paul of Franckenstein. The tenth friar, Dietrich Snicke of Lübeck. The eleventh friar, Johannes Hünler. The twelfth friar, Peter of Erdfort. The thirteenth, Diebold Husen.

See how the religious life of this observance was begun with such upstanding, honourable, proven, religious, good-willed persons.

5.24 *How the community of friars in Basel grew in religiosity* [fol. 171v]

The religious life of the Observance was initiated through the help of divine grace and these aforesaid spiritual fathers on the eve of the Feast of Saints Philip and Jacob in May [30 April] in the year recorded above [1429]. The higher authorities then ordered that all the friars in the Basel community should remain there and that the friars of the Observance should kindly indulge them and allow them to eat meat from time to time, to lie on beds, and such things. But as soon as they noted the customs of the order, placed their property in common ownership, and had remained long enough to see that it was not appropriate for them to do inappropriate things, one after the other left for convents that were not reformed. A very few remained in the Observance there until their deaths. Among those was, in particular, the honourable father and master Heinrich of Rheinfelden,[44] the honourable father Nicolaus of Landau, who was an inquisitor,[45] and the honourable father Johannes Rössner,[46] who served for many years in the Observance as subprior and lector, among many others.

There would be much to say about the virtuous, religious lives of these aforesaid friars and also of the friars who came in the beginning, but I am leaving it all out. The devout father Johannes of Mainz wrote a lovely book in Latin about how this community of Dominican friars in Basel was reformed and on the blessed and devout lives of certain friars.[47]

42. See *DDS*, 272.
43. See *DDS*, 272–273; *SOPMA*, 1: 372–373.
44. See *DDS*, 269–271.
45. See *DDS*, 315.
46. As Johannes Bötschner in *DDS*, 256.
47. See note in **4.23**.

5.25 *How the Dominican friary in Pforzheim was reformed and restored to the religious life of the Observance* [fol. 172r]

In 1429, that is, in the year that the Basel friary was reformed in May, the friary in Pforzheim was reformed in the fall. In that community also, some people committed tremendous, irreligious, incorrigible acts. Even though there was no religious life as would have been proper, there were nevertheless certain proven friars who were greatly displeased by such improper, irreligious behaviour and who wished their community to be reformed to the same religious life as the friary in Basel. Among them was, in particular, Friar Friedrich Winter, at the time prior of the community in Pforzheim, and Friar Johannes Wurmberger, who afterwards served for many years as prior of this friary's Observance. These two good-willed fathers petitioned their superiors, together with those who would help them introduce the religious life of the Observance to Pforzheim. The noble, distinguished Lord Bernhard, margrave of Niederbaden, found out about this and committed his whole energy and earnest zeal with full authority as lord of the land and the city, and petitioned the superiors that the Dominican friary in his city, Pforzheim, be fully reformed to a religious life in observance of the order. He was granted this immediately, and religious, devout friars of the Observance were sent there, who laudably reformed this friary. The first prior of this Observance was Friar Ulrich Sellatoris. Since the friary was practically falling down, they rebuilt it quite respectably and well, and profitably restored the cloister both spiritually and materially. Lord Jesus Christ, to you be the honour, praise, and thanks for this and for all good. Amen.

5.26 *How the Dominican convent of Liebenau was brought to the religious life of the Observance and enclosure* [fol. 173r]

There is an honourable Dominican women's convent named Liebenau near the distinguished city of Worms. It was founded long, long ago by an illustrious, noble prince, the count palatine, and from almost the very beginning of its institution, this convent has housed high-born women and sisters, such as the daughters of great princes, duchesses, and countesses.[48]

In the time when this holy affair was being conducted, that is, the reformation of the friary in Basel, there was a very good-willed father named Friar Peter

48. First among these was Irmgard of Oettingen (1310–1389), who entered Liebenau as the widow of Adolf of the Palatinate (1300–1327). See Christine Kleinjung, "Geistliche Töchter – abgeschoben oder unterstützt? Überlegungen zum Verhältnis hochadliger Nonnen zu ihren Familien im 13. und 14. Jahrhundert," in *Fürstin und Fürst: Familienbeziehungen und Handlungsmöglichkeiten von hochadligen Frauen im Mittelalter*, ed. Jörg Rogge (Ostfildern Verlag, 2004), 21–44, at 35–37.

of Gengenbach.[49] He was also quite diligent and when a convent of brothers or sisters was to be reformed, he helped with special faithfulness. For this reason, he was usually called upon when one wished to reform, and sometimes princes and lords both secular and religious – yea, even the papal court – appointed him to carry out important tasks in such matters, which he accomplished well and wisely. So the master general and the provincial made this father Peter their vicar over several convents because of these things and also because of his honesty. He was well-regarded and well-liked by many religious and secular people, noble and non-noble. He was held in especially high favour and love by the noble, illustrious prince, Duke Louis, the count palatine,[50] who did not withhold his intimacy.

Now this prince often heard Father Peter praise the blessed, pure, religious life of the dear sisters of Schönensteinbach and of other sisters and convents that were reformed by Steinbach, and how they upheld their order so laudably, and how the cities and lands in which such convents lay were that much happier and more blessed. This aforesaid prince heard such things and more, and gained a burning zeal and special desire that the worthy convent of Liebenau, which had been founded by his ancestors and where he also had many friends, be reformed just as Schönensteinbach had been, where the order and the religious life of the Observance were maintained. And so he petitioned with prayers and letters that this convent be reformed to the Observance. The superiors of the Dominican order granted this to the noble prince and, through the said Father Peter of Gengenbach, he obtained religious, experienced sisters from Unterlinden in Colmar, enough to reform such a praiseworthy convent. This convent of Liebenau was reformed in 1425 during Advent, which makes it one of the first reformed convents.[51]

But, just as it is written in Ecclesiasticus that the plane tree by the brook in the streets grows high[52] and brings fruit, those under the linden trees [Unterlinden] sent a little branch that had grown from the lovely stony brook [Schönensteinbach] and had been prioress there and then afterwards prioress in Unterlinden. Her name was Sister Anna Munch and she became the first prioress of this

49. See Volker Honemann, "Peter von Gengenbach OP," *VL*^{2} 7: 434–435.

50. Louis (Ludwig) III, count palatine of the Rhine (r. 1410–1436), was broadly committed to religious reform and Liebenau, although an important site of familial tradition, was only one of the numerous convents across several orders that Louis had reformed. See Bernhard Neidiger, "Standesgemäßes Leben oder frommes Gebet? Die Haltung der weltlichen Gewalt zur Reform von Frauenklöstern im 15. Jahrhundert," *Rottenburger Jahrbuch für Kirchengeschichte* 22 (2003): 201–220, at 211–215.

51. This sentence is inserted as a marginal annotation in MS 2934.

52. Ecclesiasticus 24:19.

Observance. She made the convent of Liebenau grow so great and rise so high that the duke himself placed his daughter and his sister there.[53] Duke Otto and the lord of Württemberg, as well as many other noble lords, also enclosed their children there to serve the heavenly king. Many of the old sisters left the convent, among whom were many freeborn women and countesses, who did not all want to stay nor surrender to the Observance. Nevertheless, within a few short years, a great number of sisters were there, who lived the religious life by observing the holy Dominican order so that their praise rang and resounded throughout the land. For this be praise and honour, grace and thanks, to you, oh true, superior, eternal holy Trinity, God Father, Son, and Holy Spirit. Amen.

This convent was reformed almost four years before the friary in Basel.

5.27 *How Himmelkron, the convent of Dominican sisters in Hochheim near Worms, was brought to the holy Observance* [fol. 174r]

Another worthy, great convent, also of the Dominican order, lies not far from the said convent of Liebenau in the village called Hochheim. This convent is named for Our Dear Lady of the Heavenly Crown [Himmelkron]. In Latin, it is called *Celi Corona*. Since this convent also lies in the land of the count palatine, the previously mentioned prince Duke Louis of Bavaria,[54] he spoke for it and held it under his protection, just as he did Liebenau. This prince had remarked the blessed life begun in Liebenau, and he began to desire earnestly that this worthy convent of Himmelkron also be reformed and resemble the praiseworthy convent of Liebenau in its religious life. Through Father Peter of Gengenbach, he requested and petitioned the blessed father Master General Bartholomew Texery to reform this convent as well to the Observance and the religious life for the honour of God and the great good that would come of it. When the blessed master general heard the great sincerity of the illustrious prince on account of the Hochheim convent called Himmelkron, he put his energy into reforming it. For this reason, he wrote earnestly to the sisters of Steinbach and several other reformed convents to select well-suited sisters and send them to reform this convent of Himmelkron well and in a religious manner to the Observance. Since the

53. Louis III placed his daughter, Margareta of the Palatinate (d. 1466), in Liebenau. His brother, Otto I of the Palatinate-Mosbach, placed two daughters in Liebenau, Barbara (1444–1486) and Dorothea of the Palatinate-Mosbach (1439–1482). Count Ulrich V of Württemberg-Stuttgart (r. 1433/41–1480) placed his daughter Margareta of Württemberg (d. 1479) there. See Gundolf Gieraths, *Die Dominikaner in Worms* (Worms, 1964), 75.

54. Louis was a scion of the Bavarian Wittelsbach family, but did not rule over any part of the territory of Bavaria.

dear father Friar Peter of Gengenbach, who was organizing the affair, was much in communication with the sisters of the Observance and had full authority from the master general to take sisters from certain reformed convents, this Friar Peter requested and received from St Mary Magdalene in Basel six dear sisters, three of whom were from Steinbach. And so they left Basel and were led to Schönensteinbach, where they stayed in the convent for two days. One more sister from Steinbach joined them, so that they were seven. From Steinbach they were led to Colmar and lodged in the convent of Unterlinden where they stayed for several days. From this convent, two sisters joined them. The first was named Dorothea Beheim, first chantress, a woman of such great devotion for the holy sacrament that she never missed receiving it. Often, from overflowing devotion and sweet tears she could hardly sing. She had such a good voice that it could hardly be matched and she fulfilled her office very devoutly. The other was called Sister Anna of Hornberg, a very devout, contemplative person and a strict monitor. Thus there were nine who were led from Unterlinden to Strasbourg. These two sisters were led there from the convent of Unterlinden. The others, who had come from St Mary Magdalene, had earlier been sent from Unterlinden to that convent to reform it, except for Sister Afra and Sister Gertrud of Laufenberg. And so the convent of Himmelkron is also a transplant from the spiritual garden under the lovely linden trees [Unterlinden].[55]

These sisters were led from Unterlinden to Strasbourg, where they lodged for a short time in a convent of our order that was not yet reformed, called St Nicholas-in-Undis. This convent was also reformed afterwards. From there they were led from Strasbourg to the convent of Himmelkron and were received well by many sisters there, since before the Observance they were good children and at the time had a good reputation according to their station. When the holy Observance was introduced, almost all of the old sisters stayed, and few left for convents that did not keep the Observance. They grew so much that there were afterwards almost seventy sisters where before there had hardly been thirty, even though two other convents have since been reformed by them. This Observance in Himmelkron was begun in 1429.

The names of the seven sisters[56] who began this religious life are: Sister Margretha Zorn, first prioress; Sister Truta of Polwig, bursar; Sister Mechthildis of

55. The account of the intervening stay at Unterlinden in Colmar is added on a slip of paper that is sewn onto folio 175. The main text runs "from Steinbach they were led to Strasbourg, where they lodged for a short time..."

56. The two sisters from Unterlinden, Dorothea Beheim and Anna of Hornberg, are not included here. Hence the reduction to seven.

Polwig; Sister Afra. These four sisters were previously in the convent of Schönensteinbach, but the three following were from St Mary Magdalene in Basel: Sister Anna Reinhold, first subprioress; Sister Margretha Regenstein, afterwards subprioress for a long time; Sister Gertrud of Laufenberg, a lay sister. For this and for all good may God the Lord be praised and honoured forever. Amen.

5.28 *How the Dominican convent of St Nicholas-in-Undis in Strasbourg was reformed and how it grew* [fol. 175v]

In 1431, the convent of our dear sisters in Strasbourg, St Nicholas-in-Undis in the Krutenau neighbourhood, was reformed to the holy Observance. This convent of St Nicholas is a worthy old convent of the Dominican order. In the old early days, not long after the foundation of the Dominican order and of this convent, there were also blessed, dear sisters there. But I do not wish to write about how this convent was first founded and how God spared it through his grace and eternal goodness in times of worrisome turbulence and great war before it was enclosed and encircled by the protection of Strasbourg's city wall, which now contains it, and about other matters that God the Lord worked there – only about how in our times it was reformed and restored to its former religious life by the grace of God. Nevertheless, so that you know during what time and by which pope this convent was incorporated, counted, and entrusted to the order, the following should briefly be noted.

Some years after the foundation of the convent that was named for Our Dear Lady's Meadow (afterwards for St Matthew and now for St Nicholas), Pope Innocent IV occupied the Roman See.[57] On behalf of this worthy convent, his confirmation was requested. He took counsel with his honourable regiment of cardinals and they gave their consent and will, signing the pope's bull. The sisters still have this bull and the papal letters in this convent. This confirmation took place in 1245, in the third year of his papacy. That same year, he incorporated the convent into the Dominican order for the first time. Over three years later, he incorporated it a second time. In these days, when the worthy holy father Saint Peter of Verona[58] still lived (who much later was martyred), there lived also the fourth master general, named Johannes, who had been a bishop.[59] From this, we

57. Innocent IV (r. 1243–1254).

58. Peter of Verona (1206–1252) was one of the Dominican order's early saints.

59. Johannes of Wildeshausen (master general, 1241–1252) served as bishop of Bosnia prior to this election. See Mortier, *Histoire des maîtres généraux,* 1: 295–296; Nedim Rabić, "Im toten Winkel der Geschichte: Johannes von Wildeshausen als Bischof von Bosnien 1233/34–1237," in *Die deutschen Dominikaner und Dominikanerinnen im Mittelalter,* ed. Sabine von Heusinger et al. (Berlin, 2016), 53–69.

can grasp the honourable age of this praiseworthy convent. Concerning the devout life of the first early sisters of this convent, there would surely be something to say, but since I have set out only to write about how the religious life of the early Observance in these convents was renewed, reformed, and restored again, I leave it out.

5.29 *How certain sisters of the convent of St Nicholas themselves petitioned with diligent sincerity that they be reformed* [fol. 176v]

The worthy convent of St Nicholas-in-Undis in Strasbourg has always broadly had a good reputation, an honourable life, and spiritual discipline. There has always been a respectable number of good, devout sisters, so that among the seven Dominican convents that are in Strasbourg, this convent has usually always had praise and glory above all the others because of their circumspection and their honourable behaviour. But since the enemy of the human race always strives to sow thorns among the wheat, it so happened that some young people entered the convent who did not want to pay heed to religious practice any more. They began to behave wildly and obstinately, and were quite unruly. The old sisters were worried that these wild, undisciplined, and irreligious sisters would incite a harmful, evil catastrophe that would cause the convent to lose its reputation.

At the time, there was a very blessed, dear prioress in the convent, who also had many good-hearted, devout, dear sisters with her who stood by her with help and counsel, in word and deed, in all good, divine things. This prioress was named Sister Agnes Vigin. Together with her dear sisters, she not only was serious and diligent in maintaining the convent's initial good name and reputation. She also was very intent and concerned to reform the convent fully to the holy Observance of the order and restore enclosure as it was kept in the convent of Schönensteinbach and the other reformed convents. Some of her superiors were not disposed to this, and when she asked for help and counsel in the matter, they gave her neither help nor counsel. So she and her sisters laid the divine, good matter before the honourable father Friar Peter of Gengenbach, who helped and counselled them so much that the honourable father Nicolaus Notel, who was provincial of Teutonia at the time, gave his permission and blessing and entrusted the affair to him. He made Friar Peter his vicar over the convent and gave him complete and full authority to reform the convent completely, as he earlier had laudably reformed several other convents to the holy Observance.

And so this father Peter of Gengenbach and with him the dear mother prioress, Sister Agnes Vigin, and many of the sisters of that convent went to work to plan how their convent could also come to the holy Observance. For help and counsel, they called upon both religious and secular people and their good friends, who were very powerful in the council, to help them in this holy matter. Some of the sisters said that if the convent were not enclosed and reformed, they would leave for other convents where the order was fully upheld. They had seen the gracious lifestyle and heard many good exhortations from the dear sisters of Schönensteinbach, the Basel Magdalenes, and Unterlinden, who had left the land to reform the two convents of Himmelkron and Liebenau after lodging as guests with the sisters of St Nicholas in Strasbourg. They had been greatly enflamed in love and desire for the holy Observance by the devout behaviour and religious life they saw in these sisters. The prioress and the good-willed sisters had diligently learned from them the way and the life of the Observance. From this they had gained such a great desire that they would have liked to keep these sisters in their convent or to travel with them. At that time it could not be, but their friends noticed that they persisted for a long time in this desire and no one could dissuade them from it; rather, their desire and love became ever greater. They did so much in this regard that the entire council of the honourable city of Strasbourg gave its will and blessing for it.

5.30 *Who the sisters are and from which convents they came to begin this holy work of Observance* [fol. 178r]

A great deal of effort went into the matter, and the religious and secular authorities gave their blessing and permission for it, except for certain sisters of the convent and their adherents, whom they had drawn to them through their audacity. Now the vicar wanted to reform this convent with sisters of the Observance, as he had done elsewhere and as his superiors had charged him to do with the city council's blessing. He took eight sisters from Unterlinden and four from St Mary Magdalene in Basel and brought them to the convent. There was a great crowd of their friends and relatives who wished to see them, since seven of these sisters had been born in the city of Strasbourg. Several had fathers and mothers still living there and other close friends and family, many of whom were quite distinguished citizens. Nevertheless, the sisters were so cautious that none of them was ever seen by her friends, even though they pleaded with them greatly or threatened them. The dear, blessed sisters were led into the convent in the year we recorded above, 1431, on the day after the Feast of St Thomas Aquinas, our holy teacher [8 March]. The dear mother prioress, Sister Agnes Vigin, and the good-willed sisters received them well.

These are the names of the sisters who reformed the convent: Sister Katharina Meyer, who at the time had been subprioress in Unterlinden. She became the first prioress of this Observance. Sister Verena Pfrunder from St Mary Magdalene in Basel, first subprioress of this convent; Sister Verena Riff, who as a child of four years had been raised in the religious discipline of the order and the Observance; Sister Agnes Ross,[60] chantress, a talented person; Sister Anna Ymeler, a kind sister and a person without rancour; Sister Agnes Kibiss; Sister Margred of Strasbourg; Sister Margretha Christl; Sister Gertrud Kranich. These two came from St Mary Magdalene in Basel, but they had entered the order in Unterlinden and had been sent from there to St Mary Magdalene in Basel to begin and plant the common life. Sister Elisabeth of Sesseltzheim, a lay sister. Sister Anna of Mumpelgart, who had been a secular servant and was invested as a lay sister.[61]

We may learn from this how necessary it is, when one should or must begin to reform a convent to the holy Observance, to have responsible, upright, proven, and experienced persons chosen for such a notable, great task. They must furthermore be prudent and patient, suffer love and pain for God, yea, and have such love for God's honour and the religious life that they would rather die than deviate from honour and the will of God.

5.31 *The great trouble, worry, and fear that befell this reform and how the good-willed sisters were so sorely tried by the unwilling* [fol. 179r]

The unwilling, recalcitrant sisters saw that it had gone too far and that they had not managed to hinder the Observance and enclosure of the convent through their stubborn defiance. Instead, they saw that the holy affair proceeded and they were mastered. They became very angry at this and called upon their friends, who moved against the good-willed sisters and especially against the vicar in great agitation. These friends fell upon him and treated him shamefully with great ferocity and evil slander. It went so far that they threatened to kill him and, in the great uproar, pulled their knives and weapons on him. He only barely escaped being killed on the spot. Since the disturbance was so violent and worrisome, the friends of the good-willed sisters withdrew their help and aid. Yes, even the entire city council, which had granted its blessing and will to the reform of the convent, also retreated because of the great turbulence and rage of the unwilling sisters' friends. Among the powerful, only one remained firm and steadfast – the mayor, by the name of Lord Johannes Stacheler. Even if he had not been alone, the reform could not have been brought about by human hands.

Through this great suffering and the difficult, troubling partisanship of the secular laypeople (some members of both parties were powerful in the council),

60. The processional manuscript Karlsruhe, Badische Landesbibliothek, St Peter perg. 109 (fol. 172v) preserves a scribal colophon in the form of a poem requesting God's blessing for Agnes Ross, who names herself as the copyist and dates her work to 1439.

61. If indeed there were eight sisters transferred from Unterlinden, we are missing one name here.

the good children, who in obedience to their superiors had been led into this convent from Unterlinden and St Mary Magdalene, were in great suffering. They thought that they would have to leave again, but when the almighty God had tested them and the other good-willed sisters with this suffering, it was determined that the Observance would be upheld there. When the unwilling sisters realized that they could not prevent the holy Observance with their resistance, they still did not desist and sought another way. They decided to stay in the convent but refused to surrender their property to the community, or to behave themselves according to the order's law, or even to allow the others to follow the customs of the order and the Observance. They audaciously set about resisting this good beginning in this way. The suffering and worry that arose in the convent and which had earlier reigned among the secular people cannot easily be described.

The audacious resisters saw that they still could not win out against the good-willed children of our Lord in this way, for the latter were too experienced, determined, patient, and prudent. They still could find no peace and tried yet another awful thing, with which they believed they could defeat the good work. They offered a compromise: if they were allowed to take everything from the convent that they felt belonged to them, they would leave for other convents. The good-willed children, the sisters of the Observance, accepted this offer simply and innocently, since they understood it at face value. They kindly promised them that, since they did not want to give themselves to the holy Observance of the order nor even stay, they would not keep their possessions from them. Whatever belonged to them, they would gladly let them take, as long as they would no longer hinder the good work with their obstreperous lifestyle.

There were eight sisters who wanted to leave the convent. They were given everything that belonged to them. Then they demanded everything that they had brought into the convent. They demanded that the convent repay them for the meal they had enjoyed with their friends as celebration on the day when they laid on the habit of the order, and yet more – even the rooms and cells that they had inherited from other women in the community (such practices unfortunately are a worrisome, evil habit in many convents). Because of their perversity, the convent had to pay them for all of this in cash. And yet more: they so exaggerated the good they believed they had done for the convent, in teaching children and other such things, that they wanted to be paid back wages. This was done. They withdrew everything so exactingly from the convent that some boxes and chests broke from age in the process before they were willing to cede them to the convent. Whatever they could not carry away, such as the closets and such things, was paid them. The convent had to sell its own property for them, in order to pay back what the sisters had brought in over all those years in the convent, and some of them had been there for more than twenty years. And so, these eight sisters were paid more than 1,600 florins in gold, money, and interest.

From this, the convent descended into great poverty and many said that it would be impossible for the common life and the Observance to stand. The sisters would have to separate. This had been wrought by those poor, miserable, unwilling sisters with the idea that, since they had not been able to hinder nor defeat the Observance with their resistance, they would demand so much that the convent could not pay it and the community would, in the end, have to dissolve. But God the Lord had chosen the site of this blessed convent as a place where good persons should serve Him.

5.32 *How the convent of St Nicholas-in-Undis grew so greatly and progressed in spiritual and temporal affairs* [fol. 180v]

Once these disruptive people had left the convent, there was peace, but the dear children had to suffer great poverty and lack. In other things, as well, they had to suffer so much at the beginning that it could not all be described briefly. But I have written a little, so that you may understand the great labour that goes into reforming convents and so that no one will be frightened off or become timid, if similar things happen to you during such a process. Instead, you should have great, good faith in God that if you seek his honour, God will help you in the things that belong to his praise and the salvation of souls.

After this, the dear sisters attained peace to serve God according to the law of our holy order. But since the cloister was not built according to necessity and the propriety of the Observance, the sisters built up the cloister quite laudably: a lovely refectory, which is gracious and large; a new chapterhouse; a delightful infirmary, and other office houses. The dear sisters put great labour into this building project, breaking down the old construction with their own hands and carrying the bricks for the wall themselves while the workers were eating outside. After compline, when the workers left, the sisters readied the stones and bricks near the scaffolding. The prioress herself and other dear mothers, who were more than seventy years old, helped do this work. Whatever labour the sisters could perform which would help the workers and reduce their costs, they did. This project cost one thousand florins, which honest people lovingly donated for this purpose.

And so this convent grew considerably in blessed persons and in their need for temporal goods. Counting only the persons of the order, there were fifty sisters in this convent serving God with a religious life and good practices in strict enclosure. They even abolished the custom practised not so unusually by many other convents of pushing a child through the wheel or turn so that relatives inside might see it. Their custom is also not to accept any child into the order lest regret follow with age. The great disruption and impropriety that come with youth have often resulted from this but are hereby avoided. The sisters are also seldom found sleeping all together for more than one or two hours at night. Instead, some of the sisters hold vigil and perform their prayers and good exercises late into the night before laying themselves down to rest. Similarly, some sisters get up so early before Matins that they go to their devotions as the others lay down to sleep. The same then happens again after Matins. In other good, spiritual matters, as well, these dear sisters behave laudably for the love of our dear Lord.

5.33 *Of the virtuous life of Sister Katharina Meyer, first prioress of the Observance in St Nicholas-in-Undis* [fol. 181v]

Exceptionally blessed, dear sisters have departed this world since the convent was reformed to the religious life. There would be much good, edifying material and many praiseworthy examples to write about their lives, but I leave these out for the sake of brevity. Nevertheless, I should justly commemorate the two mothers of this spiritual beginning with a brief tale for our edification.

The first was named Sister Katharina Meyer. This dear mother was the first prioress and mother of the Observance of the convent of St Nicholas in Strasbourg. She was born in Strasbourg and was an honourable, devout maiden. She led a religious life in the world with her mother, going to church, hearing sermons, and receiving the holy sacrament often. Now, she was also a very lovely maid, with a beautiful face and a straight body. She noted the danger and faithlessness of this troublesome, false world, so when she heard that sisters from Steinbach had reformed the convent of Unterlinden and brought it to the religious life, she petitioned for a long time to be received into the order in Unterlinden. She was given the habit, but since the religious life had only just begun, she was burdened not only with teaching, but also with helping in other labour, such as washing, fetching water, carrying wood, and such things. In all this, she remained humble, willing, and diligent.

With particular excellence, she practised the virtue of silence, which protects devotion and spirituality. She kept her silence so diligently and spoke so seldom that some sisters, who came into the convent after her, thought she was mute. She also pursued fasting, vigils, prayer, and all the religious practices of the order so steadfastly and behaved so well, that soon after her profession of obedience, she was made novice mistress and then subprioress.

After she had led a virtuous life in the convent of Unterlinden for a long time, the convent of St Nicholas in Strasbourg was to be reformed. Because of her proven steadfastness, this Sister Katharina was chosen to be its foundation and head. She was given to the other sisters as their mother and prioress and began the religious life in this convent well and in an orderly way with the sisters who had been sent with her. As strenuous as the initial distress was, she was quite hard on herself and those who had come with her in fasting, vigils, work, and such. She was the one who carried the first and heaviest burden of labour on the long summer days. But what this dear mother suffered in the beginning and also afterwards cannot be told in brief words. She was a long-suffering soul. Whatever happened to her or was given to her, she seldom complained to anyone but God alone. She had neither comfort nor help nor support from anyone.

Once she had borne the care of the prioress's office for six years, she was unburdened of it and practised such humility that she often served for a week in the kitchen in the place of a serving maid, if the convent was short on maids. She carried the holy water for "Asperges" and sang the "Dignare" just like the least novice.[62] When God the Lord wished to reward her toil and take her from this world, he sent her an illness such that she lay swollen for eleven weeks in great pain. She was so patient that the sisters thought it impossible that human frailty could exercise such patience. She departed this world, as we hope, blessedly.

5.34 *Of the gracious sister named Sister Agnes Vigin, prioress of the old sisters, and of her good youth* [fol. 183r]

It might be better for me to pass over in silence rather than to say so little and render such an incomplete account of the manifold graces and virtues and of the praiseworthy, devout, blessed life of the honourable mother, Sister Agnes Vigin, the former prioress, whose devotion, diligence, and labour led the convent of St Nicholas to be reformed to the religious life. Yet if we hear a little of the virtues of her good, blessed life, we may better praise God in his gifts, which he sends, and we may also take a good model from her virtues.

From childhood on, this blessed sister Agnes Vigin had a pure, innocent life. It could not be demonstrated that she ever in her entire life angered God with a mortal sin. While she was still a child in the world with her mother – who was a special friend of God and raised her very protectively, sheltering her from worldly and sinful matters and teaching her prayer and devotion – when her dear mother

62. On novices singing the chant "Dignare," see Johannes Meyer, *Das Amptbuch*, ed. Sarah Glenn DeMaris (Rome, 2015), 460.

saw that this dear child so constantly turned to God, she gave her a private chamber, even though she was only twelve years old, where she could perform her prayers and devotions day and night. We also read such things of the dear, holy woman Judith. When this wise mother noticed how very God-fearing her daughter became and how she progressed in graces and virtues, she considered how to promote her daughter growing from grace to grace, from virtue to virtue, to perfection. She knew a blessed, devout priest and brought her daughter to him to give her instruction in a good and blessed life. When this good priest interrogated this maiden's intentions as thoroughly as he could, and her whole situation, behaviour, and practices, he saw what was appropriate for her. He gave this maiden a religious rule and form of life according to which she could keep herself in God: how long she should sleep at night, when to rise for God's praise, what she should pray or contemplate, how to orient all her comings and goings well and in an orderly way in God, and to think purely of God in all affairs. The good priest told this little virgin these and other things, which she inscribed in the ground of her heart so that she would never forget her rule until her death. She lived with extraordinary diligence according to this holy teaching, and led a blessed and devout religious life with a secular appearance while staying with her dear, devout mother until she was thirty years old. She kept her virginal purity for God the Lord with a detached and serious life.

5.35 *How this Sister Agnes Vigin came into the Dominican order in the convent of St Nicholas and afterwards became prioress in the same convent before it was reformed* [fol. 184r]

After this, the dear virgin was driven by God to enter the order in the convent of St Nicholas in the city of Strasbourg. Her mother came with her but remained in secular garb. The daughter, however, became a veiled choir sister and if she had led a devout, blessed life before, she behaved in an even more exemplary way thereafter. She was a mirror and role model for the others.

Since they noticed great wisdom and holiness in her gracious person, she was appointed prioress of the convent and a mother to all the sisters. When she realized that she was to be a mirror for the others and carry all of their spiritual and temporal cares, she became very zealous to find a way to bring those who had been entrusted to her to a virtuous life. She modelled this for her sisters very kindly in word and deed, since our dear Lord had endowed her richly, both spiritually and temporally. From her youth, she had diligently exercised herself with devout contemplation of the worthy suffering of our dear Lord and wept for it daily in her devotion. However great her cares in the office of prioress or bursar, as soon as she left her concerns and gave herself to her contemplation in the choir, her tears of devotion appeared immediately, which the sisters thought a great wonder. For this reason, a sister asked her, "Dear prioress, how is it that you can always find devotion amid such great disruption and worry?" The blessed mother answered this sister, "Know, my truly dear sister, that in my youth I was taught, among other things, always to turn immediately inward after I had completed and arranged whatever outward business I had to do. Especially, as soon as I come to my usual place of devotion, I raise my heart and my hands to God and say with devotion, 'Lord, I am here and I desire your grace. If you will grant me any of your kindness, I will receive it. If you give nothing, I will still praise and honour you here.' I have always done this till now, and whenever I surrender myself thus to God, he pours out his grace upon me and gives me so much that I cannot do enough for him and I forget all temporal things."

She also spoke quite passionately, desirously, and lovingly with our dear Lord in her devout prayer, so that the sisters who sometimes noted it in her were drawn to devotion. She liked to speak of God, and also praised how noble and good it is to love God and to fulfil his dearest will. She spoke so lovingly and dearly that she drew the sisters, especially the young ones, greatly to God with her salutary language. She was also very loving and friendly in comforting the sisters in their troubles as a mother. She turned her diligence towards helping them spiritually and temporally and was as concerned for the worries of her neighbour as if they affected her own person. She was very strict on herself and disciplined herself with rods, stinging nettles, and other castigation in honour of the suffering of our dear Lord. Because of her great love, such things were often so delightful and desirable to her that she began to fear that the evil spirit was deceiving her thereby. In the office of prioress, she behaved so that all sisters liked her. They would not have desired the yoke of the common life and Observance, except for their favour and special love for her, since she behaved properly towards all of them in all things.

5.36 *How this good mother in the office of prioress brought the sisters to the point of desiring the Observance through her virtues* [fol. 185r]

Now, this honourable woman and mother was so long in the office of prioress until the convent was fully reformed. She behaved such that everyone in common held her in grace and favour – not only those who were in the convent, but also the secular people outside. No one thought he was being treated fairly unless he dealt with her personally, if he had anything to do with the convent. She was familiar with everyone and treated everyone with the courtesy and honour due his station. She was kind and loving to everyone. When she had to do something because of her office or out of obedience, she did not give priority to devotion, prayer, or contemplation, but did what she was supposed to do without any complaining or disagreeableness. Similarly, she did all her works as if she had nothing else or nothing better to do at that moment. Since she taught the sisters spirituality and virtue, she wanted them to observe common property and the order. Many learned people and other good friends of God had relationships with this prioress and her sisters because of their religious life, even though they did not maintain the Observance. They often complained of how troublesome it was to live with possessions.

After she admonished them a long time, she found that some sisters wished to follow her in all the good religious practices that pertain to the order, even though some other sisters did not want to agree to have the convent reformed to the Observance. During this time, the two convents near Worms were reformed, the ones called Liebenau and Himmelkron. So the good-willed sisters gave up all of their possessions to this devout, blessed prioress and gathered their clothes up and held them in common so that each took from there whatever came to hand. They also began to wear closed-toe shoes and wide veils and other such things that they had seen the foreign sisters do.[63] They observed silence, abstained from meat, fasted, and taught each other like children, who first must learn children's things. From day to day these practices became dearer to them. But since they would have liked to see the complete enclosure of the convent and the other sisters living like them, they were not fully satisfied. Instead, they desired for the convent to be fully reformed and for sisters of the Observance to be sent to them, who could teach them to keep the holy order perfectly and completely according to the order. And so the prioress with her good-willed sisters petitioned for this, until the convent was fully reformed, as was said before.

5.37 *How this good sister led such a virtuous life for more than thirty years in the holy Observance* [fol. 186r]

Once the holy Observance (for which this sister Agnes Vigin was the impetus) had been started in this convent by divine grace, she was relieved of the prioress's office and the offices were occupied by the foreign sisters of the Observance. This dear mother Agnes, the former mother prioress, was assigned in obedience to serve as subbursar. This was a great humiliation, since she had to submit to a lay sister who was first bursar, even though she had ruled the convent so well in spiritual and temporal matters for many years.

After the convent was enclosed and she could no longer go to the speaking window or be seen by people in any other place, her words were still so loving that

63. These foreign sisters are the reforming contingent from St Mary Magdalene and Unterlinden on their way to reform Himmelkron; see **5.27**.

whoever heard her once desired to hear more. Whoever came to the turn[64] thought he wasn't being treated justly if he did not speak with her. She had praise and glory above all other sisters. Nobody ever asked for the prioress or for anyone else if they got her.

When she reached an age where she could no longer bear such great labour and worry, she was released from this task, as loath as they were to do this. Because of her great humility, they made her refectorian and she performed this very diligently by herself for a long time. She arranged the tables, she carried water in the jug, and began right away to do even the smallest things and the work of the young when she was almost eighty years old. She sometimes served the sick. She also excelled in the virtue of diligence in the choir and in praise of God and the Divine Office. She praised our dear Lord so ardently in her singing and reading that one could catch devotion from her. When she was over seventy years old, she had such a good voice and sang so wonderfully that she could be heard over all the other sisters in the community. If you didn't know her, you would not have guessed from her voice that she was over thirty. She always went to choir day and night into her oldest age, often even on a crutch. Especially in her old age when she did not have to worry about temporal affairs any more, she frequently concerned herself with the worthy suffering of Christ in great devotion. In particular, she daily celebrated the twenty-four hours during which, from day to night, the Lord fulfilled his holy suffering for our sake, each with a special exercise. She began with twenty-four Pater Nosters in a cruciform prostration. In each she reminded the Lord of the holy suffering that he underwent in that hour. She did this often with heartfelt tears.

After she had led a devout, Christian life in the world for thirty years, and a quite edifying, strict life for twenty years in the convent before it was reformed, she had a contemplative, religious, blessed life in the holy Observance for more than thirty years before her death, filled with good days and also grace and virtues. She departed from this world, as we fully trust, for eternal peace. For this may the one God be praised, who lives and reigns in three persons eternally. Amen.

5.38 *On the blessed, gracious life of Sister Gertrud of Winterthur, the second prioress of this Observance, and how sometimes frail women surpass strong men in virtue* [fol. 187r]

As the holy pope and great teacher Saint Gregory said, and as Christianity often sings of pure, holy virgins: "Almighty God, you chose the frail stupidity of this world to shame all the disorderly temporal power and might."[65] God often

64. For an explanation of the turn or wheel, see **2.16**.
65. 1 Corinthians 1:27.

makes the feeble female sex surpass strong men in power and strength of virtue.[66] These men prove frail and stupid in devotion, in tender kindness, in mild mercy, and in other virtues such as fasting, vigils, prayers, and the like – even in the divine love, humility, serenity, and patience by which their bodily, temporal strength and power is justly shamed before God and his holy angels and also before all those who are true friends of God in this world.

We find many examples of this among the chosen holy virgins and women of former days, as we read in their holy lives. We see even now in the present age, that the female sex turns more to virtue. This is demonstrated for us by the many women's convents of the holy Observance of the Dominican order, of St Clare's order,[67] and of other orders, who are secured in the strict enclosure of God and live in devout obedience under the protection of silence. They seldom speak with people outside and never without special permission and a chaperone. Inside, they spend their time and maintain their state in silence with holy contemplation and prayers, discipline and prostrations, turning faithfully to God in complete, patient serenity. With the help of God, they conquer themselves, their sin, and all voluptuousness. They give themselves fully and humbly to God. Such things are too strict and too hard for many great, strong men – or so they think. But look, if we men diligently kept in mind how silly women staunchly prevail, we might also do something, so that their virginal frailty would not shame our manly strength before God and the world.

See how all these convents are so full of good children of God, often more than they are able to train well. See how so many women in the world beg and plead with great, heartfelt desire to enter the reformed convents. See that as soon as a convent is reformed to the religious life, it is full of those who come to them from the world or from the open convents, so that one must often turn many away because there is not enough room in the convent. See how one can hardly reform enough convents from the great desire of the female sex for the religious life and the love of God. See one more good example in this convent of St Nicholas, although there are many more that I leave out for the sake of brevity.

This good sister was called Sister Gertrud of Winterthur. From childhood on she led a blessed life, rich in perfection of all the virtues. She was an honest, gifted, steadfast, virtuous, mild, kind person. She was wise, careful, and of such cautious

66. In MS 2934 "of virtue" is added in a marginal notation. The phrase is incorporated directly into the text in Cgm 8081.

67. The Poor Clares were the nuns associated with the Franciscans as Dominican nuns were associated with Dominican friars. For a study of the Observant reform among the Clares, see Bert Roest, *Order and Disorder: The Poor Clares between Foundation and Reform* (Leiden, 2013).

speech that no thoughtless, untrue, or frivolous word was ever heard from her mouth. All sinful words and gossip were far from her. She was given to the other sisters as a mirror and became the second prioress of the Observance in this convent. Great masters, with whom she spoke on behalf of her convent, often said that they had never heard a woman speak better or more prudently and wisely. In her chapter meetings as well, she admonished her sisters with good and devout thoughts. She was humble and diligent in obedience. She had great grace, devotion, and love for the holy worthy sacrament of our Lord's body. Sisters of the Observance have the good custom of receiving the holy sacrament once a week. Sister Gertrud prepared herself every week such that for more than twenty-five years she was never seen standing still and refraining from the holy sacrament, however much worry and work she had, as a prioress must have who is in the office for twenty years. She was so devout that she was often seen in her prayers and her devotions covered in tears, although she was seldom ever seen crying over any temporal loss, suffering, sadness, or difficulty. She had such devotion and inwardness in her contemplation that she often would neither see nor notice great to-dos or commotions around or near her. She also had such a practice in vigils and prostrations that no one in the entire convent has ever done the like. From her youth on, she was careful never to upset anyone and even said to a sister shortly before her death, "I had thought that I would go to my death without ever upsetting anyone, and I trust that with the help of God I would have accomplished this if I had not had to serve out of obedience as prioress." Still she was very mild and kind in her punishments so that no one ever saw her angry. And so after her blessed life she was released from this destructive world in 1456. It is to be believed that she was received by our protector, Christ the Lord, who is blessed eternally. Amen.

5.40[68] *How the Dominican friary in Vienna was reformed and how so many other friaries came to the religious life of the Confirmation* [fol. 191r]

In 1434, the honourable, praiseworthy community of Dominican friars in Vienna was reformed to the holy Observance. This reform occurred under the honourable, blessed father Bartholomew Texery, a teacher of holy Scripture and, at the time, master general of the Dominican order. This useful, good reform was brought about by the esteemed, upright prince, Duke Albert of Austria, who afterwards became Holy Roman emperor.[69] A good, blessed friar of this community,

68. Neither MS 2934 nor Cgm 8081 has a chapter 5.39.

69. Duke Albert (Albrecht) V of Austria from 1404, then king of the Romans (i.e., of Germany) as Albert II (r. 1438–1439).

Friar Jörg Heller, initiated the matter, but the first prior of this religious life was Friar Jörg Falder.[70] The other friars who started this religious life in Vienna came from the communities of Basel and Nuremberg. This religious community flourished so greatly in way of life and in membership that no community in all of Teutonia could match this friary, especially in the number of friars. Sometimes there are up to seventy friars there together at the same time. Some of them are masters of theology, some of them bachelors of holy Scripture, some learned lectors, some masters of the liberal arts, some devout preachers of the divine word, some wise and prudent confessors, some reasonable and good advisors, and all kinds of good, dear, blessed brothers. But it is especially good and just to praise the two laudable, worthy fathers mentioned above, both named Jörg, and they should be raised as an example for us because of their virtuous lives.

The first father, Jörg Falder, was a notable, distinguished man. He was not only first prior of the Observance in Vienna, but also vicar over many friaries in Austria, some of which had been reformed through his labour. The other father, called Jörg Heller, was a gracious, good man. He led a very strict and hard life through vigils, fasting, and beating himself with heavy scourges. He scorned worldly honour. When he was master of the young friars in Basel in the first years of the Observance there, he instructed them with all diligence in virtue and religious practice through his good teaching and blessed life. He worried that he might have to become prior of the community in Vienna. For this reason, he petitioned to be sent to Lombardy, where he lived a blessed life for many years and departed from this world after many virtues.

Many other fathers and masters who worked much good were in this community in Vienna. In particular, Master Leonhard de Valle Brixiensi,[71] who was prior and, for a long time, vicar in Austria. In his time, he reformed many communities in the kingdom and province of Hungary to the religious life from his convent in Vienna. The communities in Hungary, which previously led a poor, miserable life and had almost completely collapsed both spiritually and materially, are now, by the grace of God, spiritually and temporally in good standing.

70. Georg Falder-Pistoris had been active as vicar over St Catherine's in Nuremberg. Some of the sermons and treatises he composed for religious women survive. See Barbara Steinke, *Paradiesgarten oder Gefängnis? Das Nürnberger Katharinenkloster zwischen Klosterreform und Reformation* (Tübingen, 2006), 76–79; *SOPMA*, 2: 29–30; Georg Falder-Pistoris, *Geistliche Belehrung in Dialogform und Passionstraktat für Ordensleute: Edition und Untersuchung*, ed. Petra Hörner (Berlin, 2015).

71. Leonhard Huntpichler (ca. 1405–1478). See *SOPMA*, 3: 78–80; Mortier, *Histoire des maîtres généraux*, 4: 459–480.

The fathers from Vienna, with the help of the fathers from Nuremberg, also reformed many communities in the province of Teutonia and even now send brothers to these communities when it is necessary. The names of these communities are Krems, Bolzano, Retz, Ptuj, and Neustadt. From this we may see how profitable it is when the holy Observance reforms one convent and community to the spiritual life through another. In these years, there was also a new community of our Dominican order founded called Vallis Senarum [Neukloster near Celje], which the fathers of Vienna also supplied with friars.

5.41 *A short commemoration of how the honourable, worthy convent of Tulln was reformed, and by whom* [fol. 192r]

In 1436, the distinguished, honest, beautiful, lovely communities of sisters and friars in Tulln, Austria, were reformed to the religious life. These two communities of brothers and sisters are one foundation, and the sisters manage the material affairs and provide for the friars. The sisters are enclosed in their convent and sing the hours in their choir. The friars are in their convent and celebrate the Divine Office in their choir and church. Yet some friars also hold daily mass in the sisters' church. Their two churches and convents are separated by a lovely churchyard.

Now, I am not going to recount how this honest place in Tulln was reformed and how much labour went into it and how the honourable, illustrious prince, Duke Albert of Austria, the husband of Emperor Sigismund's daughter and afterwards king of the Germans, arranged all of this.[72] I am leaving out how Master Johannes Nider, prior of Basel at the time, had to take up the holy matter and how the vicar of Austria, the honourable father Jörg Falder, did such faithful work in this godly affair. I am passing over much else that happened at the time with regard to these things. But so that some of this might be noted, I will include here a letter that was sent from St Catherine's in Nuremberg to Schönensteinbach, in which one may learn something about this reform.

The first letter was written by Sister Katharina of Mühlheim, who became the first prioress of Tulln, and who also had been sent to Nuremberg from Steinbach to reform.[73] The letter reads thus:

72. Duke Albert V of Austria married Elizabeth of Luxembourg (1409–1442), the daughter of Sigismund of Luxembourg, king of Germany (r. 1411–1437) and Holy Roman emperor (from 1433).

73. This sentence is crossed out in the manuscript. The phrase "a letter" was originally "two letters" and was corrected to the singular. There probably was initially a letter from Katharina of Mühlheim in addition to this anonymous one, but why it was not included in the end is not clear. Cgm 8081 has only one letter with no corrections or annotations.

To the honourable, spiritual mothers, the prioress and the subprioress and to all sisters in Schönensteinbach, in the good faith that I have always kept and will henceforth always keep with all of you, I must keep you informed.[74] Know, dear mother prioress, that we were sorely concerned this Easter when we sent ten of our sisters to Austria to restore and reform a convent of our order. It is located in the city of Tulln and its church is consecrated in honour of the worthy mother of God. It is also a special foundation of the lords of Austria and one hopes that much good will come from it, for Master Hans Nider is one of their reformers along with many other holy and great masters who have been appointed to it. Our honourable father, the vicar and prior of Vienna, Jörg Falder called Pistoris, went down there with the sisters himself to care for and protect them. They wrote back to us a very long letter to say that they arrived in the convent in happiness and health and were honourably received by the sisters there, who number eighteen. They also wrote much good of them and that they are taking instruction well. These are the sisters whom we sent: two from Schönensteinbach, Sister Katharina of Mühlheim and Sister Ursula Wolsack; three we found here,[75] Sister Kunigund Spatzierer, Sister Anna Kölner, and Sister Agnes Babenberger; and five who have joined during our time, Sister Elisabeth Schwert, Sister Katharina Ziner, Sister Elisabeth Steinbach, Sister Kristin Osterich, and Sister K. Rudolf. These last two are lay sisters. You should also know that Sister Katharina of Mühlheim is prioress, Sister Kunigund Spatzierer subprioress, Sister Ursula Wolsack bursar, Sister Anna Kölner first sacristan, and Sister Agnes Babenberger first chantress. The other five sisters serve as turnkeeper, monitor, and in the other offices. They are all, by the grace of God, dear children and we are very unhappy to have lost them, for they all are very talented. I commend them all faithfully to your devout prayers.

Written in Nuremberg in St Catherine's on the Friday after Pentecost [1 June] 1436.

5.42 *How the Penitents in Strasbourg were reformed and how the same sisters left again for Colmar to reform the convent of St Catherine's there* [fol. 193v]

In 1438, the convent of our dear, faithful sisters of St Catherine in Colmar was reformed to the holy religious life. This reform came about thus: The honourable father, Friar Peter of Gengenbach greatly loved helping divine honour

74. In MS 2934, the sentence continues "that God the Lord has ... me in the holy ..." This fragment, which may be from Katharina of Mühlheim's letter, is also crossed out.

75. The sense is that the three following sisters were members of St Catherine's in Nuremberg prior to its reform.

and praise spread far and wide, especially by restoring and reforming to a religious state the convents where the order was not kept and where little religious life was seen. He also sometimes helped reform to holy Observance convents that were not in his order, such as the Franciscan community in Heidelberg[76] and many other convents, as well. He was also asked to enclose and reform the women's convent of Penitents in Strasbourg, even though this convent is not of our order.[77] Nevertheless, some of the women of this convent were willing to assume reform, enclosure, and observance. Once he had the authority and commendation from the superiors who needed to give him permission to reform the convent, he took with him sisters of the Observance from our order, since he probably would not have found in this entire land any women from the Penitents who would have been fit to reform. So he took Observant sisters of our holy Dominican order from the two convents near Worms, Himmelkron and Liebenau, and tried to reform the convent in Strasbourg. Even though he had arranged through the authority of the Roman papal See that this convent would become a Dominican convent, there was such a great resistance and so much trouble from it that the dear Dominican sisters, who had been sent to these women to teach and instruct them in holy religious living, came under much suffering and stress. Father Peter was nearly stabbed to death, since some people did not think a different order should be in that convent. Even after our sisters had been in that convent for a time, there was still great discord between the two differing orders. Those who had been in the convent before did not want to assume the order of the foreign sisters, nor did the foreign sisters want to do anything other than follow the law of the Dominican order. There was so much unrest even among the powerful laity of the city of Strasbourg that the Dominican sisters left the convent.

Since they were homeless, the dear sisters of St Nicholas took these poor, disconsolate sisters into their convent, where they spent some time. When the honourable father Master Johannes Nider heard of this, he was admonished by

76. See Paul L. Nyhus, *The Franciscans in South Germany, 1400–1530: Reform and Revolution* (Philadelphia, 1975).

77. The Penitents of Mary Magdalene were an independent order of women's communities without a male branch. In the thirteenth century they were placed under the care of the Dominican friars and instructed to live according to the Augustinian Rule and the Constitutions of the Dominican convent of San Sisto in Rome. These Constitutions were an early version that was superseded for Dominican nuns but not necessarily for the Penitents. This situation resulted in great confusion about the appropriate constitutions and form of life for the Penitents both during the Middle Ages and in modern scholarship. For the complicated relationship of the Penitents to the Dominican order, see Simon Tugwell, "Were the Magdalen Nuns Really Turned into Dominicans in 1287?," *AFP* 76 (2006): 39–77.

God to reform the convent of St Catherine in Colmar with these sisters, for he had well noted that these blessed sisters were exceedingly well-suited to direct a new Observance. And so, with the blessing, favour, and permission of the honourable lord and father, Julian Cesarini, cardinal of Sant'Angelo in Pescheria, legate to all of Germany for Pope Eugenius[78] – with his full authority and the will of the Dominican superiors and the blessing of the Colmar city council, this father, Master Johannes Nider, took these sisters from Strasbourg to restore and reform the irreligious life of the disordered convent of St Catherine to a good and spiritual state.

5.43 *How the convent of St Catherine in Colmar was reformed with great trouble and suffering* [fol. 195r]

When the worthy Master Johannes Nider had accomplished all of this, the poor sisters of St Catherine's realized that the blessed sisters were being led to Colmar in order to reform their convent and so that they would learn the order's religious life from the foreign women. They became exceedingly disturbed and angered, because they had no desire to pursue any observance. Master Johannes Nider, to whom this reform had been entrusted, and the entire council of Colmar perceived the sisters' great unwillingness to accept the Observance. The women refused to accept it kindly, even though the Colmar city council and the superiors of the order earnestly begged and admonished them.

So Master Johannes Nider took the dear sisters of the Observance, who were to reform the community, and led them into the convent with an honourable company of worthy fathers and brothers. They numbered no more than four sisters, and there were twelve who had been in the convent before. When the audacious, resistant, disobedient sisters saw the sisters of the holy Observance, they behaved in so unmannerly a way and so impudently in word and gesture that it was too much. Two sisters did surrender right away to the Observance, but as for the others – in order to stir up unrest among the laity, some of them created such a ruckus outside that some of the good fathers feared for their lives. Inside the convent they showed such impolite, obnoxious disobedience, with cursing, insults, and evil treatment, that the good children were often worried and in great fear and terror from the threats and gestures of these marvellously resistant women.

78. Pope Eugenius IV (r. 1431–1447) appointed Cardinal Julian Cesarini (r. 1426/1430–1444) not legate to all of Germany, but rather to the Council of Basel. Cesarini's approval of the reform of the convent of St Catherine in Colmar must have been one of his last acts in that capacity, since he left Basel to return to Italy in January 1438. See Gerald Christianson, *Cesarini, the Conciliar Cardinal: The Basel Years, 1431–1438* (Sankt Ottilien, 1979).

A prioress of the Observance was appointed and a bursar and other officers, but still they did not desist from their misbehaviour. No matter how much virtue and friendship the dear, blessed mothers showed them, no matter how patient they were and no matter what kindnesses they did for them, none of it helped. This lasted so long that the superiors heard about their unusual audacity and had all of the guilty sisters incarcerated. After this, they agreed to let the Observance proceed unhindered, but none of them wished to be in the Observance. The majority of these sisters left the convent with all their possessions for a convent called Engelport in the city of Gebweiler.

After this great trouble, the dear mothers found peace. Yet after the former sisters had been in the convent of Engelport for a short time, God seized them and they all died but one. When she saw this, she found God's grace, and it came into her head to earnestly petition for admission to the holy Observance in her first convent. She indeed returned and lived there for many years thereafter for God the Lord and the salvation of her soul.

These are the names of the dear sisters who laudably began this great work of the reform and completed it with great patience and divine love.

5.44 *The names and virtues of these sisters who reformed the convent of St Catherine in Colmar and something of their labours and practices* [fol. 196r]

The first was called Sister Kunigund of Sponheim, first prioress of the Observance in St Catherine's in Colmar. This sister led a strict and harsh life, but nevertheless did not want the other sisters to be too hard on themselves. She was very diligent in all religious practices. She had the custom that at night after she had checked with motherly faithfulness that all sisters were sleeping, she would surrender herself to devotion and prayer, yet following the example of our holy father Saint Dominic, she was not less frequently at Matins because of this. For a long time, she suffered severe illness in great patience. She always had a cheerful face and was satisfied with the food in the refectory. She departed with a blessed, reasonable end in 1441 on the eve of the Feast of St Bernard [19 August].

The second sister was called Adelheid of Aue, the second prioress of this Observance, who served in this office for a good twenty-four years. She was a humble, peaceful, dear mother. I will briefly recount how this worthy convent of St Catherine prospered so greatly and in many ways, spiritually and temporally, in persons and buildings, during this prioress's time. When these four dear sisters were commanded to reform this convent, it was a miserable, loveless, and meagre construction, since at one point it had been burned down with everything in it. They now rebuilt this convent so beautifully, gracefully, comfortingly, and well that is a gracious sight to see. They found barely fourteen sisters there and the majority left, so there were very few of them in the convent at the time. They behaved so well, lovingly, and religiously, despite the great poverty they suffered, that during the time of this prioress more than fifty dear children lived there, always pressed in together, whether there were few or many. There was only one confessor, who provided them every week with confession and the holy sacrament and other such matters. The sisters of this convent had such a good, praiseworthy reputation that both religious and secular people held them in favour and love because of their good, blessed life.

The third sister was called Sister Agnes of Montfort, who came from a very good, noble line and nevertheless was deeply humble and submissive, willingly obedient, and an example of religious life and silence. She had such especially great devotion, love, and affection for the worthy suffering of our dear Lord, that from her true, inner compassion she could not look at an image of the crucified Lord with a cheerful face, but always regarded it with great pain. The last words that she said were to speak the "Confiteor" in full presence of mind. She received the holy sacrament and the final unction, inclined her head to the right side, and passed away softly in the jubilee year 1450.

The fourth sister was called Magdalena Franckengrüner. This sister, in addition to her other work, helped the convent greatly with writing, especially with beautiful choir books for the Divine Office. She afterwards became the first subprioress in St Gertrude's in Cologne when it was reformed in 1466. She served for ten years as subprioress there and then was made prioress in 1476.[79]

These four sisters brought a novice from Strasbourg, who helped them begin the holy Observance. What these sisters suffered in scorn, bitterness, and poverty, trouble and travail, for the sake of their strict observance, may God reward them with himself eternally. Amen.

5.45 *How the convent of sisters of St Michael's Island in Bern was reformed* [fol. 197r]

In 1439 the convent of dear children on St Michael's Island in Bern was reformed and brought to holy religious life. How this Observance was begun, by whom it was brought about, and how it began and progressed is all written in the book of the foundation and restoration of this convent of St Michael's Island, divided into fifty-five beautiful chapters.[80] Still, it should be known that it recov-

79. This sentence is added in a marginal annotation in MS 2934. Cgm 8081 does not contain this information.

80. *The Book of the Foundation and Restoration of the Convent on St Michael's Island*, which Meyer composed while confessor there (1454–1458), survives in Wrocław, University Library, Cod. IV F 194a. See Wolfram Schneider-Lastin, "Die Fortsetzung des Ötenbacher Schwesternbuchs und andere vermißte Texte in Breslau," *ZfdA* 124 (1995): 201–210.

ered from great poverty through good sisters and advantageous new constructions, but also because the religious life of the Observance is so deeply rooted there. The three first sisters were sent from the convent of St Mary Magdalene in Basel to this convent in Bern in order to start the Observance: Sister Elisabeth of Büttikon, the first prioress;[81] Sister Katharina of Eptingen, first subprioress; and Sister Ursula of Büttikon. Very shortly after they arrived, our dear Lord took the prioress and subprioress from this world, after they had suffered much toil and worry from being tested through this Observance and renewed religious life. The young sisters did not trust themselves with the new religious practices and observance, since they recognized that they did not have anyone among themselves fit to be a mother and prioress. Therefore, on the faithful advice of some honourable fathers, they chose the bursar of St Mary Magdalene in Basel, Sister Anna of Sissach,[82] to be their new prioress in Bern. This decision was respected, and with the favour, will, and authority of the superiors, she was led from Basel to Bern and installed as prioress. She was prioress of this convent for almost sixteen years and made the convent grow spiritually and materially in people and property, also in buildings and other things.

Earlier, before the beginning of this Observance, there were sometimes no more than three sisters there, who were not enclosed, did not stay in their cloister but rather in the city, and ran around the countryside. There are now twenty-six sisters, who all remain in observant enclosure, serving God the Lord with faithful devotion. Praise and honour be to you, God and Lord. Amen.

5.46 *How the convent of sisters in Pforzheim was reformed and brought to the religious life* [fol. 198r]

In 1442, the convent of our dear mothers and sisters in Pforzheim was reformed to the religious life of the Observance. The noble, worthy lord margrave of Niederbaden requested this reform from the Dominican superiors. At that time, the honourable, blessed father Master General Bartholomew Texery was still alive, as was the worthy father provincial, Nicolaus Notel. The margrave had noted the great spirituality of the blessed sisters at St Catherine's in Nuremberg. He made a humble plea before the devout father Friar Ulrich Sattler, then prior of the friars in Pforzheim, to lead ten proven and upstanding sisters from Nuremberg into his city to reform and bring a true, perfect, religious, orderly life, since Pforzheim was a worldly, open convent full of wild and wilful women.

81. See *DDS*, 628.

82. Anna of Sissach is the prioress with whom Meyer worked while he was confessor there. See Claudia Engler, "Anna von Sissach OP," *VL*[2] 11: 107–108; Claudia Engler, *Regelbuch und Observanz: Der Codex A 53 der Burgerbibliothek Bern als Reformprogramm des Johannes Meyer für die Berner Dominikanerinnen* (Berlin, 2017), 17–18.

When the dear sisters from Nuremberg arrived, the reasonable mothers well recognized that, as David the prophet says in the first psalm, the tree which is planted near running water brings forth its fruit in due season.[83] So they sent two sprigs from the Lovely Stony Brook, that is, two of the renowned mothers who had come from Steinbach to Nuremberg. One of these sisters became the first prioress and the other was also prioress there right after her.

Here are the names of these ten dear sisters who were the foundation of this holy religious life's ground and beginning: Sister Ursula Tott, first prioress; Sister Elisabeth Karl,[84] the second prioress; Sister Ursula Muntig, first subprioress; Sister Margretha Kapfer; Sister Margretha Scheuer; Sister Anna Pirckheimer; Sister Margretha Volkat; Sister Anna Huber; Sister Barbara Hoffmann; Sister Cristina Hoffmann.

When these blessed sisters came to Pforzheim, they found twenty-six sisters in the convent. Even though they had not asked for the reform of their convent – indeed, it happened against their will – very few of them left for other unreformed convents. And of those who left, some quite quickly returned. However averse they were to the Observance, before the year was out, they became so good-willed and this blessed, loving life became dear to them. They had not expected that the convent could find such religion, as wild and untamed as the sisters had been before. And so the convent grew spiritually and materially, in property and sisters, so much that there are almost fifty dear, blessed children there now. Praise and thanks be to God, from whom all good comes. Amen.

5.47 *Of the devout Sister Ursula Muntig, first subprioress of the convent Pforzheim* [fol. 199r]

The blessed sister Ursula Muntig, first subprioress of the convent Pforzheim, helped to begin this Observance. God the Lord provided her with lofty, supernatural gifts and graces. Her life was so distinguished and so blessed that it would be a great wonder if it could all be written down, but that is impossible. The Lord worked many heavenly things in her, for she was an exceptionally good person. Of all this, I wish to write only a little about her for our edification.

This blessed sister Ursula was born in the city of Augsburg and, from childhood on, had a pure life, a loving, kind heart, and an inspiring manner. God the heavenly father had planted this lovely flower from virtue's branch in his renewed and restored garden of Observance in the holy Dominican order, the convent of St Catherine in Nuremberg, where she led an edifying and perfect life before all

83. Psalm 1:3.
84. Cgm 8081 records her last name, although MS 2934 does not.

her sisters. But since she was a joyful, virtuous flower and such a fruitful branch, she was replanted from St Catherine's in Nuremberg into the convent of Our Dear Lady in Pforzheim, so that she might produce yet more fruit.

The enemy of all good things, the evil spirit, was greatly displeased by her blessed life and wished to hinder her. For this reason, he inflicted unspeakable pain upon her. Sometimes he worried and troubled her visibly, but she was one of the strong women about whom Solomon writes, who strengthen and gird themselves with the grace of divine strength and with virtue.[85] With God's help she overcame him. He sometimes came to her as a frightening animal and acted as though he would drag her from her bed.

She had great devotion and grace for receiving the holy worthy sacrament, which she did often. Usually after she had received it, she was so enraptured that she remained rapt in one place for three or four hours. Eventually, a sister was assigned to lead her into her cell after reception of the holy sacrament, for her cell was not far from the choir. She would then remain sometimes for a half or a whole day in great contemplation. When she spoke, she often uttered the most loving, sweet words and behaved so kindly towards the sisters that they gained great grace and devotion from her.

On the great feast day of the Circumcision of our dear Lord Jesus Christ [1 January], when she had received him in the holy sacrament, she remained rapt and ecstatic for the whole day until the evening. When she was brought back to herself, she went to the sisters to wish them a happy new year. The sister who cared for her wanted her to stay in her cell. She said, "I cannot stay here," and went to the other sisters. She wished them a happy new year very kindly, saying, "Whoever does not enter his new year with suffering, has not received a true new year from our Lord." She spoke so desirously of suffering that the sisters began greatly to wish that they could come to such desire for suffering and imitate her in such things. They gained great desire for suffering.

She was so loving to all people that whenever she heard someone in pain or sadness, she wished to suffer on their behalf for God's sake, even if it would mean her death. She surrendered herself willingly to all the inner torment that one could imagine suffering, as a recompense for the worthy passion of our dear Lord. When the time came for her final illness to lead her to death, she said in a loud voice, "Truly, God is mercy, and whoever contradicts this lies." She spoke lovely words of lofty, divine things and after this holy speech was silent until midnight, when she began to laugh kindly. All the sisters were gladdened and believed she was recovering and would remain with them longer in this world. But shortly thereafter, she departed and surrendered to Lord Christ her pure, clean soul,

85. Proverbs 31:17.

which she had kept unsullied from all mortal sin with his help and grace. She departed this world in 1446.

After her death, God revealed to a good friend of God these following virtues about her. The first is true, willing obedience out of pure love of God. The second is willing poverty of spirit and of body. The third is willing death to all temporal things. The fourth, that she received everything disagreeable as a gift from God himself. The fifth, that she inclined herself willingly and humbly under all creatures and served God thereby. The sixth, that she loved enemies as friends. The seventh, pure and total detachment in all things.

5.48 *On another devout sister named Katherina* [fol. 200v]

The very first person who left the world and entered the Observance of the sisters in Pforzheim was a blessed virgin, also from Augsburg, through whom God, who is wondrous in his saints,[86] worked great things. Her name was Katherina Zeller and I should also write a little about her for God's praise and our edification.

From childhood on, this sister was of humble life and good character. When she was nearly twelve years old, God the Lord sent her such a great and heavy illness that the doctors despaired of her life, because they could not help her. She surrendered herself completely to our Lord but promised, if it should be his will for her to live longer in this world, to be his eternal servant. Right away she recovered, became healthy, and soon began such a blessed, virtuous life and became such a contemplative person that all those who knew her were edified. She was greatly and ardently diligent in contemplating the worthy suffering of our dear Lord. She kept at this constantly, spoke very little, and withdrew from the company of people whenever she could. She also had a great desire for the holy sacrament, which she often received. She had a confessor in this world, who often tried and tested whether her way of life was a permissible thing or not. He could find no impropriety nor impatience in either her speech or behaviour, no matter how often she came to him.

When she turned twenty years old, she gave up the world and everything in it and came into the holy Dominican order in the convent of sisters in Pforzheim, which had just been reformed to the holy Observance. There, she led such a gracious, perfect, virtuous life that all sisters were edified and won great favour for her. She was so humble that she happily did all the disgusting tasks. She was so obedient that she never refused to do anything, even if it was too much for her. She was so patient, that she desired to be scorned and oppressed her whole life in praise and honour of the suffering of our Lord. She had such a mild, tender

86. Psalm 67:36.

heart and was so kind that she never troubled any sister with words or deeds. Whatever suffering was too harsh for her, she bore it with great patience in praise of the suffering of our dear Lord and received all things as if from God. One could hardly fully record what a blessed, devout life this holy sister led.

Now, as holy Scripture states in the person of our Lord, "Such as I love, I rebuke and chastise."[87] For this reason, he also sent great illness to his lover, so that she might cast off her sins here and prepare herself for him, and in order to increase and multiply her reward in eternal life. For two years before her death, she was sick and bedridden and yet was so patient and mild as a true lamb that the sisters often cried with her. The sisters loved to serve her because of the salutary fruit they received from her graciousness and her good, comforting words. When troubled, burdened sisters came to her for advice, they thought their suffering would be taken from them, so graceful were her mouth, her soul, and her heart. Since she had such a holy, perfect life, God granted her the grace that for a whole year before her death, she was given the holy worthy sacrament every day. The sisters loved to help her in this and both of the confessors were very willing to bring it to her, for they all knew her pure, innocent, blessed life. When the time came for our dear Lord to take her from this world to himself, there was a sweet odour around her. She began to smile very softly, and with a sweet face, she took a cross with a relic from the sacristan's hand and kissed it devoutly. She laid her hands together and inclined her head so desirously that the sisters kindly believed that our dear Lord himself received her soul, for in this moment she surrendered her blessed soul in the year of the Lord 1453.

Many other blessed, dear sisters lived in this convent, whose lives were also well pleasing to God. Those who live in this convent now still behave with such religiosity, virtue, and devotion that both religious and secular people, noble and also non-noble people praise it highly. Up to this very day, this convent brings forth the fruit of holy, virtuous life, and for this may God be praised eternally. Amen.

5.49 *How the two friaries in Worms and Eichstätt were reformed* [fol. 202v]

In the days of the worthy father Nicolaus Notel, who was provincial prior of Teutonia for twenty years, many convents of brothers and sisters were reformed to the religious life of the order, as has been recounted and recorded above. After him, the honourable father Friar Peter Wellen became provincial.[88] He was an

87. Revelation 3:19.

88. For Peter Wellen's collaboration with Johannes Meyer in reforming convents, see the numerous references in Engler, *Regelbuch*.

enlightened, wise, and learned man, as his predecessor had been, and a master of divine Scripture. This honourable father assumed the office of provincial in 1446 and served for many years. He was ardent and serious in governing all communities in the whole province well, friars and sisters alike, and he especially loved reforming convents to the Observant religious life. In his second year in the office, he reformed the community of Preachers in Worms with friars from Basel. Friar Jacob Reiser[89] became prior and Friar Nicolaus Cipriani subprior. The names of the other friars who founded this religious life are written in the Book of Life.[90] The honourable lord bishop of Worms, named Reinhard of Sickingen,[91] supported this new observance with great faithfulness and help, as did the cathedral canons and the local priests. Similarly, the city council of Worms supported and helped, as did the dear father Peter of Gengenbach, who was vicar of the two women's convents in the city, Himmelkron and Liebenau.

In the same year, the friary of Eichstätt was also reformed by this same provincial, Master Peter Wellen. The honourable father lord bishop of Eichstätt,[92] who was a learned master of holy Scripture requested it. The first prior of this Observance was Friar Egidius Schwertmann, who at the time was prior in Nuremberg.[93] The other friars who helped him start this community were also all from the friary in Nuremberg. Their names are known by God.

For the sake of brevity, I am leaving out how the restoration of these friaries to the proven state of this religious life proceeded with bitter travail. The reform of these two friaries took place in 1447.

5.50 *How another two communities of friars were reformed in Bamberg and Würzburg and how the religious life in Würzburg declined again* [fol. 203r]

In 1451 the aforementioned honourable father provincial, Master Peter Wellen, reformed the community of Dominican friars in the city of Bamberg at the request and impetus of the honourable lord bishop of the city.[94] Most of the Dominicans in this house agreed to the reform of their community, although

89. See *DDS*, 317–318.

90. Meyer probably means that there is an actual physical book that records the names of these men. For Meyer and the Bern St Michael's Island *Liber vitae*, see Engler, *Regelbuch*, 24–26. For an English-language study of a similar document, see David Rollason et al. (eds), *The Durham* Liber vitae *and Its Context* (Woodbridge, 2004).

91. Reinhard I of Sickingen, bishop of Worms (r. 1445–1482). In MS 2934 his name is added in a marginal annotation.

92. Johann III of Eych, bishop of Eichstätt (r. 1445–1464).

93. See *SOPMA*, 1: 17–18.

94. Anton of Rotenhan, bishop of Bamberg (r. 1431–1459).

very few of them remained there. The first prior of this foundation was the devout father Rudolf Goldschlager, who was sent from Nuremberg to Bamberg with other friars. He reformed this community spiritually and temporally and restored its people and grounds such that it is now in all ways a completely different friary from what it was before.

At that time, there was a God-fearing bishop in the city of Würzburg.[95] When he heard how the worthy bishops of Eichstätt and Bamberg had requested from the Dominican provincial that the Friars Preachers in both their cities be reformed, God poured great zeal into his heart. He considered how the Dominican community in his own city of Würzburg could come to such a religious life. He petitioned the worthy father provincial, Peter Wellen, to reform the community with friars from Nuremberg. Such were sent to Würzburg for this good purpose, and the lector, Friar Ulrich Messingschlager, became the prior.

Now after our dear father provincial, Master Peter Wellen, had been in his office for nine years, he desired to be relieved of this labour due to his illness and age. He petitioned the master general, Friar Martial Auribelli of Avignon,[96] who sent him a letter to be read aloud in the provincial chapter to the effect that he was freed from his office. He had the letter of his absolution[97] read in 1455 at the provincial chapter in Frankfurt and all the fathers were sorry, including the master general, who was not happy to release him. The next provincial was Friar Heinrich of Reuenach, who was inexperienced in the order and not ready for such a great office. But the old provincial, Master Peter Wellen, returned to his friary, intending thenceforth to pursue his devotion in peace.

And so it happened that in those days, the good, blessed bishop of Würzburg, who had been the impetus for the reform of the convents in his city, died and an upstanding man was set in his place.[98] The friars who had been in the convent before began plotting to get the friars who had been transferred to them from Nuremberg sent home. To this end, they lied to the bishop and the new provincial and promised loudly on pain of specific penance that they themselves would continue to uphold the Observance. The two inexperienced prelates believed them, placed them in the convent, and sent the friars back to Nuremberg, except for the one who was prior. He, however, was unable to convince them to keep the Observance and from day to day they became ever laxer in religious life. What-

95. Gottfried IV Schenk of Limpurg, bishop of Würzburg (r. 1445–1455).

96. See Mortier, *Histoire des maîtres généraux*, 4: 349–402 and 419–487.

97. "Absolution" was the technical term for being released from an office or from particular duties.

98. Johann III of Grumbach, bishop of Würzburg (r. 1455–1466).

ever was in their hearts they pursued diligently. Not long thereafter, they endeavoured to appoint a new prior among them who would not be from the Observance. As soon as this happened, they right away began leading a life such as had been before the reform, even though they had promised, contracted, and chartered that they would not let the Observance founder. It had been sealed and confirmed by the bishop, the provincial, and other notable lords and prelates, that they would uphold the order.

By this, one may note how quickly the religious life of a community may fade when one puts people who do not love the religious life together, or if one separates those who love and are practiced in observance and religious practice, or sends them away, or when such good, spiritual people die and one does not ensure that the community has some good, well-suited persons.

5.51 *How the convent of sisters in Bamberg, called Holy Sepulchre, was reformed* [fol. 204v]

Once the religious life of the Observance had stood for many years and been proven, this Observance and religious custom declined again for the reasons given above. The greatest problem was that the religious friars of Nuremberg, who had reformed the community in Würzburg to the religious life, were sent back home and that the former friars returned to govern in all spiritual and temporal offices. For this reason, the religious life could not stand, even though they had promised the provincial, and the provincial had promised and commanded them to maintain the Observance. Despite the great penance that was imposed on them should they allow the Observance to falter, and no matter how strongly and powerfully the bishop of Würzburg and other prelates insisted, nothing came of it and the Observance declined. Very many people, both religious and secular, were unhappy, insulted, and troubled. Because of the complaints that arose from this and from many other issues, this provincial, Friar Heinrich of Reuenach, was relieved of his office in 1457 on the Feast of St Dominic [5 August]. In the same year, the worthy father Peter Wellen, a master of theology, was made provincial again. As unwilling as he was, he had to resume the office of provincial in obedience.

In the very same year (that is, 1457), the women's convent in Bamberg, called Holy Sepulchre, was reformed under him to the religious life of the holy Observance. The honourable lord bishop of the city of Bamberg[99] was the greatest impetus for this Observance and brought it about through his aid and petitions. And so at the request of this bishop and with the authority of the provincial, Master Peter Wellen, four spiritual, devout, well-suited sisters were chosen

99. Still Anton of Rotenhan, bishop of Bamberg (r. 1431–1459).

from the praiseworthy convent of St Catherine in Nuremberg and were led to this convent of the Holy Sepulchre to begin the holy Observance.

These are their names: Sister Dorothea Berl, first prioress of this Observance; Sister Anna Bieber; Sister Martha Peuerl; and Sister Anna Koop. This Observance was much easier and simpler for these four sisters to begin because the other sisters who were in the convent before had already received a lot of instruction about the order and maintaining observance from the prior of Bamberg and the friars there, who themselves had been reformed several years earlier. These sisters were therefore willing to join the Observance. Now they have grown so well, spiritually and materially, that they maintain a praiseworthy, blessed, devout life according to the complete statutes of our holy Dominican order. Praise, honour, and thanks be to you, blessed holy Trinity, God the Father, the Son, and the Holy Spirit. Amen.

5.52 *How two friaries, one at Wimpfen in Swabia and one at Landshut in Bavaria, were reformed* [fol. 206r]

At that time, the city of Wimpfen in the diocese of Worms wanted the Dominican friary located there to be reformed to a holy religious life. For a long time, the citizens of this city petitioned the superiors of the Dominican order for this, so the general chapter proposed and decided that the friary in Wimpfen would be reformed. Since this general chapter was held in 1459 in the province of Saxony at the friary in the city of Nijmegen, this chapter entrusted to the worthy father provincial, Master Peter Wellen, the reform of the Wimpfen convent. And so the provincial reformed the Wimpfen friary with brothers from Nuremberg as the general chapter had commanded him. The first prior was Friar Johannes Kaufmann and the first subprior Friar Stefan Hunger. God knows the other friars in himself.

At the same time, the illustrious noble prince, Duke Louis of Bavaria,[100] petitioned the Dominican order that the Dominican friary that lies in his city of Landshut be reformed to the religious state of the holy Observance. He pushed so much and for so long through messengers and letters to the chapters and also to the prelates of the order that, through the grace of God and the diligence of our worthy father, Landshut was reformed in an orderly manner with friars from Nuremberg and Eichstätt. In the beginning, the fathers of the friary in Basel also lent help with four friars. This reform began in the friary of Landshut in 1459 on the feast of our dear Lady's Visitation [2 July]. The first prior of this new Observance was the honourable father, Friar Egidius Schwertmann, who had been prior continuously for more than twenty years in these three convents: Nuremberg, Eich-

100. Louis (Ludwig) IX, duke of Bavaria-Landshut (r. 1450–1479).

stätt, and Landshut. He had suffered much difficult labour and achieved much good and profitable fruit on behalf of the order and of other people. For this and all good things, praised be the worthiest Lord Jesus and blessed be the worthy mother Mary. Amen.

5.53 *How the friary in Gebweiler in the diocese of Basel was reformed and restored to the religious life* [fol. 206v]

In 1461 on the Feast of St Maurice [22 September], the Dominican friary of our faithful dear brothers in the city of Gebweiler in the diocese of Basel was reformed to the religious life of the holy Observance. This city lies a mile from the convent of sisters in Schönensteinbach. Now henceforth, the friary in Gebweiler and the convent of sisters in Schönensteinbach must show each other complete faithfulness in divine and brotherly love, because of their proximity but mostly because both communities uphold the holy Observance. This gracious community of friars in Gebweiler may perhaps be judged by some people as one of the least friaries. Up till now it has been small in persons and number of buildings, and aside from a very few communities in Teutonia it is the last and youngest, and it has only in the most recent years now been reformed to the holy Observance. Nevertheless, this community is not the least of the reformed friaries in the province of Teutonia with regard to the religious life of holy Observance according to the Rule of St Augustine and the Constitutions of the Friars of the Order of Preachers. These are diligently, laudably, and devoutly observed by good-willed friars with good hearts.

I will summarize briefly how and through which persons this Observance was brought about and what suffering occurred thereby. There were certain people who wished with a great desire for the reform of this community and its restoration to the religous life. There was a discussion about it among the superiors of the Dominican order and it was decided that it could not easily come to pass unless the lord of the city of Gebweiler and the noble custodians of the Dominican friary earnestly requested it from the authorities of the order. These nobles would have to actively desire it for good reasons and to promise to assist the religious life and take it under their protection.

Now, in those days there was a secular canon named Master Johannes Kreutzer[101] in the cathedral chapter in Basel who was a master of holy Scripture

101. See Natalija Ganina, *Bräute Christi: Legenden und Traktate aus dem Straßburger Magdalenenkloster; Edition und Untersuchungen* (Berlin, 2016), 113–126; Francis Rapp, "Jean Kreutzer," in *Dominicains et dominicaines en Alsace: XIIIe–XXe s.*, ed. Jean-Luc Eichenlaub (Colmar, 1996), 111–122; *SOPMA*, 2: 464.

and who had been born in the city of Gebweiler. He instructed the lord to whom the city belongs, the honourable father Lord Bartholomew Andlau, abbot of Murbach, as well as his noble subjects, the custodians, and those who have their graves in the Dominican friary, that they should request a reform from the honourable father provincial, Master Peter Wellen, whose arrival was shortly expected. And so all the nobles who were in the area gathered with the lord of the city and petitioned with great, desirous seriousness for this thing.

Now there were two noblemen not there, the Waldeners, who believed that their forebears had been the earliest custodians of the friary. Although they could not be present, the others nevertheless thought that such a good and holy matter would suit their good will. Faced with such strong petitions, the honourable provincial had to agree to reform the friary. He ordered the honourable father, the prior of the Dominicans in Basel, to introduce the full Observance to the Gebweiler community with his friars from Basel. This was done and it was reformed to the religious life.

5.54 *The great trouble and scorn that befell this holy affair* [fol. 208r]

The first prior of this religious life was Friar Caspar Maner,[102] a master of holy Scripture. The names of the other friars from Basel and Colmar who began this religious life in Gebweiler are written in the Book of Life.[103]

When this Observance began, all the friars who had been in the community before were unwilling.[104] Not a single one wished to stay, although everyone else would gladly have seen them surrender to the religious life of the Observance. Moreover, the two Waldeners returned to the country and learned of the friary's reform with pleasure, but shortly thereafter certain people convinced them to resist the Observance with all their might. They said they had been insulted and scorned since such a thing had occurred without their knowledge and permission. One in particular, Hermann Waldener, behaved so ferociously that many religious and secular people of the region became involved. He wrote an open rejection letter to all the friars of the Observance, especially those from Basel and Gebweiler. He claimed that even if he exercised his animosity against the friars

102. See *DDS*, 255–256.

103. See note in **5.49**.

104. For details on the Gebweiler friary and the very strict form of common property introduced there, see Sonia Pelletier-Gautier, "Floraison dominicaine dans la deuxième moitié du XVe siècle à Guebwiller," in *Dominicains et dominicaines en Alsace: XIIIe–XXe s.*, ed. Jean-Luc Eichenlaub (Colmar, 1996), 53–61; Bernhard Neidiger, "Der Armutsbegriff der Dominikanerobservanten: Zur Diskussion in den Konventen der Provinz Teutonia (1389–1513)," *Zeitschrift für die Geschichte des Oberrheins* 145 (1997): 117–158, at 132–139.

through manslaughter or in similar ways, he would still maintain his honour. Sometimes when the friars had to travel for necessary matters, they had to go in secret, often disguised in strange clothes. Such and similar things happened with a bit more, indeed with a great deal of trouble.

One day, the bailiff and marshal of the eminent, illustrious prince Duke Albert of Austria,[105] named Knight Thüring of Hallwyl,[106] went to Ensheim before the council of the lords of Austria. When both sides had been heard – the friars' side and also the side of the dishonourable nobleman – they were ordered to keep the peace and to suspend their animosity from a certain day until the whole matter could be decided. Yet not long thereafter, Hermann Waldener presented a case to the bailiff of the Holy Roman Empire and convinced this man. Whereas before he had repudiated the reform, he and two others now repudiated the entire order much more vehemently. He wrote insultingly and rudely and in a very threatening manner to the entire provincial chapter, which was held in Zurich in 1463 and attended by the master general, the provincial, and many other masters of theology and honourable fathers and brothers. The chapter replied to him through the messenger he had sent that what had been done in the reform of the Gebweiler friary had been for the best and in praise of God. Even though he had no right over the order, they would nevertheless agree to answer him before the bailiff and the council of Austrian lords in Alsace. This happened and there was another meeting about the affair. Even though it was clearly seen that this bizarre nobleman had no case, he nevertheless would not be content and brought the matter before the bishop of Basel.[107]

After this great conflict between the friars of the Observance in Gebweiler and the two Waldener men had lasted for nearly two years, one of them was mortally wounded but continued to live for three days after the injury with full presence of mind. He called for the bailiff and certain knights and squires and asked them earnestly that they allow the religious life of the Dominicans in Gebweiler to be entrusted to them, as well as the dear friars there. He zealously urged them to prevent the Observance from declining and to forbid that friars who did not belong to the Observance ever be transferred into the friary. Finally, he asked them to convince his kinsman and friend, the other Waldener, to do the same and to hold the friars of that community in virtuous friendship. Even though the

105. Albert (Albrecht) VI (r. 1424–1463).

106. Thüring of Hallwyl (d. 1469), son of another Thüring of Hallwyl and Margareta of Masmünster, was Duke Albert VI's marshal, his regional governor (*Landvogt*) in Ensisheim, and his representative in Freiburg im Breisgau by 1450. He will play an important role in the reform of the three Freiburg convents. See **5.60–66**.

107. Johannes V of Venningen, bishop of Basel (r. 1458–1478).

bailiff and the nobles agreed to his request, he was not satisfied until they swore their faithfulness to him on their oaths. He asked that whatever he had done against the friars be forgiven and that they pray to God for him. When he had received the holy sacrament, he died and was buried in this very Dominican friary with his ancestors. After this, the friars of the Observance lived in peace. Both religious and secular people, noble and non-noble, held them in love, favour, and grace because of their religious life, which they demonstrated and showed so virtuously. This good work was so bitterly earned that many good people worried that the newly begun religious life of the friary could not persist against this disruptive trouble. Out of temporal fear and worldly scorn, certain persons were also determined to return the site of this community to the fomer base lifestyle and to force the Observant friars to leave the convent. But they did not consider what God says through his Holy Spirit and through the prophet David in the book of Psalms, "Multae tribulationes etc.,"[108] which in German is: The friends of God must suffer so many and various afflictions, but the Lord will deliver them from all their worry and trouble when his divine grace decides it is time.

5.55 *On the reformation of the convent of sisters in Hasenpfuhl in the city of Speyer, and how at first such great suffering and trouble arose from it* [fol. 209v]

In 1463 the women's convent of St Mary Magdalene called Hasenpfuhl, which lies in the worthy city of Speyer, was enclosed and reformed to the religious life by the thirtieth master general of the Dominican order, Father Conrad of Asti,[109] a master of holy Scripture, through Friar Johannes Hohenloch,[110] prior of the friars in Worms.

It should be known that more than twenty years earlier, in the time when the holy father Pope Eugenius IV[111] lived, Father Peter of Gengenbach[112] wanted to reform this convent by the authority of the said pope, with the will of the Dominican superiors and also of the council of this city of Speyer. And when he had been granted so much favour, good will, and authority by these aforesaid prelates, he chose many religious sisters who were suited to it from the convent of Himmelkron, whose vicar he was, and through them he wished to reform this

108. Psalm 33:20.

109. Conrad of Asti, master general (r. 1462–1465); see Mortier, *Histoire des maîtres généraux*, 4: 403–418. For his role in reforming women's convents, see Engler, *Regelbuch*, 293–299.

110. *DDS*, 276; Engler, *Regelbuch*, 295 n998.

111. Pope Eugenius IV (r. 1431–1447).

112. Peter of Gengenbach's name is missing at this point in the account in MS 2934, but included in Cgm 8081.

convent of Hasenpfuhl to the Observance. This father Peter of Gengenbach brought the sisters into the city of Speyer to a lovely accommodation, which had been prepared for them to stay in until it was determined how best to lead them rightly and in orderly fashion into the convent to begin the Observance. In the evening, everyone went peacefully to sleep. Now, the women in the convent did not know that foreign sisters were in the city, even though they suspected that people were planning to improve the immorality of their lives and bring their convent to the Observance.

During the first sleep of the night, the vicar woke up the sisters who had been led there, as well as the servants whom the worthy prince, the count palatine Duke Louis,[113] had given to help him and everybody else who was with him. He thought he could reform the convent in quiet and secrecy, leading the sisters in before Matins so that it would go peacefully and not cause any trouble or outcry, since the sisters in the convent were completely unwilling to reform. Even though nobody liked carrying out the matter right away in the middle of the night, the vicar was so insistent that they had to follow him. At the convent they had to climb a little and scale the walls, until they got into the convent and into a room where they found a sister sleeping. When she noticed them and realized that they were there to begin the reform, she lifted up a loud voice and began to scream and cry out of the window so frightfully that it was heard not only in the convent but also in the city.

Now, the sisters in the convent had secular priests located nearby, since their church is a parish church. These priests had promised them that if people tried to reform them, they would help prevent it with all their might. When the priests outside and inside realized what was happening, they also raised a hue and cry as if enemies or murderers were there. There was such a tumultuous commotion throughout the whole city that the watchmen in the towers blew their horns and the churches stormily rang their bells. The townspeople did not know what was happening or why. Some thought this and others that, but the greater part ran to the convent. There reigned such an outcry, rampage, and wailing that the foreign sisters feared for their lives. In particular, those who had been in the convent before fell upon the new sisters with punches and kicks and other ferocities, but God and honest people, who understood what had happened, helped them escape.

On the advice of a citizen, the good father Peter of Gengenbach left until the great storm had passed. Otherwise, he would quickly have been beaten or killed.

113. Louis (Ludwig) III, count palatine of the Rhine (r. 1410–1436). Meyer notes in **5.26** that Louis was especially fond of Peter of Gengenbach.

He still was soon seized and arrested and led with great fury before the authorities where they were assembled. It is the practice in large cities that in such worrisome affairs and riots, it is predetermined who should run to the torturer and who should go to this or that location for guard duty. Accordingly, Father Peter was led from one to the next with torches and lanterns and blows and kicks, nearly in the same form and manner as our dear Lord was bound and led from one judge to the next. The servants of the worthy lord count palatine were taken to the towers and were almost sentenced to death. The dear honourable mayor of the city of Speyer was removed from his office over this, although he had not known anything beyond the day on which the reform was to occur. The lord councilmen of the city had also been informed that on that same day in the morning – not at night! – the sisters of the Observance would be led into the convent of Hasenpfuhl in order to reform it.

5.56 *How this convent came to the religious life in great and peaceful kindness* [fol. 211v]

Once this great uproar had passed and the sisters had been led back to their convent, Hasenpfuhl remained unreformed. This would not have happened had the matter been conducted in an orderly manner at the proper time – or perhaps the time was not yet ripe for it to be reformed at that moment.

More than twenty years later and more than ten years after Father Peter of Gengenbach's death, the praiseworthy, noble prince Duke Frederick, the worthy count palatine,[114] along with the distinguished city of Speyer wrote to the Dominican master general about the enclosure of this convent. Requesting him to institute a religious life there, they sent their own messenger south to Lombardy in order to arrange the affair with the master general of the order. He delegated complete and full authority in writing to Friar Johannes Hohenloch, prior of the friars in Worms, to reform it completely. He did as he was commanded and selected dear, religious sisters from the convent of Himmelkron and led them to Speyer and their confessors with them. The mayor and several members of the city council attended, who were to help lead the sisters of Himmelkron into the convent. It so happened that they arrived at the convent on the same day on which, many years earlier, they had been led there in the night, when the terrifying riot in the city occurred, as was recounted before.[115] But this time, all those

114. Elector Palatine Frederick (Friedrich) I became regent for his nephew Philip in 1451 and managed to retain power until his death in 1476, although the title did then pass to Philip rather than to Frederick's own children.

115. See previous chapter.

who were appointed to the matter went in all together in broad daylight, the secular with the religious persons.

They placed the foreign sisters in a room of the convent and told them to wait. They then went into another room and called the whole community of Hasenpfuhl sisters to come before them, but the local sisters did not know about the foreigners. Once they had all assembled before the fathers of the order and the lords of the city, the prioress was asked for her keys. The prioress and other sisters said, "We see well that you wish to enclose us and create an Observance here." They were kindly told to submit themselves, for it could not be otherwise. It was declared that this was being done by the order's authority, and whatever else needed to be proclaimed was read out. The prior of Worms, whom the master general had named vicar of this convent, relieved the prioress [of her office]. When she had stood up from her prostrations, she thanked him and said that he had done her a great service, since she had been relieved of a great burden.

The fathers and lords said, "Let us go into the large room to conclude the affair." They all stood up and went into the room where the foreign sisters were waiting, and the local sisters, who did not yet know anything about the foreign sisters, followed them. As soon as they saw them, the women of this convent fell upon the sisters of the Observance and embraced them. With great weeping, they fell upon their necks and welcomed them so humbly and in a very friendly manner. They showed such faith and mercy that they awakened compassion, and all received grace and joy from the sight of their sweet and peaceful surrender.

The first prioress was the honourable mother Sister Margretha Regenstein. This dear, effective, productive sister entered the order in her youth at the convent of Unterlinden in Colmar a few years after that convent had been reformed by the sisters of Steinbach. From them she learned the order so well that afterwards she was sent with other sisters to the Basel convent of Mary Magdalene. There she helped lay the foundation of the religious life so well that they sent her a third time[116] with other dear sisters to Worms to begin the Observance in the convent of Hochheim called Himmelkron. She was subprioress there for a long time and then was finally placed, as a good and fruitful tree of manifold virtues, in St Mary Magdalene's noble herb garden, the worthy convent of Hasenpfuhl. She was a virtuous mother to her children and a beneficial prioress to her sisters. For this and for all good, may praise, wisdom, blessing, resplendence, strength, and grace be to Lord Jesus, child of the Virgin Mary, with God the Father and God the Holy Spirit, now and forever eternally. Amen.

116. Both manuscripts have "for the third time" here, although Himmelkron was her second reform and Hasenpfuhl her third.

5.57 *How the convent of Sylo in the city of Schlettstadt in the diocese of Strasbourg was reformed by the authority of Conrad of Asti, master general of the order* [fol. 213r]

In the year 1464, that worthy house of God, the Dominican convent Sylo in the city of Schlettstadt, diocese of Strasbourg, was reformed. At that time, the master general, the worthy, devout Conrad of Asti, had come to Teutonia personally to inspect several communities both of friars and of sisters. Since he also visited this convent and noted that the prioress there and some other good sisters desired wholeheartedly for their convent to be reformed, he did not wish to stand in the way of their desire. Rather, he rejoiced in it and supported them kindly, since he also noted and understood that the nobles of the city requested and desired it, as well as the patrons of the convent and the city council of Schlettstadt, where the convent was located. For this reason, he gave his full authority to the honourable father, Friar Heinrich Schretz,[117] who long before had been prior in Basel. He was appointed vicar over the convent of Sylo in order to reform it with sisters from St Catherine's in Colmar, since the sisters of Sylo desired this and greatly loved the convent of St Catherine. In particular, for more than ten years the prioress of Sylo, Sister Margreta Karl, a lover of virtue, had desired and pressed the prioress of St Catherine's to come to them for the holy Observance. But this wise mother, the prioress in Colmar, as if waiting for something better, put her off with letters and other favours and asked her to suffer it, for some day her desire would be fulfilled. She promised her furthermore that she would do her very best to support Sylo by giving aid and counsel to secular and religious people alike and especially to the patrons of the convent, to whom she wrote and whom she also told in person that she would be willing.

She now let this happen, and through her good admonition, it was decided that five good-willed sisters in the convent would go. Sylo requested sisters from St Catherine's through a dear lay brother named Brother Rudolf from the Dominican friary in Colmar. He had also faithfully worked on this matter for a long time, and the sisters were encouraged by his good exhortation and prudent, religious behaviour, for they were very fond of him. By the authority and command of the superiors, he had been lent to them for a long time in order to build their convent up properly, since he had experience in this. And so, the sisters of Sylo and their advocates wrote about this to the master general, who was in the region. He entrusted the reform to the spiritual father Heinrich Schretz, to complete it with his authority by taking sisters from St Catherine's.

117. See *DDS*, 253–254.

He arrived on Septuagesima Sunday [29 January] and, as in the Gospel reading for that day,[118] recruited five sisters for the vineyard of the Lord that long had lain barren. Their names are Sister Barbara Krebs, who had been subprioress for twenty-six years and became the first prioress of Sylo, and Sister Ursula Surgend, who became subprioress and afterwards prioress. These two blessed sisters had been in the convent of St Catherine long before it was reformed. The third sister was called Elisabeth Ringler, who became sacristan and chantress. The fourth sister was Margretha Meyer, subbursar and monitor. She was talented at painting and writing whatever one required of her. The fifth sister was called Elisabeth of Rathsamhausen and was the daughter of Sylo's patron. Early on the second day, these sisters received the holy sacrament a second time and the vicar led them away with him to Schlettstadt. The patrons and advocates of the convent rode more than a mile out to meet them, along with soldiers from the city of Colmar, and escorted them in great honour on the way to the convent. Both the willing and unwilling sisters came to meet them, that is, nine of them did; the tenth ran away from the convent. The city and council have always stood by them and have sworn to give them help and support in all things, which they do faithfully. The count palatine of the city also wrote to help and support the convent in all good things.

There were four sisters for whom the religious life of the Observance was not at all acceptable. For this reason, they secretly let themselves out through the water gate. The worthy master general excommunicated them and imposed a heavy penance on them for leaving the convent without his permission. He forbade any convent from receiving them or taking them in again except under penance of two years in prison. But he left this to the discretion of the vicar because a great petition began circulating. Shortly thereafter, these sisters wished to be readmitted without the penance of imprisonment. Since nobody wanted to take them in, they ended up in an open convent in Strasbourg called St Margaret's.

5.58 *How the worthy convent of friars in the magnificent city of Cologne was reformed* [fol. 215r]

In 1464 the great, praiseworthy, and renowned community of friars in Cologne was reformed to the holy Observance through the master general, Conrad of Asti, and the provincial, Master Peter Wellen, who were both personally present in Cologne and worked very hard, about which there would be much to write. They took this great, holy affair very wisely and carefully in hand, and

118. Matthew 20:1–16.

enjoyed support and considerable aid from the honourable lord bishop (a duke by birth and the son of the eminent prince, the count palatine[119]), from a canon named Steffen (another devout and high-born duke of the same canonry), and also from the city council of Cologne. The council promoted the matter zealously and petitioned the Roman see for special bulls of confirmation for this Observance.

It was begun in the week of Pentecost [21–26 May] with a respectable, large number of friars from four reformed communities, namely Basel, Colmar, Nuremberg, and Pforzheim. Among these was also the first prior, Friar Heinrich Schretz. But soon after him, Father Peter Kirchschlag from the Nuremberg friary became prior.[120] He was an upright, spiritual, wise, learned man and a great preacher of the divine word.

5.59 *How the friary of Ulm was reformed, and by whom this was accomplished* [fol. 215v]

In 1465, the friary in Ulm was reformed after the provincial chapter, which was held in May that year in Basel. It was carried out by our worthy father provincial, Master Peter Wellen, who personally travelled from Basel to Ulm in haste, after the city of Ulm earnestly wrote to him in this regard by their own messenger. He reformed the community with friars from Basel and the first prior was Father Heinrich Schretz. The first subprior was the lector from Basel, Friar Heinrich Riss.[121]

The religious life of the Observance prospered so well that the community of city folk in Ulm were greatly pleased by it and were also noticeably improved thereby. One man in particular pushed for this great, good, holy, fruitful work and worked towards it with earnest diligence, heeding neither obstructions nor other troubles which befell him. This was the honourable master, Friar Ludwig Fuchs,[122] a master of holy Scripture in the friary of Ulm.

119. Ruprecht of the Palatinate, archbishop of Cologne (r. 1463–1480) was the son of Louis III, who has been mentioned in **5.26** and **5.55**.

120. *SOPMA*, 3: 234–235.

121. *DDS*, 277–278.

122. Ludwig Fuchs assisted in the reform of Sylo in 1464 (although Meyer only mentions Heinrich Schretz) and became the reform prior of the Ulm friary in 1465 (see **5.57** and **5.59**). He achieved his greatest prominence only after Meyer's death when he was appointed general vicar over Teutonia in 1496. The manuscript of the Rule and Constitutions that he used in his capacity as vicar survives. See Engler, *Regelbuch*, 42–44. See also *SOPMA*, 3: 94; Kurt Ruh, "Fuchs, Ludwig," *VL*^{2} 2: 998–999.

5.60 *On the three Dominican women's convents in Freiburg that were reformed together all at once* [fol. 216r]

In 1465, three convents of sisters in Freiburg were reformed to the religious life all together. Up till then it was unheard of for two in one city to be reformed together at the same time, let alone three. But this was a divine and not a human accomplishment, as is fully to be believed and may be understood from the following.

Here are the names of these three convents: the first is called Our Dear Lady in Adelhausen and lies outside of Freiburg in the suburbs. It is a princely, beautiful, large, and wide cloister, consecrated in honour of the mother of God as she received the eternal fatherly word. It is an old and worthy convent and was among the first convents in the Dominican order, founded not long after Saint Dominic's death.[123] In the beginning of the order, there was a very devout, blessed life in this convent, as is written in a special book about the holy life of the first blessed sisters of Adelhausen.[124]

The second convent is called St Agnes and is also a lovely cloister, graciously and spiritually built. As I found in its records, it was entrusted to and incorporated into the order under the sixth master general[125] and received by the entire order at three general chapters.[126] It was given to the Dominican order and confirmed by a cardinal and legate in the name of the pope.

The third convent is called the Penitents of St Mary Magdalene and is an old, honourable convent. It was already a women's cloister before Saint Dominic founded the Order of Preachers. They belonged to another order and wore white habits. For this reason, the convent still has its name ("the Penitents") from this order, even though it is now Dominican and upholds the Observance.[127]

123. On the Adelhausen convent, see Madlen Doerr, "Klarissen und Dominikanerinnen in Freiburg im 15. Jahrhundert: Sozialstruktur und Reform" (PhD diss., University of Freiburg, 2012), 124–127.

124. Meyer is referring to Anna of Munzingen's sisterbook. See Anna of Munzingen, "Die Chronik der Anna von Munzingen nach der ältesten Abschrift mit Einleitung und Beilagen," ed. Johann König, *Freiburger Diözesan-Archiv* 13 (1880): 129–236.

125. I.e., Master General John of Vercelli (r. 1264–1283).

126. The friars' Constitutions specify that any major actions, including changes to the Constitutions or the liturgy and the incorporation of new communities, needed to be ratified by three successive meetings of the general chapter. This procedure was rarely observed for women's convents and is therefore noteworthy. The relevant passage may be found in "Liber Constitutionum Ordinis Fratrum Praedicatorum," *Analecta Sacri Ordinis Fratrum Praedicatorum* 3 (1897): 26–60, 98–122, 162–181, at 98. For the incorporation of St Agnes, see Doerr, "Klarissen und Dominikanerinnen," 128.

127. From the way Meyer phrases this it might seem that the change had been fairly recent, but in fact the Penitents of Freiburg had followed the Constitutions for Dominican sisters since the thirteenth century. See Doerr, "Klarissen und Dominikanerinnen," 132–134.

5.61 *By whom the reform of these three convents was carried out* [fol. 216v]

It may be noted briefly how it came to pass that these three convents were reformed. At a holy moment before the Feast of the Annunciation [25 March],[128] the worthy convent of Adelhausen and its former holiness came to my (Father Johannes Meyer's)[129] mind very seriously. I considered how its religious life had dimmed so much that not only great barons, knights, and squires, but even a prince of the house of Austria with his army and nobles often sought worldly joy and ephemeral entertainments in this same convent. For this reason, I felt a very strong impulse to go before God and man so that this convent, as well as the other two aforementioned convents, might be restored to a religious life. I prayed to God with great earnestness and petitioned also many good friends of God that my special prayer be answered. If this matter, which lay so deep in my heart, were not from God, it could be removed from my heart, and I would desist from this impulse and find peace. If, however, the impulse to this great affair were a true divine inspiration, by which the soul's salvation and God's honour would be increased, I prayed that God would direct it through his eternal wisdom towards his highest praise and the profit of Christianity and of the holy Dominican order. When I laid my zealous intention before powerful persons, without whose help and diligent, faithful support I could not accomplish it, they were immediately willing. They promised me that however and whatever I instructed they would do it. The prince of Austria himself, Duke Sigismund,[130] was especially goodwilled, as were his councilmen, his bailiff Lord Thüring of Hallwyl,[131] and the councilmen of the lords of Austria, among many others.

5.62 *How the reformers of these three convents showed such earnest zeal through their great expense and labour* [fol. 217r]

First, the aforementioned illustrious prince, Duke Sigismund of Austria, wrote to the master general concerning this reform, as did the gracious lord and father Burckhard of Randegg (bishop of Constance),[132] the gracious lord and

128. Adelhausen's patron feast, as noted in the previous chapter.

129. The scribe has ingeniously filled in the strokes of the word *mir* (my) to turn it into *vatter* (father) and then inserted "Johannes Meger" in the margin. *Min gemüte* (my mind) has been changed to *sin gemüte* (his mind) and subsequently each *ich* (I) has been crossed out in red ink and *er* (he) is written above it.

130. Sigismund (1427–1496) was duke of Austria from 1439–1490. Although Emperor Frederick III granted him the title of archduke in 1477, Sigismund only ever reigned in Further Austria (including Alsace) and Tyrol.

131. Thüring of Hallwyl (d. 1469) first appears in **5.54** where he is named as the bailiff of Duke Albert VI, Sigismund's cousin, who died in 1463.

132. Burckhard II of Randegg, bishop of Constance (r. 1462–1466).

father Johannes of Venningen (bishop of Basel)[133], and Lord Thüring of Hallwyl, who was both bailiff and marshal as well as the mayor and a common councilman of the city of Freiburg.[134] Even though they had initially been against it because of the unjust whisperings of certain people, afterwards they supported the Observance all the more strongly. The prior and father of the Dominican friary in Basel[135] also wrote about this at the request and desire of Lord Thüring of Hallwyl.

The matter was drawn out for more than a whole year before it even could begin. Great cost and an unspeakable amount of work went into first one thing and then another. The first message was brought to the master general, Father Conrad of Asti, in Paris, France, by the prior of the Dominicans in Gebweiler,[136] who, for God and the increase of the religious life, trod this long path in the cold wintertime with only one servant at the expense of the aforesaid knight, Lord Thüring of Hallwyl. The prior brought back many letters and sufficient authority. The second message went to the provincial in Brabant[137] with a lay brother of Schönensteinbach at the expense of Friar Johannes Meyer's father.[138] He also returned with complete and full authority. The third message was brought to the papal curia in Rome by the aforesaid father, the prior of Gebweiler, at the expense of the honourable Lord Johannes Kreutzer, a master of holy Scripture and a canon of the cathedral chapter in Basel, who later became a friar of our order. Full authority also returned from Rome. The lord of Austria himself sent the fourth message through his own servant and messenger and at his own expense

133. Johannes V of Venningen, bishop of Basel (r. 1458–1478), is also mentioned in **5.54**, although not named there.

134. According to Madlen Doerr, Meyer is mistaken in identifying Thüring as mayor of Freiburg in the early 1460s. She names the Freiburg mayors for the years 1460, 1461, 1463, 1464, and 1465 in Doerr, "Klarissen und Dominikanerinnen," 247–248.

135. The prior referred to is Rudolf Bumann (r. 1464–1466, 1468–1469); see *DDS*, 255.

136. The prior referred to is Caspar Maner; see **5.54**.

137. I.e., Peter Wellen.

138. It is ambiguous whether Meyer means his own biological father, some spiritual father and mentor, or even himself, using "father" and "friar" as appositional attributions. Since Meyer belonged to a faction of the Observants that held a strict position on personal property, it is unlikely that he himself or any of his Dominican mentors had the private resources to fund a messenger. If indeed Meyer turned to his own biological family for aid, it speaks to his deep personal investment in the Freiburg reforms. For Meyer's position on voluntary poverty and his role in the extreme model of the Gebweiler friary (**5.53–54**), see Neidiger, "Armutsbegriff," 132–139.

to Lombardy to a city called Novara, where the general chapter was being held. He was also granted full authority to reform these convents as if the master general were personally present. I was commanded to complete this work, and all brothers and sisters were strictly forbidden from deterring me in any way, and other things as are contained in these letters.[139]

5.63 *How the beautiful, princely convent of Adelhausen was reformed by six sisters from St Catherine's in Colmar* [fol. 218r]

Adelhausen was reformed in 1465 on the day of our dear Lady's Visitation [2 July], in honour of which this worthy convent is consecrated.[140] The sisters of Adelhausen were extremely, inordinately unwilling to let themselves be enclosed and reformed, to allow the sisters of the Observance in, and to be governed by them, since they were accustomed to many worldly pleasures and bodily comfort and self-will. Nevertheless, the first two times they did not show the rude and rough behaviour that has sometimes been seen from sisters, although Father Johannes Meyer had to hold chapters for them over and over again, sometimes supported by the secular authority that was granted him by the order superiors in their letters.

Six sisters from the convent of St Catherine in Colmar were commanded to reform Adelhausen. When these six sisters arrived in Freiburg from Colmar, they and the persons who accompanied them, both religious and secular, were quite honourably received by the nobles of the city. Almost twenty honourable laywomen received these foreign nuns and sisters and escorted them to the convent. These six foreign sisters knelt down in the church and very devoutly sang the antiphon "Sub tuum praesidium" for our dear Lady, whose feast it was. Many people wept from devotion. Afterwards, they were led into the choir and sang the hymn of the Holy Spirit, "Veni creator." The versicles and orations and other things were duly performed, as is customary when a convent is reformed to the Observance. The first prioress of this religious life was the honourable mother Sister Edelin of Aue, who had been prioress in St Catherine's in Colmar for twenty-four years and was appointed to the same office in Adelhausen. With her came Sister Cristin of Wittenheim, Sisters Margretha and Ursula Zibold, and a lay sister.[141]

139. Here, too, a scribe has altered the first person into the third person.

140. This is incorrect. The convent of Adelhausen was consecrated in honour of the Annunciation, as Meyer states in **5.60**.

141. There appears to be a name missing here, since Meyer states that six sisters were sent but only five are listed here. Edelin appears as Adelheid in **5.44**.

Note, however, that the sisters were given a year probation, then whoever did not wish to stay could move to another convent. The prioress died before the year was out and a sister from Unterlinden was made prioress. When this happened, many sisters left for other convents that were not reformed, so that yet another prioress was appointed from St Catherine's convent in Colmar. For this reason, the beginning has been very difficult, but it may be hoped that Adelhausen will produce great fruit. Christ the Lord and his worthiest mother be praised eternally. Amen.

5.64 *How the convent of St Agnes was so graciously reformed by five sisters from St Mary Magdalene in Basel* [fol. 219r]

The convent of St Agnes was reformed that same morning by five sisters from the convent of St Mary Magdalene an den Steinen in Basel. Although these sisters in St Agnes were also not willing to submit to the Observance, they never showed any noticeable misbehaviour, neither in words nor in actions. Even the young sisters, of whom there was a good number, behaved themselves and were so well-mannered and maidenly in all aspects of the reform, that both religious and secular people were edified, even though the worthy father Friar Johannes Meyer had to suffer for it.

In the name of our order's superiors, he had commanded the sisters from Basel to come. Lord Thüring of Hallwyl, the bailiff of the city of Basel, and the Freiburg city council had also written to St Mary Magdalene in the name of the duke of Austria, zealously requesting sisters. Similarly, they had written to the city of Colmar and the convent of St Catherine there for sisters for Adelhausen. The council of Basel sent one of the councilmen and a servant with the sisters along with their priest and a number of honourable persons, who escorted them to Freiburg.

They were lovingly received by those in Adelhausen and by Father Johannes Meyer and admitted to the convent. First, the three parties of sisters from Basel, from Colmar, and from Freiburg knelt down in the choir and greeted the queen of mercy, singing the "Salve regina." Once they had delighted in their sisterly love together, more than twenty honourable women arrived to lead the sisters from Basel out of Adelhausen and into the convent of St Agnes. There they were quite honourably received and welcomed by the nobles of Austria's ruling elite and by the citizens of the Freiburg city council, who thanked them for coming. After the local sisters of St Agnes had lovingly received the foreign sisters from Basel in the presence of a great crowd, they sang the hymn of the Holy Spirit, "Veni creator spiritus," and other things that belong to the orderly fulfilment of such great affairs.

The first prioress of this Observance was Sister Anna Schneeberger,[142] a very devout, dear mother, who had also been prioress in Basel before. With her came Sister Clara Schlatter,[143] first subprioress; Sister Ursula Schlosser; turnkeeper; Sister Margretha of Bülach, sacristan; and Sister Anna of Thann, a lay sister.

5.65 *How the convent of Dominican sisters called the Penitents was reformed* [fol. 220r]

The convent of St Mary Magdalene of the Penitents was reformed by the renowned, worthy convent of Schönensteinbach with three sisters, since there were no more than ten sisters in this convent. Except for a few of these ten, they were quite impolite in word and gesture with unwomanly rowdiness in the presence of all of us – in front of knights and servants, religious and secular persons, the honourable citizens of the Freiburg city council, and the masters of the university, who in general were always present in the three convents when there was business pertaining to the reform. These sisters gravely misbehaved, worse than the sisters of the other two convents. It happened as in the Gospel reading about the ten virgins, that is, the five wise and the five foolish.[144] Five behaved wisely and stayed in their convent in religious life. Unfortunately, the other five did as the unwise virgins did, and secretly ran away at night through where the flowing water runs through the convent and cast off the habit of the order, forgetting the salvation of their souls.

When the three sisters from Schönensteinbach arrived in Freiburg on a covered wagon under honourable, religious, secure protection – just as the sisters who were reforming the other two convents had arrived similarly with honourable and praiseworthy escorts and company – these three sisters were received honourably by lords and ladies and lifted from the wagon. They were led through the city on foot, preceded by a cross and a banner. The local sisters rang their bells and received them devoutly and in festal dignity in their external church. They led them into the choir, singing the hymn "Veni creator spiritus." Afterwards, the foreign sisters called upon our dear Lady and sang "Sub tuum presidium." Then the friar priests sang an antiphon for the worthy St Mary Magdalene, the matron of this convent, "Intercede supplicans." The devout, spiritual father Johannes Meyer sang the collects that go with it. Then there was a sermon, since many common folk were also present, and finally, the aforesaid spiritual father held a chapter and made Sister Katherina Kartheuser prioress of this newly begun Observance. She had already been prioress in Schönensteinbach twice. The two

142. See *DDS*, 607.

143. Probably the biological sister of Conrad Schlatter; see **2.16**.

144. Matthew 25:1–13.

sisters who came with her were her helpers, Sister Elisabeth Toppel[145] and Sister Katharina of Mainz.

5.66 *What careful wisdom and firm prudence was used and practised in the reform of the aforesaid three convents of sisters* [fol. 220v]

Yet how these three convents were brought to the religious life with such great labour and at great cost and what trouble befell them cannot be expressed in few words. The worthy father Johannes Meyer had the permission and authority of the order to receive aid from the secular authorities in this great and holy matter of the reform of these three sisters' convents. During the first two months, when he had to enter a convent in order to hold chapter, this father Johannes Meyer ensured that he was accompanied by six powerful, good-willed knights from among the officers of the illustrious prince Duke Sigismund, along with members of the Freiburg city council, doctors, teachers, and masters of the university in Freiburg, and even the two priors and some of the fathers of the Carthusian and Augustinian communities, which are reformed there.[146] He had no one from the Dominican order with him except for one lay brother and a secular canon named Master Johannes Kreutzer, with whom he was especially close and who faithfully supported him. Master Johannes Kreutzer entered the Dominican order later that same year, abandoning great wealth and honour in the world.

Before all these people, of whom there were sometimes about thirty or forty present, I (he)[147] told the sisters that God had given it to him to speak in a pleading and admonishing way, or however else he could or would, so he was performing this speech for the sake of God and the order. Then the wise Lord Thüring of Hallwyl, bailiff and marshal, spoke on behalf of his lord, the duke of Austria, very reasonably and well. Then the city of Freiburg spoke through three eloquent, reasonable men. Even though at first the sisters were all quite unwilling to let themselves be enclosed and reformed, and especially to accept sisters from Observant convents, nevertheless this good father persisted with the help of God. He also exhorted the aforementioned lords to persist whenever he noticed some timidity.

Day by day the sisters began to soften and surrender to the religious life, and he trusted God that such a good, blessed, spiritual life would grow in these three

145. For Elisabeth Toppel (Elsbeth Töpplin) as a scribe, see Anne Winston-Allen, "Making Manuscripts as Political Engagement by Women in the Fifteenth-Century Observant Reform Movement," *Journal of Medieval Religious Cultures* 42 (2016): 224–247, at 227.

146. The Carthusian and Augustianian communities were reformed to the Observance of their respective orders, whereas the Dominican friary of Freiburg was not at the time, nor ever was.

147. *Ich* is crossed out and replaced by *er*.

convents and that God would be praised and honoured for this, the world improved, souls comforted, and the Dominican order embellished. Even though he had enjoyed much help and support from the powerful, he still had received a few scares from rowdies who wished to prevent this, such as the Dominicans who are not reformed and their adherents. If God in his mercy had not inspired him and several other persons to make sure the matter would go smoothly and be well thought out, it could not have proceeded. For this reason, it is very necessary to take up such matters very wisely and very carefully and with great resolve. One must especially call zealously and faithfully upon God with great seriousness and devout diligence, asking that he grant a salutary, fortunate, good progress to his own will, his honour, and the salvation of souls, which he redeemed and bought with his holy, dear blood.

5.67 *How the convent of Altenhohenau in Bavaria was reformed by five sisters from the convent of St Catherine in Nuremberg* [fol. 222r]

At the same time, in 1465, at the command of the superiors of our order and at the instigation and desire of the illustrious prince the duke of Bavaria,[148] a convent of sisters was reformed which lies in the countryside about seven miles outside of Landshut. It is called Altenhohenau and was reformed by the prior of Landshut, Friar Gilg Schwertmann.[149] After much work and after the matter of this reform had been negotiated for a long time, five sisters from St Catherine's convent in Nuremberg were selected and led to this convent to begin the holy Observance. The names of these spiritual sisters are: Sister Appolonia Imhof, first prioress of this Observance; Sister Barbara Schuler; Sister Margreta Kuntzelmann; Sister Elisabeth Heinlin; Sister Margretha Fock. Honour and praise be to God the Lord. Amen.

5.68 *On the convent of St Agnes in Strasbourg and how it first gained an inclination to the holy Observance* [fol. 222r]

At Strasbourg, in the meadow outside of the circuit wall, lies a convent called St Agnes. This convent is a quite honourable, rich cloister which surpasses other convents in loveliness, size, the delightful beauty of the buildings, flowing water,

148. Louis (Ludwig) IX, duke of Bavaria-Landshut (r. 1450–1479). For resources on Altenhohenau, see www.phil-fak.uni-duesseldorf.de/en/forschung/schriftlichkeit-in-sueddeutschen-frauenkloestern/altenhohenau-dominikanerinnenkloster/#c46516 (accessed 1 December 2018); Melanie Hömberg, "Wirtschafts(Buch)führung im Kontext: Der Umgang mit Schriftlichkeit in reformierten Frauenklöstern in Süddeutschland" (PhD diss., Ludwig-Maximilians-Universität Munich, 2013), 43–190.

149. This prior was named as Egidius in **5.49**; see the note there.

and other delightful comforts. Yet since without the fear of God these things serve sin more than virtue, the many inhabitants of this place forgot respect for God, for virtue, and for religion, and they lived more according to the pleasure of their bodies than for the salvation of their souls.

Nevertheless, the desire for the religious life remained in some, although very few. On their own and through their good friends, both religious and secular people, with prayers and pleading, these women petitioned their superiors for aid in beginning the holy Observance there and in starting such a life as their sisters in St Nicholas-in-Undis lived.[150] God, who begins all good things, so willed it that the prioress of St Agnes died and a prioress was chosen from among those who wished for the Observance, Sister Brida Melbrüggen. This devout prioress, although still young in years, had a firm zeal in all things divine, virtuous, and spiritual. So she put all her weight behind bringing the convent to the Observance, but did this in great secrecy from the unwilling sisters.

It so happened that the honourable master, the father provincial, Friar Peter Wellen, came to Strasbourg on visitation. The honourable prioress called together the convent's advocates and many of its best friends, who were quite notable, distinguished, and powerful in the city – knights, masters, lords of the council, and such people – and gathered them into two armies or parties, one of men and the other of women. The prioress instructed them to go to the provincial at St Nicholas, each in their appointed order and time, to request and petition for the reform of St Agnes, and they received a kind answer from him.

The honourable master father provincial wisely looked into the matter and wrote about the affair to the master general, Master Martial Auribelli, requesting his approval. In a letter commanding obedience, the master general entrusted the reform to the honourable lector of the Basel friary, Father Heinrich Schretz, who had been prior in Ulm, which had also only very recently been reformed. So Father Heinrich Schretz came to Strasbourg to learn about the situation. The sisters of St Nicholas secretly lodged him with their confessors, from whom he also received a great deal of information about how this could all be done quietly. The convent of St Nicholas provided great support with counsel and help in this holy work.

150. For the politics of Observant reform and Dominican nuns in Strasbourg, see Hirbodian, "Dominikanerinnenreform und Familienpolitik"; Sigrid Hirbodian, "Pastors and Seducers: The Practice of the *Cura monialium* in Mendicant Convents in Strasbourg," in *Partners in Spirit: Women, Men, and Religious Life in Germany, 1100–1500*, ed. Fiona Griffiths and Julie Hotchin (Turnhout, 2014), 303–337; Sigrid Hirbodian, *Geistliche Frauen und städtische Welt: Kanonissen – Nonnen – Beginen und ihre Umwelt am Beispiel der Stadt Straßburg im Spätmittelalter, 1250–1520* (Berlin, 2019).

This honourable Father Heinrich Schretz went to Colmar to take sisters from the convent of Unterlinden. Quite recently, only two or three years before, two well-known sisters called Sister Ennel and Sister Gertrud Zorn, sisters by birth, had gone there from the convent of St Agnes in order to keep the holy Observance. The prioress of St Agnes and her good-willed allies heartily desired the return of these two sisters. So the two sisters were given to this father along with an honourable old mother named Sister Margreda of Blumeneck, noble by birth and at the time serving in the office of subprioress. She became the first prioress of the Observance in St Agnes. He was also given a young sister named Sister Ennel Stockhart. With these four sisters, Father Schretz set out for Strasbourg.

5.69 *How great resistance arose against this holy work* [fol. 223v]

While the honourable father Heinrich Schretz was occupied in this holy matter, the enemy of all good was not idle. Rather, he brought it about (we do not doubt that it was done at his prompting) that this affair, which was conducted with great care, secrecy, and silence, became known to the prior of the Dominican friars in Strasbourg, who was also confessor and vicar over St Agnes as well as over the other open convents. His name was Master Johannes Wolfhard, and his deeds conformed to his name, for he was an apostate from the Observance and against all religious life. He came in a great rage to the convent of St Agnes, rang for a chapter meeting, and assembled the convent. He told them all how they had been betrayed and sold out, and that foreign women were being brought to enclose their convent. If they would help him, he would provide strong support, and so on. He used many other words to move and excite the hearts of the unwilling sisters so that they also became greatly enraged and ferocious towards the prioress. The willing sisters became very concerned and the prioress frightened and endangered, for he immediately incited great evil and cruelty, as if they had committed great injustice and harm. He even set himself against this divine affair with violence.

The prioress of St Agnes notified the sisters of St Nicholas of this great trouble. She asked them for help and counsel and instructions on how to behave, since they had previously received counsel from them quite often and done many things according to their teaching. The sisters of St Nicholas wrote back to her, comforted her, and advised her not to let any threats frighten her. Under no circumstances should she part with the keys of her office and to the gates of the cloister. If the prior Master Wolfhard wished to use violence, then she should appeal to the master general and cling to her office however she could. But the sisters of St Nicholas also quickly wrote to the advocates of St Agnes and told them all the actions and intentions of the prior and explained to them what it was appropriate to do in this situation. The two advocates immediately showed themselves willing, since they both were steadfast towards the religious life. They went to Master Wolfhard and told him firmly and seriously that he should reconsider and leave the prioress in her office. If he did not, he could expect their displeasure and wait to see what would happen to him. And so the matter was settled.

But the sisters of St Nicholas quickly sent a runner with a letter up to Father Heinrich Schretz, in which the whole situation was laid out. They explained to him all the dealings that had occurred there in the preceding days and begged him to return quickly with the sisters. But the messenger did not find him, for he and the sisters had gone a different way.

5.70 *How the sisters of Unterlinden were brought to Strasbourg and prevented by the Dominicans there from entering the convent of St Agnes* [fol. 224v]

The day after these foregoing events transpired, the honourable Father Heinrich Schretz arrived with the sisters from Unterlinden around the time for Vespers on the Feast of St Lucia [13 December] during Advent 1465. He had the driver of the cart in which the sisters rode stop at a point outside the city and he himself went to St Nicholas. On the advice of the prioress and both bursars, he decided to enter St Agnes right away. The sisters of St Nicholas asked the prioress of St Agnes to stand with her allies in the middle of the convent's gate so that Father Schretz and the sisters could drive in without resistance. But the Dominican prior had filled the streets around the convent of St Agnes with his friars to keep a lookout for Father Schretz and the path he would take with the sisters.

At Vespers, a monk named Heinrich Mennel came running furiously, calling out "The enemy is coming! The enemy is coming!" This Heinrich Mennel had also, on assignment from his prior, gone to Colmar to keep watch so that he would be forewarned. When the sisters were taken out of Unterlinden, he was to return immediately and inform him, which he had diligently done. When this cry rang out, other Dominicans were at hand, who had been waiting for this spectacle. They ran into the convent of St Agnes and tried to close the gates forcibly, but the prioress with her allies resisted them. So the monks gave the prioress an ultimatum: she could either go into the convent and allow the gate to be shut, or she could go out, for they would shut the gate either way. When the prioress and her allies saw that they could not gain the upper hand, she still would not yield until the gate was violently shut. She and three of the good-willed sisters who were with her were locked out of the convent and had to spend the night outside in the bursar's house.

The monks had not only shut the gates of the convent, but now also guarded it. Four Dominicans held watch there overnight, namely, their confessor

Johannes Mülling, Heinrich Mennel, Johannes Ortwin, and Christopholus Tegel. During the night, they kept watch so no one could go in or out. The wife of a knight, that year's burgomaster whose name was Lord Diebold of Mullenheim, was also locked into the convent, since she had gone in to visit her daughter. Since the knight, no matter his words and threats, could not get the monks to let his wife out, the city councilmen were gathered that same evening till late in the night, in order to get this knight's wife out by force. But the monks inside, after they had closed the gates of the convent, went to high windows and kept a lookout for the approach of the foreign sisters. Many other Dominicans made rounds outside the convent, calling up to those inside at the windows to keep a good watch. They did many other outrageous things that were inappropriate for them. Dominican outposts were even stationed at the gates of the city in the area. Those inside the convent rang the bells and there was immediately a tumultuous crowd running about and screaming, as if a castle were being stormed. While these things were happening, night fell.

The good father Heinrich Schretz and his driver hurried to a different gate, and since they could not get to the convent of St Agnes they turned to the sisters of St Nicholas, who received them lovingly and joyfully as friends. They took the sisters into their convent and for their sake performed the work of mercy, showing them sisterly faithfulness and also providing all necessities for the outer servants and the horses.

Right away, the sisters of St Nicholas sent their bursar to the mayor for some guards to protect the locked-out prioress of St Agnes and her allies. The mayor, named Lord Heinrich Arge, was a very God-fearing man, who earlier had also given Father Heinrich Schretz a bodyguard at the recommendation of the sisters of St Nicholas, before he took the sisters out of Unterlinden. Six city guards were sent to watch through the night and ensure that no one got hurt. While these guards were keeping their watch, they found a nun, one of the unwilling sisters inside, who had climbed out of the convent in order to pursue her usual foolishness. They captured her and escorted her to the prioress in the bursar's house.

5.71 *How great trouble and toil arose before the Strasbourg city council was convinced to permit the convent of St Agnes to be reformed* [fol. 226v]

When morning came, Father Heinrich Schretz, the advocates of St Agnes convent, and other honourable persons came to the official to ask his advice on bringing the matter to an end as peaceably and with as little friction as possible. This official was named Master Johannes of Helmstadt, who was related to a bursar in St Nicholas, Sister Ennel of Thann. As an especially good friend, she had thoroughly informed him about this holy matter before it started and told him to follow it up with our gracious lord the bishop of Strasbourg[151] and to agree with her and Father Schretz implicitly. But when he heard how the thing had gone and what had been done, he took a step back and said he could not and would not fight with anyone. They should go to the courthouse before the burgomasters and council and file a suit.

And so Father Schretz with the honourable Master Wentzel of Francken-stein, the confessor of St Nicholas, and with his companion the other confessor, Friar Peter Pflüger, went to the courthouse and filed a complaint about this afore-said matter with the masters and the city council of Strasbourg. They recounted how the honourable father provincial, Master Peter Wellen, had inspected his convents in the city of Strasbourg and found such a way of life in the convent of St Agnes that it was not proper to allow it to continue. Since many knights, squires, honourable persons, and powerful people in the city had requested it, a different life should be arranged and the convent reformed. Now, the provincial had entrusted the affair to Father Schretz and called him from Ulm, where he had been prior, and given him full authority to complete the matter, commanding him to do it out of obedience, so he had brought sisters from Colmar out of Unterlinden here; but Master Wolfhard, the prior of the Dominican friars, showed up and tasked the sisters with hindering his [Father Schretz's] authority so that he was not able to fulfil his obedient duty.

Lord Jörg Zorn, a knight, and Lord Conrad Riff were also present, both advocates of the convent of St Agnes, with other notable people. They complained on behalf of the locked-out prioress, who was also present with her three sisters, how she had been shut out of the convent unlawfully and that four friars had spent the night in the convent. They demanded to know, Was this honourable for the city? Did it please them and should it be allowed? After this complaint, they were asked to step out and the council deliberated. Once they had made their decision, the council sent two messengers. One went to St Agnes to order the monks to leave and the other went to the Dominican friary to announce the verdict to the prior Master Johannes Wolfhard. He was ordered to allow the locked-out prioress with her three sisters back into the convent, to bless them and release them from excommunication, and to leave her in the office of prioress. This all was done accordingly. And so this day was spent in much effort for this work.

151. Ruprecht of Palatinate-Simmern, bishop of Strasbourg (r. 1440–1478). He was the cousin of Ruprecht of the Palatinate, archbishop of Cologne, whom Meyer mentioned in **5.58**. Both men were named after their grandfather Ruprecht, the Holy Roman emperor (r. 1400–1410).

5.72 *How the antagonists who had obstructed this godly work defended their accomplished injustice in open court* [fol. 227v]

On the next day, the lector [*sic*] Johannes Wolfhard went before the burgomasters and council in the courthouse with some other fathers of his convent and demanded to be heard. He complained that he had been unjustly accused before them and tried to cover up his accomplished injustice with very lovely interpretations, but the story of what had happened was so well known that no one believed his embellishments. Still, he asserted that he was the vicar of the convent of St Agnes and that he knew no other authority presently overseeing the convent than himself. He had done what he had done for this reason, and no force had been exercised on anyone unlawfully, and a lot of similar blather.

When the prior had thus clearly set forth his explanation, Father Heinrich Schretz was called back before the masters and council to repeat his own claims in the presence of the prior Master Johannes Wolfhard. Once that had happened, it was decided that the prior and Father Heinrich Schretz should both produce the evidence of their authority. When both their letters of authority had been read before the masters and council, it was found that Father Heinrich Schretz had the more recent letter and greater authority and that he should pursue his affairs unhindered by the prior. And so this day also was wasted on much turmoil in this work.

5.73 *How some friends of the unwilling sisters complained before the masters and council and resisted this reform* [fol. 228r]

On the third day, the honourable Father Heinrich Schretz went again before the council and requested persons employed by some notable man who could help him to complete the godly matter and lead the sisters from Unterlinden into the convent of St Agnes and who would protect him from violence. A knight named Lord Ludwig of Mullenheim, a burgomaster of the opposing party, stood up in the council. He complained on behalf of the unwilling sisters that this monk wanted to drive the sisters out of the convent away from their old roots and to place foreign sisters there and that this was unseemly and improper. When the mayor dismissed his words, saying that the matter had been sufficiently examined, the knight became angry and made a great ruckus that they should let him speak and permit him to have his say, etc. Before he would let such a thing proceed, he would kick the monk's head until his brain leaked out his nose. It would be right and proper, since the prioress and her companions had been examined, to hear the other party also. This aforenamed knight and others publicly lodged all sorts of complaints against the good father Heinrich Schretz: that he had begun the affair so untactfully and unreasonably that murder and manslaughter would have followed if others had not gotten in the way. Many similar, weighty accusations were made against this father, which I leave out for the sake of brevity, since it would be too long to write and probably unpleasant to read or hear.

Throughout all of this and more of the same scorn, whenever he was addressed the honourable father Heinrich Schretz answered so patiently and meekly and nevertheless so wisely, prudently, and well that it was a marvel to the people who heard it.

After all this, the masters and council agreed that the opposing party should also be examined. Messengers were sent to fetch the nuns of the recalcitrant party and bring them all to the court. When the prioress with her small number of three sisters saw that the unwilling women were all being led before the masters and council and that she was left alone with three sisters, she judged her cause lost and went into the choir, exposed the holy sacrament, sang, and called upon God for aid. They filled the house of God with tears, sighs, and wails. When the messenger from the council arrived at the church and heard and saw this miserable lament, he was moved to great compassion and said, "If God does not come to help these good women, he is not a just God."

Throughout all of this, the sisters of St Nicholas were sending up great prayers, with processions and sung masses, with appeals to the dear saints and many similar prayers that God would arrange this affair for the best. With the help, advice, and facilitation of their friends, their two confessors, their bursar, and their servants, and from the very beginning till the end of the affair, they did everything in all ways, both material and spiritual, as if it were their own persons and their own convent at stake. Thus they fulfilled the words that our holy father Saint Dominic spoke at the very beginning of the foundation of the Order of Preachers. When he saw Saint Francis in Rome working to achieve the confirmation of his own order, he embraced him and said, "If we stand together, no one may stand against us." These two convents stood together in love of God and never strayed from each other in any tribulation.

Those nuns of the other party who dared to come before people for the sake of honour all came before the court and lodged a great complaint on their behalf: Father Schretz was trying to bind them too tightly to their constitutions and to impose more than the order required. They requested earnestly that they be left to their former accustomed life. The honourable Father Heinrich Schretz countered this plaint, saying that he did not desire to inflict anything imprudent or severe on them, nor to bind or burden them with anything other than what was good for them to suffer and bear, and which the sisters of St Nicholas also observed. He gave them sincere assurance of this. He then wished to lay the matter entirely before the city councilmen; whatever they proclaimed to have been justly imposed, he would enforce it; whatever they thought was too harsh and unbearable, he would accept their judgement. Through such consideration, kindness, and wise negotiation of the matter, he inclined the lords of the council to his favour. The council appointed four laymen, without whom he was neither to do nor arrange anything in this matter. The honourable Master Wentzel of Franckenstein, the confessor of St Nicholas, was also assigned to support Father Heinrich Schretz and help him complete this holy work.

When the prior saw the inclination of the council, he realized that the matter was going to proceed and said that it would be right and proper for it to be undertaken according to procedure and that he would do his best in this. The mayor responded, "So let all help one another to accomplish this."

5.74 *Of the care put into determining which articles and points should constitute the reform* [fol. 230r]

After all these things, a day was set in the chancery when the three religious men (Father Heinrich Schretz, Master Wentzel, and the prior, Master Johannes Wolfhard) and the four appointed laymen should come. One of these four was the advocate of St Nicholas, a very honourable and God-fearing man named Hans of Winterthur, who was appointed with three city magistrates. He requested thorough information from his women, the sisters of St Nicholas. They provided him with a lovely lesson, namely, that protection against visibility is the foundation of all religious life. They said that all religious people in an order are required to observe the three vows (poverty, chastity, and obedience), but he should know that neither chastity nor poverty may be fully kept in a place with windows and outside views. They explained this to him succinctly, saying, "We are all human. When I see father, mother, brother, or sister come to me in their worldly station, I hold images of them in my heart. When I should pray, contemplate good things, or serve God in singing and reading, the clothes, manner, behaviour, and gestures of secular people come to mind. This taints true chastity. When I am seen, I am ashamed of my poverty and humble clothing. I would like to have a clean, fine veil, a pretty and soft wimple, prim clothes, and such things. Otherwise I come out of the church or from my work without shame or sadness of heart and I remain thus untroubled in my spirit and in obedient poverty, etc." The God-fearing man took these and similar words so deeply to heart that he put all his energy into ensuring that the community of St Agnes would not be visible. He also coaxed and inclined the other appointed laymen to this, even though it was very hard for some. At this time, very few reformed convents were granted this at first, especially in the first year, because of the unwilling to whom one usually granted a probationary year.

When the appointed parties came together on the appointed day, Master Wolfhard, the prior, let loose with many interpretations, clever speech, and several kinds of argument that the former sisters, who were still very unused to the situation, should be left a small window, secured with three keys. Their confessor should have one, the prioress another, and the subprioress the third, so that every now and then the still unaccustomed sisters could see father, mother, brother, and sister. This proposal was rejected, and it was determined that the sisters of St Agnes should keep their windows closed and hold property in common, as did the sisters of St Nicholas. In other points, the unwilling sisters should be treated gently: those who could not go without meat were to be given meat in appropriate places; those who could not fast would be allowed to eat; those who would not wear wool would be permitted to wear linen; those who would not lie on straw would be left with their beds; and those who would not come to Matins would be allowed to sleep in. They would be given two months to try it, and then those who did not wish to stay would be allowed to take their temporal possessions, just as the Zorn sisters had been paid when they left St Agnes for Unterlinden. And so the assembly dissolved.

5.75 *How it was recorded in the Strasbourg city book that the convent of St Agnes was to be reformed and how the sisters from Unterlinden were honourably led in* [fol. 231v]

Early on the fifth day, Father Heinrich Schretz again went and requested support for carrying out his obedient duty. The four appointed laymen were asked if they believed the matter could be satisfactorily pursued by the responsible party. The four explained the previous decision wisely, saying that it was possible, and such a godly project that if it were not accomplished they worried that the honourable city of Strasbourg and its whole community would have to answer for it before God. The masters and council therefore unanimously decided that the convent of St Agnes should be reformed according to all forms and measures of the sisters of St Nicholas. Once this was finally decided and recorded in the city book, a command was given that whoever was found working against this resolution, either secretly or openly by worldly action, would be fined fifteen marks of silver and expelled from the city for ten years.

Once this had happened, Father Heinrich Schretz came with an honourable company of religious and secular people, women and men: the councillors of our worthy lord of Strasbourg, the aforementioned official, the four honourable appointed laymen, both of the advocates, and other knights, squires, and city masters, as well as the abbess of Andlau and other lordly ladies. All these wished to lead the sisters of Unterlinden into the convent of St Agnes, but the sisters of St Nicholas had provided them with a covered wagon so that no one would be able to see them. Thus, with a great crowd and honourable company, they were brought into the convent of St Agnes in 1465 on the day when the holy church sings the devout antiphon "O Sapientia" [17 December].

Once they were brought into the choir, their vicar, Father Heinrich Schretz, held a beautiful sermon for them in the presence of the whole crowd. Master Johannes Wolfhard did not want to be seen to oppose such a great crowd of people, so he also gave a lovely sermon on enclosure, how useful it is, and the eventual benefit they would receive from keeping it, even though it would be difficult in the beginning, and similar words. After the two sermons, Father Heinrich Schretz separated the four foreign sisters in one place and put them to his right. Beginning with the former prioress of St Agnes, he asked each one after another if she would willingly assume the Observance. Whoever answered that she wished to submit herself, he called her to stand on his right with the four sisters who had been brought there. The prioress and her three companions stepped to the right with the Unterlinden sisters, but the others gave strange and wild answers. Since these things had taken so long that it had become late, he told them to go to table, and the official and the others took their leave. Their vicar, Father Heinrich Schretz, and the prior, Master Johannes Wolfhard, and the four appointed laymen remained there. The sisters who had been brought there and the good-willed sisters were led into a chamber and given food, but the unwilling sisters ran around in the convent and tried by various ways and means to get their possessions out, but the six guards who had been appointed by the city prevented any of them from escaping.

5.76 *How the sisters from Unterlinden were appointed to the convent's offices* [fol. 233r]

After the meal, Father Heinrich Schretz gathered all the sisters of the convent to a chapter meeting and appointed sisters to the offices in the presence of the two confessors of St Nicholas and the four laymen. The prioress humbly surrendered her office and her keys and the worthy mother Sister Margreda of Blumeneck became prioress. The former prioress was placed in the office of subprioress. Sister Ennel Zorn became bursar and Sister Gertrud Zorn, her biological sister, sacristan and monitor. Sister Ennel Stockhart became novice mistress and cellarer. The vicar and the four laymen decided to hire a smith to install locks. They also decided to have the speaking window and other access points closed, to have cell windows and any openings in walls and doors walled up, and to pursue whatever was necessary for this without delay in order to prevent all coming and going.

But the unwilling sisters kept muttering against this. They did not want to accept the privileges they had been granted, which were described earlier, but rather to leave the convent. Their vicar and also the prior, Master Johannes Wolfhard, forbade them under pain of excommunication and by their obedience from leaving before the appointed time. Still, eight of them banded together and, at the instigation of the prior Master Johannes Wolfhard, set themselves against the religious life with all their might. Whenever Wolfhard spoke openly before many, he praised the Observant life greatly, and how good and useful it is. Secretly, he did everything in his power against it and gave the unwilling sisters advice on ways and means of resisting it. When the four laymen heard and saw their outrageous obstinacy – for they zealously demanded to leave and refused to wait even a short time – they said they all deserved to be incarcerated. But Father Heinrich Schretz, in his mildness of spirit, prevented this, hoping that it would get better in a few days.

Father Heinrich Schretz and the others had spent the day in great labour. Once night had fallen, Father Heinrich Schretz and all the outer persons, including the servants that some of the women had privately employed, took their leave and the gates were shut fast, but the sisters began to wail, scream, and weep anew when they had to part from their servants. During the night, the convent was watched from outside by the six appointed city guards who had not departed from the convent day and night. The convent had to give them food and drink and pay them one shilling in pennies every day. They not only protected the convent from the outside, but also listened to hear any screaming in the convent that might require them to go in and help.

5.77 *How Father Heinrich Schretz was arraigned before the bishop of Strasbourg for this good work and called to answer before the bishop's council* [fol. 234r]

After all these things had happened and the good-willed sisters thought that they had earned a little peace, the true battle began. Through secret messages sent daily from within the convent to Wolfhard, the unwilling sisters caused a great grievance to come before our gracious lord bishop.[152] They claimed to have been harshly restrained and bound to duties beyond their strength. They called on him to judge their affair, but our gracious lord bishop delegated the matter to his chancellor, a harsh and severe man. He wrote to Father Heinrich Schretz that he must answer to his officers at the date, time, and place he would decide.

When Father Heinrich Schretz came before the bishop's council on the appointed day, the chancellor demanded on behalf of the unwilling sisters that

152. I.e., Ruprecht of Palatinate-Simmern, bishop of Strasbourg; see note in **5.71**.

they be left to their former lifestyle and given back their cells so that they might see their friends and family and do whatever they wished according to their desires and whims. Father Heinrich Schretz responded that the matter had proceeded quite far and been confirmed by the burgomasters and city council, and so he could not and would not change it. At this, the chancellor treated him very poorly and shamefully with nasty words, called him a tyrant, and said the convent must be reopened, no matter whom it helped or hurt. He claimed that it was not his gracious lord's intention that a monk should exercise such power within his diocese and many similar things. Father Heinrich Schretz then brought before the chancellor the two advocates of the convent of St Agnes and other honourable men, who witnessed the chancellor's impropriety. They said that the convent must maintain its new religious life, that such was written in the city record, and that they would love to see whoever thought he was powerful enough to open the convent, for his property and his life must not be very dear for him to risk it in this manner. A great division arose between the lords of the city and the bishop's council, whose officers cried, "This unholy monk is undertaking to divide our merciful lord's grace and the city from one another in eternal unrest!"

The process again broke down for the time, and the affair remained with the laypeople. I could not describe briefly how three days were spent in this turbulent manner, during which Father Heinrich Schretz went back and forth between the bishop's council and the secular authorities because of his responsibility in the matter being negotiated. After this, Father Heinrich Schretz left the city and entrusted the spiritual life of St Agnes to the sisters of St Nicholas, who provided them with confession, sermons, and the sacrament through their confessors, and their external affairs to the four laymen, who also gave their best effort to assist and protect them in their newly begun religious life.

5.78 *How the good-willed sisters in the convent of St Agnes had to suffer so greatly and in so many ways during the early beginning and how they were often in fear and danger* [fol. 235r]

The fear, danger, and anxiety in which the good-willed sisters suffered day and night during this time can neither be fully written nor recounted, for the unwilling sisters constantly ran about in the convent, joining the community neither in choir, nor in refectory, nor at table, nor even at night in the dormitory. They behaved intractably and obstinately and troubled the mother prioress unceasingly about letting them leave. They jabbered to the other sisters about the unsuitability of their hearts and the displeasure they had in everything religious. They also received daily messages from the lector, Master Wolfhard, through secret means that the Unterlinden sisters did not know about and therefore could not watch out for. They had underground passages and other exits, through which they could pass notes and other things and receive answers.

On the Feast of the Holy Innocents [28 December] early after Matins, eight of them together secretly left the convent with the help of the Dominican friars. They filled the ears of an entire crowd with the sound of their wailing, spread many great lies about the sisters of St Agnes, and brought great contempt upon them. Their account perverted the sisters' lifestyle, their gestures, and their religious order, exposing them to scorn. Moreover, they encouraged their friends to make serious threats, so that the good sisters began to fear for their lives and, in their terror, did not dare to sleep. They threatened to burn the convent down and that very soon people would be saying, "The convent of St Agnes once stood here." The good sisters noticed strange persons in their cloister at night and men walking around the convent carrying covered lamps and firebrands. In the morning, their bursar found bundles of fuses, which they showed to the mayor. They also found explosives outside under the dormitory when they just happened to be sweeping there in preparation to shore up and close an unsecured spot. So many other similar hiding places with dangerous materials in them were found that it was no longer human caution but only God's power and the protection of his right hand that saved the convent from damage.

There was also unbelievable labour with daily tasks and all sorts of messages. Moreover, some of the wisest among the learned were called and the most distinguished of the noble knights and squires of the land, in order to take up the matter on behalf of the runaways with the intention of bringing them back to their old ways. This army of people was so large that the lords of the city were amazed. After these conferences, which met a couple of times because they actually accomplished nothing, the heart of the prior, Master Johannes Wolfhard, still would not rest and surrender the convent. Instead, he insinuated to the chancellor that his gracious lord bishop had the power and authority to forbid the sisters of St Agnes from building anything in the convent that would serve the religious life, or changing anything, or altering anything the runaways had used. One of the bishop's sworn notaries, Obrecht Knapp, fined them fifty marks of silver and demanded eternal submission to the bishop, since they were bound to him in dutiful obedience, as those within his diocese must observe. The good sisters of St Agnes were greatly frightened by this and sent to the lords of the city and to their advocate, Master Paul Munthart, and explained the matter to them. They then lodged an appeal against the bishop and posted it on all the doors of the cathedral chapterhouse, according to the legal custom when someone appeals against a regional lord.

Before the masters and city council, Master Johannes Wolfhard was blamed for the way this affair had proceeded at his instigation. The lords of the city asked him whether it was true that he recently had, in a matter concerning his own friary, claimed before the masters and council that our gracious lord the bishop had no jurisdiction over him. How, then, was it possible for the sisters of St Agnes to be subject to such authority and such a heavy fine, since they were also religious people of the same order? He replied that it was a special case: some bishops have powers or privileges, and in a case where a community is divided they may assume control. But he maintained under strict oath that he was not responsible, even though the time and place were named and shown to him.

So the friends of the convent of St Agnes then brought the affair before our gracious lord Duke Stephan,[153] who took the matter up. He found a way for the appeal against his brother the bishop to be dismissed, and St Agnes gave the bishop twelve florins.

5.79 *How this reform was confirmed with great trouble and labour and at great cost by the master general of the order as soon as it was requested* [fol. 237r]

After all of this, it became common knowledge that Master Johannes Wolfhard had, both in private and in public, refused to stand down from the convent of St Agnes. It was decided in the council that they themselves should send certain messengers, who knew about all the negotiations and the whole history of the affair, to the master general to speak with him face to face and explain the truth clearly. The messengers were to request confirmation of this Observance and also closure of the windows, so that in the future the convent might be more secure against Wolfhard's clever tricks.

Secular priests were chosen for this task. One of them was a foreigner named Master William, who was a canon at Young St Peter's. He was very distinguished and respected at the papal court and a special friend of the master general, with whom he had spent much time in school and in Rome. The second was a parish priest of the same community named Claus. They prepared themselves quickly for the journey and, for greater surety, took with them written affidavits from the sisters of St Agnes and their advocates. In addition, the sisters of St Nicholas wrote to provide a truthful account of the unjust, overwhelming, and diverse resistance put up by Master Johannes Wolfhard and his cronies.

Even though these messengers left the city as quietly as possible, Master Johannes Wolfhard found out about it after two days and hurried after them so

153. Stephan of Palatinate-Simmern (1421–1485) was attached to the Strasbourg cathedral and a duke by virtue of birth only. The supporters of the St Agnes sisters approached him in hopes that he would use the familial connection with his brother, Bishop Ruprecht (see note in **5.71** and **5.77**), to intervene on their behalf.

quickly that he caught up with them in Basel and joined their party. They would have liked to get rid of him and said they were making a pilgrimage, but he answered that he would like to be their companion. He never left their side until three days out of Avignon, when he started up and said, "Hey, now I see well what the story is here. I want to be the first there." So he rushed off quickly to the master general, Master Martial Auribelli, and laid forth the whole matter in a way that made the messengers who followed him seem like flatterers, bringing false news and asking for improper and impossible things.

These still came before the master general to complete their appointed task, but they could accomplish nothing further than to receive a letter from the master general confirming that the convent of St Agnes stood under the care, habit, and statutes of our order. He neither would nor should nor could bind them further to enclosure, common property, or observance of the Constitutions as long as a semblance of justice remained. Yet despite the persistent prayers of these messengers for approval to close the windows, this could no longer be accomplished because Wolfhard was constantly present. As long as he convinced the master general that he and five assistants were dealing with the matter, he knew it could not go against him on that front.

Both parties returned to Strasbourg. Master Johannes Wolfhard rejoiced in the wonderful things that had happened for him, especially bragging that he had read all the letters concerning him from the sisters of St Nicholas. He said that they had crossed him and he would get back at them or die, a promise he fully kept. Through God's foresight, while the messengers had been in Avignon, our honourable father provincial had provided the sisters of St Agnes with a confessor named Friar Johannes Bremgarten, who had been lector in Pforzheim. When Master Johannes Wolfhard returned from Avignon, Friar Bremgarten presented himself out of respect for his position as prior. Yet the prideful spirit is only raised higher when another is humbled before it, and Master Johannes Wolfhard showed this by his words, asking why Friar Johannes Bremgarten was at the convent, since it was his own prerogative to provide it with confessors. The confessor showed him the certificate from the father provincial, to which Master Johannes Wolfhard answered: "The provincial is taking too much on. The convent must be handled otherwise. They have angered me, and they will regret it." He was told that the sisters of St Agnes had the aid of the best people in the city, but Wolfhard only ranted at length about the sisters and the convent.

As he was thinking up such great things, the advocates of St Agnes became frightened and went to the sisters of St Nicholas to complain of it. These sisters comforted the advocates, saying that they would stand by the sisters of St Agnes through good and bad as long as they repudiated their ways anew and conformed to St Nicholas. They said, "If you want to have the sisters of St Agnes just like us, you should tell Master Wolfhard, and can happily do so, that our vicar should also be the vicar of St Agnes." The advocates were comforted by this and went with some of the other friends of the St Agnes sisters to Master Johannes Wolfhard and told him that he should take care to leave the sisters of St Agnes unmolested in their new Observance; this they desired of him, etc. But his words were very proud: as they would find out, the runaways would have to return and recover what belonged to them, for this had been entrusted to him and five other people. He claimed that he still had power over St Agnes and would talk to no one until this had been done. And so they left it.

After a few days, Master Johannes Wolfhard came with someone named Johannes Ortwin to the speaking window at St Agnes and demanded to speak with the whole convent. He announced his vicariate to them and asked them whether they intended to accept him. In great anxiety, the mother prioress withdrew to consider this, but quickly sent word to her sisters in St Nicholas and asked for their advice. They wrote quickly back to her that she should answer him thus: they had a vicar from the Observance who was also vicar over the sisters of St Nicholas, to whom they wished to conform in this as in all things. So Master Johannes Wolfhard again began his furious conniving and brought together four members of our order, whose names I leave out, and wrote a great treatise and many letters about how the speaking window should be opened again and the runaways should be taken back in. Again, no better counsel was found than that Father Heinrich Schretz himself should go to the master general in Avignon to beg forgiveness for the great misdeeds that Master Johannes Wolfhard had laid at his door and to work towards the confirmation of the new Observance and the closure of the window. After much labour, he fully accomplished this through God's mercy. Master Johannes Wolfhard found out about it and sent yet another message with one of his friars, this Johannes Ortwin, to the master general, with an improper letter against our honourable father provincial, Master Peter Wellen, and Father Heinrich Schretz. When the messenger arrived and realized that the closure of the window was no longer up for discussion, he nevertheless did enough to get the master general himself to come personally so that Master Johannes Wolfhard could accomplish in his presence what he was not able to bring about at a distance.

5.80 *How the master general himself came personally to German lands because of the Observance in St Agnes and the trouble that came from it* [fol. 239v]

And so after some time had passed, Master General Martial Auribelli travelled through German lands and came personally to Strasbourg. When the sisters of St Nicholas became aware of his presence, they sent good friends of theirs and of the sisters in St Agnes with a letter stating the following:

> Most worthy master and dearest father, in submissive and willing obedience, we rejoice over your worthy arrival as over a long-awaited confirmer and accomplisher of good and divine works, in particular of the newly begun and most holy Observance of our sisters in St Agnes. Without a doubt, we hurry with great hope, trusting in your fatherly kindness. He who, for the sake of the Observance, had indulged and administered to our aforementioned sisters from afar, will strengthen, increase, and expand it when close and present. We have no cause to distrust this, even though doubt may decrease our good hope through those who have been seen to set themselves powerfully and markedly against us and the aforesaid new Observance. They say that the grace and confirmation which your worthiness bestowed upon our sisters will be reduced or eliminated by your presence. Despite this, we do not capitulate, but await a future conclusion for the best. Therefore, since your most worthy person is highly praised for being zealous in seeking out the ground of the matter with complete probity in partisan affairs, most honourable master, we entrust ourselves, our convent, and all our affairs to your fatherly protection and give ourselves obediently to your will. With this, we commend your honourable person to Christ Jesus, our preserver. Amen.

In this letter, one can see the sum of the earlier missives that the sisters of St Nicholas had sent to His Worthiness many times regarding this matter. When the good friends of both of these convents – knights, squires, burgomasters, and mayors – brought this letter to the master general, they received him very honourably and worthily, and with great zeal and seriousness begged him for confirmation of the Observance and for closure of the window, but they were given no conclusive answer. When they took leave of the master general, Master Johannes Wolfhard represented them as not really invested in the matter and said their behaviour was hypocritical. But Master Johannes Wolfhard sent some of his peers, who were like him in behaviour and kept similar company, and he told the master general that these were most worthy persons, saying, "This is the cornerstone of the city," and other such things.

After this, the master general went to St Agnes to conduct a visitation with the confessor of the sisters of St Nicholas. He was named Master Wentzel of Franckenstein, an honourable master of theology, and served as translator according to the desire, demand, and petition of the sisters of St Agnes, so that the past lifestyle of the convent, which had been beyond incompatible with the religious life, could be expressed truthfully. The master general himself realized this, saying, "If I do not lend this new Observance stability, then it would be proper for me to abdicate my office."

Even though he said this openly, he still received a great complaint from the bishop's council regarding the runaways and against Father Heinrich Schretz and Master Wentzel, the confessor at St Nicholas. This became apparent when Father Heinrich Schretz was unexpectedly summoned by the master general and called before seven distinguished men, well experienced in both secular and canon law, but wholly mistaken in the present proceedings. They all treated Father Heinrich Schretz evilly in the presence of the master general, saying that he had exercised indecent force and his actions could have caused murder and manslaughter, if others had not stopped it. They were well informed, they said, and if the master general also understood the matter as well as they did, he would punish Father Schretz for it, as was just, especially since he had undertaken to reform all the convents in Strasbourg. They gave these things a solid and strong foundation and expressed pleasure both with the plaintiff of all these things, Master Johannes Wolfhard, who was also present, and with the investigator, the master general, whom they expected to dishonour the innocent Father Heinrich Schretz through a punishment without any means of forgiveness. But he who said, "When you are led before the judges, do not consider your answer, for the spirit of our heavenly father will tell you at that moment what to say,"[154] also inspired this good father with the cautious, wise, and true answer that he truly should be punished for some of his actions in the past matter. His adversaries stood dumbfounded, but while all those who stood around him could not compose themselves, the chancellor spoke with harsh words. "I trust that the worthy master general will punish this outrageous, disrespectful monk, who in my gracious lord's diocese has exercised such dishonourable violence, so that my gracious lord the bishop will see and note that you have honoured him."

So the master general organized and held the chapter of visitation at St Agnes and made confidential all of the past actions that had been brought before him, which particularly concerned Master Johannes Wolfhard. But for the two fathers who had exercised so much zeal in this work, he did not forget to increase the reward for their blessed labour by piling on more suffering, which was evident in the harsh commands the master general laid on Father Heinrich Schretz. He forbade him from going near the convent of St Agnes, deposed him as vicar, and removed him from all other offices. He also forbade him from giving counsel or help to them or to any other reformed convent, especially within the city of Stras-

154. Matthew 10:19–20.

bourg, since the citizens and the best of the city were strongly inclined to reform the other convents as well; and he commanded him to return to the friary in Basel as a novice and to remain that way unless he received express permission from the master general.

Father Heinrich Schretz remained for two years in this despicable oppression. No matter how much was laid on him by his opponents among his brethren [in the order], he bore it to cover up for the master general so that he would not seem to have punished such a good thing, even though this Master Johannes Wolfhard had bragged before the master general's arrival that this would happen by his doing. The reward of the honourable Master Wentzel, confessor of St Nicholas, was similar; he was also dismissed from his office as confessor to the sisters and exiled from the province of Teutonia with the intention that he should never return.

These two letters to Master Johannes Wolfhard were sent by the master general so that he would appear innocent of these acts. The one letter concerning Father Heinrich Schretz was read to his face by Master Johannes Wolfhard in a chapter meeting before the whole community. Mockingly, he read, "There are still two confessors behind, who must also go through." By these words and others, the sisters of St Nicholas were warned to protect their confessor, the father Master Wentzel, from such scorn and to resist any great lies when the religious practice of window closure would be addressed. The sisters of St Nicholas heard this by word of mouth from those who intended to carry it out and headed the situation off by incurring great cost and labour upon themselves, about which harsh and threatening messages were sent under the master general's seal.

But God, who can draw good from a bad thing, had brought about through this unjust violence, that the closure of the windows was finally confirmed by the general chapter that was held in Rome in the octave of Corpus Christi [17–22 June] 1468. In all the time that the reawakening Observance had stood, they had never been able to achieve this. Praise and honour be to God eternally. In this chapter, authority was withdrawn from the master general, Martial Auribelli, and entrusted by our holy father Pope Paul II to Master Leonardo Mansueti of Perugia,[155] who wholly loved the religious life. Through great zeal, effort, and labour, Master Johannes Kreutzer managed to get our holy father the pope to require this chapter to remain in Rome so that the highest dignity of the vicars and agents of Christ could thoroughly experience the disparity of all things with regard to the

155. Master General Martial Auribelli was not present at this chapter and Leonardo Mansueti, who at the time was vicar general, presided in his stead. See Mortier, *Histoire des maîtres généraux*, 4: 423.

holy Observance. The honourable Master Johannes Kreutzer had been in the Dominican order for only three years, but because of this zealous labour and his admirable and virtuous life, he was elected and confirmed as prior of Gebweiler. He gave up his life for the sake of obedience. He was at the convocation of Observant fathers in Wimpfen, and he said that the journey back to Rome, which he had just left, would be much too hard. Nevertheless, in imitation of Christ, he would rather risk his life than lose the virtue of obedience.

The honourable Master Ludwig Fuchs also worked zealously to obtain confirmation of the closure of the windows of all the Observant convents in German lands and to restore the honour and former authority of the honourable fathers Master Wentzel, confessor of the sisters of St Nicholas, and Father Heinrich Schretz, lector and vicar of St Agnes. May he be compensated by the rewarder of all good, for his work could not be summarized in human letters.

I also do not want anyone who reads or hears this record and this story to become angry, for they have not been written in order to slander anyone out of dislike or opinion but rather as a comfort and instruction for those who have the same work before them. They should be that much more cautious, for the children of this world are wiser in their schemes than the children of light.

Whoever would fully reveal the labour that went into the Observance of St Agnes's convent, and the immense amount of writing it took, first to the master general, then to the provincial, as well as to our gracious lady the countess palatine[156] and to other ladies, lords and prelates, both religious and secular – yea, the prioress of St Nicholas alone did so much writing in this affair that she was troubled day and night with the work of writing; also the great cost of the Observance: with the messengers to the master general, and the gifts, and arrangements with the runaways, the sum was not less than 1,200 florins; whoever would truthfully write word for word all these things as they actually happened would need

156. Since the marriage of Frederick I of the Palatinate to Clara Tott was still secret at the time, Meyer cannot mean the wife of the acting count palatine. This countess palatine is most likely Frederick's sister, Mechthild of the Palatinate (1419–1482), who had been widowed for the second time in 1463 and presided alone over a vibrant centre of literary activity in Rottenburg am Neckar. After Meyer had abandoned work on this chronicle, Mechthild and her son, Count Eberhard V of Württemberg-Urach (r. 1459–1496), worked together with Count Ulrich V of Württemberg-Stuttgart (r. 1433–1480) to reform all the Dominican convents in the Württemberg territories, an endeavour in which Meyer himself was also involved. See Alfred Karnein, "Mechthild von der Pfalz as Patroness: Aspects of Female Patronage in the Early Renaissance," *Medievalia et Humanistica* 22 (1995): 141–170; Bernhard Neidiger, *Das Dominikanerkloster Stuttgart, die Kanoniker vom gemeinsamen Leben in Urach und die Gründung der Universität Tübingen: Konkurrierende Reformansätze in der württembergischen Kirchenpolitik am Ausgang des Mittelalters* (Stuttgart, 1993).

more than five sexternions [120 pages]. But these are written for all those who come after as an admonishment to steadfast persistence, for all the convents up till now have not witnessed such great resistance, trouble, and labour in such works. By this it may well be noted that the closer we come to the end of the world, the greater the resistance to justice. Therefore, arm yourselves with patience. This is strongly recommended from now on, for they must suffer not less, but more. I have heard and also read in a letter that reforming the convent of St Gertrude in Cologne was carried out with even greater difficulty.

Praise, honour, thanks, and dignity to him who perfectly rewards all his servants eternally. AMEN.

[*The following three chapters survive only in MS 2934 and are not Meyer's work, but rather additions made by a Strasbourg nun.*]

5.81 *Of the growing religious life and flourishing virtues of the sisters in the convent of St Agnes* [fol. 243v]

After it was enclosed and reformed, this honourable convent and worthy community became like the good soil of which the Gospel says, "Sowing the seed of the divine word, God's help, his grace and gifts, brings fruit a hundredfold."[157] For this convent grew from day to day in religious life, in zeal for virtue, in good exercises, and in the number of its members, so that all the work that had gone into it paid off. This rightly should be a comfort and joy to all those who laboured in the matter, for the effort was little and the seed small compared to the fruit that rose and grew from it.

This blessed congregation became like the green palm standing by the flowing water.[158] Just so did this convent flourish, grow, and increase in virtue and religious life. It saw such an upswing in so short a time that within ten years it had fifty-seven people all veiled in the habit of Saint Dominic's order. Before the enclosure there were only sixteen of them, from whom moreover only eight remained.

This convent can also be compared to precious gold that is proved when it goes through pressure, suffering, and opposition and thus becomes noble gold in the fire. The Lord mildly helped them out of this, for the Lord is faithful and lets his own sink, but not drown.

To what else should I compare these good, devout sisters of the worthy house of God? I can compare them to a special little herb garden through which

157. Matthew 13:8 and 23; Luke 8:8.

158. Psalm 1:3.

the lover of pure hearts walks and plucks the lily of chastity, the rose of love, and the violet of humility to nourish himself.

With this I close the material concerning this blessed convent, lest I cause pride in the hearts of men through too much praise, for while we remain in this vale of tears, the weeds always grow among the wheat. So that the weed of vain honour does not crowd out the noble wheat of virtue and good practice, I end here the talk about this chosen convent, but the virtuous practice of its inhabitants shall have no end until they come into the state of blessedness and the word of Scripture is fulfilled that says, "Praise the sailor when he comes to land." With this, enough has been said to praise this convent and its inhabitants. Praise and honour be to God from age to age eternally. Amen.

5.82 *How the convent of St Agnes was broken up and destroyed by a regional war* [fol. 244v]

When this convent of St Agnes was in its fullest bloom, spiritually and materially, and had been reformed, and had maintained strict enclosure for four days short of ten years[159] – Now see and listen here! – the days of sorrow came during which God plagued the world and punished in particular the German lands with his fatherly rod through the gruesome tyranny of the duke of Burgundy.[160] He had inflicted much trouble, suffering, fear, distress, and sorrow on both country and city, as many are aware and as may well be seen in Neuss,[161] Cologne, and many other cities. The duke now also threatened the cities of Basel, Colmar, Strasbourg, and many others, that he would not leave one stone on top of another.[162]

The honourable city council of Strasbourg considered how they could protect and shield their city from the duke's violence. With this in mind, the lords of the city broke up three Dominican women's convents that lay outside of the cir-

159. These events took place in 1475. See Amy Leonard, *Nails in the Wall: Catholic Nuns in Reformation Germany* (Chicago, 2005), 34–35.

160. Charles the Bold, duke of Burgundy (r. 1467–1477).

161. Charles besieged the city of Neuss in 1474–1475 to put down a rebellion against the archbishop of Cologne, Ruprecht of the Palatinate, who appeared in **5.58** supporting the Observant reform of the Cologne friary.

162. In this second phase of the Burgundian Wars, Charles the Bold repeatedly attacked the Swiss Confederacy, and was repeatedly defeated, until he died at the battle of Nancy in 1477. For both a contemporary local account and a scholarly reconstruction of the events, see Eckehard Simon, "An Unpublished Poem on Charles the Bold and the Burgundian Wars Dated 1475," *Beiträge zur Geschichte der deutschen Sprache und Literatur* 97 (1975): 68–87.

cuit wall. The first convent was called St Mark's, and was the first Dominican convent ever built in the city of Strasbourg and had stood for three hundred years. It was an extraordinarily beautiful, broad, magnificent convent. The second convent to be broken down was St John's. These two were both unreformed, but the third convent was this blossoming vineyard of the new Observance, St Agnes. It is not possible to report fully in writing the sorrow, weeping, crying, and wailing the sisters of this convent raised when they had to leave. The lords and city representatives both reasonably and mercifully looked into the matter of providing them with another convent for the promotion of religious life and the salvation and profit of their souls, since the sisters had been robbed of their own. In exchange for the convent of St Agnes, they gave these good sisters the convent of St Margaret.[163]

When the previously mentioned Dominican prior was informed of this, he set himself against it with all his might. Since he was their vicar, he forbade the sisters of St Margaret, threatening interdict and punishment, from letting anyone either in or out of their convent. This met with much resistance, through which the mothers of St Agnes had to suffer, for their walls had been torn down and they could barely protect themselves from the wolves who sought their food because of the long, cold frost. The good sisters did not know where to turn, for wherever they hoped one day to find harbour, home, residence, or shelter, the next morning it was refused them, even by their nearest and dearest relatives. Their sorrow, trouble, and misery grew and multiplied daily, but at last the city lords and the good friends of the St Agnes sisters turned to our gracious lord bishop of Strasbourg[164] for aid in this matter. He took the affair wholly upon himself because of all the conflict and impediments and also because of the authority and permissions needed, whether from the papal See or from the master general of the order. He came personally to Strasbourg and remained in the city until the matter was settled.

And so, in the jubilee year 1475, on the day after the Feast of St Lucia before Christmas [14 December], between eight and nine o'clock in the morning, together with her sisters the worthy mother prioress, named Sister Anna Zorn,[165] went out of their poor convent of St Agnes into the church and stood a while

163. Sigrid Hirbodian provides contextualization and further information about the persons and families involved. See Hirbodian, "Dominikanerinnenreform und Familienpolitik."

164. Ruprecht of Palatinate-Simmern, bishop of Strasbourg; see note in **5.71**.

165. This woman is likely the Ennel Zorn encountered in **5.68**, **5.74**, and **5.76**. It was quite common for bursars to become prioresses, and Ennel could be a nickname for Anna.

there with such weeping, crying, mourning, and sorrowful gestures that all who saw and heard them were moved to tears and compassion. A great crowd of people from the city – lords, men, and women – had gathered to escort them. They went in procession, and the order of the procession was the following: First, two knights, Lord Diebold of Mullenheim and Lord Friedrich Bock, went ahead, led the way, and cleared the streets. They were followed by one of the father confessors, carrying a cross, and next to him two citizens of the city with two burning candles. Afterwards, the sisters came two by two, the youngest first and the prioress alone at the end. Each sister carried a burning light and a crucifix in her hand. After the community of sisters, the second confessor walked, carrying the holy sacrament in a box, and next to him two honourable men, the former official and the provost. After them came the entire city council with the militia. They were followed also by many honourable women, in particular, the worthy lady abbess of St Stephen and many of the sisters' friends and relatives.

It is important to note that the sisters walked with good manners and carefulness. They had so fully covered their faces with their veils that none of the sisters could be recognized and no one could look in their eyes. Moreover, even the sisters' relatives – mothers, sisters, and aunts – none of them spoke a single word to them on the way, nor stepped up to them or approached them individually. Indeed, the worthy mother prioress had a biological sister, a very honourable woman according to the world, whose husband was a knight named Lord Claus of Bülach. This lady greatly desired to go to her sister, the mother prioress, who was walking at the end alone, and say something comforting and friendly to her. But she refrained from doing this in order to avoid giving the other secular people an excuse to do this with their own friends.

Among the sisters who left the convent of St Agnes were forty-three veiled sisters and eleven white-veiled novices, children, and lay sisters – all in all fifty-four, not counting the three sick who were brought on a cart after lunch.

This honourable procession went past the canonry of St Thomas, where the sisters rested a while in the parish church, for the honourable mother prioress and many others had become so weak and faint from suffering and sorrow that they could not walk any further. After they had rested for a while, they continued past another canonry, the Old St Peter. Both parishes welcomed them by ringing all the bells. The Knights of St John did the same.[166] Once this honourable procession had reached the toll gate, the Knights of St John came out to meet them with the cross and stood under the toll gate and waited for the sisters of St

166. These Knights of St John belonged to the commandery of Hospitallers on the Grüner Wörth, founded by the mystic Rulman Merswin. See **5.13**.

Agnes. Once the sisters of St Agnes had also come through the toll gate, the Hospitallers with their cross walked before them in the procession up to the church of St Margaret.

When this honourable procession and crowd neared the convent of St Margaret, two former mayors, Lord Conrad Riff and Lord Peter Schott, separated themselves from the crowd of people and went ahead to St Margaret with some of the militia to check the state of affairs there. They found the gate, windows, and everything so boarded up and locked tight that no one could get in, and the women inside would not open for any knocking or calling. So the two former mayors sent two soldiers over the walls to break open the gate with violence, which was blocked with thorny branches from the inside. It is better to pass over in silence the fury that was seen and heard from the sisters of St Margaret, for it brings little profit to speak of it.

Once the gate had been broken open, the two old lords entered. One of the nuns said to one of the lords, "Are you Lord Peter Schott, who they say does so much good, but who creates such misfortune here for us?" Both heads of the community, the prioress and subprioress, along with many of the women, ran out of the convent. Of the sixteen women in the convent, eleven ran away. A Dominican friar came and withdrew two children from the convent by force. While he was leading them away by the hand, the children's grandfather came up and said, "Sir monk, where are you going with those children? Those children are mine!" And so he took the children out of his hands and led them back into the convent. Lord Peter Schott asked one of the children if she would like to stay in the convent and she answered very reasonably, "Yes, dear lord, I like being in the convent."

Amidst all of this, the sisters from St Agnes came up with their procession to the church. The Hospitallers entered before them and went into the choir, the sisters after, and finally the confessor with the holy sacrament. The entire city council followed him. When the holy sacrament had been set in its place and the Hospitallers had departed, the councilmen went with the sisters from St Agnes into the refectory to the former nuns, of whom only three remained with one child and the two other children who had been returned. The lords spoke with the three women, which at the moment was necessary, and entrusted the exiled women to them and then the councilmen left. By then it was lunchtime, and the servants of the St Agnes sisters came and brought them dishes with food and drink from their former, broken-down convent. The city council also sent them a lot of fish as a gift.

Now, regarding the trials, sorrow, misery, and opposition these good sisters suffered in numerous matters, now from the runaways or other people and now from various impediments, as well the great difficulty they suffered before they got used to the tiny, small place compared to their former paradisiacal habitation, ordered their things, and mourned their damages and the loss of their former, so delightful convent, only he knows who perceives and sees all secrets. May he transform their misery and sorrow into a jewel in their crown in eternal blessedness. Amen.

[5.83][167] *A conclusion to this story and all the matters concerning the convent of St Agnes* [fol. 248r]

This praiseworthy, honourable, and sadly bygone convent of St Agnes may justly be compared to the noble carbuncle, which surpasses all other jewels with its bright glow. It has the special property that it reproduces in this manner: when the carbuncle gets old, it bursts open and casts off a stone more noble than it had been, which grew inside it. This is called a ruby. Just so, this former, magnificent, and honourable convent of St Agnes was like the shining carbuncle and its destruction was not without profit and fruit, for out of it came this fine, tender, noble ruby: the humble little convent of St Margaret was reformed and restored to the religious life. Even though this convent of St Margaret is contained in a simple, plain, humble building, it is nevertheless an especially gifted and graced place, which God honours with many miracles and good deeds, for many good devout persons and sisters have lived and resided there, who have experienced God's grace.

This convent of St Margaret received from the holy father Pope Sixtus IV[168] all the rents and incomes and all the properties and persons that the former convent St Agnes had possessed. The worthy convent of St Agnes had been an earthly paradise in virtue of the location and delightfulness of its grounds, the lovely beauty of its buildings, and the ornament of virtuous persons and good, devout sisters. It was broken down and destroyed just like the burst carbuncle. For this may honour and glory be to God the Holy Trinity from age to age eternally. Amen.

[5.84][169] *How the friary in Weissenburg was reformed* [fol. 251r]

In 1466 the community of our brothers in Weissenburg was reformed by the friaries of Basel and Worms through our father provincial, Master Peter Wellen, at the behest of the city of Weissenburg as well as of the illustrious prince, Lord

167. This chapter is misnumbered in MS 2934 as chapter 81.

168. Pope Sixtus IV (r. 1471–1484).

169. From this point forward the chapters are not numbered in MS 2934 and have only the text headings. The chapter numbers here are my own addition.

Frederick, duke of Bavaria, count palatine of the Rhine, arch-seneschal, and elector prince.[170]

[**5.85**] *How the convent of Engelport in Gebweiler was reformed* [fol. 251r]

The convent of All the Angels in Gebweiler, called Engelport, was reformed in 1466 by three sisters. The first, named Sister Margretha Meyer, was from the convent of Sylo in Schlettstadt and had formerly been sent with other sisters from St Catherine's in Colmar to Sylo to reform that convent, as is written above.[171] This Sister Margretha became the first prioress in Engelport. The other two sisters were from Schönensteinbach; they were Sister Margretha Hunger, first subprioress, and Sister Elisabeth Kirchmatter. It should be noted that this convent of Engelport had greatly declined in inhabitants and holdings. The buildings were very run-down and dilapidated, and the sisters had all died. For twenty years, the convent stood empty of sisters and bereft of the Divine Office. By divine inspiration, it so happened that a rich, notable canon of the cathedral chapter in Basel named Lord Johannes Kreutzer, a master of the liberal arts and also of Scripture, came into our order with the Dominicans in Gebweiler. Since he and certain friars wished to live in voluntary poverty without any rents or incomes as our holy father Saint Dominic commanded, the blessed man Friar Peter Möhr and the other friars with him unanimously donated their properties, taxes, incomes, and rents to these sisters and their successors in the convent of Engelport.[172] This Master Johannes Kreutzer and those who helped him take on this task restored this convent in spiritual and material matters by the authority and commendation of the master general, Martial Auribelli, and Master Peter Wellen, the provincial. The Observance and this convent grew so much that in the first year fifteen people entered the order there. The Observance of these two convents, in particular the poverty of the friars in Gebweiler (that they live without rents and incomes), was confirmed by the pope in Rome, Paul II, in 1467.

[**5.86**] *How the convent of St Gertrude in Cologne was reformed* [fol. 251v]

The convent of St Gertrude in Cologne was reformed in the same year, that is, 1466, by five sisters from St Catherine's in Colmar and one from Sylo, named Sister Barbara Krebs, prioress of Sylo. She had previously been sent from St

170. Frederick (Friedrich) I, count palatine of the Rhine and elector palatine (r. 1451–1476), was "of Bavaria" only insofar as he belonged to a branch of the Wittelsbach family.

171. See **5.57**.

172. See Neidiger, "Armutsbegriff," 130–141. For Peter Möhr, see *DDS*, 275; *SOPMA*, 3: 238.

Catherine's to reform Sylo, as is written above,[173] and she was also made prioress of St Gertrude. This Observance was carried out at the request and desire of the archbishop of Cologne[174] and the citizens of the city by authority of the master general, Martial Auribelli, and the provincial, Master Peter Wellen, through Friar Peter Kirchschlag, prior of the friars in Cologne, and Friar Heinrich Lot, a master of holy Scripture who led the aforementioned six sisters from Colmar to Cologne.

[**5.87**] *How the convent of Medingen was reformed* [fol. 252r]

Medingen, a convent of sisters in Swabia, was reformed in 1467 with eight sisters from the convent of Pforzheim at the request of the duke of Bavaria[175] and by the authority of our father provincial through Father Gilg Schwertmann.

[**5.88**] *How the friary in Mainz was reformed* [fol. 252r]

In 1468 the community of friars in Mainz was reformed by the friars of Cologne, but the first prior was Friar Heinrich Riss from the Basel friary.[176] This reform was carried out with papal authority by the most worthy Lord N of Nassau, archbishop of Mainz,[177] through Master Peter Wellen, provincial, and Father Peter Kirchschlag, prior of Cologne.

[*The following accounts are found after the "Short Prologue" at the end of MS 2934, where they were written as later additions in accordance with Meyer's plea. They have been moved here for the sake of chronological continuity.*]

[**5.89**] *How the convent of Medlingen in Swabia, which had declined so much, was reformed by five sisters from Schönensteinbach* [fol. 258v]

In the year that this book was written, that is, 1468, the convent called Medlingen in the diocese of Augsburg was reformed with five sisters from the convent of Schönensteinbach at the request and impetus of the illustrious prince the duke of Bavaria,[178] in whose land it lies, and by the authority of our father

173. See **5.57**.

174. I.e., Ruprecht of the Palatinate, archbishop of Cologne (r. 1463–1480); see note in **5.58**.

175. I.e., Louis (Ludwig) IX, duke of Bavaria-Landshut (r. 1450–1479).

176. See *DDS*, 277–278.

177. Adolf II of Nassau, archbishop of Mainz (r. 1461–1475). The letter N (for *nomen* or "name") is common in medieval texts as a placeholder when the author does not know a proper name.

178. I.e. Duke Louis IX.

provincial, Master Peter Wellen, through Friar Gilg Schwertmann, prior of the friars in Landshut. The names of the sisters from Schönensteinbach, who had to travel so far, are: Sister Elisabeth Wolsack, the first prioress; Sister Elisabeth Disler; Sister Elisabeth Kels; Sister Barbara Hügler; and Sister Katherina Weingart, a lay sister.

These sisters were placed on a covered wagon and escorted by quite honourable fathers of the Gebweiler friary. The first night they stayed in Colmar, where they were well accommodated by our dear sisters there in both convents, Unterlinden and St Catherine's. The second day they came to Schlettstadt and were very devoutly received and hosted for two days by our dear sisters in Sylo. Afterwards they came to Strasbourg and were similarly accommodated by our dear sisters in St Agnes. That convent gave them a young sister who had not yet made her profession. From there they went to Pforzheim and, according to old habitual loyalty, the sisters of Pforzheim received the pilgrims from Schönensteinbach well. They stayed with them in the convent until their reformer, Father Gilg Schwertmann, came and honourably led them from there to a convent called Medingen, which lies one mile from Medlingen and had also only been reformed one year earlier. It is a lovely, large convent. They stayed there until this Father Gilg had better ordered and prepared the convent of Medlingen, which was founded in honour of our dear Lady. It also has a parish church and lies in a large village, to which this church belongs. A long time ago, it was a very honourable thing, but it had severely declined from the religious life and the number of people that it once had, and also in its material affairs and its buildings. When these sisters arrived in the run-down convent, they found in abundance the treasures of poverty and misery. The unwilling, wild sisters had not followed life according to the order; indeed they had seen very little of such a life on that estate. Here, the five sisters from Schönensteinbach had to suffer long in patience for the increase of their heavenly reward, but day by day it improves spiritually, materially, and also with regard to the buildings.

[**5.90**] *That the friary in Chur was reformed* [fol. 259v]

At the desire and petition of the honourable lord and father, Lord Ortlieb of Brandis, bishop of Chur,[179] the friary in Chur was reformed in this same year, 1468, by the authority of our aforementioned father provincial, Master Peter Wellen, through Father Heinrich Schretz of Basel, who was at the time prior of Ulm. The first prior of this reform was the lector of Pforzheim, Friar Johannes of Bremgarten, formerly the confessor of the sisters of St Agnes in

179. Ortlieb of Brandis, bishop of Chur (r. 1458–1491).

Strasbourg.[180] This community's reform was a sorely necessary affair, since Chur lies in an area of German lands that is quite far away from other friaries of this province. For this reason, it often happened that all sorts of friars from all sorts of provinces and communities would settle there and live however they wanted, and for this reason the religious life was in a very sorry state there.

The same thing happened at the friary in Bolzano, which is even further away. It was therefore only rarely subject to visitation, such that it had a very poor life before it was reformed. It was reformed about thirty years ago by fathers from Nuremberg and Vienna.[181] God be praised for the growth of the religious life in the Order of Preachers, which in our day so richly blossoms.

[**5.91**] *How the convent of St Margaret in Strasbourg was reformed* [fol. 260r]

On the Feast of St Lucia [13 December] before Christmas in 1475, the convent of St Margaret was reformed. How and by what means and arrangement that occurred is clearly described earlier in the account of the St Agnes convent.[182]

In 1474 on the Feast of St Agapitus [18 August], the Dominican friary in the praiseworthy city of Frankfurt was laudably and worthily reformed by nineteen friars, most of whom were from the honourable community of Cologne. This happened at the request and desire of the archbishop of Mainz[183] and the city of Frankfurt, by the authority and command of the master general, Leonardo Mansueti, who had been elected to the office of master general at the general chapter in Rome that very year.[184]

This holy, fruitful work was accomplished by a blessed, dear friar named Johannes Wilnow, a son of that same friary in Frankfurt, who at the time was prior of the reformed community in Mainz. He asked the former confessor of the sisters in Himmelkron and also myself, since I was at the time confessor to the

180. See *DDS*, 342–343. Eugen Hillenbrand raised the possibility that the internal lector of Chur, and not Johannes of Bremgarten, was initially appointed prior. See Eugen Hillenbrand, "Die Observantenbewegung in der deutschen Ordensprovinz der Dominikaner," in *Reformbemühungen und Observanzbestrebungen im spätmittelalterlichen Ordenswesen*, ed. Kaspar Elm (Berlin, 1989), 219–71, at 261 n182.

181. The friary at Bolzano had belonged to the Italian province of Lombardy. It was transferred to the province of Teutonia before 1449, but it is not certain whether this occurred at the same time as the 1439 reform. See Claudia Heimann, "Der Umfang der Dominikanerprovinz Teutonia im späteren Mittelalter," *AFP* 75 (2005): 233–257, at 248.

182. See **5.82** and **5.83**.

183. I.e., Archbishop Adolf II of Nassau; see note in **5.88**.

184. On Master General Leonardo Mansueti of Perugia (r. 1474–1480), see Mortier, *Histoire des maîtres généraux*, 4: 488–541.

sisters of Liebenau near Worms, if we would participate in this affair. Many of us friars came together in a reformed and religious abbey of the Benedictine order, where the monks and fathers treated us very affectionately. From there, we went by ship to Frankfurt, where we were met by many of the lords of the city council, who came out before the city to meet the ship. They escorted us honourably and led us into the city to their parish church, where the parish priests also received us very worthily. They all walked with us in procession to the Dominican friary, followed by a great crowd. When we came into the church there, the doors and gates were locked against us. The city guards had to break the doors open so that we could go into the cloister. When the bell for the chapter meeting was rung, we could barely bring the friars of the community together there so that before us and all the lords the letters confirming this holy affair could be read. A beautiful collation sermon was held, which is appropriate for such a task, and obedience was demanded of the Frankfurt friars. They were asked whether they would submit to the religious life of the order, hold property in common, and serve God in quiet peace. Furthermore, we kindly and prudently wished to hold them to austerity in fasting and food and such things.

No more than four of them submitted and the others all refused. Yet when these four had given up their keys in the chapter before all the lords, one of them gave an account of the money and books and valuables he held, and prostrated himself, saying, "All of this I willingly give up, and I have the complete and firm intention of staunchly improving my life." As willing as he was, he could not speak these words without crying, which brought tears to my own eyes and many of the other lords. And so these four came from the other side over to us in our choir and our side. When these things and more that I am not describing had laudably been accomplished and the lords had left the convent again much edified, the lay brothers had not cooked for us unworthy guests, even though it was midday.

During that first week, the choir, church, cloister, and churchyard were consecrated and rededicated by the bishop, and the common folk were especially joyous. Both rich and poor of the city of Frankfurt were pleased by this holy affair, which in the first two years has noticeably prospered, spiritually and materially. Praise and honour be to God, the Holy Trinity, *in secula seculorum*. Amen.

[*fol. 261r*][185] In 1475 the honourable community of our friars in Regensburg was reformed. The first prior of this new religious life was Friar Johannes Schwartz,

185. In MS 2934, the next three entries lack both chapter titles and numbers. Space was left between the paragraphs to add them, but this was never done. The first two of these entries, concerning Regensburg and Esslingen, are not found in Cgm 8081.

a master of holy Scripture. This reform was conducted under the master general, Leonardo of Perugia, at Pentecost not long after the provincial chapter held in Esslingen where Jacob of Stubach was elected provincial prior.[186] He is a master of holy Scripture and a lover of all religious life. The bishop[187] and the city of Regensburg were good-willed towards this reform.

[*fol. 261v*] In 1477, the honourable father provincial, Master Jacob of Stubach, a teacher of holy Scripture and a spiritual, virtuous man, visitated the community of friars in Esslingen and reformed them by the authority of the master general. The friars of this community were mostly willing and so this friary is also to be counted and reckoned among the other reformed friaries.

[*The regular order of texts in the manuscript resumes here.*]

[*fol. 252r*] In these recorded times and years, our convents and friaries were not only reformed to the religious life. Yea, many communities were newly founded and built for the order in this German province. The Roman emperor, Frederick III,[188] founded one in Graz with the favour and permission of Pope Paul, as did the count of Celje, and there is another in Brabant, also a community of friars. Now a new friary has been founded in Stuttgart in the lands of the lord of Württemberg, and similarly one in Heidelberg in the diocese of Worms, founded by Count Palatine Frederick in 1475 and confirmed by Pope Sixtus. And in Steyr.[189]

[**5.92**] *How much it hurts the evil spirit when convents are reformed to a holy religious life and how heartily he scorns them* [fol. 252v]

When a community of men or women is drawn to the religious life and reformed, the evil spirit is enormously jealous. For this reason, whenever he can

186. See *SOPMA*, 2: 321.

187. Heinrich IV of Absberg, bishop of Regensburg (r. 1465–1492).

188. Frederick (Friedrich) III, Holy Roman emperor (r. 1452–1493).

189. Count Frederick II of Celje (d. 1454) founded Neukloster in 1451 with the help of the Vienna friars (see **5.40**). The new friary in Brabant is probably Zoutleeuw, which was founded in 1471, but apparently was not long-lived. Graz was founded in 1466, Steyr in 1472. For a discussion of these late foundations, see Heimann, "Der Umfang der Dominikanerprovinz Teutonia." Count Eberhard V (d. 1496) of Württemberg and his uncle, Count Ulrich V (d. 1480), were both staunch supporters of the Observance. The lords of Württemberg not only founded Stuttgart in 1473, but they also supported the reforms in 1478–1479 of the friary in Schwäbisch Gmünd and the convents of Reutin, Weiler, Kirchheim, Steinheim, and Gotteszell. See Neidiger, *Das Dominikanerkloster Stuttgart.*

prevent and turn aside such work himself or through his messengers, he is not idle. This is also the reason why, when one wishes to reform a convent to the religious life, one must often suffer the trouble, pain, and labour by which those in the Observance are often saddened through the scorn of the enemy and his own. Evidently, sometimes the evil spirit himself struggles against the religious life, trying to destroy it, as we have often heard.

In particular, in the first book of the *Formicarius*, in chapter 10, the worthy father Johannes Nider writes about how a community of Dominican friars in France was reformed to the religious life while he was prior of the friars in Basel. The evil spirit started a great uproar among those dear friars. He broke the windows in the cloister, he threw the dishes all over the place, he broke the wine casks, he ripped the bell rope and carried it away, he rang the gong at night, and he troubled them so greatly that some of them nearly lost their minds. During the day, he haunted the cloister and refectory and other places in the friary, but at night he resided in the dormitory and behaved so monstrously that no friar of the community dared to go anywhere alone. This evil spirit ripped apart a novice's cappa. He also took a lovely Book of Hours from a friar who worked in the kitchen and threw it in a boiling pot, so that the book was completely ruined. He screamed with a threatening voice that he did not want to leave the friary and said he had long possessed it as his own home. But the blessed, devout brothers recognized that the enemy lies and is a father of lies, and so they took the newly begun reform more firmly in hand and zealously taught themselves to uphold the Observance of our holy order.

Now note from this how much the evil spirit is against restoring the praise of God, the religious life, and the salvation of souls in a convent when we drive out the sinful, irreligious, and offensive way of life, for he is an enemy of virtue. For this reason, wherever he may, he loves to disrupt the divine, pure, good life, because he knows that through this, many souls will escape him and belong to God the Lord.

[**5.93**] *How the evil spirit visibly torments the friars in the reformed communities* [fol. 253v]

In this same book and chapter, the father Master Johannes Nider describes how a good, honourable young man about twenty-four years old came into the order where this newly begun Observance was so hateful to the enemy. His cappa was ripped into twelve strips just as if a wild animal had slashed it with its claws. When this new, young knight of Christ remained unafraid in this Observance, the evil spirit appeared in the form of a black cat and said, "Unless you leave the order, I will kill you in three days." When the youth saw and heard this, he conjured the enemy in a loud voice in the name of Christ. The enemy fell upon him, and the good young man defended himself. The fight became so rowdy and noisy that the friars came running. They saw how the table, the lectern, the bed, and everything in the cell had been thrown about and overturned in their battle. When the friars saw that the dear novice was so weak, they led him to the fire, for it was wintertime during the octave of Epiphany [7–12 January] and in those lands heated rooms are not very common. When the friars held this sick novice by the fire – See here! – this same roguish evil spirit came and took this dear boy from the hands of his brothers, threw him into the flames, and held his head in the middle of the fire for a long time. Finally, with great difficulty, the friars pulled him out of the fire and carried him before the high altar in the choir. The enemy came again and took him from the hands of the friars, dragged the good youth horrendously through the entire choir, and beat him so thoroughly that they all believed he was dead. When the enemy left him, the friars began to pray for him as for the dead and commended him to the mother of God and many other saints, one after another. Finally, they called upon our holy father Saint Dominic and – Now see! – this same kind father Saint Dominic appeared in the habit of the Preachers as an upright, lovely father standing on the altar. The young friar, whom many of the brothers believed was dead and who lay in their arms as one dead, sat up with a joyful expression, turned to the altar, and devoutly took his consolation in God and Saint Dominic. In that moment, the evil spirit flew through all the buildings of the friary with raucous fury, as if all the blacksmiths in the country were hammering all together, which was an especially great wonder. As soon as the young friar had been strengthened against the enemy's spirits by the worthy holy sacrament of our dear Lord's body, he immediately became fully healthy again in all his limbs.

By this, we may well see how delightful and pleasing it is to God the Lord and also to our holy father Saint Dominic when the communities of our holy Dominican order are reformed to the religious life of the Observance.

[**5.94**] *An admonition that all brothers and sisters should willingly submit to the religious life of their order's reform* [fol. 254v][190]

We note that now, by the grace of God, many convents and friaries are being reformed to the religious life, not only in our order but also in other orders, especially the dear fathers who are called *Canonici regulares,* or Canons Regular, as well as the Friars Minor, the Franciscans.

190. The following is drawn from Johannes Nider's treatise on religious reform. This has not yet been edited but the 1611 printing is easily accessible online. Johannes Nider, *De reformatione religiosorum libri tres,* ed. Jean Boucquet (Antwerp, 1611).

Yet we still see that whenever a convent is reformed, often very few of those remain who had been in the convent before it was reformed. Instead, they transfer into other unreformed convents where the Observance is not kept. Furthermore, we also see that very few people come out of the unreformed convents into the reformed convents where they would keep their order better and more perfectly. They see young and old people voluntarily entering the convents of the Observance, yet they stay away, even though they are more obligated to go into a reformed convent or to work with serious zeal and prudence towards the reform of their own convent. They make all sorts of excuses for themselves with the sins that they fear committing, saying, "I do not have the grace for anyone to reform me or my convent. These people cannot give us grace. If we had the grace (which no human but only God may grant), then we would happily be reformed. But for this reason, we should not be reformed."[191]

Saint Anselm answers this thus: "If the sinful person does not have grace from God, it is not because God the Lord does not want to give it. It is because the sinful person will not receive grace."[192] For this reason, all the masters say that if a person zealously does what he can, God will without a doubt grant his grace, just as God says through the prophet Zacharias, "*Convertimini ad me*: Turn ye to me and I will turn to you."[193]

There are others who say, "If we were to try to maintain our order, we would be too frail, for human nature is not so strong as it was in the old days."[194] This is a foolish excuse, for everything was so prudently composed and written down by Christendom and the holy fathers who founded the orders that in many respects it is more orderly and comforting before God to uphold the order than in certain convents where the Observance is not kept. No one is so frail that he cannot live in right obedience, in a chaste and pure life, and in voluntary poverty without any property.[195] A healthy person may not excuse himself, since you are well able to suffer great and difficult labour for the sake of worldly honour, bodily health, and even for the sake of worldly, ephemeral, disorderly love! Tell me,

191. See Nider, *De reformatione religiosorum*, 7.

192. This is derived from chapters 2 and 3 of Anselm's *On the Fall of the Devil*. See Anselm of Canterbury, *The Major Works*, ed. Brian Davies and G.R. Evans (Oxford, 1998), 196–201. Meyer is citing from Nider's *De reformatione religiosorum*, where it is also directly associated with the same passage from Zacharias. See Nider, *De reformatione religiosorum*, 8–9.

193. Zacharias 1:3.

194. See Nider, *De reformatione religiosorum*, 33.

195. Poverty, chastity, and obedience are the three primary vows to which professed religious of all orders are subject.

why would you not suffer this for the sake of God's honour, for your poor soul's salvation, and for eternal joy?

Saint Paul says, "I can do all things in him who strengthens me."[196] The prophet Isaiah also says, "Those who trust in God the Lord increase in strength and grow wings and feathers like eagles and fly so that they never grow weary."[197] A teacher of the Dominican order, called Ulrich of Strasbourg,[198] also says in the great book of his *Summa*:

> It is not true what many people say, that human nature becomes ever more frail, even though in the old days long ago some people lived for many, many years through divine power. Because of this, human knowledge continuously grew, as well as their experience with things. Since this is no longer necessary, our lives now last about seventy years, as the prophet says: "The days of our years are seventy. But for the strong, robust, and powerful it can be eighty years. Nevertheless, in this time there is still nothing but labour and pain."[199]

[**5.95**] *How some people of our order, when the Observance of their order is mentioned, can give excuses but still have no reason* [fol. 256r]

Some people in the convents wear the religious appearance of a confirmed order, and yet hardly orient their lives according to the rule and statutes and barely keep the rule of their order. They give all sorts of excuses for not upholding their order or their order's rule or the confirmed, written customs that their order has prescribed and imposed and according to which they swore to God and to their order that they would live. Among other things, they say, "We do not live as is prescribed, nor keep our order's rule as our holy fathers who wrote our rule intended, although we swore to this in our profession of obedience, because we learned the lives we lead from our predecessors who came before us. The lifestyle that we found in this convent has long been the custom. We think that since we found it this way and it has been customary for many years, we are not obligated to live otherwise."[200]

196. Philippians 4:13.

197. Isaiah 40:31.

198. Ulrich of Strasbourg or Ulrich Engelberti (1200–1277) was a student of Albert the Great and provincial prior of Teutonia. See *SOPMA*, 4: 418–423. The following quote may be found in Ulrich of Strasbourg, *De summo bono: Liber 6, Tractatus 1–3,6*, ed. Sabina Tuzzo (Hamburg, 2011), 42. For Meyer's source, see Nider, *De reformatione religiosorum*, 38.

199. Psalm 89:10.

200. See Nider, *De reformatione religiosorum*, 43.

The teachers respond by saying that custom does not make law. One cannot ignore the commands of God and the promised vows of these commands and not observe them as was sworn and promised. Such custom also does not absolve one from sins; rather, the fault grows through this and it is not a custom, but a distortion or destruction. For this reason a pope wrote in canon law: "A bad custom should be as strenuously fled and avoided as an evil distortion."[201] Hostiensis and John Andreae[202] also said that just as no custom may be honest nor defensible that is against a good vow, so no custom that is against the form and command of religious life may have the force of law. Hereby may we ourselves in our own conscience and reason understand well that such custom, which is against an order's written law, cannot excuse people of that order.

Certain people within orders, who are not in reformed convents and do not wish to be reformed and drawn to the religious life of holy Observance, say, "See here, our predecessors also lived as we live now and they were so wise and learned that one can hardly find such learned, wise people today. Why should we do otherwise? If someone wants to encourage or wring something else out of us, he does us an injustice by disturbing our peace, for trouble and suffering befall every attempt at reform."[203]

Some say that the reform consists of peculiar laws, manners, and strange doings which are new statutes.[204] Some say that the reform is mostly good, but that the order should not be split or disgraced, and we should wait until all Christendom is ready to be reformed together.[205] They say many similar things, by which they intend to escape from the holy religious life, but this desertion itself may do them the greatest harm. Such excuses are best met with Scripture and the answers of the holy teachers. I recommend that the zealous reader take up the book that the devout teacher Master Johannes Nider wrote about and named after the reform of the religious state, in which he describes much other similar material.

201. Nider is quoting Pope Nicholas I according to distinction 8 of Gratian's Decretals. See Gratian, *The Treatise on Laws with the Ordinary Gloss,* trans. Augustine Thompson and James Gordley (Washington, DC, 1993), 26. See Nider, *De reformatione religiosorum,* 43.

202. These are both Italian experts of canon law associated with the University of Bologna. Henry of Segusio, commonly called Hostiensis, died in 1271; John Andreae died around 1348. This passage may be found in Nider, *De reformatione religiosorum,* 40.

203. Nider deals with these objections in book 1 chapters 10 and 15 of *De reformatione.*

204. Nider, *De reformatione,* book 1 chapter 7.

205. Nider deals with the potential split of the order in *De reformatione,* book 1, chapter 9, and the desire for simultaneous universal reform in book 1, chapter 8.

But to conclude and to bring an end to this book of the reformation, note in this final chapter the faithful teaching of our worthy holy father Saint Thomas Aquinas, the high teacher of our order.

[**5.96**] *A good instruction for all good religious brothers and sisters of a religious order and the conclusion of this book* [fol. 257v]

Saint Thomas says in the book called *Secunda secundae*[206] that a person in a confirmed religious order is bound to observe many articles on pain of mortal sin. First, the three vowed, essential articles of his order's religious life.[207]

Second, the statutes of his order, which he should not transgress intentionally in his own scorn. That is, when in possession of full reason and free will he refuses in a scornful manner to observe certain articles of his order and derides them mockingly and deliberately. Such behaviour would deviate from the path along which the religious person should tread towards perfection and it would also be against the vows of his religion and his confirmed order.

Third, all the commandments which are written in his order's Rule and Constitutions.

Fourth, the true commandments which his superiors impose and ordain, even if they are not otherwise required by the order. This is what Saint Thomas says.

The fifth thing lies in Ulrich's book[208] and addresses the case in which the superiors circulate any general call, or there is a statute from the order's written laws which is not a commandment yet he transgresses it with outrageous disdain. Even if he knew it was a true commandment, he still would not be obedient nor observe the article, no matter how imperiously it was commanded.

The sixth, all the things that all Christian people are bound to keep on pain of mortal sin by divine right and holy Christendom. All religious people of the orders are included in this.

Since we are obligated to observe these things, which we have also promised to God, we should happily serve him with a joyful heart and good free will, not like servants compelled by forced impositions, but like the free who are in

206. *Secunda secundae* refers to the second part of part 2 of Aquinas's *Summa theologiae*. The first four articles here are drawn from question 186, but Meyer gets the entire list of six points from Nider. See Thomas Aquinas, *Summa Theologiae*, trans. Laurence Shapcote (Lander, 2012), 6: 765–786; Nider, *De reformatione religiosorum*, 43–44.

207. The three primary vows of religion are poverty, chastity, and obedience.

208. See Ulrich of Strasbourg, *De summo bono: Liber 6, Tractatus 4, 1–15*, ed. Coralba Colomba and Irene Zavattero (Hamburg, 2017), 92–110; Nider, *De reformatione religiosorum*, 44.

the grace of God. God is worthy of all praise and honour. We sorely need the reward we earn by our virtues in a religious life of service to the Lord. Now may God grant that we live here well and in a religious way in this brief and ephemeral world and that we may never be separated from him in eternity. May we receive this from God the Father and the Son and the Holy Spirit. AMEN.

Explicit. Here ends the book of the reformation of the convents of the Order of Preachers in the province of Teutonia, which was created through hard work and compiled from disparate sources. It was finished and completed in 1468. May it be a praise to God. Amen.

[**5.97**] *A short prologue* [fol. 258v]

In praise of God and for the edification of humans, it is good and profitable, if afterwards more convents of our order in this province of German lands are reformed, to record it hereafter in the manner that one sees it has been written before this. This way, a reasonable, good-hearted person can read many good things.

Appendix

Masters General and Provincial Priors of Teutonia

Master General	Provincial Prior of Teutonia
Elias Raymond of Toulouse (1367–1380)	Johannes Cusin (1368–1372)
	Ulrich Wintner (1372–1384)
Raymond of Capua (1380–1399)	Peter Engerlin (1384–1390)
	Ulrich Theobaldi (1390–1397)
	Peter Florin (1398–1399)
	Peter Engerlin (1399–1402)
Tommaso Paccaroni (1401–1414)	Adam of Gladbach (1402–1408)
Leonardo Dati (1414–1425)	Giselbert of Vleytingen/Utrecht (1408–1426)
Bartholomew Texery (1426–1449)	Nicolaus Notel (1426–1446)
Peter Rochin (1450)	Peter Wellen (1446–1455)
Guido Flamochetti (1451)	
Martial Auribelli (1453–1462)	Heinrich of Reuenach/Ribenach (1455–1456)
Conrad of Asti (1462–1465)	Peter Wellen (1457–1469)
Martial Auribelli (1465–1473)	Wilhelm Roslauf/Roslöff (1469–1474)
Leonardo Mansueti (1474–1480)	Jakob Fabri of Stubach (1475–1488)
Salvo Cassetta (1481–1483)	
Bartolomeo Comazzi (1484–1485)	
Barnabas Sansoni (1486)	
Joachim Torriani (1487–1500)	Jakob Sprenger (1488–1496)
	Ulrich Zehntner (1496–1505)

Chronology of Dominican Reform in Teutonia to 1500

The houses marked with an asterisk (*) were new foundations or transfers from other provinces, not reforms of existing houses. Those houses marked with a plus sign (+) had already fallen from the ranks of the Observants or had ceased to exist altogether before 1500. This list is incomplete, since it does not include all failed reform attempts.

Year	Friaries	Convents
1389/91	Colmar	
1396	Nuremberg	
1397		Schönensteinbach*
1419	Bern	Unterlinden (Colmar)
1421/23	Marienheide*	
1423		St Mary Magdalene (Basel)
1426		Liebenau (Worms)
1428		St Catherine (Nuremberg)
1429	Basel	Himmelkron (Hochheim near Worms)
	Pforzheim	
1431		St Nicholas-in-Undis (Strasbourg)
1434	Vienna	
1436	Tulln	Tulln
	Krems	
	Retz	
	Pettau (Ptuj)	
	Vienna Neustadt	
1438		St Catherine (Colmar)
1439	Bolzano	St Michael (Bern)
1442		St Mary Magdalene (Pforzheim)
1447	Worms	
	Eichstätt	
1451	Bamberg	
	Neukloster (Vallis Senarum)*+	
	Würzburg+	
1457		Holy Sepulchre (Bamberg)
1459	Wimpfen	
1461	Landshut	
	Guebwiller	

Year	Friaries	Convents
1463		Hasenpfuhl (Speyer)
1464	Cologne	Sylo (Sélestat)
1465	Ulm	St Agnes (Strasbourg)+
	Brussels*	Altenhohenau
		Adelhausen (Freiburg im Breisgau)
		St Agnes (Freiburg im Breisgau)
		Penitents of Mary Magdalene (Freiburg im Breisgau)
1466	Wissembourg+	St Gertrud (Cologne)
		Engelport (Guebwiller)*
1467		Medingen
1468	Mainz	Medlingen
	Graz*	Imbach (Krems)
	Chur	
	Leoben	
1470	Aachen	
1471	Zoutleeuw*	
1472	Steyr*	
1473	Heidelberg*	
	Stuttgart*	
1474	Frankfurt am Main	
1475	Regensburg	St Margaret (Strasbourg)
		Marienthal Vuldep (Landshut)
1477	Esslingen	
1478	(Schwäbisch) Gmünd	Reuthin (Wildberg)
		Weiler (Esslingen)
		Kirchheim unter Teck
		Marienthal (Steinheim)
1479		Gotteszell (Gmünd)
1480		Klingental (Basel)+
		Gnadenzell (Offenhausen)
1483	's-Hertogenbosch	Holy Cross (Regensburg)
1484		St Catherine (St Gallen)
1487		Obersteigen*
1493		Penitents of St Mary Magdalene (Strasbourg)
1494	Maastricht	
1497		Zoffingen (Constance)

Alsatian Place Names

German	French
Ensheim	Ensisheim
Gebweiler	Guebwiller
Großlützel	Lucelle
Hagenau	Haguenau
Hartmannsweiler	Hartmannswiller
Kleinlützel	Petit-Lucelle
Küngersheim	Kingersheim
Masmünster	Masevaux
Mülhausen	Mulhouse
Mumpelgart	Montbéliard
Pfirt	Ferrette
Ruffach	Rouffach
Saugern	Soyhières
Schlettstadt	Sélestat
Sesseltzheim	Saessolsheim
Sulz	Soultz-Haut-Rhin
Waltwiler	Wattwiller
Weissenburg	Wissembourg
Wulferheim	Pulversheim

Bibliography

Manuscripts

Karlsruhe, Badische Landesbibliothek, St Peter pap. 9, fols 282r–284v.
Munich, Bayerische Staatsbibliothek, Cgm 8081.
St Gallen, Stiftsbibliothek, cod. 1916.
Strasbourg, Bibliothèque nationale et universitaire, MS 2934.
Tübingen, University Library, Cod. Md 456.

Primary Sources

Anna of Munzingen. "Die Chronik der Anna von Munzingen nach der ältesten Abschrift mit Einleitung und Beilagen." Ed. Johann König. *Freiburger Diözesan-Archiv* 13 (1880): 129–236.

Anselm of Canterbury. *The Major Works*. Ed. Brian Davies and G.R. Evans. Oxford: Oxford University Press, 1998.

Beutler, Magdalena. "*Erklärung des Vaterunsers*: A Critical Edition of a Fifteenth-Century Mystical Treatise by Magdalena Beutler of Freiburg." Ed. Karen Greenspan. PhD dissertation, University of Massachusetts, 1984.

Bullarium Ordinis FF. Praedicatorum. 8 vols. Rome: Typographia Hieronymi Mainardi, 1729–1740.

Dietler, Seraphin. *Chronik des Klosters Schönensteinbach*. Ed. Joseph von Schlumberger. Gebweiler: Verlag der J. Boltze'schen Buchhandlung, 1897.

Elisabeth of Schönau. *The Complete Works*. Trans. Anne L. Clark. New York: Paulist Press, 2000.

Falder-Pistoris, Georg. *Geistliche Belehrung in Dialogform und Passionstraktat für Ordensleute: Edition und Untersuchung*. Ed. Petra Hörner. Berlin: Weidler, 2015.

Ein geistlicher Rosengarten: Die Vita der heiligen Katharina von Siena zwischen Ordensreform und Laienfrömmigkeit im 15. Jahrhundert: Untersuchung und Edition. Ed. Thomas Brakmann. Frankfurt am Main: Peter Lang, 2011.

Gratian. *The Treatise on Laws with the Ordinary Gloss*. Trans. Augustine Thompson and James Gordley. Studies in Medieval and Early Modern Canon Law 2. Washington, DC: The Catholic University of America Press, 1993.

Das "Konventsbuch" und das "Schwesternbuch" aus St. Katharina in St. Gallen: Kritische Edition und Kommentar. Ed. Antje Willing. Berlin: Erich Schmidt, 2016.

"Liber Constitutionum Ordinis Fratrum Praedicatorum (iuxta codicem prototypum B. Humberti in Archivo Generali Ordinis Romae asservatum)." *Analecta Sacri Ordinis Fratrum Praedicatorum* 3 (1897): 26–60, 98–122, 162–181.

"Liber Constitutionum Sororum Ordinis Praedicatorum (ex exemplari codicis Ruthenensis in Archivo Generali Ordinis Romae asservato)." *Analecta Sacri Ordinis Fratrum Praedicatorum* 3 (1897): 337–348.

Meyer, Johannes. *Das Amptbuch*. Ed. Sarah Glenn DeMaris. Monumenta Ordinis Fratrum Prædicatorum Historica 31. Rome: Angelicum University Press, 2015.

—. *Buch der Reformacio Predigerordens*. Ed. Benedict Maria Reichert. 2 vols. Quellen und Forschungen zur Geschichte des Dominikanerordens in Deutschland 2–3. Leipzig: Harrassowitz Verlag, 1908–1909.

Nider, Johannes. *De reformatione religiosorum libri tres*. Ed. Jean Boucquet. Antwerp: Ex officina Plantiniana, 1611.

Ordinarium iuxta ritum Sacri Ordinis Fratrum Praedicatorum. Rome: Angelicum University Press, 1921.

Peuntner, Thomas. *Büchlein von der Liebhabung Gottes*. Ed. Bernhard Schnell. Munich: Artemis, 1984.

Raymond of Capua. *Die Legenda maior (Vita Catharinae Senensis) des Raimund von Capua: Edition nach der Nürnberger Handschrift Cent. IV, 75, Übersetzung und Kommentar*. Ed. Jörg Jungmayr. 2 vols. Berlin: Weidler, 2004.

—. *Opuscula et litterae*. Rome: Typographia Polyglotta, 1899.

Riccoboni, Bartolomea. *Life and Death in a Venetian Convent: The Chronicle and Necrology of Corpus Domini, 1395–1436*. Trans. Daniel Ethan Bornstein. Chicago: University of Chicago Press, 2000.

Thomas Aquinas. *Summa Theologiae*. Trans. Laurence Shapcote. Ed. John Mortensen and Enrique Alarcón. 8 vols. Latin/English Edition of the Works of Thomas Aquinas 13–20. Lander, WY: The Aquinas Institute for the Study of Sacred Doctrine, 2012.

Tschudi, Aegidius. *Chronicon Helveticum*. Ed. Johann Rudolf Iselin. 2 vols. Basel: Hans Jacob Bischoff, 1734–1736.

Ulrich of Strasbourg. *De summo bono*. Ed. Burkhard Moysisch et al. 12 vols. Hamburg: F. Meiner Verlag, 1989–2017.

"Les *vitae sororum* d'Unterlinden: Édition critique du manuscrit 508 de la bibliothèque de Colmar." Ed. Jeanne Ancelet-Hustache. *Archives d'histoire doctrinale et littéraire du Moyen Age* 5 (1930): 317–513.

Secondary Sources

Ancelet-Hustache, Jeanne, ed. "Les *vitae sororum* d'Unterlinden: Édition critique du manuscrit 508 de la bibliothèque de Colmar," *Archives d'histoire doctrinale et littéraire du Moyen Age* 5 (1930): 317–513.

Anderson, Wendy Love. *The Discernment of Spirits: Assessing Visions and Visionaries in the Late Middle Ages*. Tübingen: Mohr Siebeck, 2011.

Andrews, Frances. *The Other Friars: Carmelite, Augustinian, Sack, and Pied Friars in the Middle Ages*. Woodbridge, Suffolk: Boydell and Brewer, 2006.

Angenendt, Arnold, Thomas Braucks, Rolf Busch, Thomas Lentes, and Hubertus Lutterbach. "Gezählte Frömmigkeit." *Frühmittelalterliche Studien* 29 (1995): 1–71.

Bailey, Michael D. *Battling Demons: Witchcraft, Heresy, and Reform in the Late Middle Ages*. University Park: Pennsylvania State University Press, 2003.

Barthelmé, Annette. *La réforme dominicaine au XVe siècle en Alsace et dans l'ensemble de la province de Teutonie*. Strasbourg: Heitz, 1931.

Beebe, Kathryne. *Pilgrim and Preacher: The Audiences and Observant Spirituality of Friar Felix Fabri (1437/8–1502)*. Oxford: Oxford University Press, 2014.

Bennett, Judith M. *History Matters: Patriarchy and the Challenge of Feminism*. Philadelphia: University of Pennsylvania Press, 2006.

Berman, Constance H. "Were There Twelfth-Century Cistercian Nuns?" *Church History* 68 (1999): 824–864.

—. *The White Nuns: Cistercian Abbeys for Women in Medieval France*. Philadelphia: University of Pennsylvania Press, 2018.

Biddick, Kathleen. *The Shock of Medievalism*. Durham, NC: Duke University Press, 1998.

Blanton, Virginia, Veronica O'Mara, and Patricia Stoop, eds. *Nuns' Literacies in Medieval Europe: The Antwerp Dialogue*. Turnhout: Brepols, 2017.

—, eds. *Nuns' Literacies in Medieval Europe: The Hull Dialogue*. Turnhout: Brepols, 2013.

—, eds. *Nuns' Literacies in Medieval Europe: The Kansas City Dialogue*. Turnhout: Brepols, 2015.

Blockmans, Wim, and Anne van Oosterwijk, eds. *Staging the Court of Burgundy*. Turnhout: Brepols, 2013.

Borchardt, Karl. "Hospitallers, Mysticism, and Reform in Late-Medieval Strasburg." In *The Military Orders*, volume 3: *History and Heritage*, ed. Victor Mallia-Milanes, 73–78. Burlington: Ashgate, 2008.

Brakmann, Thomas. *Ein geistlicher Rosengarten: Die Vita der heiligen Katharina von Siena zwischen Ordensreform und Laienfrömmigkeit im 15. Jahrhundert: Untersuchung und Edition*. Frankfurt am Main: Peter Lang, 2011.

—. "The Transmission of the Upper German Life of Catherine of Siena." In *Catherine of Siena: The Creation of a Cult*, ed. Jeffrey F. Hamburger and Gabriela Signori, 83–107. Turnhout: Brepols, 2013.

Brand, Margit. *Studien zu Johannes Niders deutschen Schriften*. Rome: Istituto Storico Domenicano, 1998.

Brann, Noel L. *The Abbot Trithemius (1462–1516): The Renaissance of Monastic Humanism*. Leiden: Brill, 1981.

Brown, Rachel Fulton. *Mary and the Art of Prayer: The Hours of the Virgin in Medieval Christian Life and Thought*. New York: Columbia University Press, 2018.

Bynum, Caroline Walker. "'...And Woman His Humanity': Female Imagery in the Religious Writing of the Later Middle Ages." In *Fragmentation and Redemption: Essays on Gender and the Human Body in Medieval Religion*, 151–179. New York: Zone Books, 1991.

Caciola, Nancy. *Discerning Spirits: Divine and Demonic Possession in the Middle Ages.* Ithaca: Cornell University Press, 2003.

Caciola, Nancy, and Moshe Sluhovsky. "Spiritual Physiologies: The Discernment of Spirits in Medieval and Early Modern Europe." *Preternature* 1 (2012): 1–48.

Campbell, Bruce M.S. *The Great Transition: Climate, Disease and Society in the Late-Medieval World.* Cambridge: Cambridge University Press, 2016.

Campbell, Mary Marshall. "Sanctity and Identity: The Authentication of the Ursuline Relics and Legal Discourse in Elisabeth of Schönau's *Liber revelationum.*" *Journal of Medieval Religious Cultures* 38 (2012): 159–192.

Chèvre, André. *Lucelle: Histoire d'une ancienne abbaye cistercienne.* Delémont: Bibliothèque jurassienne, 1973.

Christianson, Gerald. *Cesarini, the Conciliar Cardinal: The Basel Years, 1431–1438.* Sankt Ottilien: EOS-Verlag, 1979.

Christianson, Gerald, Thomas M. Izbicki, and Christopher M. Bellitto, eds. *The Church, the Councils, and Reform: The Legacy of the Fifteenth Century.* Washington, DC: Catholic University of America Press, 2008.

Collins, David J. *Reforming Saints: Saints' Lives and Their Authors in Germany, 1470–1530.* Oxford: Oxford University Press, 2008.

Constable, Giles. "The Interpretation of Mary and Martha." In *Three Studies in Medieval Religious and Social Thought*, 1–141. Cambridge: Cambridge University Press, 1995.

Courtenay, William J. "From Dinkelsbühl's *Questiones Communes* to the Vienna Group Commentary: The Vienna 'School', 1415–1425." In *Nicholas of Dinkelsbühl and the Sentences at Vienna in the Early Fifteenth Century*, ed. Monica Brinzei, 267–316. Turnhout: Brepols, 2015.

Creytens, Raymond. "Manfred de Verceil et son traité contre les fraticelles." *Archivum Fratrum Praedicatorum* 11 (1941): 173–208.

Creytens, Raymond, and A. d'Amato. "Les actes capitulaires de la congrégation dominicaine de Lombardie (1482–1531)." *Archivum Fratrum Praedicatorum* 31 (1961): 213–306.

Cyrus, Cynthia J. *The Scribes for Women's Convents in Late Medieval Germany.* Toronto: University of Toronto Press, 2009.

Dahmus, John. "A Medieval Preacher and His Sources: Johannes Nider's Use of Jacobus de Voragine." *Archivum Fratrum Praedicatorum* 58 (1988): 121–176.

Debby, Nirit Ben-Aryeh. "The Preacher's Agenda: A Dominican versus the Italian Renaissance." *The European Legacy* 20 (2015): 462–476.

DeMaris, Sarah Glenn. "Anna Muntprat's Legacy for the Zoffingen Sisters: A Second Copy of the Unterlinden *Schwesternbuch.*" *Zeitschrift für deutsches Altertum und deutsche Literatur* 144 (2015): 359–378.

—, ed. *Johannes Meyer: Das Amptbuch.* Monumenta Ordinis Fratrum Praedicatorum Historica 31. Rome: Angelicum University Press, 2015.

Doerr, Madlen. "Klarissen und Dominikanerinnen in Freiburg im 15. Jahrhundert: Sozialstruktur und Reform." PhD dissertation, University of Freiburg, 2012.

Duval, Sylvie. *Comme des anges sur terre: Les moniales dominicaines et les débuts de la réforme observante, 1385–1461.* Rome: École française de Rome, 2015.

—. "*Mulieres religiosae* and *sorores clausae*: The Dominican Observant Movement and the Diffusion of Strict Enclosure in Italy from the Thirteenth to the Sixteenth Century." In *Mulieres religiosae: Shaping Female Spiritual Authority in the Medieval and Early Modern Periods,* ed. Veerle Fraeters and Imke de Gier, 193–218. Turnhout: Brepols, 2014.

—. "The Observance's Women: New Models of Sanctity and Religious Discipline for the Female Dominican Observance Movement during the Fifteenth Century." In *Religious Orders and Religious Identity Formation, ca. 1420–1620,* ed. Bert Roest and Johanneke Uphoff, 13–31. Leiden: Brill, 2016.

Ehrenschwendtner, Marie-Luise. "Creating the Sacred Space Within: Enclosure as a Defining Feature in the Convent Life of Medieval Dominican Sisters (13th–15th c.)." *Viator* 41 (2010): 301–316.

—. "A Library Collected by and for the Use of Nuns: St. Catherine's Convent, Nuremberg." In *Women and the Book: Assessing the Evidence,* ed. Jane H.M. Taylor and Lesley Smith, 123–132. London: The British Library, 1997.

—. "*Puellae litteratae*: The Use of the Vernacular in the Dominican Convents of Southern Germany." In *Medieval Women in Their Communities,* ed. Diane Watt, 49–71. Toronto: University of Toronto Press, 1997.

Elliott, Dyan. *Proving Woman: Female Spirituality and Inquisitional Culture in the Later Middle Ages.* Princeton: Princeton University Press, 2004.

Elm, Kaspar, ed. *Reformbemühungen und Observanzbestrebungen im spätmittelalterlichen Ordenswesen.* Berlin: Duncker & Humblot, 1989.

Engler, Claudia. *Regelbuch und Observanz: Der Codex A 53 der Burgerbibliothek Bern als Reformprogramm des Johannes Meyer für die Berner Dominikanerinnen.* Berlin: De Gruyter, 2017.

Erdin, Emil A. "Frienisberg." In *Die Zisterzienser und Zisterzienserinnen, die reformierten Bernhardinerinnen, die Trappisten und Trappistinnen und die Wilhelmiten in der Schweiz,* ed. Cécile Sommer-Ramer and Patrick Braun, 128–141. Helvetia Sacra 3.3. Bern: Francke Verlag, 1982.

Fechter, Werner. *Deutsche Handschriften des 15. und 16. Jahrhunderts aus der Bibliothek des ehemaligen Augustinerchorfrauenstifts Inzigkofen.* Sigmaringen: Thorbecke, 1997.

—. "Die Nürnberger Handschrift von Johannes Meyers *Buch der Reformacio Predigerordens.*" *Zeitschrift für deutsches Altertum und deutsche Literatur* 110 (1981): 57–69.

Fößel, Amalie. "Der 'Schwarze Tod' in Franken 1348–1350." *Mitteilungen des Vereins für Geschichte der Stadt Nürnberg* 74 (1987): 1–75.

Freed, John B. *Frederick Barbarossa: The Prince and the Myth.* New Haven: Yale University Press, 2016.

Ganina, Natalija. *Bräute Christi: Legenden und Traktate aus dem Straßburger Magdalenenkloster; Edition und Untersuchungen*. Berlin: De Gruyter, 2016.

Gieraths, Gundolf. *Die Dominikaner in Worms*. Der Wormsgau, Beiheft 19. Worms: Stadtbibliothek Worms, 1964.

Gilomen-Schenkel, Elsanne. *Henman Offenburg (1379–1459): Ein Basler Diplomat im Dienste der Stadt, des Konzils und des Reichs*. Basel: Kommissionsverlag Friedrich Reinhardt, 1975.

Goehlinger, Francois Auguste. *Histoire de l'abbaye de Marbach*. Colmar: Éditions Alsatia, 1954.

Graf, Klaus. "Ordensreform und Literatur in Augsburg während des 15. Jahrhunderts." In *Literarisches Leben in Augsburg während des 15. Jahrhunderts*, ed. Johannes Janota and Werner Williams-Krapp, 100–159. Tübingen: Niemeyer, 1995.

Griffiths, Fiona J. "Brides and *Dominae*: Abelard's *Cura monialium* at the Augustinian Monastery of Marbach." *Viator* 34 (2003): 57–88.

—. *The Garden of Delights: Reform and Renaissance for Women in the Twelfth Century*. Philadelphia: University of Pennsylvania Press, 2007.

Haberkern, Ernst. *Die "Wiener Schule" der Pastoraltheologie im 14. und 15. Jahrhundert: Entstehung, Konstitutionen, literarische Wirkung*. Göppingen: Kümmerle Verlag, 2003.

Hamburger, Jeffrey. *The Visual and the Visionary: Art and Female Spirituality in Late Medieval Germany*. Cambridge, MA: MIT Press, 1998.

Hamburger, Jeffrey F., and Eva Schlotheuber. "Books in Women's Hands: Liturgy, Learning and the Libraries of Dominican Nuns in Westphalia." In *Entre stabilité et itinérance: Livres et culture des ordres mendiants XIIIe–XVe siècle*, ed. Nicole Bériou, Martin Morard, and Donatella Nebbiai, 129–157. Turnhout: Brepols, 2014.

Hamburger, Jeffrey F., Eva Schlotheuber, Susan Marti, and Margot Fassler. *Liturgical Life and Latin Learning at Paradies bei Soest, 1300–1425: Inscription and Illumination in the Choir Books of a North German Dominican Convent*. 2 vols. Münster: Aschendorff, 2017.

Hamm, Berndt. "Was ist Frömmigkeitstheologie? Überlegungen zum 14. bis 16. Jahrhundert." In *Praxis Pietatis: Beiträge zu Theologie und Frömmigkeit in der frühen Neuzeit; Wolfgang Sommer zum 60. Geburtstag*, ed. Hans-Jörg Nieden and Marcel Nieden, 9–45. Stuttgart: Kohlhammer, 1999.

Hardy, Duncan. *Associative Political Culture in the Holy Roman Empire: Upper Germany, 1346–1521*. Oxford: Oxford University Press, 2018.

Heimann, Claudia. "Beobachtungen zur Arbeitsweise von Johannes Meyer OP anhand seiner Aussagen über die Reform der Dominikanerkonvente der Teutonia, besonders der *Natio Austriae*." *Archivum Fratrum Praedicatorum* 72 (2002): 187–220.

—. "Der Umfang der Dominikanerprovinz Teutonia im späteren Mittelalter." *Archivum Fratrum Praedicatorum* 75 (2005): 233–257.

Heinonen, Meri. "Between Friars and Nuns: The Relationships of Religious Men and Women in Johannes Meyer's *Buch der Reformacio Predigerordens*." *Oxford German Studies* 42 (2013): 237–258.

Heng, Geraldine. *The Invention of Race in the European Middle Ages*. Cambridge: Cambridge University Press, 2018.

Herzig, Tamar. *Savonarola's Women: Visions and Reform in Renaissance Italy*. Chicago: University of Chicago Press, 2008.

Heusinger, Sabine von. *Johannes Mulberg OP (d. 1414): Ein Leben im Spannungsfeld von Dominikanerobservanz und Beginenstreit*. Berlin: Akademie Verlag, 2000.

Hillenbrand, Eugen. "Die Observantenbewegung in der deutschen Ordensprovinz der Dominikaner." In *Reformbemühungen und Observanzbestrebungen im spätmittelalterlichen Ordenswesen*, ed. Kaspar Elm, 219–71. Berlin: Duncker & Humblot, 1989.

Hinnebusch, William A. *The Dominicans: A Short History*. New York: Alba House, 1975.

Hirbodian, Sigrid. "Dominikanerinnenreform und Familienpolitik: Die Einführung der Observanz im Kontext städtischer Sozialgeschichte." In *Schreiben und Lesen in der Stadt: Literaturbetrieb im spätmittelalterlichen Straßburg*, ed. Stephen Mossman, Nigel F. Palmer, and Felix Heinzer, 1–16. Berlin: De Gruyter, 2012.

—. *Geistliche Frauen und städtische Welt: Kanonissen – Nonnen – Beginen und ihre Umwelt am Beispiel der Stadt Straßburg im Spätmittelalter, 1250–1520*. Berlin: De Gruyter, 2019.

—. "Pastors and Seducers: The Practice of the *Cura monialium* in Mendicant Convents in Strasbourg." In *Partners in Spirit: Women, Men, and Religious Life in Germany, 1100–1500*, ed. Fiona Griffiths and Julie Hotchin, 303–337. Turnhout: Brepols, 2014.

Hirbodian, Sigrid, and Petra Kurz, eds. *Die Chronik der Magdalena Kremerin im interdisziplinären Dialog*. Ostfildern: Jan Thorbecke, 2016.

Hlaváček, Ivan, and Alexander Patschovsky, eds. *Reform von Kirche und Reich zur Zeit der Konzilien von Konstanz (1414–1418) und Basel (1431–1449)*. Konstanz: Universitätsverlag Konstanz, 1996.

Hömberg, Melanie. "Wirtschafts(Buch)führung im Kontext: Der Umgang mit Schriftlichkeit in reformierten Frauenklöstern in Süddeutschland." PhD dissertation, Ludwig-Maximilians-Universität Munich, 2013.

Hotchin, Julie. "Reformatrices and Their Books: Religious Women and Reading Networks in Fifteenth-Century Germany." In *Communities of Learning: Networks and the Shaping of Intellectual Identity in Europe, 1100–1500*, ed. Constant J. Mews and John N. Crossley, 251–291. Turnhout: Brepols, 2011.

Huijbers, Anne. "*De viris illustribus ordinis praedicatorum*: A 'Classical' Genre in Dominican Hands." *Franciscan Studies* 71 (2013): 297–324.

—. "Observant Memory and Propaganda in Johannes of Mainz's *Vita fratrum predicatorum conventus Basiliensis* (1442–1444)." *Church History* 87 (2018): 718–739.

—. *Zealots for Souls: Dominican Narratives of Self-Understanding during Observant Reforms, c. 1388–1517*. Berlin: De Gruyter, 2018.

Jones, Claire Taylor. "Rekindling the Light of Faith: Hymn Translation and Spiritual Renewal in the Fifteenth-Century Observant Reform." *Journal of Medieval and Early Modern Studies* 42 (2012): 567–596.

—. *Ruling the Spirit: Women, Liturgy, and Dominican Reform in Late Medieval Germany*. Philadelphia: University of Pennsylvania Press, 2018.

—. "Writing History to Make History: Johannes Meyer's Chronicles of Reform." In *Medieval Cantors and Their Craft: Music, Liturgy and the Shaping of History*, ed. Katie

Ann-Marie Bugyis, A.B. Kraebel, and Margot E. Fassler, 340–356. York: York Medieval Press, 2017.

Kaeppeli, Thomas. *Scriptores Ordinis Praedicatorum medii aevi*. 4 vols. Rome: Ad S. Sabinae, 1970–1993.

Kaminsky, Howard. "From Lateness to Waning to Crisis: The Burden of the Later Middle Ages." *Journal of Early Modern History* 4 (2000): 85–125.

Karnein, Alfred. "Mechthild von der Pfalz as Patroness: Aspects of Female Patronage in the Early Renaissance." *Medievalia et Humanistica* 22 (1995): 141–170.

Kern, Theodor von. "Die Reformation des Katharinenklosters zu Nürnberg im Jahre 1428." *Jahresbericht des historischen Vereins für Mittelfranken* 31 (1863): 1–20.

Kleinjung, Christine. "Geistliche Töchter – abgeschoben oder unterstützt? Überlegungen zum Verhältnis hochadliger Nonnen zu ihren Familien im 13. und 14. Jahrhundert." In *Fürstin und Fürst: Familienbeziehungen und Handlungsmöglichkeiten von hochadligen Frauen im Mittelalter*, ed. Jörg Rogge, 21–44. Ostfildern: Jan Thorbecke, 2004.

Krusenbaum-Verheugen, Christiane. *Figuren der Referenz: Untersuchungen zu Überlieferung und Komposition der "Gottesfreundliteratur" in der Straßburger Johanniterkomturei zum "Grünen Wörth"*. Tübingen: Francke, 2013.

Lehmijoki-Gardner, Maiju. "Writing Religious Rules as an Interactive Process: Dominican Penitent Women and the Making of Their *Regula*." *Speculum* 79 (2004): 660–687.

Lentes, Thomas. "Bild, Reform und *cura monialium*: Bildverständnis und Bildgebrauch im *Buch der Reformacio Predigerordens* des Johannes Meyer (d. 1485)." In *Dominicains et dominicaines en Alsace: XIIIe–XXe s.*, ed. Jean-Luc Eichenlaub, 177–195. Colmar: Conseil général du Haut-Rhin, 1996.

Leonard, Amy. *Nails in the Wall: Catholic Nuns in Reformation Germany*. Chicago: University of Chicago Press, 2005.

Lewis, Gertrud Jaron. *By Women, for Women, about Women: The Sister-Books of Fourteenth-Century Germany*. Studies and Texts 125. Toronto: Pontifical Institute of Mediaeval Studies, 1996.

Loe, Paulus von. *Statistisches über die Ordensprovinz Saxonia*. Leipzig: Harrassowitz, 1910.

—. *Statistisches über die Ordensprovinz Teutonia*. Leipzig: Harrassowitz, 1907.

Löhr, Gabriel M. "Die Dominikaner an der Universität Heidelberg." *Archivum Fratrum Praedicatorum* 21 (1951): 272–293.

—. *Die Teutonia im 15. Jahrhundert: Studien und Texte vornehmlich zur Geschichte ihrer Reform*. Leipzig: Harrassowitz Verlag, 1924.

Maier, Johannes. *Studien zur Geschichte der Marienantiphon "Salve Regina"*. Regensburg: F. Pustet, 1939.

Mengis, Simone. *Schreibende Frauen um 1500: Scriptorium und Bibliothek des Dominikanerinnenklosters St. Katharina St. Gallen*. Berlin: De Gruyter, 2013.

Mertens, Dieter. "Reformkonzilien und Ordensreform im 15. Jahrhundert." In *Reformbemühungen und Observanzbestrebungen im spätmittelalterlichen Ordenswesen*, ed. Kaspar Elm, 431–457. Berlin: Duncker & Humblot, 1989.

Meserve, Margaret. *Empires of Islam in Renaissance Historical Thought*. Cambridge, MA: Harvard University Press, 2008.

Meyer, Ruth. *Das St. Katharinentaler Schwesternbuch: Untersuchung, Edition, Kommentar*. Tübingen: Niemeyer, 1995.

Mixson, James D. "Contesting Authority and Community: Models and Practices of Monastic Reform in Late Medieval Central Europe." *Austrian History Yearbook* 41 (2010): 30–47.

—. "Religious Life and Observant Reform in the Fifteenth Century." *History Compass* 11 (2013): 201–214.

Mixson, James D., and Bert Roest, eds. *A Companion to Observant Reform in the Late Middle Ages and Beyond*. Leiden: Brill, 2015.

More, Alison. *Fictive Orders and Feminine Religious Identities, 1200–1600*. Oxford: Oxford University Press, 2018.

—. "Institutionalizing Penitential Life in Later Medieval and Early Modern Europe: Third Orders, Rules, and Canonical Legitimacy." *Church History* 83 (2014): 297–323.

Mortier, Daniel-Antonin. *Histoire des maitres généraux de l'ordre des Frères Prêcheurs*. 8 vols. Paris: Picard, 1903–1920.

Muschiol, Gisela. "Migrating Nuns – Migrating Liturgy: The Context of Reform in Female Convents of the Late Middle Ages." In *Liturgy in Migration: From the Upper Room to Cyberspace*, ed. Teresa Berger, 83–100. Collegeville, MN: Liturgical Press, 2012.

Neidhardt, Stefanie Monika. *Autonomie im Gehorsam: Die dominikanische Observanz in Selbstzeugnissen geistlicher Frauen des Spätmittelalters*. Berlin: Lit Verlag, 2017.

Neidiger, Bernhard. "Der Armutsbegriff der Dominikanerobservanten: Zur Diskussion in den Konventen der Provinz Teutonia (1389–1513)." *Zeitschrift für die Geschichte des Oberrheins* 145 (1997): 117–158.

—. *Das Dominikanerkloster Stuttgart, die Kanoniker vom gemeinsamen Leben in Urach und die Gründung der Universität Tübingen: Konkurrierende Reformansätze in der württembergischen Kirchenpolitik am Ausgang des Mittelalters*. Stuttgart: Klett-Cotta, 1993.

—. *Mendikanten zwischen Ordensideal und städtischer Realität: Untersuchungen zum wirtschaftlichen Verhalten der Bettelorden in Basel*. Berlin: Duncker & Humblot, 1981.

—. "Die Observanzbewegungen der Bettelorden in Südwestdeutschland." *Rottenburger Jahrbuch für Kirchengeschichte* 11 (1992): 175–196.

—. "Selbstverständnis und Erfolgschancen der Dominikanerobservanten: Beobachtungen in der Provinz Teutonia und im Basler Konvent." *Rottenburger Jahrbuch für Kirchengeschichte* 17 (1998): 67–122.

—. "Standesgemäßes Leben oder frommes Gebet? Die Haltung der weltlichen Gewalt zur Reform von Frauenklöstern im 15. Jahrhundert." *Rottenburger Jahrbuch für Kirchengeschichte* 22 (2003): 201–220.

Nemes, Balázs J. "*Dis buch ist iohannes schedelin*: Die Handschriften eines Colmarer Bürgers aus der Mitte des 15. Jahrhunderts und ihre Verflechtungen mit dem Literaturangebot der Dominikanerobservanz." In *Kulturtopographie des deutschsprachigen Südwestens im späteren Mittelalter: Studien und Texte*, ed. Barbara Fleith and René Wetzel, 157–214. Berlin: De Gruyter, 2009.

—. "Der 'entstellte' Eckhart: Eckhart-Handschriften im Straßburger Dominikanerinnenkloster St Nikolaus in undis." In *Schreiben und Lesen in der Stadt: Literaturbetrieb im spätmittelalterlichen Straßburg*, ed. Stephen Mossman, Nigel F. Palmer, and Felix Heinzer, 39–98. Berlin: De Gruyter, 2012.

Newman, Martha G. "Foundation and Twelfth Century." In *The Cambridge Companion to the Cistercian Order*, ed. Mette Birkedal Bruun, 25–37. Cambridge: Cambridge University Press, 2012.

Niebler, Klaus. *Die Handschriften von St. Peter im Schwarzwald*, vol. 1: *Die Papierhandschriften*. Die Handschriften der Badischen Landesbibliothek in Karlsruhe 10.1. Wiesbaden: Harrassowitz, 1969.

Niederstätter, Alois. *Der alte Zürichkrieg: Studien zum österreichisch-eidgenössischen Konflikt sowie zur Politik König Friedrichs III. in den Jahren 1440 bis 1446*. Vienna: Böhlau, 1995.

Nimmo, Duncan B. "The Franciscan Regular Observance: The Culmination of Medieval Franciscan Reform." In *Reformbemühungen und Observanzbestrebungen im spätmittelalterlichen Ordenswesen*, ed. Kaspar Elm, 189–205. Berlin: Duncker & Humblot, 1989.

Nyhus, Paul L. *The Franciscans in South Germany, 1400–1530: Reform and Revolution*. Philadelphia: American Philosophical Society, 1975.

Ochsenbein, Peter. "Latein und Deutsch im Alltag oberrheinischer Dominikanerinnenklöster des Spätmittelalters." In *Latein und Volkssprache im deutschen Mittelalter, 1100–1500*, ed. Nikolaus Henkel and Nigel F. Palmer, 42–51. Tübingen: Max Niemeyer Verlag, 1992.

Oehl, Wilhelm. *Deutsche Mystikerbriefe des Mittelalters, 1100–1500*. Darmstadt: Wissenschaftliche Buchgesellschaft, 1972.

Ozment, Steven. *The Age of Reform (1250–1550)*. New Haven: Yale University Press, 1980.

Pelletier-Gautier, Sonia. "Floraison dominicaine dans la deuxième moitié du XVe siècle à Guebwiller." In *Dominicains et dominicaines en Alsace: XIIIe–XXe s.*, ed. Jean-Luc Eichenlaub, 53–61. Colmar: Conseil général du Haut-Rhin, 1996.

Pfaff, Carl. "Bild und Exempel: Die observante Dominikanerin in der Sicht des Johannes Meyer OP." In *Personen der Geschichte, Geschichte der Personen: Studien zur Kreuzzugs-, Sozial- und Bildungsgeschichte*, ed. Christian Hesse, Beat Immenhauser, Oliver Landolt, and Barbara Studer, 221–235. Basel: Schwabe, 2003.

Posset, Franz. *Renaissance Monks: Monastic Humanism in Six Biographical Sketches*. Leiden: Brill, 2005.

Quiquerez, Auguste. *Histoire des comtes de Ferrette*. Montbéliard: Henri Barbier, 1863.

Rabić, Nedim. "Im toten Winkel der Geschichte: Johannes von Wildeshausen als Bischof von Bosnien 1233/34–1237." In *Die deutschen Dominikaner und Dominikanerinnen im Mittelalter*, ed. Sabine von Heusinger, Elias H. Füllenbach, Walter Senner, and Klaus-Bernward Springer, 53–69. Berlin: De Gruyter, 2016.

Rapp, Francis. "Jean Kreutzer." In *Dominicains et dominicaines en Alsace: XIIIe–XXe s.*, ed. Jean-Luc Eichenlaub, 111–122. Colmar: Conseil général du Haut-Rhin, 1996.

Ricoeur, Paul. *Time and Narrative*. Trans. Kathleen Blamey and David Pellauer. 3 vols. Chicago: University of Chicago Press, 1990.

Roest, Bert. "Observant Reform in Religious Orders." In *The Cambridge History of Christianity*, vol. 4: *Christianity in Western Europe c. 1100–c. 1500*, ed. Miri Rubin and Walter Simons, 446–457. Cambridge: Cambridge University Press, 2009.

—. *Order and Disorder: The Poor Clares between Foundation and Reform*. Leiden: Brill, 2013.

Roest, Bert, and Johanneke Uphoff, eds. *Religious Orders and Religious Identity Formation, ca. 1420–1620: Discourses and Strategies of Observance and Pastoral Engagement*. Leiden: Brill, 2016.

Rollason, David, A.J. Piper, Margaret Harvey, and Lynda Rollason, eds. *The Durham* Liber vitae *and Its Context*. Woodbridge, Suffolk: Boydell Press, 2004.

Rollo-Koster, Joelle, and Thomas M. Izbicki, eds. *A Companion to the Great Western Schism (1378–1417)*. Leiden: Brill, 2009.

Ruh, Kurt, et al., eds. *Verfasserlexikon: Die deutsche Literatur des Mittelalters*. 2nd edition. 14 vols. Berlin: De Gruyter, 1978–2008.

Sauer, Christine. "Zwischen Kloster und Welt: Illuminierte Handschriften aus dem Dominikanerinnenkonvent St. Katharina in Nürnberg." In *Frauen – Kloster – Kunst: Neue Forschungen zur Kulturgeschichte des Mittelalters; Beiträge zum internationalen Kolloquium vom 13. bis 16. Mai 2005 anlässlich der Ausstellung "Krone und Schleier"*, ed. Jeffrey F. Hamburger, Carola Jäggi, Susan Marti, and Hedwig Röcklein, 113–129. Turnhout: Brepols, 2007.

Schiewer, Hans-Jochen. "Die beiden Sankt Johannsen, ein dominikanischer Johannes-Libellus und das literarische Leben im Bodenseeraum um 1300." *Oxford German Studies* 22 (1993): 21–54.

Schiewer, Regina D. "Sermons for Nuns of the Dominican Observance Movement." In *Medieval Monastic Preaching*, ed. Carolyn Muessig, 75–92. Leiden: Brill, 1998.

Schlotheuber, Eva. "Bücher und Bildung in den Frauengemeinschaften der Bettelorden." In *Nonnen, Kanonissen und Mystikerinnen: Religiöse Frauengemeinschaften in Süddeutschland*, ed. Eva Schlotheuber, Helmut Flachenecker, and Ingrid Gardill, 241–262. Göttingen: Vandenhoeck & Ruprecht, 2008.

Schneider, Karin. "Beziehungen zwischen den Dominikanerinnenklöstern Nürnberg und Altenhohenau im ausgehenden Mittelalter." In *Würzburger Prosastudien II: Untersuchungen zur Literatur und Sprache des Mittelalters*, ed. Peter Kesting, 211–218. Munich: Wilhelm Fink, 1975.

—. "Die Bibliothek des Katharinenklosters in Nürnberg und die städtische Gesellschaft." In *Studien zum städtischen Bildungswesen des späten Mittelalters und der frühen Neuzeit: Bericht über Kolloquien der Kommission zur Erforschung der Kultur des Spätmittelalters, 1978 bis 1981*, ed. Bernd Moeller, Hans Patze, Karl Stackmann, and Ludger Grenzmann, 70–83. Göttingen: Vandenhoeck & Ruprecht, 1983.

Schneider-Lastin, Wolfram. "Die Fortsetzung des Ötenbacher Schwesternbuchs und andere vermißte Texte in Breslau." *Zeitschrift für deutsches Altertum und deutsche Literatur* 124 (1995): 201–210.

Schultes, Lothar. "Die Madonna im Wochenbett im Stift St. Florian." *Jahrbuch des Oberösterreichischen Musealvereins* 156 (2011): 49–73.

Scott, Tom. *The Swiss and Their Neighbours, 1460–1560: Between Accommodation and Aggression*. Oxford: Oxford University Press, 2017.

Seebald, Christian. "Ein Basler Codex mit Schriften des Johannes Meyer: Zugleich ein Beitrag zur Überlieferungs- und Textgeschichte der 'Vitas fratrum,' der 'Pabst-' und der 'Kaiserchronik.'" *Zeitschrift für deutsches Altertum und deutsche Literatur* 143 (2014): 202–219.

—. "Reform als Textstrategie: Untersuchungen zum literarischen Oeuvre des Johannes Meyer OP." Habilitation thesis, University of Cologne, 2017.

—. "Schreiben für die Reform: Reflexionen von Autorschaft in den Schriften des Dominikaners Johannes Meyer." In *Schriftstellerische Inszenierungspraktiken: Typologie und Geschichte*, ed. Christoph Jürgensen and Gerhard Kaiser, 33–53. Heidelberg: Universitätsverlag Winter, 2011.

Simon, Eckehard. "An Unpublished Poem on Charles the Bold and the Burgundian Wars Dated 1475." *Beiträge zur Geschichte der deutschen Sprache und Literatur* 97 (1975): 68–87.

Simons, Walter. *Cities of Ladies: Beguine Communities in the Medieval Low Countries, 1200–1565*. Philadelphia: University of Pennsylvania Press, 2003.

Sluhovsky, Moshe. *Believe Not Every Spirit: Possession, Mysticism, and Discernment in Early Modern Catholicism*. Chicago: University of Chicago Press, 2007.

Smoller, Laura Ackerman. *The Saint and the Chopped-Up Baby: The Cult of Vincent Ferrer in Medieval and Early Modern Europe*. Ithaca: Cornell University Press, 2014.

Springer, Bernward. *Die deutschen Dominikaner in Widerstand und Anpassung während der Reformationszeit*. Berlin: Akademie Verlag, 1999.

Steinke, Barbara. *Paradiesgarten oder Gefängnis? Das Nürnberger Katharinenkloster zwischen Klosterreform und Reformation*. Tübingen: Mohr-Siebeck, 2006.

Stump, Phillip H. "The Council of Constance (1414–1418) and the End of the Schism." In *A Companion to the Great Western Schism (1378–1417)*, ed. Joelle Rollo-Koster and Thomas M. Izbicki, 395–442. Leiden: Brill, 2009.

Sumption, Jonathan. *The Hundred Years War*. 4 vols. Philadelphia: University of Pennsylvania Press, 1991–2015.

Tschacher, Werner. *Der Formicarius des Johannes Nider von 1437/38: Studien zu den Anfängen der europäischen Hexenverfolgungen im Spätmittelalter*. Aachen: Shaker Verlag, 2000.

Tuchman, Barbara W. *A Distant Mirror: The Calamitous Fourteenth Century*. New York: Ballantine Books, 1978.

Tugwell, Simon. "Were the Magdalen Nuns Really Turned into Dominicans in 1287?" *Archivum Fratrum Praedicatorum* 76 (2006): 39–77.

Uffmann, Heike. "Inside and Outside the Convent Walls: The Norm and Practice of Enclosure in the Reformed Nunneries of Late Medieval Germany." *The Medieval History Journal* 4 (2001): 83–108.

—. *Wie in einem Rosengarten: Monastische Reformen des späten Mittelalters in den Vorstellungen von Klosterfrauen*. Bielefeld: Verlag für Regionalgeschichte, 2008.

Urfels-Capot, Anne-Élisabeth. *Le Sanctoral du lectionnaire de l'office dominicain (1254–1256): Édition et étude d'après le ms. Rome, Sainte-Sabine XIV L1*. Paris: École des Chartes, 2007.

Van Engen, John. "Friar Johannes Nyder on Laypeople Living as Religious in the World." In *Vita religiosa im Mittelalter: Festschrift für Kaspar Elm zum 70. Geburtstag*, ed. Franz J. Felten and Nikolas Jaspert, 583–615. Berlin: Duncker & Humblot, 1999.

—. "From Canons to Preachers: A Revolution in Medieval Governance." In *Domenico di Caleruega e la nascita dell'ordine dei frati predicatori: Atti del XLI Convegno storico internazionale, Todi, 10–12 ottobre 2004*, 261–295. Spoleto: Fondazione Centro italiano di studi sull'alto Medioevo, 2005.

Vargas, Michael A. "Weak Obedience, Undisciplined Friars, and Failed Reforms in the Medieval Order of Preachers." *Viator* 42 (2011): 283–308.

Voaden, Rosalynn. *God's Words, Women's Voices: The Discernment of Spirits in the Writing of Late-Medieval Women Visionaries*. Suffolk: York Medieval Press, 1999.

Webster, Helen. "Tauler and Merswin: Friends in God?" *Oxford German Studies* 36 (2007): 212–226.

White, Hayden. *Metahistory: The Historical Imagination in Nineteenth-Century Europe*. Baltimore: Johns Hopkins University Press, 1973.

Williams-Krapp, Werner. "The Erosion of a Monopoly: German Religious Literature in the Fifteenth Century." In *The Vernacular Spirit: Essays on Medieval and Religious Literature*, ed. Renate Blumenfeld-Kosinski, Duncan Robertson, and Nancy Bradley Warren, 239–259. New York: Palgrave, 2002.

—. *Geistliche Literatur des späten Mittelalters: Kleine Schriften*. Tübingen: Mohr Siebeck, 2012.

Williams-Krapp, Werner, and Ulla Williams. "Die Dominikaner im Kampf gegen weibliche Irrtümer: Eberhard Mardachs 'Sendbrief von wahrer Andacht' mit einer Textedition." In *Deutsch-böhmische Literaturbeziehungen: Germano-Bohemica; Festschrift für Václav Bok zum 65. Geburtstag*, ed. Hans-Joachim Behr, Igor Lisovy, and Werner Williams-Krapp, 427–446. Hamburg: Kovac, 2004.

—. "Eine Warnung an alle, *dy sych etwaz duncken*: Der 'Sendbrief vom Betrug teuflischer Erscheinungen' (mit einer Edition)." In *Forschungen zur deutschen Literatur des späten Mittelalters: Festschrift für Johannes Janota*, ed. Horst Brunner and Werner Williams-Krapp, 167–189. Tübingen: Niemeyer, 2003.

Willing, Antje, ed. *Die Bibliothek des Klosters St. Katharina zu Nürnberg: Synoptische Darstellung der Bücherverzeichnisse*. Berlin: Akademie Verlag, 2012.

Winnlen, Jean-Charles. "Schönensteinbach: Une communauté religieuse féminine, 1138–1792." PhD dissertation, Université de Franche-Comté, 1992.

Winston-Allen, Anne. *Convent Chronicles: Women Writing about Women and Reform in the Late Middle Ages*. University Park: Pennsylvania State University Press, 2004.

—. "'Es [ist] nit wol zu gelobind, daz ain frowen bild so wol kan arbaiten': Artistic Production and Exchange in Women's Convents of the Observant Reform." In *Frauen - Kloster – Kunst: Neue Forschungen zur Kulturgeschichte des Mittelalters; Beiträge zum internationalen Kolloquium vom 13. bis 16. Mai 2005 anlässlich der Ausstellung "Krone und Schleier"*, ed. Jeffrey Hamburger, 187–195. Turnhout: Brepols, 2007.

—. "Making Manuscripts as Political Engagement by Women in the Fifteenth-Century Observant Reform Movement." *Journal of Medieval Religious Cultures* 42 (2016): 224–247.

—. "Networking in Medieval Strasbourg: Cross-Order Collaboration in Book Illustration among Women's Reformed Convents." In *Schreiben und Lesen in der Stadt: Literaturbetrieb im spätmittelalterlichen Straßburg*, ed. Stephen Mossman, Nigel F. Palmer, and Felix Heinzer, 197–212. Berlin: De Gruyter, 2012.

—. "Outside the Mainstream: Women as Readers, Scribes, and Illustrators of Books in Convents of the German-Speaking Regions." In *Nuns' Literacies in Medieval Europe: The Kansas City Dialogue*, ed. Virginia Blanton, Veronica O'Mara, and Patricia Stoop, 191–206. Turnhout: Brepols, 2015.

—. "Rewriting Women's History: Medieval Nuns' *Vitae* by Johannes Meyer." In *Medieval German Voices in the 21st Century: The Paradigmatic Function of Medieval German Studies for German Studies*, ed. Albrecht Classen, 145–154. Amsterdam: Rodopi, 2000.

Wolf, Klaus. *Hof – Universität – Laien: Literatur- und sprachgeschichtliche Untersuchungen zum deutschen Schrifttum der Wiener Schule des Spätmittelalters*. Wiesbaden: Reichert, 2006.

Wolfs, Petrus Franciscus. "Dominikanische Observanzbestrebungen: Die *Congregatio Hollandiae*." In *Reformbemühungen und Observanzbestrebungen im spätmittelalterlichen Ordenswesen*, ed. Kaspar Elm, 273–292. Berlin: Duncker & Humblot, 1989.

Yardley, Anne Bagnall. "The Musical Education of Young Girls in Medieval English Nunneries." In *Young Choristers 650–1700*, ed. Susan Boynton and Eric Rice, 49–67. Woodbridge, Suffolk: Boydell & Brewer, 2008.

Zieman, Katherine. "Reading, Singing and Understanding: Constructions of the Literacy of Women Religious in Late Medieval England." In *Learning and Literacy in Medieval England and Abroad*, ed. Sarah Rees Jones, 97–120. Turnhout: Brepols, 2003.

Zimmer, Petra and Brigitte Degler-Spengler, eds. *Die Dominikaner und Dominikanerinnen in der Schweiz*. Helvetia Sacra 4.5. Basel: Schwabe Verlag, 1999.

Index of Names

Index of Places

INTRODUCCIÓN

Los Evangelios (Mateo, Marcos, Lucas y Juan) nos ofrecen una narrativa cuádruple de la historia de Jesús. Algunos tal vez se pregunten por qué es necesario eso, pero la fascinante verdad es que cada Evangelio habla a una audiencia concreta y enfatiza un aspecto único de quién es Jesús. Además, las áreas donde se solapan verifican la autenticidad de toda la narrativa.

Mateo escribe sobre el Rey Jesús: su autoridad, su realeza y su trono que durará para siempre. Marcos escribe sobre Jesús como el Siervo sufriente, cuyo sufrimiento servirá eternamente a todos los que invocan su nombre. Lucas, extrayendo de la humanidad de Jesús, hace hincapié en Jesús como Salvador de la humanidad, algo que parece apropiado ya que Lucas era médico. Y Juan, el autoproclamado favorito de nuestro Señor, subraya repetidamente que Jesús es Dios. Estas cuatro narrativas nos ayudan a ver a Jesús desde varios ángulos, capturando distintas facetas de su gloria: Rey, Siervo, Salvador/Hombre, Dios. Podría parecer que estas características se oponen entre sí, pero en realidad nos presentan un entendimiento más pleno de quién es Él. Los cuatro relatos no solo son necesarios, ¡sino también hermosos!

El texto de Mateo no identifica a su autor, pero los padres de la iglesia primitiva parecen estar de acuerdo en que Mateo, el discípulo de Jesús, escribió este libro. Mateo, que también era conocido con el nombre de Leví, era un judío que probablemente vivía y trabajaba cerca de Cafarnaúm junto al Mar de Galilea. Hasta que Jesús lo llamó para ser su discípulo (Mateo 9:9-13), fue recaudador de impuestos. Es difícil para nosotros entender cuán audaz fue para Jesús escoger a un recaudador de impuestos para ser uno de sus discípulos. ¡Fue algo escandaloso! Mateo, un hombre judío, trabajaba para el ejército romano, que era el enemigo opresor de su pueblo. Recaudaba impuestos para el brutal imperio de Roma, sosteniendo así al mismo ejército que amenazaba, torturaba y mataba a otros judíos. Por si eso no fuera suficiente, los recaudadores de impuestos del primer siglo eran notorios por ser corruptos, al exigir impuestos mucho más elevados de los que pedía Roma para llenar sus propios bolsillos.

La transformación de Mateo de su identidad como judío recaudador de impuestos para Roma a discípulo de Jesús fue drástica, estableciéndolo como la persona perfecta para narrar un relato de primera mano de la vida de Cristo. Y como tenía que ser meticuloso con el dinero, no cabe duda de que también fue meticuloso con los detalles de su Evangelio.

Mateo parece haber escrito principalmente para ayudar a los judíos de habla griega a ver que Jesús era el Rey que habían estado esperando. Tenemos unas cuantas pistas de que su audiencia era judía: citó el Antiguo Testamento sesenta y dos veces, más que cualquier otro escritor de los Evangelios, sin explicar las normas culturales judías como hicieron Juan y Marcos; además, usó regularmente la frase *el reino del cielo* (una expresión judía de reverencia), y comenzó su relato con la genealogía de Jesús, algo a lo que alguien que no fuera judío no habría prestado atención.

Si tú fueras una persona judía del primer siglo que creía que Dios enviaría algún día a un nuevo Rey, ¿crees que el relato de Mateo sobre la vida de Jesús te haría ver la verdad de que Jesús era y es ese Rey? ¡Vamos a descubrirlo juntos!

CÓMO USAR ESTE ESTUDIO

Aunque el estudio bíblico es vital para el caminar cristiano, una vida espiritual completa proviene de participar también en las demás disciplinas espirituales. Este estudio está diseñado no solo para equiparte con un mayor conocimiento y profundidad teológicos, sino también para ayudarte a involucrar además otras prácticas formativas que crearán una relación con Jesús más completa y satisfactoria. ¡Queremos verte prosperar en cada área de tu vida con Dios!

CONTENIDO Y PREGUNTAS

En cada una de las diez semanas de este estudio, la enseñanza y las preguntas están divididas en seis días, pero siéntete libre para hacerlo todo a la vez si es mejor para tus horarios. Si decides terminar el estudio de cada semana en un solo día, recuerda que hay aspectos que será bueno que tengas en mente cada día: la lectura bíblica diaria, la memorización de versículos y el reto semanal. Esto es mejor hacerlo durante toda la semana.

LECTURA BÍBLICA DIARIA

La lectura bíblica diaria se corresponde con nuestro estudio. Te tomará una media de tres minutos por día solamente leer (no estudiar) el texto. Si aprendes mejor de forma auditiva, tal vez prefieras escuchar una versión en audio de estos capítulos bíblicos.

Aunque decidas ver el contenido y las preguntas de la semana en un solo día, te animamos a que la lectura bíblica sea una parte de tu ritmo diario. Establecer el hábito de leer la Palabra cada día te ayudará a fortalecer tu fe y crear una mayor conexión con Dios.

Si decides repartir el estudio entre los seis días indicados para cada semana, tu lectura bíblica diaria se alineará con tu estudio. Los Días 1-5 seguirán nuestro estudio de Mateo, el Día 6 presenta un salmo que se corresponde con nuestra lectura, y el Día 7 sirve para que te pongas al día en caso que te hayas demorado.

MEMORIZACIÓN DE VERSÍCULOS

¡Memorizar versículos no es un trabajo inútil! Es una parte importante de guardar la Palabra de Dios en nuestro corazón (Salmos 119:11). Nuestro pasaje, Mateo 6:23-45, es una poderosa verdad sobre valorar las cosas eternas por encima de todo lo demás. Te animamos a practicarlo de forma acumulativa; es decir, *añadir* a lo que estás practicando cada semana en lugar de *reemplazarlo*. Citamos varias versiones en nuestros recursos, así que siéntete libre de memorizarlos en la versión que prefieras. Te sugerimos que trabajes en el versículo o versículos de cada semana a lo largo de la semana, no solo en el último minuto.

También puedes optar por algunas herramientas gratuitas en inglés para ayudarte con esto, incluyendo una canción semanal. Estas herramientas las puedes encontrar aquí: MyDGroup.org/Resources/Matthew.

RETO SEMANAL

Esta es nuestra respuesta práctica a lo que hemos aprendido cada semana. Queremos ser "hacedores de la palabra, y no solamente oidores" (Santiago 1:22). Encontrarás varios retos y te animamos a responder a todos, ¡especialmente a aquellos que te parezcan *más* difíciles! Esto te ayudará a fortalecer tus músculos espirituales y animarte en tu fe. Como ocurre con el versículo para memorizar, será bueno que comiences esta práctica al inicio de la semana, en especial porque algunos retos semanales incluyen cosas que hacer cada día de la semana (por ej., oraciones, escribir en un diario, etc.).

RECURSOS

Este es un estudio completamente basado en las Escrituras, y te verás buscando pasajes a menudo. Si eres nuevo estudiando la Escritura, ¡esta será una buena manera de profundizar y perfeccionar tus habilidades!

Te sentirás más equipado y menos intimidado a medida que avances por cada capítulo. Algunas preguntas te pedirán que consultes un diccionario bíblico, comentario o diccionario de griego o hebreo, pero no tienes que comprar estas herramientas. Hay muchas opciones gratuitas disponibles en el internet.

SEMANA 1

Mateo 1-4:
Origen del Rey

Nota: Si aún no has leído "Cómo usar este estudio" en la página 13, por favor hazlo antes de continuar. Tendrás un marco adecuado y herramientas útiles.

VERSÍCULO PARA MEMORIZAR

Por eso les digo, no se preocupen por su vida, qué comerán o qué beberán; ni por su cuerpo, qué vestirán. ¿No es la vida más que el alimento y el cuerpo más que la ropa?

Mateo 6:25

LECTURA BÍBLICA DIARIA

Día 1: Mateo 1

Día 2: Mateo 2

Día 3: Mateo 3

Día 4: Mateo 4:1-11

Día 5: Mateo 4:12-25

Día 6: Salmos 2

Día 7: Para ponerse al día

Corresponde a los Dias 275-278 de *La sinopsis de la Biblia*

RETO SEMANAL

Ver la página 40 para más información.

DÍA 1

MATEO 1

LEE MATEO 1

El Nuevo Testamento no es donde vemos por primera vez el concepto de un Rey que redimiría y reinaría sobre todas las naciones. La necesidad de un Rey que gobierne se remonta a Génesis 3, cuando los primeros humanos creados a imagen de Dios entregaron voluntariamente su realeza y dominio al enemigo, el cual apareció camuflado como una serpiente manipuladora.

Desde ese momento en adelante, la humanidad sintió la necesidad de tener un Rey para revertir la maldición de la muerte y la separación de Dios; sin embargo, Dios no estaba dispuesto a dejar que se las arreglaran por sí mismos, sino que proveyó pactos a lo largo del Antiguo Testamento que señalaban a su redención futura de la humanidad. Dios escogió a la improbable nación de Israel, con Abraham como padre, como el punto de origen de su plan de redención (Génesis 12:1-3) y el linaje del Rey (Mateo 2:2).

El Antiguo Testamento sigue a esta improbable nación durante sus tropiezos en su recorrido, con una esperanza y un anhelo de un nuevo Rey. Veremos varios de esos momentos en este capítulo.

Lee 2 Samuel 7:12-16. ¿Por qué es importante que Jesús es el hijo de David?

Lee Génesis 12:3. ¿Por qué es importante que Jesús es el hijo de Abraham?

La genealogía de Mateo tiene algunas cosas interesantes que destacar: en primer lugar, esta genealogía sigue la línea de sangre de José, que no está biológicamente relacionado con Jesús pero es su padre legal. En segundo lugar, esta genealogía incluye a mujeres y gentiles (no judíos), lo cual era bastante inusual en ese entonces. En tercer lugar, es probable que Mateo se saltara algunas generaciones por el camino para conseguir su trío de catorce generaciones.

No es que Mateo esté haciendo trampas, ya que así es como a menudo se escribían las genealogías para que fuera más fácil memorizarlas. Esta genealogía en particular también usa la suma de siete más siete, ya que el siete es el número de la totalidad o de la perfección, haciendo el total de catorce para darle el sentido de una totalidad o perfección *doble*. En esencia, a través de los números dados en este linaje, Mateo estaba diciendo que Jesús es la culminación de esta configuración completa y perfecta para la redención de la humanidad ¡como su Rey eterno!

¿Qué podría intentar comunicar Mateo al incluir a mujeres y gentiles? ¿Qué significa para ti personalmente?

El relato de Mateo del nacimiento de Jesús se enfoca específicamente en el punto de vista de José.

Lee Mateo 1:18-25. ¿Qué revela esto acerca del tipo de hombre que era José? ¿Qué características de José son convincentes o de ánimo para ti?

En la conversación del ángel con José se cumplió otra profecía sobre el nombre del Rey que vendría. Citando Isaías 7:14, el ángel dijo que el Rey nacería de una virgen y su nombre sería Emanuel, que significa "Dios con nosotros". La palabra *Emanuel* revela tanto la deidad como la humanidad del Rey que vendría:

DIOS con nosotros: deidad.

Dios ***CON NOSOTROS***: humanidad

Haz una búsqueda en la web para encontrar el significado del nombre de Jesús. ¿Cómo se corresponde con el nombre Emanuel? ¿Qué nos dice esto sobre por qué nació y qué lograría?

Lee Filipenses 2:5-11. ¿Qué aspectos particulares de este pasaje se corresponden con el tema de Jesús como Rey?

Conociendo el final de la historia, ¿cuál es tu respuesta a la persona de Jesús?

DÍA 2

MATEO 2

LEE MATEO 2

No te aferres mucho a tu belén navideño, ¡porque el estudio de hoy está a punto de poner patas arriba algunos elementos! Mateo 2:11 nos dice que los sabios encontraron al *niño* (no al bebé) en una *casa* (no en el establo donde comían los animales). Y, aunque sí hubo tres regalos, puede que no hayan sido tres sabios. Los regalos probablemente los llevaron un gran grupo de sabios, como cuando haces una colecta con tus amigos para comprar una cuna en lugar de que todos compren por separado regalos más pequeños para un *baby shower*. Así que añade una decena de reyes magos (sabios) a tu belén navideño y llévalos hasta otra habitación de tu casa, porque probablemente tardaron entre seis meses y dos años en llegar.

Los sabios de Oriente, posiblemente gentiles o judíos exiliados que conocían las profecías sobre el Rey venidero, recorrieron una larga distancia con la esperanza de encontrarlo y adorarlo. Su primera parada en Jerusalén tenía sentido porque era el centro de la vida judía; sin embargo, se toparon con un gobernador romano y líderes religiosos engañosos que sabían algo de las profecías, pero no parecían interesados en ir a adorar al Rey.

Usando un diccionario bíblico, busca los términos de abajo y escribe algunas notas sobre lo que encuentres. Puedes usar también la información de Mateo 2 para llenar la tabla siguiente.

Sabios	
Herodes el Grande	
Principales sacerdotes	
Escribas	

Los sabios, Herodes y los líderes religiosos dieron tres respuestas particulares al nacimiento del Rey. ¿Cómo respondió cada uno? **Llena la tabla de abajo.**

	Respuesta al nacimiento de Jesús
Sabios	
Herodes el Grande	
Líderes religiosos	

¿Qué revela acerca de Dios que Él mismo atrajera a los sabios desde tan lejos para que fueran a adorar a Jesús?

¿Qué se interpone en tu camino para que tú lo adores?

Mateo 2:10 dice: "Cuando vieron la estrella, se regocijaron mucho con gran alegría". La estrella que señalaba el camino hacia el Rey les dio un gran gozo a quienes lo buscaban (porque el gozo está en Él). La misma estrella que les produjo gozo y anticipación tuvo un impacto distinto sobre el Rey Herodes, ya que hizo que este gobernante sediento de poder se llenara de temor. Y no logró penetrar mucho en los corazones endurecidos de los líderes religiosos; tal vez seguían las reglas con precisión, pero no supieron demostrar el amor por Dios y su pueblo.

La segunda mitad de Mateo 2 relata tres eventos que cumplen profecías adicionales del Antiguo Testamento. Esto refuerza la identidad del Rey Jesús, incluso cuando era solo un niño.

Repasa 2:13-15.

¿Cuál era la situación y qué acción se llevó a cabo?

¿En quién confió José?

¿Cuál era el significado de la profecía (Oseas 11:1)?

Repasa 2:16-18.

¿Cuál era la situación y qué acción se llevó a cabo?

¿En quién confió Herodes?

¿Cuál era el significado de la profecía (Jeremías 31:15)?

Repasa 2:19-23.

¿Cuál era la situación y qué acción se llevó a cabo?

¿En quién confió José?

¿Cuál era el significado de la profecía?

Esta sección no parece referirse a una profecía concreta del Antiguo Testamento. Mateo usó la frase *dicho por los profetas,* lo cual puede indicar que no es una cita directa sino más bien un resumen de la expectativa profética. Los profetas dijeron que el Rey nacería en anonimato, humildad y rechazo. Nazaret, un pueblo con mala reputación, encajaría en esa definición a la perfección.

¿Qué te llamó la atención en la lectura de hoy? ¿Hay algunos pasos de acción que necesites dar como resultado?

DÍA 3

MATEO 3

LEE MATEO 3

La lectura de hoy avanza unos treinta años hasta donde se nos presenta a Juan el Bautista (lo llamaremos JEB para distinguirlo mejor de Juan el escritor del Evangelio), y vemos que inicia oficialmente el ministerio de Jesús.

En el primer siglo, la lógica sugeriría que hablaras en una ciudad si lo que querías era atraer a una multitud. Pero JEB no parecía confiar en la sabiduría humana convencional. Hizo lo contrario de lo que parecía obvio. Desde predicar en el desierto de Judea (piensa en un gran desierto con un ocasional oasis) hasta vestir ropa poco práctica hecha de pelo de camello que picaba, a JEB no le motivaban las opiniones de las masas sino el mensaje que él llevaba.

Busca Mateo 3:2-3 en un comentario bíblico y anota unas cuantas ideas sobre las siguientes palabras y frases:

- Arrepentimiento.

  ____

- El reino de los cielos se ha acercado.

  ____

- Preparen el camino del Señor; hagan derechas sus sendas.

  ____

Desde el desierto, JEB predicó arrepentimiento e invitó a bautizarse a los que confesaban sus pecados y se arrepentían. Es curioso que su mensaje de esperanza se volvió un tanto frío cuando llegaron de Jerusalén los fariseos y saduceos (un viaje de cuatro días) para investigar a JEB y sus acciones (Juan 1:19-28).

En un diccionario bíblico, busca *Fariseos* y *Saduceos*. ¿Qué características de estos dos grupos religiosos probablemente no eran agradables para JEB?

JEB sabía que realmente ellos no buscaban al Mesías Rey. Sus vidas no mostraban evidencia de ese corazón cambiado que acompaña a un verdadero arrepentimiento. Incluso dijo abiertamente que su estatus como hijos de Abraham no les concedía la entrada al reino, y de hecho estaban destinados para la destrucción. Después señaló humildemente al Rey, la esperanza del Espíritu Santo y la realidad del juicio eterno.

Hay paralelismos modernos aquí que son demasiado importantes como para pasarlos por alto. En la actualidad hay hombres y mujeres que se llaman cristianos que creen genuinamente que asistir a la iglesia cada semana y no hacer muchas "cosas malas" los califica como seguidores genuinos de Jesús. Este pasaje revela el error de pensar así. La salvación llega solamente al reconocer y confesar tu pecado y tu necesidad de un Salvador, confiando en que solo Él ha terminado la obra que el Padre requiere de nosotros. Como creyentes, nunca dejamos de necesitar el mensaje del evangelio de que la vida, la muerte y la resurrección de Jesús es nuestra única llave para entrar en el reino.

¿Dependes únicamente de Jesús y su obra completa para tu salvación? ¿O sientes que tu salvación depende de tus acciones, motivaciones, familia o cultura? ¿O incluso de alguna combinación de esas opciones?

A medida que JEB siguió bautizando, llegó un hombre de relativo anonimato y le pidió que lo bautizara. JEB había estado diciendo a todo el que le escuchaba que llegaba un Rey, ¡y finalmente había aparecido! JEB lo reconoció como el Rey y también reconoció la ironía de que un Hombre sin pecado le pidiera que lo bautizara.

¿A qué se refería Jesús cuando le dijo a JEB que "es conveniente que así cumplamos toda justicia" (Mateo 3:15)? **Usa un comentario bíblico si te resulta útil.**

Jesús no necesitaba ser bautizado para confesar su pecado, sino para identificarse con las personas quebrantadas y caídas a las que vino a salvar. Según algunas tradiciones de fe, también estaba purificando el agua para todos los que serían bautizados en el reino. ¡Y toda la Trinidad estaba presente para distinguir su bautismo del resto!

Repasa 3:16-17. ¿Qué roles distintos desempeñaron en el bautismo de Jesús las tres personas de la Trinidad (Padre, Hijo, Espíritu)?

Padre ______________________________

Hijo ______________________________

Espíritu ______________________________

¿Por qué es importante que la misión de Jesús no era algo exclusivamente individual?

Como seguidores de Jesús, reconocemos que no aportamos nada a nuestra salvación, salvo el pecado por el que Jesús murió. Es en su muerte y resurrección donde recibimos al Espíritu Santo para que viva en nosotros, dándonos acceso directo al Padre y a toda su sabiduría, fortaleza y amor. ¡Los tres obran juntos al unísono para ayudarnos a vivir para la gloria del Rey!

DÍA 4

MATEO 4:1-11

LEE MATEO 4:1-11

Al igual que Jesús se identificó con quienes vino a salvar entrando en las aguas del bautismo, también experimentó los tipos de tentación que son comunes para toda la humanidad, pero de las formas más extremas. Uno pensaría que después de un recibimiento de celebración con toda la Trinidad, Jesús tendría ímpetu para zambullirse de lleno en un ministerio activo; sin embargo, lejos de colocarse bajo el foco, el Espíritu Santo lo dirigió a tener una experiencia más privada: un ayuno de cuarenta días en el desierto que terminó con una serie de tentaciones.

Lee Santiago 1:13. ¿Cuál es la diferencia entre ser dirigido a un lugar donde habrá tentaciones y ser la fuente de la tentación?

¿Por qué el Espíritu Santo dirigió a Jesús a un lugar de tentación?

Usando un diccionario, busca la definición de *tentación*. ¿En qué se diferencia del pecado?

Lee 1 Corintios 10:13. ¿Qué dice sobre la tentación?

Este pasaje (1 Corintios 10:13) a menudo se cita erróneamente, sugiriendo que Dios no nos dará más de lo que podemos soportar, lo cual no es cierto. De hecho, la Escritura nos dice regularmente que de seguro enfrentaremos situaciones que superarán con creces nuestras fuerzas y que tendremos que depender del Rey de maneras radicales. En lugar de eso, este pasaje revela que Jesús conoce de primera mano lo que es la tentación, y Él siempre puede equiparte para que decidas no pecar si confías en su fuerza.

Antes de que el diablo tentara a Cristo, Jesús pasó cuarenta días ayunando en un lugar desierto. Aunque el Espíritu Santo lo sostenía durante el ayuno, al final del mismo Jesús tuvo hambre. Biológicamente hablando, el regreso de los dolores del hambre después de un ayuno extenso indica que la muerte no está muy lejos. Estas son las condiciones en las que encontramos a Jesús cuando el tentador entra en escena con las tres tentaciones.

Lee 1 Juan 2:16. ¿Cuáles son las tres categorías de tentación ofrece el mundo?

- ____________________________________
- ____________________________________
- ____________________________________

Cada una de estas tres tentaciones que Jesús enfrentó encaja en una de estas distintas categorías. Hebreos 2:18 y 4:15 nos dice que Jesús fue tentado en todo pero que nunca pecó. Sin embargo, Jesús es más que solo un ejemplo a seguir para nosotros: ¡Él es quien cumplió toda justicia porque sabe que nosotros nunca podríamos hacerlo (Mateo 3:15)!

¿En cuál de estas tres categorías encaja la tentación número uno (Mateo 4:3)?

En la primera tentación, ¿cómo aborda la respuesta de Jesús (citando Deuteronomio 8:3) "los deseos de la carne" tanto para su situación como para nuestros propios momentos de tentación?

¿En cuál de estas tres categorías encaja la segunda tentación (Mateo 4:5-6)?

¿Qué intentaba conseguir el diablo que Jesús hiciera en la segunda tentación? Usa un comentario bíblico si te resulta útil.

Es interesante que el diablo citara Salmos 91:11-12 para tentar a Jesús. El enemigo conoce la Palabra de Dios al derecho y al revés, pero no la citó con reverencia. Lo que hizo fue sacar dos versículos fuera de contexto para manipularlos y sacar provecho personal. Por desgracia la Escritura se utiliza a menudo de esta manera, incluso en el cristianismo. Por eso son tan importantes libros como este, *La sinopsis de la Biblia,* los estudios bíblicos y grupos de discipulado, y otros más. Cuando no conocemos lo que dice verdaderamente la Biblia, no estamos armados con la verdad para luchar contra las mentiras y las tentaciones.

En la segunda tentación, ¿de qué manera la respuesta de Jesús (citando Deuteronomio 6:16) aborda el orgullo en la vida?

¿En cuál de estas tres categorías encaja la tentación número tres (Mateo 4:8-9)?

En su última respuesta, Jesús le dijo a Satanás: "¡Vete, Satanás!", y después usó la frase del Antiguo Testamento que aparece en cuatro lugares distintos (Deuteronomio 6:13-14 y 10:20; Josué 24:14; 1 Samuel 7:3). Jesús no estaba jugueteando, sino que usaba la verdad repetidamente porque es necesario repetirlo. "Al Señor tu Dios adorarás, y solo a Él servirás". Israel necesitaba oírlo repetidamente, y también nosotros necesitamos oírlo constantemente. Es un recordatorio poderoso para que el enemigo sepa que tenemos un Dios, ¡y que no es él!

¿Por qué crees que Jesús usó la Escritura para luchar contra la tentación? ¿De qué modo esto es un ejemplo para nosotros?

De las tres categorías de tentaciones que bosqueja 1 Juan 2:16, ¿cuál te parece más difícil de combatir?

Encuentra y escribe tres versículos que se relacionen con tu tentación específica. (openbible.info/topics/ es un buen sitio en inglés para buscar si necesitas ayuda).

Cuando seas tentado	
Versículo	
Versículo	
Versículo	

El versículo 11 nos dice que el diablo se marchó y llegaron ángeles y cuidaron de Jesús. No solo vemos la victoria de Jesús, sino también la provisión de Dios. Es un gran recordatorio de que Él no nos dejará para defendernos por nosotros mismos en medio de nuestra tentación. La próxima vez que estés luchando con tu principal tentación, recuerda los versículos que escribiste arriba y declara la verdad de la Palabra de Dios para el enemigo y también para ti.

DÍA 5

MATEO 4:12-25

LEE MATEO 4:12-25

Después de oír la noticia del encarcelamiento de su amigo y primo JEB, Jesús se fue de su aldea natal de Nazaret a una ciudad cerca del Mar de Galilea. Y, has acertado, ¡se cumplió con esto otra profecía de Isaías! Isaías 9:1-2 sugiere que los habitantes de Galilea, incluidos los gentiles, verían la luz, ¡y la Luz misma resplandeció sobre ellos!

Mira el versículo 17. Escribe a continuación las primeras palabras de Jesús predicando. Subraya la palabra de acción que Jesús enfatizó a sus oyentes.

Busca los versículos escritos en la tabla de abajo. Escribe el nombre de la persona que habla. Después escribe el nombre de la persona o personas llamadas a arrepentirse.

Pasaje	Persona que habla	Llamado al arrepentimiento
Mateo 3:2		
Marcos 6:12		

Pasaje	**Persona que habla**	**Llamado al arrepentimiento**
Hechos 2:38		
Hechos 26:19-20		
Apocalipsis 2:5		

¿Qué te dice acerca del corazón de Dios el hecho de que este mensaje se repita a lo largo de la Escritura?

Mientras estaba en la región de Galilea, Jesús llamó a sus primeros seguidores: un puñado de hombres jóvenes que estaban pescando junto a la costa a las afueras de Cafarnaúm. Imagina estar trabajando mucho en el negocio familiar, pensando que probablemente es lo único que conocerás nunca, y que un rabino (maestro) llamado Jesús aparezca y te invite a seguirlo. Los niños judíos a menudo comenzaban a seguir a un rabino en torno a los doce años de edad, pero es posible que estos seguidores tuvieran algunos años más (probablemente entre trece o quince años de edad), ya que ya estaban trabajando pero aún eran lo suficientemente jóvenes para aprovechar la oportunidad de seguir a un rabino.

Repasa 4:18-22 y responde las siguientes preguntas:

Nombra dos parejas de hermanos y su ocupación.

¿Qué estaba haciendo cada pareja cuando fueron llamados?

¿A qué los llamó Jesús? ¿Por qué crees que usó la analogía de la pesca?

¿Cuál fue su respuesta al llamado y la visión que Jesús puso delante de ellos?

¿Qué dejaron atrás para seguir a Jesús? ¿Cuál es la importancia de eso?

Es interesante notar que no estaban perpetuamente sentados en casa durante horas y horas viendo su servicio de *streaming* favorito (o el equivalente a ello en el primer siglo). Estaban trabajando duro, fieles para perfeccionar su oficio a fin de poder aportar a sus familias. No eran hombres perezosos. Y su llamado de Jesús no fue "echarle un ojo" para ver si encajaba en sus horarios o personalidades. Era un llamado a tiempo completo a una educación práctica impartida por el rabino Jesús. Dejar sus profesiones y sus familias no solo era una oportunidad para probar algo nuevo, sino un compromiso profundo a una identidad completamente nueva. Ya no serían definidos como pescadores sino como discípulos del Rey.

Aunque no todos los creyentes somos llamados a dejar nuestras ocupaciones y mudarnos lejos de nuestras familias para un ministerio vocacional, *sí* somos llamados a identificarnos antes que cualquier otra cosa como seguidores de Jesús en los lugares donde Dios nos ha colocado. Podemos encontrar identidades en muchas cosas extraordinarias, pero debemos tener presente que nuestra primera identidad impacta el modo en que actuamos en nuestras otras identidades (padre, hermano, empleado, atleta, etc.).

¿Qué aspectos de tu identidad tienen el potencial de desplazar tu principal identidad como discípulo del Rey?

Describe a alguien de tu mismo campo vocacional que represente de manera auténtica su identidad como seguidor de Cristo en primer lugar.

¿Qué ajustes quieres hacer para que tu identidad principal esté en tu posición como discípulo del Rey?

Jesús y sus seguidores recorrieron toda la región de Galilea enseñando y proclamando el evangelio del reino y sanando enfermedades y aflicciones de todo tipo, ¡incluyendo la opresión demoniaca!

¿Por qué crees que "proclamar el evangelio del reino" está enumerado antes que sus sanidades y obras milagrosas?

¿Qué crees que causó que su fama se extendiera y atrajera grandes multitudes a seguirlo?

Cuando quedó inaugurado oficialmente el ministerio de Jesús, se formaron dos grupos de personas. El primero era el de quienes estaban dispuestos a dejar atrás su identidad para seguir a Jesús y ser formados por Él y por su Palabra. El segundo grupo era el de quienes vigilaban los movimientos de Jesús, buscando lo que Jesús podría darles o hacer por ellos.

Jesús estaba y está buscando personas deseosas de caminar en una identidad completamente nueva como sus seguidores. Aunque otras identidades puedan producir una felicidad temporal, la vida en el reino eterno de Jesús será muchísimo más reconfortante ahora y por la eternidad, ¡porque Él está donde está el gozo!

¿Qué es lo que más te impactó del estudio de esta semana? ¿Por qué?

¿Qué aprendiste o recordaste sobre Dios y su carácter esta semana?

DÍA 6

SALMO CORRESPONDIENTE Y ORACIÓN

LEE SALMOS 2

¿Qué correlación ves entre Salmos 2 y el estudio de esta semana sobre Jesús y su reino?

¿Qué porciones de este salmo captan más tu atención?

Termina haciendo esta oración en voz alta:

Padre,

Te alabo por ser Dios sobre todas las naciones. Jesús, ¡tú eres el Rey sobre todos los reyes! Gracias por la bendición de poder refugiarme en ti.

Padre, he pecado. Tanto Juan el Bautista como Jesús predicaron el mensaje de arrepentimiento, así que sé que hay esperanza para mí para alejarme de mis pecados. Me arrepiento de mis pecados y acudo a ti, y te pido que limpies mi corazón. Confieso que me he enfurecido y he conspirado en vano. Como los reyes malvados de la Escritura, he intentado forjar mis propios caminos en lugar de someterme a tu realeza y a tu reino. Como el rey Herodes, he querido mantener mi poder en lugar de adorarte.

Tú me has mostrado una gran compasión. Ayúdame a extender tu misericordia a otros. Cuando enfrente la tentación, empodérame para predicar la verdad tanto a mí mismo como al enemigo de mi alma. Equípame con las verdades de tu Palabra para que pueda mantenerme firme o huir, y dame sabiduría para saber qué es necesario en cada momento. Ayúdame a caminar en humildad con mis ojos puestos en tu Hijo Jesús y su reino.

Te rindo mi vida, Señor. Cada momento de mi día y en cada decisión que tome, entrego mi voluntad y mi camino a tu perfecta voluntad y a tu camino.

Yo también te amo. Amén.

DÍA 7

DESCANSA, PONTE AL DÍA O PROFUNDIZA

RETO SEMANAL

Quizá tienes un linaje marcado por la disfunción y el dolor, o tal vez tienes un legado de fe y devoción. Al margen de dónde se encuentre tu familia en este espectro, es útil mirar atrás en tu vida y en tu historia para pensar en el futuro. Dios ha estado y está actuando en tu historia, ¡pues de no ser así no estarías estudiando su Palabra hoy!

Haz un árbol genealógico de tu familia remontándote todo lo atrás que quieras (aunque solo tengas acceso a tu generación actual) y haz una lista de áreas en las que ves la redención de Dios actuando.

¿De qué manera mirar atrás te ayuda a determinar lo que te gustaría ver en las generaciones futuras?

SEMANA 2

Mateo 5-7:

Mensaje del Rey

VERSÍCULO PARA MEMORIZAR

Miren las aves del cielo, que no siembran, ni siegan, ni recogen en graneros, y *sin embargo*, el Padre celestial las alimenta. ¿No son ustedes de mucho más valor que ellas?

Mateo 6:26

LECTURA BÍBLICA DIARIA

Día 1: Mateo 5:1-16

Día 2: Mateo 5:17-48

Día 3: Mateo 6:1-18

Día 4: Mateo 6:19-34

Día 5: Mateo 7

Día 6: Salmos 112

Día 7: Para ponerte al día

Corresponde al Día 283 de *La sinopsis de la Biblia*

RETO SEMANAL

Ver la página 61 para más información.

DÍA 1

MATEO 5:1-16

LEE MATEO 5:1-16

Al inicio de su ministerio, Jesús, rodeado de sus discípulos, se sentó en una ladera cerca del Mar de Galilea para dar su sermón más conocido: el Sermón del Monte. Comenzó enumerando ocho bienaventuranzas.

Busca la palabra *bienaventurado* (5:3) en un diccionario de griego y escribe lo que encuentres. ¿Qué otros significados tiene esta palabra?

Principalmente, la palabra significa algo cercano a "felicidad", pero la ironía es que las cosas que Jesús ofrecía como el medio para llegar a esta felicidad no nos parecen cosas muy felices, cosas como el llanto, el hambre o la persecución; pero sus palabras seguro que fueron como un bálsamo para su audiencia. Eran principalmente personas judías en una sociedad rural y agraria, que vivían bajo la opresión del ejército romano que había tomado el control de su nación. Él les ofrecía una esperanza mejor más allá de esta vida. Les estaba ofreciendo algo que parecía de algún modo un retroceso. ¿El camino para heredar la tierra es ser *humilde*? Eso parece contrario a la naturaleza humana, ¿verdad?

Y eso es exactamente lo que Jesús estaba estableciendo. Como Rey del reino de los cielos, Jesús les estaba ayudando a entender que las cosas en su reino son al revés. Lo vemos en 5:3 y 5:10, donde la pobreza espiritual y la persecución son el camino para heredar el reino. Tienes que ser pobre para ser rico. Todo acerca del reino de Dios parece más bien una amenaza para nuestras sensibilidades.

Repasa Mateo 5:3. ¿Quién será bienaventurado? En tus propias palabras, describe lo que significa ser "pobre en espíritu", o espiritualmente pobre.

La pobreza espiritual es reconocer que no tenemos nada que ofrecerle a Dios, no hay razón para que Él nos escoja o nos ame. Y si somos realmente honestos al respecto, no solo llegamos con las manos vacías (con nada de dinero en nuestra cuenta), sino que tenemos una deuda. Por muy mal que suene esto o por mucho que ofenda a nuestro orgullo y autoestima, Dios dice que *ese* es el punto de partida. La pobreza espiritual es el kilómetro cero. No podemos participar en el reino de los cielos sin reconocer nuestra necesidad desesperada de Dios.

Al leer estas bienaventuranzas, es interesante considerar que podrían no ser *solo* una lista, sino una lista *acumulativa*. Si ese fuera el caso, entonces esta primera bienaventuranza es el fundamento de todo el sermón.

Según vas leyendo los tipos de personas que reciben las bendiciones que Jesús enumeró (por ejemplo los pobres en espíritu, los que lloran, los humildes, etc.), ¿qué descripciones parecen ser las que más te afectan? ¿Cuáles podrían no ser para ti ahora mismo?

Para los que estamos en el reino, el impacto del Rey sobre nuestra vida debería ser de bendición para otros, incluso para los que no están en el reino. Los versículos 13-14 dicen que la "tierra" y el "mundo" se beneficiarán de que conozcamos a Dios.

¿Hay alguien en tu vida que no conozca a Jesús como Rey que pueda beneficiarse de tu relación con Dios?

Repasa Mateo 5:16. Jesús dijo que quiere que otros vean brillar nuestra luz. ¿Quién dijo Él que recibiría la gloria cuando otros vieran nuestras buenas obras?

DÍA 2

MATEO 5:17-48

LEE MATEO 5:17-48

Nos resulta fácil convertir el Sermón del Monte en una lista de tareas. Ya sea que sintamos que lo estamos haciendo muy bien o metiendo la pata por completo, ambos puntos de vista siguen concentrándose en que seamos nosotros los que lo hagamos bien. Entonces, sin tan siquiera darnos cuenta, estamos de nuevo en el punto de partida, con necesidad de que nos recuerden nuestra pobreza espiritual. Es vital recordar que tanto en nuestros mejores días como en los peores, nuestra única esperanza es la cruz de Cristo.

Cuando se trata de tu relación con Dios y el mundo que te rodea, ¿te ves más tentado a enfocarte en tus victorias (lo que estás haciendo bien) o en tus derrotas (lo que estás haciendo mal)?

Repasa Mateo 5:20. ¿Qué se requiere para entrar en el reino de los cielos? **Compara esto con las palabras de Jesús en 5:3.** ¿Cómo pueden ser ciertas ambas cosas?

Medita en los Diez Mandamientos y en las demás leyes del Antiguo Testamento que Jesús citó en 5:17-48. ¿Qué reveló Jesús repetidamente sobre las normas de santidad de Dios?

Jesús no dijo: "Nunca serán capaces de guardar la ley de Dios, así que Dios va a bajar el estándar. Hagan lo que quieran y estará bien, porque Él es un Dios de amor". En lugar de eso, dijo que Dios no solo busca las acciones correctas sino que busca el corazón recto. Si no matas a nadie, pero odias a todos los que te rodean, eso no refleja a Dios ni tampoco su amor ante un mundo caído, y no se parece a la libertad. El Rey, por otro lado, valora la reconciliación y la paz, y alienta la humildad al perseguir esas cosas.

Cuando Jesús habló sobre la lujuria, tocó ideas que aparecen también en el Antiguo Testamento, revelando que Dios siempre se ha interesado no solo por nuestras acciones, sino también por nuestro corazón.

Lee Éxodo 20:17. ¿Cómo revela este mandamiento que Dios siempre se ha interesado por lo que está ocurriendo en nuestro corazón?

La norma de Dios no ha cambiado. Es posible hacer una buena obra con un motivo malvado, pero Dios requiere que tanto el corazón como la acción sean puros. En Amós 5:21-24 Dios le dijo a su pueblo que aborrecía sus buenas obras porque las hacían con un corazón impuro que negaba la justicia e ignoraba la rectitud.

Aunque todos pecaremos de muchas maneras, un corazón puro nos incitará a actuar contra el hecho de caer en futuros pecados. Jesús usó un fuerte lenguaje hiperbólico (cortarse la mano, sacarse un ojo) para ilustrar esto. Habló de normas que parecían demasiado elevadas para la mayoría de la gente: valorar el matrimonio, cumplir lo que prometes, y tener una honra que sea superior a un juramento. Llamó a su pueblo a amar a sus enemigos y a no tomar represalias. De nuevo, Él reveló que su reino es un reino al revés, un reino de humildad, generosidad y bondad.

Pídele a Dios que traiga a tu mente a cualquier persona que se podría considerar tu enemigo o perseguidor. Para cumplir lo que dice en 5:44, ora bendiciendo a esa persona. Pídele a Dios que te ayude a hacerlo *de corazón* para que no solo hagas la acción correcta, sino que tu corazón también sea el correcto.

La lectura de hoy termina con estas impactantes palabras de Jesús: "Por tanto, sean ustedes perfectos como su Padre celestial es perfecto" (5:48). Dios exige la perfección. Eso parece agotador como mínimo, imposible como máximo.

Busca la palabra *perfecto* (5:48) en un diccionario de griego y escribe lo que encuentres. ¿Qué otros significados tiene esta palabra?

Es útil saber que la palabra *perfecto* aquí tiene la idea de estar "completo". Nuestra única esperanza de ser perfeccionados o completados es recibiendo la justicia que Cristo nos concede. Por eso es una gran noticia que Jesús no haya venido para abolir la ley sino para cumplirla (ver 5:17). Él ha cumplido con los requisitos de la ley mediante su vida perfecta y su muerte perfecta.

Segunda de Corintios 5:21 dice: "Al que no conoció pecado, lo hizo pecado por nosotros, para que fuéramos hechos justicia de Dios en Él". Así es como puede ser cierto que estamos espiritualmente en bancarrota (Mateo 5:3), pero a la vez nuestra justicia cumple sus normas (5:20, 5:48). Es solo porque Cristo ha pagado del todo nuestra deuda mediante su muerte en la cruz, *y* la justicia que Él obtuvo ¡nos ha sido asignada a nosotros!

DÍA 3

MATEO 6:1-18

LEE MATEO 6:1-18

Jesús continuó presentando una visión de cómo es la vida en el reino: nuestras acciones deberían estar motivadas por un deseo de agradar a Dios, no a los demás. Él desafió nuestro deseo natural de ganarnos el respeto o establecer una reputación mediante las buenas obras.

Los fariseos eran un grupo de líderes religiosos estrictos en los tiempos de Jesús, y a menudo actuaban de maneras que ponían el enfoque en ellos mismos. Jesús usó una palabra interesante para describirlos; los llamó *hipócritas*, que era la palabra usada para referirse a los actores griegos en los tiempos de Jesús. Estos actores se ponían distintas máscaras sobre su rostro dependiendo del papel que estuvieran interpretando. Esta era una palabra apropiada para los fariseos, ya que hacían una especie de actuación al realizar acciones llamativas delante de los demás.

En lugar de condenar la acción por completo, Jesús dio una serie de directrices claras, diciendo: "Hagan lo que ellos hacen, pero no lo hagan *así*" seguido de: "En su lugar háganlo de *esta* forma". Él señaló un método más discreto, y aunque tal vez no erradique por completo la motivación egoísta, sí puede darle un buen golpe al ego. Sean generosos con los necesitados, dijo, pero sin fanfarria. Oren, pero no para conseguir la atención de otros. Ayunen, pero sin hacer de ello un espectáculo público. En todas estas acciones, es importante recordar "el kilómetro cero": nuestra pobreza espiritual. No hemos puesto nada sobre la mesa salvo nuestro pecado y nuestra gran necesidad de Él.

Escribe a continuación Efesios 2:10. Encuentra a quién se le atribuye en este versículo la preparación de nuestras buenas obras, luego encierra ese nombre en un círculo.

Lee Filipenses 2:12-13, después escribe debajo el versículo 13. Encuentra a quién se le atribuye en este versículo el darnos el deseo de hacer buenas obras y realizarlas a través de nosotros, luego encierra ese nombre en un círculo.

¿Cómo te sientes al leer estos versículos? ¿Cómo afecta esta verdad tus ideas acerca de Dios? ¿Cómo afecta tus ideas acerca de tus acciones?

Nuestras buenas obras, como dar, orar o ayunar, son cosas buenas que glorifican a Dios y nos producen gozo al participar en ellas. ¡Él se deleita en ti cuando das, oras y ayunas! Y es importante recordar que no está mal *que te vean* hacer estas cosas; lo que está mal es hacer estas cosas *para que te vean*. Por ejemplo, quizá tu comunidad atiende a los pobres, tal vez alguien te pide que dirijas un grupo en oración, o quizá estás soportando un largo ayuno y quieres pedirle a tu comunidad que ore por ti. ¡Dios es honrado en esas cosas!

Repasa Mateo 6:6 y 6:9. ¿Hacia quién enseñó Jesús a sus seguidores que dirijan su oración? ¿Es a Él a quien normalmente diriges tus oraciones? ¿Por qué sí o por qué no?

Jesús profundizó más en el tema de la oración cuando enseñó a sus discípulos a orar. Les dio un modelo que es teológicamente denso, y a la vez lo suficientemente simple como para sostenerse por sí solo. Enseñó a sus seguidores a hablar con el Padre y mantener una conversación real, humilde y relacional. Orar a Jesús o al Espíritu no está mal, pero no es lo que normalmente vemos que ocurre en la Palabra de Dios. La manera típica en que vemos modelada la oración en la Escritura es orar al Padre, a través del Hijo, mediante el Espíritu. Eso puede ser desafiante para todos los que tenemos padres terrenales terribles (o ausentes) o con un mal entendimiento de cómo es nuestro Padre celestial. Tal vez preferimos hablar con Jesús porque Él parece más accesible. Pero Jesús recordó a sus seguidores que el Padre les escucha y responderá generosamente a sus oraciones.

En cuanto al ayuno, Jesús habló de ello como una parte asumida de sus vidas, diciendo *cuando* ayunen, no *si* ayunan. En términos bíblicos, ayunar siempre se relacionaba con abstenerse de alimento y siempre estaba unido a la oración. Los científicos seculares elogian los beneficios físicos de ayunar, pero el enfoque bíblico del ayuno lleva al cristiano a una esfera plena de beneficios: físicos, mentales, emocionales y espirituales.

En toda la discusión de hoy sobre las disciplinas espirituales, Jesús enfatizó dos temas conectados acerca de Dios. La frase *en lo secreto* aparece hasta seis veces, reiterando que Dios se involucra con las cosas del corazón: Él está ahí, Él sabe lo que está ocurriendo, Él lo ve todo. Y la palabra *recompensa* aparece hasta siete veces; el texto siempre coloca a Dios como el dador de la recompensa.

Lee Hebreos 11:6. ¿Quién es recompensado? ¿Por qué?

¿Quién da la recompensa?

¿Cómo influye esto en tu visión del Padre?

¿Cómo modela esto tu idea de la importancia de la oración?

Mañana veremos de qué manera creer estas verdades acerca de Dios nos ayudará a desarrollar el amor y hacer morir el temor.

DÍA 4

MATEO 6:19-34

LEE MATEO 6:19-34

En la sección de hoy del Sermón del Monte, Jesús conectó repetidamente nuestros valores con nuestras preocupaciones.

Escribe los cuatro versículos en los que Jesús informó a sus seguidores acerca de algo que no quería que hicieran.

6:19–No ______________________________

6:25–No ______________________________

6:31–No ______________________________

6:34–No ______________________________

Si obedecemos el "no acumulen" del versículo 19, entonces el "no se preocupen" de los versículos 25, 31 y 34 seguirá de forma natural, porque nuestro corazón estará anclado en cosas eternas y no en cosas pasajeras.

El temor está conectado a nuestros valores y nuestra identidad. Donde basas tu identidad determina lo que valoras. Lo que valoras determina lo que temes perder o no tener nunca. Lo que temes perder o no tener nunca casi seguro que producirá temor y esfuerzo si ocupa demasiado espacio en tu corazón.

Si ves que tu identidad está en cosas pasajeras, el temor es algo natural. Pero si tienes tu identidad en las cosas eternas, en su reino, el temor mismo se convierte en algo pasajero.

Podemos aprender a crecer en la fe. Podemos aprender a hacer retroceder nuestros temores. Podemos aprender a ajustar lo que valoramos. El modo de hacerlo es conociendo más a Dios, leyendo su Palabra, viendo su carácter, y aprendiendo a confiar en Él. Al hacerlo, aprendemos más sobre lo que Él valora y podemos pedirle que nos ayude a valorar nosotros también esas mismas cosas.

El problema de intentar ser rico en lo que el mundo valora es que, al final, todo es como dinero del juego Monopolio. No puede darte nada salvo pequeños hoteles de plástico en un tablero de cartón que algún día terminará en una tienda de caridad. En realidad, Jesús les dijo a sus discípulos: *Dejen de intentar conseguir más hoteles de plástico. ¡Basta ya del dinero del Monopolio! Fijen su tiempo, sus emociones y esfuerzos en algo duradero.* En 6:21 lo dijo de esta forma: "porque donde esté tu tesoro, allí estará también tu corazón". El corazón va siguiendo al tesoro. En lo que inviertes tu tiempo, dinero y emoción es lo que realmente valoras.

Toma un minuto para hacer una pausa y ser sincero contigo mismo: ¿qué porcentaje de tu tiempo y emoción empleas en cosas de valor eterno? En un sentido muy práctico, ¿cómo podrías emplear más tiempo en cosas que tengan un valor eterno?

Si el porcentaje (en tu respuesta a la pregunta de arriba) es bajo, no lo tomes como una oportunidad para culparte por ello, sino como una invitación a una vida de más libertad y gozo. Si comenzamos a valorar las cosas eternas por encima de todo lo demás, entonces nuestras preocupaciones por las cosas temporales ocuparán el lugar que les corresponde. Por supuesto que siempre tendremos preocupaciones terrenales, pero puede ser útil verlas a la luz de la eternidad.

Cuando Jesús enseñaba estos principios, probablemente estaba hablando a un grupo de personas que eran legítimamente pobres. Habló de sus preocupaciones reales sobre la provisión con recordatorios de quién es el Padre. Dijo que es normal que las personas que no conocen a Dios como su Padre se preocupen por cosas como la comida y la ropa, pero a los hijos de Dios, Jesús les dijo: "¡Recuerden cuánto les ama el Padre! Recuerden que Él los valora por encima de todo lo demás que ha creado. Eso debería liberar su corazón para que se enfoquen en las cosas que verdaderamente importan, en lugar de ocuparse en las cosas temporales. Mientras estén enfocados en esas cosas pasajeras, estarán lleno de temor".

Jesús fue serio al enseñar a su pueblo a no temer. El temor usurpa nuestra lealtad a su reino. Fija nuestros ojos en las cosas erróneas. Nunca deja de demandar nuestra atención. En lugar de eso, ¡Jesús nos llamó a recordar quién es nuestro Padre! ¡Él nos provee!

¿En qué áreas de tu vida ves regularmente el temor? ¿Dónde compruebas que te estás esforzando? Lee el pasaje de hoy nuevamente y escribe las citas de Jesús que más te hablen.

DÍA 5

MATEO 7

LEE MATEO 7

Busca la palabra *juez* (7:1) en un diccionario de griego y escribe lo que encuentres. ¿Qué otros significados tiene esta palabra?

Repasa 7:1-5, que nos advierte sobre juzgar. **Después repasa 7:15-20,** que parece animarnos a hacerlo. A primera vista, estas dos ideas parecen contradecirse entre sí, pero ¿cómo podrían funcionar juntas?

En los versículos 1-5 Jesús nos dice que no juzguemos a los demás, pero en los versículos 15-20 parece decirnos que *sí* juzguemos a otros para discernir si alguien está dando un fruto bueno o malo. Aquí tienes tres consejos útiles para entender cómo pueden funcionar bien juntas estas dos ideas.

Primero, Dios es el juez de toda la humanidad (Génesis 18:25). Él dicta el veredicto y sus consecuencias, que son muy reales. Los humanos no tenemos ese poder, ni deberíamos, porque nosotros no conocemos el corazón de las personas como lo conoce Dios (Salmos 139:1-4, Jeremías 11:20). Si esta fuera una sala de juicios, estaríamos en la audiencia no con el mazo en la mano. Es técnicamente imposible que seamos nosotros los que pronunciemos el juicio eterno.

Segundo, lo que queremos decir la mayoría de las veces con "juzgar" (lo que los humanos *sí podemos* hacer) se define mejor como "aprobar o desaprobar". No tenemos el poder de condenar a nadie al infierno. Jesús estaba diciendo: "No intenten pesar el corazón de nadie, porque ustedes no lo conocen. Suponer que pueden es suponer que son Dios, lo cual en sí mismo es digno de condenar". Jesús también nos recordó que nuestro propio pecado nos estorba a la hora de ver a otros con claridad (7:4-5).

Tercero, Jesús nos llama a ser inspectores del fruto (versículos 15-20), lo cual es totalmente distinto a los tipos de juicio que acabamos de describir. Podemos inspeccionar el fruto, pero no podemos ver sus raíces y no somos los encargados de talar el árbol. Tenemos que discernir porque no queremos comer mal fruto. En los grandes mercados agrícolas de los maestros de la religión y gurús espirituales hay mucho fruto podrido. Puede parecer atractivo por fuera, pero si no está a la altura de la Escritura, no deberíamos buscarlo para nutrirnos. También vale la pena destacar que hay una diferencia entre una manzana *golpeada* y una manzana llena de *gusanos o enfermedad*. Aunque algunos frutos están enfermos o moribundos, otros puede que solo tengan pequeños defectos.

Jesús nos llama a la humildad y a la sabiduría. No dijo que el juicio no fuera a suceder, porque nos llegará a todos, y tampoco estaba diciendo: "¡Cada cual con lo suyo!". Pero el juicio de Dios se produce a nivel del corazón, y nosotros no tenemos ojos para ver eso, así que lo mejor es dirigir nuestro discernimiento en esta dirección: si una acción es correcta o incorrecta, en lugar de si una persona es buena o mala. Cuando nos aventuramos en ese territorio, perdemos de vista el kilómetro cero: nuestra propia pobreza espiritual. El kilómetro cero no es un punto desde el que avanzamos, dejamos atrás o superamos, sino el fundamento sobre el que está construido todo lo demás.

¿Qué te resulta más difícil, no juzgar a los demás o ser un inspector del fruto? ¿Por qué? Pídele a Dios que te ayude a crecer en sabiduría y humildad para que puedas gestionar correctamente la tensión de ambas directivas.

En 7:7-11 vemos que el Padre tiene un corazón de generosidad hacia sus hijos. Él escucha, cuida, da buenos regalos, ¡y nos invita a pedir lo que queramos!

Usando las versiones de la Biblia NBLA, RVR-60, NVI o LBLA, vuelve a leer 7:12. Escribe las dos primeras palabras del versículo aquí:

Al comenzar este versículo con estas palabras, Jesús las conectó con los versículos anteriores, mostrando la causa y el efecto. *Porque* tenemos un Padre generoso que nos escucha, nos cuida y es bondadoso con nosotros, podemos ofrecer esa misma bondad a los demás. Podemos dar lo que hemos recibido de Él.

¿Qué te resulta más difícil, pedir cosas a Dios para ti o ser generoso con los demás? ¿Por qué? ¿Cómo te podría ayudar la conexión entre estos dos conceptos a crecer en el área en la que eres más débil?

Después de que Jesús hablara sobre ser inspectores de frutos, dijo que muchas personas parecen tener buen fruto pero aún no lo conocen a Él como Rey y Salvador. Llamarlo "Señor" y hacer milagros no es la manera de entrar en el reino. Como siempre, Dios busca algo más que buenas obras, ¡busca nuestro corazón! El reino es para las personas con *corazones nuevos.*

Una persona moralmente recta que se identifica como cristiano puede parecer alguien que pertenece al reino, pero con el tiempo y las tormentas de la vida se revelará su fundamento. ¿Ha construido su casa sobre la roca que es el Rey Jesús? ¿O sobre la arena? Por muy beneficioso que pueda ser, vivir una vida buena y moral no puede salvarnos. Tanto el hedonismo como la moralidad son arena. La roca es *relación*. La roca es *cambio de corazón*. Si tu vida no está construida sobre el conocimiento de Dios, todos tus reinos son castillos de arena.

Cuando Jesús enseñaba estas palabras, la gente reconocía que Él tenía una autoridad única. Los escribas, a los que estaban acostumbrados a escuchar, citaban principalmente a otros o planteaban preguntas sin respuestas. Jesús, en cambio, hablaba como si tuviera autoridad sobre el texto. Y la tiene, porque Él *es* la Palabra (Juan 1:1, 14). ¡Él es donde está la verdad y donde está el gozo!

¿Qué es lo que más te resaltó en el estudio de esta semana? ¿Por qué?

¿Qué aprendiste o recordaste sobre Dios y su carácter esta semana?

DÍA 6

SALMO CORRESPONDIENTE Y ORACIÓN

LEE SALMOS 112

¿Qué correlación ves entre Salmos 112 y el estudio de esta semana sobre Jesús y su reino?

¿Qué porciones de este salmo captan más tu atención?

Termina haciendo esta oración en voz alta:

Padre,

Te alabo por la forma en que me has provisto y protegido. Gracias por tu Palabra y tus mandatos, porque son una bendición para conocerte mejor mediante la lectura de tu Palabra. Gracias por conocer todas mis necesidades y aun así invitarme a pedirte mis deseos.

Padre, he pecado, y apelo a tu misericordia. Me arrepiento de mis pecados y acudo a ti, y te pido que limpies mi corazón. Confieso que he caído en el esfuerzo y el temor. Confieso que a veces quiero construir mi propio reino en lugar de someterme a tu reinado y a tu reino. Pero, como tu Espíritu está obrando en mí, ¡tengo nuevos ojos para verte, nuevos oídos para oírte y un nuevo corazón para amarte!

Tú has sido generoso conmigo. Ayúdame a ofrecer tu generosidad a otros, a bendecir a los pobres así como tú me has bendecido a mí. Concédeme tener un corazón firme y estable, para que no tenga temor de malas noticias. Fijo mis ojos en ti y en tu reino eterno, no en las cosas pasajeras.

Rindo mi vida a ti, Señor; en cada momento de mi día y en cada decisión que tome, cedo mi voluntad y mi camino a tu perfecta voluntad y camino.

Yo también te amo. Amén.

DÍA 7

DESCANSA, PONTE AL DÍA O PROFUNDIZA

RETO SEMANAL

Nuestro reto semanal viene de nuestra lectura del Día 2. En 5:29-30 Jesús dijo: "Si tu ojo derecho te hace pecar, arráncalo y tíralo; porque te es mejor que se pierda uno de tus miembros, y no que todo tu cuerpo sea arrojado al infierno. Y si tu mano derecha te hace pecar, córtala y tírala; porque te es mejor que se pierda uno de tus miembros, y no que todo tu cuerpo vaya al infierno".

Como mencionamos previamente, Jesús usó aquí un lenguaje hiperbólico (arrancarte el ojo, cortarte la mano) para demostrar que el puro de corazón pasará a la acción para no caer en futuros pecados.

Escribe en un diario respondiendo a estas preguntas: ¿Cuáles son tus puntos débiles? ¿En qué trampas de pecado caes repetidamente? ¿Qué pasos prácticos puedes dar para evitar caer en esas trampas? Sé específico. ¿A quién le puedes confesar esta lucha y pedir oración o rendirle cuentas?

Mientras tratas de abordar esas áreas de tu vida, ¡resiste la desesperación! Aunque hayas fallado diez mil veces, e incluso aunque vuelvas a fallar esta semana, recuerda lo que aprendimos el Día 2 sobre nuestra perfección, que viene de Jesús y sus actos justos y no de nosotros mismos. ¡Él ya ha logrado todo lo que el Padre requiere de nosotros!

SEMANA 3

Mateo 8-10:

Autoridad del Rey

VERSÍCULO PARA MEMORIZAR

¿Quién de ustedes,
por ansioso que esté,
puede añadir una hora al
curso de su vida?

Mateo 6:27

LECTURA BÍBLICA DIARIA

Día 1: Mateo 8:1-17

Día 2: Mateo 8:18-34

Día 3: Mateo 9

Día 4: Mateo 10:1-25

Día 5: Mateo 10:26-42

Día 6: Salmos 8

Día 7: Para ponerte al día

Corresponde a los Días 280, 284 y 289 de *La sinopsis de la Biblia*

RETO SEMANAL

Ver la página 86 para más información.

DÍA 1

MATEO 8:1-17

LEE MATEO 8:1-17

Cuando Jesús terminó de dar su sermón bosquejando la vida en el reino, muchas de las personas entre la multitud decidieron seguirlo. Seguro que algunos pensaron que estaba loco, otros probablemente pensaron que estaba engañando a todos, y aun otros quizá creyeron que era el Mesías prometido.

Al descender del monte, un leproso se acercó a Jesús, se postró delante de Él y le pidió que lo sanara. La humildad del leproso es evidente. No se acercó a Jesús con derechos o exigencias; se postró y rogó. Demostró uno de los puntos que precisamente Jesús había tocado en el mensaje que recién terminó de enseñar (7:7 -11). Es posible que el leproso se hubiera quedado en la periferia de la multitud y lo hubiera escuchado dar este mensaje sobre la gran generosidad de Dios. Si es así, ¡esto no solo habría sido un acto de fe sino también un acto de obediencia!

Cuando necesitas desesperadamente que Jesús obre en ti, ¿cuál es la actitud de tu corazón hacia Él?

¿Qué actitud crees que tiene hacia ti el Rey de reyes en medio de tus necesidades?

Repasa 8:3. ¿Qué observas en la respuesta que Jesús le da al leproso?

Con compasión, Jesús extendió su mano al leproso. Como Rey de su creación, sabía que tenía autoridad sobre la enfermedad y que no se contaminaría por la afección de la piel de ese hombre. Le habló al leproso marginado y le concedió su petición, y después le dijo que se quedara callado. Esta conducta confidencial a menudo se denomina "secreto mesiánico", que simplemente se refiere al deseo de Jesús de esperar a revelar su identidad como Mesías hasta el tiempo adecuado. Aunque ya se juntaban grandes multitudes, Jesús tenía un propósito específico y una cronología que cumplir, y no quería atraer más atención hacia sí mismo; sin embargo, quería que los sacerdotes supieran de la sanidad, en cumplimiento de la ley (Levítico 13-14). Ser sanado de lepra era algo muy importante. En el Antiguo Testamento, solo dos personas fueron sanadas de lepra: Miriam (Números 12:1-15) y Naamán el gentil (2 Reyes 5:14).

Lee 2 Reyes 5. Observa las diferencias entre cómo el rey de Israel gestionó el caso de Naamán y cómo el Rey Jesús gestionó el caso del leproso.

Después, Jesús entró en Cafarnaúm, una villa pesquera donde vivían judíos y también gentiles. Un líder romano se acercó a Él y le explicó que su siervo estaba paralítico y "sufriendo mucho" (v. 6). A pesar de que este centurión romano era al mismo tiempo gentil y enemigo de Israel, Jesús le ofreció acudir y sanar a su siervo.

¿Qué revelan las palabras del centurión en los versículos 8-9 sobre su idea acerca de Jesús?

El centurión sabía de lo que Jesús era capaz. Jesús se sorprendió por su fe, y usó este momento no solo para elogiar la fe de este gentil sino también para enseñar a sus seguidores que quienes no tienen fe no entrarán en el reino de los cielos, al margen de si son judíos o gentiles. Jesús enfatizó que incluso "los hijos del reino", un término para la nación de Israel, serán expulsados a las tinieblas si no creen en Él. Después de esta enseñanza, Jesús hizo su primera sanidad a larga distancia. El Rey Jesús tiene la autoridad para ordenar a la enfermedad que huya, incluso desde la distancia.

Desde ahí, Jesús fue a la casa de Pedro, donde yacía enferma y en cama la suegra de Pedro. Cuando Jesús la tocó, la fiebre la dejó y se levantó de inmediato. Ella no necesitó tiempo para recuperarse de su enfermedad después de haber estado débil en la cama. Quedó totalmente recuperada al instante. Y cuando se levantó, no solo regresó a sus tareas cotidianas sino que también dedicó tiempo a servir a Aquel que la había sanado.

Dedica tiempo a escribir momentos en tu vida en los que la acción de Dios fue vital. Escribe una sencilla oración dándole gracias por todo lo que ha hecho.

DÍA 2

MATEO 8:18-34

LEE MATEO 8:18-34

Jesús no envió a sus discípulos a juntar grandes multitudes. Él no necesitaba un animador o un equipo de mercadotecnia. A menudo las multitudes lo encontraban, pero en esta ocasión Jesús no se quedó con la multitud. En cambio, anunció que Él y sus discípulos irían al otro lado del lago. Este "otro lado" era el lado gentil, donde vivían los no judíos, un lugar inmundo que los seguidores de Dios evitaban de modo intencional. Fiel a su costumbre, Jesús salió de otra zona de confort cultural y llamó a sus discípulos a seguirlo hasta allí. Cuando les dio estas órdenes tan audaces, dos hombres se le acercaron con preguntas acerca de seguirlo.

Compara y contrasta al escriba (8:19) y al discípulo (8:21). ¿Qué indican las respuestas de Jesús sobre lo que significa seguirlo?

Los dos hombres deseaban seguir a Jesús. Uno estaba deseoso sin considerar bien el costo; el otro estaba dispuesto, pero solo después de que pusiera en orden sus asuntos. Seguir al Rey Jesús significa darle una lealtad total, que no haya otros reyes que reinen en nuestra vida, como el confort, el dinero o las relaciones.

Jesús y sus comprometidos discípulos se subieron a la barca para comenzar su viaje. Esta barca de pesca no era nada parecido a un yate de lujo o al curioso bote pontón de tu tío. La típica barca de pesca del siglo primero en Galilea media apenas unos ocho metros de longitud, unos dos metros de anchura y metro y medio de altura. Cuando una barca frágil como esa tenía que hacer frente a las tormentas repentinas que a menudo se producían en Galilea, hasta los pescadores más experimentados temblaban de miedo. Sin embargo, en medio de este caos el Rey de la creación estaba dormido.

Lee los siguientes pasajes: Colosenses 1:15-18, Hebreos 1:3, Salmos 65 y Salmos 89:9. Escribe las frases que destacan la autoridad de Jesús sobre la creación.

Colosenses 1:15-18	
Hebreos 1:3	
Salmos 65	
Salmos 89:9	

En el transcurso de unos pocos instantes, los discípulos de Jesús fueron testigos de su humanidad al estar dormido, y también de su deidad al ordenar a la creación que le obedeciera. Jesús es la imagen del Dios invisible, concebido eternamente, gobernando y reinando sobre toda la creación, la cual Él mismo creó. Cuando Él habló, las olas no solo disminuyeron sino que desaparecieron. Los discípulos estaban asombrados ante la gran calma que se produjo.

Repasa 8:26. ¿A qué dirigió Jesús su reprimenda? ¿Qué revela esto sobre Jesús?

La frase *poca fe* en este versículo parece ser una palabra que inventó Jesús. Cada vez que aparece en la Escritura, Jesús era el único que la decía, y no se encuentra en ningún escrito secular de la época. Usó este término exclusivamente con sus seguidores (los que tenían *poca* fe, en contraposición con los que *no* tenían fe), y la mayoría de las veces específicamente con los discípulos. El contexto hace parecer como si fuera un apodo cariñoso para animarlos a tener más fe en Él. No parece que Jesús esté reprendiéndolos en este pasaje, sino animándolos. Esta historia parece mostrar que Jesús no reprendió a sus discípulos por su temor. En su lugar, reprendió a la *fuente* de su temor.

¿Qué temores estás enfrentando actualmente? ¿Cómo reprendería Jesús esos temores y te consolaría en medio de ellos?

Los discípulos estaban asombrados y aliviados de que la tormenta cesara, pero poco se imaginaban ellos que estaban a punto de hacer frente a un tipo distinto de amenaza: ¡las fuerzas espirituales de las tinieblas!

Repasa 8:29-31. ¿Cómo reaccionaron los demonios cuando Jesús llegó a los sepulcros?

Los demonios reconocieron inmediatamente a Jesús y supieron que tenía autoridad para destruirlos. Sabían que su destino final era el tormento eterno. Preguntaron: "¿Has venido aquí para atormentarnos *antes de tiempo?*". Con una palabra, Jesús los echó a una manada de cerdos y los cerdos se precipitaron al mar. Sorprendentemente, la multitud no celebró que los demonios se despeñaran y que los hombres fueran liberados. En cambio, estaban furiosos por la muerte de miles de cerdos, los cuales eran una fuente de ingresos en su sociedad agraria.

A medida que se extendió la noticia de lo que había sucedido, los lugareños rogaron a Jesús que se marchara. Dos hombres finalmente fueron liberados, pero la gente estaba más enfocada en lo que se había perdido. Su sistema de valores fue revelado, y era totalmente contrario al de Dios. Las personas de la tierra de los gadarenos no quisieron saber nada de Jesús o de su reino al revés.

¿Cuáles de tus valores son contrarios al sistema de valores de Dios? ¿De qué forma crea esto alguna tensión en tu vida?

Lo que yo valoro	Lo que Dios valora	Tensión

DÍA 3

MATEO 9

LEE MATEO 9

Después de que las multitudes gadarenas expulsaran a Jesús, sus discípulos y Él regresaron a su casa en Cafarnaúm. Dondequiera que iba el Maestro, la gente necesitaba su sanidad, y su hogar no era una excepción. La siguiente persona a la que sanó fue un hombre que ni siquiera podía llegar hasta Jesús por sí mismo, así que sus amigos lo llevaron hasta Él porque era paralítico.

Una de las cosas que Jesús le dijo al hombre nos da un destello de su estado emocional, ya que Jesús le dijo: "Anímate". Este término se usa con más frecuencia cuando alguien ha perdido la esperanza. Aunque Jesús elogió a los amigos por su fe, no condenó al paralítico por no tenerla. En su lugar, le habló de manera compasiva y le perdonó sus pecados. Jesús es un espacio seguro para tu desesperanza.

¿Por qué declaró Jesús que los pecados del hombre quedaban perdonados antes de tratar su necesidad física?

Jesús vino a sanar a los quebrantados, pero todavía más, vino para redimir por completo y restaurar *todo* lo que está quebrado. Este hombre no estaba paralítico por ser pecador, sino que su parálisis era resultado directo de vivir en un mundo pecaminoso y quebrantado. Con los escribas merodeando, Jesús decidió demostrar su poder no solo para sanar el cuerpo sino también para perdonar pecados. Al hacer eso, dio a sus seguidores un anticipo de lo que vino a hacer por toda la humanidad: rescatarnos de nuestro quebranto físico y espiritual. Los fariseos estaban horrorizados por las palabras de Jesús y lo acusaron de blasfemia, pero Él conocía sus pensamientos y les respondió.

Lee Hebreos 4:12-13 y Salmos 139:1-2. ¿De qué manera la capacidad de Jesús para conocer los pensamientos de los escribas demuestra que Él es Dios?

Solo Dios puede conocer los pensamientos secretos de los hombres. Jesús, siendo plenamente Dios, los conocía. Después de hablar de los corazones malvados de los fariseos, demostró su autoridad sobre la discapacidad. ¡El hombre cojo caminó! Aunque la multitud reconocía legítimamente la autoridad de Dios, seguían siendo incapaces de reconocer que Jesús era Dios.

¿Qué problema tenían los fariseos con las acciones de Jesús en 9:9-13? Resume la respuesta de Jesús.

Hemos visto que Jesús era atraído hacia los enfermos y destituidos, pero Mateo no estaba enfermo ni era un destituido; de hecho, estaba sano y era lo suficientemente solvente como para organizar una cena formal. Mateo definitivamente era un pecador, y aparentemente eso es lo que atrajo a Jesús hacia él. Jesús hizo referencia a Oseas 6:6 y básicamente dijo: "Los pecadores son la razón por la que estoy aquí".

¿Cómo describirías la interacción de Jesús con la mujer en 9:18-22?

El Rey Jesús no es distante. Él no gobierna y reina desde la lejanía. Él no se interesa solamente en los asuntos de personas importantes como el gobernador de la sinagoga. Él siempre ha estado dispuesto a que los más pequeños le interrumpan, incluyendo la mujer cuyo flujo de sangre la hacía ceremonialmente impura. Una marginada durante doce años, estaba destituida, desesperada y dispuesta a arriesgarlo todo para ser sanada.

A diferencia de algunos de los demás sobre los que hemos leído, ella no le pidió a Jesús que la sanara. No gritó y llamó la atención. ¿Tenía miedo de interrumpir o molestar? ¿Tenía miedo de ser avergonzada, rechazada o silenciada? Tal vez solo estaba aferrada a un hilo de esperanza. Estaba acostumbrada a que no le prestaran atención ni siquiera los líderes religiosos, porque era inmunda. Pero ella tenía una fe tenaz que le impulsó a abrirse paso entre las normas sociales y *tocar la ropa de alguien*. Ni siquiera intentó tocar a Jesús, lo cual estaba prohibido porque le podría transmitir su impureza. Podría ser apedreada por un acto tan atrevido. Pero Jesús se volteó para mirarla, y cuando habló, de inmediato ella supo que Él la había sanado.

¿Hay algún área en la que te sientas desesperado o rechazado? Escríbelas abajo. Dedica un tiempo a orar por todo ello, pidiéndole a Dios sanidad.

El Rey que vino a salvarte y restaurarte es el mismo Rey que te ve en todas tus necesidades. Él produce sanidad y *shalom*: plenitud. Cuanto mayor sea tu desesperación por Dios, mayor será tu gozo cuando tenga un encuentro contigo.

Después de sanar a la mujer que había sangrado durante doce años, Jesús fue a la casa del oficial a sanar a su hija. Aunque ella estaba muerta cuando Él llegó, tomó su mano y ella se puso de pie. Al igual que con la mujer del flujo de sangre, la muerte tenía sus propios niveles de inmundicia en la ley judía. Pero Jesús transformó la inmundicia de la muerte en pureza: *nueva vida*. Por primera vez en el libro de Mateo, el Rey Jesús mostró su autoridad sobre la muerte. Y esa no será la última vez que demuestre esta realidad de su reinado; en su reino, la muerte no es la vencedora.

Describe las respuestas de la multitud y de los fariseos en 9:33-34.

Tras salir de la casa del oficial, Jesús se encontró con dos ciegos, vio su fe y los sanó. Después, Él y sus discípulos se encontraron con un mudo afectado por demonios. Jesús los echó fuera, el hombre habló y las multitudes se maravillaron; pero los fariseos aprovecharon la oportunidad para difundir rumores acerca de Él. Básicamente dijeron: "Jesús puede echar fuera demonios porque Él es el capitán de su equipo". Veían la autoridad de Jesús en sus milagros y su enseñanza, pero en lugar de alabarlo como el tan ansiado Rey, lo acusaron de trabajar para el Príncipe de las tinieblas.

Cuando Jesús y sus discípulos recorrían la región y veían una gran variedad de necesidades, Él "tuvo compasión de ellas" (9:36). La palabra usada para "tuvo compasión" (*splagchnizomai*) es la palabra más fuerte para piedad en el lenguaje griego; sin embargo, no se conformó solo con tener compasión, sino que se puso manos a la obra como respuesta a la gran necesidad. El Rey Jesús se interesa profundamente por su pueblo, y conoce la gran cantidad de trabajo que hay que hacer para el reino. "La cosecha es mucha, pero los obreros pocos" (9:37). La petición de más obreros es tan urgente hoy como lo era cuando Jesús dijo estas palabras por primera vez.

De acuerdo con las órdenes de Jesús a sus seguidores en 9:38, "pidan al Señor de la cosecha que envíe obreros a su cosecha", escribe tu oración a continuación.

DÍA 4

MATEO 10:1-25

LEE MATEO 10:1-25

En el capítulo 9 Jesús sanó enfermedades, echó fuera un demonio y resucitó a una persona. Al final de ese capítulo, instó a sus discípulos a comenzar a *orar* por obreros; y este capítulo comienza con Jesús llamándolos a ser la respuesta a la propia oración de ellos. Mirando el modelo de Jesús, vemos que llamó a una gran variedad de personas a ser esos obreros. De hecho, la diversidad de sus seguidores más cercanos era tanto impactante como contracultural.

Consigue un diccionario bíblico, busca a los doce discípulos y llena toda la información que encuentres. (Nota: puede que no consigas llenar todos los espacios en blanco).

Discípulo	Trasfondo (nacionalidad/tribu)	Trabajo
Simón (Pedro)		
Andrés		
Santiago (hijo de Zebedeo)		
Juan		

Discípulo	Trasfondo (nacionalidad/tribu)	Trabajo
Felipe		
Bartolomé		
Tomás		
Mateo		
Santiago (hijo de Alfeo)		
Tadeo		
Simón (el zelote)		
Judas Iscariote		

Dentro de su pequeño grupo de seguidores, Jesús reclutó a personas que eran enemigas, incluyendo a un recaudador de impuestos, que básicamente traicionó a su pueblo para trabajar para Roma, y un zelote, que quería derrocar a Roma. Estos eran hombres firmes que tenían opiniones contrarias con respecto a la política, la identidad nacional, y cómo esas cosas afectaban sus propias vidas. Los discípulos también variaban en educación académica y estatus económico, ya que Jesús no solo llamó a un recaudador de impuestos sino que también llamó a la clase obrera, como los pescadores. El reino al revés es uno en el que, a pesar de su diversidad, hombres y mujeres se unen en torno a la misión principal del Rey.

Antes de que Jesús los enviara a la misión, les dio autoridad para hacer las mismas cosas que le habían visto hacer. Pero Él no *solamente* les dio autoridad, sino que también les dio instrucciones concretas sobre cómo usar esa autoridad. No fueron empoderados para hacer lo que quisieran; se les capacitó para hacer la voluntad del Padre en consonancia con el plan de Dios.

En 10:5-6, ¿con quién les dice Jesús que compartan el evangelio primero? ¿Por qué crees que les dio esa instrucción tan concreta?

El plan de Dios siempre ha involucrado llevar el mensaje primero a los judíos y después a los gentiles, así que las instrucciones de Jesús estaban en consonancia con este plan. Además de darles autoridad e instrucciones, Jesús también les puso límites. Esta era su primera misión, y sería necesario que confiaran en Él en cada aspecto de su provisión y protección. Cuando comenzaron a seguir a Jesús por primera vez, le oyeron decir que Dios cuida incluso de las aves y los lirios (6:25-34); pero cuando Él los envió, les habilitó para demostrar que también creían que esto era verdad para *ellos mismos*. Lo que hasta ahora había sido un concepto general se había convertido en un llamado personal.

En 10:16-20, ¿qué tipo de promesa o advertencia les dio Jesús?

¿Con qué animal los comparó Jesús? ¿Cuáles fueron los dos animales que les animó a imitar y de qué maneras?

Describe brevemente cómo podrías incorporar esas características en circunstancias similares. ¿Cómo se vería eso?

Jesús advirtió a sus seguidores que serían maltratados, odiados y perseguidos, parecido a como le había sucedido a Él. Quería hacer llegar el mensaje del evangelio a lugares donde lo quisieran recibir y no quería que malgastaran su tiempo en áreas donde sería rechazado. Él ya había practicado este tipo de discernimiento delante de ellos, pues le habían visto manejar las conversaciones de distintas maneras dependiendo de si estaba hablando con ellos, con gentiles o con los fariseos. Una serpiente es lo suficientemente sabia como para saber cuándo quedarse y cuándo alejarse. Una paloma puede aparecer como un mensajero de paz, o puede volar lejos y mantener su inocencia. Juntas, la sabiduría y la inocencia, ayudan a los seguidores de Jesús a saber qué batallas luchar y a qué batallas renunciar.

¿Quién dijo Jesús que iría junto a los discípulos para ayudarlos a saber cómo responder a las acusaciones?

Describe brevemente alguna ocasión en la que el Espíritu te ayudó o te guio. Si te resulta difícil pensar en una ocasión concreta, recuerda su papel en la historia de tu salvación (Juan 16:13).

Jesús recordó a los discípulos que Dios no solo era quien los llamaba, sino también quien los equipaba. De hecho, ¡Dios el Espíritu sería quien hablaría *a través* de ellos! Al margen de lo que enfrentaran, no lo enfrentarían solos, así que no había nada que temer.

Les recordó que quienes perseveran hasta el final son quienes Dios ha llamado y equipado, porque lo que Dios inicia, Él lo sostiene y lo cumplirá. Estar en una misión con el Rey exige una dependencia total de Él para completar todo lo que Él demanda, y no podemos hacerlo en nuestras propias fuerzas. Y en cada momento en el que caemos o no damos la talla, encontramos descanso en su obra terminada (Juan 19:30). Esta es la obra perfecta y terminada de Jesús que nos salva, no nuestras propias obras, y es el poder de su Espíritu el que sostiene nuestra salvación (Tito 3:5-7).

Repasa 10:39. ¿Cuánto o qué te ha costado seguir a Jesús? ¿Crees que seguirlo vale la pena el costo? ¿Por qué sí o por qué no?

DÍA 5

MATEO 10:26-42

LEE MATEO 10:26-42

El Rey Jesús siguió dando instrucciones a los discípulos diciéndoles que no tuvieran miedo a los retos de la misión a la que Él los estaba enviando. De hecho, les dijo que subieran a los tejados y gritaran sin miedo todos los secretos del reino que Él les había contado en privado. No había lugar para el temor en una misión como esta, ¡se necesita valentía para gritar desde los tejados!

Repasa 10:28. Usa un diccionario de griego para buscar la palabra *temor*, y escribe las tres definiciones. ¿Cómo modelan estas definiciones este versículo?

Cuando se trata de la frase *temor de Dios*, por lo general hay un mal entendimiento de que los hijos de Dios deberían *tener miedo* de Dios, pero no es eso en modo alguno lo que significa temer a Dios. Para los que le conocen, el temor del Señor tiene que ver más con la reverencia, el deleite y el asombro. Nos atrae *a* Dios. Para los que no le conocen, el otro tipo de temor sí es apropiado, porque la ira de Dios permanece sobre ellos (Juan 3:36). Ese tipo de temor *aleja de* Dios a una persona.

Cuando Jesús dio la tarea, recordó a sus discípulos que todo lo que sus enemigos pudieran hacerles sería solo temporal. Él sabía que llegaría la persecución, y quería que estuvieran preparados, enfocados en la misión y no dispuestos a ceder ante las amenazas y opiniones de los hombres.

Lee Josué 1:9, Deuteronomio 31:6 e Isaías 41:10. ¿Cuál es el mandato constante de Dios en cada uno de estos versículos?

El enemigo de tu alma quiere que tengas miedo de la misión *y* de Aquel que te envió a la misión. El temor es incapacitante. Nos deja sin poder ni esperanza. Pero el Rey Jesús nos capacita mediante su gran amor por nosotros, eliminando así el temor al hombre y mostrándonos cómo temer correctamente a Dios.

¿Qué significa para ti temer correctamente a Dios? Cuando te acercas a Dios, ¿con cuál de las definiciones de temor te identificas más?

Jesús les dijo a sus discípulos que la única persona a la que debían temer era a Dios, ya que *podría* enviarlos al infierno, pero *no lo hará* porque le pertenecen. De hecho, dijo Jesús, Dios estaba atento a cada uno de sus movimientos, contando cada uno de los cabellos de su cabeza momento a momento. Jesús dijo que hablaría con el Padre sobre todo aquel que lo reconociera como Rey (ver también Hebreos 7:25). Pero, para quienes no le reconocen como Rey, la idea de estar fuera de la familia de Dios *debería* hacerles temblar.

Repasa 10:34-36, después regresa y vuelve a leer Mateo 5:9. ¿Cómo crees que pueden ser ciertos ambos pasajes?

Los discípulos tal vez se quedaron perplejos cuando su Maestro de repente comenzó a decir que traía una espada. A fin de cuentas, en el Sermón del Monte bendijo a los pacificadores, pero aquí les estaba diciendo que no había venido a traer paz. ¿Te imaginas a los discípulos rascándose la cabeza y preguntándose: *¿Cuál de las dos, Jesús: somos pacificadores o llevamos la espada? ¡Aclárate!*

Lee Efesios 2:11-22. Resume cómo el Rey Jesús crea división mientras que también trae la paz.

El mensaje de Jesús es la paz, pero la misión radical del Rey Jesús tiene el potencial de crear división. Seguir verdaderamente al Rey significa que nuestra devoción a Él debe estar por encima de todo: familia, ocupación, afiliación política, denominación, nacionalidad, *todo*. No hay nada más alto que el Rey Jesús. Jesús sabía que su amor radical por los de afuera ofendería a muchos de los que estaban "dentro". Derribar los muros de hostilidad contra los "demás" en nuestro mundo puede crear nuevas murallas y enemigos incluso dentro de nuestra propia casa: las personas a las que amamos tal vez se ofenden por nuestro deseo de amar a los que no son como nosotros; sin embargo, para todos los que ven correctamente al Rey Jesús como supremo, se produce unidad incluso en medio de las divisiones sociales. La división llega como resultado de ofrecer lealtad a cualquier otra cosa que no sea el Rey.

Pídele a Dios que te muestre si hay cosas que has puesto por encima de Él en tu vida. ¿Qué identidades u opiniones podrían causar una división innecesaria entre tú y los demás en su reino? Escribe esas cosas. Arrepiéntete.

A los que lo valoran a Él por encima de todo lo demás, Jesús les promete recompensas. Prometió castigo para los que maltraten a sus hijos y bendiciones para los que traten bien a sus hijos. El Rey Jesús es un galardonador. Conocerlo es el mayor galardón ¡porque Él está donde está el gozo!

¿Qué es lo que más te impactó del estudio de esta semana? ¿Por qué?

¿Qué aprendiste o recordaste acerca de Dios y su carácter esta semana?

DÍA 6

SALMO CORRESPONDIENTE Y ORACIÓN

LEE SALMOS 8

¿Qué correlación ves entre Salmos 8 y el estudio de esta semana sobre Jesús y su reino?

¿Qué porciones de este salmo captan más tu atención?

Termina haciendo esta oración en voz alta:

Padre,

Como dice el salmista, ¡tu nombre es glorioso! Te alabo por dirigir tu corazón hacia pecadores como yo. Estás lleno de amor y generosidad. Das esperanza y sanidad al leproso, al poseído, al marginado, al desterrado. ¡Y me has dado esperanza y sanidad! Gracias por pensar en mí y amarme tanto.

Padre, he pecado y apelo a tu misericordia. Confieso que a veces he intentado establecer mi propia fuerza y gloria. He intentado darme a conocer, impresionar a otros y ganar amor, incluso tu amor. He valorado mis posesiones y preferencias antes que las cosas que tú valoras. He olvidado que tú me has provisto, protegido y me has dado un lugar en tu reino sin mérito ni esfuerzo alguno por mi parte. Me arrepiento de mis pecados y acudo a ti para pedirte que limpies mi corazón.

Ayúdame a caminar en la gloria y el honor que me has dado como tu hijo. Seas tú glorificado y honrado.

Te rindo mi vida, Señor; en cada momento de mi día y en cada decisión que tomo, cedo mi voluntad y mi camino a tu perfecta voluntad y camino.

Yo también te amo. Amén.

DÍA 7

DESCANSA, PONTE AL DÍA O PROFUNDIZA

RETO SEMANAL

En nuestra lectura de esta semana vimos la autoridad de Jesús sobre la naturaleza, la enfermedad, los demonios y la muerte. Jesús se encontró con personas en sus momentos más difíciles y fue movido por la compasión. Para amar a las personas con compasión como Jesús, necesitamos que nuestros ojos y nuestro corazón se parezcan a los suyos. ¡Su Espíritu nos equipa para esta buena obra!

Esta semana comienza escribiendo una breve oración en tu diario, pidiéndole a Dios que te dé su corazón y sus ojos para los necesitados, para hacerte ver personas concretas. Puede ser alguien que no encaja socialmente o alguien con una necesidad financiera o física evidente, o puede ser alguien que es una versión moderna del joven rico.

Al comenzar a ver a las personas con los ojos de Jesús, escribe sus nombres debajo de tu oración en tu diario, después fija una alarma de oración en tu teléfono para acordarte de orar por ellos a una hora concreta cada día. Al orar, pregúntale a Dios cómo deberías responder. Podría ser que Dios te mueva a pasar a la acción de alguna manera, pero podría ser que tus oraciones y tu corazón ablandado son el punto (en otras palabras, puede que Dios te esté retando *a ti* en este proceso porque siempre serás una persona que necesita también el evangelio). El objetivo principal en este reto no es "arreglar" a otros, sino ver la transformación de nuestro propio corazón para que a nosotros también nos mueva la compasión como el Rey al que seguimos.

VERSÍCULO PARA MEMORIZAR

Y por la ropa, ¿por qué se preocupan? Observen cómo crecen los lirios del campo; no trabajan, ni hilan.

Mateo 6:28

SEMANA 4

Mateo 11-13:

Instrucciones del Rey

LECTURA BÍBLICA DIARIA

Día 1: Mateo 11

Día 2: Mateo 12:1-32

Día 3: Mateo 12:33-50

Día 4: Mateo 13:1-33

Día 5: Mateo 13:34-58

Día 6: Salmos 84

Día 7: Para ponerte al día

Corresponde a los Días 282, 285 y 287 de *La sinopsis de la Biblia*

RETO SEMANAL

Ver la página 110 para más información.

DÍA 1

MATEO 11

LEE MATEO 11

Mateo 11 nos lleva de nuevo a Juan el Bautista (JEB), de quien no hemos oído nada desde el capítulo cuatro. Lo único que sabemos es que lo encarcelaron precisamente cuando Jesús estaba comenzando su ministerio. JEB había sido un fiel precursor de Jesús, predicando arrepentimiento y señalando a Israel hacia Él como su Rey prometido. Proféticamente, fue quien puso la alfombra roja para Jesús y habría estado ansioso por ver que el ministerio de Jesús tuviera efecto. Pero en lugar de presenciarlo personalmente, JEB tuvo que esperar pacientemente las noticias de cualquiera que pudiera visitarlo mientras estaba en la cárcel. Estos reportes probablemente habrían sido el "resumen de los momentos destacados" de la actividad de Jesús en 4:12–11:1.

Echa un vistazo rápido a 4:12-11:1 y resume esa parte del ministerio de Jesús a continuación.

Si tú fueras uno de los discípulos de JEB, ¿qué acontecimientos hubieras querido compartir con JEB?

Aunque no conocemos los detalles de lo que le dijeron a JEB, sabemos que sus reportes lo dejaron con una pregunta urgente para Jesús: "¿Eres tú el que ha de venir, o esperamos a otro?". JEB había estado seguro de que Jesús era "el que había de venir", y quería confirmar que no se equivocaba.

Repasa 11:4-6. Después lee Isaías 35:5-6, 26:19, 29:18-19 y 61:1. Compara la respuesta de Jesús en Mateo con las profecías de Isaías. ¿Qué observas? ¿Cuál es el significado de que Jesús respondiera de esa forma?

La respuesta de Jesús puede parecer indirecta, pero JEB y otros judíos que conocían bien la Escritura habrían reconocido de inmediato que Jesús estaba señalando a su ministerio como el cumplimiento de las profecías del Antiguo Testamento sobre el Mesías. Jesús estaba declarando innegablemente: "La evidencia habla por sí misma. La búsqueda ha terminado. Yo soy Aquel que había de venir".

Hay un segundo mensaje más sutil en su respuesta que JEB tampoco habría pasado por alto. Cuando Jesús mencionó que las buenas noticias eran predicadas a los pobres, estaba haciendo referencia a Isaías 61:1, pero solo a la primera parte. Jesús dejó fuera la parte sobre "liberación a los prisioneros". JEB ciertamente habría notado la parte que faltaba y captado el desgarrador mensaje: "Sí, Yo soy el que había de venir, pero tú morirás en prisión".

¿Cómo podría haber afectado esta seguridad de que Jesús era el Mesías Rey la perspectiva de JEB en estas difíciles circunstancias?

El conocimiento de que Jesús es tu Rey ¿ha moldeado tu perspectiva en las circunstancias difíciles o desafiantes de tu vida? Si es así, ¿de qué modo?

Cuando se fueron los discípulos de JEB, Jesús dirigió su atención a las multitudes que siempre estaban presentes. Puso a JEB como el ejemplo del trabajo bien hecho de un profeta. JEB había sido el campeón reinante en cuanto a grandeza humana hasta ese momento, pero a partir de entonces, incluso la persona en el último lugar del reino podría tomar ese título. ¡Jesús estaba revelando el increíble honor de ser incluido en el reino!

En la siguiente parte de su mensaje, Jesús habló de bailes y lamentos, acusaciones de posesión demoníaca y borrachos, y denunció a algunas ciudades importantes. Jesús no estaba despotricando al azar; establecía un punto consistente sobre la falta de arrepentimiento de Israel y su rechazo hacia Él. Incluso después de presenciar su ministerio y sus obras poderosas, se negaron a reconocerlo como Rey. Las señales y los milagros no cambian corazones.

Aunque Jesús tenía cosas serias que decir, no terminó la conversación con juicio y condenación. En los últimos versículos del capítulo, el tono de Jesús se dirigió hacia la gratitud. Dio gracias al Padre por cómo Él elige revelar cosas en su reino intencionalmente al revés.

Repasa 11:25-30. ¿Cuáles son algunas de las características de una persona sabia y entendida? ¿Cuáles son algunas características de una persona que es como un niño pequeño?

Después, Jesús hizo algo que no vemos en el relato de ningún otro Evangelio. Nos habló sobre su corazón. Jesús quería que no quedara duda alguna sobre quién es Él como Rey. Él es compasivo y bondadoso, amable y humilde, e invita a todos los que anhelan descanso para el alma a encontrarlo en su presencia.

Repasa 11:25-30. Piensa en tu testimonio. ¿Cómo se reveló Dios a ti misericordiosamente? ¿Cómo ha sido la salvación en Jesús una fuente de descanso para el alma?

DÍA 2

MATEO 12:1-32

LEE MATEO 12:1-32

En un día de reposo, Jesús caminaba con sus discípulos cuando se detuvieron para recoger unos granos de trigo para comer. Algunos fariseos que andaban cerca lo consideraron un quebrantamiento de las reglas que prohibían cosechar en día de reposo, así que los confrontaron de inmediato. Jesús respondió a sus críticas con palabras que les ofendieron y enojaron.

Repasa 12:3-5. Como expertos en las Escrituras, los fariseos ciertamente habrían leído los relatos a los que Jesús aludió. ¿Qué punto intentaba establecer Jesús al hacer estas preguntas?

Cuando los fariseos juzgaban, revelaban su celo mal dirigido en cuanto a la ley. Estaban familiarizados con los mensajes de Dios a través de la Escritura pero se perdían gran parte de lo que Jesús quería decir. Jesús respondió por la inocencia de sus discípulos y afirmó su autoridad sobre la ley, llamándose a sí mismo Señor del día de reposo.

Después Jesús fue a la sinagoga, donde se vio involucrado en otra controversia con respecto al día de reposo, y esta vez probablemente estaba preparado adrede. Había un hombre en la sinagoga que aparentemente tenía una necesidad física, pero en lugar de mostrar cuidado e interés por él, los fariseos lo usaron como una oportunidad para tenderle una trampa a Jesús. Le preguntaron a Jesús su opinión sobre sanar en el día de reposo, y Jesús, como hacía a menudo, respondió con una pregunta.

Señaló que ninguno de ellos dudaría en ayudar a su animal herido o en peligro el día de reposo, ya que la ley incluso hacía excepciones para eso. Como las personas creadas a imagen de Dios son más importantes que los animales, cualquiera que guardara la ley debería ser capaz de discernir que sanar en día de reposo es una forma de honrar a Dios y alinearse con sus valores, no rebelarse contra Él. Una vez más, Jesús señaló que sus estrictos sistemas creados por el hombre socavaban el corazón misericordioso de Dios hacia las personas necesitadas.

Para demostrar la falta de poder y compasión de los líderes religiosos, Jesús sanó al hombre. Sus acciones cumplieron la ley y también honraron al Padre, pero aun así los fariseos respondieron con una trama para destruir a Jesús. Jesús estaba afirmando su trono mediante sus obras y sus palabras, pero los fariseos veían que su reino de tradición y control comenzaba a derrumbarse.

A pesar de que seguimos a Jesús, también podemos tener actitudes farisaicas hacia los demás en nuestro corazón y nuestra mente. Examina tu corazón. ¿Alguna vez te has encontrado criticando a otros cristianos basándote en tus propias tradiciones religiosas o convicciones personales?

Ahora considera la pregunta desde el otro ángulo: ¿hay áreas en las que no compartes las tradiciones o convicciones de otros cristianos que pudieran ser una fuente de su crítica hacia ti?

Jesús sabía que los fariseos tramaban darle muerte, y que eso sucedería finalmente según el plan del Padre, pero Él también sabía que aún no era el tiempo apropiado. Se fue de ese lugar no por temor a los fariseos, sino para seguir cumpliendo el plan de Dios.

Muchas personas siguieron a Jesús cuando volvió a restaurar la salud y liberar a las personas. Ningún problema o aflicción estaba a la altura de su autoridad: ceguera, mudez u opresión demoniaca, ya que Él era Rey sobre todo ello.

Repasa 12:22-24. Compara y contrasta cómo "la gente" y los fariseos respondieron al milagro que hizo Jesús.

La gente	Los fariseos

Jesús no perdió el tiempo con las afirmaciones absurdas de los fariseos. Confrontó lo que salía de sus bocas e incluso sus pensamientos secretos. Dijo que toda la base de su argumento estaba equivocada: un reino dividido era una estrategia sin sentido. Aunque sabía que no lo aceptarían, comunicó claramente la verdad: Él expulsaba al espíritu de Satanás por el Espíritu de Dios. Lo que ellos habían intentado desacreditar era el poder divino en acción: el reino de Dios había llegado a ellos.

Jesús no se echaba atrás ni evitaba hacer declaraciones que sabía que causarían revuelo. Declaró una clara división entre el reino de oscuridad de Satanás y su reino de luz, sin posibilidad de partidos neutrales. Como gobernante legítimo, Él estableció las reglas: la gente debía ser exclusivamente leal a Él o estar en su contra.

Usando tu comentario favorito, resume lo que entiendes por "blasfemia contra el Espíritu Santo".

Al llamar a Jesús agente de Beelzebú, los fariseos le estaban atribuyendo a Satanás la obra de Dios. Jesús dijo que este tipo de pecado estaba en una categoría aparte: blasfemia contra el Espíritu Santo. Al difamar a Jesús, y específicamente la fuente de su poder, hablaron de manera calumniosa contra el Espíritu Santo de una forma particular. Lo que los fariseos estaban haciendo no provenía de una creencia ignorante sino de una oposición intencionada. Sabían que lo que estaban afirmando sobre los milagros de Jesús no era cierto, pero no estaban dispuestos a reconocerlo, y Él les advirtió de las implicaciones eternas que tendría esa decisión.

Repasa 12:31-32. ¿Cuál es tu reacción inicial a la frase de Jesús de que hay un pecado que no será perdonado? ¿Cuál parece ser la diferencia entre "cualquier pecado y la blasfemia" que es perdonable y la "blasfemia contra el Espíritu"?

Jesús no estaba intentando provocar el pánico en torno a la posibilidad de cometer el "pecado imperdonable" (y, de hecho, muchos creen que este pecado no es posible hoy ya que Jesús ya no camina en la tierra como Dios-hombre). A aquellos que caminaban por ese camino, Él les advirtió hacia dónde los llevaría. Aunque los que conscientemente resisten y rechazan a Jesús al final serán rechazados, Él nunca condenará al que se acerca a Él con arrepentimiento y fe.

DÍA 3

MATEO 12:33-50

LEE MATEO 12:33-50

A estas alturas del ministerio de Jesús, había en circulación mucha cantidad de pruebas acerca de que Él era el Rey prometido. Milagros por aquí, enseñanzas con autoridad por allá, y profecías cumpliéndose por todas partes. Sin embargo, en 12:38 algunos escribas y fariseos pidieron a Jesús que les mostrara una señal, como si la evidencia aún fuera insuficiente. Actualmente, tenemos incluso más evidencia para sostener el caso de que Jesús es quien dijo que era, pero vemos el mismo rechazo.

¿Qué cosas dice la gente, por lo general, que tendrían que saber o experimentar para creer en Jesús o rendirse a Él?

Jesús no se quedó de manera alguna sin saber qué decir después de las acusaciones blasfemas de los fariseos. Los llamó raza de víboras, ya que habían mostrado sus verdaderas cartas con su respuesta a su milagro más reciente. Así como los árboles dan buen fruto o mal fruto que indica su respectiva buena o mala salud, las palabras malas o justas revelan el estado del corazón del cual salen. Nuestras palabras tienen peso; importan. Aunque Jesús estaba hablando específicamente a los fariseos aquí, también estaba ofreciendo un principio general acerca de la importancia de hablar con intención e integridad.

Usa tu Biblia o una Biblia en línea para buscar cada una de las referencias cruzadas de Mateo 12:36-37. ¿Cómo contribuyen los versículos a tu entendimiento de lo que Jesús está diciendo sobre el juicio y lo que son las palabras vanas?

Como los líderes religiosos parecían estar perdiendo su altercado verbal contra Jesús, cambiaron de táctica y le pidieron que demostrara su poder. A simple vista su petición parecía sincera, pero la respuesta de Jesús dio un destello de lo que estaba ocurriendo en sus corazones.

Repasa 12:39. ¿Cuáles son las dos palabras que usa Jesús para describir a los tipos de personas que buscan una señal?

Jesús no les dio la señal que estaban buscando, pero dijo que tendrían acceso a la única señal que necesitarían ver: la señal de Jonás, lo que significa que Él pasaría tres días y tres noches en la tumba después de su muerte en la cruz.

Incluso los malvados habitantes de Nínive condenarían a estos líderes religiosos por su falta de fe en Jesús. Los ninivitas respondieron con arrepentimiento al mensaje del profeta Jonás (Jonás 3:5). Del mismo modo, la reina de Saba escuchó y alabó la sabiduría de Salomón, que era el hombre más sabio que había vivido jamás (1 Reyes 4:29-34, 10:6-9). Pero ahora les estaba hablando Alguien incluso mayor que Salomón, y no eran lo suficientemente humildes como para recibirlo.

Jesús sabía que, al margen de cualquier señal que les mostrara, ellos no creerían porque estaban espiritualmente ciegos. Dejó claro que esa generación malvada y adúltera tenía un lúgubre futuro por delante. Eran como una persona que había vuelto a ser poseída por un demonio que regresó con un escuadrón de amigos aún más siniestros porque se dio cuenta de que había encontrado un lugar seguro donde establecer su base. Jesús les estaba dando un aviso. En su resistencia a su autoridad divina como Rey, dejando los hogares de sus corazones sin ocupar, las personas estaban siendo aún más susceptibles a que las fuerzas del reino de la oscuridad pudieran llegar y asentarse.

A mitad de conversación apareció la familia de Jesús, esperando hablar con Él. Había estado llamando la atención por enfrentarse cara a cara con los principales líderes religiosos de la época, y su familia probablemente estaba preocupada por Él. Cuando un hombre fue a darle el mensaje a Jesús de que su mamá y sus hermanos estaban esperando afuera, ese hombre y la multitud a su alrededor terminaron recibiendo su propio mensaje.

Usando tu comentario bíblico favorito, busca 12:46-50. ¿Por qué estaría mal interpretar esto como una declaración de que la familia biológica no es importante? ¿Qué punto estaba intentando establecer Jesús mediante esta afirmación?

¿Cómo podría cambiar tu forma de relacionarte con tu iglesia (cuerpo local de creyentes) y la iglesia universal (todos los creyentes) si el énfasis de Jesús sobre la familia espiritual se convirtiera en una parte más importante de tu realidad?

Jesús estaba ampliando su idea de lo que es la familia, enfatizando la mayor importancia del vínculo de la familia de Dios. Aunque la familia terrenal y biológica tiene un vínculo temporal, el vínculo de la familia de Dios es eterno. Jesús llamaba a la gente a Él mismo y los invitaba a ser parte de esta familia eterna. Él sabía que esto sería un regalo muy apreciado por muchos de los que le seguirían a costa de tener a sus hermanos biológicos, padres e hijos en su contra (Mateo 10:21-22, 10:36).

La familia que Jesús estaba reuniendo sería mejor que las familias más maravillosas de la tierra, y sería redentor incluso para los que más quebrantados estaban. ¡La suya es una familia del reino unida en torno a un Rey misericordioso y justo!

DÍA 4

MATEO 13:1-33

LEE MATEO 13:1-33

Jesús era muy bueno reuniendo multitudes. Vemos repetidamente que cuando Jesús hablaba, la gente aparecía. Seguidores comprometidos, buscadores aprensivos y escépticos tenaces, todos llegaban de cerca y de lejos para escuchar al Hombre que hablaba con una autoridad asombrosa, a menudo usando parábolas.

Con la ayuda de un comentario o un diccionario bíblico, resume qué es una parábola y describe su propósito.

Este método de oratoria no surgió porque Jesús intentara usar algo nuevo. Fue un punto de inflexión intencional en su ministerio, marcando un nuevo movimiento en el concierto del Rey que pronto tendría su *crescendo* en la cruz. Las parábolas son historias sencillas que por lo general contienen solo un par de personajes anónimos que ilustran un punto principal. Puede ser tentador intentar desmembrar cada elemento de estas historias para extraer un significado más profundo, y a veces eso puede ser útil, pero es importante recordar que la mayoría de las parábolas solo pretenden aclarar algún asunto complejo.

Jesús comenzó su cadena de siete parábolas con una historia sobre unas semillas sembradas en distintos terrenos y lo que ocurre en cada situación. Después de terminar la primera parábola de la serie, los discípulos pidieron tiempo muerto para preguntarle a Jesús por qué hablaba en un lenguaje codificado.

¿Qué muestra el hecho de que los discípulos se acercaran a Jesús con una pregunta sobre su relación con Él? ¿Qué revela eso sobre su relación con su enseñanza?

Cuando Dios dice o hace algo en la Escritura o en tu vida que es difícil de entender o escuchar, ¿te lleva tu instinto a hacerle preguntas? ¿Por qué sí o por qué no?

Busca los versículos señalados abajo y escribe los que más te animen o desafíen:

Santiago 1:5-8 ________________________________

Salmos 73:16-17 ________________________________

Salmos 119:130 ________________________________

Juan 14:26 ________________________________

Los discípulos no tuvieron miedo de preguntarle a Jesús sobre cosas que no entendían. Jesús es un Rey accesible y cercano, así que aprovechó la ocasión para darles algo de perspectiva.

Su lenguaje codificado era intencional, dijo. Los secretos del reino habían sido *dados* a los discípulos, pero a otros (la audiencia general), esos secretos no se les habían revelado. Jesús hace una distinción entre sus discípulos y la multitud.

Repasa 13:13-17. ¿Qué diferencias describe Jesús entre los dos grupos?

Jesús no dijo que los discípulos eran *mejores* que quienes no entendían sus enseñanzas sobre el reino de Dios, sino que eran *dichosos*. Se les había dado un regalo, sin esfuerzo ni mérito alguno por su parte. La gente puede tener ojos, oídos y mentes funcionales en el sentido físico, y aun así no ser capaces de percibir el reino.

Lee 1 Corintios 2:14. ¿Qué dice el texto sobre la capacidad de entender cosas espirituales? ¿Qué es necesario para entender la verdad?

Aunque la verdad está oculta para algunos, la Escritura dice que todo aquel que busca, halla (Mateo 7:7). Jesús no tiene intención de rechazar a los que acuden a Él impulsados por un deseo y una curiosidad genuinos. Los líderes religiosos intentaban atraparlo, engañarlo y acusarlo, pero una y otra vez daba la bienvenida a los que acudían a Él con sus preguntas y sus dudas.

Repasa 13:18-23. Llena la tabla de abajo con los detalles sobre cada tipo de terreno.

Tipo de terreno	Versículo	¿Qué frustra o ayuda a la semilla?	¿Cuál es el resultado?

En sus siguientes tres parábolas, Jesús habló a menudo sobre cizaña, más semillas y un poco de levadura. Estas parábolas en concreto revelaban el aspecto del reino de los cielos a medida que iba creciendo. Al principio, usó la imagen de la cizaña que crecía junto al grano para representar el mal y la corrupción que aparecerían en medio del reino bueno. Dios arreglaría las cosas, pero sucedería al final y no de inmediato.

En la segunda parábola, Jesús usó la imagen visual de una pequeña semilla de mostaza que crece hasta convertirse en un gran árbol para ilustrar cómo su reino, que aparentemente tiene un inicio pequeño, avanzaría y crecería hasta convertirse en algo que superaría las expectativas y la imaginación de todos. Sería un nido de descanso y refugio ¡para *todas* las naciones!

En su última parábola usó la levadura en lo que parece ser un aspecto positivo. Del mismo modo que un poco de levadura influye en todo lo que toca, así será el reino de los cielos. Jesús y su reino son una fuerza imparable, ¡y los que están en el reino dejarán su huella en el mundo que les rodea!

DÍA 5

MATEO 13:34-58

LEE MATEO 13:34-58

En el pasaje de hoy, Mateo estaba haciendo una de sus cosas favoritas: conectar los puntos entre Jesús y las Escrituras judías. Cada vez que Mateo hacía referencia a que Jesús cumplía la profecía, no estaba tan solo dando datos divertidos, sino proporcionando pruebas de que Jesús es el Rey prometido.

A la luz de los temas de los que Jesús hablaba en sus parábolas, ¿cuál es la relevancia de establecer que Jesús es el Rey?

A medida que seguía compartiendo parábolas, Jesús aclaraba más realidades del reino; sin embargo, esta vez lo hizo en un entorno más íntimo, donde habló directamente a sus discípulos. Su audiencia era todo oídos. Volvió atrás para desglosar la parábola de la cizaña (a petición de los discípulos). Después explicó dos parábolas más: un tesoro escondido y una perla preciosa.

Repasa 13:44-46. Con el corazón del Rey y los valores del reino en mente, ¿qué punto ves que establece Jesús en la parábola del tesoro escondido? ¿Y en la parábola de la perla preciosa?

Tesoro escondido	
Perla preciosa	

Recuerda que cada parábola tiene un punto principal dominante y general. No te quedes atascado en la cizaña intentando descifrar cada detalle. No estás intentado resolver un rompecabezas, sino tan solo ver el principio.

Usando tu comentario bíblico favorito, busca 13:44-50 y anota cualquier cosa nueva que observes o aprendas.

Hay algunas interpretaciones ampliamente aceptadas de estas parábolas, muchas de las cuales ponen el énfasis en *nosotros*; sin embargo, a la luz de su tema de revelar el reino y su corazón como Rey, es probable que la parábola estuviera centrada en *Él*. Jesús es el Rey que pagaría el precio máximo para poseer lo que Él atesoraba: aquello que le brindaba un profundo gozo.

Repasa Isaías 53. Toma nota de cualquier lugar en el que veas el tema o los temas de estas dos parábolas en escena.

Su última parábola nos recuerda a la parábola de la cizaña (13:36-43), solo que usando la imagen de la pesca. Ya que Pedro, Andrés, Santiago y Juan habían dejado sus redes para seguir a Jesús, probablemente conectaron profundamente con la ilustración. Así como un pescador experto usaría una red para recoger todo lo que encontrara en su camino y clasificarlo después de subirlo al barco, los ángeles al final de los tiempos separarían a los malvados de los justos.

Dado que no todos podían entender las enseñanzas de Jesús, preguntó a sus discípulos si ellos lo habían entendido. Cuando confirmaron que sí,

Él usó una analogía para animarlos. Las cosas nuevas que estaban aprendiendo de Él deberían atesorarlas junto a las cosas que ya habían aprendido de las Escrituras. Ambas eran valiosas y dignas de guardar en el tesoro de su relación con Dios.

¿Qué cosas verdaderas sabías acerca de Dios antes de ser cristiano o de leer la Biblia por ti mismo?

¿Qué verdades has escuchado o aprendido acerca de Dios desde que comenzaste a ser cristiano o a leer la Biblia, y que han ampliado el tesoro de tu relación con Él?

Después de su conversación con los discípulos, Jesús se preparó, se dirigió a su ciudad natal y continuó enseñando en la sinagoga. Al principio, los locales estaban impresionados, pero después de rechazarlo, no hizo muchos milagros.

¿Hay áreas de duda en tu vida? ¿De qué dudas podrías necesitar arrepentirte hoy?

Dios conoce tu corazón, y eso debería producirte consuelo. Ninguna de tus dudas o temores son una sorpresa para Él. Él invita a sus hijos a hablar con Él abiertamente sobre las cosas con las que luchamos. Si las lecciones de esta semana y las parábolas te han dejado frustrado o confuso, dedica un tiempo a hablar con Él sobre ello y a profundizar a medida que intentas conocerlo más. En su reino en expansión, tú eres uno de los tesoros en los que el Rey se deleita. Acércate hoy a Él, ¡porque Él está donde está el gozo!

¿Qué es lo que más te ha impactado del estudio de esta semana? ¿Por qué?

¿Qué aprendiste o recordaste acerca de Dios y su carácter esta semana?

DÍA 6

SALMO CORRESPONDIENTE Y ORACIÓN

LEE SALMOS 84

¿Qué correlación ves entre Salmos 84 y el estudio de esta semana sobre Jesús y su reino?

¿Qué porciones de este salmo captan más tu atención?

Termina haciendo esta oración en voz alta:

Padre,

¡Tu reino es precioso! En él están bien puestas todas las cosas. Tú estás en el trono, y puedo confiar en ti incluso en los momentos más oscuros.

Padre, he pecado y apelo a tu misericordia. Confieso que he dudado de tu justicia y tu bondad. Como Juan el Bautista, mis circunstancias me han llevado a veces a la desesperación. No he confiado en tu corazón, pensando que no me estabas dando algo bueno. Me arrepiento de mis pecados y acudo a ti, y te pido que limpies mi corazón.

Concédeme oídos para oírte, ojos para verte y un corazón que te ame más según te voy conociendo más. Dame más confianza en ti, para que crea las cosas nuevas que me revelas sobre ti mismo.

Te rindo mi vida, Señor; en cada momento de mi día y en cada decisión que tome, cedo mi voluntad y mis caminos a tu perfecta voluntad y tus caminos.

Yo también te amo. Amén.

DÍA 7

DESCANSA, PONTE AL DÍA O PROFUNDIZA

RETO SEMANAL

Jesús dijo: "Vengan a mí, todos los que están cansados y cargados, y Yo los haré descansar. Tomen mi yugo sobre ustedes y aprendan de mí, que yo soy manso y humilde de corazón, y hallarán descanso para sus almas. Porque mi yugo es fácil y mi carga ligera" (Mateo 11:28-30).

Cuando te sientes cansado, cargado, ansioso o abrumado, ¿dónde acudes? Jesús nos llama a acudir a Él para encontrar un descanso que abarca mucho más que nuestro cuerpo y nuestra mente: Él quiere descanso para nuestra *alma*.

En un sentido eterno, cuando nos arrepentimos y creemos en Él estamos respondiendo a su invitación de encontrar nuestro descanso eterno en Él, pero su invitación se aplica también a nuestra vida cotidiana. Él es nuestra mejor decisión para recuperarnos y fortalecernos ante los descansos falsos o superficiales.

Escribe Mateo 11:28-30 en tu diario en la parte superior de una página en blanco. A lo largo de la semana, escribe las cosas a las que compruebas que acudes cuando necesitas descanso (tal vez incluso puedes identificar algunas de ellas de antemano. Si es así, adelante, escríbelas ahora mismo). Si esas cosas no son Jesús, pídele que examine tu corazón y te revele esto: ¿por qué acudes a esas cosas, cómo te ha impactado esa decisión en el pasado, y qué te podría ayudar a aceptar su oferta de dar descanso a tu alma?

VERSÍCULO PARA MEMORIZAR

> Pero les digo que ni Salomón en toda su gloria se vistió como uno de ellos.
>
> Mateo 6:29

SEMANA 5

Mateo 14-16:

Propósito del Rey

LECTURA BÍBLICA DIARIA

Día 1: Mateo 14

Día 2: Mateo 15:1-20

Día 3: Mateo 15:21-39

Día 4: Mateo 16:1-20

Día 5: Mateo 16:21-28

Día 6: Salmos 34

Día 7: Para ponerte al día

Corresponde a los Días 290 y 292-293 de *La sinopsis de la Biblia*

RETO SEMANAL

Ver la página 129 para más información.

DÍA 1

MATEO 14

LEE MATEO 14

Tras ser manipulado por su esposa y su hijastra, Herodes Antipas hizo que decapitaran a Juan el Bautista (JEB) en la cárcel. Los israelitas probablemente interpretarían esto como un ataque político, religioso o moral. Al fin y al cabo, uno de sus líderes fue asesinado por decir la verdad.

¿Qué verdad dijo Juan el Bautista que condujo a su asesinato?

Después de que los discípulos de JEB enterraron con mucho respeto lo que quedaba de su cuerpo, fueron a contar a Jesús lo que había sucedido. Llevaron a Jesús su ira, dolor y descrédito, producidos por las malvadas acciones de un poderoso líder político. Y cuando Jesús y sus discípulos se retiraron para procesar ellos también su propio dolor juntos, se reunió una gran multitud. Se había difundido la noticia de que el máximo mandatario romano de su región había matado a uno de sus líderes. Y el pueblo de Dios, llevando su propio equipaje emocional de desconsuelo y temor, acudió en masa en busca de Jesús, el buen Rey.

¿Cómo respondieron los discípulos ante la gran multitud de personas?

¿Cómo respondió Jesús a sus discípulos?

Jesús, que es plenamente Dios y plenamente hombre, provee tanto para el alma como para el cuerpo. En el relato que hace Juan de esta misma historia, leemos que la multitud que Jesús acababa de alimentar quería proclamarlo el rey romano (Juan 6:15). Aunque creían en su poder y habían experimentado su bondad, todavía no entendían su divinidad. Jesús no tenía intención de ser rey de los israelitas o incluso rey del poderoso Imperio romano. Él vino como *el* Rey, el Rey de todos los reyes.

¿Cómo difería la visión que tenía la gente de un rey del verdadero rol de Jesús como Rey?

La expectativa de las personas	Jesús como Rey

Mientras Jesús pasaba tiempo a solas orando, sus discípulos estaban en el Mar de Galilea. Varios de ellos eran pescadores experimentados, pero habían estado luchando contra una tormenta durante unas nueve horas y les había adentrado unos cinco kilómetros en el mar. Estaban de luto por la muerte de JEB, exhaustos tras alimentar a miles de personas, y cansados de luchar contra la tormenta. Además de todo eso, ¡pensaban que veían un fantasma que se les acercaba! Cuando Jesús reveló que no era un fantasma sino Él mismo, calmó sus temores usando parte del mismo lenguaje que Dios usó cuando se identificó ante Moisés en el Antiguo Testamento.

Lee Éxodo 3. ¿Cuál es el contexto de Éxodo 3:14? ¿Por qué usó Jesús un lenguaje similar con sus discípulos durante la tormenta?

Aunque puede ir en contra de nuestro amor por los milagros y lo sobrenatural, el punto álgido de esta escena no es que Pedro caminara sobre el agua o que Jesús acallara el viento y las olas. El punto álgido es la adoración del Rey y el reconocimiento de que Él es el Hijo de Dios. Caminar sobre el agua ocurrió *una vez*, ¡pero Jesús es el Rey *eternamente*!

Vemos esto repetidamente a lo largo del ministerio de Jesús. Al final del capítulo 14 Mateo dijo que incluso en una ciudad donde Jesús no había viajado antes, la gente lo *reconoció* y le llevaron a todo el que estaba enfermo. Rogaban a Jesús que dejara que los enfermos tocaran el borde de su manto, y los que lo hicieron se curaron. Creían que se sanarían no porque tuvieran mucha fe, sino porque el poder y el amor de Jesús eran incomparables. La fortaleza de nuestra fe es importante, pero el objeto de nuestra fe es infinitamente más importante.

¿Cómo se enfoca hoy día nuestra sociedad en la *fortaleza* de la fe de una persona?

¿Cómo puedes repeler esos mensajes y enfocarte en el *objeto* de tu fe?

DÍA 2

MATEO 15:1-20

LEE MATEO 15:1-20

Una vez más, los fariseos intentaron atrapar a Jesús y sus discípulos quebrantando la ley judía. Estos líderes religiosos viajaron desde Jerusalén hasta Galilea, un viaje de cerca de 140 kilómetros que probablemente hicieron en ocho días, solo para hacer una pregunta: ¿por qué los discípulos de Jesús no se lavaban las manos antes de comer? En ese entonces esto no se hacía por higiene, sino que era parte de la ceremonia y tradición rabínicas. En otras palabras, no era un mandato de Dios sino una de *sus* reglas. Jesús les respondió señalando su hipocresía, ya que estaban quebrantando una de las reglas de Dios por su forma de tratar a sus padres y madres.

¿Qué profecía de Isaías citó Jesús a los fariseos?

Jesús siguió diciendo que no es lo que entra en la boca lo que contamina a alguien, sino lo que sale de la misma. Sería difícil exagerar cuán confuso era eso para sus discípulos judíos. En la mente de ellos, Jesús estaba contradiciendo todo aquello en lo que habían creído desde niños sobre la ley. ¡Pedro incluso supuso que Jesús estaba contando una de sus parábolas! Pero recuerda las palabras de Jesús en Mateo 5:17: "No piensen que he venido para poner fin a la ley o a los profetas; no he venido para poner fin, sino para cumplir".

Lee Levítico 11. ¿Cuáles son algunas de las leyes concernientes a animales que los discípulos habrían cumplido durante toda su vida?

Tras este encuentro, Jesús hizo un breve comentario sobre los fariseos. Dijo a sus discípulos que aunque los fariseos tenían apariencia de ser hijos de Dios, no lo eran. Y todo aquel que no pertenecía a la familia de Dios finalmente sería desarraigado. Al añadir cosas a la ley de Dios, los fariseos, que eran los líderes religiosos del pueblo, hacían que otros también se desviaran del camino. Cuando un líder no puede ver con claridad, tanto ellos como sus seguidores terminan en un hoyo.

Es importante recordar que Jesús no estaba ignorando aquí la ley de Dios; estaba denunciando las tradiciones religiosas que esos hombres añadían a la ley de Dios. Jesús no vino para deshacerse de la ley, reemplazar la ley o ignorar la ley. Como vino a cumplir la ley, debemos interpretar la ley a través de Él. De maneras más radicales que lo que los discípulos podían entender en ese entonces, su vida y enseñanza nos muestran cómo entender el Antiguo Testamento. La totalidad del Antiguo Testamento (la ley y los profetas) señala a Él, el Rey, el Mesías que sería sacrificado (Lucas 24:25-27, 44-45; Juan 5:39-40, 46). Jesús enfatizó una vez más su proclamación en el versículo 20 como solo lo podía hacer el Rey que cumplía la ley a la perfección: "pero comer sin lavarse las manos no contamina al hombre".

Repasa 15:18-20. ¿Qué cosas dijo Jesús que contaminan a una persona?

¿Cómo has visto que las cosas escritas arriba contaminan a una persona? ¿Cómo has visto que te contaminan a ti? **(Busca la definición de *contaminar* en un diccionario para que te ayude a meditar en ello).**

Las leyes ceremoniales del Antiguo Testamento recordaban a los israelitas que su pecado era una barrera para poder tener una relación plena y próspera con Dios. La única persona que ha cumplido siempre toda la ley de manera perfecta fue Jesús. Como resultado, Él es el único que puede perdonar nuestro pecado y eliminar la barrera entre nosotros y Dios. Él cumplió la ley, pagó el precio de nuestros pecados, y nos restauró a una correcta relación con Dios el Padre. Gracias a su vida sin pecado, a su muerte y a su milagrosa resurrección, somos justificados por medio de Él y reconciliados con el Padre. ¡Gloria a Cristo! ¡Él hizo lo que nosotros nunca podríamos hacer!

DÍA 3

MATEO 15:21-39

LEE MATEO 15:21-39

En la lectura de ayer, los fariseos hicieron un largo viaje motivados por un asunto que parecía insignificante, y en la lectura de hoy Jesús y sus discípulos también hacen un largo viaje. Es interesante pensar en lo que motivaba que Jesús iniciara sus viajes.

Jesús se retiró a una zona costera a unos 65 kilómetros al norte de su pueblo natal. El distrito de Tiro y Sidón era un lugar curioso para "retirarse" porque estaba fuera de territorio judío. En regiones gentiles, Jesús podía hablar libremente sobre lo que tenía que ofrecer a la gente, porque no tenía que preocuparse de que intentaran hacerle su rey. Los gentiles no esperaban a un Rey como les pasaba a los judíos.

Y, por supuesto, Él sabía quién estaría ahí buscándolo. Una mujer cananea, una madre desesperada con una hija endemoniada con necesidad de sanidad, rogó tener una audiencia con Jesús; lo hizo de manera tan ferviente, de hecho, que los discípulos incluso le pidieron a Jesús que la despidiera.

Ella llamó a Jesús: "Señor, Hijo de David". Aunque usó la versión sencilla de la palabra *Señor* para mostrar honor, no para reconocer su señorío, que usara el término *Hijo de David* tenía algo más de peso. Parecía indicar que tenía algunas pistas acerca de su identidad. Aunque ella era gentil, había oído de sus milagros y creía en su poder.

Cuando le pidió a Jesús que sanara a su hija, Jesús le dijo que había sido enviado a las ovejas perdidas de la casa de Israel, refiriéndose a los judíos. Hasta este punto en su ministerio, su enfoque había estado en los judíos y sus necesidades espirituales. La mujer sabía esto y se humilló, arrodillándose delante de Él y pidiéndole de nuevo su ayuda.

Jesús le respondió de una manera que la gente de su tiempo seguro que entendió bien: convirtiendo un insulto usado para los gentiles en un afectuoso juego de palabras: "No está bien tomar el pan de los hijos, y echárselo a los perrillos" (15:26). La palabra común que los judíos usaban para referirse a los gentiles, *kuon*, se refería a un animal inmundo. Pero la palabra que Jesús usó fue *kunarion*, término usado para un animal doméstico, y conlleva una connotación de un término de afecto.

La respuesta de ella es extraordinaria. No reclamó tener derecho a las bendiciones que Dios prometió a Israel. No demandó una excepción al pacto de Dios con Israel. Y no argumentó que Jesús estaba siendo injusto. Más bien, humildemente pidió las migajas: "Sí, Señor; pero también los perrillos comen de las migajas que caen de la mesa de sus amos" (15:27).

Lee Génesis 12:3. Como gentil, ¿con qué promesa contaba la mujer cananea? ¿Cómo se aplica esa promesa a nosotros en la actualidad?

Jesús alabó la fe de la mujer y sanó a su hija. Vale la pena destacar que no se menciona nada más sobre este viaje. Parece que quizá todo el viaje fue para ver a esta mujer y su hija, parecido al viaje con los gadarenos para sanar a los dos hombres endemoniados de esa región gentil.

Después de esto, Jesús regresó a las colinas que rodeaban el Mar de Galilea. Más personas acudieron a Él, miles de ellos. Y según la mayoría de los comentaristas, la audiencia en esta región casi con toda seguridad estaría repleta de gentiles. Llevaron a Jesús a los enfermos, heridos e incapacitados, y Él los sanó.

Repasa 15:31. ¿Cómo respondió la multitud (probablemente gentil) a las sanidades de Jesús?

Durante *tres días* Jesús sanó a la gente de esta región. Y, de nuevo, vemos que Jesús no se interesaba solo por sus almas sino también por sus cuerpos. Se produjo una escena familiar: Jesús dijo a sus discípulos que no quería enviar a la gente a sus casas sin comer.

¿Qué preguntaron los discípulos a Jesús en el versículo 33? ¿Qué nos dice esto sobre ellos?

Al igual que hizo en Mateo 14, Jesús tomó una pequeña porción de comida, dio gracias al Padre, partió el pan e hizo que sus discípulos distribuyeran la comida. Al igual que antes, hubo más que suficiente para todos. Anteriormente, cuando Jesús había alimentado a los cinco mil sobraron doce cestas, probablemente como símbolo de su cuidado de los doce discípulos. Esta vez, sin embargo, sobraron siete cestas. En el judaísmo, el número siete simboliza completitud o perfección. Aquí vemos la abundancia del reino de Jesús que se extiende más allá de los judíos para incluir a los gentiles. Completitud. Perfección.

En estos territorios gentiles Jesús se mostró con gran paciencia y compasión, sanando a los enfermos y proveyendo para los pobres. Su reino es para todos, y en su reino ¡incluso las sobras son abundantes!

¿Cómo has visto la abundancia de Dios en tu vida?

MATEO 16:1-20

LEE MATEO 16:1-20

Nada une tanto a las personas quebrantadas como un enemigo común, y así es como comienza el capítulo 16. Apenas había regresado Jesús de su ministerio en la tierra gentil cuando los fariseos y los saduceos, que por lo general no se llevaban bien entre ellos, unieron sus fuerzas para intentar atraparlo.

Le preguntaron a Él, el Mesías, por una señal sobre... el Mesías. Así que Jesús los puso en su lugar con bastante rapidez y respondió de una manera que hoy sonaría algo parecido a esto: "Cualquiera que ve nubes oscuras y huele la lluvia, sabe que debe agarrar un paraguas".

Repasa Mateo 13:33 y 16:5-12. ¿Cuál es la diferencia entre las analogías que Jesús usó para la levadura?

Cuando Jesús explicó a sus discípulos que estaba hablando de modo figurado (¡por lo que ya debían dejar de hablar del pan!), ellos entendieron su mensaje: incluso una pequeña cantidad de pecado tiene un impacto enorme. En los tiempos de Jesús, los fariseos a menudo eran hipócritas, mientras que los saduceos eran escépticos. Ambos tenían áreas en sus vidas religiosas que no se alineaban con los caminos de Dios, lo cual les hacía desviarse aún más.

¿De qué modo has visto que una pequeña cantidad de hipocresía y/o escepticismo tiene un gran impacto?

Jesús usó la expresión Hijo de Hombre más que cualquier otra para referirse a sí mismo. En Daniel 7, el Hijo del Hombre, alguien que es tanto humano como divino, recibe poder, gloria y un reino. Aquí en Mateo, Jesús preguntó a los discípulos quién decía la gente que era el Hijo del Hombre. Es importante destacar que ningún grupo estaba confesando abiertamente que Jesús era el Mesías en ese momento. Algunos de sus seguidores tenían cierta noción de quién era Él, pero ninguno tenía aún el cuadro completo.

Como era habitual en él, Pedro respondió a Jesús por los demás discípulos. ¿Quién dijo Pedro que era Jesús?

Jesús le dijo a Pedro que solo Dios podía haberle dado un entendimiento tan completo de quién es Jesús. Jesús después le dijo a Pedro (cuyo nombre *petros* significa "pequeña piedra" en griego) que edificaría su iglesia sobre esta roca (*petra* o "montaña" en griego). La roca sobre la que la iglesia sería edificada no era Pedro. No sería posible, porque Pedro es una pequeña piedra. La montaña de roca sobre la que sería edificada la iglesia era la verdad que Pedro confesó: "Tú eres el Cristo, el Hijo del Dios viviente" (16:16).

Busca Hechos 4:11. Según Pedro, ¿quién es la piedra angular de la iglesia?

Busca 1 Corintios 3:11. Según Pablo, ¿quién es el fundamento de la iglesia?

En la albañilería de piedra, la piedra angular y la piedra fundamental es una misma cosa: la pieza más importante de una estructura. Si esta piedra se eliminara, todo el edificio se vendría abajo. Aunque Jesús afirmó la frase llena de fe de Pedro, este momento en realidad no tenía nada que ver con Pedro sino con el Rey Jesús, el Mesías, el Hijo del Hombre, el fundamento de nuestra fe.

Esta es también la primera mención en la Biblia de la iglesia. En Hechos leemos acerca del día de Pentecostés, cuando descendió el Espíritu Santo y la iglesia se formó (Hechos 2). La iglesia está compuesta por todos los creyentes, tanto judíos como gentiles, y cualquier cosa que haga dentro de la voluntad de Dios lleva su nombre. En este pasaje, Jesús le habló a Pedro como miembro de los discípulos y como miembro de todos los creyentes que vendrían, ¡y dijo que ni siquiera la muerte acabaría con su iglesia! Este sería un recordatorio importante para sus discípulos en los días venideros, cuando la iglesia primitiva enfrentaría una terrible persecución.

Repasa 16:20. ¿Por qué dijo Jesús a los discípulos que no podían decirle a nadie que Él era el Cristo? Consulta el Día 1 de la Semana 3 (página 65), donde hablamos del secreto mesiánico. Escribe cualquier idea o pregunta que tengas acerca de lo que habría supuesto para los discípulos vivir en esa tensión.

MATEO 16:21-28

LEE MATEO 16:21-28

¿Qué comenzó Jesús a declarar a sus discípulos según 16:21?

La confesión de fe de los discípulos enseguida iría seguida del viaje de Jesús a Jerusalén y la cruz. Jesús, plenamente Dios y plenamente hombre, no vino como profeta, sanador o maestro moral. Jesús el Rey vino para sufrir y sacrificarse por nuestros pecados. Nos reconcilió con Dios para que, como creyentes, pudiéramos unirnos a Él en su reino eterno como herederos. *Este* es el propósito del Rey.

¿Cómo respondió Pedro a Jesús cuando éste reveló su propósito?

Repasa Mateo 4:1-11. ¿Qué similitudes observas?

Cuando Pedro reprendió a Jesús, Jesús lo corrigió con firmeza, diciendo: "¡Quítate de delante de Mí, Satanás!". Aunque Pedro acababa de hacer una gran confesión de fe, seguía siendo plenamente humano, con un entendimiento limitado del plan de Dios para nuestra redención. En Mateo 4 Satanás tentó a Jesús para tomar la gloria de ser Rey sin el sufrimiento de ser Salvador; pero Jesús sabía que sin su sufrimiento no podía haber salvación. Sin la muerte, no hay resurrección. Sin la cruz, no hay cristianismo. Y sin el derramamiento de su sangre, no podría haber el perdón de nuestros pecados (Hebreos 9:22). Su muerte era necesaria.

¿Cuáles fueron las tres cosas que dijo Jesús a sus discípulos que hicieran en 16:24?

El camino hacia el reino glorioso es la cruz. Las instrucciones para nosotros hoy son las mismas que para sus discípulos. Nosotros también debemos dejar a un lado nuestra sensación de sentirnos con derechos, abrazar su voluntad y seguir dondequiera que Él nos guíe. Contrario a la forma trivial en que muchos de nosotros hemos llamado a pequeños inconvenientes "nuestras cruces que cargar", Jesús instruyó a Sus seguidores a someterse completamente a la autoridad de Dios.

¿En qué áreas de tu vida exiges tus derechos? ¿Qué tendrías que hacer para someterte completamente a la autoridad de Dios en esas áreas?

Jesús advirtió de dos obstáculos para caminar con Él: autopreservación y buscar las riquezas. Ambas cosas son tendencias naturales para los humanos. Algunos incluso las llaman salvavidas; sin embargo, en el reino de Jesús tienes que perder tu vida para encontrarla. Debemos negarnos a apoyarnos en nuestros propios esfuerzos y fortalezas, y debemos apoyarnos totalmente en la obra terminada de Cristo, confiando en Dios para nuestra salvación y santificación (1 Pedro 3:18, Levítico 20:7-8). ¡Gloria a Dios por el gran amor que nos tuvo al enviar a su Hijo, el Rey, para mostrarnos el camino a su reino! ¡Él está donde está el gozo!

¿Qué es lo que más te impactó del estudio de esta semana? ¿Por qué?

¿Qué aprendiste o recordaste acerca de Dios y su carácter esta semana?

DÍA 6

SALMO CORRESPONDIENTE Y ORACIÓN

LEE SALMOS 34

¿Qué correlación ves entre Salmos 34 y el estudio de esta semana sobre Jesús y su reino?

¿Qué porciones de este salmo captan más tu atención?

Termina haciendo esta oración en voz alta:

Padre,

¡Tu corazón es muy atento y bondadoso! Cada aspecto del tiempo, cada palabra dicha, cada detalle... tú estás ahí. Gracias por el modo en que cuidas tan bien de tus hijos. Intervienes cuando nuestro corazón está roto, te inclinas cuando estamos enfermos y necesitados. Lo vemos en la historia de Jesús cuando se desvía de su camino para encontrarse con la mujer cananea y sanar a su hija endemoniada. Lo vemos en su

compasión hacia los miles de gentiles hambrientos. Y lo veo en la forma en que cuidas de mí también, y te alabo por ello.

Padre, he pecado y apelo a tu misericordia. Confieso que a menudo exijo mis derechos y demando cosas. Cuando mis expectativas no se cumplen, a veces me falta paciencia o humildad. He caído en la autopreservación. Como los fariseos, he sido hipócrita y legalista, y como los saduceos, me he vuelto cínico en ciertas áreas. Me arrepiento de mis pecados y acudo a ti, y te pido que limpies mi corazón.

Ablanda mi corazón, ¡por tu gloria y por mi gozo! Ayúdame a ayudar a los que pones en mi camino en lugar de encontrar razones para acusarlos o menospreciarlos. Dame ojos para ver a la gente como tú los ves y amarles como tú les amas. Dame la sabiduría para vivir con una mentalidad de reino, no con una mentalidad terrenal.

Rindo mi vida a ti, Señor; en cada momento de mi día y en cada decisión que tome, cedo mi voluntad y mis caminos a tu perfecta voluntad y camino.

Yo también te amo. Amén.

DÍA 7

DESCANSA, PONTE AL DÍA O PROFUNDIZA

RETO SEMANAL

Los que crecimos escuchando historias bíblicas como la alimentación de las multitudes podemos tender a ponernos nosotros mismos en las historias. Aquí, pensemos en nosotros no como el niño que lleva su pequeña ofrenda y le pide a Jesús que la multiplique. Más bien, pensemos en nosotros mismos como los que son bendecidos por la extravagante abundancia de Dios. Esto servirá como un buen recordatorio de que no es lo que nosotros podamos hacer por Él, sino lo que Él ha hecho por nosotros.

Esta semana, consigue varias tarjetas o pedazos de papel. En cinco de las tarjetas, dibuja un pan. En dos de las tarjetas, dibuja un pescado. Estos dibujos pueden ser tan sencillos o creativos como quieras. Dentro de cada dibujo escribe una categoría de bendiciones en tu vida (familia, amigos, iglesia, casa, trabajo, etc.).

A lo largo de la semana, añade notas específicas a cada tarjeta a medida que medites en la gran bondad de Dios en tu vida en esa área concreta. Dale gracias por los regalos específicos que Él te ha hecho y las maneras en las que provee para tu alma y para tu cuerpo.

SEMANA 6

Mateo 17-19:

Perspectiva del Rey

VERSÍCULO PARA MEMORIZAR

Y si Dios así viste la hierba del campo, que hoy es y mañana es echada al horno, ¿no *hará Él* mucho más por ustedes, hombres de poca fe?

Mateo 6:30

LECTURA BÍBLICA DIARIA

Día 1: Mateo 17

Día 2: Mateo 18:1-14

Día 3: Mateo 18:15-35

Día 4: Mateo 19:1-12

Día 5: Mateo 19:13-30

Día 6: Salmos 131

Día 7: Para ponerte al día

Corresponde a los Días 294-295 y 304 de *La sinopsis de la Biblia*

RETO SEMANAL

Ver la página 151 para más información.

DÍA 1

MATEO 17

LEE MATEO 17

Busca *transfigurar* en un diccionario. ¿Qué significa?

Repasa 17:2. ¿Cómo se transfiguró Jesús?

Pedro, Santiago y Juan estaban profundamente conmovidos por la asombrosa escena de la transfiguración y la sorprendente presencia de los otros testigos: Moisés y Elías. Juntos, ellos dos representaban todo el Antiguo Testamento (la ley y los profetas, respectivamente), lo cual señala por entero a Jesús, el Rey Mesías. Pedro, con su impetuosidad desatada, intentó encontrar la manera de prolongar ese momento, pero rápidamente fue humillado cuando Dios el Padre le cortó a mitad de discurso y se reveló a sí mismo.

Lee Éxodo 13:21-22 y 1 Reyes 8:10-11. ¿Qué observas acerca de cómo Dios se reveló aquí? **Después repasa Mateo 17:5.** ¿Qué les dijo Dios a los discípulos aquí?

Cuando Jesús tocó a los acobardados discípulos, ellos alzaron su mirada y solo vieron al Rey. La transfiguración fue un cuadro de su gloria venidera. Jesús sabía que el momento para revelar su propósito en la tierra llegaría rápidamente, y con ello llegaría también un gran sufrimiento. También sabía cómo los discípulos responderían a eso. De hecho, unos versículos después Jesús habló de nuevo a los discípulos sobre su muerte y resurrección, y "ellos se entristecieron mucho" (17:23).

Cuando Jesús habló de su muerte, también habló de su resurrección. Pero los discípulos, que solo entendían una parte de la identidad de Jesús y no su plena divinidad, escucharon eso y se enfocaron exclusivamente en la parte que tenía que ver con su muerte. Por lo tanto, en la transfiguración Jesús les dio a los más cercanos un destello del cuadro completo: el Rey vino y se humilló para sufrir, *y el Rey volverá de nuevo en toda su gloria.*

Jesús también sabía que pronto llegaría el momento de su propósito, pero todavía no había llegado. Así que dijo a sus tres discípulos: "No cuenten a nadie la visión hasta que el Hijo del Hombre haya resucitado de entre los muertos" (17:9).

Lee Malaquías 4:5, después repasa Mateo 17:10-13. ¿Qué aclaró Jesús a los discípulos? ¿Por qué es esto importante?

Cuando Jesús regresó con el resto de sus discípulos, llegaron a una multitud, allí sanó a un niño endemoniado a quien no pudieron ayudar sus discípulos. Cuando le preguntaron por qué ellos no pudieron sanarlo, Jesús señaló su falta de fe. Les dijo que la fe del tamaño de un grano de mostaza puede mover una montaña. Este versículo es a menudo citado y malinterpretado.

Recuerda que Jesús había dado a sus discípulos el poder y la autoridad para echar fuera demonios y sanar en su nombre. Una acción bien dirigida con una fe bien colocada puede hacer cosas que de otra manera serían imposibles.

¿Cómo has oído que se saca de contexto Mateo 17:20? ¿Qué significa realmente? ¿Cómo se vería eso hoy día?

Mateo 17 termina con una historia sobre los impuestos que solo registra Mateo, el exrecaudador de impuestos. ¡Muy apropiado! Desde el tiempo de Moisés, cada israelita de más de veinte años de edad tenía que pagar dos dracmas, o medio siclo, para apoyo del tabernáculo. Mil quinientos años más tarde, la misma regla aún estaba en vigor para sostener el templo. Los fariseos fueron a reclamar a Pedro por qué Jesús no pagaba sus impuestos. Por todo lo que sabemos, Jesús no llevaba dinero encima, pero se aseguró de que el impuesto del templo se pagara por Él y por Pedro —quien tal vez ni siquiera tenía la edad suficiente para pagarlo— mediante un milagro.

¿Cómo se pagaron los impuestos del templo? ¿Cómo sucedió este milagro?

Jesús le dijo a Pedro que, aunque los hijos de los reyes terrenales no pagan impuestos para la casa del rey, Él pagaba los impuestos del templo para evitar una ofensa. Más adelante en el Nuevo Testamento, Pablo se hace eco de las intenciones de Jesús aquí: "Porque aunque soy libre de todos, de todos me he hecho esclavo para ganar al mayor número posible" (1 Corintios 9:19). Nuestro misericordioso Rey modeló para todos nosotros cómo enfocarnos en el corazón del evangelio, eliminando barreras para alcanzar a más personas.

¿Hay barreras en tu vida que podrían impedir que otros vean a Dios y su amor de manera más clara? Pídele a Dios que examine tu corazón y te revele cualquier cosa en tu vida que quisieras ajustar para tener una mentalidad del reino y no una mentalidad terrenal.

DÍA 2

MATEO 18:1-14

LEE MATEO 18:1-14

Al comenzar el capítulo 18 Jesús dibujó un retrato de su reino, respondiendo a preguntas acerca de cómo es el reino y cómo debería conocerse. Los discípulos acudieron a Él con una pregunta muy egoísta: "¿Quién es el mayor en el reino de los cielos?". Sin embargo, antes de señalar a nadie y burlarnos del orgullo de los discípulos, reflexionemos sobre nosotros mismos.

¿Cómo has equiparado tus acciones con tu salvación o con tu nivel de "grandeza" ante los ojos de Dios? ¿Qué bendiciones has esperado de Dios a cambio de tu obediencia?

Jesús hizo que se acercara un niño y lo puso en medio de ellos, y luego les dijo a sus discípulos que solo los que se vuelven como niños entrarán en el reino. El niño no representaba inocencia o pureza, sino humildad. Un niño pequeño raras veces tiene ilusiones duraderas de autosuficiencia o grandeza. El insistente "lo hago yo solito" de un niño va seguido rápidamente de gritos de frustración y pedir "ayuda". Los niños dependen totalmente de sus cuidadores para desempeñarse. Jesús no estaba diciendo a los discípulos que no estarían con Él en el cielo; les estaba señalando que su esperanza estaba en ellos mismos, los niños, y no en su cuidador, el Rey.

¿Qué advertencias dio Jesús a los discípulos sobre hacer pecar a otro seguidor de Cristo? Completa la tabla de abajo.

Versículo	**Si...**	**Entonces...**
Mateo 18:6	haces pecar a un creyente	
Mateo 18:8		córtala y tírala
Mateo 18:9	tu ojo te hace pecar	

¿Te parecen estas advertencias un poco exageradas? El pecado es grave. El pecado lleva a la muerte. Y el pecado requiere una seria solución mortal. Jesús, quien Él mismo es nuestra solución, usó deliberadamente un lenguaje fuerte para reiterar su punto: *No seas la razón por la que otro creyente decide pecar.* En esta vida nos llegará la tentación de pecar, pero el que lleva esa tentación a otro creyente acarrea juicio sobre sí mismo. Esto no quiere decir que seamos responsables de los pecados de los demás, ya que esa responsabilidad recae sobre cada persona, sino que somos responsables de considerar a los demás en nuestras acciones. Ninguno de nosotros vive únicamente para sí mismo. Nuestras acciones influyen en otros, y es sabio, humilde y amable tener esto en cuenta.

¿Qué pecado en tu vida podría estar haciendo que un hermano o hermana peque? Escribe algunas posibilidades abajo. Después lee tu lista y busca humildemente la gracia de Dios, que se dio gratuitamente a nosotros a través de Jesús, y pídele que te restaure a los caminos de su reino.

A medida que Jesús enseña sobre su reino, tenemos un cuadro de una oveja que abandona el rebaño. El pastor deja el rebaño para buscar a la que se ha perdido, se ha desviado o no ha podido seguir el paso. El pastor no solo cuida del rebaño sino también de cada oveja en particular dentro del rebaño.

Lee Salmos 100:3 y Apocalipsis 7:17. Después repasa Mateo 18:10-14.

¿Cómo es Jesús nuestro pastor?

Cuando Jesús, el Pastor Rey, deja las noventa y nueve para cuidar de una, no está abandonando al resto de las ovejas. En verdad está cuidando también a esa oveja sola, asegurándose de que el rebaño esté completo. Jesús ve todo su reino: el rebaño y la oveja, el bosque y los árboles, la iglesia y los creyentes. ¡Cada detalle es importante para el Rey!

DÍA 3

MATEO 18:15-35

LEE MATEO 18:15-35

Jesús siguió dibujando un cuadro de su reino en el pasaje de hoy, respondiendo preguntas sobre cómo es el reino y cómo debería ser conocido. Por lo tanto, después de explicar cómo responder a nuestro propio pecado, les dijo a sus discípulos cómo confrontar a un creyente cuando peca contra ellos.

¿Cuáles son los cuatro pasos que bosquejó Jesús en este proceso de confrontación justa?

Paso uno

Paso dos

Paso tres

Paso cuatro

Estos pasos son un regalo para los creyentes mientras caminamos por la vida juntos, y son aplicables en muchas situaciones en las que un hermano o una hermana peca contra otro. A medida que aprendes a perdonar como Dios enseña, tendrás oportunidades de practicar los pasos que Jesús enumeró en este capítulo, probablemente desde las dos caras de la moneda: el ofensor y el ofendido. Y, usando la sabiduría que Dios da, también sabrás cuándo buscar la ayuda de un líder de confianza para ofrecer perdón.

En la cultura judía del momento, perdonar a alguien tres veces se consideraba generoso, así que Pedro probablemente pensó que perdonar a alguien siete veces era un gesto extravagante. Pero Jesús enseñó que el perdón debería ser infinito.

Comparó su reino con un rey terrenal "que quiso ajustar cuentas". Contactó con un siervo que le debía una gran deuda, tan elevada que el siervo no tenía manera alguna de devolverla. Los ahorros de toda su vida solo serían una pequeña parte de la enorme cantidad que debía.

¿Qué hizo el rey por este siervo? ¿Qué hizo el siervo?

Cada uno de nosotros es ese siervo rencoroso. Se nos perdonará, y se nos ha perdonado, muchísimo más de lo que nosotros podremos perdonar. Cuando tenemos en cuenta la profundidad y la anchura del perdón de Dios por cada uno, deberíamos ser movidos a ofrecer a los demás un perdón verdadero.

También habrá veces en las que estés listo para perdonar, pero la persona que ha pecado contra ti no está arrepentida. En esos casos, seguimos los pasos que Jesús dio y mantenemos la disponibilidad a perdonar en nuestro corazón. Como el verdadero perdón viene del corazón, sus impactos también se sienten primero ahí. Ya sea que el hermano o la hermana reconozcan o no su pecado hacia ti, tu disposición a extender misericordia te protegerá para que no desarrolles un espíritu amargado.

Más adelante en la Escritura, Pablo volvió a repasar esta enseñanza en su carta a las iglesias en Éfeso.

Lee Efesios 4:31-32. ¿Qué instrucciones dio Pablo para la vida en el reino?

El reino de Jesús es un lugar donde los últimos son los primeros, los pobres son ricos y los humildes son alabados. Su reino debería ser reconocido por sus siervos, que seremos exigentes con nuestros propios pecados, amables con nuestros hermanos y hermanas y generosos al perdonar, ¡dando de lo que hemos recibido de nuestro generoso Rey!

DÍA 4

MATEO 19:1-12

LEE MATEO 19:1-12

Antes de comenzar, es importante reconocer que la lectura de hoy es difícil. Si se producen en ti sentimientos de confusión o frustración, llévaselos al Señor. Si surgen sentimientos de vergüenza o condenación, pídele a Dios que silencie las mentiras del enemigo y que las reemplace con su verdad. Romanos 8:1 dice que "no hay condenación para los que están en Cristo Jesús". Podemos confiarle a Dios nuestras dudas, nuestras luchas y nuestros pecados. Él es personal, relacional y soberano con todo, en medio de todo y por encima de todo. Ora y pídele a Dios que te muestre su corazón en lo que Jesús enseñó aquí.

Lee Mateo 19:1-12. ¿Cuáles son tus primeros pensamientos? ¿Sentimientos? ¿Preguntas?

Cuando Jesús terminó su ministerio en Galilea, comenzó a viajar al sur, hacia Jerusalén. Cuando los fariseos oyeron dónde estaba, aparecieron *otra vez* e intentaron atraparlo *otra vez*. Recuerda que los fariseos se enorgullecían de guardar la ley de Dios, pero eran hipócritas. A menudo añadían otras reglas además de las leyes de Dios que hacían que su "obediencia" fuera extremadamente visible a la vez que creaban fisuras alrededor de las leyes de Dios que les resultaban inconvenientes.

¿Qué le preguntaron a Jesús los fariseos?

Los fariseos sabían que, al margen de cuál fuera la respuesta de Jesús, alguien iba a quedar decepcionado. En ese tiempo, algunos grupos judíos tenían una visión muy estricta del divorcio, y no se permitía en casi ningún caso. Otros grupos judíos tenían una idea más liberal, permitiendo el divorcio en algunos casos y el volver a casarse en otros. ¿Te resulta familiar? En la actualidad, diferentes denominaciones, iglesias y líderes cristianos tienen convicciones distintas sobre las enseñanzas de la Biblia sobre el divorcio y volver a casarse.

Lee Marcos 10:2-12. Después repasa Mateo 19:3-9. ¿Qué es similar en estos pasajes? ¿Qué es único de cada pasaje?

En Mateo 19 Jesús conocía a quienes le preguntaban, y conocía sus juegos. Los fariseos a menudo justificaban sus reglas extra o sus pretextos retrocediendo todo lo posible en las Escrituras. Así que Jesús los derrota ahí mismo y se remonta directamente hasta el jardín del Edén. Citando de Génesis 1:27 y 2:24, Jesús enseñó que el diseño original de Dios era que un hombre y una mujer se unieran como uno solo, en matrimonio, como un compromiso de toda la vida.

Cuando los fariseos protestaron diciendo que Moisés había permitido el divorcio, Jesús equiparó la necesidad de provisión con la dureza de nuestro corazón. El divorcio y el adulterio no existirían si el corazón fuera blando, según Jesús.

Según la enseñanza de Jesús, ¿cuál fue la conclusión de los discípulos en 19:10?

Para los discípulos, una vida matrimonial sin divorcio o un segundo matrimonio parecía extremadamente difícil, más difícil incluso que quedarse soltero. Jesús les dijo que los que son llamados a una vida de celibato y soltería deberían aceptarla.

Siguiendo esa línea, les dio tres ejemplos de eunucos (personas que están incapacitadas para el matrimonio y los hijos): los que nacen así, los que son obligados a hacerlo y los que se ofrecen voluntarios. Pero ten cuidado de no ver algo que Jesús no enseñó aquí. Si ahora estás soltero, puede que Dios te esté llamando a una vida de celibato o puede que no. Él conoce tu corazón y tus deseos, conoce el futuro que ha planeado para ti, y obra para el bien de sus hijos.

Jesús no dijo que el celibato fuera más fácil que el matrimonio, y no dijo que el matrimonio fuera más fácil que el celibato. En ambas cosas hay alegrías y desafíos. Hay oportunidades para la santificación en ambos. La soltería entra en el reino, y hay reglas del reino para vivirla fielmente. El matrimonio entra en el reino, y hay reglas del reino para vivirlo fielmente.

La intención de los fariseos era tender una trampa a Jesús para obligarlo a establecer un mandato infiel o sin compasión sobre el divorcio; sin embargo, Jesús les respondió con arte como el Diseñador, con compasión como el Salvador y con autoridad como el Rey. Habló más allá de lo que estaba meramente permitido o prohibido en su reino. Dibujó un cuadro que nos muestra cómo es su reino y cómo debería ser conocido. Ora para que Dios te enseñe a vivir fielmente en su reino, dondequiera que te haya puesto.

Si tienes alguna lucha con la enseñanza de Jesús en la lectura de hoy, escribe abajo una oración pidiéndole a Dios que se encuentre contigo en ese espacio con su bondad, verdad, amor y esperanza.

DÍA 5

MATEO 19:13-30

LEE MATEO 19:13-30

En la mayoría de las culturas antiguas, a los niños se les valoraba no por quienes eran sino por la persona en la que se convertirían. En Israel, la idea era un poco distinta: a los niños se les celebraba como una bendición de Dios para sus familias, pero también se esperaba que no se les viera ni oyera mucho hasta que crecieran.

¿Cómo se ven evidenciadas esas creencias culturales en la reacción de los discípulos hacia los niños en el versículo 13? ¿Qué reveló la respuesta de Jesús acerca de su reino?

Tras bendecir a los niños, Jesús dirigió su atención a un joven rico que le preguntó qué tenía que hacer para obtener la vida eterna.

¿Cómo esperarías que Jesús respondiera a esta pregunta?

El hombre veía la salvación como transaccional, y no relacional. Cuando Jesús le dijo al hombre que guardara los mandamientos, tuvo la oportunidad de meditar en su fracaso. Nadie, salvo Jesús, había guardado, o guardaría siempre, los mandamientos de manera perfecta; sin embargo, en lugar de recibir convicción de sus pecados, el hombre le preguntó a Jesús qué mandamientos concretos tenía que cumplir.

¿Cuáles son los cinco mandamientos que citó Jesús a este hombre? ¿Qué tienen en común estos mandamientos en particular?

Cuando el hombre insistió en que había cumplido todos esos mandamientos, Jesús presionó un poco más para examinar su corazón, diciéndole: "Si quieres ser perfecto, ve y vende lo que posees y da a los pobres, y tendrás tesoro en los cielos; y ven, sé Mi discípulo" (19:21). Aquí, el hombre debería haberse convencido al darse cuenta de que su riqueza era su dios. Debería haber confesado que no había cumplido plenamente los mandamientos. Debería haber abandonado sus intentos de salvarse él mismo y recibir el camino de Jesús que era mejor. Pero lo único que oyó el hombre fue una instrucción que no estaba dispuesto a seguir. Así que se fue apenado.

Dios da a sus hijos regalos generosos, y a veces esos regalos llegan en forma de posesiones materiales. Pero hermanos y hermanas, oigan esto: si tu riqueza en el mundo se ha convertido en un ídolo, o si está creando espacio en tu corazón para la mentira de que no necesitas a Dios para cada respiración que das, entonces entrégala. Las bendiciones a las que tanto nos aferramos ahora palidecen en comparación con las bendiciones preparadas para quienes siguen a Jesús.

En la NBLA, vuelve a leer las últimas cuatro palabras de 19:21. ¿Qué invitación hizo Jesús que el hombre no comprendió?

Esta oferta de Jesús fue extraña, pero el hombre no estuvo dispuesto. Los discípulos de Jesús estaban entre los pocos que habían oído esta invitación antes. En Mateo 4 Jesús le hizo esta oferta a Pedro, Santiago y Juan, y como respuesta a su invitación, ellos dejaron su modo de vida y sus familias para seguirlo a Él. Y aquí en 19:27, Pedro destacó los sacrificios que los discípulos habían hecho para responder al llamado de Jesús. Pedro quería reafirmar la bendición a cambio de lo que habían dejado atrás. En lugar de castigar la precipitación de Pedro, lo cual podía haber hecho con todo el derecho, Jesús respondió con compasión.

Repasa 19:28-30. ¿Qué hay preparado para los que han sacrificado cosas como respuesta al llamado de Jesús?

La vida eterna es un regalo, no una recompensa. No nos ganamos nuestra salvación o su favor, sino que se nos dan sin esfuerzo alguno por nuestra parte. Sin embargo, Jesús nos dice que todo lo que se sacrifique por el reino será restaurado, y todo lo que se haga por Dios será honrado.

Jesús vio más allá de lo que veía este joven rico, vio más allá de lo que veían sus discípulos, y Él ve más allá de lo que nosotros vemos. Su perspectiva es más aguda, más profunda y más amplia. Él ve todo su reino, y nos invita a unirnos a Él allí. ¡Él está donde está el gozo!

¿Qué es lo que más te impactó del estudio de esta semana? ¿Por qué?

¿Qué aprendiste o recordaste acerca de Dios y su carácter esta semana?

DÍA 6

SALMO CORRESPONDIENTE Y ORACIÓN

LEE SALMOS 131

¿Qué correlación ves entre Salmos 131 y el estudio de esta semana sobre Jesús y su reino?

¿Qué porciones de este salmo captan más tu atención?

Termina haciendo esta oración en voz alta:

Padre,

Tú eres santo y justo, y todos tus caminos son rectos. ¡Tú estableces leyes que tienen la intención de aportarnos el mayor gozo! No hay Dios como tú, que bendice a su pueblo con su cercanía. Mediante la obra terminada de tu Hijo Jesús ya lograste todo lo que requieres de nosotros, y mediante el poder de tu Espíritu obrando en nosotros nos recuerdas quiénes somos, ¡mientras nos empoderas para andar en tus caminos!

Padre, he pecado y apelo a tu misericordia. Confieso que a menudo el pecado me parece más atractivo o natural que la obediencia. Cuando tus caminos parecen ser demasiado restrictivos o demasiado difíciles de entender, siento la tentación de abandonar. Como el joven rico, a veces me distraigo con las bendiciones que me has dado y fallo en seguirte. A veces me parece más fácil seguir mi corazón o pedir perdón después. Me arrepiento de mis pecados, acudo a ti y te pido que limpies mi corazón.

Dame la humildad de un niño. Otórgame fe en tu poder mientras obras en mi vida. Dame sabiduría para conocer tus caminos y andar en ellos. Y dame el tipo de paz que solo viene de estar en el reino de un Rey bueno y amoroso.

Te rindo mi vida, Señor; en cada momento de mi día y cada decisión que tomo, cedo mi voluntad y mi camino a tu perfecta voluntad y camino.

Yo también te amo. Amén.

DÍA 7

DESCANSA, PONTE AL DÍA O PROFUNDIZA

RETO SEMANAL

Esta semana entabla una conversación con un niño en tu vida, con el permiso de sus padres. Estas son algunas pautas: no le digas qué hacer y no le hagas pensar en su futuro (por ejemplo "¿qué quieres ser cuando seas mayor?"). Valóralo como portador de la imagen que ya es. Pregúntale por su día: por lo que ha hecho y a quién ha visto. Pregúntale por su vida: lo que le gusta y con quién pasa tiempo. Pregúntale por su mente: lo que está aprendiendo y lo que le asombra. Y pregúntale por su alma: qué le da miedo y quién le hace sentirse seguro.

Escribe lo que te diga el niño. Subraya ejemplos de honestidad, y rodea con un círculo ejemplos de humildad. ¿Qué puedes aprender del ejemplo del niño?

SEMANA 7

Mateo 20-22:

Tensiones del Rey

VERSÍCULO PARA MEMORIZAR

Por tanto, no se preocupen, diciendo: "¿Qué comeremos?" o "¿qué beberemos?" o "¿con qué nos vestiremos?".

Mateo 6:31

LECTURA BÍBLICA DIARIA

Día 1: Mateo 20:1-16

Día 2: Mateo 20:17-34

Día 3: Mateo 21:1-27

Día 4: Mateo 21:28-46

Día 5: Mateo 22

Día 6: Salmos 118

Día 7: Para ponerte al día

Corresponde a los Días 305 y 308 de *La sinopsis de la Biblia*

RETO SEMANAL

Ver la página 177 para más información.

DÍA 1

MATEO 20:1-16

LEE MATEO 20:1-16

El Rey Jesús siguió explicando su reino contando otra parábola. Esta vez, su historia tenía que ver con algo muy conocido en el antiguo Israel: las uvas. Tal vez pienses: *¿Uvas? Israel es la tierra de la leche y la miel. ¡¿Desde cuándo son importantes las uvas?!* Las uvas eran importantes porque son la fuente del vino. Un buen viñador sabe que para hacer el mejor vino, tienes que cosechar las uvas en su momento justo. Para conseguir este tiempo perfecto, los maestros viñadores a menudo contrataban trabajadores además de su plantilla regular.

Busca Mateo 9:37-38. ¿Qué similitudes ves entre ese pasaje y esta parábola?

Lee Isaías 5:1-7, Oseas 10:1 y Jeremías 2:21. ¿Cómo se llama a Israel en estos pasajes?

El mensaje de Jesús seguía siendo consistente: se necesitaban más obreros en el campo. Tanto en el Antiguo como en el Nuevo Testamento, Dios se refirió a su pueblo como una vid o una viña.

Usa un diccionario bíblico o comentario para identificar el tiempo exacto del día que representan estas frases.

Primera hora: ______________________

Tercera hora: ______________________

Sexta hora: ______________________

Novena hora: ______________________

Undécima hora: ______________________

Tiempo de pagar: ______________________

El primer grupo comenzó a trabajar a la hora más temprana (seis de la mañana) y acordó un salario justo de un denario, pero cuando el amo reclutó más grupos de trabajadores, no acordaron un salario exacto. Quizá el amo tenía reputación de ser un jefe justo, o tal vez los obreros estaban tan desesperados por trabajar que no les importó saber cuál sería su salario exactamente. Sea cual sea la razón, los obreros acordaron trabajar por "lo que sea justo".

¿En qué orden llamó el hacendado a los obreros del campo para recibir sus salarios?

¿Cuál fue el pago para cada obrero?

¿Cómo respondieron los obreros de la primera hora?

Lee 1 Corintios 10:6-10 y Filipenses 2:14. ¿Cuál es el resultado de la queja?

¿En qué áreas de tu vida eres tentado a quejarte?

Es común justificar la queja y es fácil entender por qué se quejaron los obreros de la primera hora, pero no hay lugar para este tipo de exigencia en el reino al revés. Dios es serio pidiendo a sus obreros que no se quejen. La queja revela un corazón que maltrata a Dios y su bondad.

Al final de esta parábola, Jesús hizo una afirmación impactante. Afirmó autoridad y dominio sobre todas las cosas, y después dijo: "los últimos serán primeros, y los primeros, últimos". Esto cambia por completo todo nuestro esfuerzo por progresar y hacer que brille nuestra reputación. Nos recuerda que la comparación es un trabajo sin sentido en el reino, porque todos estamos en el mismo equipo, ganamos más de lo que nos merecemos y se nos perdona el castigo que merecemos. En el reino de Dios, ¡su generosidad supera a su justicia!

¿Cómo moldean estas verdades la forma en que ves a los obreros que trabajan contigo en el campo?

¿Cómo modelan estas verdades tu forma de ver a Dios, sus acciones y su corazón?

DÍA 2

MATEO 20:17-34

LEE MATEO 20:17-34

Cuando Jesús y sus discípulos se dirigían a Jerusalén, llamó aparte a sus discípulos para darles unos detalles concretos de su crucifixión, más cosas secretas que más adelante podrían gritar desde las azoteas (10:27). Por tercera vez, Jesús les dijo lo que le ocurriría en Jerusalén; pero, como veremos después, ellos no entendieron lo que dijo de forma tan clara.

En tus propias palabras, describe lo que sucedió en 20:20-28.

La madre de Santiago y Juan (también conocidos como los hijos de Zebedeo, por el nombre de su padre) se acercó a Jesús con un reino terrenal en mente. Quería que sus hijos tuvieran estatus vip en el reino de Jesús: los lugares más cercanos en la mesa real. Los otros discípulos se enfurecieron por esta petición tan audaz. Quizá estaban celosos de no haberlo pensado primero pero, una vez más, Jesús reorientó a sus discípulos en cuanto a las reglas de su reino: los que quieran ser mayores tienen que ser siervos, y los que quieran ser primeros deben ser esclavos.

Cierto es que incluso estas bonitas instrucciones pueden desviarnos si nuestro corazón está puesto en nuestro propio avance. Podemos encontrarnos sirviendo a otros para que nos vean como humildes o como un medio de ganarnos respeto. Podemos tomar las palabras de Jesús como un plan de acción en lugar de un recordatorio de la clase de actitud del corazón que Dios valora.

¿Alguna vez has servido para tu propio avance o progreso? Si es así, describe abajo cómo fue la situación.

Cuando Jesús terminó de dar las duras noticias y resolver este acalorado momento entre sus hombres, les recordó que Él sería el primer ejemplo de cómo es su reino, al sacrificar su vida para servir a muchos.

Después siguió su largo viaje de ocho horas cuesta arriba desde Jericó hasta Jerusalén, más cerca de su muerte segura con cada paso que daba. Como de costumbre, las multitudes lo seguían. Cuando dos ciegos se dieron cuenta de que estaba cerca de ellos, comenzaron a gritar para conseguir su atención.

Lee 2 Samuel 7:12-13, 16. ¿Cuál es el significado del título "Hijo de David"?

Estos dos mendigos ciegos no tenían la capacidad física de ver a Dios, pero tenían ojos espirituales para reconocer al Mesías prometido entre ellos. ¡Su vista era mucho mejor que la de poder ver con los ojos físicos! Las multitudes intentaban callarlos, pero ellos gritaban todavía más fuerte.

Lee Isaías 29:18 y 35:4-5. ¿Qué esperanza tenían estos hombres sabiendo que el Mesías estaba cerca de ellos?

Según la profecía, la era mesiánica traería sanidad a los ciegos. Estos hombres sabían que el Mesías había llegado, y que era el cumplimiento de su esperanza. A pesar de la molestia de la multitud con los hombres ciegos, Jesús se detuvo en medio del caos para preguntar: "¿Qué quieren que Yo haga por ustedes?". Él no necesitaba que ellos respondieran. Él ya lo sabía. La multitud intentaba silenciarlos, pero Jesús les dio un momento para hablar. Elevó a estos hombres delante de la gente que los había menospreciado. Movido a compasión, tocó sus ojos y los sanó. Ellos vieron la cara del Mesías Rey que tanto habían esperado y siguieron a Jesús hasta Jerusalén.

El Rey Jesús sigue conociendo tus necesidades. Él conoce cada uno de tus pensamientos. Y, cuando el mundo o el enemigo intente callarte para que no clames a Él, Jesús seguirá preguntando: "¿Qué quieres que Yo haga por ti?". Recuerda: Él es quien te dice que pidas.

¿Qué quieres pedirle hoy?

DÍA 3

MATEO 21:1-27

LEE MATEO 21:1-27

El texto de hoy habla de un tema que produce malentendidos e incredulidad. Al leer, busca momentos en los que el Rey Jesús es malentendido y las multitudes siguen dudando del mensaje de su reino al revés.

Jesús, sus discípulos y la multitud, que probablemente incluía dos antiguos ciegos, seguían caminando hacia Jerusalén. Cuando llegaron al Monte de los Olivos, Jesús envió a dos de sus discípulos a hacer el recado de conseguir un asna y un pollino.

Lee Zacarías 9:9. ¿Cómo estaba profetizado que aparecería el Rey?

La mayoría de los reyes en tiempos antiguos desfilaban por las ciudades en los mejores caballos, pero el Rey Jesús apareció montado sobre un burro joven. Entró humildemente, no majestuosamente, en un animal hecho para el servicio y no para la batalla. En una demostración de su sumisión a Él, la gente arrojaba sus mantos sobre el suelo y ponían ramas de palmeras, declarando su victoria y nacionalismo judío.

Busca la palabra *hosanna* (21:9) en un diccionario de griego. ¿Qué le estaba pidiendo la multitud a Jesús que hiciera?

La multitud gritaba "¡Hosanna!" ("sálvanos"), mientras Él entraba en la ciudad del gran Rey (Salmos 48:1-2). Toda la ciudad estaba agitada, al igual que lo había estado décadas antes cuando nació el Rey (Mateo 2:3). Esperaban que un verdadero rey los salvara de la opresión de las autoridades romanas, pero su deseo era demasiado pequeño, demasiado pasajero. El Rey Jesús tenía su vista puesta en algo mucho más importante que Roma. Sí, vino para salvarlos, pero de sus pecados y de la separación eterna de Dios.

Tras este malentendido, Jesús fue al templo y encontró a personas respondiendo de manera impropia a Dios también allí.

Explica las palabras de Jesús en 21:13. **Usa un comentario si te resulta útil.**

Tres veces al año, la gente viajaba desde todo Israel hasta Jerusalén para las celebraciones santas y los sacrificios. Tener un animal perfecto era importante según la ley judía. Para acomodar a estos turistas, el complejo del templo tenía un mercado donde los viajeros podían comprar un animal sin defecto para su sacrificio. Había también una moneda concreta aceptable para el impuesto obligatorio del templo. Los cambistas actuaban como lo hacen muchos mercaderes en lugares donde hay muchos turistas: estafando a personas con el porcentaje del cambio y mintiendo sobre el valor de la mercancía.

Parece que Jesús no tenía problema con las ventas *en sí mismas*, sino con *robar* a las personas. El templo era el lugar que mejor representaba la generosidad de Dios hacia su pueblo, y los mercaderes lo estaban usando como un lugar para timar a turistas devotos.

Mucho entendimiento erróneo, mucha incredulidad, y a la vez había tres grupos de personas que parecían entenderlo. **Repasa 21:14-16.** ¿Quiénes eran estos grupos?

Los líderes religiosos judíos estaban sordos al mensaje y ciegos a la misión, pero los desesperados (los ciegos y los cojos) aún le buscaban, y los niños también le reconocían correctamente, alabándole con frases mesiánicas. Al observar esto los principales sacerdotes y los escribas, se enfurecieron. Las tensiones del Rey estaban creciendo, y salió de la ciudad para descansar una noche en una aldea cercana.

En la mañana, comprometido con su propósito, regresó a la ciudad. Por el camino vio una higuera que no tenía higos, solo hojas. No era época de higos, a fin de cuentas. Aun así, Jesús maldijo la higuera y esta se secó de inmediato. No maldijo el árbol porque tuviera el derecho de hacerlo, ni porque estuviera *de mal humor por el hambre*; lo hizo para enseñar un mensaje importante.

¿Por qué crees que Jesús maldijo la higuera? **Lee Lucas 13:6-9 para ayudarte. Si tienes tiempo, lee Jeremías 8:13 y Miqueas 7:1.**

Esta higuera representa la incredulidad entre los judíos. Los profetas del Antiguo Testamento hicieron esta comparación años antes. El Rey Jesús quería desesperadamente que Israel diera fruto, pero no lo había dado. Por supuesto que había muchos judíos que creyeron, incluyendo a sus discípulos, así que este no era un rechazo de toda una nación sino de aquellos entre los judíos que veían sus obras y no se entregaban a su reinado.

Así como las personas de la nación no le creyeron, los líderes de la nación tampoco lo hicieron. **Repasa 21:23-27.** ¿Cuáles eran las dos cosas que querían saber acerca de Jesús?

Probablemente seguían enojados porque Jesús volcó sus mesas el día anterior, y al preguntarle, el Rey Jesús *les* volcó las mesas de nuevo. Respondió a sus preguntas con más preguntas, pero ellos decidieron fingir que no sabían en lugar de reconocer que tanto la autoridad de JEB como la de Jesús venían del cielo. Los principales sacerdotes y los ancianos no pudieron aceptar ni recibir estas verdades, pero tampoco pudieron refutarlas.

La tensión aumentaba. Como vimos con la higuera, Jesús tiene el poder de maldecir al igual que el de bendecir. Pero su humildad y sumisión al plan del Padre le impidió maldecir a todos los que tramaban en contra de Él.

¿Cómo es que las respuestas de Jesús a las multitudes estimulan tu corazón para adorarlo?

DÍA 4

MATEO 21:28-46

LEE MATEO 21:28-46

Hoy continuamos con el tema de los malentendidos y la incredulidad. Jesús estaba de pie delante de la élite religiosa y les enseñó mediante sus dos maneras favoritas de hacerlo: planteando preguntas y relatando parábolas. Ambas parábolas representan la condenación para los judíos que habían rechazado a Jesús como Mesías.

Repasa 21:28-32. ¿Qué mensaje general estaba enviando Jesús en esta parábola?

Un hijo tardó un poco, pero finalmente fue obediente, y el otro fingió ser obediente pero fue desobediente. Jesús dijo que aunque las prostitutas, los recaudadores de impuestos y los pecadores quizá tarden un rato en ser obedientes, están en mejor posición que la élite religiosa que finge ser obediente pero en realidad es desobediente.

Los líderes religiosos entendieron correctamente la parábola, pero ambas parábolas y el entendimiento de las mismas tenían el mismo significado: el reconocimiento verbal de la verdad no es suficiente, ya que tiene que venir de un corazón rendido. Sus corazones rehusaron aceptar la verdad y entrar así en el reino. Y, en un insulto a todo lo que ellos creían y valoraban, Jesús señaló que incluso aquellos a quienes ellos consideraban despreciables (cobradores de impuestos y prostitutas) serían bienvenidos en el reino.

¿Alguna vez te has sentido con dudas de obedecer algo que sabías que Dios te estaba llamando a hacer?

¿Cuál fue el resultado? ¿Qué te reveló esa experiencia sobre tu propio corazón?

Él continuó con otra parábola, subiendo el tono a medida que hablaba sobre arrendatarios malvados, violencia y muerte. La historia comenzaba con un dueño de una casa que estableció cuidadosamente una viña antes de irse del país y arrendarla a unos labradores. En el momento adecuado, el dueño envió a sus siervos para recoger su fruto, pero los arrendatarios recibieron a los siervos con brutalidad. Entonces el dueño envió más siervos, y la violencia continuó.

Lee Jeremías 20:1-2 y 1 Reyes 18:4. Compara el trato de los siervos con el trato de los profetas del Antiguo Testamento.

Jesús siguió contando la historia, anunciando el plan del dueño para enviar a su propio hijo a la viña. ¡Seguro que los arrendatarios no harían daño a su hijo! Cuando Jesús compartió lo que le hicieron al hijo, los líderes religiosos se enfurecieron por la conducta de los malvados arrendatarios. Jesús estableció el escenario de forma perfecta y los invitó a la historia preguntándoles cuál debería ser la respuesta del dueño. Es como si Jesús les preguntara sutilmente: "¿Cuál debería ser el castigo de ustedes?". Y, después de que ellos le dijeran lo que *debería* suceder, Él les dijo lo que *sucedería*.

Usando un diccionario, busca la definición de *piedra angular* y escríbela abajo.

¿Cuál es el significado de que Jesús citara Salmos 118:22-23 en el versículo 42?

Jesús usó este pasaje para simbolizar que Él es la piedra rechazada: el Hijo maltratado que recibirá la posición prominente de piedra angular. Una piedra angular es la piedra fundamental de un edificio; sin ella, todo se desmorona. Para muchas personas, la piedra angular del reino era y es una piedra de tropiezo, pues no pueden aceptar a Jesús como Rey. De hecho, si usamos la comparación de la parábola, echaron al hijo de la viña de su padre y lo mataron para su propio beneficio.

¿De qué maneras has "expulsado" tú a Jesús por tu propio egoísmo?

En lugar de arrepentirse, los líderes religiosos querían arrestar a Jesús, pero no lo hicieron por miedo a sus seguidores. Siguieron con incredulidad mientras maltrataban y malentendían al mismo Mesías Rey al que estaban esperando.

DÍA 5

MATEO 22

LEE MATEO 22

El capítulo de hoy está lleno de distintos grupos que cuestionan a Jesús, pero aunque hacían preguntas, verdaderamente no estaban buscando entender. Buscaban cualquier motivo para acusar a Jesús. Al final, querían matarlo, pero el Rey Jesús conocía sus motivaciones. Conocía los lugares más hondos de su corazón. Sin inmutarse por su malvado intento, Jesús continuó proclamando el mensaje de su reino al revés.

Repasa Mateo 22:1-14. Resume la historia en tus propias palabras.

¿Qué momentos clave observaste?

¿Qué punto intentaba explicar Jesús a los fariseos y los principales sacerdotes?

En esta parábola, la élite religiosa podría compararse a los huéspedes invitados, los cuales rehusaron la invitación directa del rey de asistir a la fiesta para honrar a su hijo. Los judíos siempre habían sido los primeros invitados a la fiesta: Dios estableció primero un pacto con Abraham (Génesis 12:1-3) y declaró que los israelitas (judíos) serían su pueblo. Pero Dios siempre supo que habría algunos entre los judíos que se resistirían a su reinado, así que la invitación se extendió también a los gentiles. Esto no tomó a Dios por sorpresa ni fue un cambio en su plan sino que *siempre* fue su plan (Isaías 56:3-8, Oseas 2:23). No solo esta idea *no* fue nueva en la Escritura sino que tampoco fue nueva en las enseñanzas de Jesús.

Lee Mateo 8:10-12. ¿Quién será echado en las tinieblas? ¿Quién se reclinará en la mesa con los patriarcas (Abraham, Isaac y Jacob)?

Aunque los líderes religiosos ciertamente conocían las Escrituras del Antiguo Testamento, odiaban a Jesús por sus palabras. Se oponían a la idea de que los extranjeros fueran incluidos, pero el mensaje de Jesús sobre su exclusión fue más de lo que pudieron soportar. Los fariseos tramaron tender una trampa a Jesús usando palabras halagadoras y una pregunta engañosa.

Repasa 22:15-17. Usa algún recurso de estudio bíblico para aprender más sobre los herodianos. ¿Cuál es el significado de que los herodianos y los fariseos se acercaran a Jesús con su pregunta? ¿Cuál es su motivación al hacer esta pregunta tan peculiar?

Desesperados por atrapar a Jesús haciendo algo mal, los fariseos se juntaron con otro partido: los herodianos. Estos dos grupos se oponían totalmente entre sí, tanto políticamente como religiosamente, pero se unieron para derribar a su enemigo común: el Rey Jesús. Los judíos odiaban dar su dinero a Roma, pero no en el mismo sentido que a la mayoría de las personas les desagrada tener que pagar impuestos. Su dinero de impuestos financiaba al mismo ejército que los gobernaba, oprimía e incluso mataba a sus familiares. Estos líderes pensaban que habían encontrado una manera astuta de atrapar a Jesús: si estaba a favor de pagar impuestos al César y a Roma, perdería el favor del pueblo cargado de impuestos, y si no lo estaba, los líderes podrían acusarlo de rebeldía contra Roma.

En tus propias palabras, resume el punto de la respuesta de Jesús a sus preguntas sobre los impuestos.

¿Cómo respondieron los líderes religiosos a su respuesta?

¿Cuál es tu respuesta a la autoridad cuando no estás de acuerdo?

Jesús sabía que su meta no era establecer un reino político opuesto al de César, así que les dijo a todos: "Paguen sus impuestos, obedezcan las leyes civiles y sométanse a las autoridades que Dios ha puesto sobre ustedes, aunque sean malvados y ustedes estén en el proceso de oponerse a ellos". Jesús era el ejemplo perfecto de honrar humildemente a Dios mientras cumplía la ley y se oponía a las autoridades malvadas. En nuestro esfuerzo por imitar a Cristo, nuestra respuesta debería ser como la suya.

Escribe los nombres de líderes en autoridad sobre ti (tus jefes, líderes de la iglesia, líderes del gobierno local y nacional, etc.). Después toma un momento para orar por ellos por nombre.

Cuando los fariseos y los herodianos hicieron el intento de atrapar a Jesús, los saduceos, que no creían en la resurrección, intentaron desacreditarlo. Su plan era hacer que la idea de la resurrección pareciera ridícula. Citaron la instrucción concreta de Dios para que una viuda se casara con su cuñado para protegerse y proveer descendientes para el difunto (Deuteronomio 25:5-10), pero eso hizo que la situación fuera todavía más compleja.

En tus propias palabras, resume el punto de la respuesta de Dios a su pregunta.

¿Cómo respondió la multitud a la respuesta de Jesús?

Jesús citó Éxodo 3:6 e hizo ver la realidad de que los pactos hechos con Abraham, Isaac y Jacob no terminaron cuando estos hombres murieron. Dios tiene el poder de resucitar a los patriarcas (y a todas las personas) para que disfruten de Él eternamente. Este fue un momento decisivo. Jesús los dejó mudos.

Tras oír que Jesús había silenciado a los saduceos, los fariseos quisieron volver a intentarlo. Un fariseo, que también era abogado, preguntó a Jesús qué mandamiento era el más importante. Jesús resumió las 613 leyes del Antiguo Testamento en tan solo dos: la vertical o las leyes "del hombre hacia Dios", y la horizontal o las leyes "de los hombres hacia los hombres". Jesús no *eliminó* ningún mandamiento de Dios, tan solo los resumió. El relato de Marcos 12 nos dice que el hombre se quedó impresionado y que Jesús le dijo: "No estás lejos del reino de Dios" (Marcos 12:34). Esto era cierto tanto en un sentido espiritual como literal, porque el mismo Rey del reino estaba hablándole.

¿Cuál de estos dos mandamientos te resulta más fácil de obedecer?

[ ] Amarás al Señor tu Dios con todo tu corazón y con toda tu alma y con toda tu mente.

[ ] Amarás a tu prójimo como a ti mismo.

Si tuvieras de dejar de obedecer el que te resulte más difícil, ¿cómo afectaría eso tanto a ti como al mundo que te rodea?

Resume 22:41-46 en tus propias palabras. ¿A qué persona(s) de la Trinidad se refiere el pasaje?

Jesús siguió con su sesión de preguntas y respuestas respondiendo a algunos que estaban perplejos de que el Mesías pudiera ser a la vez un descendiente de David y alguien anterior a David. Estos versículos nos dan unas lentes para entender lo que significa que Jesús, Dios el Hijo, esté fuera del tiempo, que haya existido *siempre*. Él existía antes que David, quien murió miles de años antes, incluso aunque Jesús tenía solo unos treinta y tres años de edad en el momento de esta conversación. Jesús también afirmó que este salmo lo escribió David mediante el Espíritu Santo. No te pierdas este momento tan importante: *¡Dios el Hijo confirmó que Dios el Espíritu autorizó las Escrituras por medio de manos humanas!*

A pesar de las malvadas intenciones de la multitud y la dificultad de las preguntas, el Rey Jesús tuvo la autoridad y la habilidad para responder. Él se mantuvo humilde mientras mostraba un gran conocimiento, y se mantuvo firme en su proclamación del mensaje del reino al revés. Él nos invita a esta postura también, ¡y siguiendo su guía es como prosperamos y encontramos paz! ¡Él está donde está el gozo!

¿Qué es lo que más te impactó del estudio de esta semana? ¿Por qué?

¿Qué aprendiste o recordaste acerca de Dios y su carácter esta semana?

DÍA 6

SALMO CORRESPONDIENTE Y ORACIÓN

LEE SALMOS 118

¿Qué correlación ves entre Salmos 118 y el estudio de esta semana sobre Jesús y su reino?

¿Qué porciones de este salmo captan más tu atención?

Termina haciendo esta oración en voz alta:

Padre,

Como dijo el salmista: "Tú eres mi Dios, y te doy gracias; Tú eres mi Dios, y yo te exalto". Te alabo por tu justicia y por abrirme las puertas del reino. Tu generosidad con los pecadores revela la ternura de tu corazón, ¡y te alabo por ello!

Soy un pecador y apelo a tu misericordia. A veces me he apoyado en mi incredulidad y me he rebelado. No te he buscado a ti o tus caminos. He sido tentado a hacer preguntas sin tener un corazón que entiende de verdad. He resistido tus mandamientos de amarte a ti y a los demás, y me he enfocado en amarme a mí mismo. Padre, me arrepiento de mis pecados, acudo a ti y te pido que limpies mi corazón.

Ayúdame, Espíritu. Concédeme un corazón que te ame por encima de todo lo demás. Concédeme un corazón que ame a mi prójimo e incluso a los que podría considerar mis enemigos. Concédeme fe en los espacios donde no entiendo tu voluntad o tus caminos. Equípame con la obediencia para seguirte.

Te rindo mi vida, Señor; en cada momento de mi día y cada decisión que tome, someto mi voluntad y mi camino a tu perfecta voluntad y camino.

Yo también te amo. Amén.

DÍA 7

DESCANSA, PONTE AL DÍA O PROFUNDIZA

RETO SEMANAL

El Día 1 leímos 1 Corintios 10:6-10 y Filipenses 2:14 y notamos las advertencias sobre la queja. La queja es *muy* perjudicial para nosotros, no solo como seguidores de Cristo sino también como humanos. De hecho, las investigaciones han descubierto que quejarse frecuentemente puede dañar el hipocampo, la región del cerebro responsable de la función cognitiva.[1]

La Escritura nos recuerda repetidamente que los mandamientos de Dios son por nuestro propio bien. Su mandato de no quejarnos ¡es por nuestro bien! De maneras que Él siempre ha sabido, pero que la ciencia ha descubierto recientemente: seguir sus mandamientos fomenta nuestra salud y prosperidad. ¡Obedecer a Dios en realidad fomenta la salud cerebral!

Esta semana, ten cuidado con tus palabras. Busca eliminar la queja. Pide a las personas con las que más tiempo pasas que te digan cuándo caes en ello, y sé rápido para arrepentirte. Busca llenar tus palabras de alabanza y gratitud. Haz una lista de gratitud si te resulta útil, ya sea en tu diario o en una pieza de arte que crees tú mismo a lo largo de la semana. ¡Sé todo lo creativo y colorido que quieras!

---

1. Stephanie Vozza, "Why Complaining May Be Dangerous to Your Health", Fast Company, 12 de enero de 2015, https://www.fastcompany.com /3040672 /why-complaining-may-be-dangerous-to-your-health.

SEMANA 8

Mateo 23-25:

Discurso del Rey

VERSÍCULO PARA MEMORIZAR

Porque los gentiles buscan ansiosamente todas estas cosas; que el Padre celestial sabe que ustedes necesitan todas estas cosas.

Mateo 6:32

LECTURA BÍBLICA DIARIA

Día 1: Mateo 23

Día 2: Mateo 24:1-28

Día 3: Mateo 24:29-51

Día 4: Mateo 25:1-30

Día 5: Mateo 25:31-46

Día 6: Salmos 50

Día 7: Para ponerte al día

Corresponde a los Días 309 y 311-312 de *La sinopsis de la Biblia*

RETO SEMANAL

Ver la página 202 para más información.

DÍA 1

MATEO 23

LEE MATEO 23

Escoge tres de las cinco palabras que mejor describan las actitudes y acciones de los escribas y fariseos sobre la base de lo que has visto en la Escritura.

Las palabras que hayas escogido quizá no dibujen un cuadro muy positivo de los líderes religiosos de Israel. En la lectura de hoy, Jesús añade los retoques finales a un trágico retrato de los fariseos y escribas.

Usando un diccionario bíblico, busca los términos *escriba* y *fariseo*. ¿Cuál era el papel y la importancia de cada uno en la sociedad judía?

En tus propias palabras, resume brevemente por qué Jesús y estos líderes religiosos experimentaban una tensión constante.

Jesús pronunció públicamente un ¡ay! (una acusación profética de conducta que conduce a la tragedia) sobre los escribas y fariseos. Pero, antes de profundizar, Jesús comenzó con algo que podría haberte sorprendido, y también a ellos, dado lo que había dicho hasta entonces sobre estos líderes. Llamó al pueblo a escuchar y obedecer lo que los fariseos enseñaban, porque los fariseos se sentaban en la cátedra de Moisés.

¿Por qué Jesús habló de la cátedra de Moisés? ¿Cuál es su relevancia, y por qué debería haber motivado a la gente a obedecer a los escribas y fariseos?

No era una comparación exacta, pero los escribas y fariseos ocupaban una posición de interpretar y hacer cumplir la ley, lo cual se asemejaba al papel de Moisés, ya que él fue quien primero llevó la ley de Dios al pueblo. Jesús distinguió entre la autoridad dada por Dios y las acciones que deshonran a Dios realizadas por aquellos que están en autoridad. La ley de Dios seguía siendo buena y perfecta, a pesar de que la vida de los fariseos ofrecía una visión distorsionada de ella. Jesús expuso la injusticia de estos líderes religiosos que oprimían al pueblo con pesadas cargas espirituales y actuaban por su deseo de ser vistos y alabados por los demás. Él llamó a sus discípulos a vivir de manera diferente.

Compara Mateo 23:4-12 y Filipenses 2:1-11. Toma nota de tus observaciones debajo.

Ejemplos a evitar:

Mateo 23:4 ____________________

Mateo 23:5-7 ____________________

Cómo llama Jesús a vivir a sus seguidores:

Mateo 23:8-10 ____________________

Mateo 23:11 ____________________

Mateo 23:12 ____________________

Ejemplo a imitar:

Filipenses 2:4-7 ______________________________

Filipenses 2:8 ______________________________

Jesús era el ejemplo perfecto de todo lo que predicaba. Hablaba a las multitudes y en contra de los fariseos desde un lugar de autoridad como Rey y debido a su experiencia vivida como siervo sacrificial.

Jesús pronunció siete ayes a los escribas y fariseos, ofreciendo una lista concreta de cómo se habían desviado e influenciado a otros en el proceso.

Lee los ayes que Jesús pronunció sobre los escribas y fariseos, y resume las acciones y actitudes por las que Jesús los condenó.

1. ______________________________

2. ______________________________

3. ______________________________

4. ______________________________

5. ______________________________

6. ______________________________

7. ______________________________

¿Qué temas comunes observas?

Jesús les dijo a los escribas y fariseos que les esperaba tristeza porque actuaban como barreras funcionales, impidiendo que la gente entrara en el reino mientras ellos mismos tampoco entraban. Se centraban en minucias técnicas y enfatizaban cosas no esenciales, mientras minimizaban lo que realmente importaba para el corazón de Dios. A pesar de sus intentos de parecer externamente limpios, Jesús les dijo que por dentro estaban corrompidos. Los denunció por celebrar a los profetas y hombres justos que sus antepasados mataron, como si ellos no estuvieran siguiendo los pasos de sus antecesores. Al señalar esto, aludió al papel que ellos desempeñarían en su inminente muerte.

En la NBLA la cabecera de 23:37-39 es "Lamentación sobre Jerusalén". En tus propias palabras, describe lo que significa lamentación. **Lee Salmos 35:13-14, Jeremías 14:1-3 y Mateo 2:16-18 para ayudarte a responder.**

El último ay de Jesús dio paso a su lamento. Al reflexionar sobre el estado espiritual de Jerusalén, experimentó un dolor profundo en el alma. Mientras Él quería atraerlos a su reino, ellos querían verlo muerto. Dado todo lo que Jesús dijo con dureza hacia los líderes religiosos, podríamos esperar que tuviera una actitud fría e insensible hacia ellos, pero en cambio vemos a un Rey cuyo corazón sigue siendo tierno hacia aquellos que no están dispuestos a volverse a Él.

¿Cómo respondes a las personas en tu vida que se oponen a Dios? ¿Eres cínico? ¿Indiferente? ¿Sientes dolor?

Si la actitud de tu corazón no está alineada con el Rey y los valores de su reino, escribe una oración a continuación pidiéndole que te dé su corazón por aquellos que están fuera del reino.

DÍA 2

MATEO 24:1-28

LEE MATEO 24:1-28

Con pensamientos sobre Jerusalén probablemente aún en mente, Jesús y sus discípulos salieron del templo y se dirigieron al Monte de los Olivos, en las afueras de las puertas de la ciudad, donde Él ofreció algunos detalles intensos sobre lo que estaba por llegar. Mientras los discípulos admiraban la belleza de los edificios, Jesús les anunció que el templo se derrumbaría en un futuro no muy lejano. El templo era un enorme complejo construido con piedras macizas, la más grande pesaba más de cuatrocientos cincuenta mil kilos. No era una estructura frágil o insignificante, y sin embargo, menos de cuarenta años después el ejército romano derribó el templo, cumpliendo las palabras de Jesús.

Ya sea que estuvieran sorprendidos, confundidos o incrédulos, los discípulos seguramente habrían tenido alguna reacción ante esta información. El templo era un elemento central de la vida religiosa y cultural judía, pero Jesús pareció dar la noticia como si no fuera gran cosa.

Lee Apocalipsis 21:22. ¿Qué sabía Jesús sobre el futuro de la adoración de Israel que le permitía estar tan calmado con respecto a la destrucción del templo?

Como edificio físico, siempre fue la intención que el templo fuera temporal. Dios lo había instituido con fecha de caducidad. Nunca tuvo la intención de ser su hogar permanente, así que su destrucción era una parte necesaria para inaugurar por completo su reino inconmovible y eterno.

Cuando llegaron a su destino, los discípulos comenzaron a acribillar a Jesús con preguntas: *¿Cuándo se iba a producir esta destrucción? Él aludió a que se iría, pero ¿cuándo iba a regresar? ¿Iba a decirles cuándo sería el fin del mundo?*

Repasa la respuesta de Jesús a los discípulos en 24:3-28. Busca todos los usos de las palabras *cuando* y *entonces*.

¿Qué dijo Jesús que de seguro sucedería?

¿Repitió o enfatizó algo? Si es así, ¿qué?

¿Dio Jesús algún tiempo específico de cuándo ocurriría algo?

En lugar de decirles que marcaran una fecha en sus calendarios, Jesús explicó lo que deberían esperar que ocurriera. Acontecimientos terribles comenzarían a intensificarse y pensarían que era el fin, pero eso sería solo el principio de la prueba.

Les recordó acerca de la abominación desoladora, de la que había profetizado Daniel (Daniel 9:27, 11:31, 12:11). La palabra griega para *abominación (bdeygma)* significa algo detestable o inmundo, y se usaba por lo general en el contexto de la idolatría. Jesús estaba señalando hacia un acto ofensivo y triste de idolatría que sucedería en el lugar santo de Dios. Ese acontecimiento llevaría a la devastación y destrucción.

En el relato, Mateo insertó la frase "el que lea que entienda". Y, hasta la fecha, los lectores siguen intentando entender esta profecía. Algunos eruditos piensan que este evento ya ha sucedido (después de que Jesús dijo estas palabras pero anterior al tiempo presente), mientras que otros creen que su cumplimiento todavía no se ha producido. En cualquiera de los casos, la información e instrucción que dejó Jesús a sus seguidores sigue siendo la misma.

Repasa 24:3-28. Escribe cada instrucción dirigida a los discípulos. Si Jesús da un "porqué", anótalo también.

Jesús dijo que el fin de los tiempos sería el momento más difícil que el mundo haya visto o vaya a ver. No suavizó la gravedad de la situación, pero tampoco parece que se quedara atascado en los horribles acontecimientos que sucederían. De modo muy parecido a nosotros, los discípulos probablemente querían más detalles de los que Jesús reveló. Tal vez comenzaron a preocuparse más por las cosas hipotéticas, pero Jesús no quería que se preocuparan así.

Hay dos maneras principales en las que una persona se puede preocupar. Estar "preocupado *por*" implica inclinarse hacia la preocupación o el miedo, mientras que estar "preocupado *con*" significa estar involucrado, comprometido y prestar atención a algo.

Con estas definiciones y las enseñanzas y prioridades de Jesús en mente, ¿de qué estaba Jesús instruyendo a Sus discípulos a estar "preocupados con"?

¿De qué los dirigió a alejarse de estar «preocupados por»?

¿Qué podría significar esto para un seguidor de Jesús hoy? ¿Qué paralelismos puedes trazar con las cosas con las que Dios podría desear que te ocupes más y las cosas *por* las que quiere que te preocupes menos en tu propia vida?

Aunque Jesús hablaba de los días oscuros que se avecinaban, entretejió claros destellos de luz en sus palabras. A pesar de las dificultades que llevarían a muchos a ser engañados o a apartarse, habría personas que perseverarían en la fe. Las buenas nuevas de salvación no se quedarían en un ámbito local o regional; de hecho, se difundirían por todo el mundo, tal como los profetas de Dios habían anunciado en todo el Antiguo Testamento. Y Él aseguró que los tiempos difíciles pasarían y que regresaría por sus elegidos, ¡aquellos que perseverarían por su poder hasta el fin!

DÍA 3

MATEO 24:29-51

LEE MATEO 24:29-51

Repasa 24:29. ¿Crees que este versículo señala a un acontecimiento literal o simbólico? ¿Qué crees que significa?

Las señales cósmicas que Jesús mencionó en la lectura de hoy podrían ser figuradas, literales o ambas cosas. Pero, en cualquier caso, estaba enfatizando que habría grandes disturbios en la vida y el orden cotidianos que serían imposibles de ignorar y darían paso a su gloriosa venida. El Hijo del Hombre llevaría a cabo su tan ansiado regreso, montando en las nubes, acompañado de ángeles y al sonido de una trompeta. Sus ángeles serían enviados a los confines de la tierra para reunir a su pueblo, aquellos cuyas vidas estaban marcadas por una fe genuina.

Los siguientes versículos están todos ellos conectados con las palabras de Jesús en 24:30-31. **Lee cada pasaje,** nota la conexión y escribe cualquier cosa que enfatice o añada algo a tu comprensión.

Zacarías 12:10-14	
Daniel 7:13-14	
Apocalipsis 1:7	

Aunque Jesús no reveló los detalles concretos sobre cuándo regresaría exactamente, información que ni siquiera Él conocía, les dio a los discípulos una buena idea de cómo sería y cómo deberían esperar bien sus seguidores.

Jesús dijo que así como los brotes en las ramas de la higuera eran una señal de la naturaleza de que el verano estaba cerca, todos los eventos que describió serían el modo en que sus seguidores podrían discernir que el Hijo del Hombre estaba en camino. Más que algo que anticipar o de lo que ser conscientes, Jesús dejó claro que su segunda venida era algo para lo cual debían prepararse.

¿Qué crees que conlleva prepararse para su venida?

Para seguir pintando el cuadro, Jesús hizo referencia a los días de Noé y el diluvio, el cual llegó de forma inesperada para la mayoría. Como la naturaleza repentina de ese acontecimiento transformador, la gente viviría como de costumbre, comería, se casaría y estaría trabajando cuando Él regrese. Algunas personas se reunirían con Él, y otras tendrían que enfrentar la dura realidad contraria. A la luz de todo esto, el mandato de Jesús fue esperar lo inesperado, estar despierto y siempre preparado.

Lee 1 Tesalonicenses 5:1-11. ¿Qué similitudes ves entre este pasaje y lo que Jesús les dijo a sus discípulos en Mateo 24 acerca de su regreso y el fin de los tiempos?

En 1 Tesalonicenses 5:1-11, ¿qué dice el escritor (Pablo) sobre quiénes son sus lectores y quiénes no?

¿Qué son llamados a hacer y no hacer a la luz de esas realidades?

Está claro que Jesús no quería que sus discípulos no entendieran el corazón de lo que significa esperar bien, porque en lugar de dejar el tema del que ya habían estado hablando una cantidad de tiempo razonable, Él profundizó todavía más mediante una breve parábola. Les mostró el marcado contraste entre la vida de un siervo fiel y uno malvado, incluyendo sus acciones y los resultados finales.

Aunque vivimos en un tiempo y una cultura distintos, el llamado de Jesús a estar despiertos y preparados (24:42-44) es aplicable a todo el que viva antes de su regreso. ¿Cómo puedes vivir como un siervo sabio y fiel esperando a tu Amo?

Jesús nunca malgastó tiempo ni palabras; en cada momento que pasó con las multitudes o con sus discípulos, iluminó significativamente verdades espirituales: demostró justicia, reveló su autoridad, advirtió sobre el juicio venidero, llamó al arrepentimiento y señaló a la gente el reino por venir. Y aunque los discípulos quizá no lo sabían en ese momento, Jesús sabía que la cuenta atrás para su crucifixión estaba cerca de llegar a cero, lo que hacía que cada frase dicha y cada segundo con ellos fuera especialmente significativo.

Jesús estaba enfocado en comunicar la verdad que conduciría a la vida eterna. Su máxima prioridad era preparar a las personas para heredar su reino, y nada podía desviarlo. Jesús *regresará* con poder y gloria, y para todos aquellos que confían en Él (pasado, presente y futuro) ¡habrá valido la pena lo que hayan tenido que soportar durante la espera!

DÍA 4

MATEO 25:1-30

LEE MATEO 25:1-30

En la lectura de hoy, Jesús presentó a sus discípulos las mismas cosas para reflexionar, servidas en dos platos diferentes. Su enfoque se mantuvo en la venida del reino mientras regresaba a las parábolas como su herramienta de enseñanza preferida. Las parábolas de hoy comparten el tema de estar listos para su regreso. Como era la última semana de su vida antes de su crucifixión, Jesús quería dejar bien claro este mensaje.

Su primera lección nos presentó a diez vírgenes con lámparas. Las vírgenes de los tiempos antiguos eran similares a las damas de honor de la actualidad. Las bodas judías tradicionales tenían tres partes: compromiso, desposorio y ceremonia de matrimonio. La pareja tenía que soportar un largo período de espera entre el desposorio y la ceremonia de matrimonio.

En esta parábola, las damas de honor debían ir a encontrarse con el novio, pero cuando este tardó más de lo esperado se quedaron dormidas. Las despertaron repentinamente unos gritos a medianoche que anunciaban su llegada. De las diez, la mitad fueron llamadas insensatas y la otra mitad prudentes, según si estaban preparadas o no.

¿Qué tenían en común las diez damas de honor?

En tus propias palabras, describe cómo se desarrolló la parábola para las damas de honor insensatas.

Cuando llegó el momento de la fiesta matrimonial, solo las cinco mujeres sabias estaban presentes. Estuvieron listas cuando llegó el novio, y entraron en la fiesta con él como miembros de su fiesta de bodas. Fueron las únicas a las que el novio reconoció. Las damas de honor insensatas que no se prepararon se quedaron fuera de la celebración.

Jesús estaba enfatizando que quienes estarán con Él en su reino no son los que solo esperan su venida sino los que se preparan para Él sin importar cuándo llegue.

La parábola de los talentos envía un mensaje similar. En el antiguo Israel, un talento era un tipo de moneda, no una habilidad. Así que, para dejarlo claro, llamaremos a esta parábola la parábola de los dólares. Jesús habló acerca de un amo que se iba mucho tiempo de viaje y confió su dinero a tres de sus siervos en base a sus habilidades individuales. El amo esperaba un retorno en la inversión de cada siervo.

Llena la tabla de abajo.

	Siervo con $1	Siervo con $2	Siervo con $5
¿Qué hace mientras el amo está fuera?			
¿Cómo responde el amo cuando llega?			
¿Qué recibe del amo?			

Repasa 25:24. ¿Cómo describió al amo el siervo con un dólar?

Repasa 25:25. ¿Cómo se sintió el siervo con un dólar debido a lo que pensaba de su amo?

¿A participar de qué invitó el amo a los siervos que recibieron dos y cinco dólares?

El amo castigó severamente al siervo que no confió en su corazón, y lo expulsó. El amo nunca afirmó que su carácter era lo que el siervo temía; le planteó una pregunta al respecto. Su verdadero carácter se reveló en cómo respondió a los otros dos siervos, quienes confiaron en su corazón. Los recompensó generosamente ¡y los invitó a compartir de su abundancia y alegría!

Describe alguna ocasión en la que temiste al Amo en lugar de confiar en el gozo del servicio fiel.

En estas parábolas, Jesús dejó claro que el juicio será parte de su regreso. Deberíamos estar listos para ser evaluados.

Lee Romanos 3:23-24, Romanos 3:28, 1 Corintios 1:30-31, Gálatas 2:15-16 y Efesios 2:8-9. ¿En base a qué norma seremos evaluados cuando Cristo regrese?

Describe cómo te hace sentir eso. ¿Por qué?

Los que estamos en Cristo no tenemos por qué temer su juicio porque —aunque la norma por la que seremos evaluados es la justicia perfecta— Él ha logrado la justicia perfecta por nosotros. Nos ha entregado su justicia y ha tomado nuestro pecado y vergüenza. ¡Gloria a Cristo, porque nunca tenemos que temer no alcanzar su norma si confiamos en sus obras en lugar de las nuestras!

DÍA 5

MATEO 25:31-46

LEE MATEO 25:31-46

El regreso de Jesús será un acontecimiento grande y glorioso marcado por el gozo de algunos y el pesar de otros. El Hijo del Hombre estará sentado en su trono, rodeado de ángeles que cantarán sus alabanzas eternamente. Está dispuesto a pronunciar juicio sobre todas las naciones reunidas delante de su trono.

Sin embargo, antes de que diga una sola palabra de recompensa o castigo, comenzará la obra de separación, dividiendo a los que heredarán su reino eterno de los que experimentarán el castigo eterno. El Rey pondrá a las ovejas (creyentes) a su derecha y a los cabritos (no creyentes) a su izquierda. Esta no fue la primera vez que Jesús se describió a sí mismo usando la imagen de un pastor.

Lee Mateo 9:36 y Salmos 23. ¿Qué aspectos de Jesús como Pastor Rey te impresionan en cuanto a su relación con el juicio final?

El Rey se dirigió primero a las ovejas. En pocas palabras, habló mucho sobre la belleza de la recompensa que recibirán y la naturaleza de la salvación. La

Escritura usa varios términos para referirse a estas ovejas, incluyendo hijos, herederos y siervos fieles.

Escribe a continuación 25:34. Rodea con un círculo al que está dando la bendición.

¿Cuándo se preparó esta bendición?

Busca Efesios 1:3. ¿Quién está realizando la bendición? ¿Quién es bendecido? ¿A través de quién viene la bendición?

Busca Romanos 8:16-17. ¿Quién da testimonio de la herencia de los hijos de Dios?

La Escritura apunta a un plan y un propósito desde antes de la fundación del mundo. En el plan eterno de salvación, las tres personas de la Trinidad trabajan juntas como un equipo, pero cada persona desempeña un papel distinto a la hora de llevar a cabo nuestra salvación y otorgarnos nuestra herencia.

¿Qué enumera el Rey como evidencia de que las ovejas justas son justas?

¿Qué enumera el Rey como evidencia de que los cabritos injustos son injustos?

Jesús dijo que nuestras acciones hacia otros, especialmente los que están en una situación de vulnerabilidad, reflejan nuestro corazón hacia Él.

¿Qué revela esto acerca del Rey?

Tanto los justos como los injustos se sorprendieron cuando el Rey señaló sus acciones, casi como si estuvieran viviendo con el piloto automático, haciendo lo que era natural para su corazón. Nuestro corazón se revela en nuestras acciones, y Dios ve nuestras motivaciones, pensamientos e intenciones incluso antes de que se conviertan en acciones (Salmos 139:1-4). Él recompensa a aquellos cuya motivación no es ser vistos, sino por su corazón oculto (Mateo 6:1-4).

Lee Oseas 6:6, Salmos 51:16-17 y Amós 5:21-24. Enumera las cosas que Dios busca de su pueblo.

Incluso en el Antiguo Testamento vemos el mismo tema. Lo que Jesús reveló sobre el reino siempre ha sido verdad. Las reglas no han cambiado. El Rey siempre ha buscado el corazón de su pueblo, y en el juicio final el Rey revelará el corazón de toda la humanidad. Al terminar esta semana, seríamos sabios si examináramos nuestro corazón para ver si estamos en la fe.

Lee los siguientes versículos y escribe cualquier cosa que capte tu atención.

2 Corintios 13:5 ______________________

Juan 20:31 ______________________

1 Juan 5:12 ______________________

Romanos 8:16-17 ______________________

La Escritura dice que deberíamos examinarnos para ver si estamos en la fe (2 Corintios 13:5). Un examen implica una respuesta. Si no estás seguro de la respuesta, examina tu corazón y las Escrituras y pídele a Dios que te dé claridad. Esta es una invitación a una mayor fe, libertad y gozo, así como a un reino eterno. El Rey anhela que estés allí con Él, donde su presencia es la herencia más grande de todas, ¡porque Él está donde está el gozo!

¿Qué es lo que más te impactó del estudio de esta semana? ¿Por qué?

¿Qué aprendiste o recordaste acerca de Dios y su carácter esta semana?

DÍA 6

SALMO CORRESPONDIENTE Y ORACIÓN

LEE SALMOS 50

¿Qué correlación ves entre Salmos 50 y el estudio de esta semana sobre Jesús y su reino?

¿Qué porciones de este salmo captan más tu atención?

Termina haciendo esta oración en voz alta:

Padre,

Te alabo por tu justicia. Tú eres perfecto y justo en todos tus caminos. Aunque puede dar miedo comprender que nunca alcanzaré tu norma, estoy eternamente agradecido de que tú has provisto un camino para que se me concediera la justicia sin esfuerzo por mi parte. Jesús, gracias por vivir una vida perfecta y cambiarla por mi pecado. Debido a que se me asignó tu justicia, me puedo acercar al Padre con confianza, sabiendo que soy su hijo ¡y que soy bienvenido con celebración en su reino eterno de gozo!

Padre, he pecado y apelo a tu misericordia. Confieso que a veces te he visto erróneamente. Como el siervo con un dólar, no he confiado en tu corazón, lo cual me condujo a la autoprotección. He intentado ganarme mi propia justicia. Como los escribas y fariseos, he querido que me vean y respeten por mis acciones. He querido impresionarte a ti y a los demás. He puesto el enfoque en cualquier cosa que yo pueda hacer bien, pero hay muchas áreas en las que sigo fallando. E incluso debajo de mis buenas acciones, mi corazón sigue mirando hacia adentro. He sido egoístamente ambicioso en lugar de rendirme a la justicia de Cristo. Me arrepiento de mis pecados y acudo a ti, y te pido que limpies mi corazón.

Ayúdame a encontrar descanso, verdadero descanso, al saber que Jesús ha logrado todo lo que tú pides de mí. Ayúdame a verte correctamente. Concédeme sabiduría para saber cómo prepararme bien, como las vírgenes y los siervos sensatos. Endereza mi corazón en esos lugares en los que he tenido miedo del regreso de tu Hijo Jesús, no he tenido en cuenta sus palabras, o donde he vivido mi vida de modo insensato como si Él nunca fuera a regresar. ¡Concédeme un gran deseo por su regreso!

Te rindo mi vida, Señor; en cada momento de mi día y en cada decisión que tome, someto mi voluntad y mi camino a tu perfecta voluntad y camino.

Yo también te amo. Amén.

DÍA 7

DESCANSA, PONTE AL DÍA O PROFUNDIZA

RETO SEMANAL

En Mateo 23:5–7 Jesús habló en contra de los escribas y fariseos por estar motivados por el orgullo y el elogio, y advirtió sobre no seguir sus pasos. Aunque hoy no vivimos entre fariseos, este sigue siendo un asunto relevante. Como cristianos, podemos caer fácilmente en las mismas actitudes y acciones si no tenemos cuidado. Podemos hacer cosas espirituales por atención, aplausos o estatus, en lugar de simplemente servir a Dios y amar a los demás desde un corazón de gratitud y alegría.

¿Cómo podemos enfrentar esta tentación de vivir como fariseos? Jesús presentó una solución en Mateo 23:8–11. Cuando dejamos de buscar gloria, le damos a Dios la alabanza que le corresponde y somos humildes, de ese modo vamos caminando por la senda que Jesús estableció.

Esta semana, nuestro reto es poner en práctica la sabiduría de Mateo 23:8–11 a diario. Durante el transcurso de esta semana, pídele a Dios que te haga consciente de cualquier área en la que estés actuando por un deseo de reconocimiento o admiración.

Cada vez que sientas que tu corazón se inclina hacia ti mismo, confiésalo a Dios. Entonces, haz una oración con las palabras de Salmos 115:1: "No a nosotros, Señor, no a nosotros, sino a tu nombre da gloria, por tu misericordia, por tu fidelidad". Escribe estas palabras en una nota en tu teléfono o en una tarjeta que puedas mantener en un lugar donde la verás con regularidad. Esto te servirá como recordatorio de que Él es un motivador mejor y más adecuado que el interés egoísta.

El acto de arrojar luz sobre las motivaciones incorrectas y dirigir tu atención hacia el Señor con reverencia, arrepentimiento y adoración ¡te ayudará a reconfigurar tu corazón y tu mente!

VERSÍCULO PARA MEMORIZAR

Pero busquen primero su reino y su justicia, y todas estas cosas les serán añadidas.

Mateo 6:33

SEMANA 9

Mateo 26:

Traición del Rey

LECTURA BÍBLICA DIARIA

Día 1: Mateo 26:1-16

Día 2: Mateo 26:17-29

Día 3: Mateo 26:30-46

Día 4: Mateo 26:47-68

Día 5: Mateo 26:69-75

Día 6: Salmos 55

Día 7: Para ponerte al día

Corresponde al Día 313 de *La sinopsis de la Biblia*

RETO SEMANAL

Ver la página 227 para más información.

DÍA 1

MATEO 26:1-16

LEE MATEO 26:1-16

Repasa 26:1-2. ¿Cuáles son algunos de los detalles concretos que Jesús reveló sobre su muerte?

Lee Juan 18:4. ¿Cuánto sabía Jesús sobre su muerte antes de que sucediera?

Lee Apocalipsis 13:8. ¿Desde cuándo se había planeado la muerte de Jesús? Dada esa cronología, ¿quién hizo el plan original para la muerte de Jesús?

En la lectura de hoy, Jesús lanzó una bomba a sus discípulos, diciéndoles la línea de tiempo exacta y la manera de su muerte. De hecho las autoridades ya estaban tramando eso, lo cual les hacía alinearse con el plan que Dios tenía desde antes de la fundación de la tierra.

Lee Daniel 2:21, Romanos 13:1 y Juan 19:11. ¿A quién se le debería atribuir el establecimiento de los gobernantes responsables de la muerte de Jesús?

Los sumos sacerdotes y los ancianos puede que fueran los gobernantes de turno, pero Dios es quien está en el trono más alto eternamente. Las personas a cargo de los reinos terrenales siguen estando bajo la autoridad de su reino eterno, donde Él reina soberanamente y está llevando a cabo su plan amoroso para redimir a su pueblo y restaurar la relación rota con ellos. Estos gobernantes, sin saberlo, estaban participando en el plan de Dios para su gloria, la alabanza de Cristo ¡y nuestra libertad y alegría!

Mientras Jesús estaba en Jerusalén para la fiesta, fue a una cena organizada por Simón el leproso en Betania, un pueblo justo a las afueras de las murallas de la ciudad.

Busca los versículos siguientes y enumera a los asistentes conocidos a la cena.

Mateo 26:6 ______________________________

Mateo 26:8 ______________________________

Juan 12:2 ______________________________

Juan 12:3 ______________________________

Juan 12:4 ______________________________

¿Qué revela sobre Jesús que empleara una parte de sus horas finales antes de su muerte cenando con esta compañía de personas: un leproso, mujeres y el hombre que sabía que lo traicionaría?

Piensa en las personas con las que te juntas. ¿Hay personas en tu círculo que son diferentes a ti o que sería "arriesgado" pasar tiempo con ellas? ¿Cómo puedes discernir si es sabio o necio pasar tiempo con una persona así?

Por el relato de Juan, sabemos que María es la persona que ungió a Jesús (Juan 12:3) usando un aceite hecho de nardo puro. Este tipo de aceite se usaba con mayor frecuencia para actos de devoción, y era increíblemente caro. Judas objetó que María usara dicho aceite (Juan 12:4–7), pero Jesús respondió con compasión hacia ella. Dijo que esta historia sería contada en todo el mundo y aquí estamos, dos mil años después, todavía hablando de ello. Qué hermoso es que, en medio de esta historia sobre sus últimos días, Jesús se tomara el tiempo para resaltar la ofrenda de una mujer, alguien que tenía poco valor en esa cultura. Siempre ha sido propio de Jesús ver a los menores, a los marginados, y recordarles su valor ante Dios (10:31). Entonces, Él indicó claramente una vez más que estaba a punto de morir. Dijo que María lo estaba preparando para su entierro.

Judas sabía que los gobernantes querían arrestar a Jesús, así que aprovechó la oportunidad para ganar treinta piezas de plata entregándolo. La Pascua se acercaba, y los gobernantes acordaron no arrestar a Jesús durante la fiesta porque habría causado demasiados problemas.

Lee Juan 12:1-7. Según lo que dice Juan sobre el carácter de Judas, ¿de qué forma el hecho de que María usara un aceite muy caro habría jugado un papel importante en la decisión de Judas de traicionar a Jesús?

En las últimas horas antes de su muerte, Jesús recibió una adoración extravagante y también una profunda traición. Al margen del rango de emociones que debió experimentar, mantuvo a ambos grupos de personas cerca de Él mientras se dirigía con decisión hacia el cumplimiento del plan eterno del Padre.

MATEO 26:17-29

LEE MATEO 26:17-29

Jesús indicó a sus discípulos cómo planificar la comida que iban a tener juntos. En la mesa, anunció que había un traidor entre ellos. Se quedaron muy consternados, cada uno preguntándose si sería él. Todos sabían que tenían la capacidad de traicionar a Jesús.

Lee 26:22-25. ¿De qué forma la pregunta de Judas es distinta a la de los demás apóstoles? ¿Qué importancia tiene esto?

Los demás discípulos preguntaron: "¿Acaso soy yo, Señor?", pero Judas hizo una pregunta distinta. Preguntó: "¿Acaso soy yo, Rabí?". Llamó a Jesús "maestro". Jesús afirmó que sí, que Judas era quien le traicionaría. Pero a Judas no le asombró esta noticia, pues ya tenía la plata en su posesión.

Como ocurre con la mayoría de las cosas, hay agentes pasivos y agentes activos involucrados en hacer que suceda la voluntad de Dios. Judas fue el agente activo en esta historia en particular.

¿Qué papel desempeñaste tú en la muerte de Cristo? ¿Por qué es importante reconocer nuestro papel?

Todos somos agentes pasivos en la muerte de Cristo. En cuanto a Judas, el versículo 24 dice que hubiera sido mejor para él no haber nacido, pero su nacimiento era una parte necesaria del plan de redención de Dios. Aunque podemos ser tentados a apenarnos por Judas, es importante recordar que recibió exactamente lo que merecía, lo que *todos* merecemos, de hecho. Jesús, por otro lado, *no* recibió lo que merecía. Él llevó el castigo que nosotros merecíamos por nuestro pecado y rebeldía.

Tras su breve conversación con Judas, Jesús sirvió lo que llamamos la cena del Señor o la Comunión o Eucaristía, que significa "dar gracias", y haciendo esto les dio una acción física que les conectaba con una realidad espiritual, algo parecido al bautismo. Este sacramento nos ayuda a recordar cómo su cuerpo fue partido y su sangre vertida por muchas personas. Jesús invitó a todos los discípulos a participar, incluso a Judas. Tal vez una razón por la que Judas fue incluido fue para demostrar que la participación en la Comunión no es salvífica.

¿Con qué frecuencia tú o tu iglesia participan de este sacramento? Describe cómo es el proceso para ti espiritualmente y emocionalmente.

Lee 26:26-29. ¿Qué elementos se mencionan como parte de la cena de Pascua que comieron Jesús y sus discípulos?

Éxodo 12:1-28 cuenta la historia de cómo Dios estableció la Pascua. Lee todo el pasaje si tienes tiempo. **Busca Éxodo 12:15.** ¿Qué cosas se supone que debían evitar durante esta fiesta? ¿Cuál es el castigo por comer de ello?

Usando un diccionario de griego, busca la palabra para *pan* en Mateo 26:17 y escribe lo que encuentres.

Usando un diccionario de griego, busca la palabra pan en Mateo 26:26 y escribe lo que encuentres.

Es muy significativo que los únicos elementos mencionados en la Última Cena sean el pan y el vino. La fiesta de la Pascua consistía en varios elementos, de los cuales el más crucial era el cordero pascual. Comerlo era un mandamiento; entonces, ¿por qué estaba ausente? También es significativo que la Escritura dice que Jesús y sus discípulos estaban comiendo pan *con levadura* (griego: *artos*), que estaba prohibido durante la Fiesta de los Panes sin levadura (griego: *azymos*). ¿Dónde estaba el pan *sin levadura* que la ley requiere?

Aquí hay una teoría sobre por qué esos dos aspectos cruciales de una fiesta de Pascua parecen estar ausentes. La Fiesta de los Panes sin levadura era normalmente una celebración de una semana, pero algunos estudiosos dicen que, en la época de Jesús, en realidad era una celebración de ocho días, con el día adicional añadido antes del inicio de la semana. Durante los siete días del evento real, a los judíos no se les permitía comer nada que tuviera levadura, por lo que añadir un "día cero" al inicio les daba la oportunidad de terminar con toda la levadura existente en sus hogares antes de que comenzara formalmente el evento de siete días.

Si eso es cierto, entonces cuando Jesús y sus discípulos realizaban lo que típicamente hemos pensado como *la* fiesta de la Pascua, podría haber sido solo *una* fiesta de Pascua, donde están, en cierto modo, "limpiando el refrigerador". Es su última fiesta con levadura antes de que comience la fiesta sin levadura. Y eso explicaría por qué tampoco comieron cordero. Y sería apropiado, porque cuando Jesús fue sacrificado al día siguiente antes de que comenzara la fiesta, Él se convirtió en *el* Cordero pascual (1 Corintios 5:7, Apocalipsis 5:9). Estudiaremos este evento más a fondo la próxima semana, pero por ahora, ¡alabemos a Jesús por cubrir nuestros pecados!

DÍA 3

MATEO 26:30-46

LEE MATEO 26:30-46

Tras haber comido el pan y bebido el vino de la Última Cena, Jesús y sus discípulos cantaron un himno y después partieron hacia el Monte de los Olivos, que es una colina a poca distancia en las afueras de la puerta Oriental de los muros de la ciudad de Jerusalén. Jesús acababa de anunciar la traición de Judas, pero de repente tuvo otra ronda de malas noticias para sus seguidores: *todos* ellos se apartarían esa noche por causa de Él.

Repasa 26:31. Busca el término apartarse en un diccionario de griego y escribe lo que encuentres.

En la cena, solo una hora antes aproximadamente, todos habían preguntado si serían ellos quienes lo traicionarían, pero de algún modo parecieron asombrados al oírle decir que le negarían. Jesús también le dijo a Pedro que le negaría tres veces. Pedro se desalentó y dijo que nunca negaría a Jesús; de hecho, ¡estaría dispuesto incluso a morir con Él! Los otros discípulos que estaban allí se hicieron eco de sus palabras (podemos deducir que Judas ya no estaba entre los discípulos en ese momento, porque apareció después con los soldados que llegaban para arrestar a Jesús).

Al pie del Monte de los Olivos había un jardín lleno de olivares donde las aceitunas se prensaban para extraer aceite. De hecho, sigue estando ahí en la actualidad.

Repasa 26:36. Busca la palabra *Getsemaní* en un diccionario de griego y escribe lo que encuentres.

Este era el lugar donde se aplastaban las olivas para extraer lo más valioso de ellas; por lo tanto, es apropiado que fuera también el lugar donde Jesús experimentó el peso aplastante de su muerte inminente, en la que ofrecería a la humanidad el regalo más valioso que podríamos recibir.

Mientras Jesús oraba en el huerto, invitó a algunos de sus amigos más cercanos en su tristeza. Pidió a Santiago, Juan e incluso a Pedro, al que acababa de identificar como el que pronto le negaría, a quedarse con Él en el huerto mientras oraba. Se retiró un poco más lejos y le preguntó al Padre si había otra forma de poder llevar a cabo su plan, aunque ya sabía que la respuesta era no.

Lee Hebreos 9:22 y 10:1-10. ¿Por qué el viejo sistema de sacrificios (el que Dios estableció en el Antiguo Testamento) es insuficiente?

Los sacrificios de animales se ofrecían repetidamente y siempre estaban destinados a ser temporales (Hebreos 10:1–4). Dios siempre había estado señalando hacia el sacrificio *perfecto y final*. Mientras que un hombre imperfecto podía morir por sus propios pecados, ofreciendo un intercambio uno a uno, solo un hombre perfecto podía morir por los pecados de muchos. La única manera en que la humanidad pecadora podía reconciliarse con un Dios santo era a través de la muerte de un hombre perfecto, y solo ha habido un Hombre perfecto: Jesús, nuestro Rey Mesías.

Jesús sabía que su muerte sería increíblemente dolorosa y espantosa. La temía, pero después de pedirle al Padre tres veces si podría haber otra manera, Jesús se rindió al plan del Padre. Aunque Jesús es plenamente Dios, también es plenamente hombre. Su naturaleza terrenal tuvo que someterse a su naturaleza divina. Él oró: "pero no sea como Yo quiero, sino como Tú quieras". Esa es una buena manera de orar cuando sabes que la respuesta de Dios es no, porque Dios nos sigue invitando a compartir nuestros corazones con Él. Ningún deseo y ninguna oscuridad lo sorprenden; al fin y al cabo, Él ya conoce nuestros corazones (Salmos 139:23–24). Jesús demostró lo que es sostener la tensión de derramar tu corazón ante Dios mientras te rindes.

¿Alguna vez le has pedido a Dios algo que sabías que no era parte de su plan para ti? ¿Cómo fue el proceso de rendición para ti?

Mientras Jesús permanecía en el huerto llorando, orando y rindiéndose, miró hacia las murallas de la ciudad y vio a Judas y al grupo de soldados que llegaban para arrestarlo. Como estaba oscuro, llevaban antorchas (ver Juan 18:3) mientras se abrían camino a través del valle y entraban en el huerto. Hipotéticamente, si Jesús hubiera querido podría haber corrido en la otra dirección, subiendo a la cima del Monte de los Olivos, y haber huido al desierto de Judea, que comienza justo al otro lado de la colina. Pero no lo hizo. Se quedó. Se rindió voluntariamente mientras era traicionado en manos de pecadores.

Jesús sabe lo que es ser tú. Sabe lo que es temer al futuro, ser traicionado por tus amigos, lamentar pérdidas. No solo pagó el castigo por nuestros pecados sino que se encarnó para conocer nuestro dolor de una manera muy real. ¡Qué regalo tener un Rey como Él, que se adentra en el dolor de su pueblo!

DÍA 4

MATEO 26:47-68

LEE MATEO 26:47-68

Mientras Jesús decía a sus discípulos que llegaba quien lo iba traicionar, Judas se acercó con un grupo armado. Judas les había dicho que les indicaría quién era Jesús dándole un beso, un saludo común en ese tiempo. De nuevo, Judas llamó *Rabí* (Maestro) a Jesús en lugar de *Señor,* como lo había hecho en la Última Cena. Y Jesús respondió llamando *amigo* a Judas, pero no usando la palabra habitual para *amigo (filos)* sino la variante que implica algo más que un mero conocido *(hetairos).* Solo se usa otras dos veces en la Escritura, y ambas veces en parábolas en las que Jesús hizo referencia a personas malvadas que se aprovechaban de una persona justa. Y eso es exactamente lo que Judas estaba haciendo.

Jesús sabía lo que estaba a punto de ocurrir, y se sometió a ello. Cuando los soldados lo agarraron para llevárselo, Pedro sacó su espada para contraatacar, cortando la oreja de un hombre llamado Malco, que era un siervo del sumo sacerdote (Juan 18:10).

Lee Mateo 10:34. Es posible que Pedro estuviera recordando estas palabras de Jesús. En base a nuestro estudio de Mateo 10, explica por qué la respuesta de Pedro no se alineaba con la enseñanza de Jesús.

Jesús detuvo las acciones de Pedro y le recordó que Él podía haber pedido al Padre que enviara un número masivo de ángeles (entre 60 000 y 72 000) para luchar por Él si estuviera interesado en defenderse. En su lugar, se sometió.

Repasa 26:54 y 26:56. ¿En qué está enfocado Jesús?

Jesús sabía que la cruz era el único camino, y su deseo era que se cumpliera la Escritura. No estaba interesado en defenderse. En el relato que hace Lucas de esta historia, Jesús incluso sanó la oreja de Malco después de que Pedro la cortara (Lucas 22:51).

Lee Mateo 5:11-12. En el primer sermón de Jesús enseñó a sus seguidores cómo responder en circunstancias como esta. ¿Qué les dijo que hicieran?

¿Cómo tiendes a responder cuando las personas te acusan falsamente o te malinterpretan? Si responder correctamente te supone un reto, ¿qué puedes aprender de estos versículos o del ejemplo de Jesús que podría ayudarte a crecer en esa área?

Después de ser arrestado, los discípulos se dispersaron tal como Él había prometido. Los soldados guiaron a Jesús a su juicio ante Caifás, el sumo sacerdote, que estaba reunido con todos los líderes religiosos. Pedro los siguió guardando cierta distancia, y presenció el juicio junto a los enemigos de Jesús. Los líderes buscaban a personas dispuestas a dar falso testimonio, pero al principio nadie daba un testimonio que incriminara a Jesús.

Repasa 26:60-61. ¿De qué acusaron estos testigos a Jesús? ¿Por qué esto había sido un problema para Caifás y los líderes religiosos?

Lee Juan 2:18-21. ¿En qué se diferencia lo que realmente dijo Jesús de lo que fue acusado de decir (en Mateo 26:60-61)?

Lo que dijo Jesús	La acusación

¿A qué se refería Jesús cuando dijo la frase que estaban recordando los testigos?

Lee Isaías 53:7. ¿De qué forma fue consistente la respuesta de Jesús a Caifás en 26:62-63 con esta profecía?

Lee Mateo 16:13-17. ¿Quién es el Hijo del Hombre?

Jesús fue acusado de amenazar con destruir el templo, pero Él realmente había dicho que otra persona lo destruiría, y que Él sería quien lo levantaría en tres días. No se refería al templo donde ellos adoraban sino al templo de su cuerpo. El templo es el lugar donde Dios vino a habitar con la humanidad, así que es apropiado que Jesús (Dios encarnado) se refiriera a su propio cuerpo como el templo.

También hizo referencia al que parece ser su nombre favorito para referirse a sí mismo: el Hijo del Hombre. Les dijo que se sentaría con el Padre en el cielo. Al sumo sacerdote, que no consideraba que Jesús fuera Dios, eso le pareció una blasfemia. Los líderes estuvieron de acuerdo, dieron así el veredicto de culpable, y creían que merecía la pena de muerte como castigo. Fue golpeado, abofeteado y escupido mientras se burlaban de Él.

Soportó muchas rondas de preguntas, acusaciones y abuso, y en medio de todo ello siguió caminando en su autoridad como Rey. Declaró la verdad cuando fue necesario, guardó silencio cuando fue necesario y siguió cumpliendo el plan del Padre, dando un paso más hacia la cruz con cada conversación. Esta había sido su misión todo el tiempo, y se acercaba su cumplimiento.

DÍA 5

MATEO 26:69-75

LEE MATEO 26:69-75

Incluso en la actualidad, si caminas por la ciudad vieja de Jerusalén oirás cantar a los gallos. Es un recordatorio frecuente de las cosas que soportó nuestro Rey en las últimas horas antes de su muerte. Puede transportarte en el tiempo hasta la noche de su arresto, cuando uno de sus compañeros más cercanos cumplió su profecía negándolo tres veces.

Cuando Pedro vio el juicio de Jesús ante Caifás, se sentó afuera en el patio donde estaba teniendo lugar el juicio. Se habían reunido en ese lugar otras personas, y cuando una muchacha reconoció a Pedro como un seguidor de Jesús, él lo negó. Posiblemente por temor a haber sido descubierto, avanzó hacia la salida. Fue entonces cuando otra muchacha lo reconoció y le señaló delante de otros. Aquí fue cuando Pedro debió empezar a ponerse nervioso. No solo le habían reconocido dos veces, sino que ahora estaban difundiendo la información. Pedro juró que no conocía a Jesús, aumentando con ello la intensidad de su negación. Si alguien que juraba lo hacía mintiendo, el castigo era el juicio divino.

Lee Mateo 5:33-37. Resume a continuación las palabras de Jesús.

Busca Mateo 5:34 en un diccionario de griego. Busca la palabra original para *juramento* y escribe lo que encuentres.

Busca Mateo 26:72 en un diccionario de griego. Busca la palabra original para juramento y escribe lo que encuentres.

Una de las personas ante las que Pedro había sido expuesto lo presionó un poco más, diciendo que no le creían. A fin de cuentas, tenía el mismo acento rural de Jesús. Pedro y Jesús vivían en Cafarnaúm, una ciudad al noroeste del Mar de Galilea. Era una comunidad pobre y agraria, mientras que Jerusalén era una ciudad más sofisticada con un acento y dialecto distintos.

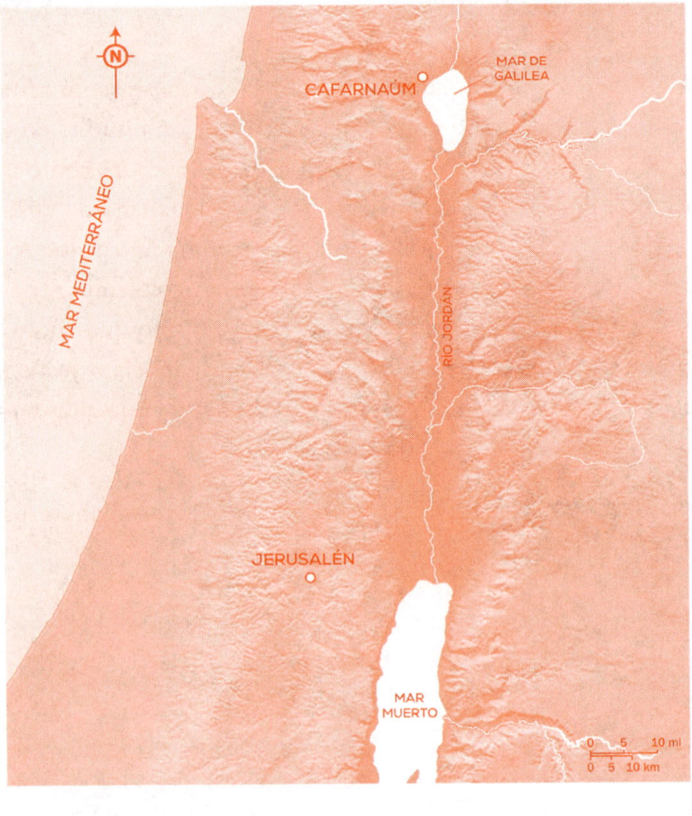

Usando un mapa o buscando en el internet, determina la distancia entre las dos ciudades. Aproximadamente, ¿cuánto se tardaría en ir caminando desde Cafarnaúm hasta Jerusalén?

Pedro negó nuevamente conocer a Jesús, y una vez más aumentó la intensidad de su negación, esta vez usando un lenguaje duro e invocando una maldición sobre sí mismo.

Busca Mateo 26:74 en un diccionario de griego. Busca las palabras originales para *maldecir* y *jurar* y escribe lo que encuentres.

Tras la tercera negación de Pedro, tal y como Jesús profetizó, cantó un gallo. Esto es importante. Dios no es solo el Dios de los grandes detalles, Él también está en las cosas pequeñas. Él es soberano incluso sobre el tiempo de los ruidos de los animales.

¿Alguna vez has intentado restarle importancia o esconder tu relación con Jesús? ¿Cómo te hizo sentir eso?

¿Alguna vez te ha preocupado que tu pecado te haya descalificado para ser usado por Dios?

La buena noticia para Pedro (y para nosotros) es que ese no es el final de su historia. La redención de Dios siempre es mayor que la rebelión de sus hijos. Él está actuando incluso en nuestras peores acciones de pecado, que son una afrenta a la relación íntima que tenemos con Él, para su gloria y nuestra alegría (Romanos 8:28).

Pedro lamentó su pecado y se arrepintió de él. Y veremos cómo Dios continuó usándolo para hacer avanzar el evangelio. ¡Los pecadores son lo único lo que Dios tiene para trabajar, y Él se deleita en darnos roles y responsabilidades en su reino! ¡Él está donde está el gozo!

¿Qué es lo que más te impactó del estudio de esta semana? ¿Por qué?

¿Qué aprendiste o recordaste acerca de Dios y su carácter esta semana?

DÍA 6

SALMO CORRESPONDIENTE Y ORACIÓN

LEE SALMOS 55

¿Qué correlación ves entre Salmos 55 y el estudio de esta semana sobre Jesús y su reino?

¿Qué porciones de este salmo captan más tu atención?

Termina haciendo esta oración en voz alta:

Padre,

Te alabo por ser soberano sobre todos los detalles, grandes y pequeños. Desde el tiempo de la muerte de Jesús coincidiendo con la Pascua hasta el tiempo del canto del gallo, tú tienes en tus manos todas las cosas y haces que sean para tu gloria y nuestro gozo. ¡Sé glorificado, Dios!

Tú has sido misericordioso conmigo, y no me has dado el castigo que merezco como respuesta a mi pecado. Me has mostrado gracia: me has dado más de lo que merezco al adoptarme en tu familia, dándome el gozo de la intimidad contigo y equipándome para servir en tu reino ¡a pesar de mis pecados y errores!

Padre, he pecado y apelo a tu misericordia. Me arrepiento de mis pecados y acudo a ti, y te pido que limpies mi corazón. Confieso que, como Pedro y Judas, he escogido mi propio camino antes que tus caminos. He sido egoísta, he mentido, y he buscado protegerme de maneras necias en lugar de confiar en ti.

Por favor, fija mis ojos en ti y en tu reino eterno, no en las personas o cosas que me vea tentado a temer. Por favor, sigue refinándome y purificando mi corazón. Revélame los motivos de mi corazón. Concédeme arrepentimiento donde me falte. Y concédeme una cercanía continua contigo en todas las cosas, para que me parezca más a tu Hijo Jesús, a medida que tu Espíritu obra en mí y da fruto en mi vida.

Te rindo mi vida, Señor; en cada momento de mi día y cada decisión que tome, someto mi voluntad y mi camino a tu perfecta voluntad y camino.

Yo también te amo. Amén.

DÍA 7

DESCANSA, PONTE AL DÍA O PROFUNDIZA

RETO SEMANAL

La última línea del salmo de esta semana (Salmo 55) dice: "Pero yo en ti confiaré". Todo el salmo está enumerando nuestros temores, horrores y traiciones de amigos, está cargado de pruebas y de tristezas. Pero David lo resume todo diciendo básicamente: "A pesar de todo esto, confiaré en ti". Está recordando a su propio corazón que Dios es digno de confianza a pesar de todas las circunstancias que podrían tentarlo a dudar de la bondad de Dios.

Esta semana, tu reto es comenzar cada día conversando con Dios sobre las cosas que te cargan, diciéndolas en voz alta o anotándolas en tu diario como un esquema de puntos. No hay necesidad de entrar en detalles para el reto de esta semana (e incluso podría hacerte sentir *más* ansioso si lo haces), así que sé breve si eso te ayuda. Después, al terminar de contarle a Dios las cosas que pesan en tu corazón, termina diciendo en voz alta: "Pero yo confiaré en ti". Tal vez incluso quieras decirlo en voz alta después de *cada* punto.

Recuérdale a tu corazón que Dios es digno de confianza. Recuérdale a tu corazón que después de todo lo que soportó Jesús, Dios estaba en el proceso de redimir el mal cometido contra Él. Recuérdale a tu corazón que después de todo el pecado y la negación de Pedro, la redención de Dios es mayor que su rebelión. Tu corazón necesita recordatorios regulares de que Dios es digno de confianza, ¡y necesita un llamado regular a poner esa confianza en acción!

SEMANA 10

Mateo 27-28:

Pasión del Rey

VERSÍCULO PARA MEMORIZAR

Por tanto, no se preocupen por el día de mañana; porque el día de mañana se cuidará de sí mismo. Básteles a cada día sus propios problemas.

Mateo 6:34

LECTURA BÍBLICA DIARIA

Día 1: Mateo 27:1-26

Día 2: Mateo 27:27-44

Día 3: Mateo 27:45-66

Día 4: Mateo 28:1-10

Día 5: Mateo 28:11-20

Día 6: Salmos 22

Día 7: Para ponerte al día

Corresponde al Día 316 y 318 de *La sinopsis de la Biblia*

RETO SEMANAL

Ver la página 252 para más información.

DÍA 1

MATEO 27:1-26

LEE MATEO 27:1-26

A veces es fácil pasar por alto el tormento desgarrador que nuestro Rey experimentó física, relacional, mental y espiritualmente en su camino hacia la victoria sobre la muerte. El estudio de esta semana nos obliga a detener nuestra mirada en esta dolorosa realidad que nos señala su máxima pasión: la salvación, redención y restauración de todos los que confían en Él como Rey.

Repasa Mateo 26. ¿Qué cosas ya ha soportado Jesús?

Tras un juicio ilegal a medianoche, Jesús fue hallado culpable de blasfemia por los gobernantes religiosos. Sin embargo, como no tenían poder para ejecutarlo, lo enviaron al gobernador romano local: Pilato. Poncio Pilato tenía la reputación de ser un gobernante brutal y corrupto, así que los líderes religiosos esperaban que conseguir de él una sentencia de muerte no sería muy difícil.

Sin embargo, antes de que Mateo nos diga lo que ocurrió con Pilato, nos enfocamos en Judas Iscariote viendo las consecuencias de sus decisiones. En pocas horas, Jesús anunció esta fractura relacional y después vio cómo sucedía, tal y como ocurrió con Pedro. Las ofensas (traición y negación) son similares, pero los dos hombres respondieron de manera distinta a su propio pecado, produciendo un resultado totalmente distinto.

¿Qué tenían en común la negación de Pedro de Cristo y la traición de Judas de Cristo?

¿En qué se diferenciaban?

¿Cuáles son las similitudes y las diferencias entre las reacciones de los dos hombres a su pecado?

Busca 27:3 en las siguientes traducciones bíblicas y escribe la frase para lo que hizo Judas (representado por la palabra griega *metamelomai*).

NBLA: ______________________________

NVI: ______________________________

NTV: ______________________________

El lenguaje original de la Escritura revela una gran diferencia entre sentir remordimiento personal por las consecuencias del pecado (*metamelomai*) y estar quebrantado por la fractura relacional que causa el pecado e ir en otra dirección para regresar a Dios en arrepentimiento (*metanoeō*, como en Mateo 4:17).

Lee 2 Corintios 7:10. ¿Qué tipo de tristeza sintió Judas? ¿Qué tipo de tristeza sintió Pedro? ¿Cómo lo sabes?

Cuando pecas, ¿te sientes más inclinado a sentir remordimiento por las consecuencias de tu pecado, o arrepentimiento y quebranto por el pecado en sí?

En la respuesta de Judas, los principales sacerdotes muestran su hipocresía; ellos son los que pagaron a Judas para traicionar a Jesús, pero después consideraron que las treinta monedas de plata estaban "manchadas de sangre". Como no querían que su dinero "limpio" se ensuciara, usaron la plata para comprar un terreno para enterrar a extranjeros fallecidos. Y con esa compra accidentalmente cumplieron Zacarías 11:12-13, reforzando que a quien ellos mataron es el verdadero Rey.

Cuando Pilato preguntó a Jesús: "¿Eres tú el Rey de los judíos?", era probablemente una pregunta irónica o sarcástica, porque el hombre que había delante de él había sido golpeado y ensangrentado por los judíos y no se parecía en nada a un rey.

Pilato no parecía querer dar muerte a Jesús, e incluso su esposa le rogó que no tuviera nada que ver con hacerle daño a Jesús de ninguna manera; sin embargo, en lugar de simplemente liberar a Jesús y arriesgarse a enfurecer a la multitud, Pilato intentó usar algunas prácticas religiosas judías para evitar tomar la decisión.

Lee Levítico 16:6-10. ¿Qué ocurrió con los dos cabritos?

Repasa 27:15-23. ¿Qué ocurrió con los dos hombres?

¿Qué paralelismos ves entre estos dos pasajes?

Lo creas o no, Mateo 27 no es un cuadro de Levítico 16, sino al revés. La práctica de matar un cabrito como ofrenda por el pecado y soltar uno durante la Pascua ¡era un *anuncio* de lo que Cristo haría en este día! En esta historia, Jesús fue quien se convirtió en ofrenda por el pecado y somos nosotros los que son soltados. Jesús fue el Salvador crucificado, y nosotros somos Barrabás. Somos culpables y merecemos la pena de muerte, pero somos liberados cuando el Justo muere por nosotros como ofrenda por el pecado.

Escribe algunas ideas o emociones que vengan a tu mente cuando verdaderamente meditas en el hecho de que *tú* eres Barrabás en esta historia.

Pilato estaba entre la espada y la pared. Mientras tanto, los principales sacerdotes y los ancianos debieron utilizar algunas tácticas fuertes de manipulación no solo para convencer a la multitud de que Jesús debía morir, sino también que debía ser mediante la crucifixión, una forma brutal de ejecución romana a la que los judíos se oponían con firmeza.

Algunos quieren usar este pasaje ahora como una excusa para el antisemitismo, pero lo que vemos en Génesis 12:3 es que Israel será a la vez bendecido y juzgado por Dios. El papel de los que siguen a Cristo es amar a la gente de una forma que les señale al Rey Jesús y orar por su salvación, no condenarlos o menospreciarlos.

Repasa 27:25. ¿Cuál fue la ironía de que la gente sugiriera que la sangre de Jesús estuviera sobre ellos y sobre sus hijos?

El estudio de hoy termina con lo que podría ser una de las escenas más desgarradoras y redentoras de toda la Escritura: el hombre claramente culpable sale libre, mientras se dan órdenes de azotar al Rey perfecto e inocente llevándolo al borde de la muerte.

DÍA 2

MATEO 27:27-44

LEE MATEO 27:27-44

Tras haber sufrido traición y golpes, el Rey Jesús seguramente estaba privado de sueño y angustiado. Sin embargo, la situación empeora antes de mejorar.

¿Cómo crees que Jesús se sentía en estas áreas?

Físicamente: ______________________________

Emocionalmente: ______________________________

Relacionalmente: ______________________________

Aunque Pilato se sentía inclinado a liberar a Jesús, parece que su guardia personal tenía sus propias ideas sobre lo que debía hacerse. Tras el brutal azote de Jesús, detuvieron la actividad en las oficinas centrales del gobernador e invitó a todo el batallón a unirse a la tortura.

¿De qué manera cada uno de estos actos intencionales de humillación (desde 27:27-29) es una afrenta directa contra su posición como Rey? **Usa un comentario si te resulta útil.**

Le quitaron la ropa ______________________________

Un manto escarlata ______________________________

Una corona de espinas ______________________________

Una caña en su mano derecha ______________________________

Arrodillarse ante Él ______________________________

"Salve, Rey de los judíos" ______________________________

Las burlas descaradas del batallón hacia Jesús tomaron la forma de una crueldad irónica, pero también nosotros somos culpables de burlarnos del Rey Jesús cada vez que vivimos para nosotros mismos, sin someternos a su reinado.

¿Qué pensamientos, acciones o relaciones específicas en tu vida podrían estar burlándose del papel de Jesús como Rey? ¿Dónde sientes un llamado a someterte a su autoridad?

Jesús fue escoltado hasta el lugar de su ejecución: el Gólgota, el Lugar de la Calavera. Pero después del dolor que soportó, no era lo suficientemente fuerte para cargar el travesaño de cuarenta kilos para su ejecución. Un hombre llamado Simón, probablemente un judío fiel que estaba en la ciudad para la Pascua desde más de mil quinientos kilómetros de distancia en el norte de África, fue obligado por los soldados romanos a cargarlo por Él.

Lee Mateo 16:24-25. Sabiendo que Jesús estaba hablando sobre este momento específico, ¿cómo sería vivir espiritualmente el llamado de Jesús a sus discípulos?

Como era costumbre, a Jesús le ofrecieron un trago para nublar sus sentidos, pero Él lo rehusó. Entre dos delincuentes comunes, el cuerpo de Jesús colgaba bajo un cartel con sus cargos: "Este es Jesús, el Rey de los judíos". La multitud le gritaba que se salvara a sí mismo, y aunque era capaz de hacerlo, contuvo su poder y se sometió al plan del Padre para nuestra salvación.

Lee Hebreos 12:2. ¿Qué palabra usa el versículo para describir en lo que se enfocó Jesús? ¿Cómo parece eso posible a la luz de todo lo que soportó en la lectura de hoy?

DÍA 3

MATEO 27:45-66

LEE MATEO 27:45-66

Aunque no se registran anomalías durante las primeras tres horas mientras Jesús estaba en la cruz (desde el mediodía hasta las tres de la tarde), una inexplicable oscuridad cayó sobre toda la tierra a la sexta hora mientras la creación lamentaba la muerte inminente de su Creador. Jesús exclamó en su lengua materna: "Dios mío, Dios mío, ¿por qué me has abandonado?".

Muchos comentarios (y un popular canto de adoración) dicen que esta exclamación es evidencia de que Dios el Padre abandonó al Hijo al volver su rostro, desconectando al Hijo del Padre, presumiblemente porque no puede mirar el pecado. Sin embargo, la Escritura nunca dice que Dios no puede mirar el pecado. De hecho, a lo largo del Antiguo Testamento Dios acampó en medio de su pueblo pecador y les dijo que se *acercaran* a Él cuando pecaran. Y Jesús, que es Dios, estuvo cerca del pecado todo el tiempo, pero se mantuvo sin pecar.

Entonces, ¿qué estaba sucediendo realmente cuando Jesús dijo esas palabras? Esta es una teoría útil: se cree que, en tiempos antiguos, las personas aludían a un salmo dado recitando su primera línea. Aún no se habían asignado números de capítulos a los libros de la Biblia, y los pasajes se transmitían oralmente como historias y canciones de una generación a otra. Por lo tanto, cuando querían cantar un salmo, no podían decir: "Cantemos el Salmo 100" o "Busquen la página 523 en su himnario". Tenían que apoyarse en la primera línea para comenzar el salmo para la multitud.

Cuando Jesús pronunció la primera línea del Salmo 22, probablemente estaba llamando la atención a todo el salmo, que era un canto profético sobre el Mesías.

Lee Salmos 22. ¿Qué podría ser profético acerca de Jesús en este salmo? Usa un comentario si te resulta útil.

Los versículos 27-28 del salmo dicen: "Todos los términos de la tierra se acordarán y se volverán al Señor, y todas las familias de las naciones adorarán delante de Ti. Porque del Señor es el reino, y Él gobierna las naciones". Nuestro gran Rey Jesús, con su último aliento, declara que su muerte es para salvarnos. Tras haber sufrido una brutal muerte en la cruz, Jesús estaba pensando en cómo su muerte nos permitiría poder estar unidos a Él para siempre. Es como si estuviera gritando: "¡Estoy haciendo esto por ustedes!".

Lee Juan 10:18, 1 Juan 3:16, Gálatas 2:20 y Tito 2:13-14. ¿Qué dicen estos pasajes sobre la muerte de Jesús?

Repasa 27:51-54. ¿Qué acontecimientos milagrosos ocurrieron, y cuál fue la implicación espiritual de cada uno?

El milagro	La implicación

¿Cómo responde el centurión a los acontecimientos? ¿Cómo crees que habrías respondido tú?

Debido a la festividad de la Pascua, un seguidor adinerado de Jesús utilizó su estatus para pedir que retiraran el cuerpo de su Rey de la cruz, a fin de poder darle un entierro adecuado. Jesús fue colocado en una tumba prestada, y se rodó una gran piedra frente a ella para sellar la entrada.

La lectura de hoy concluye con una reveladora conversación entre los líderes religiosos y Pilato. Después de decir claramente que Jesús estaba muerto, recordaron las propias palabras de Jesús sobre su resurrección y afirmaron querer frustrar cualquier intento de robar su cuerpo. Pero estos hombres acababan de presenciar los acontecimientos sobrenaturales que ocurrieron con la muerte de Jesús y vieron a sus discípulos huir y esconderse. Su miedo probablemente no se debía a los discípulos, sino al poder de Jesús mismo. Pilato les dio una unidad de guardias de élite y un sello gubernamental para asegurar la tumba. Esta gran seguridad da un mayor testimonio del poder de su inminente resurrección.

Los líderes religiosos estaban intentando usar la sabiduría, el poder y la autoridad humana para superar el poder de Jesús. Aunque esto nos pueda parecer absurdo, nosotros caemos en los mismos patrones. A diferencia de quienes conspiraron contra Jesús, nosotros tenemos acceso al poder del Jesús resucitado, y aun así a menudo nos conformamos con la sabiduría, la fuerza y la autoridad humanas.

¿En qué área de tu vida sientes la tentación de usar la sabiduría, la fuerza o la autoridad humanas cuando Dios te está ofreciendo la suya?

DÍA 4

MATEO 28:1-10

LEE MATEO 28:1-10

Deseosas de terminar los preparativos del entierro que tuvieron que interrumpir por la llegada del día de reposo, dos mujeres llegaron al exterior de la tumba antes de que el sol asomara por el horizonte. María Magdalena y "la otra María" sin duda estaban llenas de tristeza y todavía intentando asimilar la muerte de Jesús. El Evangelio de Lucas nos da algunos detalles acerca de María Magdalena: una mujer escandalosa que fue sanada por Jesús de siete demonios y que se sentó a los pies de Jesús como una discípula junto a los doce hombres y otras dos mujeres (Lucas 8:1-3). No sabemos muchos detalles de quién era "la otra María", aunque es seguro suponer que se trataba de la hermana de Marta y Lázaro.

¿Qué crees que estaban sintiendo estas mujeres después de estar a los pies de su Maestro y tras presenciar su muerte?

Imagina la sorpresa de estas dos mujeres y de los guardias romanos que vigilaban la tumba cuando un ángel apareció durante un gran terremoto para retirar la piedra sellada, dejando ver una tumba vacía. El ángel tenía una apariencia de luz (por ejemplo, brillo o resplandor), su ropa era blanca, era lo suficientemente fuerte como para retirar la piedra él solo, ¡y aparentemente era lo suficientemente alto como para sentarse encima de la piedra cuando terminó! Sin embargo, es importante notar que nadie se postró para adorarlo.

¿Cómo respondieron los soldados de élite de Roma a la aparición del ángel?

Los guardias tenían motivos para estar llenos de miedo, pues la resurrección de Jesús debería causar terror a los siervos del pecado. Pero a los fieles seguidores del Rey, el ángel les dio consuelo. Él identificó la razón por la que las mujeres fueron a la tumba y luego ajustó sus expectativas, haciéndoles saber que la tumba estaba vacía. Esto fue un cambio de paradigma para las mujeres, pero el ángel les aseguró que era mucho mejor de lo que habían imaginado.

¿Por qué crees que el ángel invitó a las mujeres a mirar dentro de la tumba con sus propios ojos?

¿Qué grandes cosas ha hecho Dios que has visto con tus propios ojos?

El ángel les dio la instrucción de decirles a los discípulos que Jesús había resucitado y que se reuniría con ellos de nuevo en Galilea. Y las mujeres no perdieron tiempo en cumplir su misión. María y María fueron las primeras en proclamar la noticia de la resurrección de Jesús: ¡las primeras misioneras designadas de lo que ahora llamamos la iglesia!

Repasa 28:8. ¿Qué revela esto sobre el estado emocional de las mujeres? ¿Te identificas con esto a veces cuando te sientes llamado a hacer algo para la gloria de Dios?

Con miedo y alegría entremezclados, su rápida obediencia fue recompensada con lo inesperado: ¡una visita del propio Rey! Con su simple saludo, las mujeres cayeron a sus pies en un momento emotivo de adoración. Las palabras de Jesús reforzaron la misión que el ángel les había dado, pero Jesús hizo que el mensaje que debían entregar fuera personal. La última vez que los discípulos estuvieron todos juntos, Jesús les dijo que todos se alejarían; y así fue. Sin embargo, aquí Jesús los llamó *hermanos* por primera vez. Su tropiezo no fracturó el afecto que Jesús tenía por los hombres. Él había invertido tres años de su vida en sus discípulos, y a pesar de su caída estaba ansioso por encontrarse con ellos en Galilea.

¿Qué revela acerca del corazón de Dios que las mujeres, que estaban marginadas en su cultura, recibieran el mensaje primero?

¿En qué otras partes del Evangelio de Mateo hemos visto a Jesús elevar a los marginados sobre las normas culturales?

¿Cómo anima tu corazón el compromiso firme de Jesús con un reino al revés? ¿Hay maneras en las que afecta tu manera de vivir? Si es así, ¿cómo?

El Rey ve y eleva a los marginados, se acerca a los humildes, es tierno con los abatidos y pone boca abajo la cultura cuando es apropiado. Él lo hizo en su vida, en su muerte y de nuevo en su resurrección.

DÍA 5

MATEO 28:11-20

LEE MATEO 28:11-20

El Evangelio de Mateo termina con un tema que hemos visto a lo largo de su relato de la vida del Rey. A algunos que ven y oyen el mensaje no les conmueve la evidencia de su autoridad. Otros que experimentan al Rey ven que sus vidas son transformadas de manera radical, obteniendo una perspectiva eterna y una misión en el reino.

Lee 1 Corintios 1:22-25. ¿Cuáles son las dos audiencias que enumera Pablo? ¿Qué impacto tiene la cruz sobre cada audiencia?

En este último capítulo de Mateo, María y María llevaron el mensaje de la resurrección a los discípulos mientras que los guardias se dirigieron a la ciudad para comunicar sus malas noticias a los principales sacerdotes. En ese momento, los líderes religiosos ya no podían negar que Jesús era el Rey, pero en lugar de doblar su rodilla buscaron la manera de encubrirlo. Este escenario revela lo que Jesús había dicho todo el tiempo: es posible conocer la verdad y que no te afecte en lo más mínimo.

En tus propias palabras, describe el plan para encubrirlo. ¿De qué manera era problemático ese plan?

Entre la plata que le pagaron a Judas (aproximadamente el salario de cuatro meses) y la "gran cantidad de dinero" que pagaron a los guardias, los principales sacerdotes gastaron mucho dinero en la trama para matar a Jesús; pero fue inútil. Otro problema es que los guardias también tuvieron que aceptar el improbable escenario en el que todos se quedaron dormidos al mismo tiempo, que a ninguno le despertó el ruido o el terremoto, y que sabían sin lugar a dudas que los discípulos robaron el cuerpo. Un entendimiento básico de los hechos supera cualquier defensa que ellos pudieran presentar.

¿Por qué crees que los principales sacerdotes se obstinaron en lugar de admitir que estaban equivocados?

¿Alguna vez eres demasiado terco para admitir que estás equivocado cuando Dios te está mostrando algo que necesitas cambiar en tu vida? ¿Cómo respondes?

Jesús se reunió con sus discípulos en la región de Galilea, tal como había prometido. Sabemos por otros relatos de los Evangelios que esa no fue primera vez que se reunían con el Jesús resucitado, pero sí fue una ocasión importante. Como es común en un encuentro con el Rey resucitado, todos lo adoraron de inmediato, pero según Mateo algunos seguían dudando. La palabra original para *duda* aquí señala a una incertidumbre y vacilación, no a una incredulidad firme. El mundo de estos hombres había sido sacudido, y es entendible que a algunos de ellos les resultara difícil aceptar todos los hechos ocurridos.

Describe una vez en la que experimentaste o supiste algo que condujo a un cambio de paradigma. ¿Cómo te resultó ese proceso de crecimiento? ¿Cuánto tardaste en procesar la nueva información?

Durante su tiempo juntos, incluso en sus dudas, Jesús les mandó difundir las buenas noticias de su resurrección.

Repasa 28:18-20. ¿Qué estaba incluido en las instrucciones de Jesús, y cuál era su promesa? ¿Cómo podría haberles dado esperanza esta instrucción a los discípulos para una tarea tan grande?

Jesús, afirmando la autoridad de Dios (porque Él *es* Dios), les ordenó ir y hacer discípulos. No estaba hablando de convertidos, partidarios neutrales o creyentes cuya asistencia a la iglesia afecta muy poco su manera de vivir. *Discípulo* significa "aprendiz". Este era un llamado a enseñar continuamente a otros sobre las cosas que habían aprendido del Rey.

Lee Génesis 17:10-11. ¿Cuál era la señal física del pacto entre Dios e Israel? ¿Cuál fue la señal dada a los discípulos para el nuevo pacto?

¿Cuál es la importancia de ser bautizado en el nombre del Padre, del Hijo y del Espíritu Santo? ¿Qué papel desempeña cada uno de ellos en la salvación de los seguidores de Cristo?

Si la Trinidad es un concepto relativamente desconocido para ti, ¡profundiza un poco más! Cuanto más lleguemos a conocer a Dios en cada una de sus personas, ¡más podemos ser como Él a la hora de cumplir esta tarea internacional de hacer discípulos!

Repasa 28:20b. ¿Se aplica en la actualidad la promesa que hizo Jesús a los creyentes? ¿Qué clase de consuelo te da esto al pensar en el llamado a hacer discípulos?

Aunque todos tenemos el llamado de hacer discípulos, nuestra motivación principal no debería ser sentirnos obligados a hacerlo ¡sino que sea un deleite! Nosotros merecemos la muerte, pero nuestro Rey Jesús experimentó la peor muerte conocida por la humanidad para que pudiéramos glorificarlo con nuestra vida y pasar la eternidad con Él. Este mensaje que comienza con nuestra depravación termina con una esperanza eterna y un reino al revés. En su reino, los más pequeños son elevados, los últimos son los primeros, los enfermos se recuperan y el Salvador de nuestra alma nos conoce y nos ama plenamente. Nuestro corazón anhela ese reino eterno con nuestro Rey, ¡porque Él está donde está el gozo!

¿Qué es lo que más te impactó del estudio de esta semana? ¿Por qué?

¿Qué aprendiste o recordaste acerca de Dios y su carácter esta semana?

DÍA 6

SALMO CORRESPONDIENTE Y ORACIÓN

LEE SALMOS 22

¿Qué correlación ves entre Salmos 22 y el estudio de esta semana sobre Jesús y su reino?

¿Qué porciones de este salmo captan más tu atención?

Termina haciendo esta oración en voz alta:

Padre,

Te alabo por tu plan perfecto para nuestra redención. Incluso antes de que crearas el mundo, tenías un plan preparado para llevarnos a tu reino eterno. Eres muy generoso, abundantemente misericordioso y audazmente compasivo. Padre, gracias por adoptarnos en tu familia. Jesús, gracias por vivir una vida justa y darnos esa justicia, cargando después nuestro pecado a cambio, y recibiendo el castigo que nosotros merecemos. ¡Espíritu, gracias por habitar en nosotros y marcarnos como miembros del reino!

Padre, he pecado y apelo a tu misericordia. Confieso que fácilmente hago caso omiso al peso del sacrificio de tu Hijo, intercambio la libertad de la obediencia por la esclavitud de los pecados que decido cometer. Como los discípulos, he tenido momentos de duda, pero tú siempre me has dado la bienvenida y me has amado a pesar de ello. Me arrepiento de mis pecados, acudo a ti y te pido que limpies mi corazón.

Después de todo lo que he aprendido sobre ti, ayúdame a hacer algo más que tan solo quedarme para mí esas hermosas verdades. Inquiétame a hacer discípulos y a enseñar a otros lo que yo he aprendido. Crea oportunidades divinas, ablanda corazones y dame las palabras que debo decir al invitar a otros a unirse a tu reino ¡o a conocer más sobre el propio Rey!

Te rindo mi vida, Señor; en cada momento de mi día y en cada decisión que tome, someto mi voluntad y mi camino a tu perfecta voluntad y camino.

Yo también te amo. Amén.

DÍA 7

DESCANSA, PONTE AL DÍA O PROFUNDIZA

RETO SEMANAL

Lee 1 Timoteo 6:11-16. Pablo escribió esta carta a su joven discípulo para recordarle seguir peleando la buena batalla de la fe. En este pasaje, vuelve a relatar los acontecimientos de Mateo 27–28 y dice que apuntemos nuestra esperanza ¡hacia el reinado de Cristo!

Tras haber estudiado cómo Mateo revela a Jesús como Rey, escribe unos párrafos en tu diario usando estas tres ideas:

1. ¿Cómo afecta el reinado de Jesús al modo en que vivo mi vida cada día? (Si no afecta, pasa un tiempo escribiendo una oración. Pídele a Dios que mueva tu corazón hacia la acción en base a lo que has estado estudiando en las últimas diez semanas).
2. Si un amigo cristiano me preguntara si realmente importa o no que Jesús sea Rey, le diría…
3. Si un amigo que no conoce a Jesús me preguntara por qué lo llamamos "el Rey Jesús", le diría…

PARA LÍDERES DE GRUPO

¡Gracias por usar este estudio y por liderar a otros a través de él! Cada semana tiene una amplia variedad de contenido (contenido y preguntas, lectura bíblica diaria, memorización de versículos, reto semanal y recursos) para ayudar al lector a desarrollar un abanico de disciplinas espirituales. Siéntete libre de usar este contenido en tus reuniones como lo veas conveniente. Los detalles proporcionados en "Cómo usar este estudio" (págs. 13–14) serán útiles para ti y para todos los miembros de tu grupo, así que asegúrate de revisar esa información juntos.

Depende de ti y de tu grupo cómo les gustaría estructurar sus reuniones, pero sugerimos incluir tiempo para dialogar sobre el estudio y el texto bíblico de la semana, el aliento mutuo y la oración. Además, tal vez quieras practicar juntos los versículos de memorización de la Escritura como grupo o en parejas. A medida que compartas con los demás, "consideremos cómo estimularnos unos a otros al amor y a las buenas obras" (Hebreos 10:24) y "confórtense los unos a los otros, y edifíquense el uno al otro" (1 Tesalonicenses 5:11).

A continuación hay algunas preguntas de ejemplo para ayudar a facilitar la discusión. Está estructurado como un estudio semanal, pero si tu grupo se reúne con una frecuencia diferente, tal vez quieras ajustar las preguntas en consecuencia. Cubre tantas preguntas como el tiempo lo permita, o siéntete libre de crear las tuyas propias. Si lo deseas, también puedes repasar los recursos adicionales en inglés que hemos vinculado para ti en MyDGroup.org/Resources/Matthew.

MUESTRA DE PREGUNTAS DE DISCUSIÓN

¿Qué preguntas te surgieron con el estudio o el texto bíblico de esta semana?

¿Qué te llamó la atención en el estudio de esta semana?

¿Qué notaste acerca de Dios y su carácter?

¿Cómo te desafió tu estudio del texto bíblico? ¿Hay algo que quieras cambiar a la luz de lo que aprendiste?

Lo que has aprendido sobre Dios, ¿cómo afecta tu manera de vivir en comunidad?

¿Qué correlación viste entre el salmo del Día 6 y el estudio de esta semana sobre Jesús y su reino?

¿Has sentido que Dios está obrando en ti a través del reto semanal? Si es así, ¿cómo?

¿Está aumentando tu amor por la Palabra de Dios a medida que avanzamos en este estudio? Si es así, ¿cómo?

¿Algo de lo que aprendiste aumentó tu gozo de conocer a Jesús?

RECONOCIMIENTOS

Fue para mí un gran gozo ser solo una más en un equipo de escritores en este proyecto. Laura Buchelt, Emily Pickell, Evaline Asmah y Meg Mitchell: gracias por su increíble investigación, creatividad, sabiduría, humildad y risas. Nunca me imaginé que una tabla de planchar podría servir como escritorio o que una manta con capucha de mapache sería el atuendo perfecto para estimular la creatividad. Y especialmente a LB: gracias por todo tu trabajo previo para dividir este estudio en segmentos y por combatir el bloqueo del escritor exigiendo un baño de agua fría.

Quien manejó todos los detalles prácticos para nuestro retiro de escritura fue Olivia Le, desde reservar vuelos hasta alimentarnos y ayudarnos a encontrar la mejor caminata cuando necesitábamos un breve respiro lejos de nuestras computadoras. También hace los mejores huevos revueltos en la verde tierra de Dios.

Sin la sabiduría y el aliento continuo de Lisa Jackson, mi agente literaria, nada de esto sería posible. Y gracias a su esposo, Rich, quien seguramente nos entregó no menos de cincuenta cajas de materiales además de una mesa plegable.

Mis editores, Jeff Braun y Hannah Ahlfield, son realmente el equipo de ensueño para mí. Gracias por compartir esta visión de ayudar a las personas a descubrir más capas de la belleza de la Palabra de Dios. ¡Brindo por muchas más bebidas energéticas de celebración!

Y al resto del increíble equipo de D-Group, Rachel Mantooth, Lindsay Ruhter, Warwick Fuller y Omar Cardenas, nuestro consejo directivo y todos nuestros líderes y miembros alrededor del mundo. ¡Me encanta estar en misión con ustedes!

ACERCA DE LA EDITORA

TARA-LEIGH COBBLE

El celo de Tara-Leigh por la alfabetización bíblica le condujo a crear una red de estudios bíblicos llamada D-Group (Grupo de Discipulado). Cada semana, cientos de grupos D-Group de hombres y mujeres se reúnen en hogares, en iglesias y en línea para el estudio de la Biblia y para rendirse cuentas.

También escribe y presenta un podcast diario llamado *La sinopsis de la Biblia*, diseñado para ayudar a los oyentes a leer y comprender la Biblia en un año. El podcast ha acumulado más de trescientos millones de descargas en sus primeros cinco años, y más de veinte mil iglesias en todo el mundo se han unido a su plan de lectura para conocer a Dios y amarlo mejor. Se ha convertido en un libro publicado por Bethany House Publishers.

Tara-Leigh es una autora éxito de ventas en la lista del *Wall Street Journal*, habla ante una amplia variedad de audiencias y lidera regularmente viajes de enseñanza a Israel porque le encanta ver a otros maravillarse con la historia de la Escritura a través de la experiencia de primera mano.

Entre sus cosas favoritas están el agua con gas y los días de 22 grados con un 55 por ciento de humedad, y piensa que cada comida sabe mejor cuando se come al aire libre. Vive en una caja de cemento en los cielos de Dallas, Texas, donde no tiene mascotas, hijos ni nada que podría morir si se le olvida alimentarlo.

Para más información sobre Tara-Leigh y sus ministerios, puedes visitarla en el internet.

Sitios web:
taraleighcobble.com | thebiblerecap.com | mydgroup.org | israelux.com

Redes sociales:
@taraleighcobble | @thebiblerecap | @mydgroup | @israeluxtours